A Primer on the Law
of Deceptive Practices

A
PRIMER
ON THE LAW OF
DECEPTIVE
PRACTICES

A Guide
for the Businessman

EARL W. KINTNER

The Macmillan Company, New York

Collier-Macmillan Limited, London

To the staff of the Federal Trade Commission, which has labored faithfully for nearly one-half century to develop the legal principles described in this book— with the author's appreciation for the privilege of working with them for thirteen years.

The Macmillan Company
866 Third Avenue, New York, New York 10022
Collier-Macmillan Canada, Ltd., Toronto, Ontario

Library of Congress catalog card number: 70–151167

First Printing

Prologue

Why Read This Book?

In our free enterprise system the allocation of goods and services is not achieved through the dictates of big government, nor do we allow such vital decision making to reside in the hands of private monopoly. Centralized decision making in either form necessarily must result in the three classical evils described by Adam Smith: high prices, a limitation on production, and a deterioration in the quality of the goods produced. For this reason we have sought another means of regulating our economic order. Economic decision making is decentralized. The allocation of goods and services is a function of consumer choice. Businessmen, spurred by the profit motive, compete for the consumers' custom, which thus dictates which goods will be produced and purchased and, in consequence, business success or failure.

With the potential rewards so great, but the consequences of failure so disastrous, it was inevitable that competitive abuses would occur. Exaggeration as to the qualities of one's products, disparagement of those of a competitor, passing off as one's own the goods of a competitor or vice versa, false testimonials, industrial sabotage, and piracy of trade secrets were but a few of the abuses that began to abound in the market place. Honest businessmen faced the necessity of retaliation or the prospect of failure. Truthful information about the goods and services offered, the *sine qua non* of an economic system predicated upon informed, intelligent consumer choice, became replaced with distortion, half-truth, and outright lies.

The latter part of the last century brought a new dimension to the spreading cancer of marketing abuses. The industrial revolution brought

v

the railroads, which in turn provided the means for the widespread distribution of goods. Coinciding with this development was the rise in literacy and the increased circulation of published material. These two conditions fostered the development of a new technique in marketing. It was now feasible to market a branded consumer product on a nationwide basis. It was now easy to market a product from a central location which, together with the tremendous growth of the publishing media, meant that it was possible to create widespread public familiarity with a brand name through advertising. The result was that what had once been a disorganized array of local marketing abuses became transformed into a national scandal.

Interestingly, the growth of literacy and the widespread circulation of published material which had made the new methods of marketing abuses possible provided the means of combating them. The muckrakers used the information media to dramatize the abuses and to marshal public support to combat them. Laws were passed in forty-four states to achieve truth in advertising; in 1914 the Federal Trade Commission was established to prevent unfair methods of competition, and in 1938 that agency was given the power to prevent unfair and deceptive practices as well.

The initial chapters in this book detail the early abuses of our consumer-oriented marketing system and the efforts of the common law courts, the state legislatures, and the Federal Trade Commission to combat them. The great bulk of the book consists of an attempt to categorize those business practices which the FTC and the courts have found to be unfair and/or deceptive and as carefully as possible to delineate the law with respect to each of them. This was no mean task. Advertising techniques and claims are bounded only by the imagination of man; it was only natural that many of the most imaginative men and women in our society should be drawn to the advertising industry. New techniques are constantly devised which must in turn be judged on an *ad hoc* basis to determine whether they violate what the truth in advertising laws seek to accomplish. Also, the laws of the states vary on these matters and the position of the FTC has changed on certain practices from time to time, making categorization and consistency of treatment a difficult undertaking. Such problems as these have made writing this book a difficult task; at times it seemed an impossible task. Nevertheless, my experience with businessmen over many years, both with the Federal Trade Commission and in the private practice of law, has convinced me that the overwhelming majority of businessmen will make every effort to comply with the law *if they understand it.* Enlightened self-interest requires no less. Further, such understanding is necessary if economic democracy is to continue to be a viable means of allocating goods and resources in our society.

With these thoughts in mind, I have attempted to state every major premise of the law of unfair and deceptive business practices and to provide meaningful examples of the application of the law to marketing practices. Where disagreements exist—as, for example, between different states or different commentators—the differing views have been indicated. This book is not, however, a comprehensive treatment of every phase of unfair and deceptive business practices law. A library of many volumes would be necessary for that task. Rather my intention is to provide a primer for the aware business executive. If the general practitioner who counsels businessmen also finds the primer helpful, as I hope he will, I shall be content with my effort.

This book is not designed to teach businessmen how to be their own deceptive business practices lawyers. The very idea is folly, because these laws are infinitely subtle and appear in an infinite variety of forms. But the businessman's awareness of these laws can be heightened, and if he is sufficiently aware to consult a specialist *before* the consequences of a contemplated course of action descend on him, a precious gain has been won.

Acknowledgment

Any book of this character is the product of many minds. I must gratefully acknowledge the assistance of three of my colleagues—Ruth P. Roland, Joseph E. Casson, and Stephen S. Mayne, who made substantial research and editorial contributions to this book. Other colleagues, Judith D. Wilkenfeld, Elizabeth M. Pendleton, Denise Davis Schwartzman, and Daniel C. Smith, also contributed valuable research.

Bernie R. Burrus, Professor of Law at the Georgetown Law Center, and my colleague in private practice, rendered invaluable research, writing, and editorial assistance as we together laboriously fashioned the shape and substance of this book during the past three years.

E. W. K.

Contents

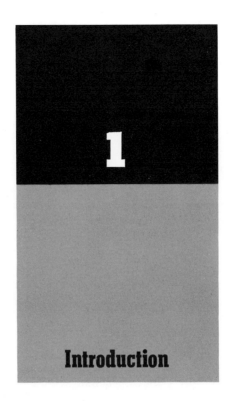

1

Introduction

THE ROLE OF ADVERTISING

The success of an economic democracy, no less than that of a political democracy, depends on informed, intelligent choice. Thus, the widespread dissemination of information with respect to alternatives is imperative; otherwise, choices would be made in a vacuum and would become meaningless, if not plainly capricious. However, there is no paucity of information in our contemporary society; the so-called mass media ensure that. Indeed, modern man can hardly escape, even if he should so desire, the constant bombardment of information from television, radio, newspapers, billboards, and other sources.

Because in our society consumer choice governs what goods are to be produced and who is to produce them, it is natural and desirable that various manufacturers should compete through the mass media for the buyers' attention. By this means the consumer is acquainted with the

1

vast variety and the relative merits and demerits of the goods and services available to him. The information thus obtained forms the basis for each individual's decision on how to spend his pay check. The cumulative effect of the choices of all such consumers is to determine what goods will be produced, what services will be performed, and who will produce or perform them, for an article that does not sell will no longer be produced. Thus, the buyer gets the merchandise he wants, and the producer who is able and willing to provide it at a price and of a quality satisfactory to the consumer is successful.

A function so vital and profitable as the dissemination of information intended to guide consumer choice cannot be performed fortuitously. Consumer acquaintance and persuasion is a matter of life or death to a producer. It is therefore only natural that specialized assistance was obtained in the marketing aspect of production, as it was in such fields as research and development and manufacturing techniques. In the process of responding to the need for expert guidance in acquainting the consumer with products and persuading him in his economic choices, advertising has mushroomed into a $12 billion per year industry, performing a service that is imperative to our free economy. Through the mass communications media, the advertiser provides the consumer with the information he needs to make economic choices intelligently and meaningfully, and thus makes economic democracy viable in practice as well as appealing in theory.

However, information *qua* information is not sufficient to sustain an economic democracy. If "a little information is dangerous," misinformation can be disastrous. For example, when goods are praised to the point of untruth, or a competitor's goods are falsely disparaged and the competitor then replies in kind, the result is not informed, intelligent choice, but rather its perversion; there is no "choice" when selection is a function of competing untruths, deceits, and misleading comparisons. Production is no longer regulated by consumer choice, and business success is no longer measured by consumer satisfaction. Moreover, the use of such deceptive techniques is not uncommon in the advertising field. The profit motive can be a powerful inducement to the destruction of principle, and control over consumer choice is a tremendous weapon in the arsenal of the unprincipled.

The valuable service performed by advertising for the American system of free enterprise and the part advertising has played in producing the highest standard of living ever achieved in the history of the world cannot be denied. Nevertheless, the power possessed by advertisers in the "battle for men's minds," as illustrated by their ability to influence the direction of our economic development, carries certain responsibilities with its use. A summary of the social responsibilities of advertising would, at a minimum, embrace these three elements:

1. To function as an efficient instrument of free and fair competition by focusing public attention on the demonstrable merits of competing products and services. .
2. To foster innovation by affording new entrants to the market place an efficient means of winning public acceptance.
3. To furnish to consumers the information necessary for intelligent choices.

The essence of these obligations is quite simply to "speak the truth," which means more than merely to avoid speaking half-truths; the advertiser must include all the facts essential to the formation of an accurate judgment concerning the qualities of the article or services described.

Most advertisers embrace the obligation faithfully and through such groups as the American Association of Advertising Agencies have established codes embodying standards of truthfulness and good taste for their own governance. However, self-regulation, as salutary and necessary as it is, cannot perform the whole task of meeting the social responsibilities of the advertising industry. There are jackals on the fringes of advertising, as there are on the fringes of any other industry, in whose ethic social responsibility takes a back seat, if it is not, in fact, left on the curbstone. Positive law and its sanctions are required to ensure that the truth will be spoken, thereby protecting the honest advertiser and providing the consumer with the basis necessary for an intelligent choice.

THE EARLY DAYS OF ADVERTISING

With the advent of the industrial revolution, education spread as did the circulation of published material. The railroad net grew and improved, providing the means for the widespread distribution of goods. These two conditions fostered the development of a new technique in marketing. It was now feasible to market a branded consumer product on a nationwide basis. It was now easy to distribute the product from a central location, and the tremendous growth of the publishing media, coinciding with the rapid increase in literacy, meant that widespread public familiarity with a brand name could now be created through advertising. Unfortunately, among the first to recognize and exploit the new marketing technique was a horde of quacks. Stewart Holbrook, in his delightful book *The Golden Age of Quackery,* describes some of the popular patent medicines, nostrums, and healing devices and the extravagant claims that were made for them. Let there be no mistake: some of these early patent medicines did have a powerful effect. Mr. Holbrook presents this analysis of one of the most popular of these sovereign remedies, Hostetter's Celebrated Stomach Bitters. At the time of the Civil War, Mr. Holbrook writes, "the Bitters contained modest amounts of cinchona bark, gentian root, orange peel, anise, and a less than modest dose of alcohol. Whether or not the alcoholic content was increased during the war is not clear, but for many years it ran to approximately 47 per cent by volume." This 94-proof compound undoubtedly warmed many a prim and temperate soul. The patent medicine king reigned supreme from the end of the Civil War to the early twentieth century. The magazines, newspapers, posters, and brochures of this period are filled with announcements of miraculous cures of persons afflicted with every disease known to man. The advertisements are replete with testimonials from Congressmen, admirals, actresses, and, most often, clergymen.

A further example may be found in Ernest Turner's book *The Shocking History of Advertising*. An American magazine published in the 1880's carried an advertisement for one Dr. Scott's Electric Corset, wherein the "Doctor" made extravagant claims for the benefits to be derived from his corset. The corset would "cure" extreme fatness or leanness "in most cases." The product should be tried by women suffering from "any bodily ailment" and by those who wished to "ward off and cure disease." The corset would "bring the magnetic power into constant contact with all the vital organs." The advertisement went on to state that "it is affirmed by professional men that there is hardly a disease that electricity and magnetism will not benefit and cure." As authority, the name of a former surgeon general of the United States was prominently mentioned.

The "Doctor" could make these assertions with impunity in the 1880's. There were no legal sanctions as such against advertising. Public education was at a comparatively low level, public taste was a factor not even to be considered, and Dr. Scott was obviously not concerned with building good will for his business for the distant future.

It was not long before the manufacturers of other branded consumer products grasped the possibilities of the new marketing technique. Soon soaps, cereals, cough drops, and canned milk all joined in the game of nationwide advertising and distribution.

As the abuses of advertising multiplied, it became apparent that legal restrictions would have to be fashioned to deal with them. As will be seen in the following chapter, the initial step in this direction was the formulation of private remedies, permitting deceived consumers and wronged competitors to sue for monetary damages or, in some cases, to seek injunctive relief against the wrongdoers. When this proved ineffective, state legislation was adopted, and finally, with the failure of state by state enforcement, the stage was set for action at the federal level.

2

Common Law Remedies for Unfair or Deceptive Business Practices

Adverising makes a valuable commercial asset of a merchant's business reputation and customer good will. These intangible factors of the business equation are as vital to success as the quality of the product itself; an assault on a merchant's character is as inimical to his success as a defect in his product.

To the extent that the early forms of commercial intangibles were capable of identification, they were afforded protection under an expanded interpretation of the law of torts. This nonstatutory body of law affords relief by way of damages or injunction to victims of civil wrongs. To succeed in a tort action a plaintiff must prove that the defendant has breached some duty owed to the plaintiff and that he has suffered injury as a proximate result of the breach of duty. By positing a duty not to interfere in the business intangibles of others, the common-law courts thus provided private causes of action to those suffering damages as a result of such interferences by others.

The earliest commercial torts focused on traditional property rights, such as a physical trade-mark, and sought to preserve the "king's peace" in much the same way as any other intentional tort of the day. As marketing techniques became more complex, the law reacted accordingly and the emphasis of commercial torts shifted to sustaining the fair operation of the competitive system. More specifically, it concentrated on preventing deception of the public, diversion of trade, and loss of business good will.

The use of traditional common law molds to form the new commercial causes of action presented a threshold problem, that of identifying the injured party. Because the tort concept essentially involved protection of immediate rights, some similar immediacy would have to be found in the commercial sphere. Under this approach it was concluded that a consumer was the only subject of direct injury for misleading or deceptive advertising and consequently was the only one entitled to sue. Similarly, a competitor was the only immediate victim of passing off or infringement, because he would suffer the diversion of trade. Commercial torts quickly were separated into two groups based on the party entitled to sue. Each category of tort developed its own defenses and exceptions, which will be discussed below, but the net effect of the bifurcation was to limit effective enforcement of commercial torts to competitive situations.

CONSUMER TORTS

A purchaser who was deceived as to the quality of goods by some affirmative representation of the seller was entitled to bring an action in deceit against the seller. The nature of the misrepresentation could be either the inherent qualities of the goods or their identification. Thus, the purchaser who sought one brand and was given another had been deceived by the seller. Deceit would also cover many statements constituting commercial disparagement—to the extent that such disparagements of a competitor falsely flattered one's own goods.

In addition, the consumer was entitled to rely on certain implicit and explicit warranties which the law stated accompanied the goods. This was fundamentally a contractual form of relief and was therefore limited to those who entered a contractual relationship with the seller, thereby eliminating any such action by a competitor.

The causes of action for deceit and for breach of warranty provided the consumer with his only remedies against a seller who endeavored to mislead him about the nature or quality of goods purchased. As initially framed, the remedies should have afforded adequate protection for any reasonable consumer. However, in addition to the elements of the misrepresentation itself, a plaintiff purchaser was faced with several debilitating restrictions in the form of procedural prerequisites and seller defenses. Chief among these inhibiting factors were *caveat emptor,* "puffing," and the necessity for privity between the consumer and the wrongful seller. Another, more subtle, inhibition on consumer protection was the fact that these other restrictions, when weighed against the actual monetary loss to the individual consumer, frequently destroyed any incentive to bring suit against the seller.

In an action for deceit a plaintiff was required to show that the seller had made a knowing misrepresentation of some material fact about his product. The misrepresentation had to be intentional and, furthermore, had to be intended to deceive the purchaser into making a purchase he would not otherwise have made. The dual nature of this element had the effect of substantially insulating two forms of deception —an innocent misrepresentation by the seller about the nature or quality of the goods and a misrepresentation that did not serve as the motivation for the purchase or was not the predominant motivation for the purchase.

The idea of reliance was substantially undermined by the common law rule of *caveat emptor.* This doctrine was formulated during a period in commercial development when the majority of purchases were for items of necessity and were made by consumers who could be expected to be reasonably familiar with the acceptable quality of the items they were buying. The rule was also a reflection of the unfortunate fact that much of the common law surrounding commercial activity was formulated at the behest of and in the best interests of the merchants of the day. Consequently, rather heavy obligations were placed on a buyer desiring to preserve his legal rights in the market place. He was expected to examine the goods or to obtain some sort of impartial advice to aid him in making the purchase, and a failure to do so constituted an assumption of the risks of deception considered inherent in the market place.

This notion of "let the buyer beware" also anticipated a certain skepticism on the part of a purchaser that would cause him to discount many of the otherwise misleading representations of a merchant. This idea found expression in the requirement for reasonable reliance by the purchaser, and the reasonableness was measured against this presumed skepticism. As a result a buyer was frequently found to have unreasonably relied on the outright misrepresentations of a seller simply because he failed to take them with a requisite "grain of salt." As an element of a cause of action the reasonableness factor was often critical, because the burden was on the buyer to prove the reasonableness of his belief in the seller's assertions.

Perhaps the greatest single barrier to a successful action in deceit was the necessity to prove a misrepresentation of a material fact. Under the traditional interpretation of this requirement a merchant was permitted great latitude in his expressions of opinion as to his product's worth. Because opinions were not facts within the definition of deceit, the seller was afforded an extensive area for exaggeration, or "puffing," of the qualities of his product. This exception for puffing was so liberally interpreted that it permitted the seller every opportunity for misrepresentation short of a direct falsehood about a purely factual aspect of his product, such as its capacity, strength, or composition. A premium was placed on broad generalities and imprecise claims; a claim of "indefinite" product life would be safer than one for a stated period of years. Courts engaged in elaborate discourses in attempting to formulate meaningful divisions between fact and opinion, but these served only to cloud further an already imprecise area.

The cumulative effect of these various burdens of proof and seller defenses was to eliminate completely any consistently effective enforcement of purchasers' rights through an action in deceit. All but the most determined or most seriously injured buyers were discouraged from even instituting a suit, and only a small percentage of those suits that were brought succeeded in surmounting the seemingly endless limitations and restrictions placed on an action in deceit.

A deceived purchaser's other remedy, an action for breach of warranty, was plagued by similar shortcomings. Because the action was in the nature of one in contract, the plaintiff had to demonstrate contractual privity with the advertiser of the deception—frequently a party other than the retailer. Once this rather substantial impediment was overcome, the plaintiff was still faced with all the other burdens and defenses available in an action for deceit, save the necessity to prove *scienter,* or fault. Like deceit, a suit for breach of warranty ordinarily involved only minimal damages.

The most serious shortcoming of the consumer-oriented causes of action was not their difficult burdens of proof but rather their inability to afford widespread and effective consumer protection. The nominal sums involved provided no incentive for individual consumers to bring suit as a policing measure for the market place, and when balanced against the difficulties and expenses inherent in any such suit, the size of the possible recovery often discouraged an otherwise justified action. Further, because the consumer remedies afforded recovery only to the individual purchaser bringing the action, they failed to prevent any future perpetration of the same deceit on other customers. The lack of any sort of general injunctive relief enabled deceptive sellers to continue calculated public deception, knowing that only a very small minority of purchasers would be able to mount successful legal responses, and then only for their individual losses. Because of this serious inadequacy the available forms of consumer protection not only provided ineffective recourse to the injured party, but contributed nothing to the effective regulation of the market place. Actions for deceptive advertising and breach of warranty soon became the rare exceptions to an otherwise consistent insulation of the retailer or advertiser from the natural and injurious consequences of his deceptive trade practices.

COMMERCIAL TORTS

In addition to a general public right not to be deceived as to the nature and quality of goods purchased, the common law also recognized a number of rights, inhering in the individual merchant, which protected innocent sellers from a wrongful diversion of their trade. Almost every form of common law protection against economically tortious competitive practices finds its source in the law of trade-marks. The trade-mark concept itself stemmed from English laws requiring silversmiths to mark their handiwork so as to ensure a proper level of precious metal. The mark of a craftsman quickly became a valuable source of clientele, and silversmiths jealously guarded their symbols from infringement. The earliest forms of trade-mark protection, however, were limited to preventing precise duplication of a mark in an effort to divert trade. This proved to be the easiest remedy to formulate conceptually because of the obvious analogies that could be made to traditional proprietary concepts with respect to the physical mark.

The common law soon came to recognize that a product's popularity was influenced by far more than the appearance of a trade-mark or the functional appeal of the article itself. Commercial intangibles, such as trade names and good will, were acknowledged to occupy much the same status, in terms of value to the merchant in marketing his goods, as the traditional form of trade-mark. The recognitional role played by product shape, color, or variety, by the slogans advertising the goods, and by the methods of servicing existing customers was essential to the establishment of a clientele which returned to the same merchant for future purchases. Similarly, the customer good will created by association with a product having a good reputation in the market place assured the merchant of a receptive purchasing public for his other wares. All of these variables affecting customer disposition were by their very nature highly susceptible to misappropriation and misuse by a seller's competitors. Consequently, a body of law developed, under the generic term of unfair competition, which sought to prevent trade practices that, although short of outright trade-mark infringement, nonetheless enabled merchants to capitalize unjustly on the labors of another. This body of law encompassed such activities as commercial disparagement, "passing off," product simulation, and misappropriation, all of which will be the subject of detailed analysis in later chapters. We shall examine them briefly at this point, however, to demonstrate the inadequacies of common law remedies and the resultant need for some form of government regulation.

Commercial disparagement is an outgrowth of slander of title, an early common law protection for the loss of a sale of realty due to the false allegations of another as to the validity of the title to be conveyed. In a general commercial context the tort covered all false statements reflecting on the quality of a merchant's products or services, where the statements were intended to divert particular trade or generally to damage the business reputation of the merchant. The statements could be made by anyone and still be actionable but usually were made by a competitor. The tort action was used to good effect, however, in preventing disgruntled customers from harassing the merchant's business establishment with derogatory campaigns, such as parking an automobile covered with lemons in front of the dealership where the vehicle was purchased. The tort also required the plaintiff to show actual injuries, but once such a showing was made, injunctive relief was available. Perhaps the most distinctive characteristic of this tort was the necessity to establish malice before any relief could be had. It was this factor, plus the special damages requirement, that distinguished this tort from that of ordinary business defamation. Despite the apparent overlap of the two torts, the inability of corporations to sue for defamation, plus the requirement that a defamation be directed against a person rather than a product, provided substantial need for the remedy afforded by commercial disparagement.

Product simulation and passing off are two aspects of the same form of common law protection. Product simulation is an intentional duplication of the nonfunctional features of a competitor's product for the purpose of creating consumer confusion about the identity and origin of the duplicate. In effect, it is an attempt to trade on some unique stylistic attraction of a competitor's product which has no relevance to the intended function of the product. Passing off involves any affirmative representations or trade-name similarities used by one merchant in an attempt to substitute his product for that of his competitor where a demand or request has been made for the competitor's product. Thus, it will not cover claims by one merchant that his product is just as good as a competitor's, but it will prevent a retailer from supplying a customer with one brand when the customer has requested another or from telling the customer that the two items are identical save for their name. The tort of passing off is intended to cover those situations, short of trade-mark infringement, where a seller has established a considerable market demand for his product under a particular brand name or because of some unique or desirable product feature. Both of these torts seek to prevent specific instances of diversion of trade, but injunctive relief is available where the passing off or product simulation has been a regular course of conduct.

The tort of misappropriation was a relative latecomer, developing in the last years of the nineteenth century as a response to new business techniques and services. As commerce became more sophisticated, industries developed that relied on timeliness, accuracy, and exclusivity for their success rather than any inherent appeal of their particular product. The information industries were the prime example of this and served as the incentive for the development of the misappropriation doctrine. Because they dealt in a service which merely communicated information otherwise in the public domain, their financial success was determined by the degree of protection available for the distribution of the data they accumulated. Problems arose when one information source would use the data of another, rather than its own independent research, in servicing a customer. The issue first arose in the stock market quotation industry and quickly shifted to the wire services as well. The judicial response was a doctrine prohibiting one competitor from using the intangible business inventory of another competitor for his own business purposes. The tort can be traced to a single United States Supreme Court decision in 1918, *International News Service* v. *Associated Press,* where it was both formulated and given its broadest application. The tort is essentially equitable and consequently defies any attempt at definition other than that afforded by the title itself—a businessman may not misappropriate the business of another.

Although this body of commercial torts recognized the valuable property rights inhering in commercial intangibles, the degree of protection afforded these intangibles suffered greatly under substantive and procedural limitations. As a general rule for all of these torts, the competitor was required to demonstrate an actual diversion of trade before he was entitled to relief. It was not enough for him to show that the defendant's present course of conduct would lead to a loss of future sales. This was a far too speculative proposition for the common law courts to accept. Consequently, competitive torts were limited to situations where at least some of the damage had already been done. Once some injury could be shown as stemming from the challenged conduct, an injunction against similar conduct in the future could be obtained, but there was no effective method of stemming deceptive trade practices before they inflicted some injury on the consuming public or the competitive market.

A merchant was also unable to act to protect the general public from being deceived by a trade practice where he could show no injury to himself. The roots of these torts were too firmly bound to protection of personal rights to permit an individual to maintain a course of action on the theory of protecting the general welfare. Although framed largely as a standing to sue question, the problem went to the source of many of the difficulties of the competitive tort—a slavish adherence to ancient notions of personal and property rights which found no meaningful parallel in the modern market place. An inordinate concern with multiplication of suits led courts to deny recovery to anyone who could not show the most direct form of injury from the deceptive conduct. The development of broader concepts of standing, or ability to sue, and better approaches to general consumer protection was left to legislatures which before had been content to ignore the problem. In addition to this general debility which afflicted all of the competitive torts, each tort itself contained several substantive and procedural limitations hampering its effective use. Commercial disparagement required a showing of special, or actual, damages before any relief whatever could be granted. Further, disparagement was addressed to the goods of a merchant rather than to the individual, thereby creating the fundamental distinction from the tort action of defamation. The substantive elements of commercial disparagement required a showing of both falsehood and malice, which was a most difficult proposition where the subject matter was an inanimate product and the milieu an aggressively competitive market place,. Finally, many courts carried over the notion from the law of defamation that equity will not enjoin a libel, thereby eliminating injunctive relief in most instances except those where the disparagement was a single, continuous course of conduct. Thus, a merchant who was careful enough to limit his misleading or disparaging remarks to a competitor's goods was reasonably safe in all but the most outrageous instances.

Product simulation and passing off were inordinately handicapped by the hazy area of secondary meaning, which required that the nonfunctional aspects of a merchant's goods had to have established a secondary meaning, reflecting their origin in the mind of the consuming public, before a duplication of those aspects could lead to a diversion of trade. The burden of establishing this secondary meaning was on the plaintiff as an absolute precondition to any relief whatever. Even where this was accomplished, the defendant could escape by showing some functional use for the copied item or by demonstrating that the diversion of trade resulted from some other aspect of his product not associated with the secondary meaning. This last factor was often referred to as the element of customer confusion, and the likelihood of its occurrence was one of the more difficult elements of a plaintiff's case.

Suit for misappropriation involved an equitable remedy that had little in the way of well-defined boundaries. It was for this precise reason that many courts were loathe to give it any meaningful application. The remedy was devised to meet the peculiar needs of the information industries, and courts made every attempt to so limit it. And even where a case could be made out for misappropriation, usually where it was clear that a lack of relief would lead the plaintiff to cease producing the valuable intangible, the relief granted was ordinarily very limited in scope and short in duration, often being little more than a requirement that the appropriator identify the source of his pirated product. This niggardly dispensation of relief stems from the judicial belief, still current, that any broader protection will invariably afford the plaintiff a monopoly of indefinite duration whereas no such monopoly is available under any of the trade-mark, patent, or copyright statutes.

This is not, of course, to exhaust the possibilities of judicial relief available at common law for unfair or deceptive acts and practices. Industrial sabotage, industrial spying to obtain trade secrets or customer lists, interference with the contractual relationships of others, and the use by a former employee of trade secrets learned while in such employ in competition with the former employer were all subject to a cause of action for damages or injunction. Such activities, however, although redressable, were atypical and actions therefor afforded no relief against the more usual types of unfair competition.

In sum, the commercial torts could best be described as well-intentioned relief which afforded very little protection in actuality. The inability of the consumer effectively to sue for injury already inflicted or to prevent further injury to other consumers relegated this aspect of commercial remedies to a secondary role. The competitive tort, although giving some individualized relief, lacked any industrywide protection or policing of the market place.

STATE LEGISLATION

By the turn of the twentieth century the shortcomings of the existing common law remedies for deceptive trade practices were becoming all too obvious. This country had moved out of the era of localized necessity purchases by reasonably informed buyers and was confronted with a marketing system that relied heavily on mass advertising techniques to sell innumerable luxury goods, as well as necessities, to a relatively unsuspecting public. It had become feasible to market a brand-name product on a national basis, because advances in transportation permitted inexpensive distribution of goods from a central location.

Soon manufacturers of soaps, cereals, cough drops, and canned milk joined the ranks of nationwide advertisers and distributors. As the impact of advertising multiplied throughout the nation, the dangers that false and misleading claims held for consumers and honest competitors became evident.

Journalists, doctors, and advertising men who were concerned with the future of advertising contributed to the exposure and condemnation of the untruthful claims of the quacks and of the inability of the common law consumer and commercial tort actions effectively to deal with them. Samuel Hopkins Adams made a monumental contribution through his famed series of articles on patent medicines that appeared in *Collier's* in 1906. In 1911 the American Medical Association began its series entitled *Nostrums and Quackery*. The response was a public clamor to which the advertising industry began to pay notice. In answer to growing public concern *Printer's Ink* magazine, a trade publication of the advertising industry formulated a model state statute which made a misdemeanor of any advertisement which was untrue, deceptive or misleading. (See Appendix II.)

Although strong in its wording and eventually adopted by forty-four states, the *Printer's Ink* statutes suffered from indifferent and inconsistent enforcement. A somewhat patronizing judiciary favored negotiated settlements under the threat of prosecution to any litigation for violations of the statutes. This tended to return the situation to an individualized approach which failed to obtain the sought-after industrywide compliance with proper trade practices. Perhaps the greatest single contribution of the *Printer's Ink* statutes was the clear demonstration that state by state enforcement, even of a uniform act, was as ineffective a restraint on deceptive trade practices as were common law tort actions. The publicity attendant to the adoption of these statutes, however, together with their ineffectiveness, presented a mandate for action on the federal level.

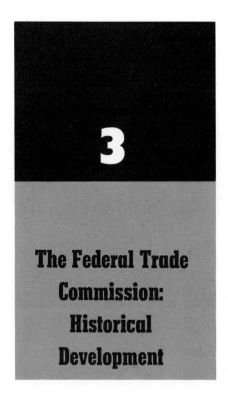

3

The Federal Trade Commission: Historical Development

THE FEDERAL TRADE COMMISSION ACT

Comprehensive federal efforts in the area of unfair and deceptive business practices began with the establishment of the Federal Trade Commission in 1914. The act establishing the commission had been preceded by the Pure Food and Drug Act of 1906, which, however, was of limited application, its principal protection being the requirement of the correct description of the contents of a medicinal product on the package.

As originally enacted, the Federal Trade Commission Act was not intended to deal with the problem of false advertising. Rather the early proponents of the act were interested in the efficient enforcement of the antitrust laws. The "rule of reason" and the apparent hostility of the courts to the Sherman Act had led men like Louis Brandeis to seek a new approach to the enforcement of the antitrust laws. An administrative agency was thought to be in order, and President Wilson vigorously supported the proposal for a trade commission. In 1914 the Federal Trade Commission Act was finally passed, containing in Section 5 this basic prohibition: "Unfair methods of competition in commerce are hereby declared unlawful."

The language employed in Section 5 suggested to many that the prohibition was limited to the enforcement of the antimonopoly policy of the federal government. As was stated in the first definitive treatise on the Federal Trade Commission, the FTC's jurisdiction over advertising was a "fortuitous by-product." If Congress had been concerned with the problem of false advertising, the author of the treatise suggested, it would have passed a different type of statute with a different procedural and regulatory scheme. Those favoring a broad interpretation of the commission's power argued that the boundaries of the statutory prohibition had been deliberately left undefined by the sponsors of the act. Mr. Justice Brandeis explained the basic theory of the proponents of a broad interpretation as follows:

> Instead of undertaking to define what practices should be deemed unfair as had been done in earlier legislation, the act left the determination to the commission. Experience with existing laws had taught that definition, being necessarily rigid, would prove embarrassing, and, if rigorously applied, might involve great hardship. Methods of competition which would be unfair in one industry, under certain circumstances, might, when adopted in another industry, or even in the same industry under different circumstances, be entirely unobjectionable.
>
> Furthermore, an enumeration, however comprehensive, of existing methods of unfair competition must necessarily soon prove incomplete, as with new conditions constantly arising novel unfair methods would be devised and developed.

Whatever the view held by the sponsors of the original act may have been, the first few Federal Trade commissioners almost immediately concerned themselves with false advertising. In its Second Annual Report, the commission stated:

> The Commission has made no attempt to define what methods of competition are "unfair" so that "a proceeding by it in respect thereof would be to the interest of the public." Unfair competition, like "fraud," "due care," "unjust discrimination," and many other familiar concepts in the law, is incapable of exact definition, but its underlying principle is clear—a principle sufficiently elastic to cover all future unconscionable competitive practices in whatever form they may appear, provided they sufficiently affect the public interest. Thus far the Commission has been of the opinion that at least those cases in

which the method of competition restrains trade, substantially lessens competition, or tends to create a monopoly are subject to a proceeding under section 5 of the Federal Trade Commission Act. *The Commission has gone further than this, however, and in some instances where these elements did not appear, as in certain cases of misbranding and falsely advertising the character of goods where the public was particularly liable to be misled, the Commission has taken jurisdiction.* [Emphasis added.]

In fact, the first two cease and desist orders isued by the commission proscribed certain false and misleading advertising practices. The commission's first formal order proscribing the deceptive advertising of a drug was issued in 1918. Moreover, the first commission order reviewed by a court involved the false advertising of food, and as early as 1922 the United States Supreme Court approved a commission order to cease and desist from deceptive advertising. It has been estimated that as early as 1925, orders directed against false and misleading advertising constituted 75 per cent of all orders issued by the commission each year.

It is interesting to note that the commission's jurisdiction over false advertising became indisputable during a period in which those commission functions most desired by the proponents of a trade commission—the antimonopoly powers—were being thwarted by judicial hostility. Thus, only forty-three commission orders out of a total of eighty-two reviewed on their merits by the courts up until 1931 were either entirely or substantially upheld, but twenty-two of the twenty-nine FTC orders concerning false advertising reviewed by the courts in the same period were upheld.

THE EXPANSION OF FTC JURISDICTION AND ENFORCEMENT POWERS

Although commission jurisdiction over false advertising was established beyond doubt, one important question remained unresolved. The statute proscribed "unfair methods of competition." Commission action was clearly authorized when a company was injured by the false or misleading advertising of a competitor; but did the commission have jurisdiction to proceed against advertising misleading to the public when injury to a competing company could not be shown? For the commission to serve as a guardian of informed, intelligent choice which, as has been suggested, is imperative to our economic order, the answer to this question would have to be in the affirmative. No answer was provided by the twenty-nine cases prior to 1931 in which commission cease and desist orders were reviewed. In none of the twenty-two cases in which an order of the commission had been upheld was the decision specifically grounded on a finding that honest competition had been injured by the proscribed advertising. On the other hand, in at least one of the cases in which the commission was reversed, the order was set aside on the ground that the misrepresentation had no tendency to injure competition.

In the famous case of *FTC* v. *Raladam Co.,* the Supreme Court was squarely confronted with the issue of whether it was necessary to show, as a prerequisite to FTC jurisdiction to take action against a false advertising practice, that the practice had an adverse effect on competition. In a unanimous decision the Court held that the commission was without jurisdiction to issue an order prohibiting false advertising without proof that the advertisement affected competitors, even though the advertisement admittedly deceived the public. The *Raladam* decision struck a hard blow because it not only limited the scope of FTC enforcement powers, but also attacked the very base of economic democracy. Agitation soon developed for Congressional action to broaden the FTC's power to enable the commission to protect the consuming public as well as honest competitors. The fruit of this agitation was the passage in 1938 of the Wheeler-Lea amendments to the Federal Trade Commission Act. Section 5 of the act now reads: "Unfair methods of competition in commerce *and unfair or deceptive acts or practices in commerce,* are hereby declared unlawful." [Emphasis supplied.] By the addition of the italicized language, the previous emphasis on protection of competition was abandoned and the commission was granted a broader basis from which to police false advertisers. As stated by the United States Third Circuit Court of Appeals, in *Pep Boys—Manny, Moe & Jack* v. *FTC:*

> The failure to mention competition in the latter phrase ["unfair or deceptive acts or practices in commerce"] shows a legislative intent to remove the procedural requirement set up in the Raladam case and the Commission can now center its attention on the direct *protection of the consumer* where formerly it could protect him only indirectly through the protection of the competitor. The logic of the present trend of the law is apparent when we realize how helpless the Commission would be under the rule of the Raladam case where all the competitors in the industry were using the same practice or where the offender had a monopoly in a field which did not compete with any other field. [Emphasis in original.]

That the commission was to have a role in guaranteeing informed and intelligent consumer choice was confirmed by Senator Wheeler, a co-author of the amendment, who said, "Broadly speaking, this legislation is designed to give the Federal Trade Commission jurisidiction over unfair acts and practices for consumer protection to the same extent that it now has jurisdiction over unfair methods of competition for the protection of competitors."

The 1938 amendments also enlarged the Federal Trade Commission Act by adding Section 12, which declares certain advertisements of foods, drugs, medical devices, and cosmetics to be "unfair or deceptive acts or practices in commerce" within the meaning of Section 5, and by providing important new procedural weapons for the commission's use in its war on false advertising. The commission's effectiveness had previously been hampered by a lack of effective penalties and by the delay involved in actually accomplishing a termination of the misleading practices whenever the advertiser insisted on contesting the commission's action. To remedy this situation, the 1938 amendments added the following three procedures and penalties, of which the last two apply only in cases involving food, drugs, medical devices and cosmetics.

1. If no court review is sought within sixty days of a commission order to cease and desist, the order becomes final; violation of a final order may result in a penalty up to $5,000. (In a 1950 amendment, each day was determined to constitute a separate violation.)

2. Where the advertisement is likely to induce the purchase of a commodity injurious to health or where there is intent to defraud, a criminal proceeding may be instituted, with fines up to $5,000 and imprisonment up to six months.

3. The commission may require a temporary injunction against the dissemination of false information about foods, drugs, medical devices, and cosmetics, pending a final determination by the commission and subsequent court review. (The FTC has no temporary injunction powers as to false advertising in general.)

Congressional action in the false-advertising field did not end with the Wheeler-Lea amendments. In 1939 Congress passed the Wool Products Labeling Act, an enactment that substantially enlarged commission authority to proceed against the false advertising of wool products sold in interstate commerce. Modeled on the Food, Drug, and Cosmetic Act, the Wool Act prohibits the introduction or the manufacture for introduction into interstate commerce of a wool product "misbranded" in that it does not bear a label as required by the act or bears a false label. The required label must remain affixed to the product until it is sold to the consumer. Cease and desist order proceedings, authority to obtain temporary injunctions in the district courts, criminal prosecution, and product seizure and condemnation suits in the federal district courts were provided for enforcement of this act. In addition, Congress in 1950 amended Section 15 of the Federal Trade Commission Act to provide that advertisements of margarine are to be deemed misleading in a material respect if "representations are made or suggested that such oleomargarine or margarine is a dairy product." A provision of general significance in the same amendment substantially strengthened the FTC cease and desist order by stating that a separate violation could be found for each day the violation of a final order continued; the penalty for each such violation could be a fine as much as $5,000.

The success of the Wool Act, together with the existence of widespread misrepresentations in the labeling of fur products, led to the Fur Products Labeling Act of 1951. This act prohibited the false advertising of fur products and required informative advertising in addition to informative labeling. The Flammable Fabrics Act, passed in 1953, authorized the commission to protect the consumer from fabrics and wearing apparel with flammability exceeding prescribed limits. Finally, in 1958 Congress enacted the most comprehensive of all the specialized product statutes enforced by the commission, the Textile Fiber Products Identification Act, which requires informative advertising as well as informative labeling and applies extensively to retail activities involving products that have been shipped in interstate commerce. Enforcement is provided by the typical means: cease and desist orders, product seizures, criminal prosecutions, and temporary injunctions.

Two recent statutes dealing with fair packaging and truth in lending have also added to the commission's arsenal of consumer protection weaponry. These statutes will be dealt with in detail in subsequent chapters, and the text of both acts are reprinted in the appendixes. As will be seen, the acts are basically disclosure statutes, requiring understandable descriptions of the size and amount of the products in the first statute and details, such as the exact interest to be charged, in the second.

It is thus readily apparent that commission authority to eliminate deception and to provide consumers with the information necessary to make intelligent choices among competing goods has changed considerably since 1914. General legislation, such as the Wheeler-Lea amendments to Section 5 of the Federal Trade Commission Act and the penalty provisions added to that act in 1950, has provided a wider jurisdictional basis and broader enforcement powers for commission action. Moreover, specialized legislation concerning such products as food, drugs, medical devices, cosmetics, oleomargarine, and wool and fur products has served to make the definition of deceptive advertising for these goods more specific, and, therefore, to make violations of Section 5 relative to such products more easily discovered and prosecuted.

As will be seen in subsequent chapters, the response of the commission, within the ambit of its expanded jurisdiction, to the challenge posed by the misuse of advertising techniques has been an impressive contribution to the elevation of business standards. Business improprieties still exist, but we have come a long way from the days of Dr. Scott's Electric Corset. Although the buyer must still beware, the seller now must also beware.

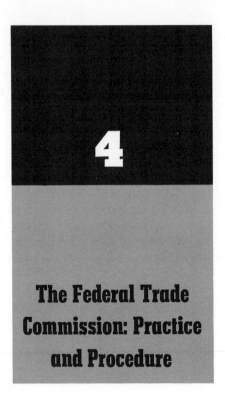

4

The Federal Trade Commission: Practice and Procedure

As we have seen, the principal enforcing agency of the laws against unfair and deceptive business practices is the Federal Trade Commission, which was established by Congress in 1914 as an independent regulatory agency. The commission is composed of five commissioners, appointed by the President and confirmed by the Senate for terms of seven years. No more than three commissioners may be members of the same political party. Since 1950 the President has by law designated one of the comis-sioners to serve as chairman. The chairman has broad authority over commission personnel, including appointments and promotions. The chairman, subject to the policy guidance of his four colleagues, also has broad authority over the use and expenditure of funds and the distribu-tion of business within the commission. Under the direction of the chair-man, the Executive Director is the chief administrative officer, exercising supervisory authority over the various offices within the commission and over the staff of the commission. The Secretary of the commission has responsibility for the commission's correspondence and records. The General Counsel is the commission's chief legal expert. His office is responsible for representing the commission in the federal courts, preparing legal memoranda, and advising the commission. An Economic Adviser, an Office of Congressional Relations, and the Office of Public Information report directly to the Chairman. There also are an Office of Policy Planning and Evaluation and an Office of Hearing Examiners. The latter office provides the FTC's independent administrative judges for the formal proceedings.

Effective July 1, 1970, the work of the commission was divided into two main areas, that of antitrust and restraint of trade matters, under the title of the Bureau of Competition, and a Bureau of Consumer Protection, which is an expanded version of the former Bureau of Deceptive Practices.

The Bureau of Competition, which largely includes the work done by the former Bureau of Restraint of Trade, is headed by a director and seven assistants who supervise the following divisions: Accounting, Compliance, Evaluation, General Litigation, Industry Guidance, Small Business, and Special Projects.

The Bureau of Consumer Protection is subdivided into nine separate areas, each supervised by an assistant director. The divisions are the following: Compliance, Consumer Education, Evaluation, Food and Drug Advertising, General Litigation, Industry Guidance, Scientific Opinions, Special Projects, and Textiles and Furs.

A third operating bureau, the Bureau of Economics, performs the same work as in the past, allocated to three divisions: Economic Evidence, Financial Statistics, and Industry Analysis.

The commission's employees total over 1,200, of which nearly 500 are attorneys and 125 are other professional personnel. The FTC's headquarters is in Washington, D.C., but more than 300 employees are located in eleven field offices throughout the country, in the following places: Atlanta, Boston, Chicago, Cleveland, Kansas City, Los Angeles, New Orleans, New York, San Francisco, Seattle, and the Washington, D.C. area. In addition to their traditional investigative role, these field offices also may handle the trial of some formal cases. They also coordinate local consumer protection work, including participating actively in consumer councils.

Violations of the law are brought to the commission's attention in a variety of ways. Letters are received from consumers, business competitors, suppliers, and customers, sometimes directly, sometimes from other agencies of the government. The procedure for filing a complaint is informal. All that is necessary is a letter to the commission detailing the facts believed to constitute a violation of the law.

The commission possesses extremely broad investigative powers under the Federal Trade Commission Act. This act provides the commission with the power of access to documentary evidence, the authority to require annual and special reports from any firm, and the power of subpoena. The power to require special reports from corporations has been exercised in several ways during the history of the commission. Reports have been used to gather information for the *Quarterly Financial Report for Manufacturing Corporations,* prepared jointly by the Federal Trade Commission and the Securities and Exchange Commission. Extensive use of this special report power has been made in connection with general economic surveys conducted by the commission. Special reports have also been used to gather data in the trial of specific cases, as well as to investigate compliance with outstanding cease and desist orders under Section 5 of the Federal Trade Commission Act. In recent years the commission has used its special report power to conduct general investigations of alleged widespread violations of the laws throughout an entire industry.

When a possible violation of the law comes to the commission's attention, either through its own investigation or through one of the media just mentioned, the procedures for enforcement are varied and flexible. The Federal Trade Commission Act provides that if it appears that a formal proceeding would be in the interest of the public, the commission may issue a complaint against the alleged offender and set a hearing date. Such hearings are conducted before hearing examiners, who serve as administrative trial judges, and the proceedings are similar to those employed in federal courts. The rules of evidence are somewhat relaxed in such hearings, yet they remain subject to due process requirements of fairness. The respondent is given an opportunity to cross-examine witnesses and to present evidence in rebuttal. After the hearings are completed and evidence has been received from the commission's lawyers and the lawyers representing the respondent, the hearing examiner makes an initial decision. This decision becomes final if not appealed or modified by the commission. If the initial decision is appealed to the full commission for review, or if the commission reviews the matter of its own volition, the commission may modify the order in any way it sees fit. If the decision is against the respondent, the commission may issue an order to cease and desist. Such an order is like an injunction and remains in effect indefinitely, unless later modified or dismissed for reasons of changes in the circumstances of fact or law. If the order is violated, the respondent may be prosecuted in a federal district court for civil penalties, which may run as high as $5,000 for each violation, with each day of a continuing violation counting as a separate offense. A cease and desist order does not become final until sixty days after it has been served on the respondent. During this period the respondent may appeal to a federal cour of appeals. Before such courts the commission's findings regarding the facts are conclusive if supported by substantial evidence. Cease and desist orders include a provision that respondents file, within sixty days from the date of the service of the order, a report of compliance setting forth the manner of compliance.

The commission seeks to encourage compliance with the requirements of the laws it administers by a number of means other than the formal proceedings just outlined, as informal techniques may be quicker, cheaper, and equally effective. These methods include administrative treatment, trade practices conferences, trade regulation rules, the issuance of guides, advisory opinions, and consent settlement procedures. It is important to note that there is a commission policy of effecting industrywide compliance, whenever possible or practicable, if alleged violations of law are extensive. This policy is a most important one in the agency's current program.

Administrative treatment is the simplest and one of the newest of the informal methods and is used by the commission chiefly in the area of misrepresentation through advertising. Letters of discontinuance or affidavits signed by responsible officials of the offending concern, accompanied by evidence of compliance with the law and assurance that the questioned practices will not be resumed, are accepted in settlement of many smaller infractions. In this connection it is important to note that currently the commission's eleven field offices have authority in proper instances to accept administrative settlements of alleged violations. However, the field office must obtain enough facts to disclose a probable violation and may not accept a settlement tendered by a businessman seeking to avoid further government involvement without regard to whether the facts indicate that a violation has occurred. The rules state, "In determining whether the public interest will be fully safeguarded through such informal administrative treatment, the Commission will consider (1) the nature and gravity of the alleged violation; (2) the prior record of good faith of the parties involved; and (3) other factors, including, where appropriate, adequate assurance that the practice has been discontinued and will not be resumed."

In 1962 provision was made for issuance of trade regulation rules applicable to unlawful trade practices. These rules are designed to express the judgment of the commission, based on facts of which it has knowledge derived from its past experience, regarding practices clearly violative of the law. Such rules may be sharply limited to particular areas of industries or to particular product or geographic areas, as appropriate. Provision is made for reliance on these rules in litigated cases if the respondent is given a fair hearing on the legality and propriety of applying a particular rule to a particular case. Also, there is the usual provision for formal due process procedures prior to the final issuance of the rules. Rules of this nature increasingly are being used by the commission to solve industrywide problems.

For many years the commission has provided procedures for trade practice conferences upon the application of businessmen and their trade associations in a particular industry or upon the commission's own motion. If the commission concludes that such a conference would be useful and proper, notice is given to members of the industry concerned. They and other interested parties appear and freely express their views regarding practices prevalent in the industry, practices that perhaps should be eliminated. Such conferences may, where appropriate, voluntarily repudiate widespread illegal practices in a particular industry. Conferences always involve formal trade practice rules with which members of a given industry may signify their willingness to comply. Recently such trade conference procedures have been merged into the industry guides program. Compliance with such rules is not permissive, because they express what the law already prohibits. Other rules, which the members of an industry may voluntarily agree to follow, condemn practices that the particular industry deems to be harmful or unethical even though such practices are not illegal. Trade practice rules, upon adoption, on occasion have become the basis for settlement of investigative matters pending against members of the industry concerned.

In recent years the commission has published a series of guides in an effort to make clear to businessmen which practices are prohibited by law and should be avoided. These guides are also useful to the consumer in educating him to the dangers of bait advertising, false guarantees, and fictitious bargain prices. Guides, unlike the trade practice rules, may deal with practices common to many industries. Although preparation of informative and accurate guides is not an overnight task, there is no necessity for hearings or conferences concerning them. The guides are not intended to cover gaps in the law by dealing with situations that have not yet come before the courts or before the commission. Rather they set forth in easily understood language the principles already established by the courts and the commission in decided cases. Their purpose is to give the businessman some knowledge of what the law requires of him. Additionally, the guides, by delineating areas of potential trouble, should alert the businessman to consult his lawyer when a problem arises and before a violation of law occurs. The commission has sought the greatest publicity for its guides in an effort to reach as many businessmen as possible. Copies are available from the commission without charge. Two of the guides, those on cigarette advertising and tire advertising, deal with deceptive practices in specific industries. Others—including the *Guides Against Deceptive Pricing,* the *Guides Against Bait Advertising,* and the *Guides Against Deceptive Advertising of Guarantees*—deal with deceptive practices that may arise in the preparation of many types of advertising copy. The reception these guides have received is a testimony to their educational value. The trade practice rules and guides, together with special conferences called by the commission staff from time to time, are all designed to educate businessmen in the requirements of the law and to encourage them to avoid illegal practices.

In this age of increasing corporate complexity it is often extremely difficult for businessmen and their legal counsel to determine accurately the legality of proposed business action. Some assistance may be obtained by seeking an advisory opinion from the commission. Informal advice may be obtained from members of the commission's staff or from its eleven field offices. Although such advice is not binding on the commission in regard to future activity of the requesting party, such advice will normally allow the businessman to proceed with greater certainty.

In connection with the advisory opinion procedure it is important to note the circumstances in which the commission will not give advice:

(1) where the course of action is already being followed by the requesting party; (2) where the same or substantially the same course of action is under investigation or is the subject of a current proceeding by the Commission against the requesting party; (3) where the same or substantially the same course of action is under investigation or is or has been the subject of a proceeding, order or decree initiated or obtained by another government agency against the requesting party; or (4) where the proposed course of action is such that an informed decision thereon could be made only after extensive investigation, clinical study, testing or collateral inquiry.

Texts or digests of advisory opinions of general interest may be published "subject to statutory restrictions against disclosure of trade secrets and names of customers and to considerations of the confidentiality of facts involved and of meritorious òbjections made by the requesting party to such publication." (Selected advisory opinions in the area of unfair and deceptive business practices are contained in Appendix XIV of this book.)

Finally, the commission may employ the consent decree procedure to halt illegal practices. Following notification by the commission of its determination to issue a complaint, a party may indicate to the commission its willingness to have the proceedings disposed of by the entry of an order. The consent decree, by which the objectionable practices may be effectively prohibited, is negotiated currently with the trial and investigative staff, advised in this connection by the general counsel. If an agreement is approved by the commission, the complaint and proposed order will be issued. If the proposed consent settlement is rejected, the complaint is issued and the matter set down for adjudication in regular course.

The commission shares with other agencies the job of enforcing many of the laws for which it is responsible. Many practices at the same time violate laws with whose enforcement the commission is charged and laws for which another agency is responsible. In such a case the practice in question could be attacked by either enforcement agency. Although many have criticized this dual enforcement, the intersection of regulatory activity by two or more government agencies need not cause overlapping of effort, undue harassment of the industries regulated, or constant jurisdictional quarrels. The Federal Trade Commission and other agencies responsible for preventing certain practices have long worked to eliminate all of these possible dangers. Thus, since World War II working agreements setting forth the primary responsibilities of each agency, the areas of sole jurisdiction, the policies governing duplication of proceedings, and the nature of liaison between the agencies have been concluded with these other agencies.

Exemplary of these working relationships is the one prevailing between the commission and the Antitrust Division of the Department of Justice in the antitrust area. This relationship has been characterized by willing interchange of information, avoidance of the duplication of effort, and careful assignment of cases to the agency whose action will be likely to do the most good. At the same time, in recognition of their mutual and separate responsibilities, each agency has preserved its individual freedom to take independent action whenever it believes it to be necessary. A closer examination of the nature of the relationship now prevailing between the commission and the Antitrust Division of Justice illustrates the practical way in which dual enforcement operates.

To avoid duplication of enforcement efforts an elaborate system of notification and negotiation has been worked out. If either agency begins an investigation, the other agency is promptly notified. If the commission schedules a trade practice conference, the division is immediately informed. If the agency notified has any objections, a conference is held to effect a workable compromise. Although each agency retains its right to initiate separate proceedings, in practice their working agreement has wholly prevented wasteful duplication. Similarly, only rarely will either the division or the commission institute action when a private suit has been brought against the same conduct.

This working relationship is obviously tailored to avoid duplication of enforcement effort. Prior expertise is utilized whenever possible, and other means of increasing the effectiveness of both agencies are readily embraced. The system has been remarkably effective in practice, and this alone is a tribute to the practical bent of those charged with the enforcement of the antitrust and unfair trade practice laws. Similar working arrangements between the commission and the Food and Drug Administration, the Federal Communications Commission, and the Post Office Department have been equally successful. It would appear, therefore, that there is little to fear from multiple enforcement and a great deal to be gained.

5

General Principles

Before turning to a consideration of the specific misrepresentations that the FTC and the courts have held to constitute unfair or deceptive business practices, it would seem appropriate to identify certain basic rules that govern all advertising. These may be summarized as follows:

1. *Tendency to deceive.* The FTC is empowered to act when representations have only a tendency to mislead or deceive. Proof of actual deception is not essential, although evidence of actual deception is apparently conclusive as to the deceptive quality of the advertisement in question.

2. *Immateriality of knowledge of falsity.* Because a basic purpose of the Federal Trade Commission Act is consumer protection, the government does not have to prove knowledge of falsity on the part of the advertiser; the businessman acts at his peril.

3. *Immateriality of intent.* The intent of the advertiser is also entirely

immaterial. An advertiser may possess a wholly innocent intent and still violate the law.

4. *Literal truthfulness.* Because the purpose of the law is to protect the consumer and some consumers are "ignorant, unthinking and credulous," nothing less than "the most literal truthfulness" is tolerated. Thus it is immaterial that an expert reader might be able to decipher the advertisement in question.

5. *Literal truth sometimes insufficient.* Advertisements are not intended to be carefully dissected with a dictionary at hand, but rather to produce an over-all impression on the ordinary purchaser. An advertiser cannot present one over-all impression yet protect himself by presenting a contrary impression in a small and inconspicuous portion of the advertisement. Even though every sentence considered separately is true, the advertisement as a whole may be misleading because factors are omitted or the message is composed in a misleading way.

6. *Ambiguous advertisements interpreted to effect purposes of the law.* Because the purpose of the law is the prohibition of advertising having a tendency and capacity to mislead, an advertisement that can be read to have two meanings is illegal if one of them is false or misleading.

TENDENCY TO DECEIVE

It is standard dogma that proof of actual deception is not essential for the invocation of FTC jurisdiction. In *Bockenstette* v. *FTC,* the respondent, a hatchery, had advertised its chickens as "R.O.P. chickens." R.O.P. had a well-defined meaning in the trade as one who belonged to a certain association, subscribed to its rules, and produced eggs and chickens according to its rules. On appeal to the United States Tenth Circuit Court of Appeals, the respondent claimed that the FTC cease and desist order was improper because there was no evidence in the record of anyone's having been deceived. In upholding the FTC order, the court said, "It is not necessary, however, for the Commission to find that actual deception resulted. It is sufficient to find that the natural and probable result of the challenged practice is to cause one to do that which he would not otherwise do."

The United States Second Circuit Court of Appeals held to the same effect in *Charles of the Ritz Distributors Corp.* v. *FTC.* The case, which involved an FTC action against a manufacturer for representing its product as capable of restoring a youthful appearance to the skin, resulted in an FTC order directing excision of the word *rejuvenescence* from the label of the product. To the respondent's argument on appeal that the FTC did not "produce customers to testify to their deception," the court replied that "actual deception of the public need not be shown in Federal Trade Commission proceedings. . . . Representations merely having a 'capacity to deceive' are unlawful."

Although proof of actual deception is not essential, testimony of dissatisfied customers is apparently conclusive as to the deceptive quality of the advertisement in question. Such testimony has also been held to satisfy two other jurisdictional requirements in an FTC action alleging unfair or deceptive business practices, first, the public interest requirement, and second, the materiality of the claim. Thus, in the *Buchsbaum* case the United States Seventh Circuit Court of Appeals, although conceding that there must be a "showing that the acts and practices sought to be proscribed are detrimental to the public interest," concluded that the testimony of a single dissatisfied customer would satisfy that requirement. The FTC had held deceptive the marketing of Vinylite, a substance resembling glass, under the name of Elasti-Glass. The customer produced at trial testified that he thought he was buying a glass product, where, in fact, he was not.

Similarly, although the representation must be of a "fact which would constitute a material factor in a purchaser's decision whether to buy," the courts have consistently affirmed broad FTC discretion in determining materiality. Perhaps the leading case on this point is *FTC* v. *Mary Carter Paint Co.,* in which the United States Supreme Court upheld an FTC order based on a finding that "buy one gallon for $6.98 and get a second gallon free" offer was deceptive. The respondent, a relatively small paint company, claimed that it utilized this marketing scheme to compete with its larger national competitors, who normally sold paint for $6.98 per gallon. It claimed that if it sold for half the price the public would not purchase its paint, which was just as good as that of its national competitors, for fear it was of inferior quality. While noting that because Mary Carter had never offered to sell paint by the single can, the representations might mean no more than "that Mary Carter has no usual and customary price for single cans of paint," the Supreme Court affirmed the FTC finding that the representation was false because it implied that the two for one offer meant that the price advertised was the "usual and customary" one for the single offer, whereas $6.98 was not in fact the "usual and customary price" for a single gallon. As in the public interest requirement, testimony of a single dissatisfied customer, although not essential, seems conclusive evidence of the materiality of a falsehood in affecting purchasing decisions.

On the other hand, if customer dissatisfaction were the sole criterion of the occurrence of an unfair or deceptive business practice, the informative function of advertising would encounter insurmountable obstacles. Products are marketed with statements of the seller's opinion which may, and often do, take the form of an overstatement of the qualities and value of the product. If every such statement of opinion could serve as the basis of a lawsuit by a dissatisfied customer, competitive advertising would be disrupted, comparative information about competing products would become unavailable, and informed consumer choice would be impossible. For this reason, and because some exaggeration is to be expected, the sales talk or *puffing* exception to the unlawfulness of false or misleading statements has become well recognized by courts and the FTC. Mr. Justice Holmes expressed the rationale of the rule as follows: "The rule of law is hardly to be regretted, when it is considered how easily and insensibly words of hope or expectation are converted by an interested memory into statements of quality and value when the expectation has been disappointed." Numerous cases affirm the exemption from the laws of unfair or deceptive business practices of mere statements of opinion, sales talk, or puffing.

Thus, the picturization of a seller's mattress that exaggerated its elasticity and resiliency by showing one end open with the filling expanding, beyond the uncut surface, some six times more than that which it could actually expand when unrestrained, was held to be "slight puffing" and a "proper trade practice."

A more concrete representation can be "mere puffery" also, when because of its generality and wide variety of meaning it would be unlikely to deceive anyone factually. A toothpaste purported to "brighten and whiten teeth" was not deceptively advertised though it could have no effect on inherent coloration or original luster. And a "common term" like *perfect,* meaning "nothing more than that the product is good or of high quality," is a permissible description of a lubricant. Although "there is nothing 'perfect' in this world," the use of the word did not have the capacity to deceive.

The superlative *best* is a good example of a claim that need not be taken literally. One commentator has observed, it refers to absolute rather than comparative quality and may be treated as "harmless hyperbole." Clearly, however, it is misdescriptive and prohibitable as "unfair" when it refers to merchandise purchased from junk dealers and which is worn, dirty, valueless, and not the "best in the market."

Even a *false* assertion of uniqueness has been dismissed as "mere puffery" where there was no evidence that the purchasing public had been led to believe that Celanese yarns and fabrics were anything but rayon. The FTC had ruled that the products of the Celanese Corporation must be classified as *rayon,* a term which it would have liked to avoid. Nevertheless, what the company did claim for its product in an attempt to distinguish it from rayon ("different from any type of fabric ever made," "like nothing you have ever known," "qualities that put it in a class by itself") was permitted as seller's expansiveness even though a functional uniqueness for Celanese yarns was unwarranted.

In some instances, "dealer's talk" is not so easily disposed of by the FTC. For example, a swimming aid, designed to be worn beneath the bathing suit, had been advertised as "invisible." The term was examined with great care before that part of the complaint was dismissed as harmless puffing. Not, however, without a pragmatic dissent which, in light of another representation that the wearer would "look like a champion" swimmer, approached the claim from the standpoint of the nonswimmer hoping to deceive the world about his lack of ability. If his hips are elevated by the device (inflated beneath his suit) and the rest of his body is depressed, he could hardly look like a champion!

The descriptive word *easy* which at common law would clearly be held to be legitimate puffing, has given the FTC some difficulty. Because it is a term of comparative or relative connotation, a weight-reducing plan based on eating the advertiser's candy before a meal to curb the appetite is "comparatively simple, comparatively easy," and must be regarded as mere puffing. On the other hand, where the descriptive *easy* is material in inducing the purchase of a home-study course in reweaving or where there might be purchasers who would be misled because what is "easy" to some is not "easy" to others, the use of the word has been condemned.

Finally, the FTC has been less prone to accept the puffing defense with regard to products potentially dangerous to health and life but represented as "safe" or "simple" to use. Thus a portable oxygen administrator, intended for sale to the general public, was found not to be safe in unskilled hands or when improperly stored, and use of the word *safe* was ordered discontinued. Many similar decisions exist with reference to power tools. Neither can *safe and simple* be held to be mere puffing when such a representation in an advertisement is inconsistent with, negates, and contradicts the hazard warnings on product labels.

IMMATERIALITY OF KNOWLEDGE OF FALSITY

Numerous cases attest to the fact that the motive or innocence of a misrepresentation is irrelevant in a suit by the FTC alleging deceptive business practices. Because a major purpose of the act is consumer protection, the government does not have to prove knowledge of falsity on the part of the advertiser; rather the businessman acts at his peril. Thus, in *D.D.D. Corporation* v. *FTC,* the United States Seventh Circuit Court of Appeals upheld an FTC order prohibiting the following advertisement: "For the itching of skin irritations such as rashes, hives . . . D.D.D. Liquid, ordinary strength, is recommended as an effective and ideal remedy." The respondents' argument on appeal that the advertisement was innocent because they did not apprehend its falsity was rejected by the court, which observed, "they must extricate themselves from it by purging their business methods of a capacity to deceive."

IMMATERIALITY OF INTENT

Similarly, intent, in the sense of an innocent motive of the advertiser, is generally held to be irrelevant in FTC deceptive advertising cases. An advertiser can have a wholly innocent intent, or innocently intend one meaning for an advertisement rather than another, and still violate the law. Illustratively, in the *Bockenstette* case a challenged advertisement read: "4 Weeks' insurance chick buyers' protection against losses up to 4 weeks." The respondent claimed that it did not intend by the advertisement to indemnify for *all* losses for four weeks and that it would require "a tremendous stretch of the imagination to give [the advertisement] . . . such a meaning." In holding the advertisement deceptive and the innocent intent of the advertiser irrelevant, the court said, "It appears to us that it would require a breakable stretch of the imagination to conclude that this language meant anything other than that it insured against all loss for four weeks." On the other hand, in a few cases the FTC has suggested that actual evidence of evil intent might be determinative in an otherwise close case.

GENERAL PUBLIC'S UNDERSTANDING

Because a cardinal purpose of the laws against deceptive business practices is protection of the consumer and because some consumers are "ignorant, unthinking and credulous," nothing less than the most literal truthfulness is tolerated. It is immaterial that an expert, or even average, reader might be able to decipher the advertisement in question so as to avoid being misled. Two leading cases illustrate this principle.

In *FTC* v. *Standard Education Society* the commission attacked representations to prospective purchasers of encyclopedias that because of the publisher's desire to place in the hands of selected representative people (for advertising purposes) encyclopedias, the publishers would as-

sess no charges for the encyclopedias themselves but only for the ten-year extension service. In fact, the price to be charged for the extension service was identical to the price for the encyclopedias and the extension service. Reversing the commission's finding of a deceptive business practice, the court of appeals said that no one could be "fatuous enough to be misled by the mere statement that the first are given away, and that he is paying only for the second."

In reversing the court of appeals, the United States Supreme Court held that "the fact that a false statement may be obviously false to those who are trained and experienced does not change its character, nor take away its power to deceive others less experienced." The Court continued:

> There is no duty resting on a citizen to suspect the honesty of those with whom he transacts business. Laws are made to protect the trusting as well as the suspicious. The best element of business has long since decided that honesty should govern competitive enterprises, and that the rule of *caveat emptor* should not be relied upon to reward fraud and deception.

Similarly, in *Charles of the Ritz Distributors Corp.* v. *FTC* the United States Second Circuit Court of Appeals rejected the argument of a respondent appealing from an FTC cease and desist order, that "since no straight-thinking person would believe that its cream would actually rejuvenate, there could be no deception." According to the court, the Federal Trade Commission Act was not "made for the protection of experts, but for the public—that vast multitude which includes the ignorant, the unthinking and the credulous," and the "fact that a false statement may be obviously false to those who are trained and experienced does not change its character, nor take away its power to deceive others less experienced." The court continued:

> The important criterion is the net impression which the advertisement is likely to make upon the general populace. . . . And, while the wise and the worldly may well realize the falsity of any representations that the present product can roll back the years, there remains "that vast multitude" of others who, like Ponce de Leon, still seek a perpetual fountain of youth. As the Commission's expert further testified, the average woman, conditioned by talk in magazines and over the radio of "vitamins, hormones, and God knows what," might take "rejuvenesence" to mean that this "is one of the modern miracles" and is "something which would actually cause her youth to be restored." It is for this reason that the Commission may "insist upon the most literal truthfulness" in advertisements, . . . and should have the discretion, undisturbed by the courts, to insist if it chooses "upon a form of advertising clear enough so that, in the words of the prophet Isaiah 'wayfaring men, though fools shall not enter therein.'"

LITERAL TRUTH SOMETIMES INSUFFICIENT

Although literal truth may be required by the FTC, even that may be deceptive, and therefore unlawful, if the truthful assertions are so combined as to impart a misleading impression on a casual reading. Thus, in *Kalwajtys* v. *FTC* the United States Seventh Circuit Court of Appeals affirmed an order directing a respondent to cease and desist from representing to prospective buyers of photograph albums and certificates for photographs that respondents sold only to selected persons, that albums were given free, and that the prices at which respondents regularly or customarily sold their products were promotional or reduced prices. The court concluded:

> A statement may be deceptive even if the constituent words may be literally or technically construed so as not to constitute a misrepresentation. . . . The buying public does not weigh each word in an advertisement or a representation. It is important to ascertain the impression that is likely to be created upon the prospective purchaser.

Thus, even though every sentence considered separately is true, the advertisement as a whole may be misleading because factors are omitted that should be mentioned or because the message is composed in such a way as to mislead.

AMBIGUOUS ADVERTISEMENTS AND INNUENDO

Commercial falsity as defined by the FTC encompasses not only the "intended assertion but also the . . . communicated meaning, should that differ." As we have seen, the mere fact that what was said was literally and technically true does not prevent its being framed so as to mislead or deceive. The dispositive question always is the impression to be gleaned from the advertisement as a whole. If the impression is false, if there is a misleading suggestion or innuendo, if two meanings are conveyed and one is false, the advertisement will be prohibited. A case involving the products of a female health-food quack gave the commission the opportunity to articulate the rule as to ambiguous statements:

> Certain of said advertisements are false for the reason that the preparations to which they relate do not possess the properties or therapeutic values and will not produce the beneficial effects claimed for them in said advertisements. Others of the advertisements are false for the reason that they affirmatively represent that certain ailments, condi-

tions, and symptoms of the body are due to deficiencies in specific minerals and vitamins which respondents' preparation will supply when such is not the case. Still others of said advertisements are misleading in a material respect, and therefore false and deceptive, by reason of the innuendos and suggestions contained therein. In referring to the group last mentioned, the Commission has in mind particularly those advertisements in which the respondents' mineral or vitamin preparations are recommended as cures or remedies for certain designated symptoms or conditions when in fact the causes of such symptoms or conditions are so numerous that their mere existence creates no reasonable likelihood that they will be benefited by said preparations. In recommending a particular preparation as a cure or remedy for certain designated ailments, symptoms, or conditions, respondents suggest not only that such ailments, symptoms, or conditions may be due to causes for which the preparation is beneficial, but also that there is at least a reasonable chance that they are in fact due to such causes. If such a representation be made in a categorical statement, and if, for example, in a very substantial percentage of cases, the ailments, symptoms, or conditions are due to causes in the treatment of which the preparation advertised will have no benefit whatever, the representation is clearly false and obviously deceptive. A representation to the same effect, made under the same circumstances, except by suggestion instead of categorically, and if it be unaccompanied by an appropriate disclosure of the possibility of other causes of the ailment, symptoms, or conditions is equally false and deceptive in the opinion of the Commission, and by reason of such falsity is subject to the exercise of the Commission's corrective jurisdiction in the same manner and to the same extent as though the representation be made by affirmative statements.

Innuendo may be, however, the only approach open to the seller of a product or device generally prohibited by law. Finding an advertisement for "Quick Kaps" to be promoting an abortifacient, the commission said:

Persons looking for such a product would not expect to find it advertised with the same clarity and directness as in the case of products not so prohibited. This advertisement seems to invite a reading between the lines . . . reminiscent of the situation existing in the bootlegging days when a knowing wink might convey to the prospective purchaser the thought that the liquid being sold as "cold tea," was in fact illegal . . . liquor.

The commission is equally ready to attack advertisements or brand names that falsely suggest medical endorsements or manufacture by the use of depictions of nurses and doctors, the American Red Cross symbol, or *M.D.* or *Dr.* or *Med.,* or a claim for a scientific sounding but medically valueless ingredient.

The ambiguous claim finds its best expression in the "cure v. relief" cases. If there is no known cure for the condition to be treated by the product and the word *cure* has been used (baldness and dandruff are commonly so touted), the FTC stands on firm ground in eliminating the false hope. The curiosity in this area is the many terms which, although they have a common meaning, have been held to be synonymous with *cure*.

Obviously, the context of use is important in the determination that a claim may be falsely understood by some while communicating another, and true, meaning to others. *Permanent* as descriptive of a hair dye, particularly to regular users of hair dyes, means no more than that it will not wash out of the hair to which it is applied. But finding that it *could* also be construed as giving color to hair not yet grown out, so that the treatment would never have to be repeated, the commission ordered Clairol to cease the unqualified use of the word.

A generic product designator also may be deemed to be so ambiguous as to demand its prohibition. The commission found that the designation of a product as a *handkerchief* or *kerchief* conveyed to a substantial segment of the consuming public some indication of the material used in its manufacture—and that it was *not* paper nor fabric of poor or second quality, poorly cut, and imperfectly sewed.

In brief, these are the broad limits within which the commission operates. By thus raising the standard of the informative function of advertising, the consumer is more likely to get that which he has chosen in the market place. Whether he is looking for quality, utility, novelty, or a particular manufacturer, advertising must give him "straight" information. Furthermore, an advertiser cannot hide behind a claim that his product is "as good or almost as good as" or "as serviceable as or almost as serviceable as" the product it attempts, by misdescription, to masquerade as. Functional or qualitative equivalence is of no legal significance in the promotion of truthful advertising, and the commission, under the two last mentioned cases, need not make any determination as to interchangeability or substitutability.

Ambiguous statements and innuendos are interpreted to effect the purposes of the law. Because the purpose of the law is the prohibition of advertising having a tendency and capacity to deceive, an advertisement that can be read to have two meanings is illegal if one of them is false or misleading.

After having indicated the basic ground rules of all advertising, we shall now turn our attention to a detailed consideration of the specific categories of unfair and deceptive business practices as found by the courts and commission. Where the development at the state and federal level has been essentially the same, the focus will be upon FTC prosecutions. Where, on the other hand, the development has not been parallel, as, for example, lotteries, warranties, and guarantees, the pertinent chapters will be dichotomized accordingly. State legislation will be treated in Chapter 23, and in the final chapter we shall consider a plan for ethical advertising.

Copyrights, Patents, and Trade-marks

The benefits accruing to an author, inventor, or merchant as a result of his efforts in artistic and mechanical innovation or in establishing a business reputation are no less deserving of protection than the more tangible creations of other manufacturers or laborers. Consequently, Congress has long afforded such protection under the copyright, patent, and trade-mark statutes. Each of these enactments creates a limited monopoly in the holder of the right which permits him to obtain maximum benefits from his property rights. Although the various statutes differ in the nature and duration of their coverage, they are collected here because they all create unique statutory rights in commercial intangibles which can be protected through an action for infringement. What follows is by no means a complete exposition of the law in these areas. Rather it is an attempt to outline those portions of the laws of copyrights, patents, and trade-marks that have significance in a study of unfair competition and deceptive advertising. Naturally, this means that the treatment will be both varied and incomplete and anyone anticipating difficulties under these laws is strongly urged to consult a more thorough treatise or expert counsel.

COPYRIGHTS

Statutory protection for original works of authorship is one of the enumerated powers of the Federal Congress. Article 1, Section 8, Clause 8, of the Constitution authorizes Congress "to promote the progress of science and the useful arts by securing for limited times to authors and inventors the exclusive right to their respective writings and discoveries." Although originally limited to books, maps, and charts, copyright coverage was eventually extended to more diverse forms of literary and artistic expression, such as dramatic compositions, works of art in all mediums, motion pictures, and scientific or technical drawings and models. An author obtains a copyright by: (1) formally publishing (2) an original, (3) artistic work (4) containing a notice of copyright designating the owner and date, (5) followed by a registration of that work at the Copyright Office. Compliance with these formalities creates for the author an exclusive right to copy, print, vend, publish, complete, perform, and record the copyrighted work for a once-renewable period of twenty-eight years. This "literary property right" created by the statute is completely distinct from any rights of ownership of the physical substance of the work, such as the paper, clay, or film.

For purely historical reasons, publication is the critical point at which statutory protection becomes available. Prior thereto, the author's rights are governed by the common law of copyright. Essentially, this consists of the right of first publication and protection against duplication of an unpublished work. So long as there is no general publication, common law protection is perpetual.

The need for prepublication protection becomes apparent when it is understood that not every distribution of a work will constitute a formal publication necessary to obtain statutory protection. Thus the submission of a manuscript to a publisher is not sufficient "publication" under the Copyright Act and would leave the author susceptible to appropriation were there no common law protection for unpublished works.

Because of the importance of publication in the securing of a statutory copyright and in the termination of common law protection, the word carries far more legal significance than its usual definition. Similarly, because of the complexity of its meaning as a term of art, it is a fertile area for unauthorized appropriation. Publication has been divided into two categories—limited and unlimited—with only the latter constituting a statutory publication. A limited publication may be defined as transmission of the contents of a work to a select, well-defined group for some limited purpose that does not include any of the exclusive rights secured by the statute. Under such a definition, advance distribution of a book or play script to critics for review would be a limited publication not divesting common law protection. An unlimited publication involves a distribution whereby the work is made available to the general public. When such a publication is made, all common law protection ceases and the work must either meet the requirements of the statute or become part of the public domain.

The notice and registration provisions of the copyirght law are particularly pertinent to any discussion of advertising. Frequently, an advertisement will prove extremely popular and a seller will wish to protect it from infringement by others. Unless the necessary preliminary steps have been taken, however, this may not be possible for an advertisement already released and used. Because use of an advertisement definitely constitutes an unlimited publication, all necessary steps to preserve copyright should be taken before any use is made of the advertising material.

The essential act necessary to preserve copyright in a published work is the inclusion of a notice of copyright on *all* copies of the work distributed to the public. Thus an advertiser should be certain that his publishers include a notice of copyright somewhere in the body of every advertisement that appears in published form. The copyright notice itself should consist of the word *copyright* or the international copyright symbol ©, or both, accompanied by the year and name of the holder of the copyright. This notice is absolutely crucial to preservation of a statutory copyright, and if some advertisements appear without it, or if it is only added at some later date, there may be a partial or complete loss of protection.

The registration of a copyright is a procedural event making the provisions of the act available to those who have preserved their copyright by proper notice. Where the copyrighted matter has received wide distribution, courts have held that registration may be delayed, so long as it precedes the institution of an infringement suit. Naturally, no damages could be recovered for infringements prior to registration, but once registration is effected, both damages and injunctive relief become available against further infringements.

This is extremely important to the advertiser because it permits him to delay the expense and inconvenience of a registration until an actual infringement occurs or until the advertisement has proved its worth and warrants complete coverage of the act. Further, registration, once obtained, will make available the automatic damages provisions of the act, which substantially decrease the burden of demonstrating actual damages when that would be difficult.

Once proper notice is given and registration is sought, the first inquiry that must be made of any tendered work is whether it is proper subject matter for copyright. This has particular applicability in the field of advertising, where art is often employed as a promotional device. The Copyright Office originally refused to register advertisements on the ground that they lacked the essential characteristics of a work of art. The issue was eventually resolved by the Supreme Court in *Bleistein* v. *Donaldson Lithographing Company,* where a colorful circus poster was declared a proper subject matter for registration. The Court concluded that a work of art is no less artistic because devised for monetary gain.

Another area of proper subject matter may be a highly functional work, such as a sculptured lamp base. Ordinarily, functional items must either qualify for patent protection or enter the public domain. However, it is occasionally possible to separate the artistic, nonfunctional aspects of a product and obtain a copyright on them. Although a lamp would not be registerable for copyright purposes, a sculpture intended to serve as a lamp base, even to the point of having the appropriate apertures for electrical attachments, may still obtain coverage as an original work of art.

Finally, the Copyright Act specifically excludes from registration all fraudulent and misleading matter. All this means is that the publisher of fraudulent or misleading material cannot prevent the unauthorized duplication of that material by others. The act does not provide any prohibitive sanctions against the original publisher of the deceptive matter but only denies him any protection of the copyright laws.

Once statutory protection has been obtained, there are two postpublication areas of significance to our discussion of unfair competition. The first involves the problem of what constitutes a "copying" under the statute. Frequently, a businessman will desire to capitalize on some copyrighted innovation of a competitor. The degree to which he can imitate his competitor's work has been the subject of considerable litigation. As an example, let us suppose that a lamp manufacturer has obtained a copyright on a figurine, as an artistic sculpture, which he then employs with considerable success as a lamp base. A second manufacturer may not make a "Chinese copy," or exact duplicate, of the figurine for his lamps. He will probably be prevented from making a "slavish freehand" copy of the figurine as well. However, he is certainly not prevented from designing his own figurines to serve as lamp bases because this does not constitute a copying. The basis for these results is the fundamental proposition of the Copyright Act that only the expression of ideas, and not the ideas themselves, are capable of protection. Thus, whenever a merchant originates a new copyrightable product, he is entitled to protection against duplication of the product but not the idea behind it. Others may lawfully use the idea to create their own expressions of it, or they may independently develop parallel expressions of it.

This limitation of copying to the tangible result of an idea, rather than the idea itself, greatly diminishes the competitive impact of the copyright monopoly. Other merchants and manufacturers may adopt and improve an imaginative artistic idea without infringing on the original work. However, this does not extend to "borrowing" or directly copying parts or aspects of a copyrighted work. The copyright protects all the component parts of an original work as well as the total entity. Thus, although an idea may be appropriated, it may not contain any of the original forms of expression. The best demonstration of the scope of copyright coverage can be seen in the case of *Nichols* v. *Universal Pictures Corporation*. Playright Anne Nichols had written a popular broadway play entitled "Abie's Irish Rose," which involved an updating of the Romeo and Juliet theme in the context of an Irish and Jewish family. A second play, entitled "The Cohens and the Kellys," adopted the same basic idea for the plot and the same general characters. The court denied an infringement on the grounds that both of these factors were ideas of the playwright not subject to copyright. The court further noted that a different result would occur if dialogue or settings had been adopted, because these items form the author's expression of his ideas.

The second postpublication area pertinent to unfair competition is that of fair use. The doctrine of fair use is essentially an equitable mitigation of the harsh application of the copyright statute in situations where the use is not excessive and the original author's rights are not adversely affected. The doctrine finds no specific support in the existing statutory framework of copyright protection. Instead, it is a purely judicially derived doctrine based on equitable principles analogous to the rule of "de minimis non curat lex." In form, it is a defense raised by an alleged infringer. In effect, it is a complete negation of the infringement.

The first authoritative exposition of the doctrine, although certainly not its American genesis, can be found in the case of *Folsom* v. *Marsh*. Although much of Justice Story's discussion of fair use can only be described as dicta because of the conclusion that an infringement occurred, the case is probably the earliest collection of the various criteria considered in determining the existence of a fair use. With only very slight alterations in subsequent cases, the doctrine of *Folsom* v. *Marsh* has constituted a judicial amendment to the statutory protection of copyrights since 1841.

In assessing whether a particular copy of a protected work constitutes a fair use, courts consider four factors: (1) the purpose and character of the use, (2) the nature of the copyrighted work, (3) the amount and substantiality of the portion used in relation to the copyrighted work as a whole, and (4) the effect of the use on the potential market for or value of the copyrighted work. The obvious case-by-case determination of fair use makes it an extremely perilous area for one desiring to copy some aspect of a protected work. A failure to maintain the defense successfully will almost automatically mean liability for infringement.

Under present interpretation of the doctrine a particular fair use is not limited to any specific amount or type of copying. Where the original work could reasonably be presumed to encourage copying, such as a book of sample contracts or wills, wholesale appropriation may qualify as a fair use. On the other hand, there is no absolute *de minimis* standard, so that mere insignificance of the copied portions will not assure a determination of fair use.

In the advertising media fair use is of extreme importance. Manufacturers often desire to excerpt laudatory passages of copyrighted works and include them in advertisements of their product. Just such a use occurred in *Henry Holt & Co.* v. *Liggett & Myers Tobacco Company*. Holt held a copyright on a scientific thesis about voice development which contained passages asserting that tobacco had no adverse effect on the vocal organs. Liggett & Myers used these passages without permission in its widely circulated pamphlet defending smoking. In a suit for copyright infringement a federal district court explored in depth the applicability of the fair-use doctrine in advertising media.

The court first noted that the size of the excerpt—three sentences—was not a controlling factor because the issue is the materiality, not the quantity, of the copy which decides the fairness of the use. Nor was it significant that the copy only paraphrased the original. Duplication need not be slavish in order to qualify as an infringement. It need only appear that the original expression of the idea was appropriated to the unauthorized use.

The *Holt* decision also rejected as irrelevant the defense that the pamphlet acknowledged the true authorship of the passages. The court correctly observed that such an acknowledgment will not serve to create a fair use where one does not otherwise exist. An acknowledgment is only a negative consideration; that is, its absence may indicate an intent to infringe but its presence is never conclusive of a fair use. Finally, the court was swayed by the fact that had the passages not been appropriated by Liggett & Myers, Holt might have realized a commercial gain by having all the cigarette companies bid for the use of the passages in their advertising. Thus, the use interfered with a potential market for the original work and could not qualify as fair.

The doctrine of fair use will also have importance where an advertisement alters, shortens, or otherwise distorts a quotation in order to have it reflect favorably on a product. The best example of this is the excerpting of reviews for use in theater or motion picture advertisements. Because the nature of a review anticipates that some copying will naturally occur without the prior consent of the reviewer, the question devolves on a determination of whether the particular use was fair. If the copy so modifies the original as to destroy the accuracy, meaning, or completeness of the author's expression, then the use is not fair and an infringement has occurred. This is also the case where permission has been obtained to reproduce the original and then some alteration is made. The cause of action for infringement does not affect or diminish any action under the Federal Trade Commission Act for unfair trade practices which might also arise from the same facts.

PATENTS

Statutory protection for the discoveries of inventors derives from the same Constitutional authorization which affords copyright protection to authors. Apart from this single genesis, however, patents and copyrights are quite distinct in the nature and scope of their coverage. A patent is awarded to an inventor for his discoveries after there has been a search of the prior art which affirms the originality, novelty, inventiveness, and usefulness of the subject matter. Upon adequate demonstration of these properties to an official examiner, a patent will issue which gives the holder a complete monopoly in the manufacture, use and sale of the invention for a single term of seventeen years.

There is, in addition to the statutory coverage, a modicum of common law protection for patentable subject matter. Such protection is limited, however, and only protects the inventor from those who improperly obtain the invention by some deceptive or improper means. The common law provides no protection against independent development of the same invention by another individual, nor does it provide relief where the invention is within the scope of some existing patent. Nonetheless, the common law will provide significant protection against many deceptive practices such as those which might result from a breach of confidence by an employee or an improper appropriation of the device by a manufacturer who obtained access under some confidential arrangement. The common law remedy can take the form of injunction or royalties or both and would be independent from any cause of action for appropriation of trade secrets or interference with contractual arrangements.

The rights created by a statutory patent are independent of the physical substance of the invention and may be contractually alienated, divided, or assigned. Thus, assuming no violation of the antitrust laws, a patentee can license one person to sell and another to use the invention, while still retaining the ability personally to perform both functions. Because of this divisibility and easy alienation of an absolute monopoly, there is considerable likelihood that the patentee might attempt to employ the exclusivity of an attractive invention as a lever to coerce greater control or competitive influence than that legitimately authorized by the patent grant. Whenever these attempts become abusive of the antitrust laws, they are the subject of prosecution under the Sherman and Clayton Acts. However, there are many abuses of the patent privilege which, although not falling within the purview of these two antitrust laws, are unfair or deceptive in nature and deserving of correction. Consequently, various legal theories have developed under the patent laws, the Federal Trade Commission Act, and the common law, in the form of causes of action and defenses, intended to remedy these improper acts and practices.

The broadest category of relief distinct from the antitrust laws and the right to contest the validity of the patent on the merits is that available under a claim of patent misuse. The misuse of a patent can consist of any activity involving a patent that is outside the scope of the patent grant. The doctrine has judicial origins and is based on the rationale that any conduct beyond that explicitly protected in the patent grant is an unauthorized extension of the patent monopoly. Naturally, any doctrine so broadly defined in the abstract only takes on accurate proportions in the context of specific factual situations. The doctrine of patent misuse is sufficiently broad that it achieves a considerable overlap of the antitrust laws while also reaching situations otherwise unassailable under any other legal theory. For example, a patent misuse occasioned by requiring the purchase of an unpatented product along with a patented one is also an illegal tying arrangement under the antitrust laws. However, where the patentee seeks to place restrictions on an unpatented machine or process related to a patented invention, his activities, although certainly unfair to competitors seeking to use the unpatented parts, might not have sufficient market significance to gain the attention of the antitrust laws. The activity would, nevertheless, constitute a patent misuse capable of denying all patent protection and royalties to the patentee until the misuse is purged.

The significance of patent misuse in the context of unfair competition can best be understood by an examination of the various remedies it affords a victimized competitor. Essentially, it is the statutory counterpart of the equitable requirement of "clean hands." A patentee seeking the protection of his invention through an infringement suit must not himself be guilty of abusing his monopoly grant. If it can be shown that he has misused the grant, he will be denied the protection of the statute. Further, a competitor can assert patent misuse affirmatively in an effort to enjoin certain conduct of a patentee. Obviously, the factual settings for a patent misuse are as varied as the imaginations of unscrupulous men.

But the doctrine, for this very reason, defies any precise definition and is generally available whenever the patentee engages in conduct calculated to extend the monopoly beyond the limits of the grant.

Besides the traditional prosecution of certain patent misuses as violations of the Sherman Act, the Federal Trade Commission recently sought to prosecute a patent misuse as an unfair method of competition under Section 5 of the Federal Trade Commission Act. This attempt seems wholly consonant with the broader philosophy of the patent misuse doctrine and injects a degree of public enforcement into areas of misuse heretofore left to private litigation. Because many types of misuse would be unlikely to come to the attention of a private defendant charged with infringement, the new approach of the FTC will provide additional protection where resort to the traditional defense of patent misuse would be realistically unavailable.

In addition to the infinite variations of patent misuse, there are several specific activities that are either prohibited by the patent laws or otherwise constitute unfair or deceptive acts and practices. Principally, they concern bad-faith threats or commencement of infringement suits and the various types of patent mismarking.

The issuance of a warning concerning the infringement of a patent, where the party threatening is acting in bad faith, has been held to constitute an unfair method of competition under Section 5 of the Federal Trade Commission Act. This activity is also specifically prohibited in the Commission's Trade Practice Rules. The critical issue, of course, is what constitutes "bad faith" in such circumstances. The clearest example is a threat of suit where no patent has been obtained. Because no rights accrue to the holder until actual grant of the patent, there can be no right to sue, or threaten suit, where a patent is merely pending or where no patent has yet been applied for. This should not be confused with invalidation of a patent. The threat of suit on a patent ultimately found to be invalid is not, without more, an act amounting to bad faith. Where the patentee knows the patent is not valid, however, a different result might obtain.

Moreover, a patentee may not threaten an infringement suit when he has no intention of instituting such ligitation. Although obviously a difficult proposition to prove, courts have been willing to infer such bad faith where there is a continuous pattern of warnings with no subsequent institution of suit. In such circumstances, a delay of one year after repeated threats has been held to be sufficient indication of bad faith. Also, where a warning is openly defied or the patentee is challenged to bring the threatened suit, a failure to do so will support an inference of bad faith.

Finally, the issuance of warnings which threaten more than an infringement suit, such as threatening to secure the intervention of the federal government, are both a misuse of the patent monopoly and an unfair method of competition. In this same respect, a premature threat of suit, as would occur where there has been no investigation or legal counseling as to the existence of an infringement, is a form of commercial harassment which violates both the patent laws and Section 5 of the Federal Trade Commission Act.

The same rationale which prohibits bad faith in threatening infringement suits will also govern the bad-faith institution of such a suit. Thus, institution of an infringement suit when a patent is merely pending, where a patent is known to be invalid, or where there is no reasonable basis to believe an infringement has occurred, all constitute unfair methods of competition circumscribed by Section 5.

The only area of patent law having direct application to deceptive advertising concerns the subject of patent mismarking. Any false allegation or indication that a product is patented or that a patent is pending is specifically prohibited under the patent laws. Such activity constitutes a fraud on the public for which the patent laws impose a fine of $500 for each offense. Concurrently, such activity has also been deemed a patent misuse which will serve as a complete defense in a suit for infringement. This would be the case where a manufacturer claimed a patent for both a product and a process when, in fact, only the process was patented. In a suit for infringing the process, an "unclean hands" defense alleging the deceptive claim as to the product would prevent recovery by the patentee.

TRADE-MARKS

Unlike either copyrights or patents, statutory trade-mark protection has no constitutional origins and confers no independent, substantive rights on the holder. Rather, the Lanham Trade-mark Act provides a system of registration which affords certain procedural advantages to the holder of a mark that were otherwise unavailable at common law. A successful registration creates presumptive notice to infringers and provides a procedure for establishing the "incontestability" of a mark after five years of registration.

The actual substantive rights which accrue to the holder of a trade-mark are those which existed at common law before our first enactment of a trade-mark law in 1844. Essentially, it is the right to prevent another person from using a word, device, or symbol sufficiently similar to the registered mark that it creates a real likelihood of confusing the public as to the origin of the product on which it is used. Insofar as the substantive rights of a trade-mark stem directly from the common law, the law of trade-marks can accurately be described as merely a part of the broader law of unfair competition. Most of the theory of unfair competition is based on protection of the commercially intangible benefits which flow from an established business reputation. Foremost among the techniques for fostering a favorable clientele is the use of a trade-mark. The marks were originally employed as quality standards by early silversmiths, and this fundamental notion of a trade-mark as reflecting superior business repute has remained to the present day.

Because of the significance of qualifying for registration and because many of the criteria of registration also form the theoretical foundation for the various types of unfair competition to be discussed subsequently, an examination of registration standards is appropriate. In simplest terms, any word, name, symbol, or device, or any combination thereof, may qualify for registration if it has been adopted and used in commerce by a manufacturer or merchant to identify his goods and distinguish them from those manufactured or sold by others. Beyond the typical procedural difficulties that might be encountered in attempting to demonstrate an adoption or a use in commerce, the applicant faces the considerable task of showing that the particular mark actually does serve to identify his product and distinguish it from others. Furthermore, because the mere existence of trade-mark rights does not permit an individual to appropriate words of common usage to his particular purpose and thereby deny them to the public at large, the Lanham Act excludes a wide variety of words, symbols, and devices from qualification as registrable marks without some express limitation on use.

In response to the inherent difficulties of any system which attempts to assign some special privileges to certain uses of the language, the Lanham Act established two registers for trade-marks—the Principal and Supplemental Registers—with varying significance given to each. The Principal Register is that which extends the greatest degree of presumptive validity and is, consequently, the more advantageous. In order to qualify, a mark must either be a technical trade-mark or have established a "secondary meaning" within the trade. A technical mark is an arbitrary word, design, or symbol which serves no other purpose and has no other meaning than to signify the origin of the goods on which it appears. Such a mark becomes a trade-mark as soon as it is adopted and used as such without ever having first established a market reputation.

The scope of a technical trade-mark can best be described by listing its exceptions. It may not be merely a descriptive word or words, a geographic name or a surname or signature, nor may it be a color or a common arrangement of colors. Finally, it may not be a numerical grade mark or a purely functional configuration of shape or color. The obvious reason for each of these exceptions is that there is nothing about them which would, apart from usage, associate them with a particular item. Also, each of these exceptions constitutes a value judgment in which

Congress and the courts have decided that it is better that they remain within the public domain and available for general usage than that they be arbitrarily appropriated by a single merchant or manufacturer to his personal economic advantage.

In addition to being a technical mark, a trade symbol may qualify for the Principal Register if it has established a secondary meaning. This category involves words or designs which have independent significance in our language or customs, but which, because of their association with a particular product, have come to designate the source of that product in the minds of those in the trade who deal in that product. Thus, the word *arrow* has a fixed definition in our language as being a type of shaft or missile, but the word takes on particular significance when associated with the manufacture or sale of men's shirts. In this respect, the word *arrow* has established a secondary meaning for those in the shirt trade which identifies it as a product source. Obviously, such a meaning is only gained after a considerable period of continuous usage within a particular industry or market. The amount of usage would vary, naturally, with the commonness of the prospective mark. The word *universal,* for example, requires a good deal more repetitious association with a product to acquire a secondary meaning than a less common superlative.

Some words, of course, are never capable of establishing a single secondary meaning, because by their very definition they always retain a predominant primary meaning which would unreasonably deprive others were it to be exclusively appropriated by one individual. Thus, the more common the word, the narrower the scope of its secondary meaning. The manufacturer of Arrow shirts would be hard pressed to prevent another from using the word *arrow* as a trade name for a bicycle or a washing machine. The word is simply too common to permit it to be completely removed from general usage by a single merchant. A similar rule applies with respect to uncommon surnames. Even though a name might be unusual, its owner should not be able to prevent others with an identical or similar name from using it in their trade or business. The solution in such cases is usually to ascribe a limited secondary meaning to the first use of the name and then require some distinguishing characteristic or legend in other, different uses.

To solve these vagaries of secondary meaning, the Lanham Act provides a Supplemental Register for those marks not capable of immediate registration on the Principal Register. Because every technical trade-mark will qualify for the Principal Register, the Supplemental Register is concerned only with the establishment of secondary meanings. Any mark capable of distinguishing the applicant's goods from those of another is capable of being registered thereon. In effect, this means that any mark capable of eventually achieving a secondary meaning may obtain supplemental registration pending acquisition of such meaning. The act specifically provides that a supplemental registration shall not preclude a later inclusion on the Principal Register. On the other hand, a supplemental registration is an admission that the mark, at that point, has not acquired any secondary meaning. Still, the fact that the act contains a provision which makes substantially continuous and exclusive use of a mark for five years *prima facie* proof of secondary meaning lends significant importance to the Supplemental Register because such usage can be most readily demonstrated by pointing to an outstanding registration for the necessary period.

Once a mark has secured registration on the Principal Register it is still not completely immune from subsequent removal. Just as secondary meaning can act to qualify an otherwise unregisterable mark, the overemphasis of that secondary meaning to a point where the mark becomes the generic term for the product can have just the opposite effect. Occasionally, a trade-mark will become so popular that it displaces all other descriptive words as a definition for the product itself. In such a case, to deny this word to the general public would eliminate the only available descriptive word for the product. Consequently, in such situations the trade-mark will be removed from the register, or denied renewal, and the word will enter the public domain. This phenomenon can involve either a technical mark or a trade-mark established by secondary meaning.

The best example of the deterioration of a trade-mark into a generic term involves the word *aspirin*. Originally concocted as a purely arbitrary description for the headache remedy of the Bayer Co., an international network of trade-marks and a highly effective promotional campaign made the word synonymous with a particular tablet headache remedy manufactured by any source. Thus, the consuming public would employ some other word in conjunction with aspirin in order to designate source. The entire function of the word as a trade-mark—identification of product origin—was completely destroyed by the popularity of the word as a descriptive term. In a similar manner, DuPont lost all trade-mark rights in the technical mark *cellophane,* because it had become a generic term for a particular type of cellulose wrapper.

Acutely aware of this danger of losing an extremely popular trade-mark because of its very popularity, businessmen frequently launch advertising campaigns to educate the public in the fact that the term is a registered trade-mark. The best recent example of this sort of "preventive policing" of a trade-mark has been conducted by the 3M Company. Afraid that *Scotch tape* might become a generic term for transparent adhesives, the company altered its advertising to state that the product is "Scotch brand cellophane tape." The most interesting aspect of this campaign is the use of another word, *cellophane,* as a descriptive term when once it was a valid trade-mark. A well-conducted advertising campaign could save Scotch tape from the same fate.

Once a trade-mark is properly registered, and assuming it avoids deteriorating into a descriptive word, it will be protected from infringement by others. An infringement of a trade-mark can be an unauthorized reproduction, counterfeit, or colorable imitation of a mark, or the unauthorized use of such copies in commerce. Whether or not a copy is an infringement will depend on the scope of the original registration. If the registered mark is a technical trade-mark, there can be no other use of that mark no matter how distinct the product. Thus, the Kodak Company could prevent use of the word *Kodak* on any product, no matter how remote from the photographic industry, because it is a classic technical mark. On the other hand, the Universal Camera Company could not prevent another use of the word *universal* on a different product, because its secondary meaning was acquired only with respect to the camera industry. Even the closely analogous motion picture industry may use the mark *universal,* and has done so for many years.

There is, however, a point at which the use of a similar term will clearly indicate the likelihood of customer confusion as to the origin of the products. In such a case, the second mark may be considered merely a colorable imitation of the first and its use will be denied. The extent of this sort of protection is extremely broad for technical marks. Under such a theory, the Polaroid Camera Company was able to enjoin the use of PolarAid as the trade-mark for a refrigerator, even though the latter was spelled differently and had a clever association with its product. Such results often turn on the phonetic similarity of the two marks rather than their actual spelling. For example, the National Biscuit Company, producer of Uneeda Biscuits, was able to enjoin the use of the word *Iwanta* for a competing biscuit but failed in its attempt to enjoin use of the word *Hava.* Although the spelling of all three words is at considerable variance, the court was persuaded to enjoin *Iwanta* because of the phonetic similarities of the two words.

In all determinations of infringement, the controlling factor is the likelihood of customer confusion as to origin of the product. For a technical trade-mark, this would be any other use because the arbitrary derivation of the mark leaves no room for any other conclusion. *Any* product sold under the Kodak mark would create some confusion as to origin because the word *Kodak* has no other purpose than to identify the camera company. Where there is more than one possible meaning for the word, then the likelihood of confusion will depend upon the similarity of products to which it is applied. The word *arrow,* having a secondary meaning in the shirt industry, would not be likely to cause customer confusion if applied to an automotive product. However, the Arrow Shirt Company was able to demonstrate the likelihood of customer confusion when a belt manufacturer sought to use the mark *Arrow.* The obvious proximity of the shirt industry and the clothing accessories industry in the mind of the consuming public would classify such a use as an infringement.

The Lanham Act provides a vast array of remedies for a trade-mark infringement, and courts have always felt free to fashion additional remedies where the situation so indicated. In addition to providing a cause of action to recover damages, profits, and court costs, the act also permits confiscation and destruction of all infringing labels, wrappers, signs, and so forth. Finally, there is provision for the broad exercise of injunctive relief. Aside from completely prohibiting an infringement, a court might permit an infringer to continue the use of the mark with some appropriate disclaimer or qualification. Or the court may exclude the infringing mark from certain geographic areas where it is likely to cause confusion. Any formulation of an injunction which is in accordance with the principles of equity may be employed by a court to remedy an infringement.

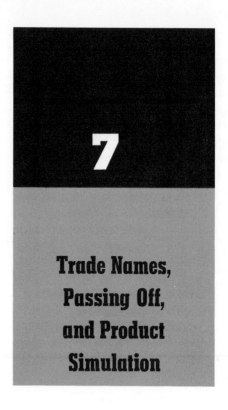

7

Trade Names, Passing Off, and Product Simulation

The commercial value of business reputation and good will is not limited to the product identification of a registered trade-mark. The various elements of a product's composition and marketing which engender a favorable customer response extend well beyond the familiarity of a particular trade symbol or design. By the same token, the ways in which a business reputation can be unfairly appropriated to another's advantage are far more numerous and diverse than the single offense of trade-mark infringement.

A business, through a continuous course of conduct and trade, will build up a reputation in a particular locale or market which is a substantial element of the total commercial enterprise. Despite its incorporeal nature, a businessman's good will is a vital proprietary aspect of his trade. Consequently, the common law has long recognized that injury to the intangible aspects of a business can be just as tortious as a rock thrown through a store window. Unfair competition, in its broadest aspects, is nothing but the extension of tort law to the area of commercial intangibles. It is a broad, often vague, category of law which attempts to prevent all forms of business conduct which abuse the business reputation of competing merchants.

It is for this reason that the law of trade-marks has been described as only a component of the far broader category of unfair competition. Beyond trade-mark infringement, that body of law circumscribes a broad range of activities, from trading on another's reputation to stealing another's trade secrets. The following two chapters will capsulize the major divisions of the law of unfair competition.

The first area to be discussed, and the one most analogous to statutory trade-mark coverage, is the fraudulent use of a competitor's name, reputation, or product characteristics to promote a competing product. Such conduct will generally fall into one of three categories: (1) fraudulent simulation or deceptive association of a trade name, (2) fraudulent substitution or "passing off" of a competing product, and (3) improper duplication of the nonessential or nonfunctional aspects of a competing product. The balance of this chapter will be addressed to a discussion of these forms of unfair competition.

TRADE NAMES

Much of the confusion and uncertainty which has surrounded the common law protection of trade names stems from the multitude of meanings which have been ascribed to the term. Thus, at one and the same time, a trade name has been variously defined as a registered trade-mark connoting a corporate name, the brand name of a product, a product name having a secondary meaning, and an unregistrable product name. Each use is valid, but the more critical inquiry is the use to which the trade name is put rather than its classification. Our discussion of trade names will be restricted to those situations where a remedy for trade-mark infringement is unavailable. This could be because the trade name is unregistered or because the use is an improper association rather than an infringement. In short, our concern is with any use of a product name, rather than a mark or symbol, which could cause confusion as to product origin but which will not create a cause of action for infringement.

Because unfair competition is grounded on a tort theory, it is not enough that two product names are similar, or even identical. There must also be a demonstrable injury flowing from the similarity in name. This inquiry has been traditionally described in terms of the likelihood of customer confusion. As a basic policy consideration, relief will be granted to protect the public from being deceived about who is making or selling the products they buy. In addition, a merchant can also show injury to his business stemming from a diversion of trade caused by the similarity of names. Either form of injury, public confusion or diversion of trade, will support a cause of action for unfair competition.

This dual basis of injury eliminates earlier confusion concerning the need for actual competition to exist between the two similar names. Under earlier interpretations, the only cognizable injury was a diversion of trade which could only occur if both parties dealt in the same goods. This reasoning contradicted the broader notions of customer good will, because it did not recognize that trade names frequently became a quality standard which consumers would associate with other related products. Later courts rejected this narrow competition requirement and recognized that an unscrupulous merchant might trade on a well-respected trade name by using it on related, but not competing, products. The likelihood of a customer belief that both products came from the same source became an alternate basis for sustaining an action for unfair competition.

With respect to an unfair use of a trade name, diversion or confusion might be achieved by one of two methods, (1) by use of a name confusingly similar to that of a competitor or some established trade name or (2) by an ambiguous association between a merchant's product and another merchant's trade name or registered trade-mark. The former method will involve unregistered trade names, but the latter might well involve a registered trade-mark because the technique is not duplication but, rather, a misleading association.

Confusingly Similar Trade Names

A mere failure or inability to register at the federal level does not completely expose a trade name to usurpation by unscrupulous competitors. However, if a trade name has not achieved the status of a registered trademark, the degree of protection afforded to it will naturally be measurably less. The notice provisions of the federal statute will serve to prevent any duplication of a mark, whereas the mere similarity of a trade name, standing alone, will not serve to create any paramount rights in the first user of it. In addition, there must be some element of culpable conduct, some degree of fraud, which indicates an attempt to capitalize on an unearned reputation. Just what facts will sustain proof of this additional fraudulent element has long troubled courts.

In *Lerner Stores Corporation* v. *Lerner* the United States Court of Appeals for the Ninth Circuit was faced with a somewhat typical factual problem involving confusingly similar trade names. Lerner Stores was a chain operation with 181 stores located in forty-one states and the District of Columbia. It operated stores in San Francisco and Oakland, California, and had purchased land for a store in San Jose. Defendant, Wilfred Lerner, opened a store in San Jose which he named Lerner's. Upon written protest by Lerner Stores, defendant set about making adjustments in his trade name to avoid further confusion. He expanded the trade name to include his first name and the qualification *home owned*. The name was written in a distinctive script and the advertisements reflected that defendant dealt in a different quality of merchandise than that of Lerner Stores. As postured by the court, the sole point of inquiry was whether the public was led to understand that the defendant's goods were those of Lerner Stores.

The court concluded that no unfair competition existed. In so doing, it examined several of the typical criteria applied to such a situation. As noted earlier, not all duplications are actionable. Rather, there must be shown an intent to appropriate the other's name with knowledge that the use would create customer confusion. As can be seen, this actually requires a double intent, to copy and to confuse. With respect to the intent to copy, the court noted that Mr. Lerner had a valid independent reason for selecting the name of his business; it coincided with his own surname. Further, insofar as the San Jose area was concerned, there was no existing Lerner Store for Mr. Lerner to copy. Although this is reminiscent of the old requirement that actual competition must exist before unfair competition can occur, its use in this context more accurately reflects the tort requirement of intent.

Concerning the intent to confuse customers, the court turned its attention to the steps taken by Mr. Lerner to disinguish his establishment from the chain stores. Every measure taken, but especially the qualifying phrase *home owned* which accompanied all advertisements, was calculated to make clear the autonomy of Mr. Lerner's establishment in the mind of the purchasing public.

Finally, the court noted that the Lerner Store chain engaged in no large-scale advertising, preferring instead to rely on pedestrian traffic for their sales. In the court's view, this meant that the vast majority of the customers of the chain store would associate its name with a particular establishment and location rather than with merely a name in an advertising media. Consequently, any lingering oral or visual similarity between the two names would be more than offset by the distinguishing physical characteristics of the two establishments and the fact that they appealed to their clientele through different media.

The *Lerner Stores* decision amply demonstrates the importance of the issue of subjective intent of an alleged appropriator. Courts will usually give strong weight to any independent basis for selecting the name, but the existence of an identical surname is most persuasive. The single characteristic which seems to typify the defendant's actions in *Lerner Stores* can best be summed up as "good faith," and this is never better demonstrated than by a showing of reasonable, alternative bases for the selection of the particular trade name.

Not all trade-name difficulties will arise in a localized geographic context, nor will they involve such compelling facts as the *Lerner Stores* case. One year after *Lerner Stores,* the same Circuit Court of Appeals was called on to interpret the allegedly unfair use of the trade name *The Stork Club.* A San Francisco cocktail lounge operated under the name *Stork Club* and employed the symbol of a monacled stork in high hat as an insignia. The New York Stork Club, an internationally known night spot, brought a suit for unfair competition alleging a fraudulent simulation of its trade name and a dilution of its business reputation.

In *Stork Restaurant, Inc.* v. *Sahati* the court enjoined the further use of the name *Stork Club* by the San Francisco enterprise. The arbitrary nature of the trade name eliminated any reasonable alternative motive for its use and strongly implied an intent to copy. The court noted that when the appropriated trade name is fanciful or distinctive, an actual showing of fraud is unnecessary, it is conclusively presumed from defendant's selection of that name from an infinite variety of other possible combinations.

Actually, defendants did not seriously contest the allegation that they had intentionally duplicated plaintiff's trade name, but relied, instead, on the argument that such a copying could not possibly result in consumer confusion as to ownership or a diversion of the plaintiff's trade. In support of its contentions, the defendant argued three points: the disparity in size and reputation of the two establishments, the geographical distance between the two, and the fact that any asserted relation to the New York enterprise was so obviously false as to be incapable of confusing anyone.

The court observed that a mere disparity in size carries with it no implications of the absence of either injury or confusion. Rather, the very smallness of the second user may be an additional motive for it to attempt to capitalize on the reputation of a better-known company. The court similarly rejected distance as a factor obviating confusion and injury. Noting the increase of chain restaurants and the fact that branches are typically smaller than the "mother house," it deemed it not unreasonable that persons might attribute identity of ownership to the two establishments.

With respect to defendant's claim that its establishment was so obviously borrowing the name of the New York night club that no one of reasonable intelligence could confuse the two, the court was unwilling to accept this narrow interpretation of customer confusion. The court considered it sufficient that the reputation of the New York club was exposed to the trade practices of the one in San Francisco regardless of whether a pecuniary loss was suffered by any actual customer deception. The likelihood of confusing even a naïve diner will suffice.

As can be seen even from this brief examination of the case law, the combination of influential factors is potentially infinite. Similar names may be used in distinct markets, or on different products and still result in unfair competition if the likelihood of confusion can be shown to exist. With respect to this likelihood, two further points should be clarified.

It is not necessary that purchasers of the fraudulently named product believe that it is the original. Rather, it is sufficient that both products appear to originate from the same source. Thus, if X Company produces ABC shirts and Y Company subsequently adopts ABC as its name for slacks, it is sufficient that consumers believe both originate with X Company, or at least with the same company that makes ABC shirts if X Company is not generally known. In this regard, the more fanciful the trade name, the greater the likelihood of a single source, because the unique characteristics of the name will carry beyond a single product. The distinction with the law of trade-marks is not based on the scope of the copying, but the subjective intent of the copier. Thus, just as a technical trade-mark is capable of preventing all unrelated uses, a fanciful, unregistered trade name can effectively prohibit unrelated uses that can be shown to be fraudulent attempts to profit on another's trade reputation. This was essentially the rationale of the *Stork Club* case, because the two restaurants involved offered widely diverse services— one dealt in fine foods and exceptional entertainment and the other focused on limited cuisine and dancing music. Obviously, product-to-product comparisons did not dictate the conclusion of potential confusion.

A second corollary of the protection of trade names is that it is not necessary to simulate the entire name if the product and market similarities are sufficiently close. As one court explained this, to permit such partial uses would permit a merchant "to break down the one trade name into two distinct segments and then destroy each segment separately." Clearly, what cannot be accomplished singularly cannot be done by such obvious indirection either. By the same rationale, one cannot enlarge a valid trade name to the point where it begins to resemble another, assuming the requisite fraudulent intent. Thus, one court concluded that a sleeping apparel manufacturer's expansion of his trade name from *Perfect* to *Perfectform*, where a brassiere manufacturer was already using the trade name *Perfect form* in the same market, was unfair competition even though the earlier use of *Perfect* alone was entirely valid.

With respect to the confusing simulation of trade names, therefore, a businessman should pay particular attention to the trade name under which he elects to market his goods. He should attempt to select as fanciful a name as possible to facilitate later protection of it until he can qualify for trade-mark coverage. Further, if he selects a fanciful name, he should attempt to discover if that name is already in use, even in a somewhat unrelated trade. If it is, the safe course is to select another name. Where the businessman elects, instead, to use some common descriptive words, a surname, or a geographic name, his investigation need only touch on related industries in competing markets, but the future protection of his name will be similarly diminished.

Confusing Association of Trade Names

As was noted earlier, the dominant theme of unfair competition is prevention of actions which cause confusion as to product origin. It is not always necessary for an unscrupulous merchant to substitute another product name for his own in order to achieve this result. Often far more subtle methods are available which accomplish the same ends. One such method which has caused a great deal of confusing and inconsistent litigation is the use of a popular trade name on a private brand label in describing the contents of the product. The opportunity for such confusion arises from the practice, current in many industries, of having merchants purchase in bulk and then repackage in smaller quantities for private-brand resale. Frequently the repackager is tempted to use the well-known trade name of the bulk product on his private label in juxtaposition with his own trade name.

The fountainhead of current law in this area is the 1924 United State Supreme Court case of *Prestonettes, Inc.* v. *Coty.* Prestonettes purchased Coty's perfume and facial powder in bulk. It reduced the powder to a compact and resold the perfume in smaller bottles. The Prestonettes label disclaimed any association with Coty, but also stated that the contents were original Coty products. Coty, having a registered trademark, brought suit for infringement and the Supreme Court concluded that when Prestonettes bought the product it also bought the right to use truthfully the product name in resale, because Coty was aware that resale was intended when it sold in bulk. Justice Holmes, who wrote the majority opinion, then cautioned that "the question therefore is not how far the court would go in aid of a plaintiff who showed ground for suspecting the defendant of making a dishonest use of his opportunities. . . ." The *Prestonettes* decision was not popularly received and later courts interpreted this language of Justice Holmes as leaving completely open the applicability of the law of unfair competition to similar factual situations.

For several years lower courts used the "escape hatch" of unfair competition to avoid the harsh results of *Prestonettes*. By noting factual distinctions and emphasizing label placement, courts inferred a dishonest or fraudulent use of the "opportunities" permitted by *Prestonettes*. In *Bourjois* v. *Hermida Laboratories, Inc.* a similar repackaging of facial powder was done with the single distinction that the dominant name on the label was the famous Bourjois name *Evening in Paris,* whereas the defendant's name as repackager was relegated to a fifth-line notation followed by a disclaimer of association with Bourjois. The Third Circuit Court of Appeals classified the differences in label as a "fatal" distinction from *Prestonettes* and found Hermida Laboratories had competed unfairly. *Bourjois* was typical of the cases which sought to circumvent *Prestonettes* and courts rather consistently employed this technique until the Supreme Court once again was presented with a name association situation, this time involving an unfair competition claim as well.

In *Champion Spark Plug Co.* v. *Sanders* the defendants were engaged in reconditioning used Champion spark plugs for resale. The word *Champion* was retained on the reconditioned plug and also on the box to identify its contents. Each plug also contained a frequently illegible stamp—*renewed.* The intermediate appellate court refused to require removal of the word *Champion* from the plugs and required that the word *repaired* or *used* be heat-stamped into the plugs. On review, the Supreme Court observed:

> We are dealing here with second-hand goods. The spark plugs, though used, are nevertheless Champion plugs and not those of another make. There is evidence to support what one would suspect, that a spark plug which has been repaired or reconditioned does not measure up to the specification of a new one. . . . But inferiority is expected in most second-hand articles. Inferiority is immaterial so long as the article is clearly and distinctively sold as repaired or reconditioned rather than as new. The result is, of course, that the second-hand dealer gets some advantage from the trademark.

Some courts have interpreted the *Champion* case as ruling out unfair competition in the association of trade names, but such is clearly not the case. The appellate court found unfair competition and the Supreme Court affirmed both its findings and its remedies. What the *Champion* decision does import, and as subsequent cases have so interpreted it, is that a legitimate purchaser of a trade-marked or trade-named product may truthfully identify the content or nature of his product even if it means a label designation of another mark or name. In effect, the fraudulent intent necessary to all suits for unfair competition can only be established by showing a misleading or patently untruthful representation as to the nature or contents of the product. Thus, if Prestonettes *diluted* the Coty perfume, a label representation that the contents were Coty perfume would still be actionable unfair competition. Similarly, a federal court applied *Champion* to hold that an auto mechanic and used-car dealer could not advertise in a manner calculated to create the impression that he was a licensed holder of a Volkswagen franchise because this intimated new-car sales and specially trained mechanics.

The precise application of *Champion* to cases where there is no alteration of the original product, save its repackaging, is not clear. Certainly a rebottler may not appropriate the other trade name without some clear and precise explanation of his own status with respect to the original. It seems equally clear that the trade-mark or trade name of the original product cannot occupy the label space on the resale that is ordinarily reserved for the brand name. To this extent, *Bourjois* would certainly appear to remain good law. Beyond these few categories of clear misconduct, the applicability of unfair competition to trade-name association remains an open factual question with the single limitation that the original product's name may be put to a truthful and profitable use by the reseller.

PASSING OFF

In the law of unfair competition, passing off can be both an activity and a result. In its broadest sense, every act of unfair competition which diverts trade succeeds in "passing off" one product for another. For this reason many courts have applied the term in the context of trade name simulation and product simulation. Such usage, although engendering some confusion, is also an accurate application of a more common understanding of the term. In a narrower sense, however, passing off connotes activity related to the actual merchandising of a product which attempts to effect an unsuspecting substitution. It is distinct from any attributes the product might have except insofar as those attributes are directly intended to facilitate the palming off of the product.

It will be in this narrower context that we will examine passing off. Our discussion will at certain times concern products of similar name and at other times products of similar construction, but these will not be the focus of our attention. Rather, we will look at the conduct of merchants who actively seek to employ such similarities in product substitution as a form of unfair competition.

The best example of passing off as a separately actionable form of conduct can be seen in the case of *William R. Warner & Company* v. *Eli Lilly & Company*. Eli Lilly produced a medicinal compound known as Coco-Quinine in which the chocolate ingredient served as a flavoring, a coloring, and a suspension medium for the quinine. Several years after Eli Lilly began marketing this extremely popular medicine, defendant Warner produced and marketed a similar drug called Quin-Coco. The salesmen for Warner suggested to various customers that the less expensive Quin-Coco could readily and easily be substituted for Coco-Quinine in prescriptions and orders for the latter. Evidence further revealed that some druggists actually followed this advice.

The two product names, although vaguely similar, are both merely combinations of descriptive words and could not serve as a basis for confusion resulting from similarity of trade names. Similarly, the chocolate served several functional purposes for which there was no satisfactory substitute. Thus, as will be seen later, there was no basis for an unfair competition suit alleging fraudulent product simulation. Thus, neither trade names nor product simulation was capable of creating a cause of action in unfair competition. Nonetheless, when faced with these facts, the United States Supreme Court concluded that Warner was guilty of unfair competition based solely on the conduct of its sales personnel in encouraging the substitution of one product for another. In the words of Justice Sutherland, "That no deception was practiced on the retail dealers, and that they knew exactly what they were getting is of no consequence. The wrong was in designedly enabling the dealers to palm off the preparations as that of the respondent."

Faced with no clear-cut theoretical principles with which to proscribe the obviously objectionable conduct of Warner, the Court resorted to the very general area of passing off. This has traditionally been the role of this area of law and offers some explanation as to why it defies precise definition. In *Warner* the traditional formula of likelihood of confusion as to origin was inapposite. The druggists were fully aware of the origin of both products, and the purchasing public was never led to believe that Quin-Coco was made by Eli Lilly. The consumer was never presented a confusing choice; rather, he asked for one and got the other without ever knowing it. Under such circumstances a court will examine conduct, rather than merely effect, to discern whether a merchant is competing unfairly.

It is also important to note that the unfair competition in *Warner* occurred a step removed from the injury. Eli Lilly was not complaining that Warner was creating injury in sales to druggists, but in the resale to the consuming public. The Court was quite clear, however, that the inducement of passing off is equally actionable as unfair competition. Although this is not unique to passing off, inducement of product substitution is a far more common sales phenomenon than inducing either name or product simulation.

The manufacturer may also protect his business reputation against passing off by noncompetitors. This is largely a quality-control effort by manufacturers concerned with product purity. Thus, in *Penn Oil Co.* v. *Vacuum Oil Co.* plaintiff Penn Oil manufactured an automotive lubricating oil. The defendant operated several retail gasoline service stations where such oil was advertised for sale. Penn Oil alleged, and the Circuit Court of Appeals for the District of Columbia agreed, that Vacuum had sold crankcase drainings as Penn's product. This constituted passing off for which Penn could maintain an action in unfair competition even though Penn did not operate at the retail level or specifically compete with Vacuum. Because it was Penn's reputation that would be damaged by the poor performance of the inferior oil, it could enjoin the activity.

On similar theories of destruction of good will and business reputation, Coca-Cola Company brought numerous actions against retailers who attempted to substitute other products or to sell a diluted variety of Coca-Cola. Although the usual case involving the individually bottled product would be handled on a trade-mark or trade name basis, passing off is frequently alleged when Coca-Cola syrup is dispensed in a diluted fashion or when another cola syrup is used in a Coca-Cola dispenser. In addition to providing the most rigorous policing of its trade-mark, the Coca-Cola Company is probably the most active enforcer of quality and purity standards in the resale of its syrup. In this latter area, the mode of enforcement almost invariably is grounded on a claim of passing off.

In addition to the more obvious forms of palming off via outright substitution or dilution of the competing product, passing off can also be achieved by far subtler means. One manufacturer might use another's product in his advertisements, or actually as part of an in-person sales promotion, while intending to deliver his own product, if a sale is effected. These are invariably close questions which turn on whether the defendant actually made representations that he would deliver something other than his own product. The case of *United Merchants & Manufacturers, Inc.* v. *Bromley Fabrics, Inc.* is typical of the difficulties encountered.

Defendant had purchased some of the plaintiff's fabrics and used them as samples in merchandising and advertising his own goods. Plaintiff sought a preliminary injunction against this practice for the duration of the trial. This request was refused by the court on the grounds that there was no indication that the defendant claimed that the sample was his product. Rather, he simply promised to deliver a product similar to the sample. The court then noted that if, at trial, it should develop that defendant had actually represented the samples to be his own product, an injunction would lie for passing off. Short of such proof, the court merely noted that "such practice may be sharp . . . but it is not illegal according to the authorities unless calculated in some manner to bring about confusion or deception." The obvious difficulties surrounding proof of such facts seriously undermine the chances of a successful suit.

However, not all courts have demonstrated the sufferance of the *Bromley Fabrics* court in tolerating "sharp" trade practices. In *Motor Improvements, Inc. v. A. C. Spark Plug Co.*, A. C. Spark Plug had lost a patent infringement suit involving an oil filter marketed by Motor Improvements. Subsequently, A. C. altered the internal construction of the filter, thereby curing the infringement, but retained the same external appearance. The noninfringing filter was then marketed under a promotional campaign which alleged that it was interchangeable with the prior, infringing A. C. filter. A. C. defended on the grounds that it never attempted to pass off its filter for the patented device and, therefore, never invaded any rights of the plaintiff.

The United States Court of Appeals for the Sixth Circuit refused to limit passing off to the substitution of one's product for that of a competitor. It noted that the successful infringement action established that only Motor Improvements had the right to sell a filter like that originally sold by A. C. Therefore, when A. C. alleged interchangeability with its earlier model it was actually claiming interchangeability with a product that only the plaintiff was entitled to market. Thus, A. C.'s advertising campaign encouraged substitution for a competing product, a practice similar to the Coco-Quinine facts discussed earlier.

The law surrounding passing off is subject to two major qualifications. The ordinary advertising comparisons and general claims of superiority involve no attempt at fraudulent substitutions and will not be interpreted as inducing palming off. Thus, mere claims of equality or even superiority are more analogous to traditional "puffing" sales methods than customer deception as to the product's nature. The court in *Motor Improvements* noted that no unfair competition would have resulted from a claim by A. C. that its new filter was better than any other on the market. The evil was its calculated attempt to have its new model used where the former one had been used without any explanation of the internal structural differences. Because most of the filters in question were factory installed on new cars, and even replacement filters would not be ordinarily subject to public inspection, the advertising encouraged a product substitution which could deceive the purchaser. In the normal advertising context, where claims are limited to the individual qualities of a product or its general comparability or superiority to the other goods marketed, there is small likelihood that a palming-off situation could arise.

A second qualification on the law of passing off involves the adaptation of popular ideas or products. As was noted earlier in the discussion of copyright law, there is no absolute property right to an idea, save a patented idea. Thus, a manufacturer is free to capitalize on a current trend or style in the marketing of his product. If manufacturer A begins marketing unpatented widgets and they catch the fancy of the consuming public, manufacturer B may also produce the now-popular widgets. In addition, manufacturer B may describe his widgets as being part of the current craze for such items, even though it was A's widgets which stimulated the fad.

PRODUCT SIMULATION

The unlimited variety of factors capable of influencing consumer tastes will often place tremendous importance on a product's configuration. An unusual shape or a pleasing design will frequently catch public fancy and ultimately determine the success of a product. Wherever possible such features are usually registered as trade-marks or covered under a patent grant. However, the registration of design patents is a very recent phenomenon in the law, and our first trade-mark statute did not exist until 1844. Furthermore, our early trade-mark statutes frequently discouraged registration of all but the most obvious technical trade-marks and trade names. Consequently, the law of unfair competition was usually the final resort of those merchants who found that their most attractive product features were being imitated by competitors. This common law protection against product simulation, although having a somewhat checkered past and an equally dubious future, nonetheless established many of the fundamental principles of the law of unfair competition which still have wide application today.

The earliest cases of product simulation limited their protection to the imitation of labels and package arrangements. There were two compelling reasons for this restricted scope. In the first place, our earliest trade-mark laws focused on trade-mark symbols and trade names rather than on the particular arrangement of those items on a product's label. Consequently, such things as the actual format or placement of a trade name and a trade-mark were protected, if at all, only under the common law. Secondly, the earliest decisions involving product simulation also evidenced a strong judicial belief in the exclusivity of the patent grant. Basically, this simply meant that the constitutional authorization for congressional protection of patents was a pre-emption of the entire field which would eliminate any common law protection for the shape of a product. Label arrangements, being more analogous to trade-mark law, were not felt to be within the prohibition of the patent grants.

The early judicial wariness about affording protection for product configurations was soon displaced by a more liberal attitude which recognized the fact that more sophisticated advertising and marketing techniques frequently hinged on a popular product appearance. Typical of the earlier cases expanding the range of protection against product simulation is the case of *Buck's Stove and Range Company* v. *Kiechle*. There the defendant had imitated a white enamel lining on stove doors which had previously served as a unique identification symbol for the plaintiff's product. The court based its decision on the traditional rationale that manufacturers have no right, by imitative devices, to beguile the public into buying their wares under the impression that they are buying those of a rival.

The *Kiechle* decision foreshadowed a vast expansion of the law of product simulation which, by the early years of the twentieth century, afforded protection for such diverse product features as unique colortones of letter files, conical shapes of bread loaves, right-angle construction of motor horns, and the shape of early acetylene gas automobile searchlights. This initial judicial enthusiasm was quickly tempered by a recognition that product features were somewhat different from other, more traditional, modes of indicating origin, consequently, specialized rules are necessary.

The ultimate composition of the rules which governed product simulation was dictated largely by the law of trade-marks and trade names because of the many close analogies which could be drawn between these areas. Secondary meaning occupied a pre-eminent position in such judicial considerations because of the focus on designation of origin. Thus, the first inquiry of any court considering a claim of product simulation was whether the imitated product feature was capable of identifying the source of the product. This necessitated the usual dual inquiry of whether the feature could identify origin and then whether, in fact, it was sufficiently well known that it actually did cause such an association in the mind of a purchaser. However, the doctrine of secondary meaning alone failed to provide adequately for those instances of product simulation motivated by some economy of production or other functional purpose. For this reason the scope of secondary meaning with respect to product simulation was further qualified by the development of the doctrine of functionality.

In simplest terms the doctrine of functionality is a judicial recognition of the fact that many unpatented product features are functionally designed to facilitate production or use of the product and, consequently, should be available to all competing manufacturers. To permit one manufacturer exclusively to appropriate an unpatented product feature would be tantamount to extending the patent law monopoly to cover that product feature. Because this would completely defeat the purpose of the patent laws, some method had to be devised to permit the widest possible imitation of essential, functional product features while still preventing unfair competition. The answer was the doctrine of functionality.

The earliest formulations of this doctrine limited its application to what can be described as the "elements of construction." If a product feature could be said to have structural value or to be necessary for the construction of a satisfactory product, it was described as functional. Naturally such an approach classified a wide range of product attributes as nonfunctional. Unless a product feature qualified as being "utilitarian" its imitation could be circumscribed. The difficulty with such a judicial theory was that it placed total emphasis on the mechanics of construction and use of a product rather than on the underlying thesis of all unfair competition—consumer confusion or deception as to product origin. So long as judicial inquiries were limited to manufacturing processes and product uses, the relationship between product simulation and customer confusion remained at best incidental.

The first case to adjust the doctrine of functionality to market realities was *Champion Spark Club Company* v. *A. R. Mosler & Company.* In that case Judge Learned Hand made the following observation on the proper scope of the doctrine of functionality:

> The doctrine was in earlier cases pressed very far, since the design of a motor lamp or horn may well be a part of the reason why the buyer chooses them. To deny the second comer the right to use that design seems rather to step beyond the principle which protects only such symbols as are representative of the plaintiff's manufacture, nor does it seem an entirely adequate answer to say that the features enjoined are nonfunctional. It is only when the mechanical operativeness of the thing is certainly all that determined the buyer's choice that such a criterion is safe.

The *Champion Spark Plug* case became a point of departure for the development of the theory of aesthetic functionality. This theory broadened the notion of functionality to include nonessential product features which stimulated customer choice or proved to be essential distinguishing characteristics between two products. If a particular attribute of a product determined the buyer's choice, then that attribute must necessarily be functional, because it accomplishes the primary purpose of marketing the goods.

It should be clearly understood that the word *aesthetic,* as used to describe a product feature, cannot be given a literal definition. Rather than meaning an artistic attribute, which might well qualify for copyright protection, the word is used to connote any arbitrary design feature not dictated by production or performance requirements. Thus, the particular shape of a pot handle is an aesthetic factor even though functionality dictates that some sort of handle exist.

One of the best examples of aesthetic functionality can be seen in *Cheney Brothers* v. *Doris Silk Corporation,* involving two manufacturers of silk patterns. The market for the products involved was seasonal and the success or failure of an individual pattern depended upon its ability to attract customer attention by its novelty and beauty. The key role played by the design itself was best demonstrated by the court's observation that only one in five patterns ever proved commercially successful. In light of these acts concerning the effect of the silk patterns, the court determined the designs to be functional elements of the eventual product, essential to their marketing, and, therefore, fully available for imitation by competitors.

Development of the theory of aesthetic functionality returned product simulation to a position analogous to other areas of unfair competition. Uppermost in all judicial considerations was the likelihood of customer confusion rather than the single fact of imitation of a product feature. Functionality now came to mean any product aspect necessary to manufacture, essential to the product's structure or performance, or critical to the marketing of the product in its consumer appeal. Product simulation, therefore, became identified with unnecessary copying irrelevant to the competitive excellence of the product.

It was at this stage in the development of product simulation as a means of unfair competition that the doctrine of functionality was formulated as a portion of the *Restatement of Torts.* According to that treatise, first published in 1938, "a feature of goods is functional . . . if it affects their purpose, action, or performance, or the facility or economy of processing, handling or using them. . . ." This definition effected a substantial shift in the focus of the doctrine of functionality. The broad sweep of its language was, in most instances, interpreted as creating a presumption of functionality which would permit imitation. The *Restatement* formulation of functional soon became the standard point of departure for courts considering unfair competition by product simulation. However, the very vagueness of the definition afforded such wide judicial latitude that the resulting case law was still far from consistent. Some courts limited the *Restatement* definition to a utilitarian or useful notion, thereby seriously curbing the influence of the theory of aesthetic functionality. Other courts read the definition very broadly, and actually extended aesthetic functionality far beyond its original bounds.

In *Sylvania Electrical Products, Inc.* v. *Dura Electric Lamp Company* a United States District Court in New Jersey was faced with the problem of applying the *Restatement* definition to the imitation of a blue dot on photographic flashbulbs which turned pink to indicate the existence of a defective bulb. Sylvania argued that the defendant could imitate neither the dot nor its placement on the bulb without liability for unfair competition. The court ruled that the dot itself was "utilitarian" and therefore could be fully imitated by other flashbulb manufacturers. As to the much closer question of the location of the dot, the court also concluded for functionality, because visibility was essential for the dot to have any utility whatever, and that utility was "greatly enhanced by the prominence of its location." The *Sylvania* decision indicates that post-*Restatement* interpretations of traditional product simulation situations remained essentially unaltered.

The same cannot be said for aesthetic functionality. Courts divided as to whether the *Restatement* definition contemplated inclusion of aesthetic functionality or was intended to be limited to the more utiliarian aspects of a product. Two cases will serve to highlight the dichotomy which resulted.

In *American-Marietta Company* v. *Krigsman* the United States Court of Appeals for the Second Circuit considered a product simulation case brought by the manufacturer of sponge floor mops. The plaintiff alleged that defendant had imitated the nonfunctional slots in the plate of the mop which served as a drain when the mop was wrung out. Agreeing with the plaintiff, the court concluded that the slots were nonfunctional, because "the mop will work as well with openings of another shape. . . ." The court would not give any persuasive weight to the fact that only a limited number of shapes were available for the restricted plate area and that certain slot shapes gave a decidedly more uniform and appealing appearance. Two years later, the same court, in *Hygenic Specialties Company* v. *H. G. Salzman, Inc.,* stated that two-piece soap dishes were all necessarily similar and therefore subject to imitation because their design was for the most part dictated entirely by function. The reason that the design features of soap dishes are functional and the design features of a sponge floor mop are not was not clarified by any subsequent court. Similarly confusing inconsistencies exist in other circuits concerning the degree to which a product design will qualify for protection against imitation.

Thus, on the eve of the United States Supreme Court's decisions in the *Sears* and *Compco* cases, the state of the law of unfair competition for product simulation could best be described as being in flux. Although the better-established aspects of "utilitarian versus fanciful" product attributes remained somewhat consistent, courts were still uncerain about the exact degree of protection to be afforded aesthetic design factors.

What did appear certain, and what is still very relevant to subsequent litigation under the unfair competition section of the Lanham Act, is that notions of secondary meaning and functionality must somehow combine to demonstrate a product feature capable of designating product origin which serves no essential purpose in the effective competitive marketing of the product other than to specify its source.

THE *SEARS* AND *COMPCO* CASES

Prior to 1964 the regulation of unfair competition involved many levels of federal, state, and local activity. Frequently the same conduct was proscribed by a federal statute, a state statute, and the common law. In other instances federal statutory protecion was supplemented by state laws of unfair competition or state enforcement of common law unfair competition. The area of product simulation is a prime example of this multilevel regulation. At the federal level, a product's structural attributes were subject to possible coverage under the patent laws, either by mechanical or design patent grants. In addition, state statutes or common law remedies would afford protection for unpatentable product configurations capable of designating origin or creating a source association. Similarly, many states afforded trade-mark protection either through specific statutes or under some general law of unfair competition. The validity of this duplication of jurisdictions was not seriously challenged until 1964, when two cases raised the issue before the United States Supreme Court.

In *Sears, Roebuck & Company* v. *Stiffel Company* the plaintiff in the lower court, Stiffel Company, had secured federal design and mechanical patents on a pole lamp, a device consisting of a vertical tube running from ceiling to floor with lamps affixed. Sears produced a similar pole lamp which the lower court described as "a substantially exact copy" of Stiffel's product. Stiffel brought suit alleging federal patent infringement and also a violation of the Illinois unfair competition law. At trial, the federal patents were invalidated on the ground that they lacked the necessary invention, but plaintiff nonetheless prevailed with the unfair competition claim under state law. The appellate court affirmed, observing that the critical issue was the likelihood of customer confusion as to the source of the products rather than the need to show any palming off of the goods. Noting the near identity of the two products, the court concluded such confusion was inevitable.

The Supreme Court, through Justice Black, reversed the decision with respect to the applicability of the state unfair competition law. Justice

Black grounded his decision on the exclusivity of the constitutional authorization allowing Congress to grant exclusive patent rights. The primary purpose of this constitutional directive was the encouragement of invention through the reward of an exclusive monopoly. Because the source of authority for the patent laws is constitutional, as enacted they are the supreme law of the land and pre-empt any state law "that clashes with the objective of the federal patent laws."

On the same day, the Supreme Court handed down the companion decision in *Compo Corp.* v. *Day-Brite Lighting, Inc.* The product feature in that case was a reflector ribbing for fluorescent lighting fixtures commonly used in commercial establishments. Again a design patent had been obtained on the product feature. Compco employed a similar cross-ribbing in its fixtures, and Day-Brite brought a federal infringement suit as well as an unfair competition suit under the Illinois statute. At trial, the design patent was invalidated and relief was granted solely on the basis of unfair competition. Relying on *Sears,* the Supreme Court reversed the determination and further observed:

> A State of course has power to impose liability upon those who, knowing that the public is relying upon an original manufacturer's reputation for quality and integrity, deceive the public by palming off their copies as the original. That an article copied from an unpatented article could be made in some other way, that the design is "non-functional" and not essential to the use of either article, that the configuration of the article copied may have a "secondary meaning" which identifies the maker to the trade, or that there may be "confusion" among purchasers as to which article is which, or as to who is the maker may be relevant evidence in applying a State's law requiring such precautions as labeling; however, neither these facts nor any other can furnish a basis for imposing liability for or prohibiting the actual acts of copying and selling, regardless of the copier's motives.

The full range of these two far-reaching decisions has not yet been accurately measured. Some commentators have speculated that the decisions virtually eliminate common law unfair competition, and others will concur that at least state remedies for product simulation are no longer viable. What is certain about the decisions is that they will dominate all future considerations of nonfederal remedies for unfair competition. Therefore, the balance of this chapter will discuss the various possible interpretations of *Sears* and *Compco.* Further, where state law appears to be abrogated by the decisions, we will consider other possible federal remedies available under the prohibition against unfair competition contained in the Lanham Act.

Any discussion of *Sears* and *Compco* must begin with an examination of the dual causes of action brought in each case. In both instances, a federal cause of action for patent infringement was coupled with a state cause of action for unfair competition by product simulation. Both plaintiffs alleged that the same facts which would support a cause of action for patent infringement would also support one for product simulation, and neither plaintiff attempted to show any fraudulent activity on the part of the defendant beyond the mere fact of copying. Both of the products involved relied for their popularity on the appealing nature of their design rather than on any trade-mark or trade name association. Thus, in the narrowest reading of these decisions, the Supreme Court was called upon to decide whether a state could afford protection for a product shape that the federal patent laws had thrust into the public domain.

The Court's negative response to this question was grounded solely on the theory of federal pre-emption. Article I, Section 8, clause 8 of the Constitution, which authorizes federal legislation covering patents, is a comprehensive grant of power intended to reach all potential areas of patentable products without respect to state borders or interstate commerce. Because of this sweeping grant of authority, the pre-emption which accompanies the patent and copyright laws must be distinguished from the more typical federal pre-emption which occurs when a statute is enacted pursuant to the commerce or taxing powers of Congress. Under the commerce clause, a specific basis in interstate commerce must first be established before the federal law becomes applicable to a particular transaction. Thus, the federal statute will only pre-empt *conflicting* state enactments, that is, those which have an influence or an effect upon the interstate characteristics of the subject matter. In sharp contrast, the constitutional patent and copyright authority recognizes no state exceptions which would permit local regulation of patents or copyrights. This total exclusivity or complete "occupation" of the field would invalidate not only state laws which limit rights granted under federal statutes, but also state laws which extend rights to the subject matter beyond that offered by the federal statute.

Returning to the specific facts of *Sears* and *Compco,* the subject matter under both the federal and state laws in question was clearly the configuration of the goods, the actual substance of the product itself. In such circumstances, the only state law which would not conflict with the federal enactment would be one which neither expands nor contracts the rights available under the patent laws. Because this would be a type of legislative redundance equally prohibited by federal pre-emption, it would be effectively impossible for a state to pass any law addressed to an area whether the federal grant of authority is constitutional in origin and comprehensive in scope. This was the literal holding of *Sears* and *Compco.*

The precedential impact of *Sears* and *Compco,* however, far exceeds its resolution of the issues before the Court and it would be naïve to limit the interpretation of these decisions to a prohibition on state remedies for product simulation. In speaking for the Court, Mr. Justice Black formulated several broad pronouncements which far exceeded the issues immediately before that tribunal. In so doing, he raised serious doubts about the validity of other, related areas of unfair competition analogous to product simulation. As was noted earlier, the one continuous theme permeating all aspects of unfair competition is the attempt to prevent customer confusion about the origin of the goods. It was this rationale that provided the sole foundation for the product-simulation action brought in the *Sears* and *Compco* cases. In striking down this cause of action, the Court also dismissed the judicial concern about confusion as to the source of the product as a meaningful basis for independent action at the state level. Thus, the broader language of *Sears* and *Compco* seriously undermines other areas of unfair competition which, although not involving the imitation of product shapes or designs, nonetheless rely on source association as the motivating factor in their determinations. Consequently, it is essential to re-examine each of the areas of unfair competition already discussed to measure the impact of *Sears* and *Compco* on the future availability of these remedies.

Product Simulation

Obviously, the most immediate impact of *Sears* and *Compco* is on the area of product imitation. The Court was quite clear that a state could not afford protection for the imitation of product features that were themselves unpatentable. However, the Court did specifically note that a state was still entitled to formulate statutory requirements with respect to the identification of products by means of labels. Thus, the very considerable area of product labeling and packaging, commonly referred to as "trade dress," is still open to state supervision. This would seem to return the law of product simulation to one of the earliest stages of its development, namely, preventing simulation of those aspects of a product which, although not an actual part of its structure, nonetheless constitute part of the final product package as presented to the customer.

Much of the area of trade dress protection is more analogous to trademark law than to patent law, which may explain the Court's different approach to it. By limiting the scope of product simulation protection to trade dress, the area becomes closely analogous to the law of unfair competition with respect to trade names. Because trade dress cannot be, and was never intended to be, registered under the patent laws, it does not impinge on the exclusivity of the federal patent system. Nonetheless, it does focus on the prevention of consumer confusion and may, therefore, have been affected by the broader language of *Sears* and *Compco*.

To the extent that trade dress protection at the state level prevents improper product identification, rather than confusing identification, it will be within the exception provided by the Court for labeling. In essence, this means that state laws must be concerned with the objective truth or falsity of labels and label arrangements, and may not focus on the misleading aspects which derive solely from similarities between competing labels. Thus, a state may require a certain label format in order to identify the product but may not prohibit a certain label format simply because its similarity to another will tend to confuse such identification. Obviously, close questions will arise and the exact dividing line is still uncertain.

At least some elucidation, however, was provided in *Double Eagle Lubricants, Inc.* v. *FTC,* wherein a Texas labeling statute imposed stricter disclosure requirements than a Federal Trade Commission cease and desist order. The product involved was re-refined used oil, and the Texas law required explanatory labeling on the front and back of every can, whereas the commission order gave a choice of either location. The district court rejected a federal pre-emption argument on the grounds that the state regulation was a safety measure pursuant to its police power. Although containing obvious distinctions as to the basis of the state law and the extent of federal "occupation" of the field, the case does clearly indicate that a state law founded on some basis other than protection of competitors will be more readily sustained in a suit alleging federal pre-emption.

What is certain, however, is that states may still formulate legislation either to require labeling where none presently exists and product features are similar or to require more informative labeling where a deceptively similar label arrangement is being employed.

Even in the area of regulating deceptive labeling practices, however, the state must be conscious of federal pre-emption. Thus, some recent decisions have indicated that a state law must recognize the existence of federal regulation of deceptive advertising insofar as it may conflict with the state's rules on labeling and trade dress. The simplest resolution of this dilemma was employed in *Metropolitan New York Retail Merchants Association* v. *City of New York.* A New York State Supreme Court there reviewed a New York City ordinance regulating false advertising. Acknowledging the possibility that this local law might "clash" with federal advertising regulation by the Federal Trade Commission, the court judicially amended the local ordinance by enjoining its enforcement where compliance could be shown with the federal law. In effect, the court read a defense of federal compliance into the local law. *Sears* and *Compco* would seem to countenance such a result and courts have so interpreted it.

Passing Off

The narrower description of passing off, that pertaining to conduct whereby one product is substituted for another, remains relatively undisturbed by the *Sears* and *Compco* decisions. As the Court noted in *Compco,* "a state of course has power to impose liability upon those who, knowing that the public is relying upon an original manufacturer's reputation for quality and integrity, deceive the public by palming off their copies as the original." Once again, a lack of conflict with the patent laws is self-evident. Palming off is *activity* unrelated to comparative product compositions, and equally unrelated to patentability, which results in deceptive substitution of products rather than in any confusion about their origin.

However, passing off in its broader sense—that is, a successful confusion of one product for another—has been completely invalidated where achieved solely by the means of copying product characteristics. The lower courts in *Sears* and *Compco* indicated that it was the product simulation alone, without any reference to passing off, which accomplished the unfair competition under the Illinois statute. In rejecting this, the Supreme Court considered it irrelevant that there might be confusion among purchasers when caused solely by product similarities. Thus, the fact that a passing-off result is achieved by product simulation will not alter the fact that product simulation may no longer be a separately provided state remedy for unfair competition.

Trade Names

It is in the area of trade names that the precise impact of *Sears* and *Compco* is most difficult to measure. To understand properly the problems involved, we must re-examine the fundamental rationale of *Sears* and *Compco.* In those cases, the Court rested its decision on the comprehensive grant of patent and copyright authority contained in the Constitution. Because this grant of authority transcends all state borders, it is capable of reaching every aspect of potentially patentable products. Thus, everything relating to product structure and its protection from imitation is within the scope of the patent laws alone. Such is not the case with the federal trade-mark laws. That legislation was enacted pursuant to the commerce clause of the Constitution and, consequently, only affects those trade-marks and trade names which can be found in interstate commerce. In addition, the commerce requirement of the trade-mark laws has been somewhat more narrowly interpreted than other commerce requirements. For this reason many restaurants have been unable to register their trade names simply because they have been unable to demonstrate that their services—that is, their provision of dining facilities and meals—are "in commerce" within the meaning of the Lanham Trademark Act. Because the scope of federal trade-mark coverage is limited by a commerce requirement, it is not as comprehensive as that of the patent and copyright laws. Rather, there will be many instances of an intrastate use of trade names and trade-marks totally outside the ambit of any federal trade-mark statute.

The pre-emptive declarations of *Sears* and *Compco,* when applied to the trade name situation, must be read in light of the federal pre-emption that otherwise exists in that area. This federal pre-emption pertains to the trade-mark statutes rather than to the patent and copyright legislation and will extend only so far as the reach of the commerce clause. For this reason, purely localized trade name protection, and even local trade-mark statutes, have not been invalidated by *Sears* and *Compco.*

A more difficult question, of course, is the type of protection that such local remedies can offer. Where neither use is in commerce, as where both litigants are local merchants with limited clientele, the state courts can obviously fashion effective protection. However, where only the party seeking the protection can manifest a purely intrastate business, there is grave doubt that any state remedy can be given. For example, if merchant A and merchant B both sell only in a single county, a state court could give effective protection against trade name simulation, because there is no interstate commerce warranting federal involvement. However, where one of the merchants is in interstate commerce, he may well be able to simulate a local trade name without state interference, because any attempted enforcement by the state would have the requisite effect on commerce.

One final area where the limitations of *Sears* and *Compco* will have significant effect pertains to those trade-marks and trade names presently listed on the Supplemental Register under the Lanham Act. It is a prerequisite of such registration that a use in commerce be demonstrated; therefore, such a registration automatically precludes state protection for the mark or name. As will be noted in the final discussion in this chapter, this does not preclude all protection for such marks, but only invalidates whatever state protection which might have existed prior to *Sears* and *Compco.* By the same token, trade-marks or trade names that are rejected from registration because of a failure to demonstrate the necessary commerce requirement would seem to fall automatically outside the possibility of incurring federal pre-emption with respect to their protection under state law. In this sense, the effect of *Sears* and *Compco* can be readily and quickly determined—registration being the key to whether or not a federal pre-emption will occur.

UNFAIR COMPETITION UNDER THE LANHAM ACT

Thus far our discussion has focused on the availability of state and common law remedies for various types of unfair competition. The extensive limitations on these remedies occasioned by the decisions in *Sears* and *Compco* have lent increased importance to federal statutory prohibitions on similar conduct. The possibility of federal protection for commercial intangibles previously covered by the law of unfair competition has greatly expanded with recent liberalizations in trade-mark and copyright registrations for product designs and configurations, but the central source of federal protection against unfair competition remains Section 43(a) of the Lanham Trademark Act of 1946. By its provisions,

> Any person who shall affix, apply, or annex, or use in connection with any goods or services, or any container or containers for goods, a false designation of origin, or any false description or representation, including words or other symbols tending falsely to describe or represent the same, and shall cause such goods or services to enter into commerce, and any person who shall with knowledge of the falsity of such designation or origin or description or representation cause or procure the same to be transported or used in commerce or deliver the same to any carrier to be transported or used, shall be liable to a civil action by any person doing business in the locality falsely indicated as that of origin or the region in which said locality is situated, or by any person who believes that he is or is likely to be damaged by the use of any such false description or representation.

The section provides a single cause of action for unfair competition without reference to the various categories previously existing at common law. The section constitutes a major departure from traditional remedies for unfair competition and, consequently, requires close scrutiny in order to determine its precise scope.

The nature of the wrong described by the section is simply a "false designation" or "false description" of the origin of a product or service. Within this description are two critical factors, the nature of a false representation and the meaning of the word *origin*. As to the first factor, false representations have not been limited to literal falsehoods. It is sufficient that the activity creates a false impression in the mind of the consumer. Thus, both express and implied falsehoods are covered by the section. Further, the false description need not directly relate to the origin of the product if the implication reasonably inferred therefrom pertains to origin. Thus, in *Parkway Baking Co.* v. *Feihofer Baking Co.* it was sufficient that the defendant had falsely asserted his product was authorized or approved by another. The court held this a sufficient implication of false origin.

The word *origin* itself has generated extensive judicial discussion. Its use in conjunction with *locality* in the latter part of the section has led some courts to entertain the argument that the section only concerns representations as to geographic origins. However, more recent judicial interpretation has rejected this narrow view in favor of having the section apply to any representation as to the originator or origin of the product. Thus, a particular manufacturing source, as identified solely through a product or business name, is sufficiently related to origin to come within the section. This would seem the most logical interpretation, because the section proscribes the use of words or "symbols" in this regard, and symbols can only have significance in identifying production sources rather than geographic origins.

The section has been held to apply to more than misrepresentations involving trade-marks and trade names. Although the precise language refers to "words or other symbols," this has not been read to confine the section to trade name "words" and trade-mark "symbols." In *Glenn* v. *Advertising Publications, Inc.* a brochure and film alleged to contain false and misleading representations were held to be a description within the section's meaning. According to the court, Section 43(a) "forbids 'any' false description or representation in connection with goods or services." This would seem to indicate that the essential wrong, deception as to origin, can be accomplished by such tangential means as misdescribing either a product's attributes or those of a competing product. Just how far the "any" language can be stretched is still far from settled.

The commerce requirement of Section 43(a), as with all portions of the Lanham Act, is narrower than traditional notions of that legislative authority. The section literally requires that the offending goods "enter into commerce" as a prerequisite to federal jurisdiction, and this rather harsh formulation proved a substantial limitation in the earlier interpretations of the section's scope. Read alone, the section appears to focus solely on the interstate character of the unfair copies without regard for the character or status of the resulting injury. Early courts so interpreted the section and it became necessary to tie the unfair competition claim with a substantial trade-mark or trade name infringement allegation in order to ensure the requisite showing of actual involvement in commerce.

However, later courts began to read Section 43(a) in conjunction with Section 45, the proviso enunciating the intended purpose of the Lanham Act. Section 45 lists, *inter alia,* the following legislative intent: "The intent of this Act is to regulate commerce within the control of Congress . . . to protect persons engaged in such commerce against unfair competition. . . ." This language appears to manifest a dominant congressional desire to prevent injury from unfair competition *in interstate commerce* rather than simply to prevent the insertion of misleading or deceptive product descriptions into interstate commerce. Later courts began to read the commerce statements of the two sections together and developed the notion that Section 43(a) created a federal tort *sui generis* of unfair competition where an "effect on commerce" can be shown under the more traditional interstate commerce standards.

Although the effect-on-commerce rationale represents a considerable liberalization, it still will not extend the section to activities involving only an indirect influence on interstate commerce. Thus, if either of the products involved is in interstate commerce, the jurisdictional basis would be available, but if both products are local and the sellers or manufacturers have other dealings in interstate commerce, this alone will not provide an adequate connection with interstate commerce to come under the scope of the section.

Perhaps the greatest single legal innovation wrought by Section 43(a) is its tremendous broadening of the "standing to sue" requirements. Under common law, only those persons who could demonstrate a vested interest or right in the appropriated name or mark were entitled to sue for its unfair use. Thus, *standing* was limited to those who could establish some sort of "property right" being injured by the defendant's conduct. As was noted earlier in the chapter on common law remedies, courts would not entertain the notion that a competitor can be the "vicarious avenger" of the general public. A real, immediate, and tangible injury had to be shown before a suit for unfair competition would be entertained.

Section 43(a) rejects all references to any "property right" notion of unfair competition and offers civil relief to "any person who believes that he is or is likely to be damaged" by the misrepresentation. The effect of this sweeping category of those entitled to sue is that the section has effectively eliminated the need to show any vested interest in the subject matter of the suit as a precondition to judicial consideration on the merits. This notion of standing seems to direct the section as much to preventing public deception as to preventing competitive injury. The "public" orientation of the section is further magnified by the provision which affords a cause of action for "any person doing business in the locality falsely indicated as that of origin." This proviso avoids any mention of actual or possible damage and creates a presumptive standing to sue through the mere geographic location of the plaintiff. Clearly, this overreaches the farthest extensions of common law competitive torts in affording a general theory of relief.

For more than a decade after its enactment in 1946, Section 43(a) was used only infrequently by plaintiffs seeking relief from unfair competition. This paucity of litigation can generally be ascribed to the then existing strict judicial interpretation of the commerce requirement plus the ready availability of state remedies. However, the decisions in the *Sears* and *Compco* cases, coupled with a liberalization of the commerce standards, have thrust the section into the vanguard of remaining remedies for unfair competition. The willingness of courts to expand notions of "origin" and "representation" to encompass many areas abrogated by *Sears* and *Compco* can best be seen by an examination of some of the recent litigation under Section 43(a).

In *General Pool Corp.* v. *Hallmark Pool Corp.* the United States District Court for the Northern District of Illinois was urged to extend Section 43(a) to cover defendant's use of a photograph of one of plaintiff's pools in defendant's advertising brochure. Defendant claimed that *Sears* and *Compco* permitted him to copy plaintiff's pool in all respects and, therefore, the picture's use was not objectionable unless it was copyrighted.

Disposing of the commerce requirement with the observation that "both parties are engaged in interstate commerce," the court then proceeded to examine whether the acts complained of fell within the scope of Section 43(a). This involved the resolution of two issues, (1) whether the photograph was a "false description" and (2) whether its use could create confusion as to origin, without contradicting *Sears* and *Compco*.

Noting that neither the picture nor the pool itself were eligible for statutory protection, the court observed that a third factor was involved, the *conduct* of the parties in the use of these items. Conduct alone, without a proprietary attachment to any particular tangible, is sufficient to support a cause of action under 43(a). In this case, the conduct was advertising and the photograph only provided the vehicle for the "false description" in the advertisements. Because of the frequency with which advertising proves to be the medium for unfair competition, Section 43(a) has been described as a federal remedy for false advertising.

In finding that the use of the photograph in advertising constituted a false description under Section 43(a), the court applied the following logic:

> This result is reached by attaching to the defendants' brochure the only reasonable construction that can be made; that is, that the defendant corporation installed the pools pictured in its brochure. To the extent that the defendant corporation did not install the pool represented by the picture of plaintiff's pool, there is a false representation and hence false advertising.

The conclusion that false advertising exists is not, without more, a *prima facie* showing under 43(a). In this respect judicial observations that Section 43(a) is a false advertising law are somewhat incomplete. Section 43(a) only provides a private cause of action for certain types of false advertising, namely, that which deceives as to the origin of the product. Thus, even though false advertising is fully established, this only satisfies the "false description" element under 43(a) and confusion as to origin must still be demonstrated. It will be remembered from earlier discussions that source association can relate to either confusing one source with another or confusingly indicating that both products originate from a third unidentified source.

In *General Pool* the court was faced with the additional problem that many other manufacturers made the same pool as plaintiff, so that a secondary meaning would be most difficult to establish. Absent the proof of this secondary meaning, the false advertising would not sustain a Section 43(a) suit. Acknowledging the plaintiff's "particularly great" burden of proof with respect to this element, the court nonetheless refused to dismiss the action on defendant's motion. In so doing, the court found that the possibility of a secondary meaning being shown, even in the highly fungible business of popular design pool construction, would not be ruled out as a matter of law.

The court also took a particularly narrow view of the "origin" requirement of Section 43(a) by noting that the false description "must involve the misuse of some distinguishing characteristic of a manufacturer's product or the manufacturer himself." This is far narrower than the literal reading of the section, which implies that any description which misleads as to source is actionable by anyone at that source *or* anyone likely to be damaged. This would seem to eliminate the necessity of showing a secondary meaning in the plaintiff's product so long as it can be shown that the defendant represented falsely an origin identical to plaintiff's. In spite of this apparently strict construction of the origin requirement, the court was unwilling to deny the likelihood of a secondary meaning even though the plaintiff had only used the photograph a short period of time and the model in question was a "standard" in the industry. The court found that "it would not be unreasonable to find upon proof of the fact that the picture has become distinctly associated with the plaintiff and that there has in fact been a misdesignation of origin. . . ."

The *General Pool* decision typifies the approach of federal courts to Section 43(a) after *Sears* and *Compco*. Prior to those decisions suits under 43(a) usually involved a "borrowing" of plaintiff's product to promote inferior goods or the assertion of an attribute possessed by plaintiff's goods but lacking in defendant's. In both situations a showing that the goods were of substantially the same quality would negate the falsehood. Relief against sheer trade name or product simulation was left to state courts.

Subsequent to *Sears* and *Compco,* the focus of the "falsehood" shifted to origin and a description became false if it misrepresented its source, regardless of the relative quality of the two products. This is highlighted by the *General Pool* decision. Both parties agreed that defendants could probably produce a substantially identical pool to that of the plaintiff's, so comparative quality did not even enter into the considerations. Rather, the conduct, not the product, occupied the court's attention. Thus, although courts will still prohibit the unauthorized marketing of inferior goods under 43(a), the section's scope has been expanded along source association lines to fill the void created in this area by *Sears* and *Compco.*

The decision of the United States District Court for the Southern District of New York in *Geisel* v. *Poynter Products, Inc.* is an excellent example of this dual application of Section 43(a). Plaintiff was the famous Dr. Seuss, a well-known artist-author of children's books. The plaintiff had illustrated a 1932 story in the now defunct *Liberty Magazine.* Plaintiff also had current licensing agreements with manufacturers for toy reproductions of his various cartoon characters. Defendant purchased all rights to the 1932 illustrations from a survivor corporation of *Liberty Magazine* and immediately contracted with a Japanese toy manufacturer for production of toys derived from the 1932 illustrations. The toys were inferior in quality and deviated substantially from the illustrations. They were sold under the names *Dr. Seuss Merry Menagerie* and *From the Wonderful World of Dr. Seuss.*

The defendant argued that the absence of any trade-mark or copyright rights in the 1932 illustrations necessitated dismissal of the action. The court disagreed and determined that defendants had violated Section 43(a) on two separate grounds. First, the advertising of the products was a false representation that they were authorized by and originated with Dr. Seuss. This was a false description or designation of origin within the meaning of the section.

Further, the court noted that plaintiff was entitled to relief against the *type* of toy being sold by defendant because of the great disparity in quality with respect to his initial work: "The defendants do not possess the right to represent that their goods were sponsored or authorized by the plaintiff; nor do they have the right to represent as copies, goods which are poorly made and deviate materially from the originals." The *Geisel* decision by no means represents an extreme extension of Section 43(a). It essentially concerns very traditional areas of trade names and palming off. What is significant about it and similar recent case law is the complete willingness of courts to interpret the "origin" requirement of the section broadly so as to achieve the most expansive application of it to undesirable modes of competition.

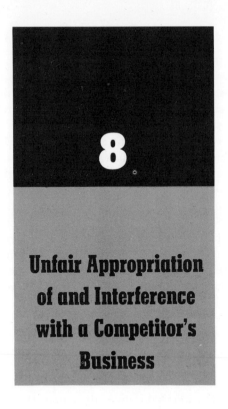

8.

Unfair Appropriation of and Interference with a Competitor's Business

In the modern market place the various elements that contribute to the commercial success of a product are often far more than the various components which constitute the physical structure of the product. Efficient methods of production, effective distribution systems, and competent personnel are frequently valuable ingredients in the ultimate popularity of a consumer good. To the businessman each of these factors constitutes valuable commercial intangibles essential to his continued functioning in a competitive market.

Each of these intangibles can be the subject of unfair use by a competitor. An unscrupulous businessman can seek to exploit the valuable commercial intangibles of a competitor without authorization or compensation. To prevent such an eventuality, the law of unfair competition affords a wide variety of remedies calculated to inhibit business practices which exploit or disrupt the commercial activities of a competitor. Although these remedies will vary greatly, they all concern forms of business conduct whereby one competitor attempts unfairly either to use or to destroy a favorable commercial arrangement of another. Specifically, these remedies will involve the categories of relief traditionally denominated as misappropriation, trade secrets, covenants not to compete, and interference with contractual relationships.

MISAPPROPRIATION

Unlike tangible property, intangibles are inexhaustible with respect to their potential exploitation. The single good will factor of a particular merchant may apply to any number of goods he sells and will not be exhausted upon the disposition of a particular inventory. However, the market value of intangibles lies in their relative scarcity and their identification with a particular source. Herein lies their great susceptibility to unfair exploitation by third parties.

In order to be of any value whatever, an intangible must be used, it must be exposed to the public, and the public must come to identify it with a particular product or service. At the same time, its public exposure must be controlled or else the source association so critical to its market value will be destroyed. Where a competitor attempts unfairly to confuse this source association, the law of unfair competition provides relief in the form of actions for passing off, trade name simulation, and product simulation. This does not, however, exhaust the methods in which a commercial intangible could be competitively abused. A competitor might simply exploit a commercial intangible to his own advantage without creating any confusion as to source. For example, a merchant might structure his product to conform to a well-established distribution system in order to capitalize on the attractiveness such a system might have for the consumer. It is to this type of competitive exploitation—that is, the unauthorized use, adaptation, or enjoyment of the efforts of a competitor—that the law of misappropriation addresses itself.

A misappropriation can be as varied an act as the intangible being exploited. It is very difficult, therefore, to abstract the legal principles which will support an action for misappropriation. Being an equitable form of relief, the particular facts and circumstances of each situation will govern the legal outcome. There are, however, certain broad legal notions which must be kept in mind when considering the area of misappropriation. It will be well to examine these principles before turning our attention to the various factual situations which will support a claim of misappropriation under the law of unfair competition.

As an initial proposition, it must be understood that not every appropriation of a scheme or arrangement of a competitor is actionable, or for that matter even unfair. An appropriation which merely consti- tutes a copying, duplication, or imitation of a competitor's conception of a favorable business scheme will only provide grounds for a cause of action where it can be shown that the originator of the intangible had some vested property right in it. It will be recalled that such vested in- terests in intangibles are created by the copyright, patent, and trade- mark statutes and, to a limited extent, by the law of unfair competition where a secondary meaning has been established. Beyond these various forms of protection, however, any competitor is free to capitalize on an intangible promotional idea by simply duplicating it and applying it to his own uses. However, where the method of exploitation is not copying but rather simply using an already established scheme or arrangement of a competitor, somewhat different legal principles will apply. Although no businessman is entitled to the exclusive possession of an idea or con- ception, he does enjoy certain rights to the exclusive use of the manner in which he selects to express or structure that conception physically. For example, if a manufacturer has an idea for a national distribution system of automobile parts, he may not preclude others from establish- ing similar distribution systems for such products. But he is entitled under certain circumstances discussed hereafter to prevent a rival from using his system to market competing goods.

The earliest formulations of the doctrine of misappropriation paral- leled the emergence in American business of industries which dealt with intangibles as an ultimate product. As the business community became more sophisticated, it fostered an increasing number of business enter- prises concerned solely with the marketing of tangible products belong- ing to others or to the public at large. The "advertising and informa- tion industries" became distinct entities in the market place, offering such intangible products as advertising campaigns and current stock market quotations. The obvious susceptibility of these products to mis- appropriation by competitors led the courts to formulate unique forms of relief under a general theory of unfair competition.

One of the earliest applications of the doctrine occurred in the *Ticker* cases, a collection of decisions involving the telegraphic communication of news and business statistics to major Western and Midwestern cities for redistribution to local subscribing newspapers. The obvious value of the entire news transmittal system was the exclusivity which the infor- mation might have at its destination. The cases in the *Ticker* collection all concern unauthorized appropriations of the transmitted informa- tion by local competitors through resale to nonsubscribing newspapers. The facts presented obvious difficulties to courts accustomed to resolv- ing problems of unfair competition along traditional tort and prop- erty law lines. Consequently, these early judicial efforts at affording some protection for news communication often drew analogies to the more traditional common law concepts. Thus, in one of the earlier *Ticker* cases, *National Telegraph News Co.* v. *Western Union Telegraph Co.*, the United States Circuit Court of Appeals for the Seventh Circuit first established that the news matter collected for transmission was a distinct and valuable business property and that the service of purveying this information was a legitimate commercial enterprise "partaking of the nature of property in a sense that entitled it to the protection of a court of equity against piracy."

Once a court was able to establish the proprietary nature of the subject matter of the appropriation it was an easy step to afford some form of equitable relief in the form of an injunction. This proved to be the typical approach for a court faced with the problem of providing protection for a business system or method of operation. Later cases, involving such things as the emergence of trading stamps as a form of product promotion, stimulated similar judicial responses. Courts viewed the trading stamps and their system of distribution as independent proprietary elements deserving legal protection.

Perhaps the first step toward a more general theory of misappropriation was the *Prest-O-Lite* cases. Prest-O-Lite manufactured an acetylene gas for automobile searchlights which was distributed in a uniquely shaped container particularly suited for a Prest-O-Lite receiver. Only containers of the prescribed shape would fit the Prest-O-Lite receiver, and Prest-O-Lite maintained a nationwide distribution system for the replacement of these acetylene tanks when their gas supply was depleted. This network of depots was a major factor in the commercial success of the Prest-O-Lite Company. The defendant, Searchlight Gas Co., in an effort to enjoy some of the advantages of the Prest-O-Lite system, engaged in a practice of refilling old Prest-O-Lite tanks with Searchlight gas. The justification offered for such a practice was that the tanks, once purchased, became the property of the purchaser and could be put to whatever subsequent use the purchaser desired without in any way impairing any of the legal rights of Prest-O-Lite. Because the actual product of Prest-O-Lite was not being appropriated by the defendant, the courts were finally presented with the situation wherein the sole subject matter of the appropriation was a commercially intangible distribution system.

The initial difficulty faced by the courts in attempting to resolve the *Prest-O-Lite* cases was determining when a distribution system ceased to be an idea and commenced being a product. Certainly the actual Prest-O-Lite depots were tangible product elements, but these were not being appropriated by the defendant. Rather, the defendant was trading on the fact that its customers would be able to use the Prest-O-Lite depots at some later time because of the exchangeability of the Prest-O-Lite containers. The issue was eventually resolved by determining that the product marketed by Prest-O-Lite was not simply acetylene gas but rather a composite product consisting of the tangible fuel coupled with a right to participate in the business system which the plaintiff had established for replenishment of that fuel. Because this right and the system to which it related was a creation of Prest-O-Lite, the court concluded it was a product quality, rather than simply an idea, which could not be appropriated by others to the detriment of Prest-O-Lite. Even at this stage of the doctrine's development, courts felt an obligation to establish some nexus with a tangible business commodity before affording relief against misappropriation.

The final step in the establishment of misappropriation of commercial intangibles as a distinct form of unfair competition, and the acknowledged headwaters of the doctrine, was the decision of the United States Supreme Court in *International News Service* v. *Associated Press*. Associated Press operated a news wire service to newspaper affiliates throughout the United States. It was a cooperative organization and only the members of the cooperative had access to the news distributed over the wire-service facilities. The defendant was a competing news service with a far less extensive network of members. The gravamen of the complaint was that the defendant, by various means, copied plaintiff's news stories when they appeared on the East Coast and immediately transmitted them to its Midwestern and Far Western subscribers. Because of the time delay caused by the various time zones in the country, defendant was able to compete with plaintiff in the subsequent distribution of plaintiff's own news stories in the later time zones. The defendant argued that once the plaintiff had published its news information in any form without copyright protection, the material had entered the public domain and was available for use by anyone for any purpose. Associated Press responded that the news in question was a commercial intangible of the type which should be afforded protection under the laws of unfair competition.

In sustaining the plaintiff's position the Court acknowledged that a commercial intangible in and of itself could constitute a sufficiently distinct element of property to warrant independent protection against misappropriation. The Court further held that the existence of a competitive situation involving the intangible could sustain its proprietary aspects as between the competitors, even though it is otherwise fully available to the general public. Here the Court acknowledged that the plaintiff could assert no pre-eminent rights as against the general public in its news once that news had been released without copyright protection. However, as between the plaintiff and the defendant the news took on an additional characteristic, that of stock in trade, out of which both parties sought to realize a profit. The Court concluded that "as between them, it must be regarded as *quasi* property, irrespective of the rights of either as against the public."

Having determined that the news matter in question had sufficient attributes of property to be protected against misappropriation, the Court then turned its attention to whether the conduct complained of amounted to a misappropriation of plaintiff's property. In addressing this issue, the Court focused on the two major aspects of commercial intangibles which had previously prevented the formulation of any general theory of misappropriation—the inexhaustibility of plaintiff's property and the necessity of publicizing the intangible in order to capitalize on its value. With respect to the first point, the intangible had to be described as a component product consisting of intangible information plus the premium of exclusivity. Although the information itself was inexhaustible to the plaintiff, because it would be retained even after the appropriation, the exclusivity was diminished in each instance in which an unauthorized retransmission of the information occurred. Thus there could be conduct which caused injury to property even though that property might aptly be described as inexhaustible.

The necessity to reveal the news information in order to realize a commercial advantage was interpreted by the Court as highlighting the fact that, as between plaintiff and defendant, the wire service reports were competitive inventory rather than the original works of authorship they otherwise might be to the general public. Thus duplication and redistribution of the news reports was the appropriation of a product rather than the copying of an uncopyrighted work. In describing the effect of this conduct, the Court observed that:

> [I]n doing this defendant, by its very act, admits that it is taking material that has been acquired by complainant as the result of organization and the expenditure of labor, skill, and money, and that defendant in appropriating it and selling it as its own is endeavoring to reap where it has not sown, and by disposing of it to newspapers that are competitors of complainant's members is appropriating to itself the harvest of those who have sown. Stripped of all disguises, the process amounts to an unauthorized interference with normal operation of complainant's legitimate business precisely at the point where the profit is to be reaped, in order to divert a material portion of the profit from those who have earned it to those who have not; with special advantage to defendant in the competition because of the fact that it is not burdened with any part of the expense of gathering the news. The transaction speaks for itself and a court of equity ought not to hesitate long in characterizing it as unfair competition in business.

This language has been described as the highwater mark of the doctrine of misappropriation. In fact, it has supplied the basic posture for all subsequent cases of misappropriation of commercial intangibles by describing the wrong to be prevented as "reaping where one has not sown."

The *INS* decision held the potential for one of the broadest expansions of traditional notions of unfair competition, but its application to future decisions was seriously limited by two sharp and cogent dissents by Justices Holmes and Brandeis. The former Justice was of the opinion that value, even the value of exclusivity, could not, without specific legislation, create property because property was essentially a creature of law. The only protection to which the plaintiff was entitled for its news information was protection against falsehood. Justice Holmes argued that the only potential for falsehood was the creation of the mistaken belief that the defendant, rather than the plaintiff, was the source of the news information. Therefore, he concluded that the plaintiff's only remedy should have been required acknowledgment of the actual source of the news information. The dissent of Justice Brandeis went even further, challenging the fundamental precepts relied on by the majority opinion. It was the contention of Justice Brandeis that if news information was property at all, it was literary property and subject only to those protections afforded by the copyright laws. In the absence of a similar statutory provision protecting literary property too ephemeral in value to be copyrighted, the plaintiff must surrender whatever property rights it might have in the news upon plaintiff's publication of such news to the public.

Although potentially there is no limit to the situations in which the *INS* rationale could be applied, its actual application has proved to be rather limited. Subsequent courts were not completely willing to extend the theory of misappropriation to factual settings which varied from that in *INS*. Consequently, misappropriation actions have met with limited and erratic success. With few exceptions, relief has been confined to factual situations closely analogous to the information industries.

Typical of those instances in which a theory of misappropriation has prevailed is *National Exhibition Co.* v. *Martin Fass*. There, defendant rebroadcast the play-by-play description of a baseball game to which the plaintiff had all exhibition rights. Relying on *INS,* a New York State Supreme Court concluded that broadcast rights to such an event was "a valuable property right of the plaintiff." The court further observed that the value of this right depended, in part, on the exclusivity of the broadcast and any immediate rebroadcast would sufficiently dilute the right to be actionable. Similar judicial interpretations served to protect the broadcasts of the Pittsburgh Pirates baseball team, the New York Rangers hockey team, Fred Waring's Pennsylvanians Orchestra, the Metropolitan Opera Association, and the 1941 Baseball World Series.

Beyond the limited sphere of electronic communications and broadcasting, the doctrine of misappropriation found scant judicial acceptance. By 1940, Judge Learned Hand was moved to observe in *RCA Manufacturing Co.* v. *Whiteman* that the *INS* decision "held no more than that a western newspaper might not take advantage of the fact that it was published some hours later than papers in the east, to copy the news which plaintiff had collected at its own expense." Other courts expressed similar disaffection for the theory and courts often strained to find sufficient facts to distinguish their decision from that otherwise dictated by the rule of *INS*.

This slow erosion of the doctrine continued until 1964, when the Supreme Court decided the *Sears* and *Compco* cases, discussed in the preceding chapter. Many commentators interpreted these decisions as dealing a mortal blow to the theory of misappropriation. Because they prohibited state relief respecting rights available for protection under a federal copyright or patent, all forms of misappropriation relief appeared obviated. Commentators were quick to note that the Supreme Court in *INS* had acknowledged the copyrightable nature of the news information in question, and therefore such material should not be afforded protection from any other source.

Although a quick analysis of the origins of the misappropriation doctrine would appear to support the contention that the *Sears* and *Compco* cases effect a total pre-emption of the area, closer examination reveals several important distinctions. In the *INS* decision the Court was not directly addressing itself to the protection of the news in question, but rather to the temporary value created by the *currency* of that news. In this regard the business machinery established to transmit rapidly the news information created a value, apart from copyright, deserving the protection of equity. This separately created intangible value was neither patentable nor capable of copyright and was therefore not subject to the federal pre-emption of *Sears* and *Compco*.

This theory has been sustained in the cases decided subsequent to *Sears* and *Compco*. Perhaps the best example of this recent and surprisingly liberal judicial approach to the protection of commercial intangibles can be seen in the case of *New York World's Fair 1964–1965 Corp.* v. *Colourpicture Publishers, Inc.* The developers of the New York World's Fair sought to prevent the defendant from making and selling postcards and other photo souvenirs of the exposition. The defendant claimed that copyright was the only protection against photographing, and no copyright had been obtained on the World's Fair. Therefore, no other form of state protection should be available. A New York State Supreme Court rejected this rationale on the grounds that the value expropriated by the unauthorized photographs was the public interest created by plaintiff's efforts in promoting and assembling the fair rather than the physical structure of the buildings. Because this intangible was not copyrightable subject matter, the rule of *Sears* and *Compco* would not apply.

The *World's Fair* court went on to point out that neither the *Sears* nor the *Compco* decisions contained any reference to the *INS* decision. It would be a most unusual circumstance if the Supreme Court had intended to eliminate misappropriation as a form of unfair competition. Clearly, its silence on the *INS* decision cannot be attributed to ignorance so it must have been the result of design. And the only possible intent of such silence would be to perpetuate the doctrine of misappropriation as formulated in *INS*.

The *World's Fair* decision not only reaffirms the continued viability of the doctrine of misappropriation, but does so in a factual context substantially different from the more traditional applications of the rule. The case is not alone in this regard and reflects a developing trend toward expanded application of the theory of misappropriation. It is impossible to predict the extent to which misappropriation will receive general acceptance in the courts, but it is unquestionably still a viable form of state protection against unfair competition.

TRADE SECRETS

The *Restatement of Torts* defines a trade secret as consisting of "any formula or pattern, any machine or process of manufacturing, or any device or compilation of information used in one's business, and which may give the user an opportunity to obtain an advantage over competitors who do not know or use it." Whenever such a secret is obtained and used by a competitor without authorization, the original owner will have an action for injunction and damages.

The theory of trade secret protection originally addressed itself to a far narrower subject matter than that covered by the present definition. As was the case with most areas of commercial common law, the earliest formulation of trade secrets was based on traditional property notions. Only those secrets were given protection that could be classified as some sort of tangible asset of the plaintiff businessman. The net effect was to create a type of common law patent for industrial property that did not qualify for ordinary patent protection because of some lack of statutory prerequisites. This approach was already well developed by 1865 when the Supreme Judicial Court of Massachusetts observed in *Peabody* v. *Norfolk:*

If one invents or discovers and keeps secret a process of manufacturing, whether a proper subject for patent or not, he has not, indeed, an exclusive right to it as against the public or against those who, in good faith, acquire knowledge of it; but he has a property in it which a court of chancery will protect against one who in violation of contract and breach of confidence, undertakes to apply it to his own use or to disclose it to third persons.

Such a theory involved proof of two essentials: (1) that the property was eligible as a trade secret and (2) that it had in fact been maintained in secrecy. The first requirement was distinct from the second, and mere secrecy alone would not create trade secret protection. Thus if a certain manufacturing method, although known only to a limited group, is an essential part of the know-how of a particular industry, it will not qualify as a trade secret regardless of the general confidentiality accompanying its use. This rule developed in the context of the early trade guilds and can best be explained in that setting. Under the guild system, trades required specialized knowledge learned through an apprenticeship system. Thus the special skills of a cabinetmaker were known only to those who had served an apprenticeship, but by the same token were fully known to the whole industry of cabinetmakers. Therefore these skills, although known only to a special few, were the know-how of the trade and could not be afforded trade secret protection no matter what confidential restrictions a manufacturer placed on the cabinetmakers in his employ.

This know-how limitation has survived to the present day as the major qualifying factor in identifying which industrial property may receive trade secret protection. Just where the know-how of a particular industry leaves off and its trade secret property begins is a particularly close question, which will often govern the outcome of the case. One of the most succinct definitions of know-how was offered by the United States District Court in *Mycalex Corp. of America* v. *Pemco Corp.* In attempting to determine whether knowledge of the desirable proportions necessary to produce mica and glass insulators was industry know-how, the court characterized it as

factual knowledge not capable of precise, separate description, but which, when used in an accumulated form, after being acquired as a result of trial and error, gives to the one acquiring it an ability to produce something which he otherwise would not have known how to produce with the same accuracy or precision found necessary for commercial success.

Of similar significance under a property theory of trade secrets is the tangibility of the property in question. The early common law approached the trade secret area in two stages. First, the subject matter was identified as property and then as a secret. Obviously, early courts gave strong emphasis to the physical attributes of the alleged property. If the secret could be mastered as a skill and was incapable of reduction to a tangible form, such as a writing, then it most probably would not qualify as property. Although this appears to be nothing more than a technique for determining know-how, it did create a certain amount of confusion in areas such as compilations of information. The customer list of a route salesman might well be appropriate property for trade secret protection, but a different conclusion might follow if the route salesman makes his rounds from memory. Although such anomalies have to a large extent disappeared, they still recur with sufficient frequency to leave the area of tangibility completely unsettled. Almost every jurisdiction has its own peculiar rules on the "laundry list" or "route slip" problem in trade secrets law.

Once the property has been identified as qualifying for possible trade secret protection, it must then be shown to have actually been a secret. Secrecy has properly been described as the *sine qua non* of trade secrets and its existence must be independently proved. The ordinary method of demonstrating secrecy is by showing that precautions were taken to prevent general disclosure. The extent of these precautions and the scope of those individuals privy to the information are critical factors in establishing secrecy.

The most common single proof is an employment contract placing restrictions on the revelation of certain trade information by employees. The greatest shortcoming of such instruments is that they are frequently worded so broadly as to overstep the bounds of legitimate subject matter and attempt to restrict know-how as well. The more particularized the restriction, the stronger is the presumption of secrecy.

Many other methods are employed to establish the necessary secret. Limiting access to the information is strong evidence of attempted secrecy. Ordinarily, this limit will be in the form of a restricted list of persons authorized to use the trade secret in question. Obviously, the smaller the category of authorized persons, the greater the inference of secrecy. The classic example of this is the protection from disclosure given to the formula for Coca-Cola. Apparently, only a very limited number of executive personnel in the entire corporate structure of the Coca-Cola Company have access to the formula.

There is actually very little else in the way of affirmative measures that a manufacturer can take to establish the secrecy of his property. Consequently, many cases will turn on the degree to which the imposed restrictions were adhered to and enforced. If an employer permits certain former employees to use trade secrets despite restrictive employment contracts, then he may well be destroying the secrecy of his property and thereby effectively precluding later trade secret protection. Similarly, if access is technically limited but the restrictions are ignored in practice, then there is little likelihood that the secrecy requirement will be sustained. The lesson for the businessman is that he must actively police his security arrangements and fully enforce his restrictive employment contracts to ensure against an unintentional relinquishment of the confidential status of a trade secret.

In addition to the property theory of trade secrets, courts have developed a second rationale for affording trade secret protection based on a theory of proprietary information. Under such a theory the gravamen of an action for breach of a trade secret is violation of the confidential relationship that accompanied revelation of the secret information. This theory is not a substitute for a property concept of trade secrets, and obviously will have no application to a stolen or accidentally obtained trade secret. It was intended to expand the law of trade secrets beyond the artificial restrictions of tangibility and thereby provide a modicum of protection for industrial information that, although clearly intangible, was competitively advantageous.

The notion that a form of proprietary information could be protected apart from any property attributes of the trade secret was fully expounded in 1917 by Justice Holmes in his decision in *E. I. duPont de Nemours Powder Co.* v. *Masland:*

> Whether the plaintiffs have any valuable secret or not the defendant knows the facts, whatever they are, through a special confidence that he accepted. The property may be denied, but the confidence cannot be. Therefore the starting point for the present matter is not property or due process of law, but that the defendant stood in confidential relations with the plaintiffs, or one of them.

The doctrine represents an extension of the law of agency to provide the principal with a continuing protection against revelation of information transmitted to the agent because of the confidential nature of the agency relationship. Thus an employee entrusted with knowledge of a secret process may not violate that confidence by using his knowledge of the process in competition with his former principal.

It has been this aspect of trade secrets that has received the greatest degree of expansion in recent years. The notion of secrecy has been reexamined in the context of confidential communications, and courts have held that the information in question need only be secret with respect to the industry involved and not the world at large. The most startling example of this broadened notion of secrecy can be seen in the Maryland federal district court case of *Head Ski Co.* v. *Kam Ski Co.* The owner of Head Ski Company employed a wood and metal bonding process in the production of snow skis. This process was very well known in the aircraft industry, where plaintiff first learned of it, but was completely unheard of in the ski industry. Two employees left and set up a competing ski company manufacturing wood and metal bonded skis of similar, but not identical design. These latter skis clearly employed the bonding process, but defendants claimed a right to use the process because it was well known to any aircraft engineer. The court found the process to be a secret in the ski industry, largely because it had been imparted to defendants in a confidential relationship.

The obligation of confidentiality has been interpreted to exist apart from any contract embodying the obligation. In ascertaining whether specific data will be covered by this fiduciary duty, courts look to the circumstances of the information's transmission and use. If the material in question is obtained by the employee by reason of his occupying a position of trust and confidence, if its communication to him is understood to be confidential, and if the usual and ordinary industry status of such information is that of confidentiality, then protection will be granted.

Obviously, there are certain limitations on the type of information that can be protected by reason of a confidential relationship. An employer cannot unreasonably restrict subsequent use of ordinary information by the simple expedient of confidential communication. Consequently, the know-how limitation already discussed will have application to confidential information as well. It will not, however, be as broad an exception because the creation of a strict confidential relationship might well restrict subsequent use of know-how information. For example, the practice in a particular industry might well be to maintain certain know-how in secrecy, and a properly established confidential relationship would preserve such secrecy. Aside from the limitations against undue restrictions on know-how, there must also be a reasonably well-established industry practice of maintaining this *type* of information in confidence. Thus, if the data in question is pricing information and the industry generally does not keep such data secret, there is a presumption against concluding that such information is received in confidence.

Under either of the presently accepted theories of trade secrets, a plaintiff is only entitled to relief against unauthorized competitive uses of the information. The law of trade secrets creates no exclusive use in a manufacturer as against the whole world and anyone is free to develop independently the subject matter of the secret and put it to a competitive use. The possessor of a trade secret will only be protected against unauthorized competitive uses of his secret where knowledge of it was improperly obtained or obtained pursuant to a trust which the user breached. Thus the theft of a trade secret by *anyone* will afford a basis for an injunction prohibiting its use in competition with the original owner. Further the use of a trade secret in competition with its owner by someone who originally had proper access, such as a former employee, will also support an injunction. Naturally, whenever a competitor induces an employee to reveal such a secret improperly, an injunction will lie against use of that secret. Whenever there has been an improper competitive use, a plaintiff is also entitled to an accounting of profits for the period of the use.

COVENANTS NOT TO COMPETE

Whenever an employer's particular business situation gives rise to a legitimate need for the protection of its confidential internal affairs, an employer is entitled to restrict the future competitive conduct of his employees to an extent reasonably calculated to afford the requisite degree of protection. Similarly, when an employer's business depends, in major part, on the continued patronage of an established clientele, that employer is entitled to take reasonable measures to ensure that employees, at some future time, do not exploit their past position to subvert the employer's good will and induce away his clientele. In each of these instances an employer is entitled to include in his employment contract reasonable restrictions on employee conduct after termination of employment.

The critical consideration in any covenant not to compete is the reasonableness of the restrictions placed on postemployment conduct. There is an obvious danger of involuntary servitude or deprivation of livelihood in any restrictive employment contract and the terms of such agreements are, therefore, construed most strictly by courts. Three factors are usually considered in assessing the reasonableness of a postemployment restriction: (1) the duration of the restriction, (2) the geographic scope of the restriction, and (3) the necessity for it in relation to the employer's need for protection.

Ordinarily competition can only be prohibited for a period long enough to dissipate any advantage that might be obtained from the prior employment. This will quite naturally depend on the nature of the business and the quality of the employee which could competitively damage the former employer. Where it is skill rather than customer contact that is in issue, then the restriction will ordinarily run a little longer. Thus, the restriction on a salesman who only knows the customers would usually be shorter than the restriction on a sales manager who knows the entire sales operation. A good standard for measuring a proper term of restriction is the time necessary to train or develop a replacement capable of assuming the duties of the departed employee. Courts have held that restrictions of from one to five years are reasonable, depending upon the nature of the job in question.

The permissible geographic scope of the restriction is also dependent on the nature of the employment, although there are certain absolutes. A national prohibition will rarely, if ever, be supported unless it is for an extremely short duration. As a rule of thumb, the restriction should cover the market area in which the employee could competitively injure his former employer. This must relate to the particular employee's competitive impact rather than the size of the company involved. For example, a salesman for a national company can only competitively injure it in his sales area, and that would be the reasonable area of prohibition.

Covenants not to compete are not looked upon favorably in the law; consequently, an employer's need for such protection must clearly justify the breadth of the restriction. If a covenant is found to be too broad, courts will frequently reject it altogether rather than adjust it to reasonable proportions. In making such a determination, the courts will often give controlling weight to the nature of the employment involved and the susceptibility of the employer to special injury through competition with a former employee. Consequently, where the employee would be capable of offering no greater competition than any other new entrant into the market, there is no judicial incentive to afford special protection against one particular individual. On the other hand, where the employee has gained some special knowledge or clientele by reason of his employment, then the employer is entitled to protection against having an employee use his work experience against him.

In addition to contractual protection against employee competition, the common law also recognizes one area where a former employee will be restricted from competing with his employer regardless of the existence of a contract to that effect. Where the employee, at the time of his departure, is engaged in a continuous or protracted course of dealings with a particular customer, he may not solicit that customer in competition with his former employer for a reasonable period or until negotiations are terminated. This follows the confidential relationship rationale of trade secrets law in that it is calculated to prevent an employee from capitalizing unfairly on a special customer relationship established solely by reason of the position he occupied in his former job.

INTERFERENCE WITH CONTRACTUAL RELATIONS

The common law has long recognized the tort of intentionally inducing a breach of contract. Briefly stated, one who, without a privilege to do so, intentionally causes a third person not to perform a contract with another is liable to the other for the resulting harm. To succeed in an action based on this tort, a plaintiff must prove (1) that a contractual relation existed between himself and the party induced, (2) that the defendant knew or should have known of the contract, (3) that the conduct of the defendant was the direct and proximate cause of a breach of the contract, and (4) that the breach resulted in damage to the plaintiff.

In the leading case of *Lumley* v. *Gye,* the plaintiff was lessee and manager of an opera theater and had contracted with one Johanna Wagner to perform in his theater "with a condition, amongst others, that she should not sing, nor use her talents elsewhere during the term without plaintiff's consent in writing." Knowing of the contract, the defendant "enticed and procured Wagner to refuse to perform" for the plaintiff. In holding the defendant liable in damages, the court said, "He who maliciously procures a damage to another by violation of his right ought to be made to indemnify." Moreover, the argument that the defendant did not induce the breach out of malice but only in pursuance of his right to compete will not exonerate a defendant. As the Massachusetts Supreme Court stated in a case in which a tourist agency induced a hotel to breach its exclusive contract with another tourist agency, "No case has been cited which holds that a right to compete justifies a defendant in intentionally inducing a third person to take away from the plaintiff his contractual rights." The court further noted that where money damages are inadequate "equity will issue an injunction" against further acts of interference.

In addition to inducing a breach of contract, interference with contract performance is a tort recognized by the common law. Thus, where the president of a corporation "engaged in a systematic course of conduct having for its design and purpose to strip plaintiff [the treasurer and secretary of the corporation] of his duties being performed by him for" the corporation as provided in his contract of employment, a New York court held the president liable in damages. According to the court, "where a third party unlawfully interferes with contractual rights existing between two other parties or improperly interferes with the performance of duties by one of the parties to the contract, he is guilty of a tort for which he must respond in damages to the aggrieved party."

Occasionally plaintiffs attempt to recover the loss of "reasonable business expectancies," claiming that "but for" the interference of the defendant they would have been able to enter into advantageous contractual relations. The North Carolina Supreme Court described the rationale of such a suit as follows:

> Every one has a right to enjoy the fruits and advantages of his own enterprise, industry, skill and credit. He has no right to be protected against competition; but he has a right to be free from malicious and wanton interference, disturbance or annoyance. The right to make contracts is both a liberty and a property right. . . . [U]nlawful interference with the freedom of contract is actionable, whether it consists

in maliciously procuring breach of contract, or in preventing the making of a contract when this is done, not in the legitimate exercise of the defendant's own rights, but with design to injure the plaintiff, or gaining some advantage at his expense.

Thus, where a plaintiff's former employer threatened suit against third persons should they accept plaintiff's patent, the court held that the defendant had "wrongfully interfered with his freedom of contract and use of his trade and occupation," and was, in consequence, liable in damages.

The problem with recovery for interference with "reasonable business expectancies" is that before the contract is entered into, competitors should be free to compete, and, by definition, successful competition is an interference with the expectancies of the unsuccessful. As a New York court said, "The interference of a competitor creates no cause of action." The case involved competitors for the advertising to be placed on an elevated railway company. The unsuccessful bidder claimed that the contract was let to his competitor because of the latter's derogatory statements concerning the plaintiff. The court conceded that an interference had occurred, but ruled, "To entitle the plaintiff to recover in an action like this it must prove that it would have procured and received the contract *but for* the wrongful and illegal interference of the defendants." Thus, even if the defendants' statements were malicious lies, a plaintiff still may not recover unless as a matter of near certainty the contract would have been let to the plaintiff but for the interference. The court explained, "The courts will be a little slow in permitting juries to speculate upon what a competitor had reason to expect or might reasonably suppose would happen."

Crucial to recovery under any one of the three theories previously discussed is the intentional act of the defendant. Courts uniformly have denied recovery for unintentional interference with contractual relations by negligent conduct which prevents performance or makes it more difficult. Thus, where an employee of a plant destroyed by fire as a result of the negligence of a third party sued the third party to recover for lost wages, an Ohio court dismissed the action on the grounds of remoteness. Fearing an overloading of court dockets if such suits were allowed, the court ruled that the injury, to be compensable, must be the "natural and proximate or immediate and direct result" of the wrong.

One final point should be made with respect to interference with contractual relations. If a defendant can show justification for the interference, he enjoys an absolute defense. The leading decision in this area is the English case of *Brimelow* v. *Casson*. The secretary of an actors' association persuaded the owners of theaters with whom the plaintiff, who managed a burlesque troupe, had contracts to cancel them. As a result, the troupe was stranded in the town of Maidenhead and the manager brought suit against the actors' association for intentional interference with his contractual relations. In fact, the manager so underpaid the girls that many of them were forced into prostitution. The court acknowledged that a *prima facie* case had been stated, but held the interference to be justified as a legitimate attempt by the labor union to improve the condition of the working girl in England.

9

Deceptive Nondisclosure

In order to eliminate advertising that is false, deceptive, or misleading, the Federal Trade Commission may prohibit absolutely any faulty representation or require the disclosure of certain additional information.

The "disclosure order" would seem to serve either one of two purposes: (1) to clarify or qualify a representation which, although truthful, has the capacity to mislead, or (2) to supply a material fact which previously had been omitted. The explanatory or qualifying disclosure is discussed in other chapters. The problem to be dealt with here is the deliberate concealment of certain aspects of the product or offer which, though less appealing than the ones already revealed, are considered to be highly important—that is, "material"—as affecting the likelihood of purchase.

With respect to advertising in general, the FTC has never posited an affirmative duty to "tell all." Even under Section 15 of the Federal Trade Commission Act, concerning the advertising of food, drugs, cosmetics, and devices, which gives the FTC a clear mandate to look to facts undisclosed as bearing on the falsity of an advertisement, there seems to be a question whether such a duty exists. With respect to other products, originally the courts were reluctant to characterize the nondisclosure of material facts as an unfair method of competition or commercial practice. Thus, in *Berkey & Gay Furniture Co.* v. *FTC* the United States Sixth Circuit Court of Appeals refused to require disclosure of the fact that furniture was veneered in the absence of a representation that it was "solid," and the Second Circuit Court of Appeals reversed an FTC order requiring disclosure that a testimonial for Cutex fingernail preparations had been paid for by the advertiser. Because the testimonials had been found to be neither exaggerated nor untruthful, the failure to disclose the fact of payment was not deceptive and no presumption of falsification of the opinions could arise therefrom.

Subsequent cases, FTC Guides and trade practice rules, and particularly the labeling "disclosure" statutes of which the commission is guardian, have hacked away at the judicial fustian denying the FTC an affirmative function. Clearly it is "in the interest of the public" to make available to the consumer better and more information upon which to base his economic choices. Moreover, the Supreme Court has held that an advertisement may be "completely" misleading "because things are omitted that should be said." The only question is, "What things should be said?"

Generally speaking, an advertisement should set forth whatever the purchaser would normally want to know about the nature and use of the product. If certain information could affect the tendency to buy or not to buy, then it is a safe bet that such information should be disclosed in advertising.

Two recent cases illustrate the type of facts which the commission feels the consumer needs to make an informed purchase. In *J. B. Williams Co., Inc.* v. *FTC,* the Sixth Circuit Court of Appeals affirmed a commission order requiring that Geritol advertising affirmatively disclose the negative fact that a great majority of persons who experience the symptoms of tiredness do not experience them because there is a vitamin or iron deficiency. The court said, "while the advertising does not make the affirmative representation that a majority of people who are tired and run-down are so because of iron deficiency anemia and the product Geritol will be an effective cure, there is substantial evidence to support the finding of the Commission that most tired people are *not* so because of iron deficiency anemia, and the failure to disclose this fact is false and misleading because the advertisement creates the impression that the tired feeling is caused by something which Geritol can cure." [Emphasis supplied.]

In *S.S.S. Co., Inc.* v. *FTC* a similar product was involved except that the iron tonic was "aimed principally at the rural and urban poor." Typical of the advertisements was the following radio broadcast:

> Do you find yourself *missing out* on the fun in life? Do you feel, dull, draggy . . . just "too tired" to do things? Then maybe you're suffering from Iron Deficiency Anemia—*low blood power*. If so, what you need is Three-S Tonic! New formula Three-S Tonic—now with B vitamins—is rich in iron to help *build back* your blood power . . . *restore* your energy . . . help you *feel better fast!* Three-S Tonic goes to work within 24 *hours*. And if you don't feel better in just *six days* the Three-S Company will refund your money . . . every cent of it! So don't *miss out* on the fun in life. Don't *let* yourself feel "too tired" to enjoy things. If *you're* suffering from Iron Deficiency Anemia, take Three-S Tonic! Yes, yes, yes, . . . get S.S.S.! Get started on new-formula, iron-and-vitamin-enriched Three-S Tonic . . . in liquid or tablet form . . . *right away!*

Objecting specifically to suggestions of self-diagnosis and the fact that the advertising was addressed to the poor, the commission had directed that such representations "must be accompanied by the affirmative disclosure that the great majority of persons experiencing tiredness symptoms will derive no benefit from such preparations." The Sixth Circuit agreed, noting that otherwise "the objects of petitioners' advertising campaign will *not* be fully informed of the material facts."

These and other cases, as well as proposed guides and public comments of individual commissioners indicate that the FTC is leaning toward a more exacting standard as to what the consumer needs to know. Although "the practice of less than half-disclosure" has not yet been construed as misleading, the commission is "coming to a turn in the road," as one of its staff has publicly suggested, and more and better information has become the governing principle.

DANGER IN THE USE OF A PRODUCT

Probably the most closely scrutinized advertisement is that which has reference to a product whose use might endanger the public health or safety. The product is most often a food, drug, cosmetic or "device" with respect to which the FTC is authorized by Section 15 to take into account "the extent to which the advertisement fails to reveal facts material in the light of such representations or material with respect to consequences which may result from the use of the commodity . . . under the conditions prescribed . . . , or under such conditions as are customary or usual." As has been pointed out elsewhere, however, an advertiser of these commodities must examine the FDA's requirements as well. Because of the overlapping of the jurisdictions of the FTC (advertising) and the FDA (labeling), an advertiser's responsibility does not stop with Section 15.

This is not to say, of course, that the FTC has no interest in the labels affixed to foods and drugs. Clearly a label which fully discloses the potential danger in the use of the product, in addition to a cautionary warning, is considered the best insurance against deceiving the purchasing public. It is not necessary, however, that advertising contain a full explanation of the possible effects resulting from injudicious use. It appears sufficient if the advertisement contains the warning *Caution: Use only as directed on label,* providing the label bears the warning and adequate directions for use.

It is obviously improper to characterize something as safe when it is not, but the commission's orders and stipulations go even further and require the advertisement to reveal "clearly and conspicuously" that users should "follow the label" and "avoid excessive use." If a product is advertised as "harmless," it must be so in every respect.

To what extent the advertiser must make himself knowledgeable as to the possible effect, and on whom, is not entirely clear. About all that can be said is that a complaint from the FTC will outline the limits rather well. Illustratively, an advertiser of shaving cream had to reveal its harmful propensities to those "with tender skin" and the effects if allowed to get into the eyes, and the manufacturer of an asthma remedy was required to disclose its possible harmful effects if used by those with goiter or tuberculosis. FTC procedure has had the effect, to the partial relief of the manufacturer of Carter's Little Liver Pills, of deflating the fish wife's tale about the potential danger in the use of laxatives by persons suffering from abdominal pains, nausea, vomiting, and other symptoms of appendicitis. The FTC stated that it had been unable to find that the potential danger to the public health inherent in the use of laxatives "so serious" as to require a disclosure in the advertisements.

Patent medicines and therapeutic devices are not alone in their potential danger when used by the uninformed. The ingestion of a nonfood product or the breakage of a toy are examples of obvious hazards not requiring disclosure. Where, however, such risks are likely to occur and would not be apparent or obvious to a consumer, nondisclosure is considered deceptive and, therefore, unlawful.

Much of the effort of the FTC in this area of potentially dangerous commodities complements legislative control—for example, the Flammable Fabrics Act and the Hazardous Substance Act. To illustrate, the combustible nature of balloons, furniture polish, and certain cleansers must be revealed, as well as the possibility of harm if a product is permitted to come into contact with the skin or to be inhaled. The commission has also required the disclosure of possible electric shock and directions for use and/or installation in connection with electric water heaters and welders, and, of course, the requirement that packages of cigarettes contain the statement *Caution—Cigarette Smoking May Be Hazardous to Your Health.*

PRODUCT MAKE-UP

Unless a consumer is otherwise informed, he expects that the object of his purchase is new, available in unlimited supply, flawless, effective for the use intended, and, in general, as it appears to be. Where the opposite is true and such fact has been concealed, the consumer has been misled. That which was omitted is, of course, the less appealing aspect of a product, its "shortcomings," as one judge has commented. No one could argue reasonably, however, that disclosure is not necessary to eliminate the deception.

Accordingly, the FTC requires the disclosure of a product's old, used, secondhand, rebuilt, or reconstructed status. The rule has been applied to everything from films to ladies' finery. One product that often has been deficiently labeled and advertised is lubricating oil. Of no moment is the argument that oil drained from crankcases and lube guns is as effective as the oil right out of the well as long as impurities have been extracted therefrom. A reprocessed product is not what the purchaser expects when he chooses oil. The fact of "prior use" must be disclosed in advertising, on the front panels of the containers and in sales promotional material. Furthermore, neither the term *reprocessed* nor the phrase *guaranteed re-refined* is sufficiently informative.

Granted there may be a market for seconds and rejects or unused government supplies. Nevertheless, the deterioration and imperfections of such products must be revealed on the articles themselves, on their containers and in advertisements, invoices, and shipping memos. With respect to the placement of the disclosure statement, the commission has not specified a particular location so long as it complies with the "well-established principle that [the affirmative disclosure] must be made with such clarity that it will likely be observed by prospective purchasers making a casual inspection of merchandise prior to, not after, the purchase thereof." Accordingly, the manufacturer of "irregular" men's shirts was advised that a disclosure made on the shirttail would not be acceptable. Because prospective purchasers look at the neck band for size and fiber identification, a legible disclosure there would be "the best possible location."

A change in the composition of an old-time favorite commodity also demands disclosure of such fact. To continue advertising Royal Baking Powder without revealing that phosphate has been substituted for its primary ingredient, cream of tartar, would lead the public to believe it was the same product, when, in fact (as any baker will attest), it is a radically different powder. However, the commission's concern that the public should get that which it has purchased will not be limited to a "different" product or one where the quality has been reduced; a disclosure order is equally appropriate in connection with a product which is "better" than that which was shown in a sample from which orders were taken.

Where the appearance of a product deceptively conceals the actual composition, the product's make-up must be affirmatively revealed. This area covers such things as rayon which looks like silk, plastic which looks like leather, paper or metal which looks like wood, copies which look like the "real McCoy," glass which looks like natural gems, and base metals which look like gold or silver or stainless steel. Although much of the subject of simulation is covered by trade practice rules, cease and desist orders and stipulations in this area are numerous.

Another example of "deceptive appearance" is the abridged or condensed book. Here again the FTC has required that any such shortened publication bear an affirmative disclosure as to its true nature. Advertisements must do the same. The FTC has also set forth a rule governing the location of the disclosure for both hardbacks and paperbacks. It must be in immediate connection with the title or "in another position adapted readily to attract the attention of a prospective purchaser." For paperbacks the location must be the front cover and title page. Hardback editions will make use of the front flap of the jacket or dust cover as well as the title page.

FOREIGN ORIGIN

The Federal Trade Commission and the courts have found in many cases not only the existence of a general consumer preference for American products but also a specific preference for particular products made in the United States. Moreover, it has been found that a consumer believes an unmarked product to be of domestic origin. Hence, as a general rule, it is unfair to sell or offer to sell a foreign-made product without disclosing the country of origin.

On April 4, 1968, the FTC made public its conclusions resulting from a general review of the subject of foreign-origin disclosure. Resolving that it was "neither necessary nor desirable to announce any new or changed rule or statements of general policy . . . [t]he Commission

reaffirms its adherence to the rules and principles which have been announced in prior cases."

As recently as 1962 the commission had reviewed its "general policy"
in the case of *Manco Watch Strap Co., Inc.* Where a foreign-made
product is shown not to be clearly marked, two additional findings are
necessary to justify an affirmative disclosure of national origin: "(1) a
belief or assumption by a substantial segment of the buying public that
the product, not being clearly marked otherwise, was made in America;
and (2) a preference by such buyers for the American-made product."
Moreover, these facts may be presumed and officially noticed, where
their existence has been shown in prior foreign-origin decisions, dispensing with the need to reprove them in each new proceeding that is
brought. The burden of showing in rebuttal that a particular product or
circumstance is "exceptional" and not within the general rule of disclosure rests on the respondent in each case.

One exception to the rule is the foreign product that is not produced
in the United States. With no competitive domestic business to protect,
the "public interest" statutory requisite to FTC action is absent. An
example would be imported cultured pearls.

Another exception is to be found where the imported product gets so
lost in the domestic manufacture of another commodity that marking is
either impossible or misleading. The imported alabaster bead around
which domestic imitation pearls are formed so loses its identity as a foreign
product. Where, however, the foreign product remains substantially as
imported and constitutes a significant component of the product as it is
sold to the consumer, disclosure of national origin must be made.

With respect to the application of the general rule of disclosure to imported components, the commission has said:

> In the absence of any evidence to the contrary, the Commission be-
> lieves that the question of foreign-origin disclosure largely depends
> upon the importance which prospective purchasers would attach to the
> fact that, if known, a substantial number of the components of the
> finished product are of foreign origin.

The commission then determined that imported barrels, cylinders, and
hammers "represent such an integral and essential part" of revolvers and
automatic pistols that prospective purchasers would in all probability
manifest a deep concern over their origin. Accordingly, the failure to
disclose the origin would play a vital, if not decisive, role in the customers' selection or purchase.

Where the significance of the imported components, or of foreign
labor or assemblage operations, is not so clear, the commission will base
its decision on the percentage, of the total cost of the finished unit, represented by the foreign part or service. Decisions and advisory opinions

indicate that componential-origin disclosure will not be imposed up to one third of the total production cost, providing that the finished product is not affirmatively represented as having been made in the United States.

A generality of *exceptional* may be made, also, for the unmarked foreign product for the American counterpart of which there is no public preference. The commission has pointed out that cigars, perfume, caviar, and Scotch fall into this category, intimating that disclosure of origin would not be required if, as an affirmative defense, the seller can establish that the domestic product is not preferred.

At one time a foreign product priced lower than a comparable American product was excepted from the disclosure rule for unmarked foreign goods on the ground that no preference for the higher-priced domestic product existed. The current view of the FTC is that the burden is on the seller to prove that the purchasing public does not prefer the American product over the lower-priced foreign-made commodity, thus subordinating the price differential distinction to the larger issue of buyer preference.

Commissioner MacIntyre, speaking for the commission in *Oxwall Tool Co., Ltd.,* specifically rejected the "lower price" defense advanced by respondent—that because its tools were to be for home use, a low price was the most important factor. He said:

> Although the tools sold by respondent are undoubtedly, for the most part, purchased by nonprofessional users such as homeowners, it does not follow that such purchasers are interested only in the price of the tool to the exclusion of all other factors. There is reliable testimony in the record that certain members of the public will not buy foreign-made tools no matter how cheaply they are sold. There is evidence that a lower price will not serve to identify a tool as foreign. The record also discloses that some domestic tools sell at the same price level as respondents. As a matter of fact, the respondents themselves mix domestic and non-domestic tools in "kits" and sell them as a single unit, thereby seriously weakening their arguments that domestic tools are not sold in this low price class and that foreign tools can be identified by price alone. . . . The fact that an imported article has no domestic competitors in its price class does not force the conclusion that consumers who purchase such an imported article unmarked as to foreign origin have no preference for domestic goods.

Thus, it would appear that the fact that a foreign-made product is marketed at prices substantially below the price of comparable merchandise made in the United States will have little bearing on the question of the advertiser's duty to disclose the country of origin.

The general disclosure requirement for foreign goods is directed only to the problem of origin markings on the products themselves, on their containers and packaging, and on point-of-sale promotional pieces like wall charts and other display materials. Advertising per se has not been the subject of a disclosure order. In fact, in dealing with *marked* imported watchbands which were packaged before sale in such a way as to conceal the disclosure, Commissioner Elman, in *Manco,* specifically excepted as "significantly different" the burden of requiring disclosure of foreign origin in all advertisements, assuming adequate disclosure is made on the package and product. However, the commission has recognized the need for such information in advertising where the consumer would not have an opportunity to examine the product or package prior to purchase. Mail-order vendors have been directed to disclose country of origin in advertisements, catalogs and other promotional material.

Disclosure is necessary also where a trade name suggests, contrary to fact, a domestic origin or an origin other than the real one. The FTC has ruled that under those circumstances, the foreign origin would have to be revealed in conjunction with and *wherever* the trade name appears.

MISCELLANEOUS

Finally, there are a few disclosure cases which avoid neat classification. For instance, a toy manufacturer must disclose that its battery-operated toy does not include batteries. Curiously, this revelation need not be included in a TV commercial. On the other hand, it would be an unfair practice to leave the impression that the toy is operated by something else, as for example the command of a child's voice. It is sufficient to imply that the movement of the toy is battery-driven by showing the controls. Apparently even a child would then "get the picture."

The incidents of a sales transaction have also come under FTC scrutiny. For example, it is unfair to procure the signature of a purchaser to a promissory note, conditional sales contract, or other instrument without revealing the terms. Although disclosure of such facts is now required by the 1968 Consumer Protection Act, the FTC rule encompasses another practice which had become widespread with the increased use of credit for the purchase of consumer goods.

Having found that, by and large, installment buyers prefer to deal with sellers who do not discount their negotiable paper, the commission has held that it is unfair not to disclose that this may be done. The rule is aimed at eliminating the situation where, at the seller's option and without notice to the purchaser, the contract is sold to a finance company or other third party to whom the purchaser must make full payment, including finance charges, without regard to any personal defenses the purchaser might assert against the seller. Even a seller who does not routinely assign the contract must disclose with such conspicuousness and clarity as is likely to be observed, read, and understood by the purchaser. Phrases such as *dealers nonrecourse assignment* or *assignment with recourse,* accompanied by words describing the transfer, have been held to be insufficient notice to the buyer of a possible assignment and its consequences. And where a "cooling-off" period, during which a sales contract may be canceled, is imposed, the seller may not negotiate or assign the contract during that time. A recent cease and desist order utilized this remedy against a seller, who used bait-and-switch techniques in selling sewing machines door to door, and also required that a notice of such a period be disclosed in a conspicuous place on the contract.

In ruling that purchasers need to know that their sales contracts may be assigned, the commission recognized that the average consumer is not aware of the legal implications of signing a negotiable instrument. Another recent disclosure case would appear to have contemplated similar consumer enlightenment. Although usually involving relatively small sums of money, the merchandising plan which encourages sales by mailing to potential customers merchandise "on approval" has always created for the recipient some confusion as to his obligation for the unsolicited goods. Repackaging and returning the merchandise is an inconvenience. On the other hand, keeping it and not paying for it may provoke a stream of correspondence from the seller, implying that money is due and that there is some contract or agreement to pay for or return the merchandise. The commission's recent order would clarify the situation by requiring the seller to disclose that there is no obligation either to return the merchandise or to preserve it and that the recipient must pay only if he decides to purchase it. On respondent's appeal to the Tenth Circuit Court of Appeals, these disclosure requirements were modified to add *or uses it* as a condition precedent to payment, but not even then "if the law of the recipient's state permits him to use unsolicited merchandise without payment."

The FTC has also taken the position that it is deceptive not to disclose the purpose of skip-tracer forms. Usually, this issue is included among a large number of other allegations of improper collection practices and, thus, has rarely received extended discussion in the courts. In 1962 the United States Seventh Circuit Court of Appeals refused to follow the commission on this point where, notwithstanding that the forms did not disclose the purpose, they were not otherwise deceptive. However, in two later decisions of other Circuit Courts of Appeals, the Federal Trade Commission's orders requiring affirmative disclosures of purpose in skip-tracer forms were upheld.

One final example involves an apartment complex in Arlington, Virginia. The practice complained of was its failure to disclose in advertising the apartments the fact that racial restrictions were imposed. The initial decision was to dismiss on the ground that the Civil Rights Act of 1968 had rendered the issue moot. Although the commission supported the complaint with a quotation from *P. Lorillard Co.* v. *FTC:* "To tell less than the truth is a well-known method of deception," it ordered dismissal upon the parties' assurances that the restrictive rental policy had been discontinued, necessarily eliminating the deceptive nondisclosure charged in the complaint. However, the commission was constrained to answer the hearing examiner and noted that Section 5 of the Federal Trade Commission Act proscribes *any* advertising matter which creates a misleading impression in the mind of the ordinary purchaser and that the Civil Rights Act would not render lawful any act or practice which would be otherwise unlawful, thus underscoring its authority to regulate advertising and to require affirmative disclosures when needed to avoid deception.

10

Product Description, Composition, and Origin

Having discussed the question of deception resulting from a failure to disclose matters necessary to informed consumer choice, we now turn to deception from misdescription. In particular, we shall be concerned with deceptive claims relating to product description, composition, and origin.

DESCRIPTIVE AND DESIGNATIVE TERMS

Abstract Claims of Superiority or Uniqueness

As mentioned previously, at common law and under the Federal Trade Commission Act, a seller may overstate the quality of his product for the sake of persuasion under the "puffing privilege." *Greatest, purest, best,* and *perfect* are common examples. From the standpoint of the informative function of advertising, however, such claims may be so unwarranted as to demand their prohibition.

Obviously, *best* misdescribes dirty secondhand merchandise, and a reclaimed paint is not "superior in quality," and the FTC has so held. But how would these claims fare in connection with secondhand merchandise that is not dirty or reclaimed paint for which a comparative quality has not been claimed? Would the decision have been different had the source of the products been disclosed? The FTC has not yet taken a position on this issue, but there does not seem to be a permissible claim of *quality* for dealer's junk or the salvage from a spray gun, although there is apparently a market.

One wonders, however, if there is even a market for a cigarette holder made of cellulose acetate which disintegrates when exposed to heat. Nonetheless, one cannot argue with the decision that *extra fine* was misdescriptive when the product was compared to a nonburning bakelite holder that it closely resembled.

Such qualitative judgments can hardly be avoided when dealing with substandard products or when the advertiser has invited a comparison. For example, *as good as the best, better than the rest* was condemned by the commission when it found the off-brand radio did not contain many of the features regularly included in a "standard first-class radio." The designation of a timepiece as a "railroad watch" also called to mind a quality standard as to accuracy and dependability that was not to be found in the advertiser's inferiorly constructed watch.

But what of products which do not vary substantially from competing products? Is there a "fair" assertion of superiority for them?

Top quality will be prohibited when there are similar products of "better" quality, and *truly superior* will be condemned where there is a standard that the commission will recognize and the product does not satisfy it. Similarly, *unique* or *utterly unlike* were held to be deceptive when used to describe Palmolive soap: because it is not essentially different from other toilet soaps on the market.

How much "difference" is required is not clear because the *Celanese* decision must be reckoned with. Celanese is rayon, yet it may be advertised, to differentiate it from rayon, as "different from any type of fabric ever made." This claim was deemed to fall within the privilege to puff. Under common law, *purest* was similarly categorized. However, it has failed to get by the commission as such where the aspirin so described was not the "purest obtainable in America."

About all that one may conclude is that product-differentiation claims, particularly if material to the consumer's selection or purchase, will be on safer ground if made in more factual, rather than abstract, terms. That is not to say that there are not problems there as well. Some will be dealt with here; others are raised in the chapter on disparagement and comparisons.

New

The character of a claim of novelty connoting *never before available* is dependent, in part, upon compliance with the FTC's six-month rule. After that period, presumably, a product is no longer new.

Recently, however, the commission advised that the rule did not apply to the bona fide test-marketing of a new product so long as the test-marketing program was confined to not more than 15 per cent of the population and was conducted in good faith for test purposes only and for less than six months. The six-month rule would be applicable only after the testing period had come to an end and the product was introduced to the general market.

For products that are generally unavailable but that have been reintroduced to the buying public, such as a book long out of print, *new, modern,* or *up-to-date* will be misdescriptive if the reprint contains no revision of the original text. Falsifying the date of publication to give the appearance of newness or selling a previously published book or film under a different name or title for the same purpose is also prohibitable.

New also carries a connotation of *unused.* As such, the term is deceptively used in connection with secondhand, renovated, rebuilt, reconditioned, or restored merchandise. The commission has also advised that it would be misleading to use the term to describe ten-year-old equipment, even though it has never been used, is still in the original shipping cartons, and has undergone no model changes since the equipment was produced. Furthermore, such merchandise must be identified by the term or phrase which most aptly describes its current condition.

Genuine

In the sense that the descriptive term *genuine* connotes that the composition of the product is "pure," the "real thing," its fair use will depend upon whether the composition is as it is generically described or as it appears to be. Thus, the commission has held that *genuine* leather is properly used only in connection with top grain leather or the hairy side of the hide. The phrase, as well as the unqualified term *leather,* would be misdescriptive of the split or subsequent layers from the hide and products made therefrom. The commission has advised also that it would be objectionable to use *genuine* in connection with a product composed of pulverized or ground leather, notwithstanding that the product is otherwise truthfully described.

Genuine may also be used to suggest origin, either in the sense of "only" source or "original" source, or to imply that the particular source of the product permits qualitative differences not to be found elsewhere. If the product, of same or similar quality, is available from several sources, the commission will give short shrift to such attempts to misrepresent its uniqueness.

Origin may be *falsely* designated by modifying an accurate generic description with the word *genuine*. To illustrate this point, *Danish pastry* has been used time and time again. *Swiss cheese* is another example. Both phrases accurately describe a particular kind of food, and it matters not whether it is domestically produced or imported. *Genuine,* however, stamps the pastry as having been imported from Denmark and the cheese as having been imported from Switzerland.

Copy or Reproduction

Unlike the fact that a product has been imported, which, if material, may have to be disclosed, there is no requirement that a product which imitates an established and preferred product must be labeled and advertised as a *copy* or *imitation*. Although the use of these terms might be encouraged as a means to better product differentiation and, thus, to a more rational exercise of consumer choice in the market place, the commission's standard makes this difficult to accomplish.

For example, *replica* is defined as "a duplicate, that which resembles or corresponds to something else" and *reproduction* is "a counterpart or reconstruction of something else." Moreover, the word copy represents the product so designated to be a replica or reproduction. Accordingly, none of these three terms, without qualification, may be used on rugs resembling Orientals unless the rugs are in fact duplicates of genuine Oriental rugs *in all respects,* including structure, method of manufacture (meaning, presumably, handmade), and material used (wool, not cotton). The use of Oriental names on American-made rugs, such as *Kirman* and *Karashah,* taken from the rugs copied, is also prohibited, because the implication is that the rugs were made in the Orient and possess all the essential characteristics of Oriental rugs. The fact that the label discloses the place of manufacture will not be sufficient to dispel the false impression.

But how may machine-made rugs, which resemble the true Oriental so closely as to be indistinguishable, be described? *Oriental-type rug* may be unacceptable in light of an FTC order against a textile manufacturer who had described his product as *Madras-type*. However, later the commission tentatively approved the use of *Oriental-style* on rugs, which may be a distinction without a difference. Another possibility is to be found in the answer given by the FTC to American producers of silver plate patterned after the old English Sheffield plate.

Because true Sheffield plate was available only as an antique, American manufacturers, to meet a widespread demand, reproduced the old designs and patterns from various base metals coated with silver by the electroplating process. The problem was that such plate could not be designated as a reproduction—in the sense of being the same in structure, method of manufacture, and material—because true Sheffield plate consisted of a copper base with a *welded* silver coating.

For more than twenty years the FTC balked at the use of *Sheffield* in any way by American manufacturers of electroplated silverware. Finally, in 1947, the FTC approved calling such silver plate *Sheffild design reproductions,* provided *made in the U.S.A.* was used to qualify any inaccurate implication as to origin in the use of *Sheffield.*

Special-Feature Description

Generally, this discussion contemplates utilitarian or functional claims which serve to differentiate otherwise similar products. Identifying the method of manufacture, or even a particular source, may accomplish the same thing. *Custom-made, Indian-made, imported,* and similar claims are discussed in the chapter on business and trade status.

Here, as elsewhere, the product description must accord with the understanding of the ordinary member of the purchasing public. If words are used other than in the ordinary sense, an explanation will be required. For example, the number of tubes (or transistors today) in a radio receiver fixes the quality of the set in the mind of the ordinary buyer. That measure of quality so indicated is understood, however, to be dependent upon a *functioning* tube. It will not do, then, to advertise a radio kit as a *two-tube* when one is a nonfunctioning, or rectifying, tube. Its special features have been overstated.

The "proof" claims account for a considerable amount of the special-feature claims in advertising. It may seem incredible that there are women who would expect to find hosiery which will not snag or clothes that will not wrinkle, but apparently there are. The FTC has been active against such claims.

Waterproof is controlled by trade rules for the paper industry (asphaltic type), the masonry industry, and the watch-case industry. If a product does not measure up to the standard therein promulgated for the use of such a representation, the FTC may issue a restraining order. Otherwise, it would seem that *waterproof* is misdescriptive unless the product is impervious to water.

Washproof can only describe a product which can be washed without discoloration or damage. *Shrinkproof* represents that *no* residual shrinkage remains in the product, although the claim may be qualified, and it must be with particular reference to both the warp and the filling, by designating the amount in percentages.

Non-Krush misdescribes a linen which wrinkles or creases. Hose cannot be described as *snagproof.* Equally false is "indestructible" carpeting. A floor may be described as *skid* or *slipproof;* but if this special feature obtains only when the floor is free from water, this must be disclosed.

Locks are not pickproof if they can be picked, and are not thiefproof unless they will indefinitely withstand all attempts to open by picking or use of special tools or keys or other devices. And a key may not be described as *defies duplication* when it is possible, although difficult, to do so.

The FTC has found that no watch can withstand shock, and thus *shockproof* or *shock protected* are misdescriptive of any watch. *Shock resistant,* however, has been upheld.

Soundproof and *breakproof* are absolute assertions under all conditions. *Mothproof* means *permanent* immunity from attack or destruction by moths. *Pill-proofed,* in connection with a sweater, implies that no balls or pilling will appear even under conditions of rough use. The FTC, however, has permitted a qualifying statement if normal wear and usage was what was intended in the guarantee.

Claims of durability and "lasting and eternal protection" are, apparently, highly effective in the sale of caskets and grave vaults. The commission, in recognition that nothing lasts forever, has issued an enormous number of orders against such representations as *centuries of protection, endure forever, eternal beauty,* and *permanently free from the inroads of water and rodents.*

Claims of Function and Efficacy

In naming his product or otherwise attributing to it particular qualities and value, an advertiser has told the consumer much about what he can expect it to do. More often than not, however, elaboration is necessary to make the point. Neither approach will invite FTC approbation where the product's capabilities have been overstated.

Modern technology has perhaps made it easy for the consumer to assume that anything is possible. Until, however, losing weight becomes as simple as taking a bath, as one advertiser claimed, the FTC has acted to ensure that the consumer's hopes and expectations are not transformed into disappointment.

In other areas of deceptive-practices law, the sheer fatuity of a claim has precluded the application of a strict test of deception. Although the FTC seems less disposed to overlook improbable claims of function, they are given, nonetheless, "comparatively short shrift." An obvious example is the case of a "violet-ray" machine that was touted as having treated and healed eighty-four alphabetically listed diseases (from *abscess* to *writer's cramp,* with *red nose, brain fag,* and *felons* in between) and "should heal all other diseases." Obviously, the commission did not test the machine, but neither had its inventor. The curative claims being unfounded, an order to cease and desist was issued.

On the other hand, lack of conformity with the truth was easily determined for the assertion that a set of reference books would provide information on "Everything you've ever wanted to know—on every conceivable subject."

The Darling Dimple Company held out false hopes, however improbable, to those consumers who had always desired a dimpled cheek. The deception was found in the extent to which the device was said to be effective—"permanent" dimple.

Similarly, Helena Rubenstein claimed she had a preparation which would cause eyelashes to grow. Apparently so convinced was she of its incredible properties that the claims continued after one cease and desist order, only to be finally eliminated by another order in which the FTC found the claims to be "entirely unwarranted."

The FTC has also concluded that rejuvenation is medically impossible and that nourishment results only if something (commonly called food) has been ingested. The decisions operated to deny to advertisers the implication arising from the use of *rejuvenescence* and *food* in the brand names of skin preparations.

If an advertiser wishes to claim or suggest capabilities arising from the content of his product, obviously the ingredients must be there. What constitutes "substantial amount" (the usual language of the commission) so as to warrant an ingredient being touted at all, is discussed elsewhere in this book. What is here contemplated as an advertising problem is the association, often improbable, between a named ingredient and its generic product as though such ingredient holds some special utilitarian value for the consumer. The content is truthfully represented; its functional effect is either doubtful or nonexistent.

Truthfully labeling soap as Butt-R-Milk Soap or as Egg Complexion Soap, as if the named ingredients had some magical power beyond ordinary cleansing has been held to be deceptive. Similarly, to use *asbestos* to describe a liquid roofing material, thereby suggesting greater insurance against fire than was available from ordinary roof paint, was misleading when the asbestos content was insufficient to accomplish the inferred advantage.

The FTC has found that both *nonfattening* as a product description and *Lite Diet* as a product designator means low caloric content to the consuming public. When, however, a beer is truthfully (because all beers have a relatively low caloric content) described as nonfattening, it must be amplified to point out that this effect obtains *only* when the product is consumed *in substitution* for foods of equal or greater caloric value.

Similarly, although a more thinly sliced piece of bread would, in truth, give the consumer a "lite diet" of bread, the brand name misleadingly described the weight-reducing effects of its consumption when the bread, pound for pound, had the same calories as other breads.

As pointed out in another chapter, pictures may speak louder than words. Where efficacy claims are thereby exaggerated or falsely implied, pictorial advertising will be prohibited also.

Comparative picturizations are fairly common gimmicks to show the before-and-after effects to be expected from the use of a product. To the commission, the question is frequently, "is it 'cure' or mere 'relief' that is being suggested?"

No doubt, to go from a pictured situation characterized by pain to the obvious pleasure of a golf course is ambiguous when the product is offered to arthritics and rheumatics. Although, undoubtedly, they have been told by doctors they cannot be cured, the commission requires that no false hope will arise from advertising, or that an established effect is not overstated by suggesting speedier results than is actually the case.

Similarly, a before-and-after commercial by Geritol depicting the "transformation of a wan, lackadaisical housewife into a veritable tigress," was held to be misleading when it created the impression that "Geritol is a generally effective remedy for tiredness." Because the number of people experiencing tiredness symptoms as a result of deficiency of the ingredients of Geritol was "infinitesimally small," the suggestion in the commercial that tiredness was equatable with iron deficiency anemia and, therefore, curable by Geritol was false and misleading. Furthermore, the commission concluded that

> in advertising in which an affirmative disclosure is required [here, that Geritol would aid only that small number of people suffering from tiredness because of iron deficiency] respondents may make no representations, directly or by implication, which in any way negate or contradict the facts which are affirmatively disclosed. In other words, if despite the affirmative disclosure, any advertising conveys the impression that Geritol will be of benefit in relieving tiredness generally or in other than a small minority of persons with such symptoms, such advertising will be deceptive.

Because "there are none so credulous as sufferers from disease," therapeutic claims for medicinal preparations constitute an area of enormous activity for the FTC, and reasonably so. The difficulty is not only that the product may disappoint, it may also be harmful. Precautionary measures are commonplace now, but to protect the trusting who do not analyze, the use of the word *safe,* for example, is strictly controlled. Unqualified, it means "harmless for indiscriminate use by laymen." So even a deodorant is misdescribed as safe if it will cause irritation, even among people *without* allergies and skin idiosyncrasies. Moreover, *safe use* means "in accordance with directions on the label," unless the directions caution certain persons against use except as a physician might direct.

The larger concern is the claim that a cure may be expected when only temporary relief can be obtained. To assert affirmatively a cure for a condition to be treated with the product when medical science has provided none is, obviously, false representation.

Moreover, there is little doubt that the advertiser invites problems for himself where he offers his product for many specified conditions and then slips in an omnibus clause. Most particularly will such an advertisement render itself suspect where the word *cure* or its synonyms are also used. And where the "tone" of an advertisement appears to stress the effect of a product on systemic conditions as distinguished from symptoms, some courts more closely scrutinize a "relief" claim as connoting "permanent removal" of the disturbance rather than mere "alleviation of discomfort."

To other courts no implication of permanency follows from the proper use of *relief*. In addition, it has been held that *temporary* is a word of such uncertain meaning—anywhere from a few minutes to a few hours—that to require a seller to use it to describe the effect of his product might limit him in truthfully representing his product.

REPRESENTATIONS OF COMPOSITION OR INGREDIENTS

The unfair representation of product composition may be accomplished in several ways. One is the application of a term to a product which does not come within the accepted definition of that term. *Chamois,* for example, has been defined by the FTC as including the leather from both the Alpine antelope and the oil-tanned split sheepskin, but not to include the sheepskin which is tanned with chrome salts before splitting. Another is by the use of a trade name which implies a composition other than the true composition. The subject of an early FTC order is illustrative. The respondent had designated his candy confection as an Ice Cream Bar. It did resemble the popular chocolate-covered Good Humor and other ice cream bars; it did not, however, contain any ice cream.

Composition of a product may be misrepresented also by the failure to disclose the true composition. Disclosure is compelled by legislation for some products, particularly those whose composition would not be recognized by most consumers. Furs and textiles are examples. In addition, such things as the artificiality of the flavor and color of a food product is illegal under the Federal Food, Drug and Cosmetic Act. Such practices are, also, deceptive and unfair under Section 5 of the Federal Trade Commission Act.

Disclosure of composition is not compelled for every product, however. Simulation is an ever-extending fact of modern technology. Close resemblance to an ingredient which the product does not contain is a situation repeated again and again in the market place. Consumers too often must rely upon their own sense of value or upon the sales clerk, who may not himself know.

The saleswoman may point out the latest fashion item, a "turtle" handbag. "Real *turtle?*" "Yes, and only $13.95." However, it is real patent leather, stamped to resemble the characteristic markings of turtle skin. Did she know or did she assume you knew the difference? Only the price indicated simulation.

But to the trusting, price may be only the "marvelous bargain" won for a "72K. Alexandrite." A genuine gem, the size of a pea, retails for over $1,000. The stone here described could be properly designated only as "Alexandrite-like Synthetic Sapphire."

The accomplishments of the FTC in this area are numerous, but seemingly only skim the surface. A few examples will show the range.

One rule, now firmly established, cuts directly across the examples given. Silk, according to the commission, is the product of the cocoon of a silkworm, and ladies purchasing dresses and underwear prefer it. The problem, of course, is that, for many purchasers, it is impossible or difficult to distinguish silk from its poor cousin, rayon. If the item is made wholly or in part from rayon, it must be labeled as rayon. Any other component may be indicated also, but the predominating fiber must be given first (as in *Silk/Rayon* or *Silk & Rayon* and *Rayon/Silk* or *Rayon & Silk*).

Similarly, of course, to advertise furniture as "walnut" when its exposed structural parts were made from pecan is misdescriptive. As with other terms, the unqualified use of a name of a wood means that the product is made exclusively of the wood named. It does not, however, carry an inference that the furniture is *solidly* constructed of the named wood. An order requiring a furniture manufacturer to label laminated or veneered furniture as "veneer" was set aside and "held for naught." The record having disclosed that *solid* or *genuine* had not been used in connection with the name of the wood used to describe the furniture, the court concluded that "to all but the grossly uninformed of the public" the use of the unqualified wood name would have no tendency to mislead.

It is the application of "accepted definitions" which needs more amplification here. These determinations are the key to nondeceptive naming of a product for advertising purposes. An advertiser would do well to consult, in addition, the rulings of the Food and Drug Administration defining various foods, drugs, and cosmetics and determining what should be revealed and what should not be used on labels. Both the FTC and the FDA seek "truth." What may satisfy one, however, may be insufficient for the other.

The FTC Trade Practice Rules will be helpful also. The naming and designation of metal products, for example, is particularly well covered. And the FTC's definition of *handkerchief,* a product seemingly difficult to sell or advertise as something it is not, is directly attributable to the rule promulgated for the handkerchief industry.

There is some indication, however, that these "accepted definitions" may be more restrictive than those which consumer understanding has established. Price, being an effective product differentiator, would alone tell a purchaser much about the composition to be expected from the product he had chosen as a handkerchief. But the commission has ruled it must be silk, linen, or cotton. It is to avoid a misdesignation that the definitions are important.

We now turn to a consideration of the conditions under which the ingredients of a product may or must be named or their presence suggested. A few special rules notwithstanding, as a matter of general application there are some well-established precedents.

A few terms, standing alone, have been found to connote purity. *Wool, woolen, worsted* are examples. Each one means not only that the product is composed 100 per cent of wool, but that the fiber has been made from the fleece or hair of a sheep; that it is virgin, or unused; and that it is *not* reclaimed. *Gold* and *silver,* too, unqualified, indicate pure metal.

No such purity of composition is suggested by the use of other terms. Unfortunately, there is no easy rule of thumb. Accepted consumer understanding, industry practice, and the like will operate to dilute, in time, an otherwise "true" definition. *Castile* is an example. It is still properly designative of a soap or shampoo, but it no longer means a 100 per cent olive oil composition. *Shellac* is another. It is properly affixed to a product which is less than pure shellac gum dissolved in alcohol. Furthermore, the common procedure of indicating the percentage of other ingredients found in a product was not ordered, provided some means was used to indicate that it is not pure shellac. (*Substitute* or *imitation* was suggested in one case.)

Where purity is not implied or intended, there remains the problem of how to indicate ingredients to avoid a charge of deceptive use under Section 5. Industry rules may preclude naming an ingredient at all. For example, it is customary within the paper stationery industry to omit any reference to rag content when it is less than 25 per cent of the paper. The FTC has recognized this rule and issued an order against a manufacturer whose paper was labeled as having rag content when it was only 10 per cent. In general, however, if an ingredient is to be named or suggested, as in a brand name (*Ice Cream Bar*) or trade name (*Silk Skin, Inc.*), the ingredient must be there. It need not be 100 per cent, however. It must be only in "substantial amount." The Fair Packaging and Labeling Act requires that to warrant being mentioned in the specification of identity of a product, an ingredient or component must be present in a "substantial or significantly effective amount."

The purpose of giving any play to an ingredient (beyond legislative requirements) may be to suggest practical efficacy of the product, its relative value or absolute quality. Then the question is whether the ingredient obtains in that amount as will substantially bring about the promised effect. It may be as little as 1 per cent of the weight of the product (naphtha in soap chips, powder, or bars). However, it is doubtful that 1.5 millionth of a gram would effect any purpose for which the use of the ingredient's name may have been intended. Accordingly, the FTC held that there was no justification for using the ingredient as a distinguishing part of a brand name.

What is perhaps less easy to understand is the prohibition of names suggestive of product content which might very well be descriptive of something other than "effect" or quality. Although it has apparently escaped FTC censure, Glass Wax would be a good example. The name is accurately descriptive of its purpose if not its content (that is, not a wax made *of* glass but *for* glass). The FTC, however, did catch Silverglo on aluminum pots and pans. The name endured excision on the ground that it falsely suggested a silver content, notwithstanding, apparently, no specific representation as to actual composition, as had been the case with Silver Seal cooking utensils. There a representation that the pots contained no appreciable amount of aluminum invited the FTC to investigate and to find that they did not contain any appreciable amount of silver either. Both names are, nonetheless, accurately descriptive of the appearance of the products.

And appearance has been given at least judicial sanction as a permissible frame of reference in false description cases. *Glass* was the word in question. Having found that to the purchasing public *glass* meant common glass—that is, the product made from silica such as is found in windowpanes and bottles—the FTC had prohibited the use of *Elasti-Glass* on plastic suspenders, belts, and garters as grossly misleading. It was found to leave the impression that a new discovery had made it possible to make pliable glass that is ordinarily found in windows and the like.

In setting aside the order, the United States Seventh Circuit Court of Appeals pointed out that no one had bothered to consult the dictionary, which clearly included any substance that resembles glass. Because the garters and belts in question had a "perfect" resemblance to those articles made from common glass, the descriptive brand name was properly, not misleadingly, used. Again there is no hard-and-fast rule.

A partial listing of FTC definitions for descriptive and designative words includes the following:

Air Conditioner: an electrical device that mechanically controls indoor temperature, humidity, and air circulation and removes or filters dust from the air.

Automatic: "completely" automatic is erroneous. The term is properly used only in reference to such operations as actually are performed without manual effort.

Bristle: describes a product made exclusively from hog or swine bristles provided, however, that other fibers used may be truthfully designated.

Buck Skin: connotes oil-tanned skin of deer or elk.

China: describes a nonporous, vitreous, translucent material.

Compost: decomposed organic matter.

Copperback or *-backed:* with reference to a mirror, describes the solid sheath of copper on the back of mirror deposited by an electroplating process.

Copy: unqualified or in combination with *true* or *perfect* represents the product so designated to be a replica or reproduction, a duplicate of the original *in all respects,* including structure, method of manufacture and material used.

Crepe: unqualified, means 100 per cent silk. As with *satin,* it may be used to describe a type of weave, providing the constituent fibers are designated.

Crepe de chine: unqualified, means 100 per cent silk. It may be used to describe weave or finish so long as component fibers are given.

Danish, Danish Modern: descriptive only of furniture produced entirely within the Kingdom of Denmark.

Danish Designed: properly used only in connection with furniture entirely designed or styled within the Kingdom of Denmark.

Down: indicates feathers of any aquatic bird, not to include chickens.

Eider: either alone or in combination with *down* indicates a content obtained from the Eider duck.

Full-fashioned: deceptive if used in connection with a *seamless* product, be it hoisery or girdles.

Gem: unqualified, designates a natural or genuine precious or semi-precious stone.

Genuine: as descriptive of a wood product means that no wood other than the one named has been used.

Glass: essential ingredient is silica, hence prohibited in *Liquid Glass* as a name for an auto polish.

Golden: alone or with accompanying explanatory phrase, *electroplated with real gold,* is deceptive designation for a thimble which is neither 24-K gold throughout nor coated with a substantial thickness of gold. Less than 7/1,000,000 of an inch was too thin to be called gold electroplate.

Grand Piano: accurately descriptive only of a piano with strings placed horizontally, with gravity action and possessing the "tonal qualities associated with" such a piano.

Hair: unqualified, means hair content, not burlap or other vegetable fiber. *Horsehair* means hair from the horse.

Heirloom: as used on furniture, permissible only if previously owned for several generations by the same family.

Hollandaise: describes a product made from eggs, lemon juice, vinegar, and butter.

Invisible: concealed or susceptible of being worn out of sight.

Ivory: or *genuine ivory,* must describe product made from tusks of elephants.

Jewel: with reference to a watch movement, describes the synthetic stones therein serving a mechanical purpose as a frictional bearing. With reference to a product to be used for decoration or personal adornment, it designates a natural stone. If used in connection with a synthetic stone, the fact that the product is not a natural stone or natural jewel must be clearly disclosed.

Jeweled: describes a watch movement containing at least seven jewels, each of which serves a mechanical purpose as a frictional bearing.

Kapok: describes a product or part obtained from the seeds of the Javanese kapok tree.

Kid: normally descriptive of leather made from hide of both old and young goat.

Leather: unqualified, means top grain leather.

Leather-lined: means *completely* lined with leather.

Linoleum: designates a product which is composed of oxidized oil and gums mixed "intimately" with ground cork or wood flour.

Mahogany: unqualified, used only to designate genus *Swietania.*

Name of an animal: unqualified, or in combination with *skin* or *hide* indicates a leather made from the top or grain cut (or layer) of the hide.

Names of fruits: unqualified, only if product is wholly composed of the natural fruit or its juice.

Naphtha: descriptive of a cleaning product containing kerosene.

Natural: with reference to photographs, describes only those made from color film.

Nestle Down: indicates a content consisting *wholly* of down.

Onyx: implies genuineness, natural stone; misdescriptive to use on manufactured or composition product looking like onyx but lacking the properties of cryptocrystalline variety of quartz.

Peat: a natural product, one that is formed naturally where vegetable matter has decomposed over a long period of time. The term may not be used in connection with decomposed municipal refuse.

Porcelain: may be used to describe only a product that is made of porcelain or vitreous enamel.

Preserves: or *pure preserves* describes a product consisting of "sound" fruit mixed with sugar in a proportion 45 pounds of the fruit named to 55 pounds of sugar and cooked to an appropriate consistency.

Replica: a duplicate, that which resembles or corresponds to something else.

Reproduction: a counterpart or reconstruction of something else; a copy.

Ruby: unqualified, means natural stone.

Safety: with reference to matches describes only those which ignite when head thereof is drawn across a specially prepared coating on the box in which the matches are sold.

Sapphire: unqualified, means genuine, natural stone; not synthetic.

Satin: unqualified, means 100 per cent silk unless it is used to describe the type of weave and then the fibers from which the product is made must be designated in order of their predominance by weight beginning with the largest single constituent.

Seal or *sealskin:* describes only the pelts obtained from the earless or true seal family or from the eared fur seals or sea bears.

Sectional overlay: in association with silverware describes the extra deposit of silver at points of wear, indicating additional value and increased use.

Silk: product of cocoon of silkworm and, unqualified, means "unweighted"; that is, it has not been subjected to a bath whereby a metallic substance is permanently absorbed by the silk fiber.

Silk Rayon Crepe: has no acceptable meaning, because there is no such material as "silk rayon." The fabric consisting of mixed fibers must be designated in order of the predominance by weight beginning with the largest single constituent, such as *silk/rayon* or *rayon-and-silk.*

Silverware: as descriptive of a product, means the composition is solid silver.

Simulated: see *synthetic.*

Solid: as descriptive of a wood product means that no wood other than the one named has been used.

Swansdown: down of the swan, misdescriptive of marabou feathers.

Synthetic: as defined by the FTC, refers to the jewelry industry. Accordingly, the term is properly affixed only to artificially produced stones which have essentially the same physical, chemical, and optical properties of the natural stone which such products simulate.

Taffeta: unqualified, means 100 per cent silk.

Towel: deceptive and misleading when applied to unwoven cotton and rayon fibrous product, closely resembling paper toweling, because term conveys impression that product is similar in texture, appearance, and thickness to the textile product customarily used in the home.

Vanilla: unqualified, describes only that which is obtained from the vanilla bean.

Wool: 100 per cent composed of fiber made from the hair obtained from the sheep, virgin or unused and not reclaimed.

QUANTITATIVE CLAIMS OR DESCRIPTION

A statement of the size or weight of the product offered to the consuming public at once conveys an indication of the quality and effectiveness to be expected therefrom. In addition, a quantitative description will serve as a means of making price comparisons and of making a selection relative to the needs of the consumer.

A quantitative description in mathematical terms or translatable into a mathematical designation is to be preferred. Not only would such a standard ease the task of the FTC, and others, in ferreting out any aberrational use thereof, but it should make unnecessary the use of such superfluous and obscure terms as *giant, family-size,* and *economy-size,* all, of course, for the purpose of giving the consumer better information.

This argument is now largely academic since the enactment by Congress of the Fair Packaging and Labeling Act. Such is now required. This law is treated in detail in another chapter, but a brief discussion to cover the old law under Section 5 of the Federal Trade Commission Act is appropriate at this point. The question is whether a deceptive meaning has been communicated—by whatever means quantity claims and descriptions have been made.

Obviously, a misrepresentation of the actual size or weight is deceptive, and a warning that the quantitative statement may be inaccurate —by, for example, *all sizes approximate*—will not eliminate the deception when the actual size is invariably smaller than that described approximately. The phrase reasonably implies that occasionally, at least, the actual size will be larger. Beyond that, the ingenuity of advertisers has accomplished the same thing in strange and varied ways.

One device is to set out the size in two different terms of measurement as, for example, "Approx. size 2 x 3, actual size 20″ x 30″." The first may be incorrect and the second correct or approximately so. It is, as the FTC has stated, confusing and has the tendency to give dealers the means by which size can be misrepresented.

Huge misdescribes a book that is no more than "ordinary size"; and *giant* may not be used in connection with a set of reference books consisting of fifteen volumes of less than comprehensive coverage. An "average" count is misleading when the actual number of crackers in the box is always substantially less. Because the actual size is of primary importance to the consumer, *cut size* is not an adequate quantitative statement when the variance is as great as 5 inches in length and 3 inches in width.

A brewer of beer had always sold his product in 12-ounce bottles. Later he was to advertise that a new federal tax on his product was being absorbed by him in order that he could continue to offer the beer at the same low price and quantity. His gimmick was to use a deceptive, and largely indistinguishable, new 11-ounce bottle.

A diagonal measurement to describe the *actual* viewing area of a television screen is a deceptive overstatement of size unless, as is permitted by a trade practice rule, the diagonal measurement is so designated.

The advertising of fabric as "Dress goods—15 running feet" was found to be false representation of quantity where the remnant was too narrow to be usable for cutting a dress pattern. The length measurement was accurate but the width had been split.

To claim for a coffeemaker an eight-cup capacity, the FTC has ruled that the cups must be at least 5 ounces. Similarly, for a golf cart that is advertised as being capable of holding two adults, the sitting arrangement must be "comfortable" or the claim is deceptive. A handkerchief is falsely described as "men's" if it is less than 17 x 17 inches in size.

A common device for suggesting greater quantity or size than is actually the case is the use of oversized containers. Children's toys are usually packaged in this way. In June 1967, the commission triggered some relief by issuing consent orders against ten toy manufacturers and, simultaneously, asking the industry to examine their packaging practices and bring them into line with the "non-functional slack-fill" provisions of the Fair Packaging and Labeling Act.

Similar orders have been issued against sellers of gift-wrapping paper. The width of the paper was always correctly stated; the deception was in packaging a 20-inch roll in a 24-inch box with a window only 19 inches long, so as to hide the end of the roll of paper. The customer, it was found, was more apt to be influenced by the length of the box than the statement of width. The same problem was found in packing 14 ounces of butter in a carton closely resembling the standard 1-pound size.

Section 500.22(b) of the Fair Packaging and Labeling Act deals with the variance, if any, between the quantity packaged and that ultimately received by the customer. Recently, the commission advised that it was proper to state the net weight as "32 oz. (2 lbs.)" when the weight might vary as much as 2 ounces at the point of sale, provided the package contained the stated amount when it was packed. In arriving at this conclusion, the FTC said that it assumed that good distribution practices would be followed which often unavoidably result in a change of weight.

STATEMENT OF ORIGIN

The disclosure or suggestion of the origin of a product may refer to either a particular business or a particular geographic locality. The means whereby a particular business source may be misrepresented are discussed in the chapter on business and trade status. The discussion herein will treat only of the situations in which the country of origin has been affirmatively asserted or suggested. The topic, from the standpoint of a Section 5 violation when the fact of origin is *not* disclosed, is treated in detail in the chapter on deceptive nondisclosure.

Beyond what is imposed by the Bureau of Customs under the Tariff Act for imported goods or components, or other legislation such as the Textile Fiber Products Identification Act, the FTC has no general requirement for marking goods as to the country of origin. The Section 5 prohibition against unfair trade practices is interposed where affirmative misrepresentations or nondisclosure as to the origin of a product constitutes deception of the consuming public. It is consistent with the general rule that a consumer has the "right to know" any material fact that might influence his purchasing decision.

Thus, where various means are used to obscure the domestic source on articles which the public prefers from abroad or to conceal the foreign origin where domestic goods are preferred, the proscriptions of Section 5 will be levied. Whether or not any preference exists in the case of a particular product, and whether or not the failure to disclose the origin of an imported product or substantial component constitutes a material or actionable deception warranting FTC action is, of course, a question to be determined on the basis of the facts and circumstances involved.

On April 4, 1968, the FTC released a general review of the subject which had been undertaken as a result of numerous inquiries. The commission concluded that it was neither necessary nor desirable to announce any new or changed rules or statements of general policy and that it would continue, as before, to deal with origin matter on a case-by-case basis, in light of the particular facts presented.

It is well established that a product unqualifiedly marked as "made in the U.S.A." constitutes an affirmative representation that the finished product was made *in its entirety* in the United States. It would appear to be equally settled that, absent any representation or suggestion (as, for example, by picture or symbols or use of foreign words in the brand or firm name) that might mislead the public as to the country of origin, if the product *has* been made entirely in the United States, disclosure of domestic origin need not be made. The only question remaining is whether to mark the product as domestic if it contains foreign components. There are two answers, apparently.

Assuming nothing else in the packaging or labeling might suggest the product is wholly domestic, the label may disclose the foreign origin of the substantial or significant part and, *also,* indicate the domestic contribution as illustrated by stating "made in the U.S.A. of impregnated cloth imported from _____." This identification was suggested for a polishing cloth consisting of two cloths sewn together, only one of which was imported. The qualifying words must be made as conspicuously as the claim *made in the U.S.A.* and in close proximity thereto.

On the other hand, and again assuming no device with a tendency to mislead has been used, a picture, consisting of a frame imported from one country, the picture motif from another, and a domestic glass and mat need not be labeled as to the origin of the imported elements. Nor would it be necessary for a picture of which all the components, except the picture motif, are domestically produced.

In the case of small imported FM tuners that are domestically disassembled and, for some of their components, American-made counterparts installed in order to change the tuning frequency and narrow the bandpass, the FTC approved a plan to omit any statement of origin on the label and to include with each unit a brochure that would accurately explain its origin. Equally proper would be the use of a legend, *Assembled in the U.S.A., [name of country] components,* where appropriate or to make a factual disclosure of the percentage of both the American-made parts and the imported parts.

Apparently, the use of the word *imported* without disclosing the specific country of origin is an inadequate statement of foreign origin, and if the product is *entirely* imported, it is necessary to disclose the country or countries of origin, whether or not *imported* is used. Moreover, the use of an *unqualified* company name which suggests an origin different from the actual source is improper. Under those circumstances, the origin of the product must be disclosed in conjunction with the company name wherever it is used. Equally improper is the use of names of cities and states in connection with products which do not originate there. For example, *Virginia* misdescribes the origin of hams that are not the product of hogs raised in Virginia and cured by the old Virginia process.

There are no specific regulations as to the size, material, and location of a required statement of origin. The FTC has said that any rule would have to be stated in general terms because the facts of each case may be different. The basic requirement is that of conspicuity (as to *location* and *legibility*) to assure its observation by prospective purchasers making casual inspection of the merchandise and of such degree of permanency so as to remain thereon until the product is sold to the consumer.

This raises the question of how to mark a product as to its imported status when, because of its container or packaging, a customer may not or would not normally inspect the product. Obviously, a mark on the product itself is insufficient under these circumstances. Beyond that, proper marking depends upon the packaging or display at the point of sale.

For imported fishing rods packaged for resale in the United States in a vinyl zipper case and then placed inside a cardboard carton, disclosure on the carton is necessary if that is the means used for display. A similar disclosure on the vinyl case would be required if the reels are displayed only in the case. On the other hand, it follows that the disclosure on the reels would be sufficient provided that the reels are displayed in such a manner that the disclosure may be readily observed prior to, not after, the purchase.

Finally, the FTC has advised as to the location of the statement of foreign origin of false eyelashes that are mounted on a card and packaged in the United States with directions for use and adhesive in a plastic box. It found the *back of the mounting card* acceptable, provided the disclosure is prominent and conspicuous.

11

Endorsements, Testimonials, Tests, and Surveys

THE LAW IN THE STATES

Private Causes of Action

As with many types of false advertising, misrepresentations concerning endorsements, testimonials, tests, and surveys, as such, were not actionable by a competitor at common law. But this is not to say that an injured party is bound to sit idly by while a business rival unfairly diverts customers to his own products by the use of such devices. In many cases the use of false endorsements and testimonials is tied in with other deceptive practices actionable at common law. For example, one who, for the purposes of passing off his article, falsely claims medals, awards, or endorsements legitimately conferred on another, will ordinarily be enjoined. Thus, in *Friedman* v. *Sealy, Inc.,* the appellee was able to prevent the appellant from attaching to its mattresses a sticker bearing the motto "As Advertised in Life" when such a claim was untrue and from using the Good Housekeeping Seal of Approval when it had not in fact been awarded. Sealy, who had rightly used both the Life and Good Housekeeping emblems in its own advertisements, demonstrated that the use of such false promotional materials was part of a broader scheme to divert trade by means of passing off and trade-mark infringement. The court enjoined these unfair practices including the use of false endorsements. Similarly, in *Girl Scouts of the United States of America* v. *Hollingsworth* the plaintiffs were successful in their private action to enjoin a false endorsement. In that case the defendant had used the words *Safety Scout* and a emblem similar to that of the Girl Scouts in marketing various products. This term was found to suggest, if it did not actually indicate, that these articles were sponsored by the plaintiffs. The false endorsement was, therefore, enjoinable as an infringement of the plaintiff's trade-mark.

At least one court has treated the use of false endorsements as coming within the broad purview of the tort of unfair competition. In *Thomas A. Edison, Inc.* v. *Shotkin* the defendant, who did business under the name Edison Power and Light Company, misleadingly used the significant phrase *Certified by Edison* in advertising his electrical products. The plaintiffs' so-called family of nationally known companies sold appliances similar to those of the defendant. The court found that Shotkin's acts, although not amounting to trade-mark infringement, constituted "unfair competition and unfair trade practices" by deceiving the public into believing that the goods were actually approved by the nationally known Edison. The defendant was, thus, enjoined for making these claims of certification.

It is possible, also, that the use of deceptive endorsements and test results may be actionable as part of a conspiracy in restraint of trade. At least the result in *Eastern Railroad Presidents Conference* v. *Noerr Motor Freight, Inc.* suggests this possibility. In that case the defendant railroads and others engaged in a publicity campaign against the trucking industry in an attempt to encourage the adoption of laws and law-enforcement practices that would have destroyed the long-haul trucking business. The truckers charged that the defendants had conspired to restrain trade and monopolize long-distance freight business in violation of Sections 1 and 2 of the Sherman Act. The key to the controversy was the defendant's use of the so-called third-party technique. Briefly, this scheme involves the circulation of publicity materials which appear to be spontaneously expressed views of independent persons and civic groups, when, in fact, these materials are propaganda prepared, produced, and paid for by the party in interest, in this case the railroads. The defendants had reactivated an organization known as the New Jersey Automobile Owners, Inc., and formed a new group, the New Jersey Citizens Tax Study Foundation. Their representatives and others like them in neighboring states, under the guise of independent public-spirited citizens, traveled extensively delivering speeches before associations such as the Lions and Rotary clubs. They attacked the trucking industry for increasing highway construction costs, for not paying their own way in taxes, and for creating safety hazards on the highway. The United States Supreme Court reversed the lower court decision and held that the use of the third-party technique alone could not constitute a violation of the Sherman Act. But the Court left no doubt of its opinion of this type of conduct. It agreed with the district court characterization of the use of third-party "front men" as involving "deception of the public, manufacture of bogus sources of reference, [and] distortion of public sources of information." In the Court's view, "this technique, though in wide-spread use among practitioners of the art of public relations, is one which falls far short of the ethical standards generally approved in this country." The way has certainly been left clear for possible further private litigation of similar matters.

Though to a great extent immune from suits by competitors at common law, the advertiser who employs false endorsements, testimonials, surveys, and so forth, runs the risk of being sued by the person or organization whose name he falsely used. Many courts have recognized that a person has a property right in his name and have allowed causes of action for misappropriation or invasion of privacy. These are the most common grounds upon which suit has been brought. But two additional bases for relief have been recognized.

First, the false advertiser might be sued for disparagement. For example, in *Consumers Union of the United States, Inc.* v. *Admiral Corporation* the controversy arose out of the defendant's use of the following statement upon cartons in which its air conditioners had been packaged: "Rated America's *Best Buy* By Independent Research Organization." (Emphasis added.) The plaintiff was an independent research organization which tests various products and publishes the results in its monthly magazine *Consumer Reports*. For many years it has rated products and has designated the superior ones as a "best buy." No other independent research organization rates products with this description. The plaintiff argued and the court agreed that the defendant's advertisement tended to give the reader familiar with the magazine the mistaken impression that the plaintiff had labeled the defendant's product as superior. Because of the court's interest in protecting the plaintiff's most valuable asset, its good name and good will, the motion for a preliminary injunction was granted.

There is no mention in the case on the basis upon which relief was granted. The case could possibly be read as recognizing a cause of action for false endorsement. But the safer interpretation would be to identify the cause of action here as one for commercial disparagement. By using the term "Best Buy" in connection with a product that evidently did not merit such a claim, the defendants were indirectly attacking the quality of the plaintiff's product, that is, its reputation for accuracy and fairness in product evaluation. If consumers had been dissatisfied with the air conditioner's performance, after having relied on Admiral's misrepresentation, the good will and reputation of plaintiff's product would have been impaired. Thus, it appears that disparagement offers another legal peg upon which an action for false endorsement may be hung.

Second, the use of a forged testimonial might result in the advertiser being sued for libel. For example, in *Foster-Millburn Co. v. Chinn* a drug manufacturer published a letter claiming it to be a testimonial by a famous horseman, Senator Chinn, that his back pains had been cured by Doan's Kidney Pills, produced by the defendant. Alleging that the statement was false, forged, and published without his consent, the plaintiff's complaint that he was held up to contempt and ridicule by the public was held to warrant the award of damages.

Additionally, a producer may be inhibited from engaging in false and deceptive advertising because of the consequences that could attend such practices should he himself go to court to seek relief against a competitor. One who has misrepresented testimonials or endorsements may be barred from recovery against an unfair competitor by the defense of *unclean hands*. For example, in *Gynex Corp. v. Dilex Institute of Feminine Hygiene* the plaintiff had advertised that its product had been tested and approved by "The Bureau of Feminine Hygiene, Inc.," a corporation controlled by the plaintiffs. Because the public had been deceived into thinking that the bureau was an independent organization qualified to test the product on its merits, Gynex was held not entitled to relief against the defendant's trade-mark infringement and unfair competition. The court refused to be used in furtherance of a deception upon the public.

The common law also presented the traditional problems of proof and defenses which added to the difficulty of maintaining an action for false advertising. *Caveat emptor* and puffing afforded great latitude to a would-be deceiver. The need to show special damages in a suit for commercial disparagement, and the general difficulty of privity and standing with regard to suits by competitors, made common law remedies anything but comprehensive. For the most part, successful suits were limited to unusual situations of obvious deception and well-demonstrated injury.

The State Statutes

The state statutes have not remedied the inadequacies of the common law. Though some statutes specifically forbid false advertising with respect to testimonials and regulate the registration of misleading firm names, ineffective enforcement has left the competitor and the consumer exposed to the unfair practices of an unethical few. The Uniform Deceptive Trade Practices Act specifically prohibits behavior likely to cause confusion as to "sponsorship, approval, or certification of goods or services" or "as to affiliation, connection, or association with, or certification by another." Also, one may not represent that his goods or services have sponsorship, approval, and affiliation, or a certain connection when such is not the case. The extent to which the Uniform Act will operate to remedy common law deficiencies must await further development. Thus far, the Uniform Act has not received the broad acceptance originally anticipated and has been adopted by only eight states.

FEDERAL TRADE COMMISSION REGULATION

Endorsements

Generally speaking, the FTC has been successful in its attempts to bar the use of fictitious testimonials and unauthorized endorsements, at least when direct assertions of product approval are involved. Thus, the use of testimonials and recommendations that in fact were never written by their alleged author in connection with the publication and sale of an encyclopedia was properly prohibited in *FTC* v. *Standard Education Society,* and the respondent's representation that its product had been advertised in *Life* and *McCall's,* when such was not the fact, was barred in the *Royal Sewing Machine* decision. In the same vein, it is obviously unlawful falsely to claim that one is associated with or a representative of a well-known company because it amounts to an implication that the company has endorsed the good standing and reliability of the one making the claim. Consequently, in *Consumer's Sales Corporation* v. *FTC* the respondent's salesmen, engaged in selling kitchenware, were prohibited from falsely representing to prospective customers that they were making a survey for prominent soap manufacturers who desired to obtain from housewives soap box tops, and that they were authorized to offer the utensils at a special low price in return for the box tops.

The knotty problems arise, however, when the advertisers rely on more subtle techniques such as endorsements by implication. In determining whether an advertisement misleadingly creates the impression that a particular product is associated with or approved by a noted person or group, the commission is necessarily reduced to making a decision based primarily on the facts and circumstances in each case. This piecemeal approach creates difficulties for those desiring to make precise conclusions about the state of the law in this particular area. What behavior is either permissible or prohibited must be derived from an examination of the cases themselves.

If one has some actual relationship, contractual or otherwise, with a highly regarded person or corporation, it is natural to expect that he will attempt to extract some benefit from the latter's good name, but there are limits to the inferences he is allowed to draw from the association. In one case the FTC ordered a burial vault company to cease from advertising an agreement with a well-known insurance company to underwrite the vault's guarantee, because such was tantamount to an endorsement of both the vault and the organization behind it. The respondents claimed that the insurance company would not have undertaken the risk of underwriting a fifty-year guarantee against air and water seepage unless it had been convinced of the products' high quality. However, the FTC found that the insurance company's decision to issue the policy did not constitute an endorsement based on the probable performance of the vault, but was principally motivated by the fact that in the normal course of events there would be relatively few disinterments. Thus, the public was being deceived.

Often the attempt to capitalize on another company's good will amounts to an attempt to pass off one's product as that of a better-known corporation. In two instances, at least, misuse of the Westinghouse name was found to create a likelihood of consumer deception. In both cases the respondents were distributors of electrical products equipped with a Westinghouse thermostat. As a part of its sales campaign for the appliances, one of the parties prominently displayed the Westinghouse name. The other had packaged the products in cartons bearing the words *Westinghouse thermostat;* but this term had not been preceded by the qualifying words *equipped with.* Both of these practices were found deceptive in that the name Westinghouse had been used to induce the belief that the entire appliance was manufactured by or somehow associated with the well-known company of that name. Also, in the *Niresk* case, the respondent was found to have unlawfully implied that a particular endorsement it had received was more extensive than it actually was. The court sustained the commission's conclusion that Niresk, in describing an electric cooker by the phrase *Stainless Glass Cover as Guaranteed by Good Housekeeping* had stressed the seal of approval awarded to the cover in such a way as to deceive the public into believing it referred to the complete cooker.

In another recent case the commission successfully challenged an advertisement making an offer of employment in which reference was made to the employer's listing in a well-known financial encyclopedia. "How do [you] know that [our] company is reliable? We are listed by Dun and Bradstreet. . . ." The FTC said that this was tantamount to an allegation that the respondent's integrity was vouched for by the fact they were listed in the publication, and as such was false. A listing in Dun and Bradstreet was found to signify nothing more than that a company has a certain financial rating and a certain estimated financial worth.

The FTC restriction on misleading inferences of private endorsements are also applicable to implications of endorsement by government bodies. For example, in *Mytinger and Casselberry, Inc.* v. *FTC* the controversy arose out of an earlier suit brought against Mytinger by the Food and Drug Administration which was disposed of by a consent decree in a federal district court. Although the decree barred certain claims made by the petitioners for its vitamin-mineral supplement, Nutrilite, it did set forth certain allowable claims that might be made as to the need for, or usefulness of, Nutrilite. The respondent published pamphlets describing the decree as a tribute for which petitioners "are sincerely grateful." Other literature referred to the decree as one of the "strongest sales tools a Nutrilite distributor could use, an official document bearing the signatures of officers of the federal government, thereby supporting the claims made for the product." The court sustained the commission's charge that these advertisements unlawfully misrepresented the decree as amounting to an endorsement or approval of Nutrilite by the United States government, the United States district court, and the Food and Drug Administration.

However, the FTC has not always been successful in its attempts to secure court enforcement of its orders barring allegedly false implications of product approval. In the recent case of *FTC* v. *Sterling Drug Company, Inc.*, for example, a dispute arose over an issue of the *Journal of the American Medical Association,* which carried an article written by medical experts on the comparative merits of five analgesic compounds or pain relievers—Bayer Aspirin, Saint Joseph's Aspirin, Bufferin, Anacin, and Excedrin. The research team found that there were "no important differences among the compounds tested in rapidity of onset, degree, or duration of analgesia." The respondent embarked on an extensive advertising campaign in an attempt to capitalize upon its findings. The following statements were representative: "Government-Supported Medical Team Compares Bayer Aspirin and Four Other Popular Pain-Relievers." "Findings reported in the highly authoritative journal of the American Medical Association reveals that the higher priced combination-of-ingredients pain relievers upset the stomach with significantly greater frequency than any of the other products tested, while Bayer aspirin brings relief that is as fast, as strong, and as gentle to the stomach as you can get."

The commission alleged that these advertisements falsely represented: (1) that the findings of the medical research team were endorsed and approved by the United States government and (2) that the publication of the article in the A.M.A. journal was evidence of endorsement and approval thereof by the association and the medical profession. Conceding that none of the statements was literally false, the commission contended that they were ambiguous half-truths having the capacity to deceive the "hypothetical, subintelligent, less-than-careful reader." In the commission's view, the reference to the "Government-Supported Medical Team" gave the misleading impression that the United States government endorsed the findings of the research team. Conceding the point that the word *supported* might be alternatively defined by a dictionary as, among other things, the equivalent of *endorsed,* the court hoisted the commission by its own petard by rejecting the dictionary definition and looking to the manner in which the ordinary reader would interpret the word. Stated differently, the court viewed the words as would a member of the gullible general public. It then found no impression conveyed that the product itself was being endorsed by the government. And because the FTC had selected the research team, supported the study with a grant, and authorized the publication of the report, the words *Government-Supported* could not be characterized as false or misleading. The alternatives to this statement would have been either "complete omission of the admittedly true statement or longwinded qualification and picayune circumlocution." In the court's view neither remedy was contemplated by Congress when it created the Federal Trade Commission Act. In addition, the commission's attack on the reference to the A.M.A. journal as a misleading connotation of endorsement was held to be unfounded. In the words of the court:

> To assert that the ordinary reader would conclude from the use of the word "authoritative" that the study was endorsed by the Journal and the association is to attribute to him not only a careless and imperceptive mind but also a propensity for unbounded flights of fancy. This we are not yet prepared to do. If the reader's natural reaction is to think that the study, because of publication in the Journal, is likely to be accurate, intelligent and well-documented, then the reaction is wholly justified, and one which the advertiser has every reason to . . . seek to inculcate.

The court felt that there was no reason to believe that the lay observer

would tend to construe the views expressed in the article as having secured the wholehearted endorsement and approval of the authoritative
periodical in which it appeared.

Misleading implications or inferences of endorsement arise, also,
through the use of company and product names that suggest a connection with, or an endorsement by, reputable businesses or the government.
Thus, the use of *Army and Navy* in the name of a dry-goods store was
successfully challenged by the commission in *FTC* v. *Army and Navy
Trading Company*. When the respondent's store was first established
soon after World War I, close to 90 per cent of the merchandise offered
for sale was military surplus. Because of the sharp curtailment by the
government in the quantity of goods offered for sale, the percentage of
surplus goods in the store declined to only 10 per cent. The FTC decided
that the continued use of the name Army and Navy by the respondents
was misleading the public in that they expected to buy inexpensive,
quality goods that had been produced for and met the specifications of
the United States government.

The respondent offered to use with its name the qualifying phrase *we
do not deal in Army and Navy goods*. The court rejected this and other
qualifications because the clear import of the trade name was that a
major portion of the merchandise offered for sale was in some sense
Army and Navy goods, and the suggested contradictory statement would
only tend to engender more confusion in the public mind. However, the
FTC did permit the store to use the words *formerly Army and Navy
Trading Company* for two years in connection with its new name.

A somewhat similar situation arose with a private publication called
the *U.S. Navy Magazine*. The commission reached the conclusion that the
use of an apparently official name for an unofficial private publication
was misleading in that it created an impression with the public at large
that the magazine was an official organ of the United States Navy Department. Once again deferring to the commission's wide latitude for
judgment in selecting the remedy reasonably necessary to correct the evil
and protect the public, the court sustained the finding that no qualifying
words would wholly eliminate the deception and allowed excision of the
trade name.

But this is not to say that the commission always demands the excision
of misleading trade names. For example, the brand Mayo Brothers Vitamins was held deceptive as tending to create the impression that the
product was connected with the highly regarded Mayo Clinic of Rochester, Minnesota. The commission's finding that the name was deceptive
is especially understandable in light of the respondent's claims in its
promotional materials that there was "no need to tell you that a line of
vitamins bearing this name means . . . more profits for you," and that

"months of scientific research was carried on before these vitamins were worthy of bearing the name and trademark of Mayo Brothers." The commission required the respondents clearly and conspicuously to disclose in immediate conjunction with the words *Mayo Brothers* that they were in no way connected with the Mayo Clinic.

Similarly, the commission's order in a recent case involving the United States Testing Company did not require excision but did place effective limits on the company's right to use its own name. The respondent was engaged in the business of testing products for manufacturers. Once the tests were completed, the results were usually incorporated into extensive advertising campaigns of which the following two are typical: (1) "Official Report from U.S. Testing Company, on 1962 Chevrolet, Ford and Plymouth" and (2) "Parliament is tested for uniformity, month after month by the United States Testing Company. . . ." Through the use of *U.S.* in its trade name, accompanied by either its "seal of quality" or the seal of the U.S. Testing Company, the respondent was alleged to have placed in the hands of others means and instrumentalities by and through which they could mislead the public into the belief that the respondent was connected with an instrumentality of the government or that the tests were approved by the government. Under the commission's order, the U.S. Testing Company was prohibited from furnishing a test report under the corporate name or with any seal containing *U.S.* to any firm for the use in advertisements aimed at the general public. Also, the U.S. Testing Company was required to include in any report to or contract with any firm the express provision that under no circumstances could the respondent's corporate name or insignia containing the terms *U.S.* be used in any advertisements.

It is unlawful to use the words *doctor, M.D.,* or any other expression which falsely suggests that a product has been made by or under the supervision of a medical doctor, or has been manufactured in accordance with a medical prescription or formula. For example, in *Stanley Laboratories* v. *FTC* the petitioner called its product MD Medicated Douche Powder, the letters *MD* being the core of the controversy. Generally, the advertisements for the powder featured either a young woman in a nurse's uniform extolling its virtues or a person saying, "Thank you . . . for your advice, Doctor!" In most of the ads the initials *M.D.*, with or without the periods after the letters, were prominently displayed. Basing its conclusions on the testimony of both medical and lay witnesses, the FTC found the use of these letters to be deceptive, either alone or in conjunction with a picture of a doctor, nurse, or cross similar to the emblem used by the American Red Cross (an act in and of itself a violation of Section 5) in connection with a medicated powder sold by the petitioners. The use of the letters *M.D.* was prohibited as tending to lead the public into the belief that the powder was either made or endorsed by the medical profession.

It would seem that the use of the symbol *RX* in marketing various cosmetic products would be objected to for reasons similar to those advanced in the *Stanley* case, but the use of the term has been found not unlawful in at least one FTC case. There the complaint noted that *RX* has been used as the heading on physicians' prescriptions for many centuries and thus had become associated in the minds of the public with medical preparations. Thus, the respondent's use of such symbols was alleged to have misled the public into thinking that the product was of a medicinal nature and that each parcel was individually compounded in accordance with a specific prescription. The commission held that the record failed to substantiate this claim, but it did suggest that the use of *RX* might be misleading on other grounds not alleged in the complaint.

It may well be that the use of this symbol has become so firmly associated in the minds of a substantial number of the public with physicians and their prescriptions that its use in connection with or reference to cosmetics, and perhaps other products as well, may have the capacity and tendency to engender an erroneous belief of some sort concerning the relationship of a physician to a product.

Use of the emblem associated with a well-known organization of high repute is also a method of implying endorsement by that group. In one case a green Greek cross was used in advertising safety glasses. Because it is the trade-mark of the National Safety Council, its use was thought falsely to imply that the council had endorsed the glasses. Similarly, in *FTC v. A.P.W. Paper Co.* a paper products manufacturer was challenged for his use of the name Red Cross and an emblem consisting of a red Greek cross as identification for his products. The respondent's defense was that, as a pre-1905 user, he was allowed under the American Red Cross Act of 1905 to continue to use the words *Red Cross* and the symbol. The United States Supreme Court, however, recognizing the danger of consumer deception, allowed the commission to modify this right to the extent of requiring the following notice of differentiation or disassociation on the respondent's labels: "This product has no connection whatsoever with the American National Red Cross."

Testimonials

As was seen in the beginning of this chapter, the *Standard Education Society* case unsurprisingly outlawed the use of testimonials that in fact had never been given. Remaining to be discussed, however, are the following problems: solicitation of and payment for testimonials, recommendations by nonusers, and misrepresentation through testimonials.

Prior to the decision in the well-known *Northram-Warren* case, the commission had successfully conducted a vigorous campaign designed to prevent nondisclosure of payment for testimonials. Several respondents had stipulated that they would not use paid-for testimonials without revealing that fact in an equally conspicuous manner. If this pattern had continued, its effect would have been to eliminate all paid testimonials and endorsements.

The *Northram-Warren* decision has severely curtailed the ambit of FTC regulatory authority over testimonial advertising for at least two decades. The important issue presented was whether or not it was a violation of Section 5 to use admittedly truthful testimonials without disclosing that payment had been made for their use. The dispute arose out of the petitioner's use of testimonials and endorsements of well-known theatrical personalities in advertising its toilet articles and preparations. The commission argued that the failure to state the price paid for the testimonials amounted to a deception concerning the petitioner's product. The court responded by saying the FTC had no right to presume that endorsers of commercial products falsify their statements because they have received compensation. If the testimonials represented the honest beliefs of the endorsers, there was no misrepresentation concerning the product. To substantiate its conclusion that no one was deceived by these truthful endorsements, the court also expressed doubt as to whether the public was gullible enough to believe that such testimonials are given without compensation. Stated differently, these testimonials came within the purview of the "puffing" privilege because they were nondeceptive. However, at least one noted commentator has shared the commission's view that it is "inconsistent to assume that the public realizes that such payments are common and, at the same time, to say the sponsors would not be willing to cooperate if payments were disclosed."

With due regard to the impact this case has had on the regulation of testimonial advertising, it is of doubtful validity today. First, the case was decided prior to the Wheeler-Lea Amendment to the Federal Trade Commission Act. Before that time, the commission was regarded primarily as an instrument of federal antitrust law. It was largely concerned with eliminating unfair competition, consumer benefit being only an incidental concern. The Wheeler-Lea Act of 1938 was the manifestation of a congressional intent to broaden FTC jurisdiction to cover not only acts which are unfair to competitors, but practices which tend to mislead and deceive the consumer. Today, the commission's consumer orientation and its congressional mandate to protect the public interest could well result in a judicial acceptance of the restrictions the FTC urged on the United States Court of Appeals for the Second Circuit in 1932. Additionally, the concept of puffing has been altered drastically since the

Northram-Warren decision. What was viewed as harmless exaggeration in that case might well be considered deceptive today. In fact, as early as 1942 there was evidence of judicial acquiescence in the commission's restrictive view of the privilege.

In the *Moretrench* case a court allowed the commission to require the most literal truthfulness in advertising. A claim that "contractors all over the world testify" that the maintenance "cost of [a particular machine] is 50 per cent lower than that of any other" was held misleading because, in fact, contractors all over the world had not testified as quoted. Even though the court found it hard to imagine how any one reading the advertisement could have understood it as more than puffing, it sustained the commission's cease and desist order.

Even though an advertiser may be able to use a testimonial without revealing the existence of consideration therefor, he may not represent that it was voluntarily given. For example, in one case the FTC questioned the use of the medical findings of a group of doctors who purportedly found the respondents' cigarettes to be less irritating. Philip Morris was found to have represented that these results were published for the sole benefit of the medical profession. In fact, the studies were financed by the respondents for the purpose of providing a basis for their advertising claims, and the results were given directly to the respondents and not to the medical profession. Though its decision was later reversed on other grounds, the FTC did order these advertisements to be dropped.

In another case a soap manufacturer advertised that leading automatic washing machine companies and their dealers had recommended the respondent's detergents, soaps, and bleaches and had inserted free samples of these items in their machines. Furthermore, it was claimed that these appliance manufacturers and dealers had voluntarily selected the respondent's products to be placed in their respective machines and had recommended they be used exclusively in these machines. In reality, Proctor & Gamble had entered into exclusive "free-sampling" contracts with these manufacturers and dealers under which the latter received substantial sums of money in return for recommending the respondent's products and using them in demonstrations. The commission required Proctor & Gamble to disclose on the sample packages that the samples in the machines were supplied free and at its initiative. Also, where those demonstrating the appliances had been paid for using and recommending the respondent's soaps and bleaches, they were required to disclose that fact at the time of the demonstration.

The effect of these and other cases had been to demonstrate clearly the limited application of the *Northram-Warren* decision. There can be no doubt that once an advertiser makes any affirmative claims suggesting an absence of consideration, he steps out from under the *Northram-Warren* umbrella into the realm of FTC regulation. Furthermore, in *FTC v. Inecto, Inc.* it was held unlawful for a hair dye manufacturer falsely to imply that testimonial letters were received from users or consumers or that the testimonials were unsolicited. Similarly, a yogurt distributor agreed not to publish testimonials attributing good health and other benefits to the yogurt when they falsely implied that they were based on the testimonialist's actual use of and personal experience with the product. More recently, a dairy company agreed to cease using testimonials to the effect that Mickey Mantle preferred and regularly consumed its milk products when such was not the fact. Thus, not only is a nonuser prohibited from testifying as to a product's benefits, apparently he may not even create the impression that he uses the product when in fact he does not do so. The *Northram-Warren* obstacle has been neatly circuited. Though the payment of consideration need not be revealed, the statements used must represent the testimonialist's own views or opinions based on actual use of the product. Gone are the days in which testimonials are signed without even having been read.

There have been many attempts in the past to use testimonials as vehicles for the conveyance of false claims to the consuming public. It is now a basic proposition of the law that a statement otherwise objectionable under Section 5 is not sanctified by being put forward in a quotation as the opinion or testimony of others. Thus, if in a burst of exuberant enthusiasm a satisfied customer makes an extravagant claim for a particular product, the manufacturer of that product may not lawfully quote him if he knows the statement is false.

As early as 1929 the courts recognized that testimonials have a stronger appeal to members of the purchasing public than other types of advertising. For this reason, in the language of one court, such statements may be more, not less, obnoxious to the law. In the *Fulton* case instead of making direct statements or representations that its drugs were of curative or therapeutic value, the defendants reprinted many letters from physicians reporting that the drugs had afforded relief from diabetes for many of their patients. In fact, the drugs were worthless. The court denied the defendant's contention that these reports and letters constituted a complete defense to the misbranding charge, whatever the character of the drugs. The court reasoned that to accept these contentions would be to permit by indirect means that which would be unlawful under the Food and Drug Act if done directly.

The commission's approach in dealing with testimonials extolling the virtues of medicinal products of dubious therapeutic value was revealed in the years following the *Fulton* decision. Basically, the attack is two-pronged. First, a mass of expert testimony is introduced to demonstrate that it is scientifically impossible for the products in question to achieve the results attributed to them by the satisfied users. Second, "it is shown that the users of the preparation did not subject themselves to accepted diagnostic methods" prior to using the allegedly miraculous medicine. The purpose of such a demonstration is to show that there frequently is no conclusive proof that the recovered patient ever actually had the disease from which he thought he had recovered. Once the falsity of the claims is established, the FTC prohibits the advertisers from further public deception through the use of these testimonials. In other words, a testimonialist's sincere belief that a particular medicinal preparation which he has endorsed actually cured his disease or sickness does not give advertisers a blanket license to use these claims as they wish. They must first be able to withstand the onslaught of exacting scientific scrutiny. Thus, in two early cases, one involving claims of cures of various ailments by electromagnetism and the other arising out of advertisements for a stomach medicine preparation called Pepsotalis, the advertisers were prevented from circuiting the FTC's proscriptions against false advertising by the use of testimonials from well-intentioned but misguided customers. There was no discussion of the puffing privilege in either of these cases. It would appear that the commission's attitude toward this historical common law right is the same here as in other areas of the law. That which has a tendency to mislead or deceive is not a "puff," and few such false statements are not deceptive.

In the more recent *American Paint Co.* case the commission specifically adopted the court's language in the *Fulton* case to the effect that the use of testimonials containing false statements are more, not less, obnoxious to the law because of their stronger appeal to members of the purchasing public. Accordingly, "the efforts by the commission to prevent false advertising would be rendered ineffective" if it permitted publication of good-faith testimonials making unquestionably untrue claims for certain products. In this case a medically related product, a plant hormone called Rootone was in controversy. The respondent based its advertising claims for Rootone on testimonials received from various farmers who in good faith claimed substantial increases in crop yields per acre. Not only did expert scientific testimony establish the product's inability to achieve the results claimed, the commission noted the respondent's failure to demonstrate that the testimonialists' increase in productivity was not attributable to one or more of the many factors that influence crop yield, such as temperature, rainfall, and soil fertility. Thus, despite the presence of good faith on the part of both the advertiser and various satisfied users, further publication of these testimonials was prohibited because they were in fact false.

The *R. J. Reynolds Tobacco Company* case provides a recent example of unlawful misrepresentations through testimonials. The respondents used statements from various personalities and average men in the street:

> When the pace I go gets me fatigued, a Camel gives me a "lift."
>
> I like . . . Camel's for "digestion's sake." There's something about Camels that agree with me—all around.
>
> [B]ut after a quick bite I always grab a Camel, because Camels seem to smooth the way for digestion.

Because expert testimony established that these cigarettes did not relieve fatigue and aid digestion, the FTC banned the use of testimonials containing any of these representations. But the commission went further. It prohibited the use of representations that were "not factually true in all respects." On appeal, the court eliminated this last phrase from the commission's order. The court said:

> It seems to us that this all-inclusive language is too broad and goes beyond any concern of the Commission. A testimonial, for instance, might not be "factually true in all respects" but still be immaterial to the subject matter of the instant proceeding in that it bore no relation to public interest, and it would virtually make petitioner an insurer of the truthfulness of every statement contained in a testimonial, no matter how immaterial or beside the issue in controversy it might be.

Thus, while there is no absolute prohibition against the use of testimonials containing inaccurate representations, there seems to be a little life left in the advertisers' puffing privilege.

Tests, Awards, Certification, and Surveys

The publication of test and survey results has been a popular advertising practice because it graphically illustrates either the minimum performance levels of a particular product or its merits compared to those of competing products. The potential for abuse being significant, the commission has carefully scrutinized this type of advertising device. One of the earliest examples of FTC regulation in this area is the famous case involving *Good Housekeeping* magazine. There the respondent had engaged in the practice of issuing its Good Housekeeping Seal of Approval, containing the words *tested and approved,* to various household products it deemed deserving of this award. Manufacturers were not required to advertise in any Hearst publication as a condition of qualification for receipt of the seal. In fact, a majority of the certified products were not advertised in *Good Housekeeping* magazine. Once awarded, the various manufacturers were permitted to use these emblems or shields in advertising the recipient product.

The FTC challenged the issuance of these seals on the ground that the accolades were often not preceded by tests and that even when tests were performed, they were not sufficiently thorough to assure the fulfillment of the advertisers' claims for its product. The unwarranted issuance of seals of approval based on performances that had never occurred was unlawful in that the purchasing public had been misled into believing that all products bearing the *Good Housekeeping* shield had been thoroughly tested and approved.

It is clear that a manufacturer will be prohibited from falsely representing that his product has been tested in comparison with competing products. It is equally clear that the published results of the comparative tests must not be deceptive. For example, the tests must be made in comparison with products readily available to the consumer. In one case the respondent tested its Crest toothpaste against a "regular toothpaste," the results demonstrating that those using Crest received fewer cavities. In fact, Crest had not been tested against competitive brands as the advertisement implied but against Crest minus an ingredient known as stannous fluoride, a formula not commercially available. The use of test results involving a nonexistent product was, of course, held to be deceptive. Stated differently, in order to make the use of comparative test results legitimate, competing products must be afforded an opportunity to compete.

References to the standards by which the products were compared or the conditions under which tests were conducted should be included in the advertising of test results. The failure to do so may well invite FTC inquiry. For example, a manufacturer was challenged for advertising his "Crown" product as "Crown Tested and Approved Rayon Fabric," when the commission found that no specifications or standards had been recognized by competent authorities as being adequate for testing rayon. Thus, even though products have been honestly tested (which in this particular case they had not been), apparently no claim should be made that the products meet consumer standards unless certain minimum test requirements have been generally recognized by the industry. In a somewhat related case an automobile manufacturer recently agreed not to claim that its trucks averaged 30 miles per gallon in certified tests without disclosing the conditions under which the tests had been conducted.

Though the tests relied upon are apparently legitimate, their results, and consequently the use thereof, may be tainted by an affiliation with, or a failure to disclose the identity of, the test conductor. For example, claims of "certified" in describing a product have been prohibited unless the certifier's identity has been clearly and plainly disclosed. And if the certifier is someone other than the seller, any connection between them must be shown. Furthermore, claims that products are "certified" have been prohibited unless the certifier is qualified and competent to know the truthfulness of what he testified to.

Assuming that the tests in question have been fairly conducted by qualified personnel whose identity has been disclosed, the advertiser is still not home free. Not only is it unlawful to claim product superiority on the basis of tests which, though technically favorable, demonstrate no significant difference between the products tested, it is a violation of Section 5 to misrepresent product quality by publishing incomplete test results. In *Country Tweeds, Inc.* v. *FTC* the petitioners, who were engaged in the manufacture of cashmere wearing apparel, submitted two samples of cashmere fabric to the United States Testing Company with the request that they be subjected to various comparative tests. One sample was a leading cashmere, the other a fabric labeled *Country Tweeds Elegant Cashmere*. After the tests had been completed, a two-page report setting forth the results was submitted to the petitioners, who then reduced it to a single page. The altered report was then used in an advertising circular, replete with the testing company's official letterhead and the signature of two of its employees.

The controversy arose over two aspects of the altered report: First, the original report had set forth the results for the abrasion portion of the tests in terms of the number of abrading cycles necessary to produce a given degree of wear for each sample. Elegant withstood 715 cycles, whereas the competing cashmere lasted for only 673. The testing company added the following comments: "Test results indicate no significant difference in abrasive resistance between the two submitted samples." In the altered report, Country Tweed omitted the qualifying statement and expressed the test results in the form of a claim that its product lasted 6.3 per cent longer than the leading competitive cashmere. Second, the results of the breaking-load test were expressed by the testing company in the original report in terms of a given number of test pounds. The results were broken down into the strength of the warp and the strength of the filling for each sample. Elegant was clearly stronger in one category but slightly weaker in the other. Instead of reporting the results in terms of test-pound strength, the petitioners claimed in its advertisements that its cashmere was 56.5 per cent stronger than the leading competitive product. This figure as it applied to the phase of the test in which Elegant proved superior was accurate. But the altered report completely ignored that part of the strength test that demonstrated the competitive product's slight advantage.

In defense to the commission's allegations that these representations were deceptive and misleading, Country Tweeds contended that their altered report was a fair summary of the original, framed in less technical terms. The court did not agree. "Even if we were convinced [which we are not] that framing the tests results in percentage terms did not cause [them] to appear more [favorable] to the fabric [which] petitioners were interested in promoting, we would still be compelled to refuse to hold the altered report a fair summary." In deleting the original report's important qualifying statement of the lack of significant difference in the abrasion test results, the petitioners had attributed to the United States Testing Company the opinion that one of the fabrics tested would last longer than the other. Unsurprisingly, the court found the summary of the breaking-load test even more misleading. Though the partial results were technically true, the omission of one half of the test findings resulted in a deceptive and misleading advertisement.

The use of survey results is, of course, permissible, but the accuracy of the sampling process in estimating public opinion or practice must be demonstrated. As the *Bristol-Myers* case demonstrated, a failure to do so may lead to an FTC ban on the use of the survey results. In that case the corporation sent questionnaires to a random selection of 10,000 of the 66,000 dentists in the United States. Each was asked to name his own toothpaste plus the one he recommended to his patients. There were 1,983 questionnaires returned. Bristol-Myers made many advertisements for its Ipana brand on the basis of the results. The following claims were typical: "Do you know that the 1940 National Survey conducted among thousands of dentists revealed the following remarkable fact—Twice as many dentists personally use Ipana Tooth Paste as any other dentifrice preparation." "[I]n a recent nationwide survey, more dentists said they recommended Ipana for their patients' daily use than the next two dentifrices combined."

Technically, these representations were correct. Of those responding more dentists recommended Ipana for their patients than any other brand. But the court sustained the commission's finding that these ads were deceptive and misleading. The claims suggested to the casual consumer that a careful inquiry among the members of the dentistry profession had disclosed that a large majority endorsed Ipana. In other words, the average reader would not infer that the positive proof in the hands of the advertiser disclosed the personal preference of only 621 dentists and the customary recommendation of toothpaste to patients of only 461 dentists out of the 66,000 in the United States, or that less than 20 per cent of those who had been questioned had taken the trouble to reply. The court did not reject the notion that an accurate estimate of public opinion or practice can be obtained by a sampling process or survey, "but the record is devoid of information on this subject and in the absence of the proof of the scientific principles, if any, which underlies the practice, we must rely upon the impression which the advertisements would be likely to make on the mind of a man of ordinary intelligence."

Thus, the advertisements failed quantitatively for insufficient statistical data, not qualitatively because of the nature of the advertisement itself.

As is the case with endorsements and testimonials, it is possible to create through the use of misleading trade names the implication that a particular product has been given an award or has been proven superior in tests with other products. For example, one company used the trade name First Prize Bob-Pins superimposed on the picture of a blue ribbon. As an issue of fact it was determined that through the use of this trade name, the respondent had implied that his product had received an award for its quality or design. Deciding that language of explanation would only contradict and therefore confuse the public, the FTC ruled that no remedy short of excision of the respondent's registered trade-mark would be adequate. Similarly, in *Re Neuville, Inc.* the use of the trade name Academy Award for a line of hosiery products was held falsely to imply that they had received a meritorious award based on comparative tests. The respondents were prohibited from using this name or any phrase of similar import.

12

Pricing and Savings Claims

Because buyers love a "bargain," sellers may seek their custom through various pricing practices that misrepresent the value or worth of merchandise or the special conditions of the offer to sell. Although such practices are not new, since World War II it has become an even greater temptation for the merchandiser competing against the new man on the scene, the discount retailer. Largely eliminating customer service and operating on a "low markup high volume quick turnover" basis—and, what's more, boldly inviting comparison of its prices with those in the competitive department stores—discount stores have become a place to shop for everything from major appliances to toys.

Not that the traditional retailer has ever been at a loss for counter-measures; every conceivable excuse for bestowing on his customers "special" offers has been exploited, sometimes deceptively. When, however, he cuts prices to meet the competition of discount houses, the basis for genuine price comparison is gone. The obvious answer, of course, is to *create* a price, either deliberately or arbitrarily—just as special conditions may be invented—upon which to base a savings claim. It is a game anyone can play. The seller, often assisted by his distributor, has only to choose his weapon and the war is on to attract the bargain hunter.

Undoubtedly, bargain-price advertising may serve a legitimate business purpose. Seasonal items have to be pushed and business reverses have to be resolved. The farsighted (and not necessarily improvident) buyer is only too happy to oblige. Moreover, when not in contravention of trade regulation laws, advertising of bargain prices is a well-recognized competitive practice. Price will always be *an,* if not in many instances *the most,* effective choice maker in the market place. The question is whether the buyer's choice has been fairly induced.

Even assuming that today's buyer is sufficiently sophisticated to know that he rarely gets more than he has paid for and, hence, views all savings claims with a wary eye, or that the various consumer research services have had the effect of replacing the casual buyer with the "shopper," a significant segment of the consuming public is still misled by price advertising. Indeed, the essential nature of the "bargain" offer contributes to the disadvantageous position of the uninformed buyer. Because the true value of the bargain is dependent on a former price of the advertiser or the current price of other sellers—or on other things which neither the advertising nor the merchandise reveal—it is difficult, if not impossible, for the buyer to evaluate the advertised price. Accordingly, the buyer must rely on the integrity of the advertiser. To assure that this reliance is justified is a particular province of the Federal Trade Commission.

The subject of unfair pricing practices is one of several in which the commission has buttressed its pronouncements on what constitutes a violation of Section 5 with guidelines to assist the businessman who wishes to conform to the requirements of the Federal Trade Commission Act. With the incidence of deceptive price advertising apparently on the increase, the FTC promulgated its *Guides Against Deceptive Pricing* in 1958 and *Guides Against Bait Advertising* in 1959. They were a codification and simplified restatement of the relevant principles arrived at in adjudication over the years. Moreover, they consolidated for the benefit of advertisers everywhere the two classifications of rules found in most sets of trade-conference rules. Framed in the negative "no statement . . . shall be used unless," the guides clearly set forth the violative acts. When, however, in 1964 the *Guides Against Deceptive Pricing* were revised (reprinted in the appendixes), the approach was softer. Written in easy-to-read narrative form, the current guides only enunciate the standard for permissible conduct. Moreover, the standard would seem to have been relaxed to some extent. To some commentators this indicates an easing of the commission's attitude on bargain advertising. The revision, of course, may have been intended to give the commission greater flexibility in defining unfair pricing practices. To at least one member of the agency, however, the new guides are "so loosely worded that it will take an unprecedented number of cases until both the Commission staff and the business community know what the guidelines . . . are."

MEANS OF DECEPTIVE PRICE ADVERTISING

Former Price Comparisons—Guide I

A seller seeking to increase his business may appeal to a buyer's desire to make a good buy by offering a reduction from his own former price. Seasonal sales are probably the best known example. If such an offer is truthful, it is a benefit to buyer and seller alike. All too frequently, however, the purported bargain is illusory and, to the extent it induces sales, benefits only the seller. The advertiser, then, is advised to "shun sales gimmicks which lure the consumer into a mistaken belief that they are getting more for their money than is the fact."

The question with respect to bargain advertising is always the genuineness of the price on which the savings are based. As the guide points out with respect to the advertiser's own price,

> Where the former price is genuine, the bargain being advertised is a true one. If, on the other hand, the former price being advertised is not bona fide but fictitious . . . the "bargain" being advertised is a false one; the purchaser is not receiving the unusual value he expects.

Accordingly, the FTC has said that there are but two legitimate bases for a former price savings claim: (1) the regular price customarily charged by the retailer or (2) the price at which the advertised article was offered for sale actively and openly in good faith for a reasonably substantial period of time in the recent, regular course of business—in other words, a former selling price or a former asking price. In the following discussion it will be assumed that neither of these bases has been deliberately invented for the purpose of a subsequent savings offer. This would be per se a fictitious former price.

Former Selling Price. If a price at which sales have been made is to support a subsequent bargain offer, it may have to pass a test of substantiality. Indeed, throughout the several guides the term *substantial sales* modifies any reference to the regular selling price of the advertised article. It is, however, difficult to state to what extent it will be determinative of the genuineness of a *former selling price* of the advertiser. For example, with respect to every other deceptive pricing practice outlined in the guides, some attempt is made to define *substantial* more clearly.

Guide I, on the other hand, uses the term almost as an afterthought, albeit specifically in order to distinguish *selling price* from *asking price*. Moreover, the cases do not help. Those that are directed to the question of substantial sales deal with savings claims which invite comparison with the prices of other retailers or those of nonretail distributors, and will be discussed when we turn our attention to Guides II and III. They may shed some light on the meaning of the term in this context of an advertiser's own former price; it is apparent, however, that they are not controlling, nor were they meant to be. It would have been easy enough for the commission to include a parenthetical explanation in Guide I as well when, in promulgating the 1964 guides, it chose to create an evidentiary problem which did not exist under the 1958 guides.

What all this appears to add up to is that substantiality of sales, at least as to an advertiser's former "selling" price, will not be wholly dispositive. It will be measured as well by facts which are consonant with a bona fide effort to sell at a price which reflects customary and usual markup and business methods, rather than a deceptive purpose. For example, Guide I points out that a price which was not used in the regular course of business or not openly offered to the public would be a fictitious, that is, not genuine or bona fide, former (selling) price. Moreover, that guide and the cases clearly impose a temporal test as further indication of the advertiser's honesty in inviting comparison between a currently advertised price and a former selling price. *"Reasonably substantial period of time* in the *recent,* regular course of business" is the traditional phrase. Where *no* sales have been made, time alone will bear out the legitimacy of an asking price that is used as the basis of a bargain offer.

Former Asking Price. The price which, having failed to entice sales, never became a regular selling price is a permissible basis for a bargain offer. The guide only admonishes the advertiser to "scrupulously avoid" any implication that it is a selling price and to be "especially careful" that it has been used in the *recent,* regular course of business for a *reasonable* length of *time.*

Reasonable time is nowhere defined, and, undoubtedly, for the traditional reason: it depends upon the circumstances. Although one commentator has attempted greater precision, the commission apparently prefers a flexible approach to *recent* course of business as well. Its meaning was fully explored in the context of the Washington, D.C. Metropolitan area's traditional Washington's Birthday Sale.

Recognizing that the general public in Washington expects that merchandise advertised for sale during this event may be limited in number, age, style, and color and may be soiled and outdated, the commission agreed with the examiner that the fact that no sale of an advertised item had been made more recently than six months prior to the "sale," did not constitute a misrepresentation of a former price and the savings to be afforded by the discount price. The time element alone was not a fair and reasonable test. Under the circumstances of the particular sale and the items offered, to demand a sale within a short time immediately preceding the advertisement in order to establish, in fact, a regular price was said to put a "strained and unrealistic interpretation" on "recent, regular course of business."

Bargain-Pricing Techniques Which Imply Advertiser's Former Price. Drawing a line through the higher figure in a dual price representation is the means very frequently utilized to imply that a bargain is being offered. Assuming that the figure has not been invented for the occasion, according to the guide, "the mechanics used are not of the essence." Indeed, there may be no reference at all to a former price, and/or the amount or percentage of the reduction, as when the ad merely states, "Sale" or "Save $_____" or "Reduced to $_____." With respect to this type of dual-pricing technique, the guide warns the advertiser that he "must take care that the amount of reduction is not so insignificant as to be meaningless. It should be sufficiently large that the consumer, if he knew what it was, would believe that a genuine bargain or saving was being offered." The guide illustrates this point with an otherwise unexplained $9.99 "reduced" price on an item that had previously sold for $10. Such would be misleading, because the consumer would expect the claim to mean that a much greater reduction was being offered.

Of seemingly greater significance to the FTC where the source of the savings is not indicated is the fact that it could be understood to be either the advertiser's usual and regular price or that of his competitors. Consistent with its usual view of ambiguous representations, such an ad is considered deceptive. An advertiser who claimed "Yours for only $149.88. *Save* $60.00" was ordered to use "descriptive means that clearly and truthfully describe both the higher and the lower price."

"Descriptive means" are unncessary with other terminology which appear with considerable frequency in savings ads. *Regularly, reg.* or *usually,* for example, all carry definitive connotations. They have been held to be descriptive of the *advertiser's* own regular, former price. As the commission has said, it is "the only reasonable and logical interpretation possible." And those terms may not be used to indicate the regular price of the advertiser's competitors even where the amount of the savings offered is correctly stated. To permit two contrary interpretations would be confusing and "detrimental to buyers and sellers alike." Moreover, these terms must refer to the previous price of the *identical* product that is offered at a reduced price or savings. It is "false, misleading and deceptive" to contrast a current price with a price at which similar merchandise, even merchandise by the same manufacturer, has been sold previously. *Originally* carries this specific connotation as well and would be deceptive in connection with merchandise specially purchased by the advertiser for the bargain event.

Other terms which have been held to represent the advertiser's former price are *sold for; Was $*_____, *now $*_____; *formerly; were; off;* and *now $*_____.

The terms *value* or *worth* are used at times to give the impression that the value of the article is greater than the price at which it is advertised, thereby implying that the advertised price is a bargain. One authority defines *value* as the price or amount at which the article may be bought in the retail market in the usual course of business. When, however, that term is used with a dollar figure that is otherwise undesignated (which is usually the case), it would seem to present a classic case of an ambiguous, hence deceptive, representation. And because the FTC apparently prefers to have the retailer nailed down as either the advertiser or his competitor, the unexplained use of *value* would fail for specificity, as would *save,* or even *sale,* when used alone in conjunction with a current selling price. The problem must remain conjectural, however; neither the commission nor the courts have directed their attention to the ambiguous nature of the term *value.* Nonetheless, the commission has said that where an advertisement, read as a whole, leaves no doubt as to the source of the savings offered; for example,

> $50–$55–$60 VALUES During Bond's Big Celebration Sale—You can Save Up to Twenty-one Dollars on a Suit—During This Sale Only— Priced at Just Thirty-eight Ninety.

the only question is whether the base price or "value" is bona fide, so the savings are not misrepresented. It must be the regular and customary price *of the advertiser.* Again, the fact that the amount of the savings may actually represent a reduction from the price at which the merchandise is customarily sold by the advertiser will not cure the deception which occurs by reason of the fictitious "value" that has been ascribed to the merchandise offered as a bargain.

The preceding discussion touches on one of several aspects of the law of deceptive price advertising which appears to raise as many questions as it provides answers. The commission is apparently as concerned over a misrepresentation of the source of the purported savings as it is over a misrepresentation of the savings to be obtained by buying at the advertised price. But what purpose is served by identifying *the* source as long as there is a source (which has not been misrepresented)?

One could argue and subscribe to the rationale that customer evaluation (and that of the FTC as well) of the bargain is more easily made thereby. Yet the commission gives no indication that this is behind its orders directed against bargain advertisements which may be deemed to be ambiguous with regard to the source of the savings. One respondent agreed to cease representing any price as a "sale" price unless such price constituted a reduction from the *generally prevailing price* at which the merchandise is sold at retail *in the trade area* where the representation is made or "sale-priced" unless the price so designated constituted a reduction from the price at which the merchandise was *sold by the advertiser* in the recent, regular course of business. It would seem extremely doubtful that the buying public would read a distinction into these bargain-event designations, or even care that there might be one, inasmuch as *a* reduction from the price they would have to pay *somewhere* is that in which they must be primarily interested.

Retail Price Comparison; Comparable Value Comparisons— Guide II

The *Guides Against Deceptive Pricing* recognize as a permissible form of bargain advertising the offer of a reduction from the price charged by others in the advertiser's trade area for either the *same merchandise* or *comparable merchandise.* Again the genuineness of the higher price that is contrasted with the "bargain" price is of primary importance and will be discussed at length. There are, however, several other factors which will affect the legitimacy of this advertising practice.

Although the guide does not so advise (and the 1958 guides did not cover the subject at all), presumably *same merchandise* means *identical merchandise.* Thus, *Brand X Pens, Price Elsewhere $*————, *Our Price, $*———— would be a legitimate advertisement if, in fact, Brand X pens are made available to the customers. In this way an advertiser may combine the self-propelling nature of a brand name with the lure of a bargain. Moreover, because he need not bother establishing the higher comparative price by his own prior sales (assuming it has been so established elsewhere), he may introduce the article to his customers at the lower price and maintain it on a temporary or permanent basis.

Comparable merchandise presents a more difficult situation. "Like grade and quality . . . competing merchandise" is the definitive language of the guide, which goes on to state, "Such advertising can serve a useful and legitimate purpose when it is made clear to the consumer that a comparison is being made with other merchandise and the other merchandise is, in fact, of essentially similar quality and obtainable in the area." *Comparable value $*———— or *Comparable retail $*———— in juxtaposition with the advertiser's lower price is the manner in which this type of savings claim is made most frequently. Presumably the word *value* alone, because of its ambiguous nature, and *regularly* and *formerly,* because of their specific connotation, could not be used even if the implied savings is accurate and the merchandise is "comparable or competing." Conversely, if the merchandise is not comparable, the consumer does not realize the savings advertised.

The FTC has held that, because *comparable* is a relative and not an absolute term, the merchandise need not be identical. It may be enough, as a hearing examiner has said, that the merchandise is "fit to be compared with or worthy of comparison." But this means to be of "like grade and quality in all material respects" as the merchandise to which it is compared. Size alone, therefore, is enough to render rugs not comparable where the advertiser's rug was a full five inches smaller in all dimensions. Other construction differences were found to be conclusive against the advertiser even though his rug was designed to, and did in fact, resemble the higher-priced rug. That rug was flat braided and sewn with nylon thread (for greater durability), the advertised rug had a braid effect but was achieved by a tubular wrap-around process and was sewn with cotton thread. To the commission, these rugs were not worthy of comparison.

The guide (paragraph 3) also permits the advertiser to relate a bargain price to one "being charged" by him for other merchandise of like grade and quality. Apparently, the guide intends the contemporaneous availability of the competing merchandise in his place of business, at the higher price, throughout the trade area, as is essential where the merchandise of other retailers is compared. If this speculation is true, Guide II does not provide a loophole, as it may seem to do at first reading, through which an advertiser may escape the rigid rule in Guide I providing that, where an advertiser "marks down" his own merchandise, the higher price in the dual-price representation (that is, his own price) must refer to the *same,* not merely similar or comparable, merchandise that is being offered as a bargain.

Undoubtedly a situation that is contemplated by this guide's specific references to the advertiser's price is the comparison of the advertiser's own brand with a higher-priced nationally advertised brand which he also carries. Even though it might be difficult to come up with material differences between Safeway's apple juice and Del Monte's, in designating its juice as a "bargain," Safeway would be on tenuous ground unless its glass bottle held substantially the same amount as Del Monte's #10 can.

As mentioned, the factor of greater concern to the legality of bargain advertising based on prices other than the advertiser's own is the genuineness of that other, higher price. It has been consistently held that it must conform substantially to the price at which the merchandise (be it "same" or "comparable") whose price is being compared is regularly sold at retail in the trade area where the savings claim is made. Where it does not, or where it is fictitious (not a price at all but an arbitrarily fixed amount) or excessive (unreasonably related thereto), the comparison is deceptive, because it suggests a bargain where there is none or misrepresents the amount of the savings to be afforded by the advertiser's selling price.

Although the 1964 guides do not define *regular retail price,* they do say when a *retail price should not be used* as the basis of a bargain offer: when that price is based on isolated or insignificant sales. Number of sales has been made the test of fair price comparisons by retailers, and of the legitimacy of retail prices that are merely suggested (by "list pricing" or preticketing) and advertised or otherwise disseminated by manufacturers and then used by retailers as the basis for savings claims. This aspect of bargain advertising is covered by Guide III. What is said here will be equally applicable there, however. Indeed, in the *Revco* case, the one decision which discusses the revised guides at length—and within the context of a Guide II advertisement—readily reads Guide III into its discussions of "substantial sales" and liberally cites cases which deal with deceptive list and preticketed prices.

Substantial Sales. It should be noted at the outset that the topic of substantial sales does not lack for either adjudicated cases or interpretative comment. Although the commission has characterized the 1964 guides as making "no change in the substantive law applicable to the advertising of price comparisons by retailers, but do attempt to explain and elaborate the standards summarily stated in the old guides," a degree of uncertainty in the law has been dispelled by the new concept of substantiality of sales. In recognition that there is rarely a single price at which all sales of a product are made in a retail trade area, the higher price will be deemed a legitimate basis for comparison with the advertiser's selling price if it can be supported by concrete selling experience.

Of course, the guides do not state how many sales will be sufficient to establish the genuineness of the higher price, only that it must be enough "so that a consumer would consider a reduction from the price to represent a genuine bargain or saving" (Guide II). And *Revco* points out that "no exact quantitative measure of substantiality, applicable to all products and markets is possible." In general, however, "unless the higher advertised price is in fact the price being charged by many if not most of the principal retail outlets in the trade area, a price comparison will be misleading." Stated another way, as Guide III provides,

> It will not be deemed fictitious if it is the price at which substantial (that is, not isolated or insignificant) sales are made in the advertisers trade area. . . . Conversely, if the list price (or other comparative price) is significantly in excess of the highest price at which substantial sales in the trade area are made, there is a clear and serious danger of the consumer being misled by an advertised reduction.

Thus will a showing of substantial sales at the higher price in the advertiser's trade area be a sufficient defense to a charge of deceptive pricing (as would a showing, per Guide II, that that price did not "appreciably" exceed the price at which substantial sales were made), and deception will be established if there has been a meaningful volume of sales at prices substantially less than the price that the advertiser claims to be comparative. Clearly, it is difficult to draw a line between fictitious pricing conditions and acceptable pricing conditions. The guides confirm earlier indications that if only a few retailers were selling at less than the higher comparative price, that price would not be considered misrepresentative of the regular retail price. Nevertheless, the problem is in large part a matter of proof, and for that, the *Revco* decision would seem to be dispositive.

Revco is a discount retail drugstore chain operating in the Cleveland, Ohio, area. A typical Revco newspaper advertisement would list some 400 nonprescription drug items and in connection therewith a column of prices designated as "retail," "retail list," or "value" and another column of prices designated "Revco's everyday low prices." The complaint against the company charged that, because a substantial segment of the Cleveland drug retailers did not charge the comparative price advertised by Revco, Revco had not truthfully and fairly represented the regular retail price of the articles advertised. Hence, the bargain or savings to be afforded by Revco's price had been misrepresented. The commission reversed the ruling of the hearing examiner and dismissed the complaint for insufficiency of proof, because the evidence competent to support the complaint had come from chain stores like Revco. In so doing, the FTC adhered to the rule of proof laid down in the *Giant Food* case, which had found it sufficient to elicit the prevailing retail price charged from a representative cross section of the advertiser's competitors. Because Revco operated in an area dominated by independents (518 out of 600 drugstores), the commission found it "questionable whether the prices of the chains are likely to be representative." Although the dissenter's point, that the chain stores with fifty outlets constituted a "substantial segment" of the Cleveland drug market, was reasonable, the majority of the commission relied on its decision in the *Giant Food* case.

Giant Food had advertised certain small appliances with the traditional dual-price representation, designating the higher price as "regular price" or "manufacturer's list." With fifty branch stores in its market area, Giant contended that the evidence against its pricing practices, elicited from three large retail department stores in the same area, proved no more than that *some* retailers sold the advertised items for less than the higher price advertised by Giant as comparative. The commission noted that complaint counsel did not have to show that no retailer in the trading area sold at that price and that the course chosen, "that of questioning representatives of businesses competing with Giant on a large scale," was "eminently sensible." Of seemingly greater significance, however, was the fact that great care had been taken to elicit from the competition's witnesses an explanation that they continually study the prices of other retailers in order to keep their prices "competitive." The commission felt that if *their* lower prices *are* competitive, it was unlikely that any "preponderant or even substantial segment of the . . . retailing community was charging the inflated . . . [comparative] prices advertised by [Giant]".

Evidence of this continual study of retail prices by the competition was lacking in *Revco*. Therefore, the commission was of the opinion that "there is scant basis for inferring from the [chain store] prices alone that a preponderance or substantial segment of the Cleveland retailing community *did not charge* the comparative prices advertised by Revco." [Emphasis supplied.] Anyway, Revco had conducted a survey to determine the prevailing retail prices of the items it sold and the results of its investigation were corroborated by the fact that the challenged prices were either fair-trade prices or "chart" prices. This evidence, everything else failing, clearly would have absolved Revco, because now, under the revised guides, an advertiser is permitted a "good-faith estimate" of the higher price that he advertises as the basis for his bargain claim.

Good-Faith Defense. Before the issuance of the 1964 guides there was no room for error by one who represented a comparative figure as being the usual and customary price of the advertised article. He was responsible for any deviation therefrom because the old guides made him "chargeable with the knowledge of the ordinary business 'facts of life.'" The correctness of the representation was determinative of its legal acceptability. The new guides suggest a relaxation of this rule by advising the advertiser that he be "reasonably certain" (Guide II) and "act honestly and in good faith" (Guide III). And this, according to the *Revco* majority, is not a subjective test. The advertiser has a "duty" to make certain that the higher price is one at which substantial sales have been made. If it is, he has acted in good faith and may assert price comparison claims with relative assurance. Bad faith is much easier to establish, as, for example, the deliberate fabrication by a manufacturer of a preticketed price to accommodate retailers bent on deceiving the buying public. The advertiser who knows his comparative figure does not reflect the price that the advertised article would command in the retail market can hardly be considered as having made a bona fide estimation of the regular, retail price. A representation made in total disregard or ignorance of the "going" price is on the same footing. But from there to the point where assertion of good faith will relieve the advertiser of responsibility is a broad area. In the words of the FTC,

> A retailer is liable for the deception he creates if in fact his comparative prices do not accurately represent the regular retail price in his trade area. "Good faith" requires him to ascertain the truth, by whatever investigation may be appropriate, before making price comparison claims. And where he so ascertains the truth, his claim should not

be untruthful or dishonest. Price comparisons that are objectively false or deceptive cannot be defended on an assertion of "good faith" not supported by a responsible effort to determine the actual prices being compared.

Guide III suggests a "market survey" as a possible source for the information upon which such claims may be predicated and not render the advertiser chargeable with having engaged in a deceptive pricing practice. Similarly, the FTC approved Revco's "continual study" of local pricing conditions and its use of locally prescribed retail pricing charts. For the advertiser operating on a large regional or nationwide scale, more may be involved. Nevertheless, he need not investigate all prices throughout his marketing territory. "It is enough if he ascertains the price at which substantial . . . sales . . . are being made by principal retail outlets in representative communities." But if such information is not available, the commission has advised that price-comparison claims should not be made. It would seem that this would be the most sensible course to follow, because an investigation of representative communities may not be sufficient.

In connection with the FTC decision in *Revco,* in reading Guides II and III together for a discussion of "substantial sales" and "good faith," no distinction has been made thus far between retailers who advertise bargains and manufacturers (or others) who advertise or otherwise disseminate prices which may be used as the source of retail bargain advertising. Generally, a distinction is unnecessary because both must make that "responsible effort" to ascertain whether the price, suggested or compared as the case may be, conforms in fact with the regular retail price of the article advertised. A distinction becomes essential, however, to cover the situation where that responsible effort *by a manufacturer* (because he has investigated the prevailing prices in a "substantial number of representative communities"—Guide III) results in handing to a retailer an instrument of deception because of the pricing conditions in that retailer's trade area. It will be remembered that a retailer is "liable for the deception he creates if in fact his comparative prices do not accurately represent regular retail prices in his trade area." But the question remains whether the disseminator of the comparative figure may avoid liability on what is, by the previously described tests, a good-faith estimate and leave the retailer to establish his own defenses.

These two categories of price advertisers are not by any means inextricably combined in a deceptive pricing practice simply because the manufacturer presumed to suggest a price, knowing it might not be followed in retailing his product and/or used for a deceptive purpose. On the other hand, an illegal combination may be said to exist to the extent a manufacturer will be responsible, following the pretext well established as a Section 5 violation, for placing in the hands of others the means by which deception may be practiced on the buying public. There would seem to be little doubt that the price which was established in good faith by the manufacturer by means of a survey of "representative communities" may be rendered fictitious by the pricing conditions in an area that he did not investigate because it was unrepresentative. Will his good-faith investigation protect him there? We can only conjecture a weak "maybe not" on the basis of two cases, neither of which dealt directly with the good-faith defense.

The *John Surrey* case was decided under the 1964 guides which initiated the good-faith defense. Although the decision that the company had engaged in deceptive pricing practices turned on invented comparative prices, the commission discussed the company's contention that complaint counsel's evidence of the retail price was insufficient. Noting that its trade area covered the whole United States, the company pointed out that proof of the actual price at which the merchandise sold at retail came only from New York City, which represented 10 per cent of its retail sales. Although the commission agreed that a stronger case against the company would be found in a showing that the advertised price exceeded the actual retail price "in different sections of the [respondent's] trade area," it referred to Guide III's suggestion of the extent to which a retailer must investigate, implying, thereby, that complaint counsel need do no more. Guide III states that an advertiser who disseminates his prices over a large area "cannot be required to police or investigate in detail the prevailing prices throughout so large an area." However, as the commission suggested, if he does so, he will have a stronger good-faith defense. Moreover, he will be more apt to cover that gullible, unsophisticated, unsuspecting purchaser whom the FTC is bound to protect.

It was upon such customer consideration that the *Baltimore Luggage* case turned. Decided under the 1958 guides, this company lost on the basis of pricing conditions in a specific area, notwithstanding proof of substantial sales (62.5 per cent) generally at the higher comparative figure. The challenged price, the commission held, could not be judged on an entire national market because a customer in the smaller area would not be interested in a bargain available in another section of the country. Such deference to a countervailing consumer interest is, of course, absolutely inherent in the FTC's regulatory role. The degree to which this primary concern may be expected to be accommodated by an advertiser's duty to investigate must remain speculative, however. No cases on point exist and the guides neither define *representative* nor suggest the consequences which could enure to the manufacturer-advertiser beyond the representative community situation. It may be that the answer is contained in *Revco,* where the majority warned that the good-faith defense is not absolute. However, it was there addressing the *retailer* with respect to his liability "for the deception he creates." Deception is unlawful. Under the circumstances hypothesized, the manufacturer, with honest purpose and good faith, has done everything to avoid that result.

Advertising Retail Prices Which Have Been Established or Suggested by Manufacturers (or Other Nonretail Distributors)—Guide III

A manufacturer will not be in violation for having merely suggested a resale price. To some extent, particularly with respect to a new product, publication of a "suggested retail price," "list price," or "manufacturer's suggested price" may serve a useful purpose. Wholesalers and retailers are informed by the manufacturer of his opinion that the product will probably sell best at that price and consumers will be apprised of the product's availability at that price. For "old-standby" items or for products manufactured under many brand names, a "suggested" price may serve as a ready product identifier.

Clearly, however, not much of a case can be made for the other way in which a manufacturer becomes involved in retail pricing, that of pre-ticketing his product with a price that he hopes will be followed. In an age where discount retailing is closer to the rule than the exception, it is not enough to say that it is a form of protection to the manufacturer who fears loss of his traditional retail outlets and/or prestige by price cutting. The extent to which he can influence the actual resale price is limited. The practice would seem, at best, to be suspect as the means for introducing a fake bargain.

The "bargain" offer which uses a manufacturer's "list" or "suggested retail" price is more subtle than the other type discussed. In a literal sense, it is completely truthful: the "suggested" price is stated accurately for what it is, and the "sale" price is, likewise, correctly designated, leaving the shopper to draw his own conclusion. Such a representation is no less vulnerable to interdiction, however, because the FTC has determined that a substantial segment of the buying public reads a great deal more into a manufacturer's "suggestion," regardless of how he presents it to the buying public (mass-media advertising, direct-mail advertising, catalogue, catalogue inserts, brochures, instruction booklets, price lists, point-of-sale promotional material designed for display to the public). The buying public is said to view a "suggested" price in the same way that it views preticketed prices, as a representation that it is the price at which the advertised article is generally sold. Therefore, to prevent any misuse of these prices at the retail level, the manufacturer will be restrained from placing them in the hands of retailers unless they do, in fact, correspond to the regular retail price.

However, as noted earlier, prediction of that price is, at best, difficult. And even where his published prices may rest on a responsible effort to establish their genuineness, the manufacturer is at the mercy of market fluctuations. Absent evidence of an intent to deceive, fluctuations arising from temporary pricing conditions should not result in liability. However, where there has been a breakdown in the retail price structure and where the formerly regular prices are adhered to by only a few isolated or atypical sellers and are no longer representative of the general price level in a section of his trade area, the manufacturer would appear to have to alter his prices accordingly or suffer the consequences.

Control over preticketed or suggested prices in manufacturing and warehousing a product creates a number of difficult problems. Where a wholesaler distributes into two trade areas with two different prevailing prices, the question arises of whether the manufacturer should police the distribution into those two trade areas. To the extent he has created the instrumentality by which deception may be practiced subsequently at retail, the answer, of course, must be yes. He must remain reasonably alert to any misuse of his preticketed or suggested price, at whatever level of distribution. This is what is proscribed. On the other hand, any efforts he makes to prevent illegal use may result in liability under the antitrust laws or Section 5 of the Federal Trade Commission Act.

Although price fixing as a violation of the antitrust laws is not within the scope of this book, it should be noted that under some circumstances an improper resale-price-maintenance system might be inferred by courts from activity at the distribution level by a maufacturer who pretickets or suggests resale prices. A manufacturer may, without liability, refuse to deal with a wholesaler who resells his product into a fictitious price area. Practical considerations, however, would appear to dictate against this type of policing, particularly where a good wholesale customer is involved. On the other hand, if he enters into an agreement with the wholesaler not to sell in one area at a given preticketed price, the agreement could fall afoul of the antitrust laws as vertical price fixing or differential pricing under the Robinson-Patman Act—an agreement to resell in one area at one price and in another area at another price. Even efforts by one manufacturer to remain apprised of pricing policies in the various resale trade areas, and thus to satisfy his responsibilities under the deceptive practices law, if too frequent and comprehensive, may suggest to a court evidence of a conspiracy under the antitrust laws, that is, affirmative action to achieve adherence to the resale price suggested or prefixed to the product. To paraphrase Gilbert and Sullivan, the life of the businessman in these circumstances is not an easy one.

On the other hand, the mere preannouncement of a desire that customers resell at suggested prices and actual sales at those prices should not violate the antitrust laws. The United States Supreme Court has so held in the landmark *Colgate* case. Where a manufacturer, with proper motive, merely seeks to offer price guidance without compulsion to dealers, the law permits him to do so.

In summary, an estimation of the regular retail price is absolutely essential to the advertiser who offers a reduction from a price that has been established by sales or merely suggested by the manufacturer. It is, moreover, the basis upon which the "suggestion" must be made if it is to be used for something other than retail pricing guidance. As Guide III points out, "[t]his general principle applies whether the advertiser is a national or regional manufacturer [or other non-retail distributor], a mail-order or catalog distributor who deals directly with the consuming public, or a local retailer." Substantiality of sales will be sufficient generally to establish the genuineness of the price compared or suggested, and some affirmative action on the part of the advertiser, such as a market survey, will provide evidence of his honest and good-faith effort to arrive at a price which will be neither false nor deceptive when used as the basis for a "bargain" claim. Moreover, if the price is found to have been established by a fair-trade pricing system, it will not be deemed to be "meaningless and therefore fictitious or misrepresentative." Price fluctuations brought about by brief semiannual sales of seasonal goods and which affect the actual retail price should not alter the responsibility of an advertiser who has attempted to determine the "going" price of the article that he advertises or offers at a "sale" price. Consideration will also be given to defining the trade area in which the price representation is made. For the retailer competing in a local area the limits will be circumscribed by the outlets whose selling practices would have a "real significance" to the retailer's customers. The advertiser who does business on a large regional or national scale, on the other hand, must look to a "substantial number of representative communities" and the pricing practices which prevail therein. However, the existence elsewhere of customers who might be deceived by reason of conditions not reflected in the representative survey could impose a greater responsibility on this advertiser. Finally, liability for fictitious pricing may be avoided where the manufacturer can show that his prices were published for, and used by, dealers only and were not displayed to the public.

Bargain Offers Based upon the Purchase of Other Merchandise—Guide IV

The subject of free goods and offers as a deceptive practice has been given comprehensive treatment in another chapter. It should be sufficient here to summarize only.

The law as it is currently applied to bargain offers based upon a purchase stems from Guide IV of the 1964 guides. It gives due notice to the "powerful incentive to purchase" which derives from an opportunity to receive something free in addition to the article paid for. However, because the seller "literally . . . is not offering anything 'free' [that is, an unconditional gift]," he is advised to take care so as not to mislead the customer. The guidelines announced in 1964 are essentially a reiteration of the practices which had been condemned earlier in the so-called Free Good Rule. They are

1. Failure to disclose fully the terms and conditions of the bargain offer "at the outset."
2. Increasing the usual and regular price of the article to be purchased.
3. Reducing the quality of the article to be purchased.
4. Reducing the quantity or size of the article to be purchased.

The guide contemplates that all bargain offers based upon the purchase of other merchandise will be so judged whether designated as "free"; "buy-one, get one free"; "two-for-one sale"; "half-price sale"; "1¢ sale"; or "50% off." The unconditional gift, although not specifically mentioned in the guide, would not be in violation of the Federal Trade Commission Act, providing, of course, it is really a gratuity. As the FTC has said, "if a merchant thinks that his business will be benefitted by the distribution of gifts . . . to his customers, that is his affair."

It should not be overlooked, of course, that proper attention to the guidelines suggested by the commission will not necessarily preclude a complaint that the bargain offer is deceptive. The *Mary Carter Paint Co.* case presented a practice that was not covered in detail by Guide IV. That case, discussed in detail in another chapter, is particularly curious because it recalled a rule that had been set forth in the 1958 guides and left out in the revision. A "two-for-one" offer was involved.

The original guides had specifically warned that such an offer should not be made unless the advertised price for the unit of two was the usual and customary price for a single item as previously charged by the advertiser or, if he had not sold the item, by his competitors in his trade area. The establishment of a single article price was, therefore, absolutely essential to a subsequent offer of a unit of two at the single price. This was where the Mary Carter Paint Company lost. Because it had never sold a single can of paint at any price, the commission was constrained to conclude that it had never established a single-can price and that the cost of the second can must necessarily have been included in the price paid by the purchaser for two cans. Accordingly, the second can was not "free" as advertised.

It would be difficult to quarrel with the commission's conclusions. Of greater importance, however, to other advertisers, if indeed they are to be guided, is the route by which the FTC arrived at its decision. As noted, the revised guides did not include the old rule with respect to a "two-for-one" offer. In fact, it did no more than announce that any and all bargain offers would be judged by the standards enumerated above. None of them, however, covered Mary Carter's offer. The terms had been fully disclosed and the quality and quantity of the paint as well as its advertised price had been the same from the beginning. Only with reference to the old 1958 rule could a basis be found for determining the deceptiveness of the offer. What is more, the FTC was to add substantially to this legal basis when it subsequently modified the cease and desist order.

The case had provoked dissents all along the line, from the commission right up to the Supreme Court. Perhaps in recognition that some truth lay behind them, the Supreme Court granted the commission's request to clarify its order. The modification was to prohibit any representation that an article is "free" in connection with a sale of merchandise unless the advertised price is the "same or less than the usual and regular price at which the merchandise has been sold *separately* for a substantial period in the recent regular course of business." (Emphasis supplied.) In the future, and beyond the guides, an advertiser would be required to establish a "regular price" before advertising a "free" item in addition to the purchase.

The new guides were issued to "supersede" the 1958 guides, yet we find here an instance of a case supplying a rule which can only be said to have been deliberately omitted. It lends some support to Commissioner MacIntyre's criticism of the revision as "loosely worded." It also leaves in doubt the extent to which the guides (be it the 1958 version as read into the 1964 revision or the revision all by itself) still control. If they do, it would appear that what the FTC requires for compliance cannot be gleaned solely from its guidelines. However, as noted in another chapter, new guides for the use of the word *free* are under consideration. They are particularly significant in as much as they incorporate pertinent aspects of the deceptive pricing guide, underscoring the necessary relationship between pricing and so-called free offers.

Miscellaneous Price Comparisons—Guide V

Having covered those bargain pricing practices that are most frequently employed, it remains only to mention a few which Guide V calls "variations." The same general principles discussed previously will be applicable here as well. Truth in advertising a bargain is what the FTC hopes to achieve.

An unusual event or manner of doing business is very often the means by which a savings will be represented or implied. The "special purchase," "clearance sale," "manufacturer's close-out," "introductory sale," "limited offer" are well-known examples. If, indeed, each event is as it is represented, the advertiser will have no problem, providing, of course, that it results in a genuine bargain to the consumer. Where the price remains the same beyond the period set aside for the special offer, or the offer is extended to every prospective customer, or the price is the usual and customary price of the article rather than "sacrificed" or "forced" as advertised, the buying public has been duped into believing it is obtaining something for less than its real value.

"Far-sighted planning," "cooperative buying," "weaknesses in the market," "factory outlet," and "wholesale" have all been used to justify what is represented as a special price. "Marketing surveys" have been another effective gimmick. They give an aura of credibility to the offer. Too often, however, they are only devices for misrepresenting the actual retail price.

The advertised article, too, may be described in such a way as to infer that the price represents a saving to the customer. Repossessed merchandise, even "odds and ends," are definitely marketable; but where it is priced the same as new merchandise or is part of regular stock, no bargain is received, nor was it intended. The customer has been effectively forestalled from "shopping around" and misled into a purchase believed to be a "good buy."

Imperfect or irregular merchandise is commonly offered at a special price. The guide advises that, where a dual-price representation is used, the advertiser must disclose that the higher comparative price refers to the "perfect" price. Where the merchandise is only described as to its imperfection in conjunction with a selling price, it may be assumed that an evaluation of the bargain may be left to the consumer, providing, of course, that the advertised price represents an actual reduction from the price of the merchandise if perfect. On the other hand, an advertiser cannot get away with implying a reduction which does not exist in fact by describing new merchandise as "irregular."

There are, of course, other situations "too numerous to mention" (Guide V) in which prices may be misrepresented. To make assurances of a stable price at a time when costs, taxes, and prices generally are rising is deceptive if the quality and quantity of the product are changed. Similarly, to provoke immediate sales by representing that the current price cannot be maintained when no increase is contemplated is a tactic which cannot be sanctioned. It is analogous to an advance "sale" price, of which the guide speaks. Where, however, additional stock has been purchased at a higher cost, presumably the advertiser could show that good-faith expectation of an increase in price at a later date.

BEYOND THE GUIDES AGAINST DECEPTIVE PRICING

As was stated, the guides are "not intended to serve as comprehensive or precise statements of law" or "detailed statements of the Commission's enforcement policies," and since their promulgation, advertising practices have been found that are not clearly or adequately covered. The Mary Carter Paint Company practice of marketing "twins" is one such example that has been discussed.

Another possibility that comes to mind is the manufacturer-sponsored "sale" effected by temporarily cutting his own price to facilitate his retailer's price reduction. The manufacturer may also be helpful by printing on the package or container a "cents off" representation or by advertising his "sale" price nationwide. The problem, of course, is that there is no assurance that the manufacturer's claim will be made meaningful at the retail level. This aspect of the subject recently has been debated within the context of its rather prevalent use by the coffee industry. It is one of the marketing abuses corrected by the Fair Packaging and Labeling Act.

The status of the manufacturer-sponsored sale under the guides and the Federal Trade Commission Act is another matter. Clearly, there should be no problem where the retail "sale" price is lower than the price customarily and regularly charged during the rest of the year. In the *Kreiss* case this had been decisive. The decision was not reached, however, within the guidelines suggested for determination of the regular retail price. As the dissent pointed out, 95 per cent of the manufacturer's sales to retailers had been made at the brief low price, thus establishing the fiction of the higher price by the test of substantiality required by the guides. But the commission apparently had been persuaded that, in the light of the number of retail sales at the higher "regular" price, there was no intent to deceive or possibility of deception. Nevertheless, such manufacturer-sponsored sales could mask a fictitious pricing scheme, and the guides offer little or no help in their resolution.

Many other practices do not fall neatly within the scope of the guides. That is not to say that they will not be reached under Section 5 of the Federal Trade Commission Act. Nevertheless, businessmen should not be lulled into reading the guides too precisely or narrowly.

Misleading computations, best exemplified by the 6 per cent finance plan used in the automobile industry, are certainly a deceptive pricing practice. The giants in the field have been called to task for use of the "lumped markup" ruse whereby purchasers have been kept ignorant of an installment plan's cost, and in 1951, the FTC issued a trade conference rule requiring a complete presale disclosure of the cost. Both failure to itemize finance and insurance charges and the use of installment sales contracts with blank spaces to be filled in after execution are branded as unfair trade practices. These standards are now, of course, imposed by the Consumer Protection Act.

Another example can be found in an offer which represents a savings percentage in conjunction with a price figure. The guides warn only against use of a fictitious base for computing the savings or percentage thereof, that is, one that is not the regular retail price of the advertised article. What is contemplated here as both false and deceptively misleading is just the reverse, the use of an advertised price which does not reflect a customary trade-in allowance, the computation of which would necessarily reduce the savings percentage claimed. A representation that a dollar figure is the "total cost" is similarly unfair when the seller fails to disclose that there will be additional charges or that the offer to sell at the advertised price relates only to volume purchases.

Finally, the commission has also taken a position on the structure of a "sale" advertisement. Having found that ads which feature both sale-priced items and merchandise at regular prices have the tendency to cause consumers to believe that every item is "sale" or "bargain" priced, the FTC announced in January of 1969 that such multiproduct ads, including catalogues, may not use the word *sale* or words of similar import unless (1) items not reduced are clearly set off and identified, and (2) the "sale" or bargain representation is clearly qualified by a statement which indicates all items offered are not reduced.

In summary, the business community cannot be too cautious in its approach to pricing practices. Besides the fact that the consumer is very sensitive to any injury to his pocketbook, a continuing attack on deceptive pricing is certainly consistent with the current drive for consumer protection. Admittedly, a note of skepticism has been injected here with respect to both the scope of the guides and the current attitude of the FTC toward deceptive pricing practices. That the commission's pronouncements on what is a violation of Section 5 carry great weight cannot be doubted, however. As the Supreme Court has said, the Federal Trade Commission Act

> necessarily gives the Commission an influential role in interpreting Section 5. . . . As an administrative agency which deals continually with cases in this area, the Commission is often in a better position than are the courts to determine when a practice is "deceptive" within the meaning of the Act. This Court has frequently stated that the Commission's judgment is to be given great weight by reviewing Courts.

This admonition is especially true with respect to allegedly deceptive advertising since the finding of a Section 5 violation in this field rests so heavily on inference and pragmatic judgment.

If the Supreme Court is going to tell the FTC it has all that power, "the Commission is likely to use it."

"BAIT-AND-SWITCH" ADVERTISING

"Bait" advertising is an alluring but insincere offer to sell a product or service that the advertiser in truth does not intend or want to sell. Its purpose is to interest the consumer in the advertised product in order to sell something else, usually at a higher price or on a basis more advantageous to the advertiser. The primary aim of a bait advertisement is to obtain leads to persons interested in buying merchandise of the general type offered.

At this point we must recognize a distinction between bait advertising and the attribute of salesmanship popularly known as "trading up"; that is, legitimately trading a customer up from the advertised merchandise to higher-priced merchandise. In the trading-up situation the advertiser has a sufficient stock of the advertised item to meet the reasonably anticipated demand. Although he may extol the virtues of the higher-priced goods, he does not disparage the advertised item to those customers who are unimpressed with his salesmanship.

The Federal Trade Commission has actively prosecuted and exposed a great number of bait schemes. This form of advertising is particularly prevalent in such commodities as used automobiles, combination storm windows, furs, furniture, home appliances, jewelry, pianos, radio and TV sets, sewing machines, upholstery, and vacuum cleaners. As an illustration of illegal bait advertising, let us take a look at a typical FTC case in which the respondents advertised a sewing machine, purported to sell for as much as $119.50, for prices as low as $38.88. The advertisements, published an average of three or four times a week in most of the newspapers in Washington, D.C., invited interested parties to call for a home demonstration and to reserve a machine. Usually, when a person called in response to the advertisement, an appointment was made for a salesman to call at the customer's home to demonstrate the machine. The salesman, in almost every instance, brought with him a more expensive machine in addition to the advertised machine.

The testimony of most of the witnesses at the hearing described how the salesman discouraged the sale of the advertised machine by advising the customer not to purchase it, by disparaging its performance, by stating that it did not perform certain operations—although such operations were among the advertised features of the machine—and by displaying a general attitude of reluctance to sell the machine. This was followed by an inducement to buy the more expensive machine. Most of the witnesses referred to the unusually noisy performance of the advertised machine and in some instances mentioned that this had been emphasized by the salesman as an indication that the machine was undesirable. Contrary to the claims made in the advertisement, it was pointed out to the customer that the machine did not sew backward and forward, that it skipped stitches, that the stitch could not be regulated, that it did not sew over pins, that you could not get parts for the machine, that it was a toy, and that it had a long bobbin, which was less desirable than the round bobbin on the more expensive machine the salesman just happened to have with him. After the customer had been sufficiently discouraged by the disparaging remarks of the salesman and noisy performance of the machine, the salesman then tried to sell a more expensive machine.

None of the witnesses had been successful in their efforts to obtain the advertised machine. They were given various excuses and were shunted back and forth between the salesman and persons at the store, all to no avail. In several instances the salesman would not take a deposit, but told the customer to telephone the store or that a driver would get it. The customers who telephoned the store were given some excuse, such as the fact that the advertised machines were "oversold" or that the machines in stock had certain attachments which the customer would have to take at additional cost. Several witnesses who did get the salesman to accept a deposit were later told, upon telephoning the store, that the machines were sold out. Some customers who went directly to the store in response to the advertisement were told that none of the advertised machines were in stock.

With regard to the noisy operation of the machine, the hearing examiner stated:

> There are undeniably a number of instances in the record where customers rejected the . . . machine because of its deficiencies in performance, particularly its unusual noise in operation, and where there is no evidence of any overt criticism or disparagement by the salesman. However, this does not necessarily impugn the testimony of those witnesses who claimed that the salesman had discouraged them from purchasing the machine, nor does it necessarily disprove the bait advertising charge. In the first place, the examiner is not convinced that the noisy performance of the . . . machine was due entirely to the fact that it had a long bobbin, as contended by respondents. The testimony of so many of the witnesses on both sides concerning the unusually noisy performance of the machine suggests that the demon-

strated models had been tampered with in some way so as to accentuate the noise.

From these facts the hearing examiner concluded that the offer was not a bona fide effort to sell the advertised product. The commission agreed with him by adopting his decision and issuing an order against the practice.

The essence of a bait-and-switch practice is a scheme to switch the consumer from the advertised product to a product that the baiter actually wants to sell. This can be done blatantly or subtly. An experienced shopper would recognize an obvious bait situation where the advertised product is "nailed to the floor" and its qualities are disparaged by the salesman.

Because of increased efforts by government and voluntary groups to combat this evil, the baiter has resorted to a more sophisticated approach. This involves "switch after sale." The ridiculously low-priced vacuum cleaner or sewing machine will be willingly sold to the consumer without any disparagement whatsoever on the part of the salesman. In service the vacuum cleaner will not pick up dust because a cardboard insert has been placed in it. The sewing machine will operate, perhaps with the efficiency of a machine gun, but also with as much noise, because of tampering by the baiter. When the consumer's expected dissatisfaction has ripened, a second call by the salesman is made, at which time Mrs. Housewife is more than delighted to know that she can return the product she purchased. But her relief is tempered when she is told that the first machine can be returned only as a trade-in on a more expensive machine. This is not to say that any attempt to adjust consumer complaints is a bait practice; however, such a technique has often been used as a part of a bait scheme.

In its effort to eliminate deceptive bait advertising the commission in 1959 issued its *Guides Against Bait Advertising*, covering definitions of bait advertising, standards controlling the advertised offer itself, examples of acts which constitute discouragement of purchase of the advertised bait, and rules dealing with the switch after sale. In addition to the guides, the commission has covered the subject of bait advertising in its trade-practice rules for five specific industries: the musical instruments and accessories industry, the hearing-aid industry, the combination storm window and door industry, the metal awning industry, and the rabbit industry.

Since it is the insincerity of the offer to sell that the FTC condemns, the 1959 guides enumerated six acts or practices which would indicate to them such lack of good faith. They are:

1. Refusal to show or demonstrate the advertised product.

2. Disparagement, by acts or words, of the advertised product or of any of the advertised conditions or terms of the sale.

3. Failure to have at all outlets listed in the advertisement "a sufficient quantity of the advertised product to meet reasonably anticipated demands," unless the advertisement states that the supply is limited or available only at a designated location.

4. Refusal to take orders for merchandise to be delivered in a reasonable length of time.

5. Demonstration of a defective product.

6. Use of a sales plan in which the salesmen are motivated to prevent or discourage sales of an advertised product.

The guides recognized that, notwithstanding sales of the advertised merchandise, a bait-and-switch scheme may nevertheless exist. Several more practices are listed as indications that a strategem to sell other merchandise has been employed rather than a sincere effort to conclude the sale of the advertised product. For example:

1. Acceptance of a deposit for the advertised product and then switching the customer to a higher-priced product.

2. Failure to deliver the advertised product within a reasonable time or to make a refund.

3. Disparagement of the advertised product and/or the terms of the sale, availability of service for the product, and so on.

4. Delivery of the advertised product that is defective or unusable for the purpose represented in the advertisement.

The commission has indicated that the failure to disclose material facts in advertisements designed to lure prospects for the purpose of obtaining leads or switching may also be used against the advertiser. One who painted automobiles was ordered to disclose all the material details of the low-priced job which was advertised, including the small range of colors and the comparative quality of the paint. On the other hand, the failure to disclose the age of the sewing machine used as "bait" was *not* standing alone a sufficient basis for a finding that the offer to sell old machines was not genuine.

13

Free Goods and Offers

As a device to attract customers, offering and giving free goods is a very effective and totally accepted merchandising and advertising method. There is hardly a consumer alive who cannot be lured by the opportunity to get something for nothing. Because an offer that is "truly free in fact as well as description" will be rare, the word *free* most often refers to an offer involving something other than an unconditional gift for which the customer pays nothing and/or does nothing. The usual "free deal" will be an offer to give or the giving of something for nothing contingent upon the purchase of goods or services for a price. The legal issue, then, is whether there has been any deception in the use of the word *free*. In this context, the offer of something "free" is viewed solely from the standpoint of the consumer. Typical vehicles of deception to be discussed here include conditional free offers, two-for-one deals, free samples, free trial offers, and free services incidental to the sales transaction.

Premiums and trading stamps also will be discussed briefly, although questions as to their legality usually stem from an anticompetitive effect rather than any deception in their use or essential nature. Furthermore, some states outlaw their use absolutely, and to the extent that they indirectly constitute, as something "given away," an abatement in price, they may violate fair-trade statutes or laws prohibiting sales below cost. As a gratuitous trade practice, however, premiums and trading stamps do contribute to the general law of free goods and offers.

Contests and lotteries are discussed in the following chapter. Although facts in advertisements designed to lure prospects for the purpose of their commercial efficacy is related to a free offer, any alleged "unfairness" and illegality are attributable to something other than deception.

FTC REGULATION OF "GRATIS OFFERS"

As early as 1919, "free" transactions were recognized as a source of competitive unfairness. The commission has consistently prohibited businessmen from giving away their wares, where the intent and effect thereof is anticompetitive. In subsequent cases, the law of free goods and offers was extended to give protection to the consumer.

Such a case-by-case development logically presupposes, at the very least, an assumed standard, some persistent requirement which can be asserted time and time again and by which each future event can be measured and the business community guided. This the law of free goods and offers does not reflect. Its evaluative content has varied from inflexible and stringent conformity to the truth to "a little inaccuracy with a lot of explanation."

The number of definitions of the word *free* is considerable. That is not the crux of the problem, however, because its use in economic or commercial reference is limited to "without charge," "furnished without cost or payment," "gratuitous." But within this fairly acceptable definition the FTC has groped for a meaning of *free* that would more nearly approximate what the consuming public understands when it is confronted with free goods and offers.

A group of early cases involved the sellers of encyclopedias who, without exception, utilized a sales plan whereby prospective customers were offered a set of the books "free" with the purchase of the loose-leaf extension or supplemental service for ten years. Customers were variously lured with representations that they had been specially selected, that their "connections" were good, or that an original owners' list was being compiled prior to offering the encyclopedia to the public. The stated price for the loose-leaf services was found to be in every case the regular standard price for *both* the encyclopedia and the yearly supplements. It followed that the books were not in fact free. As the Supreme Court observed in the *Standard Education Society* case, to fail to prohibit such a practice "would be to elevate deception in business and to give to it the standing and dignity of truth."

One court had found such a promotional plan to be so obviously false as to preclude the possibility of finding anyone "fatuous enough" to be misled by it. In another situation the false representation had been deemed to be too "petty" to be unfair. Nevertheless, the Supreme Court was prepared to give greater conclusiveness to the findings of the commission, suggesting a position against limiting the scope of "unfairness" with respect to representations that are false in fact.

The evil of these practices was lack of conformity with the truth. The recovery by the seller of any portion of the cost of the so-called free goods directly from the immediate transaction constituted the necessary deceptive element because the goods were "not in any sense free."

But what about goods that are in that sense "free" but are restricted by the offeror to those who buy from him? The FTC's answer is the full-disclosure rule found in the *Samuel Stores* case. The truth of the representation was not violated by the imposition of conditions precedent providing these were fully disclosed "in the initial stages of the transaction, that is, in the advertisement first attracting the customer's attention to the 'free goods' offer." Lawfulness or fairness would "depend on the terms of the offer and the underlying and surrounding facts." Stores' offer to give clothing "free and without cost" with the purchase of $25 worth of merchandise was not deceptive where the cost of the free goods was charged to the general advertising budget, the disclosed terms of the offer were fulfilled and no others imposed, and the prices of the merchandise to be purchased were based on a standardized mark-up and did not change before or after the period of the free offer.

By the close of the 1930's, the commission had established two propositions in connection with the commercial use of *free* or such phrases as *paid in full gift, at no cost or obligation, with our compliments,* and *included free of extra charge:*

1. The goods that are directly or by implication offered as free must be in fact without cost or obligation to the offeree.
2. A conditional offer may be free, as per the rule in No. 1, but the terms and conditions must be fully disclosed.

About this time, however, the commission began to exhibit something less than full devotion to these precedents. Some orders which had involved conditional offers without the requisite disclosure were modified and no reasons assigned. The language was the same in all:

> the Commission having further considered said order . . . and being of the opinion that the public interest requires that a modified order to cease and desist be issued . . . the Commission . . . issues this its modified order to cease and desist . . . representing articles or goods as free when (1) their receipt is conditioned upon the purchase of another, (2) their delivery is not without cost or condition, (3) they are offered as compensation for the distribution of the offeror's merchandise, or (4) such merchandise is not a gift or gratuity.

On January 14, 1948, the commission released what it called an Administrative Interpretation of advertising making use of the word *free*.

> The use of the word "free," or words of similar import, in advertising to designate or describe merchandise sold or distributed in interstate commerce, that is not in truth and in fact a gift or gratuity or is not given to the recipient thereof without requiring the purchase of other merchandise or requiring the performance of some service enuring directly or indirectly to the benefit of the advertiser, seller, or distributor, is considered by the Commission to be a violation of the FTCA.

Clearly, as an interpretative ruling, this pronouncement was intended to do no more than clean up the waters muddied by the recent revised orders. It had neither the force nor the effect of law, although as a practical matter, that might have been the case. The Supreme Court has spoken on the subject of interpretative bulletins:

> We consider that the rulings, interpretations and opinions of the administrator . . . , while not controlling upon the courts by reason of their authority, do constitute a body of experience and informed judgment to which courts and litigants may properly resort for guidance. The weight of such a judgment in a particular case will depend upon the thoroughness evident in its consideration, the validity of its reasoning, its consistency with earlier and later pronouncements, and all those factors which give it power to persuade, if lacking power to control.

The 1948 rule is now considered to be the "extreme position of the commission" and at the time of pronouncement, in light of its effect of unsettling what was considered settled law, it was characterized by a very disgruntled commissioner as satisfying the agency's "emotional 'id'." Nevertheless, in the *Book-of-the-Month Club* case, the rule easily met with judicial approval as a "rough restatement of the Supreme Court's decision in the *Standard Education* case." Furthermore, the rule toppled a long-standing practice of that giant of the book clubs in which the introductory free book had always been conditioned upon an agreement to purchase four books during the first twelve months of membership. To the commission, this of itself was sufficient to negate the representation that the offeree would receive a free book. The fact that the offeror demanded and expected to collect the retail price of the introductory book upon failure of the condition settled the question. The book was not offered as a gift or gratuity.

The commission did say of the rule, however, that "it must be applied realistically and hypertechnical applications designed to condemn the use of the word 'free' in advertising under all conditions must be avoided." Accordingly, the following advertising plan was upheld: a publisher engaged in the sale of a set of encyclopedias offered one volume "free," provided the offeree remitted 10 cents to cover mailing and reserved the remaining volumes at the regular retail price. After receipt of the first volume the offeree could cancel the balance of the set or expect to receive them on a predetermined schedule. Neither the act of cancellation nor the 10 cents was deemed to constitute a "service enuring to the benefit . . . of the advertiser."

The rationale behind the 1948 rule probably can be found in the language of the commission's *Book-of-the-Month Club* decision which characterized the word *free* as that "powerful magnet that draws the best of us against our will 'to get something for nothing'." It was felt that the in the mind of the reader that it "can never be completely eradicated by meaning of the word, because of its power to attract, remains so fixed any other words of explanation or contradiction" in the advertisement.

Such was not, however, the panacean finale that the commission must have contemplated. It had, after all, considered the two broad areas in which the word *free* is used commercially and had rejected one as unfair. The commission, apparently, was to realize in a very short time that the one-word, one-meaning official definition was not sufficient for adequate consumer protection or flexible enough to avoid evasion. Nor did it meet the needs of honest advertisers.

In 1953, with another book club's free deal before it, the commission reversed its policy (essentially to its initial full-disclosure doctrine in the *Samuel Stores* case) with respect to the word *free,* in a decision which three times referred to a desire to make its position as "clear as possible."

Walter J. Black, trading as the Classics Club and The Detective Book Club, had offered a "free" enrollment book in return for an agreement to purchase books in the future.

The commission outlined the following question: May a businessman in commerce be charged with engaging in an unfair act in violation of the FTC Act if he uses the word *free* in advertisements to indicate that he is prepared to give something to a purchaser free of charge upon the purchase of some other article of merchandise? Recognizing that the practice had long endured and that "the businessmen of the United States are entitled to a clear and unequivocal answer," the commission voted no, upheld the practice, and dismissed the complaint.

It is very clear that this new policy, which would remove a major interference with a substantial number of advertisers, was announced because the commission had been persuaded that the consuming public could not be deceived by a "genuine offer to give something away free of charge in order to induce a person to buy something else." According to the commission:

> It is commonplace that persons may be induced to buy if they think they are getting a bargain. An opportunity to receive something free in addition to the article paid for is a powerful incentive to purchase. If a merchant thinks that his business will be benefitted by the distribution of gifts, prizes, or premiums to his customers, that is his affair. His customers may gain by his apparent generosity. *They cannot lose, and they are not deceived.* [Emphasis added.]

External conditions in the regulated activity not having changed appreciably, the policy change reflected the commission's new understanding of what the consumer thinks *free* means. The commission said:

> They [the customers] know that the purpose of the gift is to induce them to purchase another article, and *they assume* that the donor expects ultimately to recover the cost of the gift in increased return from sales. . . . [Emphasis added.]

> But if the regular price of the article sold without the premium is the same as the price with the premium, the premium does not cost the customer anything. It is FREE TO HIM regardless of whether or not it is ultimately included in the purchase price.

But Black and other businessmen must use *free* honestly; that is, "there must be truth in advertising to support the use of the word 'free'."

The *Black* opinion announced the guidelines for the "honest" use of *free,* claiming any other use to be unfair. Subsequently, the guides were promulgated as the so-called free-goods rule of 1953, which was, in addition, to answer some of the objections Commissioner Mead had raised in his dissent in *Black.* (Where, the commissioner had asked, would the advertiser place the words which would qualify *free,* because it was highly unlikely that he would use the headlines if he could help it!)

A businessman could still give "fairly" an unconditional gift or gratuity to his customers. The free-goods rule only prohibits four practices where the "free" goods or service are offered and given upon a condition:

1. Failure to disclose fully the terms and conditions "at the outset," meaning in close conjunction with the word *free* wherever it first appears in each ad or offer. The use of a footnote for disclosure to

which reference is made by use of an asterisk or other symbol placed next to the word *free* is not regarded as compliance.

2. Increase of the ordinary and usual price of the article to be purchased in order to obtain the "free" goods, even though full disclosure has been made.

3. Reduction of the quality of the article to be purchased, even though full disclosure has been made.

4. Reduction of the quantity or size of the article to be purchased, even though full disclosure has been made.

More guides and rules were to follow, perhaps in an effort to answer further the commission's dissenter who had also commented in *Black* that because an advertiser may now use a "literally untrue statement provided he uses it reasonably . . . [the policy has] the virtue of flexibility and the vice of uncertainty." But any uncertainty which may have existed seems to have been covered fairly well in the subsequent announcements.

In 1958, a guide advised businessmen that in offering "two-for-one" bargains, the sales price for the two articles would have to be the usual and customary price for the single article. Then on January 8, 1964, the FTC issued its *Guides Against Deceptive Pricing* which included a less detailed reiteration of the 1953 free-goods rule. Guide IV contemplated that *all* "bargain offers" based upon the purchase of other merchandise should be covered, whether designated "free," "two-for-one," or whatever. The guide also made a hitherto unannounced admission:

> Literally, of course, the seller is not offering anything "free" [i.e., an unconditional gift], or ½ free, or for only 1¢, when he makes such an offer, since the purchaser is required to purchase an article in order to receive the "free" or "1¢" item. It is important, therefore, that where such a form of offer is used, care be taken not to mislead the consumer.

The guide, of course, suggested that consumers may be deceived if the practices condemned in the 1953 rule are used.

SPECIFIC OFFERS OR MERCHANDISING METHODS INVOLVING USE OF THE WORD *FREE*

Unconditional Gifts

The unconditional gift, the simplest type of free offer, is not prohibited by the Federal Trade Commission Act. It is contemplated, of course, that it be truly a gratuity, no strings attached—the "true in fact as well as description" situation. There are many day-to-day examples: toothpaste in the mail (including a redeemable coupon for your next purchase), paper towels hung on the front doorknob, balloons and lollipops for children at the local liquor store or barber shop.

Otherwise, the public must request the object of the free offer by visiting the advertiser's place of business or mailing in a coupon. The inclusion in the offer of a request for a small sum "to cover handling and mailing" should not invalidate its essential nature if the amount is no more than the actual cost to the offeror. A recent case and advisory opinion of the FTC may shed some light on the scope of this general rule.

The distributor of a vitamin product invited radio listeners to respond with a post card to his offer to receive "Free vitamins! Yes, absolutely *free* . . . $5 worth of vitamins without a single penny cost." In addition, the offeree would receive an "extra" month's supply *on approval.* The "free" bottle was to be used first and if it did not "delight" the user, he was simply to return the extra bottle. On the other hand, this bottle could be purchased for the "low introductory price" of $5. "The free bottle is yours to keep, regardless!"

The facts did not support the representation that the vitamins were free and without cost to the offeree. First of all, said the commission, misrepresentation existed as to the "free" bottle because postage must be paid to return the second bottle. Furthermore, by paying $5 for the second bottle, the offeree was paying for the "free" bottle, because the advertiser's usual price for two bottles was $5. The advertiser was ordered to cease and desist representing that any product is given free "when a payment of any nature is required of the recipient," unless the necessity of such payment and the amount thereof are disclosed at the outset.

Recently, the Federal Trade Commission was asked to consider the propriety of "It works . . . or we'll fix it free" in advertising and on boxes containing products of the manufacturer. Having taken into account the facts that the manufacturer customarily repairs without question and without charge for "parts, labor, 'handling,' or return postage" and that the products are received directly from owners or through retailers, the commission advised that the representation was not objectionable.

This raises a question of the status of the "small service charge" which accompanies most guarantees. One commentator rejects the argument that a guarantee is an implied unconditional offer to replace or to repair inadequate merchandise free or as qualified. To that author it is a condition of the sales contract and does not constitute an aspect of "free" goods and offers. The Federal Trade Commission, however, would seem to view guarantees otherwise. A refusal to make refunds to dissatisfied customers who purchased a product on a "money-back guarantee" basis was held in one case to constitute a failure to fulfill an offer to replace without charge, that is, free. In another case, the refusal to replace hoisery guaranteed as "holeproof and snap-proof" for a fixed period of time unless the purchaser remitted the original receipt (a condition not previously announced) was held to be tantamount to a falsification of an implied representation that the replacement would be free.

Furthermore, it seems clear that, to the FTC, *guaranteed lifetime* (or any other length of time) *service* implies *without cost* to the purchaser. A manufacturer sold his fountain pens with this guarantee, but repaired the product only upon the payment of a charge for postage and insurance. The cease and desist order read "when *any* charge is made for such service." Although "small service charge" would seem to nullify the representation inherent in an unconditional "free" offer, it will be valid, of course, under the free-goods rule if the necessity of such payment and the amount are disclosed at the outset.

Similarly, the express offer to give free services auxiliary to a sale must be, in fact, free or the conditions must be disclosed. A seller of fur coats advertised free repair service to "rips and seams" for three years. It was a false offer when material that might be needed was not included. The representation that storage of fur garments was free was likewise false when a charge was made for insurance against fire, burglary, and theft. Because *free storage* was understood among members of the trade to include proper refrigeration space where the garment was hung and adequate insurance, the charge for insurance abrogated the necessary implication arising from the use of the phrase.

We erect all monuments at no additional cost could not be used by a manufacturer and seller of tombstones and monuments where the erection was made only upon a foundation provided and paid for by the purchaser.

Finally, the failure to fulfill the offer to give away goods is only a shade different from a charge for so-called free goods and services. A seller of dry-goods remnants included the following representation in his advertisement: "Special offer 5 yards EXTRA." To the commission, it was inescapable that a purchaser was being offered an additional amount without charge, that is, free. The seller was ordered to cease using the "extra" offer until and unless the purchasers' orders would be filled as represented.

Conditional Free Goods and Offers

The legality of offers to give so-called free goods which are conditioned upon the offeree making a purchase or otherwise performing some service inuring to the benefit of the offeror depends upon, first, a full disclosure of the conditions and, second, due diligence to the technicalities relating to price, quality, and quantity set out in the 1953 rule and subsequent guides. It is that honest use of the word *free* which will reasonably ensure the offeree of getting the bonus or premium without cost to him.

Examples are numerous and well known to purchasers and prospective purchasers of all ages and personal tastes. Children learn very early the pleasure of reading the cereal-box copy and expend early efforts in the grocery store locating the breakfast foods which deliver a plastic toy or game along with the flakes, chips, or squares of grain. The word *free* imprinted on these boxes—and in comic books soliciting children to sell salve, seeds, and Christmas cards—may or may not be the beginning of a life-long vulnerability to commercial handouts. It does, nonetheless, sell a great deal more of the product to which the "free" offer is tied than might otherwise be the case.

Adults are plied with free offers from vendors of rubber gloves (one national advertiser frequently offers an extra right one at no extra cost) and dog food, banks (one institution offered trading stamps for an initial savings deposit of a prescribed minimum), and record and book clubs. Although it has been said that "the American book-buying public hardly needs to be protected against such promotional tactics," there are "unwary and undiscriminating" buyers of books, as well as various other things.

The free offer that is conditioned upon the purchase may be extended by such come-ons as, "buy one and get another free," "buy one and get another for 1¢," or "two for the price of one." They are legitimate if the stated price for the one article or for the unit of two is consistent with the 1953 rule and subsequent guides. Where the necessity of a purchase is concealed, however, the full-disclosure rule is violated.

A rather sophisticated example involves two individuals who serviced television sets. They advertised shop estimates, as opposed to home estimates, as free. What they failed to say was that after receiving the estimate, the owner of the television set must leave the set for repairs in order to avail himself of the servicemen's largesse.

A seller of trading cards to retail merchants represented that the latter's customers receiving the cards could redeem them without cost for silverplate tableware. The fact was that they were not redeemed except and unless customers also remitted a sum of money, which was found to approximate the cost of the silverware to the respondent. The cease and desist order required the respondent to disclose this condition in conjunction with the offer. Similarly, one engaged in the sale of Christmas cards was prohibited from representing to prospective sales representatives that sample cards would be sent free, when in fact they either had to remit 50 cents for the sample box, return the cards, paying postage therefor, or sell the cards.

Mail-order conditional offers, generally, have provided a fertile source of FTC action. They at once bore the reader and effectively preclude a careful reading with a great deal of surplusage and, while highlighting the gratuitousness of the offer, fail sufficiently to enlighten. The typical conditional book and record club offer of a "free" enrollment book is now valid, providing disclosure is made at the outset. The order against the Book-of-the-Month Club has been modified to permit again the practice used by many and prohibited to them under the previous rule. Similarly, a mail-order seller of jewelry may offer a "watch included free with every ring purchased," but if he intends to withhold the gift until all installments on the purchase are paid (and promptly), similar to the condition imposed by the book clubs, he must disclose that fact.

The mail-order offers which condition the receipt and retention of the free goods upon the rendering of services to the offeror are flagrantly misleading by reason of that which is not said. The motive of the offeror would seem to be obvious; it will not, however, validate the duping of children and others who have unknowingly ordered a shipment of the advertiser's product by signing and mailing in a coupon and thereby obligating themselves to become salesmen for the advertiser.

A notation at the bottom of one advertisement indicating a need for sales help and the ease with which one could sell the "lovely styles we supply" did not constitute disclosure of the fact that the receipt and retention of a dress "absolutely free" was only as compensation for selling services.

A similar scheme, directed at children who would sell salve door to door, employed the following come-on:

> Win a Beautiful Signet Ring—It's Fun—It's Easy—All you do is Name These Famous U.S. Presidents. Just Get All 4 Right. We'll Send Your . . . Ring ABSOLUTELY FREE! Also—we'll send salve, picture and Big Catalog [of prizes to be earned]. . . .

The offeree got his ring, and fourteen cans of salve to be sold at 65 cents.

Another solicitor of sales help was found to provide the proffered "free" camera only after the salesman had procured a sale and a picture of the buyer with his purchase.

The second unlawful practice set out in the 1953 rule exists where the offeror increases the usual price of the article to be purchased during the period of the free offer.

The cases are really little more than a matter of arithmetic. A purchaser lured by the opportunity to get three cans of dog food in a handy single package for the price of two cans can easily compare the price on the single cans sitting next to it on the shelf, and multiply by 2. Almost without exception the problem with the "two-for-one" deals is that the so-called special price for the two items is the regular and customary price charged for two. As the commission said in *Standard Distributors, Inc.,* "If he buys anything, he pays for everything he gets"; so one cannot be free. This comparison is not available where a 400-day German clock is offered with a $23 membership in a Shoppers' Club, unless one had previously read an advertisement, when the clock was not offered and remembered that membership then cost $18. Moreover, the club imposed a charge of $5 for the special handling of the "free" clock which was found to be more than two thirds in excess of the actual cost of shipping the clock from Germany.

It all depends upon the facts, as the commission recently advised a retailer who proposed to offer a stereophonic record player for "absolutely nothing" with the purchase of one stereo record each week for fifty-two weeks. The company asserted that the records to be purchased were regularly and customarily sold by them, and others, for $4.98. Thus, the customers would spend $249 for records and the record player, which was the price normally paid for the record player alone.

So far the arithmetic holds up; but as the commission said, it would not if the records offered for sale, although ticketed at $4.98, were those known in the trade as "low cost," "cut-outs," or "budget line," which generally command a lower price. The price paid by the offeree for such records would go a long way in defraying the cost of the record player, in which case it would not be free. The standard was expressed in the following language:

> When a seller offers to supply one article "free," or "at no extra cost," or for "absolutely nothing," in conjunction with the purchase of another article, he is thereby representing to prospective customers that the article required to be purchased is being sold at no more than the price at which it is usually sold in substantial quantities.

In this case, the commission advised that more facts would be needed in order to render a "categorical opinion."

To deny a well-established pricing practice in connection with the sale of an advertiser's product may have the same effect as the price increase prohibited in the free-goods rule. For example, for some time Schick had given a trade-in allowance on an old shaver when a new Schick shaver was purchased. In 1957 the company inaugurated the "Lucky Lady Special Offer" with the slogan "Buy his—get hers free." Contained in the carton of the man's Schick 25 was a certificate entitling the purchaser to a Lady Schick without extra cost. The price of the man's shaver remained at its usual and customary price during the period of the offer. But to get the ordinary trade-in allowance, the purchaser had to forfeit the "Lucky Lady" certificate. He could have one or the other, but not both. The practice resulted, effectively, in increasing the price of the Schick 25 which had to be purchased in order to become entitled to the "free" lady shaver and in rendering the advertised "free" offer both false and misleading.

Another interesting example involved a "mailer" offer, by a retailer, of a "free gift box" of three pairs of a nationally advertised hosiery in return for an agreement to purchase one box of nylons each month for three months at the regular price. The customer was warned that she would be charged for the initial gift box should the three-box subscription be canceled before its completion. The commission, finding the offer consistent with the rule, dismissed the complaint. The argument of counsel supporting the complaint, however, sheds some light on the scope of the price-increase prohibition. The fact that was urged as salient was that retailers who agreed to utilize the respondent manufacturer's promotional plan obtained the hosiery at a lower wholesale price than retailers who did not. In simple arithmetical terms, argued counsel, by selling the hosiery at the price regularly charged everywhere, these retailers got more than their customary mark-up. Moreover, since a lower retail price was possible, by not passing the advantage on to the customer but offering him a "gift" instead, the retailers were including the cost of the gift in the price charged for the hosiery sold under the subscription plan.

The commission was not impressed and rejected the fact of two different wholesale prices as controlling. What was important was that the price of the hosiery to be purchased was the same as would have been charged by any source and the gift hosiery, too, was available otherwise only at the price charged everywhere.

The case just mentioned is the typical "combination deal," differing from "two-for-one" offers only in that the arithmetic is not as easily computed, particularly where the two or several items in the unit are not the same. Accordingly, it may be some time after the fact of purchase or agreement to purchase before the purchaser will realize that he was misled.

Consider the offer of a photograph album and a certificate for photographic sittings and positive prints. The special price of $39.95 was represented as the cost of ten portraits to be taken at "associated" studios at the rate of two per year. The album was "free." The commission disagreed when it found that the respondent had no financial interest in the photographic studios and that it, consequently, retained the entire purchase price. It was a sale for $39.95 of one album plus certain contract rights set out in the certificate. Furthermore, the purchaser was required to pay a small amount at the time of each sitting.

An example of a case where the price of "free" services is included in that paid for the combination offered is provided by a complaint against an undertaking establishment. An advertisement offered "every privilege" of the funeral home, from plastic surgery to burial permit, with the purchase of a casket. If a vault was purchased, a wooden box was "furnished free." The facts were that the prices for caskets substantially reflected the cost to the company of the use of their cars, chapels, and floral arrangers.

Similarly, a seller of correspondence courses was prohibited from representing that employment and consultation services were free to graduates when the cost thereof was included in the amount paid for the course.

Beyond the 1953 Rule

All the commentators agree that the FTC is free to find unfair trade practices other than the four outlined in the 1953 rule and that *Mary Carter Paint Co.* is a case in point.

From the beginning the Mary Carter Paint Company had offered, and usually sold, "every second can [of paint] FREE, gallon or quart." The problem was that the usual and customary price for a single can of paint had never been established. A customer paid "$6.98 per gallon" or "$2.95 per quart" and either accepted or rejected the additional "free" equivalent quantity. As the commission saw it, the cost of the second can of paint must necessarily have been included in the price paid by the purchaser; accordingly, the second can was not given free of charge.

The dissent by Commissioner Elman called his peers to task for "explaining" and "distinguishing" the *Black* decision and thus introducing uncertainty and confusion into an area of business activity where advice, guidance, and constructive information were needed. Commissioner Elman reminded the commission that *Black* had been intended as a "self-contained exposition" of the commission's position on the subject of free goods and offers. Because it clearly permitted a "free" offer to be predicated upon a purchase, in that sense, of course the purchaser always pays for the free goods. Mary Carter had done no more or less.

This would seem to be a reasonable understanding of the offer as made and explained by the company. Nevertheless, it had not been permitted to support its claim that it indeed had established single-can prices of $6.98 and $2.95 and had done so because its paint was comparable in quality to other paints in those price categories. Because such evidence was the only basis upon which the commission could base its decision that the $6.98 or $2.95 price as regularly and usually charged for the two cans was deceptive, Commissioner Elman concluded that the case was consistent with *Black*.

The Fifth Circuit agreed, adopted the dissenting opinion, and reversed the order. A concurring opinion noted that the commission had denied to Mary Carter what earlier pronouncements in *Black* and the 1953 rule clearly permitted, and advised that agency to make up its mind.

To recapitulate, what had *Black* and the rule permitted? They had permitted a conditional "free" offer, providing its conditions and terms were disclosed. With respect to price, the rule cautioned only that the price of the article to be purchased should not be increased.

The history of Mary Carter's practice compelled the conclusion, as the Supreme Court was to express it, that it was and had been "marketing twins." In setting the price charged, it must have considered the second can because it never sold a single can for less money. It was a variation of the problem so often challenged in "two-for-one" deals: that is, the stated price for the unit of two, including the so-called free item, is found to be the price a customer would have to pay if he chose to purchase two under normal conditions. As noted, ordinarily it is a matter of comparison and simple arithmetic as to whether one item in the unit is "free" in the sense that the purchaser is buying or paying for only one item in the unit. The "sense" suggested by Commissioner Elman is something else altogether: the permissibility of representing one item as free when a purchase is required. That, as he noted, is clearly a fair-trade practice under *Black*. The question raised in the Mary Carter practice is, "How free is 'free'?" It must be answered by an examination of the ordinary and usual price of the article required to be purchased.

Having no history of selling single cans of paint, there could be no comparison of Mary Carter's stated price for the unit of two with anything but the ordinary and usual price of a unit of two. There had never been a free can of paint.

The Supreme Court found "ambiguity" in the commission's opinion but voted to reinstate its order, and in addition granted the commission's request for remand to clarify its order.

In his dissent, Mr. Justice Harlan found the "basis for the commission's action is too opaque to justify an upholding of its order." The commission's subsequent modification probably sheds little more, if any, light; however, it does appear to add to the "price" standard of the 1953 free-goods rule some language from the 1958 *Guides Against Deceptive Pricing*. Mary Carter was required to cease and desist representing that

> an article is given "free" or as gratuity or without charge in connection with a sale of merchandise unless the stated price of the merchandise to be purchased is the same or less than the usual and regular price at which the merchandise has been sold separately for a substantial period in the recent and regular course of business.

Separate sales of the paint, which was not available elsewhere, would provide the foundation upon which to base an offer to give "free" an additional can of paint. Had the paint been sold by others in the trade area, presumably it would not be misleading to use the usual and regular price prevailing for the merchandise to be purchased. But, again, this is a pricing standard, and prior to *Mary Carter,* pricing had been related only limitedly to the conditional "free" offer permitted by the free-goods rule. However, this interrelationship between pricing and "free" offers was implied in a 1968 proceeding against Spiegel, the large catalogue retailer. The "dollar-sale" practice challenged was strictly a pricing problem, but counsel for the Federal Trade Commission had contended that both *Mary Carter,* a "free" goods case, and the *Guides Against Deceptive Pricing* were controlling. Although the commission disagreed, stating they were "relevant" only, a few months later it seemingly responded to the suggestion that the two be united, with a new set of "do's" and "don'ts" concerning the use of the word *free.*

With the old 1953 rule as its core, the *Proposed Guide Concerning the Use of the Word "Free" and Similar Representations* (see Appendix XI) incorporates relevant provisions of the deceptive pricing guides as well as suggestions for the use of practices similar to the Mary Carter and Spiegel offers. The pricing sections are easily identified. The Mary Carter-type situation would be covered by the guide's provision for an introductory "free" offer, permitting the advertiser to offer one unit in a combination deal as "free" if he expects "in good faith, to discontinue the offer after a limited time and commence selling the newly introduced merchandise separate from that which was described as 'free' at a price which is not in excess of the price that prevailed during the introductory period."

Although the prescription would not provide the consumer with the means to evaluate the bargain offered, because the basis can be established only after the purchase, *after* the "limited time" of the offer, it has, of course, the advantage of providing the commission with a relatively easy formula for determining the "freeness" of an introductory offer which, like *Mary Carter,* never ceases to exist. As such, it is a fair warning to the commission's attitude toward "free" offers which go on for so long that single sales of the merchandise to be purchased virtually disappear or are so insubstantial as to fail in establishing an ordinary and usual price apart from the combination price. However, this section of the proposed guide must be read in conjunction with another.

The guide's section on "continuous offers" contemplates, analogously, the Mary Carter practice and, specifically, the Spiegel "dollar sale" that had been advertised with such great frequency as to eliminate single sales and, thus, to render misleading the claim that the second item would be "only $1 more." The guide advises that such offers are misleading because "the advertiser's regular price for merchandise to be purchased by consumers in order to avail themselves of 'free' merchandise will, by lapse of time, become the regular price for the 'free' merchandise together with the merchandise required to be purchased." Under such circumstances, "any offer of 'free' merchandise is merely illusory."

It is not clear whether the guide is intended to preclude the continuous or frequently repeated use of the word *free* in connection with minimum purchases of regularly priced items as, for example, when a seller continuously offers a toothbrush with the minimum, regular-price purchase of five tubes of toothpaste. It would seem, however, that such an offer, though continued for a long period to time, should not establish a new price for the combination if both items are concurrently sold at regular prices. As the commission observed in the *Black* case, "If the regular price of the article sold with the premium is the same as the price with the premium, then the premium does not cost the customer anything. It is FREE TO HIM regardless of whether or not it is ultimately included in the regular price [i.e., the increased volume at the regular price]."

If adopted and promulgated by the commission, the provisions of the proposed guide will supersede those contained in the 1953 free-goods rule on use of the word *free* and would considerably contribute to the constructive information and advice for which Commissioner Elman expressed a need in the *Mary Carter* case.

STATE LAWS

Although the principal control of the use of *free* and words of similar import lies within the jurisdiction of the Federal Trade Commission, some states have statutes which affect the commercial use of free goods, including gifts and premiums. Among them are those which prohibit the sale of merchandise at or below cost and those which prohibit the sale of a fair-trade commodity at less than the price stipulated in the governing contract. As herein discussed, along with antitrading stamp and antipremium statutes, the subject will be summarized only to the extent to which such legislation affects the offer to give or the giving of gifts and other free deals.

Central to the thrust of this legislation is the status of trading stamps and the free goods exchanged for them. Whether or not they constitute the unlawful "abatement" of price is the basis of a substantial number of cases predicated upon an alleged violation of the pricing statutes. The answers, as well as the legislative support thereto, are historically based in the antipremium statutes and the 1916 decision of the Supreme Court in *Rast* v. *Van Deman.*

Beginning around 1880, state after state passed legislation to outlaw premiums and trading stamps. Such prohibition was seen as promoting the welfare of the buying public (because premiums "may be thought to be" a "lure to improvidence" and an appeal to the desire to get something for nothing) and/or the welfare of competing sellers and of the economy as a whole. The various statutes encompassed a multitude of commercial practices and aims, ranging from attracting customers initially to stimulating sales of a specific product. The use of trading stamps is the prime target in some statutes; others prohibit the use of premiums, in connection with the sale of specific merchandise, and unconditional gifts. For purposes of the Federal Trade Commission Act, unlike the use of lotteries to promote sales, the giving of a premium is not an "unfair method of competition." It, nevertheless, may be prohibited as a deceptive, hence unfair, trade practice. Because premiums are given only in connection with or in addition to the sale of another article (gifts being those free articles which are distributed to everyone without condition), they are controlled by the current free-goods rule.

A premium may be the same or similar to the main article or it may be entirely different. The latter category encompasses the trading stamp or trading card plans to which the legislatures have directed their attention. The Federal Trade Commission, too, was constrained to announce its position on the trading stamp plans that are so pervasive in the commercial world. It did so on October 3, 1957:

> Although deciding not to take action as to stamp plans at this time . . . changing circumstances or methods may reveal that some plans may be operated in violation of specific provisions of the law. For that reason, the Commission intends to continue to study stamp plan operations and will take action where necessary to prevent deception of customers, price discrimination, illegal exclusive dealing, boycott, conspiracy or any other conduct in violation of the Federal Trade Commission Act or Clayton Act.

Not until 1968, however, in its *Sperry & Hutchinson Company* decision, did the commission find it necessary to take action against a stamp plan operation. In order to determine that anticompetitive practices existed, recognition was given to trading stamps as a viable and substantial competitive tool which has "stood the rigorous test of time" and is "worth preserving against limitations and restrictions." Accordingly, the commission ruled that the nation's oldest and largest trading stamp company unlawfully restrained trade when it required retailer licensees to restrict their offer of trading stamps to a maximum of one stamp for each 10-cent purchase. Also held to be a Section 5 violation was the company's restriction on exchanging its stamps for other trading stamps.

There was a dissent by Commissioner Mary Gardiner Jones, who felt that the order did not prohibit S & H from fixing a designated rate of exchange. She characterized the decision as "permit[ting] a little bit of price fixing provided it is the fixing of the minimum price but not a maximum."

State courts have wrestled with the subject of commercial "handouts" in much the same way as has the Federal Trade Commission. Positing the presupposition that an owner of property may give it away or sell it on any terms acceptable to him, these regulatory bodies, nonetheless, have recognized that in making a sale or in giving a gift the owner may employ a device with the capacity to deceive the purchaser as to the true character of the transaction and to injure competitors or destroy competition.

Against this latter possibility stand the laws prohibiting sales below cost and price cutting of fair-traded merchandise, some of which incorporate a prohibition against doing indirectly what is directly forbidden. For example, the Indiana Fair Trade Act to prevent "evasion of resale price restrictions . . . [except to the extent authorized by . . . contract]," prohibits:

> (a) The offering or giving of any article of value in connection with the sale of such commodity;
> (b) The offering or making of any concession of any kind whatsoever (whether by giving coupons or otherwise) in connection with any such sale; or
> (c) The sale or offering for sale of such commodity in combination with any other commodity. . . .

Another example is California's Unfair Practices Act which prohibits any person engaged in business in the state from (1) selling below cost and (2) giving away a product for the purpose of injuring competitors or destroying competition.

A state may have, also, a law, of general application or with respect to specific merchandise, prohibiting trading stamps and premiums.

It would appear that the commercial offer of merchandise which is, in truth, a gift (that is, not tied to a purchase) is not apt to be encompassed by any of these statutes. The intent to injure competitors or to destroy competition is not likely to be found under circumstances where the customer is really getting something for nothing. The offeror is more interested in increasing his own business than in destroying his competitors.

Where, however, a state has not taken a position on the commercial giving of gifts, premiums, coupons, and the like, whether such devices will amount to a violation of the unfair-practices and fair-trade laws is largely a question of statutory interpretation and the willingness of the court to extend a statute beyond its express language.

Where trading stamps have been questioned as an unlawful abatement in price, the courts seem to agree that they constitute a method of giving discounts. The point of departure among them is whether they can be considered as essentially given in consideration of the cash paid by the customer (that is, a mere term of payment) or "practically," as the Supreme Court said in the *Rast* case, "a rebate upon the price."

The cases do not pinpoint a definitive rational basis for either viewpoint. The courts agree that trading stamps are a method of advertising, a device to draw trade to the user and away from his competitors. But, as one court pointed out, that would be no less true of any violation of these pricing statutes; "the greater the discount or price cut, the greater the lure." On the other hand, the courts permitting the use of trading stamps with fair-traded commodities or other protected merchandise compare them to the many services that are commonly available to and confer benefit on customers. In the words of a Pennsylvania court, "They cannot be regarded as cutting prices any more than free delivery or free parking could be so regarded although these are practices which obviously save money for the customers of the stores offering such advantages." Such is the view also of courts upholding the practice of giving gifts to stimulate trade. Recognizing it as a common method of advertising, a California court has stated,

> For more than a quarter of a century merchants in America have occasionally displayed staple articles at reduced prices, offered gifts and prizes, issued trading stamps, paid rebates, and resorted to other cut-rate methods of advertising their commodities to stimulate trade in the hope that a slight sacrifice on a few staple articles would be more than compensated by an increased bulk of business.

A gift to all, without regard to purchase and not dependent upon the sale of articles covered by fair-trade contracts—as are parking, in-store music, and delivery—will not be illegal. On the other hand, if either the premium or the revenue article is the subject of a fair-trade contract, the transaction may be deemed a combination sale of both products for a single price, thus unlawfully reducing the price already established on one of the products. The same result has been reached where a retailer allowed a 10 per cent discount to his employees on purchases made by them of fair-traded commodities.

Even in states where premiums and stamps enjoy a fairly free use, however, promotional schemes which practically amount to a "palpable subterfuge" to evade the law will be dealt with less liberally. Accordingly, to limit the receipt of trading stamps to specific items of merchandise or to conduct a carefully planned campaign "to get their bread in [a particular town] and the sky was the limit" could negate an intent to merely promote and to advertise. Rather, it establishes a scheme designed to give one dealer an unfair advantage over others, which is the very practice to which this legislation is directed.

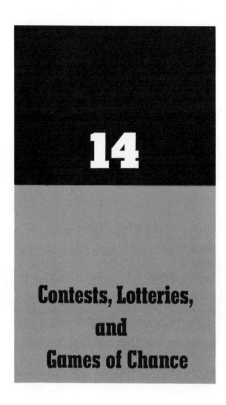

14

Contests, Lotteries, and Games of Chance

Most businessmen utilize an advertising program which, at least to some degree, extols the merits of their product or service. Notwithstanding the pressures which emanate from government and the commercial community itself to maintain this preferential standard, there would appear to be a very practical basis for doing so. Assuming customer satisfaction is the ultimate goal, the most successful promotional plan will be one which incites consideration of quality, price, and the like, of competing offers. The purchase which reasonably satisfies the customer's needs or whims and fairly corresponds to the representation made to him is most likely to be repeated.

In recognition, however, of the proclivity of many to be attracted by an opportunity to "get something for nothing" or to "take a chance," sales are often fostered by contests and lotteries and various other gaming devices. Stimulation of the purchasing desire is not the aim of such promotional gimmicks. The appeal is to the gambling instinct, and the rationale is obvious—the offer of a chance to gain back more value than was given. Although by their very nature suspect, merchandising schemes involving an element of chance are not on that ground alone illegal.

LOTTERIES AT COMMON LAW

At early common law, gaming was not unlawful so long as it did not tend to immoralize the innocent or affect the interests of those not similarly engaged. The proviso clearly states the subsequent, and now firmly established, public policy against lotteries "as a vice to be prevented and suppressed in the interest of the public morals and the public welfare." The risking of money or other property on an event, chance, or contingency in the hope of realization of gain was not to be encouraged in the citizenry. At the present day, both state and private lotteries are forbidden, or at least regulated in some manner, by constitution or statute, or both, in probably every state in the union. Congress has closed the mails to such schemes and has barred them from interstate commerce.

The term *lottery* has been defined variously by courts, statutes, and authors. It seems clear, however, that it embraces all schemes for the distribution of prizes by lot or chance, short of the gratuitous distribution of property, and is composed of three elements: consideration, chance, and prize. To constitute a lottery these three elements must coexist and "their joint presence is enough to vitiate a scheme, no matter how innocent or attractive it is otherwise." Every aspect of the scheme, from its purpose to its form, is legally irrelevant. Absent an enabling statute, an eleemosynary lottery will be just as vicious as one which lures children to part with their pennies. If consideration, chance, and prize are found to be present, the "game" will be within the prohibitory scope of public policy regardless of its "name."

Elements of a Lottery

Consideration. Lottery involves a chance for a prize, with the price as consideration. The requirement that a participant risk or hazard something for the chance to gain raises the question of the public policy behind lottery statutes. Judicial decisions demonstrate uniform objection to lotteries and similar schemes. Condemnation is evidenced, as noted, by state and federal legislation and a continuous referral to the policy established by the common law. There is no clear consensus, however, as to what is to be accomplished by the suppression of lotteries except that it is, without question, for the general welfare and benefit of society.

If the purpose is to preclude impoverishment of participants in lottery schemes, then only those schemes involving valuable consideration should be prohibited. That evil is effected only when the participant has paid something of value for his chance to win, like buying a ticket or making a purchase. Consideration, then, is measured by the value to the participant of what he gives, because only on this basis can it be said that the participant has risked something in the hope of chance gain.

Frequently, however, lottery legislation is purported to have another purpose: to prevent the general promotion of the gambling spirit, to discourage "gain by other than one's own efforts." Because chance and the prize are rarely in doubt, the concept of lottery consideration has been extended to "include more than money passed from participant to sponsor" in order to invalidate schemes where value has not been given for the chance to gain. The rationale most frequently advanced is the benefit accruing to the person offering the prize by reason of the participation of those who have been lured to play the promotional "game." Courts have spoken also of the detriment or inconvenience or disadvantage suffered by the participant. When he or she, for example, must register or be at a particular location for the drawing, these being deemed the conditions and terms of the sponsor's offer to award a prize by lot or chance, something *sufficient*, albeit not value, is found to move from the participant to the sponsor. "Benefit" and "detriment" constitute the so-called indirect consideration, and this has divided the courts when a merchandising scheme is questioned as an illegal lottery.

Indirect consideration is not new to the law. Study of the lottery cases reveals a reluctance, nevertheless, to employ it in this context. Interestingly enough, even a statutory definition of consideration as "paid or promised," which would seem to have greater reference to direct consideration, has not resulted in an agreement of the courts as to its precise meaning.

In 1963 an Illinois appellate court reviewed a declaratory judgment which had approved an advertising project. The judgment was reversed on the ground that the scheme was a lottery within the meaning of the state statute, even though participants were not required to pay for a chance or to make a purchase from the sponsor. Relying on a 1937 decision of the Illinois Supreme Court which had dealt with a movie theater's "Bank Night" scheme prior to the enactment of the statute, the appellate court found the necessary consideration in the benefit accruing to the merchant because even "free ticket seekers" became potential customers. In its opinion, the advertising promotion was not legitimate because the controlling inducement to become patrons of the merchant was the "lure of an uncertain prize." Apparently, the court felt that "consideration" was in no way qualified by "paid or promised," as used in the statute, and it was free to decide that actual pecuniary loss or actual pecuniary benefit was immaterial.

A year later, the Supreme Court of Illinois had an opportunity to construe the same statute and to reverse the appellate court, which had again accepted the "benefit theory." The scheme to increase patronage by a retail grocery store required, once more, only a visit there to obtain numbered cardboard coins which entitled the holder to cash awards when certain combinations of numbers turned up. The Supreme Court was of the opinion that the statute contemplated that consideration flow from the one who is given the opportunity to win a prize by chance and that *paid* or *promised* has no reference to the mere physical inconvenience in going to the store. Furthermore, because the "purpose of lottery legislation is to prevent people from being cheated of their money," the court held that the statute clearly contemplated money or a thing of some value. Two judges dissented on the basis of their own prior ruling in a 1937 bank night case.

The existence of three different situations in which prize and chance concur seemingly has added to this judicial difficulty with lottery consideration. The three schemes have been designated appropriately as open participation, closed participation, and flexible participation. The descriptive adjective, in each case, refers to the existence or absence of direct consideration.

The first type is open and free to all who care to participate. It stands to reason that a merchant may promote his business by giving away prizes or premiums, because he alone stands to gain or lose thereby. Participants, or more appropriately the recipients of the merchant's largesse, part with nothing and no offer of a chance to gain is extended as an inducement. Such a scheme will always be legal for lack of consideration as required for a lottery.

It would seem that a free distribution of merchandise would be fairly obvious. A Washington jeweler recently extended a typical offer: to the purchaser of a service for eight in a famous-brand sterling silver flatware a "prize" of a pair of sterling silver candelabra worth $100 would be awarded. The absence of chance must, of course, be kept in mind. When such a sales plan is questioned chance is a factor and consideration is always the point in issue.

A recently proposed sales scheme which evoked the disapproval of the Federal Trade Commission is illustrative. The plan involved little more than an invitation to the general public to specify on an entry form contained in the advertisement a preference among the sterling silver flatware featured therein. Sometime later, a winner would be "drawn" from among the entries submitted, and the prize would consist of a four-piece place setting in the preferred pattern. Because no purchase or promise to purchase was exacted from the entrants, the commission would not have found the scheme to be objectionable if it had stopped there. The sponsor, however, proposed to donate to a winning purchaser additional pieces in the chosen pattern equal in retail value to those purchased during the period of the contest. The plan fell on this "matching provision." It created the element of consideration that was lacking when the scheme was free to all.

The courts have been unwilling to extend the concept of consideration in an "open" plan so as to include such things as window shopping or watching television, even though prizes might be distributed, by lot or chance, for doing so. Such activities, without any additional requirement, do not encourage gambling and the participant has risked nothing. It is the requirement that participants in an "open" promotional scheme do something beyond mere acceptance of the sponsor's free prizes that has given rise to the only notable exception to the legality of such a sales gimmick. This exception falls more appropriately under direct consideration and will be discussed later in conjunction with the "flexible-participation" schemes.

The "closed-participation" scheme contemplates that every person gives up something as a condition precedent to obtaining a prize to be distributed by chance. Although the "price" will have been induced by the offer of a chance of gain, it need not have been given exclusively for the ticket or card which evidences the change. The more usual sales plan involves a transaction in which goods are sold and the purchaser is, at the same time, "given" a chance to win a prize. Where a chance on an automobile is distributed with a six-months' subscription to a magazine, it is not difficult to "pierce the thin disguise" and see these so-called gift enterprises as a lottery under a new name. Although the consideration is given ostensibly for the goods purchased and not for the chance, and the benefit to the merchant is from the "lawful sale of goods, not the unlawful sale of chances," the fact that the purchaser gets something of value for his consideration—or has risked nothing for a chance to gain—does not negate the existence of a lottery scheme. Several recent FTC advisory opinions have re-emphasized this point. Part of the consideration for each transaction consists of a contribution to the maintenance of the scheme, thus furthering the sponsor's pecuniary interest.

With consideration as no insurmountable problem in the "closed-participation" schemes, they, assuming chance and prize are present, are almost never legal. The price of the goods or services purchased supplies the illegal consideration. An absolute condemnation is not possible in light of a case which held a sales plan promulgated by a businessmen's association to be legal even though the merchants distributed tickets to buying customers only. Distribution was at the rate of one for every dollar spent, similar to the use of trading stamps. Obviously, the greater the aggregate amount purchased, the greater the chance of winning when the eight winning tickets were drawn at the end of the "trades day." The court, apparently with the question of consideration in mind, because chance and prize were present, held the scheme to be legitimate because the customers had "paid nothing for the chance to win and had no chance to lose anything." Furthermore, because the plan was calculated to stimulate business, it was not deemed to be detrimental to public morals.

It would seem that the preceding case indicates a judicial preference for "trades days" rather than a deviation from the ban against gift enterprises as lotteries, because "bank nights," "cash nights," and such are also calculated, indeed designed, to stimulate business. Without a statutory definition of *lottery* to guide it, the court obviously felt something had to pass directly for the chance to win. Without it, and without a chance to lose, there could be no gamble, hence no lottery.

The "flexible-participation" promotional scheme is the troublemaker and the one most frequently used to stimulate sales because its condemnation is not at all uniform, absent a statute which embraces it specifically. Some participants pay for the offered chance to win a prize, some do not. Accordingly, courts are divided as to whether lottery consideration is to be found flowing from the nonpaying participants for the promised chance to win a prize. It is this particular type of merchandising scheme which has given rise to the most prevalent authority for the proposition that indirect consideration is sufficient to constitute a lottery. As noted, the absence or presence of giving up some value on the part of the participants is rather clear-cut in the other two chance schemes. Where payment as a condition to participation is flexible, however, indirect consideration is a necessary implement if illegality is to be impressed upon a scheme which, except for the lack of consideration on the part of some participants, is in every other respect the vice which the common law and lottery statutes seek to suppress.

Ordinarily the "no-charge" aspect of a "flexible-participation" scheme is played up prominently in its promotion. Thus, it professes to be free and open when, in reality, it is more closely related to the "closed-participation" scheme. The essential difference is that the restrictions inherent to the "closed" game are relaxed sufficiently to include some nonpaying participants. Registration to acquire a ticket representing the chance (or tickets may be given to anyone who requests them and to some who do not) is the usual term of the offer to distribute prizes. A food sales scheme is a situation in point. A drive-in dispenses both hamburgers and potatoes, for a price and a chance, free of charge, to be the child who will be given the opportunity to take home all the toys he or she can gather together in fifteen minutes at a well-supplied toy store. To be sure, a name and address on a form provided at the drive-in is essential for the drawing. Could there be doubt, however, as to the appeal of that specific establishment over the drive-in down the street when hamburgers and potatoes are to be the luncheon or supper fare?

There may be, however, some restrictive conditions which make the "game" more favorable to the paying participant. Thus, the rule in most movie theater "cash-night" schemes that the winner claim his prize inside the theater within a very short time, usually two to five minutes, gives the participant who paid the admission fee a decided edge over the participant who chose to await the drawing outside the theater. Thus, it is not difficult to understand why some courts looked to the expansion of the lottery consideration concept, from "value given" to "benefit received" or "detriment suffered," as the means of invalidating schemes which were unworthy of legal approbation.

The rationale behind this expansion was expressed well by the Michigan Supreme Court:

> While patrons may not pay and the [theater] may not receive any direct consideration, there is an indirect consideration paid and received. The fact that prizes of more or less value are to be distributed will attract persons to the theater who would not otherwise attend. In this manner those obtaining prizes pay consideration for them, and the theaters reap a direct financial benefit.

In other words, an option to get a chance without paying for it should be immaterial when there is a reasonable probability that most will pay consideration, whether lured (1) by the chance to participate in the distribution of prizes, (2) by the desire to see a movie or make a purchase, or (3) by embarrassment in requesting a "free" chance. The dissent in a theater bank-night case felt that the question should be, in fact, whether the scheme induced the payment of consideration and not who acquired tickets. This point, however, is not really in conflict with the rationale supporting indirect consideration. The benefit theory only sidetracks the question of inducement by an assumption, based on man's known propensity to take a chance, that more people were attracted to pay than would have had no chance been offered. Furthermore, the theory is intended to, and does, reach the schemes which promote gambling generally without the attendant risk of loss. The others, where money is hazarded, are rather uniformly proscribed.

Where money is not risked at all, however, the courts who do not accept indirect benefit as supplying the element of consideration hark back to the other evil connected with a lottery. Unless money or something of value is mulcted from the unsuspecting public expecting to get something for nothing, then one element is missing. The benefit, through advertising, derived by the sponsor is, by the weight of authority, too "remote" to be labeled illegal consideration.

Before leaving our discussion of consideration, something should be said about the cases which shall be characterized as "do something" and "do nothing." As a general rule, the schemes involved have been open to all without the requirement of purchase or payment for the chance. The cases present the "detriment suffered" aspect of indirect consideration. The primary interest, however, lies in the fact that it is the only pronouncement on lottery consideration by the Supreme Court of the United States.

By federal statute, radio and television are prohibited from broadcasting lotteries. The Federal Communications Commission, therefore, sought to enjoin the broadcasting of such give-away programs as "Stop the Music" and "Sing It Again," which procured their participants, without charge, from the listening and viewing audiences. Agreeing with the commission, but without deciding that substantial commercial benefit accrues to the sponsors of these programs and that the courts have not limited consideration to money or a thing of value, the Supreme Court held that listening to the radio or viewing television at home did not constitute the element of consideration essential to a lottery. In dispensing with the cases which have found consideration in registering free for a chance in a store or awaiting a drawing at a specified location, the Court distinguished the type of participation in the case before them. No one had paid anything, bought anything, or done anything except sit and listen.

A similar "do nothing" participation scheme was decided the same way in Alabama in 1955. A furniture dealer awarded prizes to contestants whose names were drawn on a weekly television program without any requirement of a purchase or payment. The court was careful not to say that no consideration moved to the sponsor or that consideration must be valuable. What it did say was that the consideration, if any, was not sufficient to label the scheme a lottery. Because the effect of the sales scheme was not to attract people to the furniture store where they might be subjected to a sales pitch and, hence, a purchase, no detriment or disadvantage was sustained by the participants.

This detriment, however, is present in the "do something" cases, where the courts find the essential consideration moving indirectly from the participant to the sponsor. The necessity of registering, as in the theatre "bank night," or in attending a public auction in order to be eligible for a chance on an automobile, is that disadvantage which will supply the element. Similarly, going to the store of a sponsor, not only once to obtain the free card, but weekly to have it punched for a drawing from among all the punched cards, has been found to constitute legal detriment. The participants clearly did more than sit at home and await their chance. They gave of their time and effort to participate, were effective in advertising the promotional "game," and subjected themselves to the attraction of merchandise once in the store.

In April of 1965 the state of Wisconsin amended its constitution so as to remove any doubt as to lottery consideration which until that time had been left to the courts for definition. The amendment narrowed consideration so as to permit certain types of activities theretofore classified as lotteries, namely: "[T]o listen to or watch a television or radio program, to fill out a coupon or entry blank, whether or not proof of purchase is required, or to visit a mercantile establishment or other place without being required to make a purchase or pay an admittance fee." The amendment also gave the legislature permission to "cut back the constitutional definition if it wishes." In July 1966, the legislature in revising its lottery laws enumerated the previously described activities as being insufficient for purposes of lottery consideration with the exception of the last one, the visit to a store. The omitted activity subsequently was held to be without the Constitutional exemption in Wisconsin, provided it is combined with a chance game and a prize.

For the sponsor with second thoughts about his plan to increase sales, a word of caution. He may be successful in arguing his point that there is no consideration in registering for the chance to participate in his chance scheme, but he may lose in a suit by the "winner" to collect his prize. To those courts which hold that even "doing something" is not that value which will support a lottery, it can be, nevertheless, sufficient to support the sponsor's promise to award a prize.

Chance. Chance, as an element of a lottery, refers to the attainment of certain ends not by skill or any known or fixed rules, but by the happening of a subsequent event, incapable of ascertainment or accomplishment by means of human foresight or ingenuity. Although consideration and the prize may exist in a contest requiring skill, chance always converts a game into a "lottery" or a "gamble."

As stated by the Nevada Supreme Court: "The test [however], of the character of a game is not whether it contains an element of chance or an element of skill, but which is the predominating element." Hence, if chance, in the "causative sense," is determinative of who wins the prize (or what the prize will be as with punchboards and pushcards), the fact that it might have been accomplished by research or calculation will not be sufficient to circumvent the laws and public policy against lotteries. For example, the Missouri Supreme Court held that where only two contestants, who were not puzzle experts, out of over 45,000 gave the correct answers to the entire eighty-four puzzles to be completed, skill or judgment was not involved. Also, where there exist so many factors which could make a given result unforeseeable, as in a promotional gimmick requiring the nearest estimate of the total popular vote to be cast for the office of the United States President, chance was held predominant in the scheme to increase the circulation of a newspaper. In the same manner, referral-type sales programs have been held to be permeated with chance. The cash or credit "prize" to a customer is dependent upon subsequent sales to persons who have been referred as "live" prospects. Even assuming judgment was exercised in the selection of names, so much depended upon chance (from contact of the referrals by salesmen to the decision to buy) that such a promotional plan was deemed to be prohibitable as a lottery.

Chance must inhere in the game and not be merely incidental. It must control and determine the award of the prize, whatever it may be, as, for example, where a company offered a watch to everyone who completed each of seven different puzzles found in the unmarked boxes of the sponsor's food product. Although some skill was involved, the dominant element was the chance of finding in the package purchased the puzzle needed to complete the set. A variation on this "chance find" dealt with coupons distributed in boxes of Mother's Oats. One of the letters in *Mother's* was imprinted on each coupon. The trick was to spell the word with the appropriate coupons. The "chance" was in obtaining the *one* "o" coupon that was distributed.

On the other hand, chance does not inhere in an offer to pay a substantial cash prize to any person shooting a hole-in-one on the offeror's golf course. Although swayed by the fact that the contestant could not lose, hence no gamble to him, the court was convinced that it took skill to get the ball within the area of the green where a hole in one was feasible. The element of luck thereafter did not convert this scheme to sell more green fees into an illegal lottery. Similarly, where the prize is to be awarded on the basis of the aptness or originality of the slogan submitted, or for the "neatest correct solution" of a puzzle, or the "best" essay on a certain breakfast food, a standard such as would guide a contestant in the exercise of skill had been provided. Selection of the winner on that basis could not be said to be the result of chance.

The use of trading stamps is not illegal in itself, absent a prohibitory statute, because the ultimate premium or gift, or prize, is not procured by chance. A similar result obtains, in a promotional scheme where each purchaser is given a ticket and the number of tickets held at the termination of the contest is determinative of the prize. Chance clearly is not controlling. Because the purchaser got only, and no more than, what was specifically offered, it could not be said that the appeal was to "take a chance" or that his gain was a result thereof. Moreover, legality is not affected by a choice of several gifts or prizes of like kind and quality because the purchaser is free to choose before he makes the purchase.

A subterfuge to avoid the element of chance, however, will be rejected. Illustratively, a Georgia court "saw through" a scheme utilizing a coin-vending machine. A nickel produced a nickel's worth of gum or mints. After each operation the machine would indicate whether on the next operation the customer would receive, in addition to the gum or mints, "premium checks" which could be traded for merchandise or redeposited into the machine. Although there was clearly no chance involved in each operation, because the customer always knew in advance whether he would get the prize, he could not forecast as to any succeeding operations until after he had paid his nickel and, in effect, taken his chance to become entitled to a prize for the expenditure of another nickel.

Prize. The prize is the motivating factor or inducement which accounts for the success of all forms of gambling. The possibility of gain, of getting something for nothing, is that upon which the offeror relies to attract participants. Anything of value will be sufficient for a prize. Its intrinsic worth, obviously, will vary, depending upon the sophistication, or even the potential size, of the group to be attracted by the specific offer.

The element of prize presents no problems generally. There are a few aspects, however, that are worthy of brief attention. As noted, the removal of the possibility of loss to the participants will not change the character of the game as one of chance, nor will it affect the existence of prize if there is any inequality in value resulting from chance in the distribution of money or property paid back to the contributor to the chance scheme. Distribution to everyone of property of equal value is not the prize that would motivate a gambling scheme.

A distribution of value equivalent to that contributed will not constitute "prize" either. Accordingly, a scheme to stimulate sales by means of a pull-tab device (which universally is deemed to be a means by which chances are sold) which revealed both the article to be purchased and the purchase price thereof was held not to offer a "prize" within the sense of lottery. Absent findings that some of the articles were of greater value than the prices assigned to them—hence disparity among the values of the property to be paid back to the contributors to the scheme—each participant received something equivalent to the contribution made.

However, even the possibility of gain, by itself, is insufficient to invalidate a scheme. It is only when this advantage accrues to some, and not to all, participants that it properly can be labeled lottery "prize."

It is, of course, this type of scheme which is most prevalent among the lottery cases. It has proved successful in luring not only participants initially, but repeated attempts by them in the hope of being the one to win. Children have been attracted to part with their pennies for "choco-late penny men" candy, until there were none, to obtain from among the 120 candies in the box those four which concealed a penny within the wrapper; or for the ten peanut bars out of sixty which would sell, as indicated within the wrapper, for 1 cent as compared with 2 cents or 3 cents for the others. Housewives, also, have been lured to make repeated purchases of food products advertised as having been packaged with coupons of either no value or of varying redeemable cash value. In one case, the FTC advised a processor of a grocery item that the free dis-tribution to the general public of equivalent coupons did not cure the proposed plan to insert them in the containers of its product for pur-chase because, standing alone, the latter were prizes in a lottery scheme. Assuming, of course, chance and consideration coexist, lottery prizes have ranged from automobiles and large amounts of cash to a free hamburger at the local drive-in. The cases reveal how amazingly little will attract so many or will induce so much effort, time loss, and possibly discomfort and inconvenience, all in the expectation that someone *must* win.

LOTTERIES AND THE FEDERAL TRADE COMMISSION

Scope of FTC Jurisdiction

In the words of a federal court of appeals, "If it is unfair competition to tempt buyers by misrepresentation of the quality of goods, it may be regarded as likewise unfair to them to buy goods not upon their merits but upon the chance of securing something for nothing." This is a precise statement of the policy to which the Federal Trade Commission has been committed since its inception in 1914, or more appropriately since its first orders to cease and desist in the use of lottery schemes in commercial transactions in 1918. During June and July of that year there were twenty-three orders to the distributors of coffee and tea who concealed within the container, thus employing chance as a factor, premium coupons which were redeemable in varying cash amounts. By 1925 the first of many penny-candy lotteries had come to the attention of the commission. In the administration of its enabling statute and under the mandate of Section 5 to prevent the use of unfair methods of competi-tion in commerce, the commission condemned these schemes. It was not until 1934, however, that the Federal Trade Commission Act was judicially construed so as to prohibit them.

In *FTC* v. *R. F. Keppel & Brothers, Inc.* the United States Supreme

Court declared merchandising by means of lottery or similar chance schemes to be unfair methods of competition, and thus within the Federal Trade Commission's injunctive sanction. What had been frequently condemned and prohibited as unfair in the past was, henceforth, to be so as a matter of law.

In striking down the scheme which lured children with an offer of a chance to get something more than one piece of candy for their penny, the Court, in addition, recognized a wide ambit of jurisdictionally permissible action in the Federal Trade Commission, where chance was a factor in competitive sales. Having no doubt that the statutory requisite of "unfair method of competition" was intended to be more flexible than the common law "unfair competition" and that its definition depended upon the "gradual process of judicial inclusion and exclusion," the Court concluded that the commission's authority must embrace trade practices prior to that time never regarded as unfair because they tended neither to restrain trade, create monopoly, or involve fraud and deception. So long as the practice was "of the sort which the common law and the criminal statutes have long deemed contrary to public policy"—that is, having the tendency to encourage gambling—FTC jurisdiction did not depend upon technical violation of the narrower confines of state and federal lottery laws. To force competitors either to adopt a practice which, although not criminal, "it brands as unscrupulous" or to suffer business loss was deemed to be the kind of unfairness at which the Federal Trade Commission Act was aimed.

The commission had found competition to be adversely affected by Keppel's sales methods and had in fact found that Keppel itself had experienced a decrease in sales during a period of selling "straight." The question remained, nevertheless, as to why competitors did not adopt a chance scheme when free to do so in order to stem the diversion of trade to Keppel. The Court settled on the injury to consumers, the exploitation of children "who are unable to protect themselves." The use of a device "whereby the amount of the return they receive from the expenditure of money is made to depend upon chance . . . [had] met with condemnation throughout the community." Thus, the commission's authority to prevent unfair methods of competition could be predicated, apparently, upon the "moral injury" to consumers vis-à-vis a financial injury to competitors when trade and patronage were induced by an appeal to the gambling instinct.

The cases which followed revealed clear utilization by the commission of this generalization adduced from *Keppel*. Thus, in *National Candy* v. *FTC* the United States Court of Appeals for the Seventh Circuit stated that, "A violation of public policy is an injury to the public, and it is in the public interest to prevent the use of a method of competition which is contrary to an established policy of the Federal Government, even if injury to competitors be not alleged or proved." The introduction of the element of chance in the selection of the candy which revealed, when broken, the colored center entitling the purchaser to a larger, free piece of candy was found to be a sound basis, on the ground of public policy, for FTC jurisdiction. This was deemed sufficient even though the court was of the opinion that the sales plan had the capacity to divert trade away from competitors and to exclude existing and potential competitors who did not use such methods.

The point is largely academic, however, because in 1938 the Federal Trade Commission Act was amended so as to broaden the commission's jurisdiction to include "unfair or deceptive acts or practices in commerce." There would seem to be no doubt that the amendment constituted a nod by Congress to the public-injury generalization in *Keppel*. As the Seventh Circuit noted in 1963:

> It seems clear, that by thus broadening the Commission's jurisdiction, Congress did not intend to give the Commission any lesser jurisdiction over trade practices which, while not directly related to competition, are unfair because of their effect on the public or on public morals. Consequently, a method of competition which appeals to the public's baser gambling instincts would seem to clearly fall within the Commission's jurisdiction, irrespective of whether it technically constitutes a lottery or otherwise violates the penal laws.

Sales of various articles of merchandise by means of a mechanical gaming device (pull tab) was, by this rationale, found to be an illegal game of chance in the context of actual use as promoted by the salesmen and as accepted by the purchasers, although a "no obligation to buy" feature might remove the device from the operation of the state lottery laws.

An examination of the cases reveals that the commission approaches a trade practice alleged to constitute merchandising by a "game of chance, gift enterprise or lottery scheme," hence per se "unfair" under *Keppel* as a competitive device and not as a penal offense. The question remains, however, as to what is necessary to prove the scheme. It does not help that most, if not all, questioned practices have contained the three elements of a lottery, or that one commissioner has pointed out that the existence thereof should not be within the concern of the commission. What is clear is that the "unfairness . . . lies in the fact that [the scheme] employs the element of chance as a factor in the sale of merchandise." Hence the proof must exist in its inherent appeal, by design or effect, to the instinct to gamble, to take a chance, to get something for nothing rather than to the purchasing desire of a customer.

Schemes Condemned

The *Keppel* case did not end the use of lottery schemes in the sale of candy. In fact, during the ten years that followed, a myriad of candy sales were effected by a number of variations on that particular chance scheme.

On one day in 1934 the commission made forty-eight findings and/or orders in candy lottery cases, including three involving the sale of chewing gum. Twenty of the cases involved assortments of candy in which the "colored center" method was employed. A typical come-on was "Pick a Pink Center and Get a Five Cent Bar of Candy Free." The chance selection of a piece of candy in the box differing in color from the majority entitled the purchaser to a prize in the form of a larger piece or article of merchandise. Often the purchaser of the last piece in the assortment was also a prize winner. The report of children discarding nonwinning candies until the pennies or candies were gone clearly "proved" the scheme's appeal to the gambling instinct rather than to the desire for candy.

Ten cases involved the sale of candy from an assortment which varied the price per piece (from no cost at all to 3 cents), depending upon a slip of paper concealed within the wrapper. In other cases, the fact that the purchaser was entitled to a prize of more candy was condemned. "Winnabar" and "Winnanegg" were some of the slogans calculated to attract children.

Punchboards and pushcards also sold a good deal of candy. The offer varied from a penny to a nickel a "push" or "punch" for a penny or a nickel's worth of candy, or several times that amount for the same penny or nickel, depending upon the chance selection of the right tab to be pushed or punched. As noted, the fact that everyone got something did not change the character of the game as one of chance.

The so-called prize-package candy was another merchandising method to be condemned by the FTC. Candy was sold by the box. Each contained the same number of pieces of candy and a prize. The variance in the value of the prizes from as little as 1 cent to as much as $3 was the chance appeal and was the factor played up in the promotion of sales. This, no doubt, is what saves Cracker Jack, an old-time favorite which distributes "prizes" of the same insubstantial intrinsic value in all boxes.

The sale of penny-candy in coin-vending machines which allowed for the mixture of small toys and charms with the candy has been prohibited. The insertion of a coin in the machine occasionally gave the purchaser one of the toys in addition to the commodity selected. Both the receipt of the "prize" and the nature thereof was determined wholly by lot or chance and as such was held to constitute an unfair merchandising practice. That its chance appeal was effective was proclaimed in literature by the distributor of the machine. It was said that adults were "intrigued" and children had been known to drop from ten to fifteen pennies in the hope of receiving the one toy which appealed to them most.

Even money has been packaged with foodstuffs to promote sales. The penny in *Keppel's* candy has already been mentioned. Coffee consumers have been lured with the promise of a penny to $25 packed in each bag or can. One promotor employed the chance factor by limiting the "prize money" to certain packages of his salted nuts.

The mechanical device by which chance is merchandised has been employed in the sale and distribution of almost every conceivable small appliance, houseware, and leather product. There appears to be no exception to prohibition by the FTC as unfair lottery schemes. The orders have been upheld, also, by the courts with one curious exception, previously mentioned in connection with prizes. In a case involving the J. C. Martin Corporation, the Seventh Circuit had vacated the commission's order on the ground that the essential "prize" was lacking, because everyone got an article of merchandise equivalent to the amount contributed for the use of the pull-tab device. Several years later the same company was charged with selling merchandise by means of a "chance or gaming device." "Lottery scheme" was omitted from the second complaint. The United States Third Circuit Court of Appeals upheld *per curiam* the commission's order to cease and desist a "solicitation" which clearly gave the impression that pulling a tab meant taking a chance, a scheme which could not "be found to be other than a flagrant appeal to the gambling instinct of the public." With the element of prize unchanged, the commission had found solace in the rationale used by the Seventh Circuit which it quoted: "A reading of the cases does not reveal a pinpointing of lotteries as the only method by which the public gambling instinct may be aroused. Other methods are comprehended within the more general terms 'merchandising by gambling.' " The commission concluded that, "Merchandise [sic] by gambling should not be divided into insulated acts which appear innocent when examined separately."

The usual method of operation where punchboards, pushboards, and the like are involved is to supply these devices to members of the public (apparently retailers are used to a lesser extent), along with literature describing the merchandise which can be sold in this manner. Both the article and the price to be paid may be determined by the chance "push" with a written assurance on the boards as to the maximum purchase price, or the distribution of merchandise may be limited to chance "winners," with other customers risking only the price to be paid for the "push."

A novel variation on the more common mechanical device is the "fortune board" which sells fortunes and the chance to win articles of merchandise. The device is a small box containing slips of paper folded much in the way that Kleenex tissue is packaged; that is, when one piece of paper is pulled out, the edge of the next one is raised so that it can be easily grasped. Each slip contains a fortune and a number. The numbers, which are not in consecutive order, determine whether the purchaser of a "fortune" will receive the prize merchandise at no additional charge or only the "fortune." Thus, it was deemed that the sale and distribution of merchandise to the purchasers was wholly by lot or chance.

Frequently, the prospective customers may buy the merchandise at straight sale, that is, without taking the chance "push," but the commission has found that this alternative purchasing method was rarely utilized. Another ploy used by the distributors was to give all customers an option to reject the purchase of the merchandise after the chance was taken, hence to risk nothing. This also was a rare occurrence, but is of no consequence because the commission has rejected summarily the "no obligation" feature as a "mere subterfuge intended to avoid responsibility for obvious illegality" of a device designed, and in fact used, to encourage merchandising by gambling. As had been said in the first *Martin* case, "The objection to the pull-tab scheme cannot be removed by offering the individual an unobjectionable alternative."

So-called club plans have been prohibited as an unfair lottery gimmick. Each participant is solicited to purchase men's clothing at a fixed sum to be paid in weekly installments and is given a "purchase agreement" to this effect. The chance involved is the offer to procure the merchandise for less than the fixed sum; the amount of this discount is determined by certain figures published in a well-known newspaper. If these figures correspond to the serial number on the contract, the holder thereof either is entitled to a cash prize or is relieved of further payment on the contract. Purchasers who did not "win" prior to the end of the contest received the merchandise for the contract price.

A similar "club" scheme to sell radios and phonographs was the subject of a 1966 advisory opinion in which the commission rejected the proposed plan. Noting that the participant "clearly . . . would be motivated by the chance of receiving something of more value than the amount they contributed, . . . [the commission advised that] the nature of the appeal is unmistakable."

Because trading stamps cannot be condemned as a game of chance, there have been several attempts to devise a legal variation on this proved sales stimulator. One distributor of food products under the label "Plee-zing" provided booklets for the use of retail purchasers. One hundred receipts representing $25 worth of "Plee-zing" products could be pasted in the book. The completed booklet entitled the holder to a redemption of 15 cents and a cash award to range from 50 cents to $5. The amount was concealed beneath a seal which had to remain intact until the completed booklet was submitted for payment. The same gimmick with a slight twist was proposed to the FTC and rejected. The holder of a completed booklet could chose to take $2 in cash or $2.15 in merchandise rather than break the seal at all. The minimum chance award was $1.50 and the maximum was $100. In both cases the absence of risk, providing the purchaser stuck with the scheme and filled the book, did not negate the overwhelming appeal to the gambling instinct. Not only was there a possible contingent gain, but as the commission stated with reference to the proposed plan, "the amount of return would vary greatly with [the] willingness to 'take a chance'."

A "profit-sharing plan—in appreciation of your patronage," with trade cards to be punched according to the dollar amount purchased, fared no better. Again the card had to be completely punched and the seal, concealing the amount of the award, kept intact. The same chance distribution of a cash prize was found to exist in the distribution of numbered coupons to purchasers of grocery products on the basis of one for each 25-cent purchase. A weekly drawing from among coupons corresponding to the ones distributed was determinative of the winner.

Gambling Devices

The commission has had no difficulty in prohibiting the separate sale of punchboards and pushcards. The facts that the seller had no expectation of ultimate "unfair" use in commercial transactions or that the device might be incomplete in itself as a game of chance were rejected as immaterial where the unfair practice of "merchandising by gambling" was viewed as a whole.

The defense under these circumstances has been that the commission is without authority to restrict interstate shipment of gambling devices as such, that its restraining power extends only to shipments which amount to unfair trade practices.

There is no doubt that of necessity the ultimate sale to consumers of the "push" or the "punch" always takes place within the border of some state. Additionally, it is quite possible that the sale of merchandise by these means would not adversely affect trade of the same kinds of merchandise by "straight" sales. But neither injury to competition nor the purely intrastate nature of the ultimate use of the device is to the point where the commission's jurisdiction over "merchandising by gambling" is questioned. The important fact is that the use of these devices is a means of selling or distributing merchandise which is opposed to the public policy.

A device that is obviously intended to be used as a lottery device and that, when used, facilitates the encouragement of gambling, makes the separate sale thereof an unfair trade practice subject to the commission's jurisdiction. The distribution of these devices to others is "thus aiding and abetting, inducing and procuring manufacturers and wholesalers and retail dealers . . . to use unfair or deceptive acts or practices and unfair methods of competition."

This is not to say, of course, that the Section 5 bar on lottery schemes, in order to prevent gambling, will operate as a proscription on everything that might be used for gambling. That products or methods may be employed in violation of the laws, where such is not their intent and where other lawful uses exist for them, should not infect the product or method with illegality. Poker chips and playing cards, bingo and lotto games, and certainly the roulette wheels currently enjoying popularity in toy stores are intrinsically connected with gambling, but their sale is not prohibited. Something more is required than the intrinsic inducement to gamble contained in a given product or method.

A case before the commission will be useful in understanding the distinction. A complaint was issued against a distributor of punchboards and merchandise alleging merchandising by means of lottery devices and a cease and desist order ensued. On appeal to the commission the distributor was concerned primarily with the impact of the order on the separate sale (that is, without a punchboard) of his so-called deals, described as large boards upon which was mounted merchandise for display purposes. Admittedly, the deals were occasionally used by retailers in conjunction with punchboards obtained elsewhere. The distributor maintained, however, that he disposed of them as a single sale of merchandise and frequently for use as door prizes or for some other legitimate purpose not involving a subsequent commercial transaction.

Although the commission refused to modify the order as to the "deals" (on the ground that its comment thereon would preclude any doubt as to the scope of the order and, thus, would facilitate its enforcement), it recognized the "neutrality" of the device and its usefulness for purposes which did not involve the element of chance or lot. Hence, where a deal's obvious utility for legal use would not be negated by a design or legend which indicated an illegal use—or if it were not sold in conjunction with a punchboard—it would not fall within the scope of the cease and desist order.

Accordingly, it seems clear that FTC jurisdiction over gambling devices as well as schemes which utilize chance as a factor in the promotion of sales is dependent upon their appeal to the gambling instinct as a method of merchandising products and services.

CONTESTS

At Common Law

The vice in most gaming is the risking of something of value induced by the possibility of chance gain. As mentioned, the name of the game as well as its purpose are of no legal significance. The gravamen of the public policy against gaming is the adverse effect on the citizenry. Accordingly, the applicability of the lottery laws to a sales promotion plan characterized as a "contest" is a matter of inquiry into its essential nature.

To recapitulate, *lottery,* as a generic term to describe gaming which is unlawful, embraces all schemes for the distribution of prizes by chance among persons who have paid a consideration. It follows that if prizes are distributed on some other basis, as for example by gratuitous donation or by vote or by the exercise of skill and judgment, the scheme is not a lottery. The policy target of gaming laws, the incitement of the gambling instinct, is untouched, although the element of chance may be involved to some degree.

To illustrate, there may be a number of answers that will be equally appropriate in a guessing or puzzle contest so that the selection of the "right answer" is a matter of chance. It is not, however, "every conceivable chance which makes a transaction illegal" or which will "convert into a lottery that which had no resemblance to a lottery." For example, the "chance" that the judges would not choose the entry that was actually the "neatest correct solution" was held not to constitute the chance essential to a lottery. On the other hand, where a scheme is deemed to be an attempt to evade the lottery laws, a legal status will not be granted to a "voting contest." The fact that winners were determined by the votes cast by holders of purchased tickets was held not to eliminate the element of chance in a scheme designed to arouse the gambling instinct, in a case wherein the promoter agreed, upon the sale of 25,000 tickets at $1 each, to distribute $15,000 cash in various amounts to persons elected at a monthly meeting of the ticket holders.

As mentioned under the discussion of the element of chance, the question centers on the dominant factor in a given scheme. If chance controls, it is a lottery; if skill, knowledge, and judgment predominate, it is a legal contest. The prescriptive standard has been stated as follows: "Whether the element of chance is present so as to bring a contest within the lottery laws must be determined, not by any absolute or technical standard, but with reference to the capacity of the general public to solve the problem presented." Thus, one with knowledge as to the relative weight of soap and the ability to judge size is more likely to be able to guess the nearest correct weight of a large block of soap. Similarly, a contest requiring the nearest correct estimate of the number of cigarettes subject to federal tax within a given month was not a matter of chance. Certain facts were given to every contestant; beyond that the court felt that the winning answer was susceptible of intelligent study and forecast.

Another scheme in which skill was found to be the dominant factor involved a punchboard. For a dime a participant could punch the board to determine in which of the many partly-played checker games he would compete for a box of candy. The degree of skill needed for each game varied and this clearly rested upon the chance "punch." The successful completion of the checker game, however, being the condition precedent to the prize, was dependent upon forces well within the control of the contestant. It was thus not a "chance" game. To summarize, the legal significance of a contest lies in the substitution of knowledge, skill, and judgment for chance as the controlling element.

That its consequential nature thus would preclude the application of the lottery laws and the public policy against gaming, as well as condemnation and prohibition as an "unfair lottery scheme," does not in any way diminish the interest or authority of the Federal Trade Commission if a "contest" is otherwise an unfair method of competition or unfair or deceptive act or practice in commercial transactions. Contests have a legitimate position as an advertising gimmick; their position as a trade practice is subject to inquiry.

Contests and the FTC

The thrust of the commission's power to restrain unfair and deceptive business practices when a contest is questioned is the capacity of the scheme to deceive and mislead the general public. An illegal lottery is deceptive because participants do not get something for nothing. But there the deception is only secondary to the evil of a calculated appeal to and promotion of the gambling instinct to sell goods. A contest will be prohibited only if it is not all it is represented to be. Therein lies the unfairness. In other words, a "contest" must be a bona fide competition and the rules appertaining thereto fully disclosed and truthfully represented.

The efficacy of a contest as an advertising gimmick, and hence a sale stimulator, cannot be doubted. It offers, as do lotteries, the attraction of getting something for nothing. To be a contest (that is, bona fide), however, the prize offered must be awarded on the basis of an affirmative standard of skill such as would be clearly competitive. Where substantially everyone, if not all, may qualify and win because the putative puzzles and quizzes "are . . . so simple of solution, or the winning thereof so easy, as to remove them from the categories of competition, skill or special selection," the scheme to acquire leads to prospective customers may not be represented as a contest.

To procure sales representatives has been another purpose of a so-called contest. The solution to a simple problem depicted in a newspaper advertisement plus $2 entitled the "contestant" to a prize of an automobile, cash, or both and an introductory assortment of cosmetics. But, as the FTC found, in fact, the solution and the purchase only qualified the entrant to become a contestant for the same prizes to be determined by the amount of the sponsor's toiletries sold to friends and neighbors. The get-acquainted offer had been represented as a "sensational advertising campaign." Because, however, there was nothing in the advertisement to indicate that the contestant had to do anything except solve the puzzle, the sales effort disguised as a contest had to cease. Sewing machines, magazines, and cosmetics are popular subjects of such schemes.

The nonexistence of prizes or the misrepresentation of their essential nature or value has been another problem area in advertising contests. The deception is patent where the prize is represented as a free sewing machine when in fact the "winner" receives only a discount certificate on a specific machine, usually an inexpensive one, and certificates are given indiscriminately to other entrants. Similarly, there was deception where to the winner of a "first dance lesson" or a "$35 dance course," the sponsor threw in, without charge, a sales pitch for more lessons or a previously undisclosed condition that any lesson after the first must be purchased.

A "family puzzle contest" advertised as a means of introducing a "fine, dependable, and precision-made" watch offered a free watch and the possibility of sharing in large cash prizes for an entry fee of $11.25. The watches did not even exist at the time a substantial number of entrants had paid the fee. Those who actually received a prize got a watch which was neither fine nor distinctive, costing the sponsor less than $3. This was found to be another promotional scheme to obtain the names of people who would be encouraged to sell the sponsor's product.

GAMING AND THE FTC

In recent years, games of chance have developed into a major form of retail sales promotion. Long-running games which require repeated participation in order to win have become a major device for ensuring consistent retail patronage. Once a customer has been persuaded to participate in a game, there is a strong impetus for him to return to the same retail establishment without regard to the quality or price of merchandise available there. Consequently, such games have proved a highly successful device for establishing consumer buying patterns, in fungible product markets, which do not necessarily reflect price consideration.

In the early 1960's the use of games became a major promotional factor in the food and gasoline retailing industries. Major gasoline manufacturers and chain grocers would conduct national or regional games which encompassed large numbers of retail outlets. The games and the prizes were advertised nationally as well as locally, and each local outlet advertised the total volume of the national game.

The concern of the Federal Trade Commission over certain advertising practices connected with these games was finally aroused late in 1966, when the commission announced an investigation into the use of such games in the food-retailing industry. Less than two years later a subcommittee of the House Small Business Committee commenced an investigation of games as a device to increase consumer traffic in gasoline marketing. Both of these investigations revealed a number of abuses connected with such games and even stimulated some state legislatures to outlaw any use of games as a promotional device.

The investigations revealed six major deceptions practiced in the use of such games:

1. Prizes were allocated or "seeded" to various outlets most in need of the promotional assistance.
2. Winners were programed for the early weeks of the game to have greatest effect.
3. "Dummy" boxes, containing no winners, were supplied after all prizes had been given out.
4. Large prizes were advertised out of proportion to their availability.
5. The games could be "broken" by the local retailer, who would cash in the winners or give them to favored customers.
6. Often the games would terminate before all prizes were awarded.

In addition to these specific evils, there was considerable evidence that local retailers were coerced into offering the game and that the net effect of such games was to raise the retail price of the product, because the local retailer had to bear the expense of the game.

In response to growing consumer alarm over the use of such games, the Federal Trade Commission, in August of 1969, promulgated the *Trade Regulation Rule Relating to Games of Chance in the Food Retailing and Gasoline Industries,* which appears in Appendix XII. The rule was the result of more than six months of proceedings conducted by the commission; during that time comments were received from all sectors involved.

Demonstrating a disinclination to legislate morality by banning such games altogether, the commission instead sought to make such games as honest as possible. Essentially, the rule is based on three simple principles, randomness, security, and disclosure. Under the rules all prizes must be distributed on a totally random basis. This is referred to as the problem of the game mix, and such mixture may not be calculated to favor localities, retailers, or time periods.

The requirement of game security is intended to prevent detection of winning game pieces prior to their distribution. This will mitigate the problem of having local retailers remove major prize pieces for personal gain or for special patrons. The requirement that winning pieces not be detectable will also aid in the prevention of "seeding" winners after the games leave the manufacturer.

The final, and most comprehensive, principle underlying the new rule is full and complete disclosure. The commission, in its statement of policy accompanying the new rule, expressed particular concern over the lack of information concerning the odds of winning any of these games. The length of the games, the number of prizes in each category, and the total number of game pieces available were all unknown to the consumer. Frequently, the odds against winning a top prize exceeded one in 1 million, although the advertising for the game created the impression of a far better chance of winning.

Assuming that a consumer who is fully informed of such contingencies will be better able to decide whether he wishes to participate in such a game, the commission required that all advertising of such games must contain full disclosure of all information relevant to the likelihood of winning. Thus, disclosure of the odds of winning, the number of participating outlets, the length of the game and all other information relevant to reaching an educated decision as to whether to participate in the game was required.

Because of the relative newness of this rule, there is no real body of case law available which affords an accurate interpretation of many nuances present in the regulatory language. However, this rule was adopted as an alternative to prohibition (rather than no regulation at all); consequently, it can be expected that the commission will read its terms strictly.

CONCLUSION

It has been said that the public is entitled to get what it chooses. This choice is qualified, however, where the bargain involves a possibility for contingent gain. Owing to the human propensity to take a chance, the sale and distribution of products and services which make an appeal to the gambling instinct are unlawful business practices. In 1850, the Supreme Court of the United States outlined the public policy which underlies the prohibition of merchandising chance: "Experience has shown that the common forms of gambling are comparatively innocuous when placed in contrast with the widespread pestilence of lotteries. The former are confined to a few persons and places, but the latter infests the whole community; it enters every dwelling; it reaches every class; it preys upon the hard earnings of the poor; it plunders the ignorant and simple."

15

Warranties and Guarantees

Williston, a leading authority on the subject, begins his work on warranties with the bold statement, "There is no more troublesome word in the law than the word 'warranty.' It is constantly used in different senses." He defines it as "a representation of fact which induces a bargain."

The use and misuse of warranties and guarantees must be approached from two directions: first, through the common law, which grants the consumer some protection and imposes on the seller some duties to stand behind his bargain; second, through FTC regulation of deceptive advertising under Section 5 of the Federal Trade Commission Act, which declares unlawful "unfair methods of competition in commerce and unfair or deceptive acts or practices in commerce."

COMMON LAW AND THE
UNIFORM COMMERCIAL CODE

The action for breach of warranty was originally in tort; that is, the law imposed a duty on the seller irrespective of whether he had made a contract with the buyer or whether the one damaged by the goods was the buyer or a stranger with whom he had had no dealings. The earliest reported case is *Fitz. Abr. Monst. de Faits.,* decided in 1383. This was a century before the action of assumpsit, from which the modern contract action emerged. It was not until 1778 that the first decision regarding an action in warranty brought in assumpsit was published, so for 400 years the action rested not on an enforceable promise, but on a civil wrong, or tort.

The courts, however, have come to view the warranty action as one in contract, primarily because of a nineteenth-century decision, and the language of Lord Abinger in *Winterbottom* v. *Wright,* who foresaw "the most absurd and outrageous consequences, to which I can see no limit unless we confine the operation of such contracts as this to the parties who entered into them." This was originally interpreted to mean that the original seller was liable only to the immediate buyer; all others on the chain of distribution were not in privity with him. As we shall see, the privity doctrine has been eroded—necessarily so, because of modern techniques of multilevel distribution and national advertising. However, for many years the doctrine impeded effective consumer protection.

An action for breach of warranty goes hand in hand with actions for negligence and deceit as the three methods for consumer recovery for defective products. A warranty is a seller's affirmation of a material fact about the goods he is trying to sell. If the buyer has relied on the statement, it creates a promise that the goods will conform to the description or be suitable for the general or particular purpose the buyer had in mind. If the goods fail to meet the description or are unsuitable for the use intended, the seller has not lived up to his side of the bargain and is liable to the buyer for the breach of warranty. A breach of warranty action has advantages over the other two. First, the consumer need not prove the element of negligence required for a negligence suit. If a consumer has to prove someone was negligent in producing a car, for example, he seldom has the money to pursue all the possible persons along the production line from the ingot of steel to the boy in the service station who last looked into the engine. Even if he could use depositions to bring all the testimony into court, he would not necessarily have access to the records which might reveal negligence. Deceit is an intentional tort, which means that the consumer must prove that the seller knew that his representation was false and that he made it with the intention that the buyer rely on it to his detriment. This is known technically as *scienter*. Such is seldom the case with defective-products injury, and even if it is more common in misrepresentations in advertising, it is often hard to find sufficient evidence to sustain the burden of proving it.

Therefore, a breach-of-warranty action is called an action in strict liability because the seller's knowledge or negligence in making a representation are immaterial. He will be held liable even if he acted carefully and in good faith.

The buyer must still establish (and these factors will be further elucidated) that there was a warranty, that there was a breach of it, that the defect caused the breach, and that the defect was in the product when it left the hands of the defendant. The buyer must show that he was the one to whom the warranty was addressed, that he relied on the warranty and relied justifiably, and that he did not know of the existence of the defect when he purchased the product. The representation must be one of fact, not of opinion, and it must be part of the bargain, in that it must cover the injurious defects in the goods. If it is an express warranty, the seller must have made it or it must have been made by someone who was an agent or authorized by the seller in order for the statement to be held against the seller. The buyer must hear it and act in reliance on it. The damages must be substantial, not nominal, and many courts still question whether it can apply to pecuniary loss alone without personal or property damage. Generally, courts apply rules similar to those in negligence actions as to the interpretation of terms such as *normal use, normal user, obvious defects, prompt warning, instruction for use,* or *failure of an intermediary to discover the defect.*

The law of warranties is treated extensively by the Uniform Commercial Code, which is now in force in all states. The UCC recognizes express warranties and two implied warranties, one of merchantability and a second of fitness for a particular purpose.

Express Warranties

Section 2-313 of the Uniform Commercial Code (UCC) provides:

(1) Express warranties by the seller are created as follows: (a) Any affirmation of fact or promise made by the seller to the buyer which relates to the goods and becomes part of the basis of the bargain, creates an express warranty that the goods shall conform to the affirmation or promise. . . . (c) Any description, sample, or model of the goods which is made part of the basis of the bargain creates an express warranty that the goods shall conform to the description sample or model.

According to Comment 3, "In actual practice affirmations of fact made by the seller about the goods during a bargain are regarded as part of the description of those goods, hence no particular reliance on such statements need be shown in order to weave them into the fabric of the agreement."

Some examples of express warranties emerge forcibly from farm cases. A farmer bought some cows from a seller who knew that the cows were for milking and in striking the bargain warranted that the udders of the cows were sound and that the cows would give a decent flow of milk. The cows turned out to have mastitus, which ruined their ability to give milk and eventually infected the rest of the farmer's herd. The case was originally submitted on the theory of a breach of an implied warranty of fitness for a particular purpose, that is, to give milk, not for beef or breeding. The court found an express warranty in the seller's representations, but said that it was not prejudicial that the case had been submitted on the theory of implied warranty. It allowed recovery not only for the benefit of the bargain, but also for the consequential damages resulting from the spread of infection to the other cows.

Seed is often sold warranted to be a particular kind or grade. If it turns out not to be—as in a case of a tomato grower who discovered that his seed labeled as special, early-ripening tomato seed produced a motley crop which matured late and was of a mixed, inferior quality—the grower is unwilling to receive only the refund of the price of seed. If there is an express warranty of the kind and quality of the seed, the measure of damages is the difference between the reasonable market value of the crop and the theoretical value of the crop that the grower assumed he was growing when he bought the warranted seed. This case, which arose in California, demonstrated the number of persons involved along the chain of distribution in that the tomato grower sued the immediate supplier of the seed, who cross-claimed against the intermediate supplier, the broker, and the seed producer. The court found that the warranty agreement was in no way limited to a price refund of the seed and that the grower could recover both on the seller's express warranty and on implied warranties of merchantability.

The seller need not use formal words, such as *warrant* or *guarantee,* and need not have a specific intention to make a warranty, but an affirmation merely of the value of the goods or a statement purporting merely to be a sales opinion or commendation of the goods does not create a warranty. Comment 8 of the UCC adds, "There are statements or predictions which cannot fairly be viewed as entering into the bargain. Even as to false statements of value, however, the possibility is less open that a remedy may be provided by the law relating to fraud or misrepresentation."

For example, a seller represented that a ring with a yellow stone in it was as good as a ring with a white and blue stone and said that it was worth twice the price he was asking. This was held to be merely stating an opinion and an estimate.

It is not a big step from representations a seller makes directly to a buyer in a store to representations a manufacturer makes to a consumer in an advertisement. In *Baxter* v. *Ford Motor Company* Ford had distributed literature saying that the glass in its windshield was shatter-proof. A purchaser bought the car and was injured when a pebble which struck the windshield shattered the glass. The company was held liable without knowledge or negligence in its statement. Some twenty jurisdictions follow this theory.

Implied Warranties

Implied warranties are more troubling because they arise out of factual situations and assumptions and are imposed on the seller as a matter of law. The implied warranty of merchantability is the seller's promise that the goods will be fit for their ordinary use—food will be edible, a car can be driven, an air conditioner will cool. The words of the statute are

> Unless excluded or modified, a warranty that the goods shall be merchantable is implied in a contract for their sale if the seller is a merchant with respect to goods of that kind. Sec. 2-314(1). . . . seller must be a merchant to warrant merchantability. . . . [(4) adds] although a seller may not be a "merchant" as to the goods in question, if he states generally that they are "guaranteed" the provisions of this section may furnish a guide to the content of the resulting express warranty.

This has particular significance in the case of secondhand sales and has further significance in limiting the effect of fine-print disclaimer clauses where their effect would be inconsistent with large-print assertions of "guaranteed." Therefore, although the statue is directly applicable to the car dealer as a merchant, the man who sells his car to his neighbor comes under the statute only by analogy.

This section also states that "the serving of food or drink to be consumed on the premises or elsewhere is a sale." This is to allow persons who have been injured by harmful food to recover. Earlier cases held that serving food was a "service" not a "sale." This distinction still appears in other "service areas." Thus, in a case where someone received an injurious blood transfusion, he could not recover on an implied warranty, because it was not for a sale. And where a purchaser tried to recover for faulty repair to his camera, it was held that repairs are services, not sales, and the UCC implied warranties were not applicable.

Cases of implied warranty of food should make a carefree diner tremble. Thus, a Massachusetts court held that there is no implied warranty that fish chowder will be free of fish bones. "They are not a foreign substance and do not render chowder unwholesome. Their presence is to be anticipated because no recipe calls for their removal."

In Pennsylvania, however, you can ask the jury whether the seller of chicken pie impliedly warrants that the pie would be free from bones. Should you be so unfortunate as to break a tooth on a cherrystone in a pie in Oregon, you will discover that because the stone is not a foreign substance in the pie, there has been no implied warranty of use or ordinary consumption. On the other hand, if your tooth is broken by a "hard unyielding substance" in a hamburger bun in Georgia, you can maintain an action.

Thus, the supplier of food is not a full insurer of the diner's digestion. He does extend the implied warranty of merchantability, but only for its wholesomeness. If some dangerous part of the raw produce, such as a pit or bone slips in, it is in several jurisdictions considered natural rather than foreign, and recovery is disallowed.

An article on the subject of air conditioner warranties states the general rule to be, "even in the absence of an express warranty, the seller of an air conditioner warrants impliedly that it will operate properly and that it will reasonably cool the area for which it was designed." Cases to this effect are found in nine jurisdictions. Where a contract stated that the unit was guaranteed to be fully satisfactory for five years and the motor for one year, it was held that the express warranty did not avoid the implied warranty of fitness. The court said that "satisfaction" could have no other meaning than satisfaction for the purpose intended by the buyer. However, courts have held that "unconditionally guaranteed to maintain a certain temperature" did not make the manufacturer liable for the cost of repairs necessitated by a flood which submerged the machine. In an Arizona case the company had allegedly warranted health benefits from the air conditioner. The court found, however, that there was insufficient evidence of the warranty and of the breach of it to allow recovery.

Section 2-314(2) describes some of the attributes of merchantability: "Goods to be merchantable must be at least such as . . . (c) are fit for the ordinary purposes for which such goods are used; and (f) conform to the promises or affirmations of fact made on the container or label if any." This paragraph applies:

> wherever there is a label or container on which representations are made, even though the original contract, either by express terms or usage of trade, may not have required either the labeling or the representation. This follows from the general application of good faith which requires that a buyer should not be placed in the position of reselling or using goods delivered under false representation appearing on the package or container.

Section 2-315 covers the implied warranty of fitness for a particular purpose. "Where the seller at the time of contracting has reason to know any particular purpose for which the goods are required and that the buyer is relying on the seller's skill or judgment to select or furnish suitable goods, there is, unless excluded or modified, an implied warranty that the goods should be fit for such purpose." The crucial distinction between the implied warranty of merchantability and the implied warranty of fitness lies in the manner in which they may be disclaimed. The warranty of merchantability covers ordinary use; warranty of fitness covers a particular use. This is generally a question of fact. For instance, is the use of a logchain to tow cars an ordinary or a particular use? Moreover, the buyer's reliance on the seller's judgment must be proved. For example, when a buyer wanted a scale which would be certified by the state to be used in state contracts, he wrote the seller demanding a specific model. The buyer made his own choice and was relying on his own judgment in his request and could not recover against the seller when later the state refused to certify the scale.

Under prior law the existence of a brand name or a patent was sufficient to exclude warranty of fitness for a particular purpose. This is no longer true under the UCC. "The mere fact that the article purchased has a particular patent or trade name is not sufficient to indicate the non-reliance if the article has been recommended by the seller as adequate for the buyer's purposes. It is merely one of the facts to be considered in determining whether the buyer relied on the seller's judgment."

Any article may carry one or more of the three warranties: express, implied of merchantability, and implied of fitness for a particular purpose. The seller has traditionally defended himself by three lines of argument: (1) exclusion and modification of warranties, (2) cumulation and conflict of warranties, and (3) absence of privity. The UCC is more consumer-oriented than the prior case law, and courts now seem to be liberalizing their approach. The UCC comments, "the whole purpose of the law of warranty is to determine what it is the seller has in essence agreed to sell." It adds,

> expressed warranties rest on "dickered" aspects of the individual bargain and go so clearly to the essence of that bargain that words of disclaimer in a form are repugnant to the basic "dickered" terms. The implied warranties rest so clearly on a common factual situation or set of conditions that no particular action or language is necessary to evidence them and they will rise in such situations unless unmistakably negated.

Section 2-314, Comment 1, continues, "the warranty of merchantability, wherever it is normal, is so commonly taken for granted that its exclusion from the contract is a matter of threatening surprise and therefore requiring special precaution."

The present language of the code is confusing, however, in that Section 2-316(2) says "to exclude or modify the implied warranty of merchantability or any part of it the language must mention merchantability and in the case of a writing must be conspicuous, and to exclude or modify any implied warranty of fitness the exclusion must be by a writing and conspicuous." Whereas Section 3 reads, "unless circumstances indicate otherwise all implied warranties are excluded by expressions such as 'as is'." Commentators have questioned whether an "as is" statement would exclude the implied warranty of merchantability when Section 2 calls for the use of the word *merchantability;* they suggest that the cautious seller, if he wishes to exclude that warranty, still include the word *merchantability* in his disclaimer.

A Pennsylvania case held that to exclude or disclaim the warranty of merchantability, the person who is disclaiming must use statutory expressions or clear and definite words revealing that the warranty of merchantability is being excluded.

The purpose of Section 316, Comment 1 adds, is "to protect the buyer from unexpected and unbargained language of disclaimer by denying the effect to such language when inconsistent with language of expressed warranty and permitting the exclusion of implied warranties only by conspicuous language or other circumstances which protect the buyer from surprise."

The following Section (2-317) states that warranties, whether expressed or implied, shall be construed as consistent with each other and as cumulative as possible. If not, the intention of the parties shall prevail. This is to prevent the seller from drafting such a clause as, "this warranty being expressly in lieu of all other warranties expressed or implied," when his representations have led the buyer to assume he has received a warranty of merchantability, that is, the implied warranty of fitness for ordinary use.

Car Warranties

Probably the most extensive litigation on disclaimers and conflict of warranties has involved the standard New Motor Vehicle Warranty. This document was drafted by the Automobile Manufacturers Association and has subsequently been adopted by all the major manufacturers and the majority of dealers. The pertinent part of the warranty is the following:

We warrant each new motor vehicle sold by us to be free from defects in material and workmanship under normal use and service, our obligation under this wararnty being limited to making good at our place of business without charge for replacement, labor, any part or parts thereof, including all equipment or trade accessories (except tires) supplied with the motor vehicle which shall within ninety (90) days after making delivery of such vehicle to the original purchaser or before such vehicle has been driven four thousand (4,000) miles, whichever event shall first occur, be returned to us with transportation charges prepaid, and which our examinations shall disclose to our satisfaction to have been thus defective, this warranty being expressly in lieu of all other warranties expressed or implied and of all other obligations or liabilities on our part, and we neither assume nor authorize any other person to assume for us any liability in connection with our sale of motor vehicles.

Older cases held, and in some jurisdictions it still seems to be the law, that this standard warranty was the exclusive basis for recovery and the buyer could not recover on any implied warranty, whether or not it was inconsistent with the express warranty.

Because the express warranty was only to replace any part for the first ninety days, the harsh and illusory quality of the disclaimer came to light in personal injury cases or in cases where the consequences of the damage were far greater than the replacement of a particular defective part. Courts were generally unwilling to impose such a narrow reading and avoided the literal terms by saying that it was not sufficiently conspicuous, that it was not brought to buyers' attention, that it was against public policy, or that any warranty may exist contemporaneously with the express warranty unless wholly inconsistent with it.

In *Sutter* v. *St. Clair Motors, Inc.* an Illinois court found nothing in the express warranty or its "in lieu of" clause which specifically disclaimed the implied warranty of merchantability. The unlucky purchaser of an Edsel that broke down on the day of delivery, finally towed the car to the dealer's place of business and demanded his money back. The disclaimer, which the dealer argued excluded him from liability, was either inconspicuous or hidden. This attempt to negate an implied warranty, the court said, was contrary to public policy and unconscionable.

In another case of simple pecuniary loss, the owner of a Rambler claimed that he had been induced to buy the car because of advertisements in magazines, in newspapers, and over television and radio, all proclaiming the Rambler as "trouble free, economical and built and manufactured with a high quality of workmanship." The plaintiff's car, however, had a defective oil pump and its doors were out of line. Its estimated worth was $1,200 and had been bought for $2,700. The court allowed recovery, saying, "the defenseless consumer who has suffered substantial pecuniary losses by national advertising of false claims should be protected, regardless of lack of privity."

An Iowa court also read the express warranty and disclaimer as not inconsistent with the implied warranty of merchantability, and therefore the standard car warranty did not relieve either the manufacturer or dealer of the duty under the implied warranty. In this case, the new car caught fire ten days after it had been bought and was totally ruined. The manufacturer tried to argue that his warranty would be effective only if the purchaser paid transportation costs for shipping the car back to the factory. Under these circumstances the court found this futile and said that after total destruction of the car the purchaser is relieved of the condition of returning the defective parts.

A Missouri court concluded that the question of whether the disclaimer in the warranty was part of the bargain was an affirmative defense that the dealer had to plead and prove. It went on to find a complete failure of proof that the parties had done so when it found that the dealer's warranty was delivered not with the contract for sale, but two days later, with the delivery of the car.

In South Carolina the dealer had the burden of establishing that the disclaimer in the standard warranty was shown to the purchaser at the time of the sale, if he, the dealer, wished to protect himself by adopting the manufacturer's warranty and its limitations. This he was unable to do.

A landmark case in this field is *Henningson* v. *Bloomfield Motors,* in which a New Jersey court allowed the ultimate purchaser to recover regardless of the lack of privity of contract between the purchaser and the manufacturer or the existence of the express warranty. The injured party was the wife of the car owner, and the new car came with the standard warranty. The court struck down the disclaimer as void and against public policy, "because the automobile purchaser's capacity for bargaining is so grossly inequal and the disclaimer to this warranty is a studied effort to frustrate the protection afforded by an implied warranty of merchantability." It based its reasoning on modern marketing practices which left the buyer completely dependent on the manufacturer, unable to bargain for a warranty, no sale being possible except under the limited uniform warranty of the manufacturers' association. It said that the controlling principle was, "When the manufacturer puts a new automobile in the stream of trade and promotes its purchase to the public, an implied warranty that it is reasonably suitable for use as such accompanies it into the hands of the ultimate purchaser from the dealer."

In *Rose* v. *Chrysler Motors* the purchaser of a new car sued the manufacturer and the seller for breach of a standard new-car warranty when the car was severely damaged by fire. The manufacturer tried to argue that the vehicle itself was not warranted in its entirety. Only each separate part was warranted individually and independent of any other part. Therefore, the cost of dismantling the car and the damage to other parts caused by the defective part, or the loss and destruction of a part were not the manufacturer's responsibility, but were costs to be borne by the purchaser. The California court rejected this argument, saying, "The standard manufacturer's new vehicle warranty must not be given an interpretation which will provide only an illusory protection, and which considered in context with the basic warranty made would be tantamount to a fraudulent defeat of the purchaser's natural understanding." The court added, that a standard warranty which excludes all implied warranties does not exclude the obligation which flows from non-performance of a written agreement to replace or properly adjust all defective parts. The district court of appeals, in affirming the judgment against the manufacturer and the seller, agreed that the warranty of the manufacturer and the seller extended to restoring all parts that had been damaged by the fire from the defective wiring, so that the plaintiff could recover the full amount of the damages, not simply the cost of replacing faulty wire.

In another California case the purchaser of a truck discovered that it suffered from "galloping." The court found an express warranty in the purchase order which was insufficiently disclaimed by the standard car warranty. Having found the express warranty, the court did not have to reach the questions of privity. The plaintiff had assumed that the dealer, not the manufacturer, was the one giving the warranty, but this, according to the court, was sufficient reliance, even if he was mistaken as to who was giving the warranty. Moreover, the court found that the purchaser had given sufficient notice of the defect to the defendant by repeatedly complaining of the defect and returning the truck to the shop, requesting repair. Because the manufacturer had had ample opportunity to make good its warranty and had failed to do so, the purchaser could recover for breach of warranty. The court measured the damages so as to cover lost profits as well as purchase price, but stated that the recovery was in breach of warranty and was measured in contract terms, not an action in strict liability, which would be measured in terms of tort damages.

In breach-of-warranty cases courts have differed in their interpretation of the written terms of the warranty. A Missouri court held that it was a fatal failure to comply with conditions of the warranty when the purchaser did not return the defective parts to the factory for inspection. In a North Carolina case, the purchaser could not recover because he had disregarded the terms of the warranty when he failed to give the dealer adequate notice and refused to allow him to repair the defect.

In *Haas* v. *Buick Motors Division, General Motors Corporation,* it was held incumbent on the purchaser to demand that the manufacturer determine the cause of the fire to establish that the defective part was the cause. Failure to do so prevented recovery in a case where the purchaser's wife saw a fire coming from the dashboard which proceeded to melt the dashboard, smoke the windows, and render the car a total loss. The court found no evidence proving that the defect caused the fire. This information would only be supplied by the dealer's or manufacturer's inspection.

On the other hand, the condition precedent was disregarded in *Allen* v. *Brown,* where the standard warranty required that the buyer locate the defective part and return it to the manufacturer. It was sufficient that he complained of its violent vibrations and noise and returned several times to the dealer for repairs. Such action by the buyer made it the dealer's duty to find and replace the parts.

The statement "acknowledgment by the Ford Motor Company to be defective" has been read to mean that "it does leave the matter to the uncontrolled judgment of the manufacturer, but should be understood to include any defect which actually existed regardless of the manufacturer's determination to the contrary."

The measure of damages, the possibility of consequential damages, and the extent of liability of the manufacturer and dealer under the warranty varies from court to court. In *Norway* v. *Root* the warranty was held to be only to repair or replace the defective part, so that the manufacturer had only to replace the starter switch, not to pay for the damage from the fire started by the defective switch. In *Payne* v. *Valley Motor Sales, Inc.* the warranty was specifically limited to replacement, so the general rule of allowing consequential damages did not apply. The court said that the plaintiff failed to meet the burden of proof and concluded with respect to interpretations of limitations on warranties that any change must come from the legislature. The general measure of damages as stated in *Rose* v. *Chrysler Motors* is the difference between the value of goods at the time of delivery and the value of goods if they had been what they were warranted to be. This is called the benefit-of-the-bargain measure, as opposed to a tort concept of reimbursing the plaintiff for what he has suffered.

Courts in general have held that the dealer has adopted the manufacturer's warranty with its burden and its benefits.

Limitation on Recovery

If it appears from the foregoing that the courts most often allow disgruntled purchasers to recover from every dealer and manufacturer, we should correct the impression with some examples of vital elements to a buyer's cause of action. The buyer must prove that the warranty covers the defect that caused the injury. It is insufficient to purchase a bar of soap warranted 99.44 per cent pure and then sue for an eye injury if the buyer does not establish that the soap was the probable cause of the injury. That is, the buyer must prove that the soap was less than 99.44 per cent pure, and that it was this broken promise of purity which was the cause of the eye injury. The buyer must also prove that the goods were defective when delivered. For instance, one plaintiff was mowing his lawn with a mower purchased at defendant's store. An unknown object thrown out by the mower hit his son in the eye, causing injury and later loss of sight in that eye. In his suit recovery was denied because the court held he failed to meet his burden of establishing that the mower was not of merchantable quality when delivered.

Similarly, the seller can defend by showing that the loss resulted from some other event occurring after he delivered the goods. Care in the manufacturing process, or selection of the goods is evidence relevant to the question of whether the warranty was, in fact, broken. Buyer's steps, following an examination of the goods, which ought to have indicated the defect complained of, can be shown as matter bearing on whether the breach itself was the cause of the injury. Buyer's action, such as retention of the article or delayed and insufficient notice, may be grounds for waiver of the warranty or grounds for contending that the conditions of the warranty were not met.

The seller's other defense is lack of privity. Privity was a creation of the nineteenth century, still firmly entrenched in case law but under heavy judicial attack, which required a party to be under contract to allow recovery between a buyer and a seller. Therefore, if the manufacturer had sold to a dealer who resold to a purchaser, there was no direct contract from seller to buyer and the buyer could not recover directly from the manufacturer. His route was to sue the dealer and recover, and then have the dealer sue the manufacturer to indemnify him. The history of the "assault on the citadel" of privity is beyond the scope of this chapter, but it is apparent in the present marketing situation that the buyer does rely on the manufacturer's ads and brochures and that the duty of the manufacturer to provide safe products does not stop with the purchaser but extends to others reasonably intended to use them.

Courts have differed widely in the extent to which they adhere to or disregard privity. Section 2-318 of the UCC reads, "A seller's warranty whether express or implied extends to any natural person who is in the family or household of his buyer or who is a guest in the home if it is reasonable to expect that such a person may use, consume or be affected by the goods and who is injured in person by breach of the warranty. A seller may not exclude or limit the operation of this section." Comment 2 explains that the purpose of this section is to "give the buyer's family, household or guests the benefit of the same warranty which the buyer received in the contract of sale, thereby freeing any such beneficiaries from any technical rules as to privity." Except for the relationships listed in Section 2-318, the UCC is neutral with respect to privity, and states follow prior law. Generally courts have liberalized the protection toward the consumer and restrict it when a nonconsumer has sought recovery. Employees are often held outside the bounds of privity, as not reasonably foreseen to be intended users. A corporate successor is definitely not one for whom the UCC extends exceptions to privity. The critical thing is that the injured plaintiff bring himself into the category of relationships to the buyer listed in Section 2-318. Then he must demonstrate that the buyer had a warranty from the seller.

The courts do not have to reach the question of privity if there is a warranty like the standard car warranty, which accompanies the product and by its express terms runs in favor of the injured person. Privity is also not necessary when the action is based on fraud, deceit, misrepresentation, or other torts by the seller, because these actions do not involve contractual duties.

The prevailing view is that in an action for breach of warranty, privity is a necessary prerequisite for recovery. There are, however, three major exceptions. Privity is immaterial where the defect causing the injury was in a food. This is mostly based on the public sentiment that the consumer can do little to protect himself from harmful food, and it is in the interest of all to protect human life, by imposing a duty on the supplier of food to give the public pure and wholesome products.

Some courts have extended this exception to cases involving defective containers of food, such as Coca Cola bottles. Second, privity is unnecessary when the consumer relies on the manufacturer's express representation in advertisements and labels, which have been held to be an express warranty directed at him, the ultimate purchaser. Third, where articles are dangerous to life if defective and are used in or near the body, such as soap or beauty products, the same public policy that has been applied to food is extended to protect the consumer against them.

The most liberal extension of the doctrine of privity is found in Connecticut, where a repairman who was servicing the taillights of a car in the gas station was injured when the owner of the car pushed the reverse button of the automatic transmission. The court found in the massive advertising campaign sufficient material directed at those, like the repairman, to be included in the category of "intended users of the seller and dealer." Similarly, the renter of a golf cart which collapsed was allowed to sue the manufacturer.

In *Randy Knitwear,* a case of economic loss, not personal injury, a New York court decided that traditional privity limitations would be dispensed with in an action for breach of an express warranty by a remote purchaser against a manufacturer who had used advertisements and labels to represent the quality of its shrinkproof goods, which the purchaser read and relied on and which persuaded the purchaser to buy:

> The warranties made by the manufacturer in his advertisements and by the labels on his products are inducements to the ultimate consumers, and the manufacturer ought to be held to strict accountability to any consumer who buys the product in reliance on such representations and later suffers injury because the product proves to be defective or deleterious.

In *Randy Knitwear* v. *American Cyanamid* a New York court said that "the cause of action turned on the representations of the manufacturer, not on the character of the product," so that the likelihood of personal injury was not the basis for granting recovery. Rather, it was the representations in the advertisements and on the labels that the fabrics would not shrink.

Both cases involved express statements in advertisements directed at the ultimate purchaser, who relied on the specific attribute represented to be warranted, and both purchasers were harmed when the attribute was missing. "The existence of a defect means a violation of the representation implicit in the existence of the article in the stream of trade, that it is suitable for the general purpose for whch it is sold and for which such goods are generally appropriate." Good faith or willingness are immaterial. The court found no need to distinguish cases where personal injury resulted from cases where a manufacturer had put a worthless article in the hands of an innocent purchaser who had paid the required price for it. Here, where the defect was unusual lines in the carpet, the damages were only partial, because the purchaser had used the carpet several years.

New Jersey has been willing to extend *Henningson* and *Santor* to cases involving mass-produced housing. Thus, in *Schipper* v. *Levitt & Sons, Inc.,* a court disregarded the traditional rule that warranties of sale are not to be implied in real estate transactions, finding instead an exception in the sale of new housing where the vendor is also the developer and contractor, because the purchaser did rely on an implied representation. The New Jersey court has also extended the breach-of-warranty action to bailment cases. Traditionally, the bailee was liable only for negligence. The court, however, held that leasing agreements give rise to an implied promissory warranty that the leased trucks would be fit. Here an employee of the lessee of the truck sued the lessor for breach of warranty and negligence in maintaining the truck in which the plaintiff was injured because of brake failure. An illustrated booklet provided by Hertz and advertisements by Hertz that Hertz guarantees uninterrupted service and that Hertz provides the first "rent-a-car" guarantee were placed into evidence. Absence of negligence was held no defense to an action in breach of warranty or strict liability.

Strict Liability

California courts, with Chief Justice Traynor writing most of the opinions, have championed the cause of the consumer by imposing strict liability on the manufacturer without regard to privity. Strict liability is a tort concept, but it is closely related to actions for breach of warranty. The seller is not an insurer. To allow recovery the buyer must prove that the product was defective and unreasonably dangerous and that his injuries were caused by the defect. He must also connect the defendant with the product. Some courts require proof that the manufacturer had reason to know that its product would be used without inspection and that the buyer had no reason to be aware of the defect. In *Greeno* v. *Clark Equipment Co.,* where the defendant sold a defective forklift to the plaintiff, the court, in allowing a recovery, commented that the old confusion of the law of warranty should be abandoned and the action for recovery for products liability should be given a new name. Among the jurisdictions adopting strict liability, the courts in several cases have reasoned in terms of a breach of implied warranty of merchantability, but have circumvented the defenses of lack of privity, disclaimers, failure to give notice, and failure to show reliance on a warranty, with the result that we may classify these actions as a separate tort of strict liability, not as a breach of warranty action where recovery has been allowed under one of the exceptions. The practical result of changing the name of the action, then, may not alter the outcome of many cases, where the courts have felt a need to impose liability, but it will simplify the procedure and dispense with the intricacies of the law of warranty.

In the case of *Greenman* v. *Yuba Power Products* a California court said, "The representations that the goods are suitable and safe for their intended use must be regarded as implicit in their presence in the market, not conditioned upon advertisements. Therefore, the manufacturer's liability is 'an enterprise liability' and does not depend upon intricacies of the law of sales, so that the makers of products bear the cost of injury or damage."

The theory behind abandoning such defenses is that a tort duty is involved, not a contract one. The seller cannot contractually alter or disclaim a duty that the law imposes upon him. Moreover, inconsistent express warranties cannot "dilute the seller's duty to refrain from injecting into the stream of commerce goods in a defective condition." This reasoning goes beyond *Randy Knitwear* because it is not the representations in the advertisement which give rise to the cause of action, but the placing of the defective article in the stream of commerce.

On the theory of strict liability, a retailer of cars was held liable even when he had restricted his contractual liability to the immediate purchaser, and even though there was not timely notice under a theory of breach of warranty. It was immaterial for recovery in strict liability because it was a tort concept. Similarly, no privity was necessary for recovery in *Mitchell* v. *Miller* when the defendant dealer's automobile killed the decedent because its transmission failed to lock in park. Section 402A of the *Tentative Draft of the Restatement of Torts* reads as follows:

(1) One who sells any product in a defective condition unreasonably dangerous to the user or consumer, or to his property, is subject to liability for physical harm thereby caused to the ultimate user or consumer, or to his property if (a) the seller is engaged in the business of selling such product, and (b) it is expected to and does reach the user or consumer without substantial change in the condition in which it is sold.

(2) The rule stated in Subsection (1) applies although, (a) the seller has exercised all possible care in the preparation and sale of his product, and (b) the user or consumer has not bought the product from or entered into any contractual relation with the seller.

Depending on the circumstances, proof of the defect occurring after the product left the defendant's hands may shift the liability from the manufacturer to the dealer or to the retailer. A manufacturer, however, may be held strictly liable if he was responsible for discovery of the defect and did not discover it.

Strict liability actions have mostly been for personal injury and wrongful death cases. To a lesser extent they have been used to recover damage to property other than the product itself. In New Jersey strict liability has been used to recover the amount of payments on the product, but in California it has been stressed that damages for the amount of payments on the purchase price and lost profits can be awarded only in breach of warranty, not in an action in strict liability.

Dean Prosser, a leading expert on the law of torts, who is very much in favor of a judicial policy which protects consumers, thinks that the concepts of warranty introduce intricacies of the law of sales into what is more reasonably considered a tort liability. He prefers to discard the word *warranty,* with all its contract connotations, and speak in terms of strict liability. He comments that if a consumer is injured because of a product, it should be immaterial whether the defendant actually represented the product to be something in an advertisement that the plaintiff read and relied on. Instead, in Judge Traynor's words, it is the "presence of the goods in the stream of commerce" which carries with it the implied promise that the object is fit for the general use intended.

But until most of the courts in the nation adopt his viewpoint, the action of breach of warranty is hindered by the complexity of the law of sales.

FTC REGULATIONS

Guarantees and warranties are widely used to attract customers to a sale. They are more than the seller's representations of the qualities of his goods. They are held out as a form of buyer's insurance for continued satisfactory performance of the article. The consumer considers them to be one more reason to pick a particular brand. The words *guarantee* and *warranty* imply the reliability of the manufacturer or seller and durability of the product. They lull the purchaser into a sense of security, providing the cautious with the impression that he need lose nothing if he discovers that he is not pleased with the product. For that reason guarantees are extensively advertised and used competitively in sales promotion campaigns. But, as with any effective sales technique, guarantees are often misused and manipulated by the unscruplous at the expense and frustration of the hapless consumer, who discovers too late that he has bought inferior goods and then cannot get satisfaction from the illusory guarantee.

The FTC, in its regulation of deceptive advertising, has uncovered and prohibited many deceptive guarantees. In addition to its orders, stipulations, and advisory opinions, it has issued *Guides Against Deceptive Advertising Of Guarantees* (reprinted in Appendix VIII) to outline its policy. Basically, its policy is one of truth in advertising, but imaginative layouts, fine print, and ambiguities of the English language have required the commission to outline more fully what it means by deception and truth in advertising guarantees.

The Nature and Extent of the Guarantee

The most common deception is the large advertisement stating or implying an unconditional guarantee followed later by the disclosure that there are many restrictions preventing the person claming the guarantee from qualifying under the terms of the guarantee. The guide states, "In general, any guarantee in advertising shall *clearly* and *conspicuously disclose—the nature and extent of the guarantee.*"

Car dealers have been notorious in their exploitation of guarantees. For example, several Washington, D.C., car dealers advertised such slogans as "Guaranteed 100% parts and labor for one full year at no extra cost," "Positively guaranteed 100% to your satisfaction," "Famous warranty," "This 90-day, 100% no cost parts or labor warranty is offered to you," "Up to 10,000 mile warranty available on all cars." The cars were actually sold "as is," with provisions to that effect in each purchase order and bill of sale. If there was a purported guarantee, the purchaser was generally charged additionally for it. The purchaser would not realize this because it was disguised as a handling or delivery charge. Other undisclosed limitations include the requirement that all the repair work be done in the dealer's shop. One dealer advertised a 100 per cent guarantee and a nintey-day guarantee for parts and labor but did not give it on its used cars. Occasionally, it was given on its late models. Often the guarantee and a ninety-day guarantee for parts and labor were not given on uniform terms, varying with the amount paid for the warranty and the demands made by the individual customer.

Hidden costs can make the guarantee illusory. A burial vault company guaranteed the durability of its vaults. But the guarantee was good only if the customer disinterred and returned it to the manufacturer at his own expense.

A television repair shop advertised that it serviced television sets in the home for only $1 and that its repairmen were factory-trained and all work and repairs were fully guaranteed. However, the shop did not repair television sets in the home for any amount. Instead it removed them to its shop, and if the owner did not have repairs made there after receiving the cost estimate, the company refused to redeliver the set unless the owner paid $13.50 for pick-up, redelivery, and estimate.

A guarantee accompanying home building materials which only replaces parts and does not cover the cost of installation can leave the owner with a large bill. A television ad said, "each Coral Stone [used in the renovations] is backed by the manufacturer's lifetime guarantee not to chip or crack." What the ad did not disclose was that the guarantee merely obligated the company to provide the owner without cost with new materials to replace any which had cracked or splintered from the weather. No provisions were made to install the new material in place of the defective material in the house wall.

A sprinkler cannot be advertised as guaranteed in catalogues or even proclaimed as guaranteed on its cartons if the guarantee inside the package accompanying the sprinkler is for one year only and requires the purchaser to pay the transportation costs of returning the sprinkler to the company for repairs. The purchaser is entitled to think that the word *guaranteed,* without words of limitations, means an unconditional guarantee, and manufacturers must not mislead him by insufficient disclosure.

A more ingenious scheme was invented by a maker of watch bands. The respondent had attached his watch bands to cards covered with transparent plastic that in turn were attached to display placards or racks. On the display material, in a large and prominent manner, the bands were promoted as unconditionally guaranteed or fully guaranteed, without words of limitation. When the purchaser read the fine print on the back of the card within the package after it had been removed from the placard or rack, he was informed that the guarantee lasted for one year only and that a 35-cent service charge was required for repairs. The fact that the back of the cards attached to the watch bands contained the guaranteed limitations was held not to constitute sufficient disclosure, because the prospective purchaser would have to remove the watch band and card from the display before he could examine the back of the card. The commission agreed that the broad guarantee claims were misleading and rejected the defenses that the volume of sales from the placards was insignificant and that the false statement was obviously false, saying, "The fact that a false statement may be obviously false to those who are trained and experienced does not change its character or take away its power to deceive others less experienced."

Another case involving insufficient disclosure of the nature and extent of the guarantee is *Clinton Watch Co.* v. *FTC*. This company advertised a lifetime guarantee without disclosure of the $1 service charge. The advertisement had read, "all movement parts guaranteed for life never to break." The slips accompanying the watches stated on their faces "Guaranteed All-Inclusive," and on the reverse they printed the service charge.

An advertisement addressed to catalogue houses that accompanied watches and costume jewelry guaranteeing in writing for one full year and guaranteeing "imported Swiss movement," was held to be deceptive where the ultimate purchaser from the catalogue had to pay a service charge.

Another deceptive practice occurs when the manufacturer advertises its products as unconditionally guaranteed but the purchaser receives neither a guarantee certificate nor information of the nature and conditions of the guarantee and the manner in which the guarantor will honor it.

The commission does not prohibit guarantees which include service charges if the amount of the charges are clearly and conspicuously disclosed in immediate conjunction with the guarantee. Proximity of the disclosure and the words of limitation are important. A television station was advised that it would be improper in commercials for local car dealers to mention a manufacturer's guarantee; instead, such advertisers should refer the viewers to the manufacturer's national advertising for a description of the guarantee, because all material terms must be conspicuously and clearly stated in the same advertisement.

Initial Deception

The courts and commission are now faced with the question of whether any discrepancy between the advertised guarantee and the guarantee certificate is a deception. A prevalent practice is to advertise an unlimited guarantee to attract customers and to enhance the corporate image, and then, when the customers have responded to the bait by ordering by mail or arriving in person, to disclose the true limitations of the guarantee. This has been termed *initial deception*. Difficulties arise in proving whether any consumer was induced to purchase in reliance on the guarantee, and whether the company honored the terms of the advertised guarantee or of the guarantee certificate.

Montgomery Ward Company was recently sued by the commission on this question and was found to be advertising deceptively. It had advertised in forty-three newspapers between 1957 and 1964 that its products, such as drills, sewing machines, automobile parts, and shrubbery, were unconditionally guaranteed. The certificate of guarantee which accompanied the purchase, however, contained limiting terms that were not disclosed in the advertised guarantee. For example, a sewing machine advertised as being guaranteed for twenty years had a certificate showing a repair guarantee for one year and a replacement guarantee for nineteen years, with charges for transportation and labor. A water heater advertised as guaranteed for ten years or fifteen years had a certificate which prorated the guarantee during the last half of the guarantee period and only guaranteed the water tank for the first year. Labor and installation were charged to the purchaser and the purchaser had to adhere to certain maintenance requirements. The automotive parts guarantee advertised remanufactured engines for 4,000 miles or ninety days. The certificate disclosed that the installation, the check-up, the type of vehicle, and the use to which it was put were all limitations on the guarantee. The certificate for the brake shoes called for a fee of $2 for installation, and the guarantee went only to the person for whom the original installation was performed and only applied when the customer had obtained a complete brake overhaul. Further, the shock absorbers required a service charge.

The company had an internal policy to honor the guarantees in whatever form they appeared in the advertisements, and they reminded their employees to comply with the *Guides Against Deceptive Advertising*. The hearing examiner found a discrepancy between the advertisement and the certificates, but granted a motion for dismissal because he found no evidence of deception. The commission adopted the hearing examiner's finding of a discrepancy but disagreed with the examiner's finding of no deception, concluding that Wards had violated the act by its advertisements. In an opinion by Commissioner Jones, with Commissioners Elman and Riley dissenting, the commission said,

> A company cannot advertise a product as guaranteed and attach to the product the actual text of the guarantee, which covers that prod-

uct and which contains numerous limiting terms and conditions not disclosed in the advertisement, and then defend the proceeding brought by the FTC against the deceptive ads by asserting that as a matter of practice, not disclosed to its customers, it would, in fact, honor the ad guaranteed if the claims that were presented to it fell outside the limitations fixed by specific guarantee certificate. The test is capacity to deceive, not actual deception.

The Seventh Circuit unanimously affirmed the commission, in an opinion by Judge Hastings, holding that a willingness to live up to an advertised unconditional guarantee broader than the one actually provided with the product does not make the advertisement true and is no defense to the charge of discrepancy between advertised guarantees and the guarantee certificate. Overstatement of a guarantee in one's ad is illegal deception, even if the guarantees are honored as advertised and even if this policy of performance is communicated to the buyers. The court believed that buyers are still apt to be deterred from attempting to enforce the rights going beyond the warranty certificate limitations. The burden of proof was on Montgomery Ward to show that prospective customers were not deceived, and the company failed to present evidence of no deception. The court repeated that actual deception was not necessary, that it was the likelihood of deception that was important.

In another case on initial deception, *Western Radio* v. *FTC,* the hearing examiner said that because magazine ads that the public saw induced the purchase, the first impression of the prospective purchaser is the determining factor on the question of deception with reference to the guarantee even if later material mailed to the purchaser disclosed all the conditions and limitations. Here the company had advertised a one-year guarantee on a radio transmitter, neglecting to mention a $1.50 service charge.

A third case on initial deception was *Sibert* v. *FTC.* A seller of a water filtration system advertised a ten-year guarantee, but disclosed in circulars to the customers responding to the ad that the guarantee was conditioned upon a $30 service charge. The $30 approximated the amount the respondents had paid for the materials, so the seller did not lose much. In addition, the customer had to take the trouble and bear the expense of dismantling and shipping this 100-pound, 4-foot water filtration unit. The guarantee, therefore, was of little value to him. Commissioner Jones, in an examination of the entire record said, "the initial deception was not cured by the fact that the respondents disclosed the limits elsewhere."

In *Interstate Builders, Inc.* salesmen of a company selling aluminum siding were making oral guarantees broader than the written terms.

Commissioner Jones found two possible violations: (1) where the customers heard an oral guarantee and then received a second written one, (2) where the customers heard an oral guarantee and received no written guarantee. The commission held that the salesmen had actual or apparent authority from the company, with the result that the company was responsible for their representations.

In the first instance the salesmen spoke of an unlimited guarantee, whereas the written guarantee was unconditional with respect to labor and materials. This was held not to be a deceptive practice, because although conceivably a guarantee could be more extensive, guaranteeing a time of completion or guaranteeing against accident, it could be reasonably expected to provide only labor and materials.

In the second instance, because the written contracts stated that the company was not responsible for any representation not contained in the contract, it was a deceptive practice to give an oral guarantee but no written one. The company provided proof that on one instance it honored the oral guarantee, but that was considered insufficient to establish a defense. Moreover, in light of *Montgomery Ward,* it is no defense to a charge of a deceptive discrepancy between the guarantee as advertised and as written in the guarantee certificate that the company claimed to honor all oral guarantees as spoken. The commission ordered the company to cease and desist misrepresenting guarantees and to take affirmative steps to prevent its sales personnel from overstating the guarantees.

The courts have occasionally expressed doubt about the commission's standards of deception. In *Benrus Watch Co.* v. *FTC* the ad said "fully guaranteed watches," and the certificates of guarantee stated the terms, but not clearly. Prior to 1959 the company had imposed a $1 service charge, but then it abandoned its policy and proceeded to grant a three-year guarantee without a service charge. The hearing examiner found no deception. The commission reversed, holding that there was deception, and ordered that the nature and extent of the guarantee and the manner in which the guarantor would perform must be clearly and conspicuously disclosed. The court on appeal accepted the commission's findings "even though [it] maintained some doubt as to whether the matter complained of had any real tendency seriously to deceive anyone. We think the Commission might well have upheld the examiner in dismissing the charge relating to guarantees."

In *Brite Manufacturing Co.* the guarantee charge was dismissed because there was no substantial evidence establishing that respondent's watchbands were not fully guaranteed. Some affirmative evidence in the record demonstrated that the respondent had honored the guarantee without qualification. The case is distinguished in the *Montgomery Ward* case because the ads in *Brite* were at the point of sale, whereas the ads in *Montgomery Ward* were an initial deception followed later by disclosure of the limitations in the guarantee.

Product, Part, and Characteristics

Disclosure of the nature and extent of the guarantee means disclosure of what products or part of the product is guaranteed, and what characteristics or properties of the designated product or part are covered by, or excluded from, the guarantee. For example, between 1959 and 1961, Sand & Streiffe, Inc., importers of binoculars, opera glasses, and telescopes, furnished printed insert sheets to be distributed in catalogues. These sheets advertised lifetime guarantees without any language of modification disclosing which characteristic or properties of the binoculars were covered and what one claiming under the guarantee must do before the guarantee was honored. This the hearing examiner found deceptive in that the respondents were representing directly or by implication that their products were unconditionally guaranteed. The commission adopted the hearing examiner's initial order to cease and desist.

The advertisements of a sewing machine suggested that the entire machine was guaranteed, whereas, in fact, only the motor and the motor accessories were guaranteed for one year, and other parts were not guaranteed at all. The advertisements were terminated by a consent order.

Duration

The Sand & Streiffe guarantee was also deceptive on not disclosing its duration. The company advertised a twenty-five-year money-back guarantee that was limited by small print reading "if returned during sale." Because most sales last only a matter of hours, the purported twenty-five-year guarantee was limited to a few hours time. Further, a dealer or manufacturer cannot advertise his wares as unconditionally guaranteed if he limits the guarantee to three or six months.

Claimant's Duties

The guarantee must also set forth what, if anything, anyone claiming under the guarantee must do before the guarantor fulfills his obligation under the guarantee. In the *Champion Products* case the company's advertised guarantee was deceptive in that it had not revealed that a dissatisfied purchaser must submit performance data concerning the operation of the motor vehicle in which the products were used before a refund was considered. The consent order stated that the company must stop advertising "money-back guarantee" unless it clearly described all the terms and conditions of the guarantee and the manner in which the guarantor will perform.

The Guarantor's Manner of Performance

The guarantor must make clear how he will honor the guarantee. Does he intend to repair the article, to replace it, or to refund the purchase price, to the purchaser's satisfaction? Often the purchaser assumes a guarantee means replacement or refund at his option, only to discover that the guarantee is narrow and hedged by conditions precedent. The Montgomery Ward certificates and the car dealer's practices described previously are only two examples of the many times a discrepancy occurs between the purchaser's assumption of the guarantor's promises and the guarantor's actual performance.

Identity of the Guarantor

Another omission on many guarantees is the guarantor's identity. This becomes an increasing problem with a proliferated chain of distribution. The consumer can waste time and even be delayed beyond the time limit of the guarantee because he does not know whether to pursue the retailer, the wholesaler, or the manufacturer. Courts require notice for breach-of-warranty actions and often find that failure to give notice to the proper party is fatal for recovery.

Where the proper identity of the guarantor was not disclosed in many of the ads, the commission has issued cease and desist orders.

Name Brand Distributors advertised its merchandise as unconditionally guaranteed, but admitted in a FTC hearing that neither it nor the manufacturer guaranteed these articles unconditionally. It was required to cease and desist the practice.

Another practice involving the identity of the guarantor is the use of endorsements by major magazines. *Good Housekeeping* advertised "Good Housekeeping Seal," "Good Housekeeping guarantee," "every product guaranteed as advertised" extensively throughout the magazine. Readers were alleged to believe that the guarantee in question was an unlimited one, but inconspicuously, on page 6 of the magazine, the guarantee was stated to be an undertaking to investigate any advertised product and to replace or refund any product found to be defective. Also, where manufacturers used the *Good Housekeeping* insignia in their advertisements, purchasers were said to assume the product to have been tested by *Good Housekeeping,* and this was not the case in several instances.

Unauthorized use of insignia and emblems of *Good Housekeeping* and *Parents' Magazine* occurred in *Tri-State Sewing Machine.* The purchaser assumes that the magazine is backing up the product and that he can turn to the magazine if he is dissatisfied, whereas the magazine has in no way put its name behind the reliability of the product. This deception also occurs when an unknown company imitates the name of a well-known company. The consumer, relying on his familiarity with the name, purchases inferior goods and then finds that he was mistaken as to the identity of the manufacturer. By this sleight of hand all his assumptions of the existence of a guarantor vanish.

Pro-Rata Adjustments

If the guarantees are to be adjusted by the guarantor on a pro-rata basis, the advertisement of these guarantees should clearly disclose the fact. For instance, a guarantee was advertised as "All Champion customer built recapped tires carry a 9-month unconditional guarantee." Any tire failing to give satisfactory service, regardless of the cause, within this time would be replaced at half the list price. The commission found that the guarantee was merely an agreement to supply another tire at half the price, and because practically all the tires were of inferior quality, supplying a second tire was of little or no practical benefit to the purchaser; this was particularly true because he was compelled to pay an additional sum to obtain the second tire.

In *U.S. Bedding Company* a respondent was ordered to cease and desist from placing in dealers' hands newspaper mats representing falsely that the mattresses carried ten-year guarantees, when actually they were only fully guaranteed for one year. After the first year an adjustment charge had to be paid for the time the mattresses had been used.

A pro-rated guarantee must not only state its terms clearly, it must also be based on a real, not fictitious, list price. The commission attacked the automobile battery industry's wide practice of deceptive advertising, which failed to reveal that the value of the guarantee was reduced each month after the battery had been sold. The ads misled the consumer by saying, "50-month guarantee," "fully guaranteed," "wherever you go a registered guarantee," "full 3-year guarantee," none of which suggested pro-rata adjustments.

Attempts to correct pro-rata deceptions in the tire industry have been handled in a guide. Thus, the *Tire Advertising and Labeling Guides* provide for adjustment based upon a predetermined price which fairly represents the actual selling price of a comparable new tire at the time of adjustment, provided such predetermined price is the price at which at least 85 per cent of the retail sales of the replacement tire are made.

A dealer in water heaters represented that his water heaters were unconditionally guaranteed when actually there were numerous limitations and conditions not disclosed in the ads. Moreover, from the sixth to tenth year, there was a pro-rata adjustment on one of the models based on a fictitious list price. To add insult to injury, the respondent frequently failed and refused to honor the written guarantees he had furnished to the purchaser. A consent order was issued to cease and desist the practice.

Satisfaction or Your Money Back

If a guarantee reads "satisfaction or your money back," it should be construed as a guarantee that the full purchase price will be refunded at the option of the purchaser.

In *Towel Shop* the partners were ordered to cease and desist representing "satisfaction guaranteed or money back" when they did not refund the postage, because *satisfaction or money back* means all your money, including the postage.

In *B. R. Page Company* the respondents had represented in catalogues and advertisements that under their money-back guarantee the full purchase price of any article of merchandise sold by them would be refunded at the option of the purchaser, whereas in reality the guarantee was subject to many conditions and limitations, so that usually the purchaser got only credit vouchers which could be used toward the purchase of other merchandise sold by the respondents.

A facial cream was advertised as offering "10-day trials, satisfaction guaranteed." The FTC gave qualified approval to the advertisement if there were no limitations or qualifications attached to it.

When a reupholsterer advertised its repairs as "guaranteed satisfactory to the customer," the commission held that unsatisfied customers were entitled to adjustments to meet their satisfaction. There were numerous instances of upholstery sagging soon after repair, and almost as many instances of the upholsterer refusing to make good his guarantee.

Life

There are innumerable guarantees using the word *life*. If they relate to any life other than that of the purchaser who is the original user, the life referred to should be clearly and conspicuously disclosed.

The best-known case in this field is *Parker Pen Co. v. FTC*. The Parker Pen Company advertised a lifetime guarantee on its pens. At the bottom of the ad, in small type, was a statement that there was a service charge of 35¢ to cover insurance, postage, and handling if the pen was returned for repair. It was sufficiently inconspicuous to escape the attention of the ordinary reader. Parker was ordered to cease and desist from using the words *guaranteed for life, life guarantee, guaranteed life contract, life contract guaranteed,* or any word or words of similar import alone or in conjunction with any other word unless the company would in fact make, without expense to the owner, repairs during the lifetime of the owner. There was nothing in the order to prevent the company representing that the service on the pens, as opposed to the pens themselves, was guaranteed. Words of limitation, such as *35¢ service charge,* should appear in the advertisement close to the words *guaranteed for life* and in the same size print. The court said, "a guarantee *per se* negatives the idea of a further consideration." It could not find a case where a guarantee of satisfactory performance attached to an article for sale needed to be supported by further consideration.

There have been several other cases involving lifetime guarantees on pens. All the companies were ordered to cease and desist making un-qualified representations that their pens were unconditionally guaranteed for the life of the user or for any other designated period, when a service charge was made for repairs or adjustments. Sheaffer advertised "guaranteed for life"; Parker, "guaranteed for life," "life contract guaranteed"; Eversharp, "guaranteed forever"; Waterman, "the 100-year pen," "guaranteed for a century." Phonograph needles were also subject to an agreement to consent to cease and desist advertising an unconditional lifetime guarantee which was actually subject to undisclosed limitations.

If an advertisement of a guarantee for the life of the "vehicle" is to be understood as meaning only for the time that the original purchaser owns the vehicle, that must be clearly stated and the expression *life of the vehicle* without words of limitation may not be used.

In the car muffler industry, International advertised its muffler as un-conditionally guaranteed for life and backed by a lifetime written guarantee. Midas advertised, "You can keep your car forever and never have to buy another muffler—that's what Midas's guarantee means. A guarantee in writing for the life of your car." Actually, the guarantee was not for the life of the car, but only for the time that the purchaser owned it. An order to cease and desist was issued.

Savings Guarantee

The guides state that a savings guarantee "should include a clear and conspicuous disclosure of what the guarantor will do if the savings are not realized together with any time or other limitations that he may impose." The example given is "Guaranteed lowest price in town," which should be accompanied by a disclosure, such as, "If within 30 days from the date that you buy a sewing machine from me, you purchase the identical machine in town for less and present a receipt therefor to me, I will refund your money."

Food and freezer plans are replete with such statements and implications of savings. The consumer is flooded with ads, circulars, brochures, radio statements, and statements by the salesmen that the purchaser will receive a freezer and food to stock it for the same or less money than he has been paying for food alone; that he will save enough on food to pay for the freezer; that he will be able to enter the plan on a trial basis (he soon discovers, if he tries to give up after the trial, that he is bound by the original contract to go through with the purchase); that he will be able to purchase food under this plan for a lifetime; that he will realize savings of 25 to 40 per cent by this method. Also, in one case, the guarantees were advertised to be backed by a reserve fund or posted bond to ensure the purchaser continuous service. None of these representations was accurate.

A company was ordered to cease and desist advertising its guarantee as follows:

> Every installation guaranteed. Fully guaranteed for installation. Fully guaranteed for life. Can you spare $4.92 per month to guarantee yourself lowered household expense? Better Living, Inc. unconditionally guarantees to lower your household expenses. We unconditionally offer to install all windows for only $4.92 per month. Why can we fearlessly, unhesitatingly publish such a guarantee in black and white? Who is the authority behind the guarantee? The U.S. government.

The hearing examiner found the guarantees to be deceptive and designed only to draw customers. Savings were not forthcoming and the United States government had made no such representations. The commission upheld the hearing examiner, and the Third Circuit, in a memorandum decision involving no question of law, found the facts to be as the commission had stated them.

Guarantees Under Which the Guarantor Does Not or Cannot Perform

"Cannot perform" is usually a matter of financial incapacity, when neither corporation nor owner are financially equipped to give performance. A company claimed that its watches were bonded and accompanied by a guaranty bond. The watch company, however, had executed neither a bond, an insurance policy, nor an agreement supported by a fund to permit it to live up to its representations. The commission ordered it to cease and desist and to disclose fully the nature and extent of its guarantee.

A heater company guaranteed its heaters for five years of normal usage. Frequently, however, the company refused to replace, repair, or make adjustments for breakage or defects growing out of normal use of the heaters. The commission adopted the hearing examiner's order forbidding the company to represent any merchandise to be guaranteed, if any provision of the guarantee was not fully complied with. In addition, it ordered that any conditions or limitations must be set forth clearly.

It has come to the Federal Trade Commission's attention that mail-order insurance policies often involve deceptive practices, several of which involve guarantees. One company advertised its accident insurance with the following come-on: "You get an iron-clad guarantee which pays you at the rate of $1,000 cash a month beginning the first day of your full stay in any hospital due to accidental injury—there are no gimmicks, no exceptions, no exclusions, no limitations, no waiting periods, no ifs, ands, or buts." Nevertheless, the policy contained a provision, that any claim filed in the first two years could be denied on the grounds that the insured had a physical condition which existed before the date of the policy. Following a head of "guaranteed continuable," one policy reduced benefits after the age of sixty-five; another, although requiring no medical examination, was drafted so that the insurance company could waive liability on the grounds of a pre-existing condition if the questions on medical history in the application form were not filled out in strictest accuracy.

Advertisements proclaiming "guaranteed lowest premium" often hide the fact that the low premium is only for a few years and then the premium payments increase sharply.

A Material Fact

Guarantees are often employed in such a manner as to constitute representations of material facts. If so, the "guarantor not only undertakes to perform under the terms of the guarantee, but also assumes responsibility under the law for the truth of the representations made." For instance, if an automobile-polishing mitt is advertised as unconditionally guaranteed for three years, the purchaser can expect it to last for three years, not for the three months that this mitt lasted. This product also proved to be little better than an ordinary soft cloth.

In yet another case involving watches, the complaint alleged that the identity of the guarantor and the obligations he would undertake were inadequately disclosed. Also, although the watches were guaranteed for two years, few if any operated for that time; therefore, the guarantee failed to live up to its representation of material fact. Other deceptive practices involved name simulation, preticketing, and concealment of the fact that the watch cases were base metal.

A guarantee of "1st class" craftsmanship and materials is more than "puffing," it is a material representation in a field or industry in which "grade and quality are of prime importance." One advertisement read: "We at Youngstown, Ind., unconditionally an unequivocally guarantee in writing '1st class craftsmanship and materials.' We further agree to furnish especially trained mechanics to insure proper installation. Absolute satisfaction shall be yours."

When a profit guarantee is used, as when a company guaranteed that its customers' profits would be increased by exclusive handling of its beverage syrups, the statement must be a fact or else it will be prohibited, even if the company refunds the money.

Following a series of cases involving aluminum siding, the commission issued Advisory Opinion Digest No. 100, stating that it is illegal to represent a lifetime guarantee for aluminum siding when a seller's test showed that no aluminum siding will last a lifetime and that twenty years is a more accurate estimate of its durability. Also inconsistent with a claim for a lifetime guarantee are provisions for pro-rated cost of replacement and an exclusion from the guarantee of damage resulting from weathering of the surfaces. Having represented that its product lasts a lifetime, by the use of the advertisement "lifetime guarantee," the company deceives the purchaser both by concealing the material limitations on its guarantee and by manufacturing a product that will not last a lifetime.

CONCLUSION

Modern marketing practices are a far cry from the classic bargain at arm's length between the buyer and seller of equal bargaining power, in which the buyer had the time, knowledge, and opportunity to inspect the goods and the seller was in a direct contract with the buyer. Today it is a picture of a large corporation telling the consumer the terms of the sale with any number of middlemen along the chain of distribution. The consumer is deluged by advertising on television and in newspapers and is solicited with offers, comparisons, and representations of maximum psychological value, if of minimum objective validity. The complexity of the manufacturing processes and of the finished commodities; the lack of time, knowledge, and opportunity to inspect; the dangerousness of certain machines and food, if defective; and the impossibility of chasing down who is responsible for a defect all transform the classic bargain.

A seller has been held for a long time to give certain warranties to the buyer with the article he is selling, and he is held to be in a contractual relationship with the buyer, who has an action for breach of warranty if the article fails to live up to the seller's representations. The development and restrictions on this action, primarily complicated by theories of "privity," have been partially remedied by two approaches in the twentieth century. The New Jersey courts have abandoned privity, and the California courts have promulgated the idea of strict liability. The Uniform Commercial Code has codified the law of warranty with a more liberal approach toward protection of the consumer. The reasons for the extensions have been many, but primarily the courts speak in terms of the new pressures of advertising which impose responsibility on the manufacturer to provide the ultimate consumer with satisfactory products. Through the courts the consumer can recover substantial damages for breach of warranty, but such involves a lawsuit. Courts are only slowly extending the remedy and abandoning the classic restrictions. Personal injury is still, in many courts, the prerequisite to recovery. The fact that the gullible consumer has been badly cheated because he did not read the fine print and has lost many dollars on a car, major appliance, or household improvement has been held an insufficient injury to permit recovery.

The second route toward expanding consumer protection has been the FTC and its regulations. These proceedings do not give damages to the aggrieved consumer, but they do bring to bear government power on deceptive industry-wide practices and improve the lot of a large number of consumers. Both routes are still needed.

16

Business and Trade Status

The word *status* connotes a relative rank or preferred position. It calls to mind such things as connections with or approval by recognized organizations and individuals. With reference to a trade or business, its essential nature, size, age, and prominence or reputation will be important points in fixing status as the hallmark of integrity and reliability. Many members of the buying public, be they ultimate consumers or intermediate dealers, have demonstrated purchasing habits which can be explained only in terms of the "status" attributable to a particular business. The buying public is attracted by, indeed influenced by, appearances and general impressions. Because many people assume that there is a definite correlation between the nature and character of a business and the prices and quality of its goods or services, these considerations have been used by, and to the advantage of, certain members of the commercial community to accord to a business, through advertising or choice of its corporate name, a status which will entice customers but which is false or misleading. Such deceptions have been condemned frequently as unfair trade practices under Section 5 and enjoined as incidents of trade-mark infringement and unfair competition.

In its 1938 annual report, the Federal Trade Commission listed twenty-seven methods of competition that had been declared illegal under the Federal Trade Commission Act. Four of the twenty-seven involved practices that properly can be included in a summary of misrepresentations of trade status. These are

1. *False advertising.* This includes a wide diversity of fraudulent practices and mendacious claims and is the vehicle by which status may be misrepresented most efficaciously.

2. *Business status.* The commission describes this deceptive practice as "concealing business identity in connection with the marketing of one's products, or misrepresenting the seller's relationship to others" (for example, agency).

3. *Advantage of dealing with seller.* Included are such things as misrepresentation of: seller's alleged advantage of size, endorsement by government or nationally known organizations, being an importer, or being the manufacturer or producer or grower, all contrary to fact.

4. *Bogus independents.* This type of misrepresentation has been described as "using concealed subsidiaries, ostensibly independent, to obtain competitive business otherwise unavailable, and making use of false and misleading representations, schemes, and practices to secure representatives and make contacts."

It should be clear that the connecting element of these trade practices and any variations thereof is that the essential character of the business enterprise from which the product or service allegedly originates is not as it has been described or suggested. Admittedly, a partnership may produce a rug as fine as, or superior to, that produced by a corporation; a domestic blending of French essences may result in a pleasing perfume; two or more firms lawfully but secretly bound by a trade agreement may be able to offer advantages not otherwise possible. These are, nevertheless, immaterial when this trade practice is questioned. Consumer understanding alone must be examined. Because the source of goods and the reputation of that source are to the buying public some index of quality and price, and, therefore, demand stimulators, it is sufficient if the offer and sale be other than as it was represented.

The Federal Trade Commission has been active in eliminating falsely designated business status, although it is very often only one of several acts and practices of a given business that are prohibitable under its broad mandate to protect the consuming public and to keep competition open. As a specific misrepresentation commonly found in advertising, it is, however, often ignored by the courts or prohibited only incidentally in an action to enjoin passing off or misappropriation of a reputable trade name. The following two cases are illustrative.

Mantle Lamp Company of America had marketed kerosene mantle lamps and accessories under the trade-mark *Aladdin* for twelve years when Aladdin Manufacturing Company began to manufacture portable electric lamps using the same trade-mark. Eleven years later, Mantle began to use *Aladdin* on portable electric lamps, as it had on its kerosene lamps. In an infringement action, the trial court enjoined Mantle's use of the trade-mark with reference to portable electric lamps and Aladdin's use in connection with its kerosene lamps. On appeal, the decision was reversed giving the first user, Mantle, an exclusive right to the trade-mark for a lamp "regardless of the method by which light is produced therein." In addition, the appellate court faced the question, ignored in the lower court, as to Aladdin Manufacturing Company's use of the word *Aladdin* in its corporate name. Concluding that the corporate name had been adopted with the deliberate intention of utilizing the advertising and the good will of the Mantle Company, the court issued an injunction, stating that, "The continued use of the trade-mark of [Mantle] in the corporate name of [Aladdin] will inevitably confuse the buying public and place an instrument of deception in the hands of the unscrupulous or overzealous salesman." The same extension of the scope of an injunctive decree so as to restrain the use of a corporate name was the result of an appeal involving cigar manufacturers. The defendant company had been organized by two cigar manufacturers and a third person whose name furnished a plausible excuse to use a corporate name very similar to that of a well-established cigar manufacturer. To the court, the inference was "irresistible" that the name was not adopted in good faith and for an honest purpose; the court quoted the Supreme Court in its discussion of the right to use one's own name in one's own business: "But although he may thus use his name, he cannot resort to any artifice, or do any act calculated to mislead the public as to *the identity of the business firm or establishment,* or of the article produced by them, and thus produce injury to the other beyond that which results from the similarity of name." [Emphasis added.]

MISREPRESENTATIONS OF SIZE

There would seem to be little room for doubt that there is a direct correlation between the size of a business and its trustworthiness, its available stock, its efficiency, and the price it will charge to the consuming public. An exaggeration thereof is, in consequence, highly significant and has been treated as such by the FTC and, to a more limited extent, by the courts.

Although *Corporation, Corp., or Inc.* suggest substantial size, this representation apparently has not been a major problem. It does, after all, represent a legal status; however, it deceptively designates a business which is operated by one person.

It would seem reasonable to assume that even the most credulous consumer would know that an incorporated business may be no more complex structurally than a partnership. That the latter, however, is susceptible of considerable size is possibly less well recognized. This may explain a complaint which alleged misrepresentations in the use of *Co.* by a partnership. The defendants (Standard Distilling & Distributing Co.) urged that relief be denied the complainants (Standard Distilling Co.) on the ground that the latter represented themselves to the public as a corporation in the use of their firm name when in fact they were doing business as a partnership. This argument was rejected, however, for the reason that the mere use of *Co.* did not give a false impression of substantiality such as would warrant an inference of intent to mislead or that the public was thereby misled. In another case a temporary injunction to suppress the use *by an individual* of *Wallack Brothers* or *Wallack Bros.* as a trade name so similar to that of the plaintiff's *Wallach Brothers* in connection with the same type of business was denied. The practical effect of granting the injunction would have been to put the defendant out of business and could not be countenanced by the court, especially where doubt existed as to plaintiff's right to enjoin use of the similar name for a business which had originally been a partnership and to which the defendant, individually, had succeeded.

Although *Co.* is not synonymous with *corporation* and is permissible to designate a partnership, it may be deceptive to use it in connection with a sole proprietorship. The use by an individual of *Carl Flora Shirt Co.* as a trade or corporate name raised a reasonable presumption that honesty and good faith were lacking when the Flora Shirt Co. was already well established in the same city. Interestingly, the question of unfair competition was not even involved here because there was neither an allegation nor evidence that the defendant had commenced to make or sell shirts. Evidence suggested only that he intended to transact business and to form a corporation for the purpose of deceiving the public into a belief that his business, as listed in the telephone directory, was that of the operating concern. The appellate court, nevertheless, affirmed the decree to enjoin Carl Flora's use of words (*Shirt Co.*) identical with words used by the original company in conjunction with his own name.

The word *works,* too, suggests an industrial plant of some size, as do a variety of other words frequently found in a trade or corporate name. *Stores* in conjunction with *Safeway* and used to designate a single business unaffiliated with the well-known concern was held to have created a false impression of size as well as an illegal attempt to capitalize on the business and reputation of a national concern. Similarly, *federated* imports a size in excess of what a single-office, unaffiliated collection agency can justifiably claim.

Association and its derivatives, *Assoc.* or *Ass'n,* suggest an organization of people with similar interests or goals banded together for mutual benefit of the members. Thus, a single-office collection agency which collects delinquent accounts by mail without benefit of representatives located elsewhere was prohibited from using its trade name, U.S. Association of Credit Bureaus, Inc., to represent its business to be a group of credit bureaus. Similarly, a dunning device whereby, in correspondence to defaulting debtors, clients who subscribed to the services of a collection agency were referred to as "members" did not cure the false impression left by the agency's trade name, U.S. Retail Credit Association.

Association has been prohibited also as a misrepresentation of the sale for profit, through door-to-door canvassing, of cheap colored photographic enlargements as though they were the product of an art studio or group of photographers. The fact of the matter was that the business did not even maintain equipment or personnel for enlarging and tinting photographs. *Master Artists' Association, Inc.* was a mere trade name for a business enterprise which sold a service performed by someone else. Similarly, Educators Association, Inc., attempted to capitalize on the false impression left by its corporate name to sell its reference books to parents. It gave to its sales representatives an instrument of deception in that it suggested a group of teachers or educators with the common purpose of furthering the cause of education. Furthermore, it stamped the books offered for sale with an endorsement which did not exist in fact. The company, however, was permitted to continue use of the corporate name provided it was coupled with other words which would reveal the true character or status of the business conducted.

The terms *institute, university, academy,* and *seminary* have been used to suggest an organization of higher education with the power to grant degrees. Accordingly, the Federal Trade Commission on many occasions has issued orders to cease and desist the use of these words in connection with correspondence courses, a business with considerably less status than is suggested by the words prohibited. A business which offers instruction in a large number of professional and educational courses (from veterinary science to petroleum engineering by a "faculty" consisting of the petitioner, who had graduated from law school, eight translators to assist a preponderance of foreign "correspondents," and a small office staff) but which imposes no entrance requirements, maintains no library or laboratories, and has no resident students cannot call itself the Joseph G. Branch Institute of Engineering and Science. The court agreed that an unfair trade practice existed in so conducting this "diploma mill." Similarly, the use of *Institute of Hydraulic Jack Repair* in advertising and as a trade name for a business which only sells a manual instructing in the repair of hydraulic jacks was held to be deceptive because it created a false impression of a bona fide institution of higher learning. A consent order required a "school" to cease selling its instructional courses in so-called specialized training for commercial airlines positions through the deceptive use, among others, of its trade name (Sun Valley Air College, Inc.) and describing its salesmen as "registrars" when there were no classrooms or dormitory facilities and the corporation did not constitute a college of higher learning. The same misrepresentation of substantiality was apprehended in the use by The Colonial Academy, Inc., and The Pioneer Theological Seminary of their trade names to sell courses in Bible, theology, and philosophy because they suggest residence schools with residence instruction by trained and competent faculty members, which was not the situation.

On the other hand, the use of *university* by LaSalle Extension University was not enjoined because it does maintain residence courses in accounting. One case apparently never reached the point where a decision could be made regarding the use of *Post Graduate School of Nursing, Inc.* to designate a business which sells a correspondence course in auxiliary nursing, that is, all nursing positions below the level of R.N. The trade name clearly would suggest an institution of higher learning as well as the source of courses for those who had already received a degree in nursing. However, the initial order was dismissed for failure of proof of the alleged false representations in advertising the correspondence course.

One final example in this area involves the sale of cosmetics as being the product of the Dorothy Jay Beauty Institute. The well-known Dorothy Gray Cosmetics had another complaint, obviously, but the court additionally enjoined the use of *institute* where no beauty institute existed and the designation was adopted, rather plainly, it was felt, to confuse the customers of the better-known concern.

Legal problems involving private vocational and home study schools are more fully discussed in Chapter 18 of this book. As there noted, the FTC has proposed guides for the conduct of such schools. These proposed guides are reprinted for reference in Appendix XIII of this book and should be available in final form at the FTC or in the *Federal Register* by early 1971.

The adoption of trade names which import to a business a size or substantiality which it cannot justifiably claim is, perhaps, a more sophisticated unfair trade practice. The more commonly used vehicle is advertising claims. To be sure, puffing, boasting and exaggeration are the stock-in-trade of advertising. On the other hand, to characterize a business as the "largest" is much more precise than to claim for an article of merchandise that it is the "best," because the latter is largely a matter of individual taste. *Largest* is measurable by extrinsic facts and therefore should be permitted only in connection with a business which can live up to all that such a claim reasonably implies. The FTC has so held in issuing orders requiring companies to cease the use of *largest* in advertising where such was not the case and of such other representations that suggest a business to be so large and the quantity of its stock so immense as to require a complex organization.

Furthermore, the commission leaves no room for doubt as to the scope of its order. A manufacturer of stationery and business forms had to cease representing itself as both the "world's largest manufacturer" and the "world's largest manufacturer engaged solely in the manufacture of business cards." Similarly, a manufacturer of children's cribs and other furniture could not advertise itself as the "largest crib manufacturer in the world" or the "largest manufacturer of low price children's cribs in the world" until and unless it was in fact. In another case, the complaint alleged misrepresentation of size in the use of "largest exclusive retail army goods store in the country." The cease and desist order, however, did not include a specific reference to the use of *largest* because it was found that the company did not deal in army goods exclusively. The clause prohibiting any representation as to exclusive dealing must necessarily eliminate the false representation as to size.

Use of the phrase *Dept. 48* on printed forms is deceptive unless the business is divided into forty-eight departments. The listing, on letterhead and stationery, of offices and warehouses in five locations which do not exist also gives a prohibitable false impression of size, as does the use on order forms of the phrase "shipment to be made from Kansas City or your nearest branch factory" by a company which only affixed its own label to and sold uniforms manufactured by others. Again, the statement "you save because we operate on a volume basis" was found to be a false claim of substantiality requiring a Washington, D.C., mail-order seller of drugs to eliminate this phrase from its advertisements. *Volume* certainly suggests a business at least substantial enough to support the savings offered. The evidence, however, failed to establish that the drugs were available at a reduced rate that would justify the exaggerated claim.

Representations in advertising and on printed material which give a false impression of the size or scope of a business establishment are fairly common. *National and regional offices,* for instance, implies a great deal without getting specific. It, nonetheless, precipitated a cease and desist order respecting that false claim.

The use of specified locations and addresses to give an exaggerated impression of size has occurred under curious circumstances. For example, a business, which canvassed house to house to sell hosiery, imprinted *Dallas Office* on its order blanks to convey the belief that it was established and substantial. As a matter of fact, there was no company at all and no office anywhere, only a trade name. The only connection with Dallas was the respondent's residence from which he filled orders by purchasing from those local merchants who would give him the most advantageous price.

The American Bank Machinery Company repairs and rebuilds perforating and check-endorsing machines in Philadelphia, Pennsylvania. Yet letterheads used by the business represented falsely an establishment of such size as to require several places of business as evidenced by a Chicago address, an Atlanta address, and the Philadelphia address designated as the Eastern Service Center. Chicago and Atlanta were mailing addresses only.

Philip Morris & Company indulged in a similar trade tactic in connection with the sale of its English Oval and Player's Navy Cut cigarettes. Although manufactured in its only factory, in Richmond, Virginia, the company exaggerated its size and import by representing on the cigarette package the existence of factories in three foreign locations, including England. This was an obvious attempt to palm off its product as that of an English cigarette with a similar name. The same supposed preference for sewing needles manufactured in England caused a company to claim a factory and address in England although the needles were produced elsewhere in Europe and only packaged and sold in the United States by the respondent. Another pretended "manufacturer" of wooden furniture claimed factories in four locations, "executive offices" with a New York City address, and "shipped F.O.B. our N.Y. state plant . . ." or "our Missouri plant." In truth, however, orders were merely placed with a manufacturer who affixed respondent's labels and tags and shipped the furniture under respondent's bill of lading. Similarly, the claim "in one of our Tampa factories" implies a manufacturing status which could not be used by a mere retailer and distributor of cigars.

The use of *nationwide* or *national* to describe falsely the scope of a business also has frequently fallen under the injunctive ax of the Federal Trade Commission. It is difficult to determine from the cases the range of activities or renown that will justify the use of these adjectives. It must suffice to say that a corporation which does not have and maintain a selling organization through which "sales are made by the corporation *generally throughout the United States"* cannot represent itself as being "national in scope." A respondent trading as Consumers Bureau of Standards and representing his publication as the product of a "national consumers' research organization" obviously intended to capitalize on an impression that it was connected with the National Bureau of Standards of the Department of Commerce. The cease and desist order, nevertheless, specifically included *national* or any representation that the business is greater in size or scope than is in fact true of one which has no employees or labs or equipment and only one location at a time (which is changed frequently).

When a product is represented to be "nationally known," again there is only a hint as to the standard used to determine the extent of its reputation, hence the character of the claim. If an innerspring mattress is sold as a "Dr. Sealy," which is "nationally known," the intent of the advertiser and the possible deception is rather patent. "Dr. Sealy" mattresses may or may not be well known; mattresses produced by the Sealy Company are, however, nationally known. The combination of an exaggerated claim with a trade name so similar to a well-established concern cannot be tolerated. In connection with the sale of a rodent and insect poison, there was no apparent design to palm off the product. Yet a respondent agreed to cease and desist the practice of representing the preparation to be "nationally known." Again the respondent was found to have indulged in other practices deemed to be unfair; the representation of a status which it apparently could not rightly claim simply fell along with it. It would seem to be fair to say that the commission does not regard the use of *national* or *nationwide* where the facts do not support the boast as too serious a violation. It is not, first of all, susceptible of satisfactory definition. (For example, will contact with one state in each time zone suffice, or must there be sales in a majority of the states?) But more importantly, such claims are usually coupled with more serious infractions of the fair-trade-practice laws. A recent case before the commission has shed some light on the extent to which it views *national* as a prohibitable misrepresentation.

The National Research Corporation had been charged, among other things, with the deceptive use of its corporate name in that its business of selling drug preparations did not include a nationwide organization or scientific (or any other kind of) research. The hearing examiner dismissed on the ground that there was no indication that the corporate name had ever misled anyone or was likely to do so. The commission subsequently modified the order to prohibit the word *research* in the corporate title because a mere high school graduate was the only employee of the "research" department and the name had the capacity to mislead the public into the belief that back of respondent's products stood an organization with personnel for scientific and medical research. On the other hand, the order did not require the respondent to delete *national* from its corporate name. In the opinion of the commission, the word has been so widely used and, in connection with the sale of drugs, is so innocent as to make it unnecessary to infer a tendency or capacity to mislead.

The state courts have dealt also with misrepresentations of size where it appeared to be part of a design to palm off a product or service as that of a better-known competitor. The display by a potato chip manufacturer of a large sign on the roof of his place of business reading "The Hunt Potato Chip Co., Worcester Branch" was found to have misled the consuming public into believing that the business was operated as a branch of the well-established concern and first user of the trade name, The Hunt Potato Chip Company. The facts established that the sign designated the only place in which the appropriating manufacturer conducted his potato chip business and was not a branch at all. In another case, the defendant was enjoined from affixing to his place of business three signs reading "Main Entrance" when in fact there was only one real entrance.

Before concluding our discussion of misrepresentations of size, it should be noted that pictorial misrepresentations have been used to satisfy the consumer's preference for dealing with businesses which operate on a large scale in the expectation of getting better quality, prices, and services. Some exaggeration may not be illegal, but there is some doubt as to whether a business occupying one or two floors of the Empire State Building, for example, may properly picture the entire building. That some semblance of truth is required is clear. Accordingly, the use upon letterhead and stationery of a depiction of the purported place of business showing a large two- or three-story building was a prohibitable exaggeration when the business occuppied two office rooms and a loft on the second floor of a moving picture theater. It was equally misrepresentative of the nature and status of the business conducted to portray the size of a manufacturing plant through a composite picture upon which a portion of the building appeared twice so as to give the appearance of greater length and width than was actually the fact, or to use a whiskey label picturing a distillery which did not exist except in the imagination of the lithographer who designed the label, or to use on printed forms pictures of buildings which have absolutely no connection with the business, or to display composite depictions of a factory and two offices which in fact were several miles apart but, as pictured, appeared to be one place of business.

The other side of the substantiality coin is a "going-out-of-business" sale representing a status commonly associated with bargains. Competitors of a business in Paterson, New Jersey, obtained an injunction in order to be relieved of the detrimental effects of a distress sale which seemed to go on perpetually and well beyond the period provided in the license issued by the city for that purpose. The court agreed it was a tactic prohibitable as competitively unfair and a fraud upon the general public.

MISREPRESENTATIONS OF AGE

Statements which exaggerate, falsify, or mislead with reference to the duration of corporate existence or length of time in business are deemed to be unfair trade practices for the reason that they import a reputation upon which consumers tend to rely in making their trade choices. If it is claimed for a business that it is well-established or implied in a statement which sets forth its number of years in business, the consuming public assumes a concomitant reliability and trustworthiness.

Clearly, some license is permissible; this is not freedom, however, to claim the "power of thirty years' progress" when the business is four years old, or to state that "we are a well-established firm and have been in business for over 19 years," when in fact the firm has existed for much less time.

Because reference to an early date of establishment or a long period of existence is designed to suggest experience and reliability borne of long stableness, the issue arises as to whether the business has continued essentially unchanged. Clearly, not every change in the status of the business breaks the continuity of the founder's reputation. On the other hand, the independent establishment of a new line by one formerly connected with an old business cannot succeed to the status of stability enjoyed by the old business. Thus, an injunction issued against the use of *Mfg since 1875* by a recent member of a manufacturing family whose line is dog food and not the family's malted milk business established around 1875. There had been a break in continuity as far as the dog food manufacturer was concerned. It was unfair for him to use the representation; moreover, extreme confusion had prevailed among customers, some of whom reportedly had fed, without success, malted milk to their dogs and cats. Similarly, a business cannot advertise *Incorp. 1913* when in fact it did not engage in the current business until 1921, although a prior business under a different name had been established at the earlier date.

Successorship to a status cannot be claimed unless the business which earned the reputation somehow goes on in its entirety. A case concerning a renowned manufacturing concern will make this point even clearer. The original Waltham Watch Company of Waltham, Massachusetts, was founded in 1849 and continued producing watches and clocks until the mid-1950's. In 1957, the Waltham Watch Company of Delaware was organized as a result of a "spin-off" of the original company, which from that point was to be known as the Waltham Precision Instrument Company. The new Delaware corporation acquired, among other things, the trade name *Waltham* but no inventory of timepieces. Moreover, the new company never manufactured any. Whatever clocks it (and its licensee of the name *Waltham*) sold were imported from Europe. Yet "Waltham" clocks and watches were offered for sale in advertisements which claimed "Famous 109-year firm," "Product of Waltham Watch Co. since 1850," "You know Waltham . . . your grandfather did, too," and other similarly misleading statements. The Federal Trade Commission issued an order requiring the Delaware company to desist from placing in the hands of others any means whereby the public would be misled as to the source of the clocks it sold or as to the age, experience, and reputation of the manufacturer. As the court later said, the "109–150 year old company" had reference to the original Waltham Watch Company, which was totally disassociated from the clocks that were the subject of the proposed sale of franchises by the licensee. In other words, the transfer of the trade name *Waltham* from its original user to the new company and subsequently to a licensee did not carry with it a claim to the reputation built up by the old Waltham company as a *manufacturer* of precision timepieces. *Waltham* to the subsequent users was a mere trade name for a business enterprise engaged only in the sale and distribution of clocks and watches. A substantial change in the essential nature of the business had taken place. The founder's reputation, therefore, could not be juxtaposed to a timepiece produced by another, albeit rightfully a "Waltham" clock.

The sale of a business in its entirety, however, will justify use of whatever reputation or status is implicit in a trade name to which one succeeds. Upon this principle, the Emerson Electric Manufacturing Company was denied an injunction against the buyer, in bankruptcy sale, of the old Victor Emerson business to prohibit the use of the trade name Emerson Radio and Phonograph Corporation. The defendant company's interest in the name was upheld even though the plaintiff company's interest in the same name stemmed from its long continued use, first as a manufacturer of electric motors and only later of radios in competition with the defendant company. The Supreme Court had much earlier zeroed in on this aspect of a sale of a business when it said that the use of a trade-mark by the transferee "only indicates that the goods to which it is affixed are manufactured at the same place and are of the same character as those to which the mark was attached by its original designer."

Even if the "place" is not the original location, use of "Manufactory established in 1812" on a building that is of more recent vintage is not fraud as would require elimination of that status designation. It was held that the public could have reasonably concluded that the current manufacturer had succeeded in some way to the rights of those who began the business in 1812. Since, in fact, it had, the business continued unchanged and its founding date could be used.

One other aspect of misrepresenting status by means of capitalizing on an unearned reputation borne of age and experience should be mentioned. It involves the continuing use by subsequent transferees of an old firm name which contains a *personal name* in it. Where such practice has been upheld, the thrust of the argument is that the name has become a business designation of no personal significance. So where one buys the entire business which manufactures a liniment, he may properly use labels which state the name of the originator, A. Johnson, and may maintain a suit to enjoin another from using the facsimile of his own name, F. E. Johnson, on a liniment label in a manner so closely resembling the former that the public is likely to be deceived. The sale gave the buyer the right "to use what was found to have become an impersonal designation which had become a trade name and which was transferable with the good will of the business."

It does not follow, however, that the widow of a long-time manufacturer of "stogies" that were sold under his name and label bearing the legend "none genuine without my signature _____ (signature)" could continue the business without some indication that the stogies were no longer made under the personal supervision of the old master. Consequently, a bill by the widow to restrain an alleged infringement of trademark was dismissed because her use of the name was calculated to deceive the public. The most persuasive evidence adduced by the putative infringer concerned a letter mailed to the trade two years after the manufacturer's death, using his name and signature as if he were still living.

The Federal Trade Commission also has prohibited practices which, although devoid of reference to age, imply a prominence or reputation or stability which the business did not deserve. An advertisement which falsely claimed for a seller of furs a "$500,000 stock" had to be stopped until such time as the inventory would have a market value of the amount represented, because its use designated the business as being more financially stable than was the case.

To advertise for a manufacturer of electrical appliances that its products had been featured as gifts or shown on each of twelve named television "give-away" programs when such was not the fact tended to upgrade the acceptance of these products and, hence, to mislead consumers. It was the subject of a consent order. The same deception was apprehended in the use by two seed-distributing companies of misrepresentations to the effect that their supply was limited and prospective customers were specially "selected," "chosen," or "designated."

MISREPRESENTATIONS AS TO CONNECTIONS

Because a substantial number of consumers look to the opinions or beliefs of others as a guide in making their economic choices, a represenation by a business that it is affiliated with or has been endorsed by an individual or organization whose judgment demands respect is of considerable significance in the marketing of a product or service. That consumer deception can result where a seller represents or otherwise adumbrates a connection which does not exist has been recognized repeatedly by the commission and, under the doctrine of confusion of sponsorship, by the courts.

The government is rather frequently the endorser or affiliate falsely claimed for a business or its product. The following examples are representative only of this not uncommon trade practice, *unfairly used.*

- To do business as the Army & Navy Trading Co. gave a false impression of connection with these branches of the government when less than 10 per cent of the goods sold were G.I. surplus.
- The similarity of Civil Service Training Bureau, Inc. to the United States Civil Service Commission was sufficient to intimate that this private correspondence school had governmental connections or was an adjunct of the federal government. Additionally, it suggested that assistance was given in preparing for civil service exams and in getting a government position. The same unfair trade practice was deemed to be inherent in the use of the following trade names with Washington, D.C., addresses for businesses which distributed "skip-trace" forms to obtain information concerning the whereabouts of defaulting debtors: The National Service Bureau; National Clearance Bureau; and National Research Company.
- Adoption of the trade name Consumers Bureau of Standards precipitated trouble for the appropriator from the Federal Trade Commission. The commission intervened in a private action for the reason that the trade name was deceptive and misleading in the implication that its publication was compiled, issued, and sold under

the direction of a bureau or agency of the United States government. Similarly, the words *world's fair* in the title of a privately owned magazine, *World's Fair News,* were prohibited because they implied an official connection with the organization planning the fair.

A business trading as the Aviation Institute of U.S.A., Inc., in the sale of correspondence courses in aviation was enjoined from using *U.S.A.,* and in conjunction therewith an insignia resembling the one used by the Army and Navy Air Forces, because an official connection or close affiliation with government departments was clearly, but falsely, implied thereby. The corporation changed its name to the Aviation Institute of America, Inc., which was accepted by the commission as a compliance with its order.

A slight twist to this form of deception occurred in a case concerning a publication entitled *U.S. Navy Weekly.* The editors objected to an order that required them to cease and desist the practice of representing that ownership and editorial policy resided in "naval" personnel. It was denied that such a representation had ever been made; "navy" personnel was the claim made for its staff, and this, the respondents said, was true in that the corporate president was a permanently retired chief warrant officer and the secretary-treasurer was a civil service clerk employed by the Navy. The court, nevertheless, upheld the order, stating that "The FTC need not concern itself with a distinction between the two terms, since the public would not be aware of such a distinction and would be deceived by either term."

A rather recent innovation which suggests falsely a government affiliation has been the subject of a FTC complaint and a commission report entitled "Pitfalls to Watch for in Mail Order Insurance Policies." The complaint, issued September 19, 1967, charged a company engaged in the sale of general merchandise to the public with the unfair misrepresentation of business status under the following circumstances. Advertising material consisting of a credit voucher in the sum of $2 which could be used to make a purchase in stores operated by the respondent was printed in such a way as to have the appearance of a check issued by the United States government. It was, moreover, enclosed in a window envelope similar to ones used by the government for the transmittal of its checks. The words imprinted thereon, *OFFICE OF THE TREASURER, Accounting Division* (with a Georgia address), furthered the deceptive design. It was found that the use of these forms misrepresented to recipients "that the contents of the envelope is a check sent by a government agency and so cause the recipient to open the envelope and read the contents, which he might not otherwise have done."

The "pitfall" warned against by the commission concerned the mail offer of insurance to veterans or service personnel contained in similar official appearing brown window envelopes. The envelope identified the sender by some designation such as *Veterans Insurance Division* and contained other words like *Important Business* or *Special Armed Forces Policy Enclosed.* To complete the deceptive façade, a postage meter number was used rather than a stamp. Apparently, the enclosures usually make it clear that the offer is being made by a private, commercial insurance company in no way connected with the United States government. The report, nevertheless, went on to point out that caution should be exercised in responding to the insurance offer because it would be either a duplication of a regular G.I. policy or substantially inferior thereto.

Another misleading adumbration of government approval or endorsement has been apprehended in advertising distributed by some insurance companies using envelopes that are imprinted with the term *MEDI-CARE,* with only the hyphen distinguishing it from the Medicare program offered by the federal government. Again the offer is from a commercial insurance company and would be in addition to the government benefits, and at regular commercial rates.

The name of well-known organizations, too, have been used to accord to business enterprises a status that they do not enjoy. The American Marketing Associates, Inc.—or AMA, as was used at times—a door-to-door retailer of encyclopedia and other reference books, hoped to mislead the public into believing that it was the American Marketing Association, an "old, non-profit, long-established, highly-respected and nationally active" association primarily engaged in marketing research. The hearing examiner concluded that the corporate name suggested a status that was not warranted and that should be stopped. Similarly, an FTC order required an independent organization to cease calling its tabloid-sized newspaper the *United Labor Management Press,* because of the natural tendency of the name of the paper to represent falsely an endorsement by or affiliation with a labor union in soliciting business concerns to buy advertising space.

Making use of the status earned by a competitor is also a deceptive trade practice under Section 5. Accordingly, a manufacturer which used the word *Champion* on its automotive spark-plug-cable sets was held to be unfairly trading on the reputation of the well-known Champion Spark Plug Company, even though the manufacturer had copyrighted the label containing the word. A cease and desist order was also issued against the use of a format similar to the reputed *Who's Who in America* by the publisher of *Who's Who in the Law* (. . . *in the Clergy; . . . Among Physicians and Surgeons,* and so on) because the title conveyed the impression of compilation and publication by the first user of the phrase *Who's Who.* Having found that a large portion of the buying public associated *Who's Who* with a single and exclusive publishing source, the commission directed the respondent to cease the use of the phrase in the title of any book of biographical reference. Subsequently, however, the phrase was permitted in the title of a similar reference book, *Who's Who Among Students in American Colleges and Universities.* Although clearly contrary to the earlier decision, the use of the phrase on this book can perhaps be explained by the disclaimer found on the title page: "This Publication Is Not that of A. N. Marquis & Co. or The Publication Known as *Who's Who in America.*"

As previously stated, the courts pursue their antideception policy by frequently employing the so-called confusion-of-sponsorship doctrine against the use of representations (often through the trade name) which falsely claim for a business an association, approval, endorsement, or recommendation by a better-known competitor or by a well-known, though noncompetitive, concern. The principle is said to be just another means (along with those against "palming off" and confusion of source) by which the identifying function of trade symbols is safeguarded. Nevertheless, the likely confusion of customers is also the touchstone in these cases. As one court defined the doctrine, it is a misleading of the public by the imitation of

> an attractive, reputable trade-mark or trade-name . . . not for the purpose of diverting trade from the person having the trade-mark or trade-name to the imitator, but rather for the purpose of securing for the imitator's goods some of the good-will, advertising and sales stimulation of the trade-mark or trade-name.

Deception can result, because it is the "fine reputation for the high quality of its products, for financial responsibility, and for business integrity and fair dealing" which may be implicit in a trade name (even one embodying a corporate name, and upon which a consumer frequently relies in making his economic choices). Accordingly, an injunction will issue against the "borrower" of the senior user's reputation.

For example, in *Hanson* v. *Triangle Publications, Inc.* the publisher of the magazine *Seventeen* was successful in prohibiting the use of *Seventeen* or *17* in connection with the sale or advertising of teen-age wearing apparel and girdles, because there was a likelihood that these items would be thought to have been sponsored by the magazine.

In *Stork Restaurant, Inc.* v. *Sahati,* it was held, contrary to a lower court judgment that the trade name *The Stork Club* applied to a large cafe and night club operated in New York and publicized at some expense, and, together with a well-known insignia, was entitled to protection by injunction against the use of *Stork Club* by a small bar and cocktail lounge in San Francisco.

In *Ambassador East, Inc.* v. *Orsatti, Inc.* the owner of a Chicago restaurant using the widely advertised name *Pump Room* was deemed entitled to injunction against the adoption of a similar name for a Philadelphia restaurant and a New York restaurant. In the case of the Philadelphia establishment, the appellate court did not agree with the lower court that use of the appropriator's name in conjunction with the trade name would sufficiently erase the "likely" confusion, so long as the first user did not establish himself within ninety miles of Philadelphia.

And in *Esquire, Inc.* v. *Esquire Bar* the popular magazine was granted an injunction against the use of its name to designate a restaurant in Miami and a men's clothing store in Pittston, Pennsylvania, because to some extent the magazine could be said to be "blessing and obliquely branding" the men's fashions displayed in the store.

MISREPRESENTATIONS AS TO ORIGIN OF PRODUCT OR SERVICE

Consumers usually select the source of the product or service that they intend to buy by depending upon the considerations that are then and there most important. If the concern is for a wide variety or for better service or for the convenience of location, the purchase will be made where these are available, regardless of the status of the seller. If, however, the prime consideration is price, the consumer's preference may be for a very particular source. Many assume that by dealing directly with the originator, the manufacturer, of a product, lower prices accrue to them. This preference has been repeatedly recognized by the Federal Trade Commission in its pursuit of commercial acts and practices which are unfair; as the Supreme Court said in the *Royal Milling Co.* case, "this right [to prefer to purchase a given article because it was made by a particular manufacturer or class of manufacturers] cannot be satisfied by imposing upon them an exactly similar article or one equally as good but having a different origin."

The origin of a product—or, more specifically, the particular services rendered by a seller—has been falsely represented in a variety of ways. The cases would seem to permit two broad categorizations: (1) misrepresentation through use of a trade name and (2) misrepresentation through advertising.

Before getting into the examples, however, some generalizations appear to be in order. For instance, since the word *mill* or *mills* so often has been used falsely to suggest a manufacturer of textiles, the Federal Trade

Commission, in September 1965, promulgated a Trade Practice Guide with respect to its use by the textile industry. It would appear that the general rule as to what constitutes legal use of *mill* is equally applicable to the use of other words which designate a manufacturing facility, such as *refinery* or *manufacturer*.

The guide says in essence that *mill* should not be used in corporate, business, or trade names of concerns or persons handling textiles unless there is actual ownership and operation or direct and absolute control of the facility in which all the textile materials sold under that name are produced. The guide goes on to explain what control is not:

(1) contracting for milling operations to be performed by others;
(2) furnishing yarns for the manufacture of garments according to distinct specifications;
(3) leasing 5 looms in a mill for their exclusive output; and
(4) contracting for the entire output of a mill.

To this can be added a few others gleaned from commission cases. Thus, "direct and absolute control" is *not* to be found in the

(1) Acquisition by corporate-respondent of less than $\frac{1}{6}$ of the outstanding stock of a hosiery mill and the placement of one of its officers as one of 7 directors of the mill.
(2) Acquisition of the majority of the shares of the company found to be identical with the mill for which the "Stephen Rug Mills, Inc." purchased all of its raw material, made all determinations with respect to the nature of the product which was manufactured exclusively for them, had a mortgage on much of the property of the mill, and leased the premises on which the mill was situated.

Nor is there "actual ownership and operation of a mill" when the corporate respondent maintains only a single carpet loom that is used infrequently and is productive of only a minute portion of their carpet stock. The commission has also indicated that a business which only "technically" rather than "substantively" operates as a manufacturer cannot properly represent itself as such.

The guide lists exceptions to the general rule whereby a nonmanufacturing concern might continue to use *mill* so long as an accompanying phrase qualified the implication of ownership and control of a facility which manufactures textiles. The exceptions are (1) where a trade name has become a valuable business asset, and (2) if a qualifying phrase would eliminate all possibility of deception.

When the value of a trade name is to be determined, several things are suggested as guides: time in use, funds expended to promote, extent of good will, and adverse effect on the company to be expected if the word *mill* is excised.

Misrepresentation Through Use of Trade Name

As stated earlier, one of the functions of a trade symbol is to identify either a product or service or to designate its origin or source. Accordingly, it is clear that, as to those consumers or dealers who prefer to buy directly from the original source in the expectation of eliminating the middleman's profit, the law of fair-trade practices will not permit a business to masquerade under a trade name which identifies it as something it is not. Case after case demonstrates the deception: purchasers are misled into buying an article which they do not wish to buy and might not buy if correctly informed of its origin.

The following is a representative listing of the deceptive trade names which have been suppressed or modified:

1. Companies deceptively using *mills* in their trade name have been the object of many cease and desist orders and stipulations. Concerns designating themselves as a "mill" have run from retailers of hosiery and rug and carpets to converters of textiles and to operators of a chain of thirty-four discount department stores called the Atlantic Mills Thrift Centers.

2. *Smithsonian Institution Series, Inc.* was considered to be a deceptive trade name for a business which publishes and distributes books even though the books are written and edited by scholars of the institution of Washington, D.C., and the name was suggested by one of its members. The name falsely suggested that the commercial enterprise was a part of or directly connected with the Smithsonian Institute.

3. *The Primfit Textile Co.* falsely implied a manufacturer when, in fact, respondent was a jobber and distributor of hoisery to department stores.

4. The use of the abbreviation of *distributing* to *dist.* in the corporate name on printed material by the Pennsylvania Whiskey Distributing Co. was found to be a false representation that it is a distilling company and that the whiskey sold by it was manufactured through the process of distillation.

5. The trade names *Federated Wholesalers Services, Nationwide Wholesaler Services,* and *Nationwide-Federated Wholesaler Services* were subject to a complaint in 1964 because they created a false impression that the respondents were wholesalers when, in reality, they were engaged in the retail sale of items listed in a catalogue.

6. Finding a preference among the purchasing public to buy directly from a nurseryman (the "manufacturer" or grower of nursery products), the FTC charged Lakeland Nurseries Sales Corp. with misrepresentation of business status, because the concern merely distributed nursery products and did not own, operate, or control a nursery, farm, or property on which these products were grown or propagated.

7. Use of *Atlantic Packing Co.* or *Atlantic Packing Co., Distributors* on goods that are not packed, but only distributed by respondents was held to be deceptive with respect to their business status and origin of the product they sell.

8. Use of the word *motel* in conjunction with the trade name *Trave-Lodge* was held to be misrepresentative of the services rendered by an establishment which, as an adjunct to its private club, maintained only thirteen rooms, had no lobby, took no reservations, was closed on Sunday, and took in an average daily income of $20. In granting injunctive relief to TraveLodge Corporation, the court had no problem particularly where the defendant "not only offers inferior services but its establishment tolerates questionable activities."

9. *Club* has been held to be suggestive of the nature of the business conducted and could not be used by an organization which sought the patronage of the public, but did not offer services usually provided by clubs.

10. Companies in the business of selling encyclopedias are notorious for attempts to conceal their true status in order to eliminate sales resistance. *World Wide Educational Services* had to be eliminated from the letterhead of one company. In another case, involving three affiliated concerns, the commission affirmed an examiner's findings that their trade name, Educational Foundation, was a false designation because it suggested an organization operated on a nonprofit basis and engaged in educational work.

11. *Weavers' Guild* as a trade name for a business engaged in the sale of weaving courses was held to be misleading in that *guild* suggests a nonprofit (which it was not) association of persons engaged in the same craft for mutual assistance (which it also was not).

12. Two Chicago real estate advertising firms could not represent themselves as a *cooperative* organization of real estate and business brokers through the use of trade names *Business Co-op, Inc.* and *Affiliated Brokers, Inc.*, nor could one man represent himself as a cooperative association in the publication of the *Business Broker's Bulletin.*

13. Businessmen have even attempted to capitalize on the natural sales lure of products produced by and sold for the benefit of the blind. The trade name *National Blind Industries* for a business engaged in the sale of luminous house numbers for profit had to be stopped because of its similarity to the name of a nonprofit institution, the National Industries for the Blind, which serves as a coordinating agency for numerous workshops for the blind. Similarly, a manufacturer of rugs for profit had to cease and desist the use of the corporate name *The Light House Rug Co.* and the label depicting a lighthouse, even though some rugs were produced by blind people. The word *lighthouse,* as applied to rugs,

had acquired a secondary meaning that the rugs were made by the blind in charitable institutions, called lighthouses, and hence was misrepresentative of the nature of the respondent manufacturer's business.

14. A wholesaler of shoes made to his specifications could not sell his shoes under the trade name *Dr. Florence Scientific Shoes* when the shoes neither were designed by a doctor nor contained orthopedic features for the alleviation of foot problems.

15. Because *claim adjusters* in a trade name suggests an organization of liquidators, authorized adjusters, or agents engaged in the sale or disposition of bankrupt estates, salvage, or other distressed or surplus merchandise for the purpose of settling an indebtedness or claim, the words could not be used in the trade name for a business which buys merchandise from a manufacturer and sells it at retail for its own account.

16. *American Research Society for Better Management* was prohibited as a trade name for a clipping service (from previously published materials) because it designated the business as being engaged in research or operating or maintaining a society (a collective group).

17. *Gold Tone Studios, Inc.* could not be used as a trade name by a photographic finishing company unless and until it made substantial use of the finishing process which involves the use of a toning or developing bath consisting of salts or chloride of gold. A court reversed that part of the order forbidding the company from identifying itself under a new name as having been in business formerly under the prohibited name.

18. *Hospital* had to be excised from the trade name *Post Graduate Hospital School of Nursing* as suggestive of some kind of a medical center in connection with the correspondence courses in practical nursing which the respondent sold. However, *clinic* could be retained in the corporate name *Hair & Scalp Clinic, Inc.* for a business engaged in the sale and distribution of medicinal preparations for the hair and scalp. Because *clinic* was found to have been commonly used to designate organizations and activities having no connection with medical science (child welfare clinic, sales clinic), it would not necessarily represent the corporate respondent as operating an institution for the diagnosis and treatment of diseases of the scalp.

19. *American Registry of Doctor's Nurses* was the subject of a cease and desist order in that it deceptively suggested a nonprofit organization. The order required the use of a statement revealing that the business was private and operated for profit in immediate conjunction with the trade name.

20. A final example demonstrates how far afield a business will go in choosing a trade name. *National Laboratories of St. Louis* was prohibited for a company engaged in the business of operating and servicing vend-

ing machines. No laboratory existed for, or did research in connection with, the services rendered.

Suppression or Modification of a Deceptive Trade Name

In 1933, in the *Royal Milling Co.* case, the Supreme Court agreed that to conduct a business under a trade name which falsely identified the nature thereof was an unfair method of competition. The use of *milling, millers,* or *mills* by a company which, in preparing flour for marketing, only mixed and blended different kinds of flour purchased from the grinder of wheat was properly prohibited by the commission. The Court did not agree, however, with that part of the six orders involved which required the excision of *milling* from the trade name. It amounted to the destruction of a valuable business asset and should not be ordered if the evil could be corrected by the use of an explanatory phrase in immediate conjunction with the trade name; *not grinders of wheat* was suggested.

In the years to follow, the FTC frequently found it necessary to interdict the use of trade names suggestive of activities not followed by the user. Almost as frequently, the courts of appeals were constrained, under the doctrine of *stare decisis,* to modify the remedy selected. Purchasers and prospective customers had to be informed of the true nature of their vendor's business. Indeed, as one court said,

> The accuracy of representations implicit in a trade name indicating whether a concern is a manufacturer, converter or jobber is in general important and it cannot be denied that a misleading trade name may lead to injurious misapprehensions on the part of customers, actual or prospective, and damage to competitors. We think that the Commission is authorized to guard the public against such dangers. Indeed, it exists to promote fair rules of trade and in so doing to curb practices that involve a likelihood of injury to the public, even if in a particular case the acts complained of are, as here, innocent in purpose and may thus far have done little harm.

The commission, however, could go no further than to avoid the false impression which use of a descriptive word created. Accordingly, an order requiring a company which purchased unfinished cotton and rayon goods from a mill and dyed, bleached, and printed the fabric for resale to a clothing manufacturer was modified by the court to add to the misleading corporate name the words *Converters, Not Manufacturers of Textiles.* Where members of the purchasing public were not apt to have an occasion to deal with the company, the abandonment of a well-known trade name was deemed to be too drastic a method of remedying a "slight infraction of a proper trade practice."

A modicum of deference to the expertise of the FTC was accorded from time to time. In one case a qualifying phrase was deemed proper and one was suggested by the court. However, because there were other possibilities, remand was ordered so that the commission could make the choice which would sufficiently convey the true facts.

For the most part, however, the commission was held to a tight rein. In one case, where it was not clear whether the cease and desist order was intended to prevent the use of the misleading trade name, "for sake of clarity" the court modified the order to provide for its use if it were coupled with other words which eliminated the false impression by revealing the true character of the business conducted. The judicial power to modify an administrative remedy, too, led Judge Augustus Hand to abrogate an order requiring English translations which would have erased the false impression of an "import" status left by French words, characterizing it as a "fantastic requirement."

This situation was drastically changed in 1944 by the *Herzfeld* decision in which Judge Learned Hand begrudgingly bowed to the commission's "skill which comes of long experience and penetrating study" to decline to order an accompanying explanatory phrase. The decision was compelled by several cases involving the NLRB in which, it was felt, the Supreme Court had "circumscribed our powers to review the decision of administrative tribunals *in point of remedy,* as they have always been circumscribed in review of facts [Emphasis supplied]." Judge Hand went on to explain:

> In controversies about trade-marks, and particularly about trade-names and make-up, the question is always one of degree; i.e., how far the chance of deception outweighs the inconvenience, or worse, to the merchant inevitable in compelling him to change his mark, his name, or his package. The decree marks the compromise which the court thinks adequate and necessary; it is the resultant of those unexpressed determinants which collectively we conceal under the term "discretion."

Henceforth, the discretionary measure of relief, once an illegal commercial practice has been found, would be up to the Federal Trade Commission and would include a determination of whether qualifying words would eliminate the deception. This consideration is apparently the crux of the matter, although it is not necessarily express, in *Herzfeld.* There *Stephen Rug Mills* had been used in conjunction with *Importers & Wholesalers of Floor Coverings* to identify a business which sold, to the trade, rugs manufactured in a mill in which the company held a majority interest. Having found that the corporate title in full conveyed the impression that the company did not exclusively consist of importers and wholesalers—that is, it was also a "mill"—the commission ordered suppression. The commission had ordered the same remedy in *U.S. Navy*

Weekly, Inc. v. *FTC,* wherein it was determined that only prohibition of the name could eliminate the false impression that the publication had some official connection with the U.S. Navy; and in *Perloff* v. *FTC,* wherein it was held that because packing and distributing are two different activities, the characterization of Atlantic Packing Co. as "distributors" was not a representation that it was not a packer of those goods which it did not pack or can.

In *Herzfeld,* however, the commission had considered the effect of a qualifying phrase, and having ruled against it, the court would not interfere (though it felt that the company was near enough to being a manufacturer to justify the title if the chance of deception were removed). And in *Deer* v. *FTC* the Second Circuit Court of Appeals affirmed an order which denied use of the proposed *distributors only* because it would not negative the false effect of *manufacturing* in the trade name of a company which had manufactured nothing for the last ten to fifteen years. The court said it was up to the commission to determine whether the explanatory clause would be adequate to prevent deception.

Where the commission orders excision without considering the possibility of qualification, it will be deemed to have abused—or, at least, not exercised—its discretion and remand will ensue. Thus, in *Jacob Siegel Co.* v. *FTC* the Supreme Court named the commission as the "expert body" to determine the remedy and limited the role of the courts to ascertaining whether the commission has made "an allowable judgment in its choice."

In summary, it is clear that to designate falsely a business's activities by a misleading trade name is an unfair commercial practice, and that the primary responsibility in fashioning the cease and desist order rests with the FTC. The question remains, however, as to the standard used in its decision to require suppression or modification of a trade name. In this regard, the FTC has continued to customize its remedies and, apparently, leans toward the rationale gleaned from an appellate decision prior to *Herzfeld.* Thus, in the *Army & Navy Trading Co.* case the commission had ordered excision of *Army & Navy* from the trade name because it falsely and misleadingly represented the origin of the goods sold by respondent where only about 10 per cent of the total inventory originated from the Army and the Navy although at an earlier date, the respondent had carried as much as 90 per cent surplus goods. In a proceeding to enforce the order, the Trading Company argued that suppression of its trade name was unlawful where use of qualifying words would eliminate the deception, citing several qualification cases (including *Royal Milling*) as postulating that "orders should go no further than is reasonably necessary to correct the evil and preserve the rights of competitors and public." The court agreed that qualification is a permissible remedy "where qualification is possible; [the cases, however] . . . do not justify contradiction."

Using the cases urged by the Trading Company, the court carefully showed how the representations therein could be qualified to eliminate any deception. *Royal Milling Co., Not Grinders of Wheat* clearly indicated that the grain from which Royal's flour was made had not been ground by Royal; nevertheless, *Milling* was left to describe Royal's blending and mixing activities. Similarly, *Good Grape, Artificial Color and Flavor* to identify a soft drink was possible because the color and taste were, indeed, grape though fresh fruit had not been used. *White Shellac, Shellac Substitute* was upheld because the product had the qualities and uses of shellac though it was not composed of genuine shellac gum dissolved in alcohol. And *Satinmaid* or *Satinized, a cotton fabric* eliminated the misrepresentation that the fabric was made of silk but left the truthful description of it as having a silk weave. In each instance, there was a truthful representation to be preserved; hence, qualification was feasible. This was not the case with the "Army & Navy" claim. It was untrue as to both the origin and the nature of the goods sold by the Trading Company. The court might have added that it was equally untrue as to its status as importing a connection with the United States government or an agency thereof. The point is, however, that any of the proposed explanatory phrases—*not connected with the Army and Navy, not connected with the government, not a government store, not affiliated with the United States government*—would not effectively eliminate the misrepresentation that the company sold Army and Navy surplus or goods of that character and quality. The use of the trade name with qualifying words would be contradictory and, hence, an improper remedy.

The commission has adopted this principle in two recent cases involving misleading trade names. In the first case, corporate respondent operated thirty-four discount department stores. It was, therefore, a retailer; yet the stores were identified as Atlantic Mills Thrift Centers. Although in some advertisements, the respondent has disclaimed any manufacturing status, on all occasions *Mills* or *Atlantic Mills* was prominently displayed, and *our usual Mill* price was a common vehicle to entice sales.

The examiner, however, found no preference on the part of members of the purchasing public to buy directly from a manufacturer, and, correspondingly, no deception on the part of the company in the use of *Mills* as part of the trade name. To use the abbreviated trade name without further explanation or qualification, however, was deemed to be deceptive and the order required a conspicuous disclaimer that the store is a factory or a mill.

Disagreeing with the examiner upon the findings of fact, the commission declined to adopt the order and substituted a requirement of excision. *Mills* in the trade name as well as in advertising represented to the public the ownership of a mill or factory, and in light of a preference found to exist on the part of many consumers for the price advantage supposed to flow therefrom, its use by a retailer constituted an unfair trade practice.

The choice of remedy discussion made use of the *Army & Navy* case. Where milling or converting activities were carried on, the words of qualification or explanation would dispel the deception imparted by *mill* and modification would be appropriate. If, however, the company engaged only in nonmanufacturing activities, any words of qualification would only contradict the word which conveyed the deceptive impression, and excision would be the proper measure of relief. Moreover, the commission felt that the situation, involving as it did wide use of radio advertising and direct contact with the purchasing public, precluded a *practical* method of disclaimer and necessitated an accurate portrayal of the company's true business status.

A little later, the commission remained true to this rationale and (reversing a contrary ruling of the examiner) permitted the use of words of qualification in conjunction with a trade name. Apparently, *Not Textile Manufacturer or Mill Owner* was deemed not to contradict *Standard Mills, Inc.*, the name under which a textile converter and jobber traded.

MISREPRESENTATION OF SOURCE
THROUGH ADVERTISING

Seeking to satisfy the consumer's supposed preference for a particular source as securing him, in his belief, better prices or superior quality, some businessmen make full use of the power of the written word on labels, in ads, and in catalogues to falsify the "status" which will engender sales.

An ad which identified stores as "Factory Showrooms in the East" and claimed "factory showroom prices" as being substantially less than the "nationally advertised prices" created in the minds of the purchasing public the impression that the same clothing that was sold nationwide at higher prices could be purchased in these stores at lower prices because the clothing could be obtained from the manufacturer. Such an advertisement would bring the public in droves, but when the store is not a factory outlet and the clothing is sold at regular retail prices, it is unfair competition and enjoinable.

Again, an intimation of a false status will not be condoned by a distributor of cigarette holders who claims "when buying from us you buy from the manufacturer . . . Buy Direct—Save Money." Nor will such an intimation be condoned by a tombstone and monument cutter who advertised, "Buy directly from the quarry owner," when he used granite produced in quarries not owned or controlled by him.

Similarly, a company could not capitalize on its status as a successful *manufacturer of firearms* to suggest a lower price was being offered for razor blades which it sold under its trade name, but did not produce. And a manufacturer of parts adapted for use in Ford cars could not advertise the parts as Ford articles, because in common acceptance, *Ford* indicated articles manufactured by the Ford Motor Company. Nor could the imprinter of the name of the customer on a pen claim, for whatever advantage he hoped to obtain thereby, the status of manufacturer. Furthermore, a company which produces only some of the articles which it sells is deemed to be a middleman with reference to products purchased from other manufacturers and it may not represent, in connection with the sale of the latter, that the quoted price is possible because the articles are furnished direct to the consumer from the company's own factories. Such phrases as *direct to you, from factory to you,* and *factory prices* all suggest that price advantage sought by many consumers and will be prohibited unless the business has attained the status of manufacturer.

If a company cannot claim to be a manufacturer, it may assume a comfortable competitive position by a claim to the status of wholesaler. There is also a substantial portion of the buying public that prefers to deal with a wholesaler in the hope of saving an amount equal to the retailer's profit. But the company must be wholesaler, that is "one who sells to the trade for resale and seldom, if ever, to the purchasing public," with the possible exception of industrial concerns and similar organizations which purchase in quantity. If the sales are to ultimate consumers, the company is in the retail trade and it may not represent itself as a wholesaler or a jobber or even an "industrial jobber." In the *Helbros* watch case, the District of Columbia Circuit Court of Appeals said, "the transaction by which the merchandise comes into the possession of the ultimate consumer [is a retail sale], *regardless of the title by which the vendor may choose to denominate himself.*" [Emphasis added.]

To the purchasers of such things as perfume, caviar, and vodka, imported products are often preferable to domestic products. Hence the status of "importer" is an enviable position for the vendor of these, and other, products.

One who blends French essences with domestic alcohol and bottles the resulting mixture is not, however, an importer of French perfume. He is a manufacturer, and to represent himself otherwise is an act of unfair competition, infringing upon the interest of consumers who think they are getting French perfume, upon the trade of those who import the mixture (of concentrates and French alcohol) blended in France, and upon those who import only the concentrates to blend with domestic alcohol and represent it accurately as a domestic product. And because "the American public is more easily beguiled when the article has a French name," use of French words like *un air embaumé* or *Paris* to suggest a foreign origin or import is an unfair commercial practice, although the country of origin of various ingredients may be stated if it is accompanied by a statement that the *product* was made domestically.

One final status, that of agent, has been frequently misrepresented because such a relationship suggests to the consumer sufficient control running from the prime source to justify a conclusion that the interest of the manufacturer in good will extends to the retail level. However, because an agency relationship is based on a contract, it will not do at all for one to claim to be an "agent" when such is not the case. Accordingly, a general automobile business, although it sells genuine Ford cars, cannot designate itself as *Ford agents* or *Ford Auto Agency*. Similarly, use of *VW* or *Volkswagen* in a manner calculated to mislead the public into belief that a retailer is an authorized dealer for Volkswagenwerk constitutes a threat to appropriate the manufacturer's good will and justified a temporary injunction pending trial.

Use of *Yale* in a trade name for a locksmith and *Yale Lock Service . . . Mfg's Agent for Yale* on a sign and in the telephone directory was prohibitable as tending to mislead the public into thinking that service was controlled by the manufacturer of Yale locks; and no justification could be found therefor in the use and sale of Yale locks by the locksmith. A *former* (because he breached the contract) member of a chain of stores, however, could use the type of store front and colors used by the member stores, but not the trade name, provided there was clearly shown to be no connection with the chain store.

"BOGUS INDEPENDENTS" AS MISREPRESENTING TRADE STATUS

A bogus independent has been defined as an "organization, nominally or apparently independent, which in reality is secretly controlled and operated by another concern in order to destroy independent competition." It is said to be more commonly utilized than any other method of unfair competition. The creation of a bogus independent may be part of a scheme to drive a competitor out of business and prohibitable at common law. According to one commentator, it is this "monopolistic character of the practice [which] brings it clearly within the [Federal Trade] Commission's jurisdiction." Other authorities would seem to base FTC jurisdiction more on the deception of consumers wrought by the concealment of a subsidiary's factual dependence upon a parent company. An example would be a buyer who is adverse to purchasing from firms bound by any trade agreement, lawful or unlawful. In order to obtain his business, a bogus independent is formed. There is no doubt that such a scheme would permit many of the particular trade practices that the FTC traditionally prohibits as unfair—price cutting and "spying" on competitors at a local level by the "independent" seem to be two obvious ones. It is this overlapping, however, which makes for some hesitation in giving "Bogus Independents" such an elegant label as *Misrepresentation of Trade Status*—except insofar as such a business is, in truth, masquerading as something it is not, that is, independent. Nevertheless, irrespective of the other malefactions a bogus independent might be guilty of, the commission will prohibit its capitalizing on a status (as with descriptive trade names) that is not supported by the facts.

To many buyers of fertilizers, a farmers' cooperative company would be the best source for that product because quality and a price advantage would seem to flow therefrom. A different set of values may be attached if it is known that the Farmers' Coop Fertilizer Company is directed and controlled by Armour & Company. The FTC thought so and issued an order to cease and desist the sale of fertilizers manufactured by the Coop without fully disclosing to purchasers and the consuming public that Armour controls the distribution and sale of fertilizers sold by the Coop. *Armour owned* was placed upon bags, tags, stationery, and advertising material used by the Coop Company in the conduct of its business. Apparently, the misleading nature of the independent's trade name was to be eliminated by the disclosure of Armour's control.

Another well-known concern, Fleishmann Company, which manufactures about 90 per cent of the compressed yeast used by bakers in the United States formed a bogus independent, apparently in an attempt to get that last 10 per cent or to retain trade that it was in danger of losing. Fleishmann was required to disclose its control of and affiliation with the Bakers' and Consumers' Compressed Yeast Company.

Bogus independents have been formed frequently to lure back dissatisfied customers. A manufacturer and vendor of children's cribs and bassinets who has, in the past, padded orders is not very likely to get repeat orders. A bogus independent might, however; at least it could be used to make collections on unordered goods sent by the parent company.

One company tried a similar scheme when its mail-order sale of inferior seeds resulted in a loss of customers. A separate company using a separate catalogue was organized; the seeds, however, for both came from the same stock.

A manufacturer of lightning rods secretly organized and "operated" two other companies with fictitious addresses for nonexistent offices and manufacturing facilities as independent manufacturers and competitors in whose name it solicited business and sold its rods. This practice was ordered to be stopped.

The same inferior retreaded and recapped tires were sold by respondent's salesmen using order blanks and other literature bearing one of three different corporate names to solicit persons who had unsatisfactory dealings with respondent under one or another of the trade names. The general practice of shipping to the purchaser tires of a different and inferior (at times, worthless) quality from that of the sample shown continued, however, until respondent was discovered, and a cease and desist order ensued.

A recent case involved the seller of encyclopedias. The company was alleged to have utilized the "services" of two fictitious companies by sending collection letters under their names to create the false impression of a bona fide business engaged in financing, servicing, and credit reporting—or to dun customers who had not paid for the reference books purchased. The "independents," however, were fully owned and operated by the corporate respondent.

MISREPRESENTATION OF PRODUCTION METHODS AND PROCESSES ACCORDING TO A BUSINESS A FALSE STATUS

Misrepresentation of production methods and processes has been employed time and time again to embellish a business with an aura of exclusivity or speciality. If a company may imply that it is the only source of a particular product because of some right that it owns to a production method or that its methods and processes are productive of an article of merchandise with some particular appeal, its competitive position is a fairly comfortable one. As with other commercial claims, however, it must be supported by the facts. Again, the failure to disclose material facts concerning a business or its product or service, which if known to prospective purchasers would influence their conduct, is an unfair trade practice.

False Exclusivity

A patent, trade-mark, or copyright gives to its owner varying degrees of exclusiveness in the use of the thing protected. A claim to such protection at once raises a cautioning flag to would-be competitors and suggests to prospective purchasers a primacy or superiority either as to the source of a product or the product itself.

Ordinarily, one who lays false claim to a patent right, a trade-mark, or a copyright will be subject to statutory penalty. Such is, in addition, however, deemed to be an act of unfair competition and enjoinable as such, providing, of course, the public has been deceived or there has been an attempt to "palm off" at the expense of a competitor. A claim to a monopoly or exclusivity which does not exist in fact tends "to stifle competition" by deterring others from the manufacture or handling of such article, in other words "to bulldoze the trade."

Pat. No. _____; *made under U.S. patent rights; under our new patents* or *cannot be successfully imitated because . . . amply covered by U.S. Patents; Reg. U.S. Pat. Off.; registered under U.S. laws; Mfg. of Patented Protected Devices;* and, of course, *patented, Pat., Pat. Pend.,* all seek to capitalize, undeservedly where there is no patent or none pending upon the popular assumption "among wholesalers, retailers and members of the purchasing public" that a patented article is of superior quality and one to be preferred over a nonpatented article or one for which application for a patent has not been made.

It follows, also, that to continue use of any of the previously mentioned variants of *patented* after the protection has expired operates falsely and unfairly to extend the monopoly granted beyond the period of such a grant. Furthermore, the registration and use of a trade-mark that is based upon and refers to a patent subsequent to the expiration of the patent gives the registrant no exclusive right and he may not, therefore, interfere with another's prior (but not exclusive) right to use the words that had been descriptive of the manufactured article. In the words of one court, "Of necessity when the right to manufacture became public, the right to use the only words descriptive of the article manufactured became public also." Moreover, where many inventions and mechanical advantages of a manufacturer's device either are used by competitors under licenses granted by the manufacturer or have been independently developed, it is misleading, deceptive, and false to represent that, "Every important development of . . . equipment and technique has been accomplished by LUX engineers" or that they "are responsible for every worth while improvement made." The devolution to the manufacturer of certain patent rights from the original Swedish patent holder and subsequent major improvements thereon did not justify the claims made for the product by the manufacturer.

Moreover, a corporate vendor of the paraphernalia used by banks in the conduct of "Christmas Clubs," with the purpose of importing some uniqueness to itself, may not represent ownership of and exclusive right to use the phrase *Christmas Club* for the reason it is trade-marked. The words were registered for use as a title for a magazine. And, it is false and deceptive to claim any exclusivity for them in connection with the Christmas savings system.

But an advertiser need not indulge so baldly in misrepresentation. He can hedge a bit, and still get caught! *Secret Process* to suggest unusual longevity in hosiery will influence purchases by many women, at least initially. Such representation must be ceased, however, when it is discovered that the actual process is in fairly common use among manufacturers of hosiery.

The "bud-selection method" of grafting in the propagation of trees may sound unusual to many purchasers of nursery products. It is not, however. The commission found that it has been used since the sixteenth century and held that a nurseryman employed a deceptive trade practice by intimating exclusivity to himself.

Pioneers of the First . . . imports to the advertiser a unique position among all those who use the process or method so represented. Such a claim cannot be justified, however, by one who was not the developer. Moreover *sole purveyor* cannot be used to designate the source, nor can *only genuine* be used to describe a product where others are entitled to sell it and/or use the name. Where there are two with equal rights to sell a proprietary article, either may enjoin the other from representing himself as "sole proprietor."

The words *authorized* or *only authorized* have come in for their share of adjudication as vehicles of commercial falsity. Where a famous newspaperman wrote a war history for one publisher and subsequently contributed to a multivolume history of the war for another, absent a finding of deceit or fraud as would justify the putative palming off of the second history for the first, an injunction would not lie to restrain the later publisher's use of advertising claiming it was the only history written by the famous man. Similarly, where the plaintiff does authorize certain dealers to copy and sell the copies of creations designed by the House of (Christian) Dior but denies such authorization to the defendant department store, it is not an act of unfair competition by the defendant to advertise garments as "Copies of Dior Models." They were, in truth, copies and anyone might reproduce the design. The court called attention to the fact that the defendant had not used *authorized* to qualify *copy;* for that matter, neither did the dealers who had the blessing of the couture house. There was, then, neither deception of the purchasing public nor appropriation of exclusive property of the plaintiff.

Because *authorized* is defined as "possessed of authority, acknowledged as authoritative," it may not be used on a book by Culbertson describing his bridge game system in such a way as to imply that any other book on the subject would be unlawful or, at least, defective. Since a system is an idea, the public may use it and the originator will be restrained from representing that he has "exclusive rights in the Culbertson system" so as to scare off those who would wish to interpret his system.

Authorized may be used to inform the public that the product so represented is the only one on which its creator has put his stamp of approval or consent. However, where the names of famous dress designers are used as a brand name for hosiery that was not designed or created by the designers, it is false, and therefore an unfair commercial practice. Such practice must cease even though the vendor obtains the right to use the names of the designer. Similarly, it was immaterial that it was a common practice in the hosiery trade to use as trade-marks the names of fashion designers.

The nature of the working force behind a particular product or service has been used to accord a status which will appeal to a particular class of consumers.

For collectors or connoisseurs of primitive art, silver jewelry made by Indians utilizing their traditional designs and production methods is a popular item. The product has been sold for some time as "Indian" or "Indian Made." Thus represented, the silver jewelry was understood by the public to have been made not merely by Indians, but by Indians using exclusively hand processes. Accordingly, the FTC charged misrepresentation in the labeling of a product as "Indian made" by "Navajos," where machinery was used in the fashioning of the silver as a partial or entire substitute for hand hammering and hand ornamentation. The fact that the workmen operating the modern equipment were all Indians did not cure the deception of those purchasers who wanted hand-crafted Indian jewelry, or the anticompetitive effect on jewelry manufacturers who use only *Indian design* to describe their machinery-made product. *Indian made* could not be used unless the product was handmade by Indian workmen.

The commission's order requiring truth in describing the production of silver jewelry was modified, however. In recognition of the widespread use, even by independent Indian craftsmen, of certain modern equipment not known to their predecessors, the court permitted *Indian made* to describe jewelry that had been hammered, shaped, and ornamented in substantial part by machinery, *providing* labels and other advertising clearly stated the method of manufacture. Subsequently, the same court held that *press cut and domed blanks* was effective in informing the purchasing public of the use of machinery in the production of jewelry said to be "Indian made." No confusion was likely to result in the context of the advertising material which clearly outlined separate and distinctive steps in the productive process. Even if *press cut and domed blanks* is not very meaningful to some consumers, where it is followed by *filed, decorated, shaped and finished entirely by hand,* it must indicate a machine process.

Union made, or such words as would simulate a union label, strongly suggests that the product, in connection with which the representation has been used, has been made by workers affiliated with a labor union organization. It, not surprisingly, is an unfair trade practice if such is not the case.

Blind-made is a selling point to those consumers who would wish to contribute to the welfare of blind workers. Exaggeration, however, will not be tolerated. Accordingly, a distributor of house signs and a chair recovering service could represent his one-man unsighted working force as "blind"; he could not claim, however, that "contributions" from sales maintained a rehabilitation and training program for blind workers where there were no facilities for the program, no blind person had ever been trained by him, and the "contributions" defrayed operating expenses like those of any other commercial enterprise. Where a business was engaged in the door-to-door sales of rugs woven by blind workers as well as machine-made rugs with only the fringes knotted by the blind with no attempt to distinguish the two samples (although an advertising pamphlet did so), the use of the corporate name, Rugs of the Blind, Inc., was deemed to convey the impression that all rugs offered for sale were made by the blind. The company was required to distinguish conspicuously the origin of the two classes of rugs. In keeping with the current rationale regarding misleading trade names, the corporate name was not subjected to excision. Admittedly, the question of an appropriate name was difficult. But because the one in use contained a representation that was partially true, absolute prohibition was not ordered. A qualifying phrase on the machine-made, blind-tied rugs was held to erase the tendency of the business name to mislead.

A misrepresentation of the qualifications or particular competence of employees is equally unfair. Cosmetic houses are quite apt to make an appeal to the purchasing female with claims of a production and development staff consisting of beauty experts, all with French names, or of the services of a "famous" or "well-known Parisian cosmetician." This is impermissible if those named are fictitious or are trained only in giving facial treatments. Moreover, the fact that a staff member is a commercial chemist and consultant for certain cosmetic concerns will not justify the representation that he is "one of the world's leading cosmetic scientists."

Similarly, a company engaged in the manufacture, sale, and installation of warm-air furnaces may not permit its *salesmen* to characterize themselves falsely as heating engineers. And an enterprising promoter of the sale of mushroom spawn to "do-it-yourselfers" cannot counteract the expectable doubt for success among the nonprofessional planters by falsely claiming a "staff of experts to advise you on every phase of the [mushroom] industry."

A product that has been made by hand is to many purchasers preferable to its machine-made counterpart. Thus, *handmade* has been frequently the subject of alleged unlawful trade practices. As we noted earlier with respect to Indian jewelry, the phrase is understood by the purchasing public to mean "made by manual, not machine, processes." In that industry, however, a qualifying phrase is permissible where, as a practical matter, some machinery is used.

Pursuant to its policy of eliminating in their inception trade practices that violate the Federal Trade Commission Act, the commission has promulgated some trade-practice rules as to the use of *handmade* by a few specific industries. Thus *hand-braided* for braided rugs can only designate the procedure whereby the strands are braided by hand; furthermore, *handmade* means entirely by hand. *Hand-engraved* in connection with engraved stationery means that the markings on the metal plate have been incised by hand. With respect to the jewelry industry (apparently not to include Indian jewelry), it is unfair to represent a product as handmade unless the entire shaping from the raw material and the finishing and decorating were accomplished by hand labor and manually controlled methods which permit the maker to "control and vary the type, amount and effect of the operation."

A hand-rolled handkerchief must include an entire hem that has been rolled by hand labor.

Hand-sewn may be used to describe *such part* of a shoe as may be sewn by hand or that product which embodies hand operations in its manufacture. Yet a vendor of barber tools agreed to the requirement that he cease use of the descriptive *handmade* unless the product was made "entirely by hand from its inception."

A consent order was issued against a distributor of a domestic fabrics represented as *Madras* since the word connotes a fabric produced in India made of "fine *hand loomed* cotton." The following are other descriptive phrases deemed to suggest a handmade product and which may not be used if machine processes are employed: *bench-made,* with respect to clothing; *compounded by hand,* with respect to cosmetics; *cut and traced by manual operations,* in connection with jewelry.

The cases and the trade-practice rules concerning the artificial limb industry and the bedding industry clearly posit the unfair use of *custom made, custom built, custom crafted,* or *customized* unless the product so represented has been made in accordance with specifications furnished *prior to the manufacture* by the individual purchaser (it could be the consumer's vendor) and/or the user of the product.

In the auto seat-cover trade, however, *customized* is commonly used to define a set or series of seat covers that are made in advance to fit specific models of automobiles. A complaint alleging commercial falsity on the ground that the covers were not made to order for the car of each customer was dismissed.

It remains to be seen whether *custom-tailored* means to a respondent's customers that his ready-made uniforms are "custom-made." In a suit to collect damages for violation of an FTC order, the vendor claimed that his use of *custom-tailored* did not violate the order requiring him to cease the use of *custom-made,* because the substituted phrase indicated the particularly fine stitching and other tailored finishing which made the uniforms so represented substantially different from ordinary ready-made military uniforms. The court denied to the government summary judgment on this point and ordered a jury trial on the question of the meaning of *custom-tailored.*

Tailor-made or *made-to-measure,* of course, may not be used in connection with the sale of ready-made garments that are only altered (when necessary) to conform to the measurements shown on the order blank.

False Speciality

A tablecloth is not just a tablecloth to the purchaser who desires a woven pattern rather than a printed one. The processes productive of each are different. Accordingly, any speciality which can be imported to an article of merchandise by virtue of its method of manufacture must stem from a true representation of the facts. The FTC's antideception policy demands no less even though the printed tablecloth is as good as the woven one.

Damask, then, to describe a fabric in the production of which a pattern is stamped thereon after weaving is an unfair trade practice. It falsely represents the pattern as having been *woven into* the fabric by changing the direction of the thread.

Embossing is generally understood to involve the distension of paper (or other appropriate material) through the use of a die to form a pattern. The resulting raised surface would be impractical (if not disastrous to a golfer's game) for a golf ball, yet a manufacturer of a golf-ball marking device represented that the device "embossed" the name upon the ball. Had more of his potential customers been aware of the significance of *emboss* the manufacturer might not have sold many gadgets. The FTC required the manufacturer to cease the use of *emboss* in any manner calculated to mislead the public into a belief that the letters formed by the device are of an "embossed" or raised type when such was not the fact. Printing processes described previously, under "embossing," and the similar thermo-type process have frequently been the subject of a complaint alleging the false use of *engraving*. To use *plateless engraved* is no better, because the engraving process as defined by the commission was not employed, although *plateless* was true. *Dri-engraved, Hand grav,* and *heliograving* or *heliograved* have been held to be equally misrepresentative.

Cloisonne describes a long-established method of producing artistic designs by fusing enamel, enclosed in cloisons or cells outlined by metal strips, upon a metal base. To use *cloisonne* alone or in conjunction with other words (*cloisonne top, cloisonne enameled*) to describe an article which either contains no enamel (only plastic) or no metal strips so characteristic of the traditional process was deemed to be misrepresentative.

Braided, also, as used in the rug industry, connotes a process productive of a rug which is superior to a tubular rug in regard to construction and wearability. Thus, the commission promulgated a definition of braided rug as "sewing together flat braids or plaits into desired shapes" to be distinguished from a tubular rug produced by braiding yarn around a core to form a tube that is thereafter sewn into desired shape.

Mercerized has a specific meaning also; the article so labeled has been treated with a caustic solution whereby the tensile strength and microscopic appearance thereof is changed and the sensitivity to dyeing is enhanced. Thread is usually subjected to the process of mercerization for obvious reasons and people are willing to pay more for it. Such a representation must be supported by the facts, however. Thus, a wrapper on shoe laces describing the *untreated* product as *Mercerized Broadway Brand* was unfair and deceptive.

To many men, *Milan* as descriptive of a hat has come to mean a "quality" and "luxury" hat manufactured in Italy of wheat straw in a distinctive weave or braid. In other words, the term designates at once origin, material, construction, design, and workmanship. It is not surprising that the FTC pursued an American manufacturer of hats constructed of a braid manufactured in Japan of Philippine hemp and sold as "Genuine MILAN" or "Genuine Milan Imported Braid." On appeal, however, the court was not convinced that the prohibition of *Milan* should include any geographical restriction, because even Italian manufacturers now use wheat straw grown in China. It was felt that *Milan* had acquired a secondary meaning generally indicative of a type of weave or braid. It could not be used to describe a hemp hat, but the commission was directed to consider whether or not qualifying words like *hemp-Milan* or *imitation-Milan* would ensure against consumer deception when braid hats made of hemp in the United States are offered for sale.

Ply, as it is generally used to describe the construction process of a given article, imports several layers which have been fused or bonded together as one. The manufacturer of asphalt roofing material invoked the FTC machinery when *ply* was used to designate the (unlayered) thicknesses of their product. *One ply* was used in connection with the lightweight material (and was not misrepresentative), *Two ply* indicated medium weight, and *Three ply* indicated the heavy weight. Although the practice at one time had been industry-wide, some manufacturers had discontinued its use because of its ambiguous and misleading nature. The others ultimately were required to cease and desist the deceptive use of *ply*.

17

Disparagement and Comparisons

COMMERCIAL DISPARAGEMENT IN THE STATE COURTS

Disparagement and Defamation

The tort of commercial disparagement, often referred to as trade libel, is another in the succession of deceptive tactics available for the diversion of customers. It consists of a false assertion of fact about the quality of another's product or services by one intending to injure the other's business which directly results in financial harm.

Closely associated with, but distinguishable from disparagement, is the tort of defamation. Defamation includes, but is not limited to, situations where false statements are made which tend to injure one in his business by impeaching his integrity, skill, diligence, or credit. Simply stated, it impugns the integrity or credit of a person in connection with his business, as opposed to the quality of the product. Both disparagement and defamation are subject to attack as common law torts.

Though in practice the division between the two torts is hazy, the consequences of the distinction are often critical to the success of a suit. Defamatory statements which are prejudicial in a pecuniary sense to a person engaged in a profession or trade are actionable per se. In most states this means that no actual financial damages need be proved because economic injury is conclusively presumed to flow from the statement itself. In contrast, in an action for disparagement "special damages" must be both alleged and proved before recovery is possible. In other words, an actual pecuniary loss must be demonstrated with considerable specificity. Moreover, in disparagement the plaintiff must prove the defendant's statement false; in defamation the defendant bears the burden of proving truth. Finally, only in disparagement is "malice" a requisite to recovery. Stated differently, in defamation the defendant's state of mind or intent is immaterial, the only defense being the truth of the matter asserted by him. It can be seen, then, that a cause of action for disparagement presents many technical hurdles not found in an action for defamation.

Although every aspersion cast upon the goods of a business may reflect upon its integrity to some degree, the courts in many cases have had no trouble in distinguishing between consumer deception through attacks upon integrity and credit, on one hand, and upon product quality, on the other. An allegation that a particular rifle has a faulty ejection mechanism is an example of the latter, whereas an accusation that a corporation traded with the enemy during a time of war clearly exemplifies the former. But great difficulties are to be found in the gray areas in which statements malign both integrity and quality. For example, a statement in reference to a tradesman that, "He has nothing but rotten goods in his shop," attacks both the quality of the goods used and the shopkeeper in the conduct of his business. In *Burnet* v. *Wells* these words were held to be actionable per se—that is, defamatory—but generally the courts have vacillated in their willingness to find an impugning of business integrity in similar circumstances. Although the courts have displayed a reluctance to infer a defamatory charge, the best view seems to be that the greater the likelihood of a crippling injury to the plaintiff's trade or business, the more likely it is that a given assertion will be held to be actionable per se.

An examination of the case law substantiates these observations. In *Hopkins C. Co.* v. *Read Drug & C. Co.* the defendant, in endeavoring to sell a particular brand of toothpaste, said to a customer that a competing brand of toothpaste made by the plaintiff was "nothing else but grit, was very harmful to the gums, and also would take the enamel off your teeth." Though it would not take much imagination to find that those words impugned the plaintiff's integrity, especially because of the allegedly deleterious nature of the product, the court found no aspersion of the plaintiff as an individual.

Similarly, in the New York case of *Frawley Chemical Corp.* v. *A. P. Larson Co. Inc.* the defendant wrote to the plaintiff's foreign customers that the plaintiff had available neither an export license nor the drugs that he was to deliver, and that therefore it would be impossible for the plaintiff to deal with them. The court held those statements not to be actionable per se and required a showing of special damages. It seems clear, however, that even without innuendo, these remarks in effect charged the plaintiff with deceitful dealing and misrepresentation. Clearly, Frawley's integrity had been attacked, yet, as in the *Hopkins* case, the court refused to allow a cause of action for defamation.

The following two cases demonstrate that some courts at least will find defamation if the very existence of the business is imperiled. The case of *Larsen* v. *Brooklyn Daily Eagle* involved a newspaper report that a child had been seized with convulsions and died after eating ice cream manufactured by the plaintiff. The article stated that the ice cream was directly responsible for the death and for the illness of several other children. The court said the article was libelous per se because it implied that the plaintiff was intentionally and continuously placing injurious ingredients in its ice cream. The similarities with the *Hopkins* case are apparent in that it, too, involved an allegedly deleterious product. But the *Larsen* case is different in that the disparagement was more likely to imperil the very continuation of that business because the statements had been widely communicated, not uttered only to a few customers, as in *Hopkins*. Moreover, considerably more attention would be paid by consumers to remarks about a product's lethal qualities than about its propensity to harm the gums.

One court has gone so far as to hinge its findings squarely on the likelihood of ruination of the plaintiff's trade or business. In the case of *Greyhound Securities, Inc.* v. *Greyhound Corp.* the defendant transportation corporation sent to regulatory bodies letters which stated that the plaintiff securities dealer was improperly using the name *Greyhound*. Because of the similarity in names, the court took the position that if a publication disparages some aspect of a person's business in such a manner as to prejudice directly the successful conduct of or to imperil the very continuation of that business, then he may maintain a cause of action for defamation without an allegation of special damages.

Lest anyone be misled into thinking that the preceding rationale is applied in every case, there are two apparently irreconcilable decisions by a New York Supreme Court which serve as reminders of the inconsistencies which plague the defamation–disparagement dichotomy. In the 1960 case of *Drug Research Corp.* v. *Curtis Publishing Co.* the defendant published an article in its magazine concerning a product manufactured by the plaintiff called Regimen. The article was entitled, "Don't Fall for the Mail Frauds," and contained the following statements: "The hottest gimmick . . . today is the alleged weight reducing pill. . . . [S]o common is the desire to get something for nothing—in this case slimness without diet—that some schemes promising this impossibility have taken in over a million dollars a year." The author went on to mention Regimen by name in connection with these schemes. Because the plaintiff was not specifically mentioned in the article, the controlling issue was whether or not the complaint alleged a libel against the Drug Research Corporation as well as against its product. The implication of the article was that the pill does not reduce weight at all. If this is true it would seem that no manufacturer could have produced it without intending it to be sold under false pretenses. In other words, the plaintiff alleged that the published matter gave the impression that the plaintiff was a swindler and was engaged in obtaining money by fraud and misrepresentation. However, the court said that there was no defamation of the plaintiff, only a disparagement of its product. Therefore, the complaint was deemed insufficient for failure to allege special damages.

A different result obtained a year later in *Harwood Pharmacal Co., Inc.* v. *National Broadcasting Co., Inc.* The suit arose out of a televised comedy skit parodying what was thought to be a completely hypothetical sleep-inducing product called Snooze. The performer displayed an object to the audience that was purportedly a package of Snooze, saying, " 'Snooze,' the new aid for sleep. 'Snooze' is full of all kinds of habit forming drugs. Nothing short of a hospital cure will make you stop taking 'Snooze.' You'll feel like a run-down hound dog and lose weight." Unfortnuately the plaintiff was engaged in the manufacture of a sleeping pill of the same name. The court held that this language could be understood by a television audience as charging the manufacturer "with fraud and deceit in putting on the market an unwholesome and dangerous product." Thus, the allegation of this unintentional disparagement by a comedian was found to be sufficient to state a cause of action for defamation, making a plea of special damages unnecessary.

The court made an unimpressive attempt to distinguish these two cases by restating the conclusions reached in both cases. But there was no attempt to distinguish the substantive differences between the allegations and no attempt to explain why the plaintiff was defamed in one case but not the other. Apparently the judge's visceral reactions to the facts of each case were different. But there is a deeper explanation for these conflicting results. As we shall see, unlike defamation, "intent" to do harm in some form or another must be proved in an action for disparagement. The damaging remarks in the Snooze case were concededly unintentional. In fact, the existence of Snooze was not known. A successful cause of action in disparagement was therefore impossible. Yet not wishing carelessness before a television audience to go unpunished, the court found the parody defamatory per se.

Elements of Commercial Disparagement

Motive or Intent. Technically, the element of intent involves two questions: (1) Did the defendant know his statement was false? (2) Did he know it would disparage another's product? For our purposes, however, there is no need to differentiate between the two. Suffice it to say that there are problems of proof that may arise that are unique to each area.

The general rule has been that in addition to untruth, a plus element (described as "something in the way of an improper intent or motive or of bad faith") has been required. This plus element is frequently characterized as "malice," but one must not be misled into equating malice as used in this context with the intentional infliction of harm, though some courts have done so.

In the context of disparagement, malice can be described as the equivalent of fault of one sort or another. In cases involving competitors, malice is almost invariably present and a jury seemingly draws such an inference quite readily. However, in cases involving noncompetitors, the requirement may cause difficulties. In the event the defendant is not a competitor, the plaintiff will most likely succeed in proving the defendant's knowledge or fault only when the offending statement blatantly disparages a product which has an easily determined quality, or when the defendant falsely maligns a technically complex product about which he is well informed. In both situations the disparager would be hard pressed to show an honest mistake.

Generally speaking, proscriptions against deceptive advertising are based upon the belief that the free flow of accurate product information is essential to the proper functioning of an economic democracy. False statements are subversive of this system regardless of the speaker's state of mind as to the truth of his statements or his estimate of their consequences. Because the law of commercial disparagement has as one of its avowed purposes the protection of the consumer, it has been suggested that mere untruth plus proof of special damages should permit recovery. The disparager's state of mind is of no consequence to the consumer; his only concern is that he has not been misled. Historically, however, more than untruth has been required.

The *Restatement of Torts,* a leading text on the subject, avoids to some extent the criticism of being too lenient with the unintentional disparager. It suggests that the basis for relief should be foreseeability of harm, thereby obviating the necessity of showing either knowledge or negligence as to falsity. Despite this improvement *Restatement of Torts* has one major flaw. Among the most important sources of accurate information for the consumer are the professional product evaluators and commentators. Under the preceding rule, this group would be subjected to absolute liability for false statements about the products tested. Because it is generally known that thousands of consumers act upon the information contained in these publications, it must be said that the evaluators are aware that their detrimental statements are likely to cause injury. Thus, the foreseeability-of-harm test would be satisfied. In the interest of providing accurate information with which a consumer can make an intelligent choice, a general exception should be carved out of the restatement law. The best rule in this limited situation would be to make reasonable belief in the truth of the statement a defense, conditioned upon the exercise of considerable care.

Nature of the Statement: Falsity and Statement of Fact. In an action for commercial disparagement the plaintiff must allege and prove that the defendant's statement was both factual and false. The false assertion of fact must refer to some facet of the plaintiff's trade or business in a way that is likely to influence or interest prospective customers.

Special problems have arisen with respect to statements of opinion. Pure opinion cannot be measured by the objective standard of falsity because it is based on the subjective values of the utterer. The *Restatement of Torts,* Section 627, however, holds the publisher of a pure opinion liable for resulting pecuniary loss if he did not hold the opinion he expressed. But pure opinion is rare. Just as statements of fact are seldom free from expressions of opinion, the opposite is true. Assertions of objective fact measurable against the standard of falsity are generally present in every utterance. Where the factual portions of such statements are false, such mixed statements of fact and opinion are actionable. For example, in *Shevers Ice Cream Co.* v. *Polar Products Co.* the defendant alleged that the plaintiff produced an "inferior grade" of ice cream. Such statements were enjoined by the court without any discussion of the "opinion" problem. Most likely the general standards of the ice cream industry as to what constituted quality provided an objective standard by which to measure the accuracy of the statement.

As previously noted, it has been suggested that malice, even in the broad sense, be eliminated as a requisite to recovery for disparagement. Because of the extreme importance of assuring that the consumer receive only accurate information about products, there are some who would make an even more radical departure from the present law by eliminating truth as an absolute defense. There are times when a statement technically true has the capacity to mislead the consumer. For example, in the case of *P. Lorillard Co.* v. *FTC* a cigarette manufacturer truthfully stated that its cigarette contained less nicotine than other brands. In fact, the difference in nicotine between the various brands was medically inconsequential. Thus, this statement was held to be proscribed by Section 5 of the Federal Trade Commission Act. As we shall see later in this chapter, the point of view of the consumer rather than the standard of technical truth has been adopted by the FTC in judging whether a statement is misleading.

There is another type of unjustifiably harmful but technically true statement which, in the interest of consumer protection, some maintain should also be brought within the purview of commercial disparagement —namely, true assertions of facts irrelevant to the objective quality of goods. It has been urged by some observers that the American courts accept the doctrines employed by the European countries which disallow truth as a defense in cases where the controverted statements have the effect of diverting customers for reasons completely unrelated to the quality of the products or services involved. The European courts have developed rules to protect the consumer from his own economic irrationality by prohibiting references by competitors to all irrelevant criminal and immoral conduct, past and present, on the theory that such statements have no place in a system of fair competition. It is felt that the personality of the rival traders is a collateral issue which has no place in a properly functioning economic democracy. Significantly, the Continental law goes even further; it also prohibits comparative references to a competitor's goods and business practices. The rationale for this rule is that there exists no fundamental or uniform standard to provide criteria for a proper product appraisal. Features which appeal to some consumers may be regarded as inferior by others. Thus, in the interest of honest competition, it is argued, comparisons must be left to the public.

The American courts have consistently refused to relax the requirement of falsity or change the rules governing the use of irrelevant information. They may well have anticipated the pitfalls that could possibly accompany a change in these standards. The complexities involved in trying to adjudicate whether a statement is deceptive, albeit true, are apparent. Additionally, a businessman would be required to stumble down the path of truthful competitive advertising without any warning signs as to whether a particular trail will lead him into a violation of the law. It would appear that any significant changes in this area will have to be by the legislatures. Until the laws are changed, however, the responsibility for following the lead taken by the Continental countries in these areas will fall upon the business and trade associations. Although many of these associations have established standards of conduct higher than those required by the courts, they are limited as to the sanctions or policing methods that can be employed to enforce these codes because of the antitrust consequences of such activities.

Special Damages. Special damages can best be defined as compensation for actual financial injury such as a loss of sales or a drop in market value of the plaintiff's product. The requirement that special damages be specially alleged and proved is the major obstacle to recovery for disparagement. It has been suggested by a noted commentator that this requirement of proof is tantamount to a denial of legal protection. Consequently, there has been a great pressure exerted in a number of cases for the defendant's statement to be categorized as defamatory per se in order to eliminate the special damages obstacle. It should be noted that, unlike a suit for defamation, general (injury to reputation or good will or to an individual's feelings) and punitive damages are not obtainable.

Historically, in order to satisfy the specificity of damages requirement, the plaintiff had to append to his claim a list of customers who had refused to trade with him because of the defendant's statements. Most present-day courts have sought to relax the specificity requirement by allowing the plaintiff to make a precise claim of loss of receipts or decrease in product value. Included within the purview of special damages today are expenditures incurred in issuing circulars "to ease the minds of prospective purchasers" and losses resulting from necessary price reductions. The *Restatement of Torts,* Section 633, states that the reasonable expenses of litigation may be awarded also.

A few examples will illuminate the problems in this area. In *Fowler* v. *Curtis Publishing* the plaintiff alleged that his taxicab business had been damaged by the defendant's magazine article, but was unable to prove the loss of particular customers by name. The court, in finding that the plaintiff had failed in his burden of sufficiently pleading special damages, set forth the requirements for proof of a general diminution of business. "If the plaintiff desired to predicate his right to recover damages upon general loss of customers, he should have alleged facts showing an established business, the amount of sales for a substantial period preceding the disparagement, the amount of sales subsequent thereto, facts showing that such loss in sales was the natural and probable result of such publication, and facts showing that [the] plaintiff could not allege the names of particular customers who withdrew or witheld their custom."

It must be shown that the disparaging matter was a substantial factor in causing the pecuniary harm, or that such harm was the natural and probable result of the disparagement. This requirement has proved troublesome. In the *Houston Chronicle Pub. Co.* v. *Martin* case it was shown at trial that agencies and factors in addition to the publication of the disparagement had contributed to the injury suffered by the plaintiff. The plaintiff's failure to apportion the damages among the various causes led to a reversal of the jury's $14,000 verdict. Despite the fact that the undisputed evidence showed the plaintiff's loss to be over $44,000, or three times greater than the amount awarded by the jury, the award was deemed too speculative and conjectural.

At least one court appears to have ignored the requirement of specificity. In *Advance Music Corp.* v. *American Tobacco Co.* the defendant misrepresented the relative popularity of the plaintiff's songs on a radio program which listed the top ten songs in sales during the previous week. The judge jumped the obstacle of specificity by emphasizing *how* the plaintiff was injured and ignoring the *extent* to which he suffered an actual loss. The defendant's moral turpitude appears to have influenced the court also. Because of the nationwide nature of the disparagement and its indeterminable effect on both past and future sales, a strict adherence by the court to the conventional view would have been tantamount to a denial of recovery. Evidence of prior sales would have been of little value, because it would have been impossible to determine how much each song would have sold but for the disparagement. There is no objective method by which one can measure the impact that the appearance of a song on the top-ten list has on its future popularity. Consequently, the plaintiffs could only claim that its revenue was diminished and its business prestige was impaired. The recovery here appears to have been based on general damages.

Another court gave similar treatment to a cause of action for disparagement. In the famous case of *Pendleton* v. *Time, Inc.* the publisher of a magazine, after negotiating with the plaintiff for the right to reproduce the first portrait of President Truman ever made, published a different portrait, labeling it as the first portrait of the President. The plaintiff alleged that the publication was made maliciously, with knowledge that the statement in the magazine was false, and with an intent to injure the plaintiff. There was an allegation of loss of prestige and a reduction in the value of the plaintiff's right of reproduction, plus a claim for loss of commissions from some named customers to do other portraits. The court, apparently influenced by the defendant's intentional wrongdoing, allowed the plaintiff to sue for the $100,000 damages despite a paucity of specific allegations of financial loss. Again we have an example of a court being satisfied with allegations of general damages. Here, however, there was at least a modicum of specificity.

Despite the departure by courts from the strict specificity requirements in the area of *pleadings,* it is not at all clear whether or not this trend has been followed with respect to the amount of *proof* required. Avoidance of a defendant's motion to dismiss the suit does not necessarily mean that the plaintiff has won his case. It has been observed recently that except for eliminating the requirement that loss of specific sales be shown, the quantum of proof required to permit the plaintiff to recover damages has not diminished to a great extent. A jury award still may not be based on speculation and conjecture.

To summarize, if a causal relationship can be proved, a plaintiff can recover for a drop in sales or loss of specific customers following a disparagement. But this limitation on the relief available at common law leaves the plaintiff dangerously vulnerable in several distinct situations: (1) Where he has not been in business long enough to establish a valid earnings history prior to the disparagement, the specificity requirement will preclude recovery. (2) The general rule creates an unduly onerous burden for the plaintiff where there has been widespread dissemination of the falsehood to unknown future customers. No business using general advertising instead of personal solicitations of customers could satisfy the specificity rule. If the rule allowing recovery of expenses for counteracting circulars as a part of special damages is extended to allow reimbursement for general advertising costs, the harsh result is partially ameliorated. On balance, there is little protection against loss of future sales, often referred to generally as good will, although loss of good will is a well-recognized ground for recovery in defamation and other tort actions. (3) With the exception of a few cases, the plaintiff cannot recover for nonpecuniary harm such as loss of business prestige or mental distress. (4) Finally, the law makes no provision to recompense one whose sales not only would not have declined but would have increased over previous levels absent the disparagement. Evidence to this effect has been called "manifestly speculative and argumentative."

In view of these weaknesses it might be advisable to follow the English lead and pass a statute which eliminates the necessity for alleging or proving special damages in those cases where the defendant's language is calculated to cause pecuniary damage. The English statute has been criticized for its breadth, but at least it is more sensitive to the problem of present-day economic realities and the frequently savage competition in the advertising arena.

Though for one reason or another the plaintiff may be unable to hurdle the special damages barrier, and therefore be without a remedy at law, he still may have available the equitable remedy of injunctive relief. Protection through injunction raises its own set of problems, which we shall now examine.

Injunctive Relief

Can Equity Take Jurisdiction? The traditional rule has been that equity will not enjoin a defamatory or disparaging utterance. The English abolished this rule by statute in the nineteenth century, but it lingers on in the United States. This denial of jurisdiction has been based on two fundamental principles, the first of which is thought to be the most formidable barrier to a change in the law: (1) the unconstitutionality of prior restraints on speech, and (2) the defendant's right to a jury trial.

The free-speech argument is tenuous at best, at least where competitors are involved. The basic thrust of the First Amendment to the Constitution is to protect political and social comment. Advertising which contains disparaging material certainly occupies the lower ranks in the hierarchy of types of speech deserving protection. In fact, the United States Supreme Court, in *Valentine* v. *Christensen,* held that advertising may be controlled without abridging free speech. However, the Court has never passed on the specific question of whether or not it is unconstitutional to enjoin defamatory or disparaging statements which do not contain political or social comment. A law review article by Mr. Justice Black expresses an absolutist theory of interpretation of the First Amendment's free-speech guarantee which would prohibit any legal action against any type of speech. Although this concept has not been adopted by the Supreme Court as a whole, it prevents anyone predicting with absolute certainty the position that the Court will ultimately adopt with respect to injunctions against disparagement.

A strict adherence to the traditional rule barring such injunctions leaves the unethical few free to disparage continually their rivals so long as they are willing to make periodic payment of court-awarded damages. While giving lip service to this rule, most courts have been able to avoid its effect by finding other wrongful or tortious conduct in addition to disparagement lurking in the facts of each particular case. Where fraud, illegal conspiracy, threats and intimidation, unfair competition, and breach of contract provide an independent ground upon which an injunction can be based, the courts enjoin all the wrongful conduct, including disparagement.

In most cases involving disparagement by competitors, the courts readily find conduct which constitutes unfair competition, a tort distinct from disparagement which provides the necessary peg upon which the injunctive hat can be hung. The decisions in at least two cases, *Maytag Co.* v. *Meadows Mfg. Co.* and *Royer* v. *Stoody Co.,* have found unfair competition in the form of widely disseminated advertising circulars which contained false statements about the plaintiff's goods. In other words the courts appear to have treated disparagement or defamation involving competitors as the basis for a cause of action for unfair competition.

Threats, coercion, and intimidation are frequently encountered in the area of alleged patent infringements and provide an independent ground for injunctive relief against disparagement in that area. In *Emack* v. *Cane* the plaintiff sought to restrain the defendants from making threats intended to intimidate the plaintiff's customers. The defendants threatened to sue them under the pretext that their patent was being infringed by the plaintiff's goods. It was found that the defendants had no intention of prosecuting these suits at the time the threats were made. The court enjoined the defendants' disparaging assertions of patent infringement along with the coercive threats and intimidation which provided the necessary independent grounds for relief. It should be noted that the presence of bad faith was critical to the outcome in this case, because without it, no injunction would have issued. A patentee has a right to protect his property interest in his patent, but he must be in good faith in charging infringement. In *Emack* the defendants displayed their bad faith by a failure to prosecute their claim.

One court has gone so far as to reject outright the old rule that equity would not enjoin disparagement. In this case, *Black and Yates, Inc.* v. *Mahogany Ass'n Inc.*, the defendants falsely claimed that the plaintiff's "Philippine mahogany" was not mahogany but was inferior wood. In granting the injunction, the court emphasized the injustice which would have resulted from a denial of jurisdiction. The defendant was insolvent. The precedential value of the decision may be open to serious question today because it was a pre-*Erie* case. A federal court today, under the *Erie* doctrine, no longer retains the power to decide the appropriate remedy but has to follow state law of unfair competition.

Where unfair competition has not been available as an independent ground in which to root equitable relief, injunctions have been granted against noncompetitors in certain cases, generally those involving suits against dissatisfied automobile owners who had affixed disparaging signs on their automobiles. For example, in *Carter* v. *Knapp Motor Co.* the purchaser painted a white elephant on his car when the dealer refused to replace the allegedly defective car with a new one. The court found this tactic irreparably harmful to the dealer's business and the good name of his product. The disparager's demands were found to be legally unjustified and an injunction was issued. The court in *Menard* v. *Houle* went even further. The defendant in this case found fault with the steering mechanism of his new car. Finding the apparatus to be in good condition, the dealer refused to replace it, whereupon the defendant wrote on his car: "Don't believe what they say, this car is no good; . . . they can't fix it and they will do nothing about it." Emphasizing the absence of an adequate remedy at law, the court enjoined the defendant's activities because of the "continuing course of unjustified and wrongful attack upon the plaintiff motivated by actual malice and causing damage to property rights."

At least one court has refused relief in a situation similar to these. In *McMorries* v. *Hudson Sales Corp.* the dealer sought to enjoin the purchaser from displaying on his car a sign reading, "Frame out of line when purchased. Hudson refuses to make good." In denying a temporary injunction the court emphasized the constitutional guarantees of free speech and noted the absence of allegations either that the statement was untrue or that the defendant sought to extort money from the plaintiff. The impression was given by the court that the defendant has the right to speak as long as he is willing to pay damages.

Is the Remedy at Law Inadequate? The Special Damages Problem. Assuming that the plaintiff presents the type of case over which equity does exercise jurisdiction, the plaintiff must also demonstrate the inadequacy of his remedy at law before qualifying for equitable relief. A continuing publication or the threat of renewal of the objectionable activities by the defendant creates the specter of periodic suits by the plaintiff to collect damages. The threat of a multiplicity of suits tends to make the legal remedy inadequate. The defendant's insolvency is recognized as an important factor in many jurisdictions. Difficulty in ascertaining money damages is another generally recognized ground. An allegation of unascertainable damages, however, can create problems in that such an allegation constitutes an admission that special damages, an essential element in an action at law for disparagement, cannot be demonstrated. Because many courts will not provide equitable relief unless the plaintiff could also state a cause of action at law, anyone who relies upon the absence of ascertainable or special damages as a basis upon which to secure an injunction against disparagement may, in effect, preclude himself from obtaining such equitable relief. In *Marlin Firearms Co. v. Shields,* for example, the defendant seriously disparaged the plaintiff's rifles in an effort to coerce him to continue advertising in the defendant's magazine. In demonstrating the inadequacy of the legal remedy, the plaintiff negatived the claim of special damages. Despite the malicious nature of the defendant's actions, the court refused to enjoin them.

The harsh result of the *Marlin Firearms* case has been mitigated to some extent, however, particularly where there exists in addition to disparagement an independent cause of action for unfair competition, a tort which, as previously noted, has become so broad as to include nearly all wrongful conduct between competitors. But the *Marlin Firearms* decision still retains its vitality with respect to cases involving noncompetitors where the tort of unfair competition is not available as an independent basis for injunctive relief.

So far we have seen that where a competitor has disparaged the plaintiff's products, the courts tend to find the separate tort unfair competition, and thereby circuit the rule against enjoining disparaging statements. It has been found, too, that strict proof of special damages is no longer a requisite to injunctive relief. Some courts have gone so far as to reject the notion that the loss of good will has no place in the law of disparagement. They have protected the intangible, but real, relationship existing between a merchant and his customers—his good will —by enjoining the defendant's wrongful activities. Additionally, when seeking an injunction, the plaintiff need only *assert* rather than *prove* the falsity of the defendant's statement; the burden then falls upon the defendant to vindicate his actions.

The full import of injunctive relief can now be appreciated. It compensates for the indaequacies in the law of commercial disparagement by ignoring its harsh requirements. In fact, the courts of equity today appear to be treating disparagement in the same manner as they have been dealing with defamation—that is, protecting good will, obviating the necessity of proving special damages, and placing the burden of proof as to the truth of the statement on the defendant.

Privileged Statements

Opinion of Noncompetitors. Though not technically categorized as privileged statements, some types of opinion, though disparaging, are not actionable and therefore are properly included in this section. As we have already seen in our discussion of the fact–opinion dichotomy, statements of pure opinion are rare. *Opinion* as used in this context will include statements of subjective opinion uttered by a noncompetitor which contain an element of fact measurable against the objective standard of falsity. The questions raised by expressions of opinion by competitors will be covered in the following section.

According to the *Restatement of Torts* view, statements of opinion are not actionable unless the publisher did not hold the opinion he expressed. This rule correctly emphasizes the role of intent in determining whether or not one is privileged to utter his opinion. The *Restatement* view appears to protect against the sham opinion in that one who intentionally disparages a trader or his product would be hard pressed to demonstrate an honest belief in what he said.

The significance of this rule can best be seen in a comparison of two cases involving the Federal Trade Commission, *Scientific Mfg. Co.* v. *FTC* and *Perma-Maid Co.* v. *FTC.* In the former, Scientific published and sold pamphlets containing two articles by its president, Force, that were intended to expose alleged dangers to health attendant the use of aluminum utensils in food storage and preparation. The articles were prefaced by the question, "Did you ever find maggots in your aluminum pans?" They then claimed that aluminum was a disease-producing, and death-dealing metal. "Almost daily you read in the press of hundreds being poisoned by eating food cooked in aluminum." The company had no business interest in cooking utensils of any sort. Force, who unquestionably believed his statements to be true, was a graduate pharmacist and chemist.

The court reversed the commission's cease and desist order on basically the same reasoning adopted by the *Restatement,* Section 627, referred to previously. Without reaching the constitutional free-speech issue the court stated that Section 5 of the Federal Trade Commission Act did not prohibit the assertion of honest opinion, even though unfounded and untrue, by one not engaged or financially interested in the particular trade involved. Under Section 627 the result would have been the same because it also protects expressions of honest beliefs.

The importance of the honest opinion privilege can be demonstrated by contrasting the result in *Perma-Maid,* where the disparaging statements were identical to those in issue in the *Scientific* decision. In fact, Force's articles were distributed by the respondent's salesman. But in this case the utterances were by a competitor and not of the type protected by the competitor's privilege. Absent the broad privilege available to a noncompetitor, the commission's cease and desist order was upheld.

The honest opinion rule is not without its weaknesses. Noncompetitive experts are frequently looked to for guidance by the consumer because of their apparently disinterested position. Because of this influence these experts are, in a sense, trustees of the public interest. As to them, the opinion privilege should be less forgiving. In order to foster fairness, the better rule might be to require the expert to base his opinion upon at least "some" evidence, thus eliminating the honesty-without-more approach of the present law.

The Competitor's Privilege. Though some statements by competitors, otherwise disparaging, are privileged, two different rules have been applied in determining whether or not the privilege exists. Under the less popular view there is a privilege for a competitor to disparage his rival's products in good faith. Because malice is one of the elements of a cause of action for commercial disparagement, this privilege appears to accomplish little if malice is equated with an intent to do harm. However, where the malice element of disparagement is broadly drawn so as to include not only intentional inflictions of harm, but also negligently caused economic injury, this privilege becomes meaningful. Though the plaintiff may be able to prove the defendant's negligence, the defendant may still be able to escape liability upon showing his good faith. In other words, the existence of the privilege means that the plaintiff will be required to prove an intent on the part of the defendant to injure.

The more widely accepted rule, found in *Restatement,* Section 649, is different in that it extends the privilege only to unduly favorable comparisons made by a competitor about his own products. The comparison may not "contain assertions of specific unfavorable facts." This view protects normal exaggerations, known as "puffing" or "dealer's talk," made by a person in selling his own product, and distinguishes such "talk" from a false utterance about a competitor's product, the type of statement that is generally actionable as disparagement. In other words, a competitor can claim that his toothpaste "gets your teeth whiter, brighter, and freer from decay and odor-causing bacteria," but can't state that his rival's toothpaste "is just like grit and will take the enamel on your teeth right off."

There are at least two rationales for this privilege. One is that puffing in superlative language is such a frequent occurrence in American advertising today that the consumer is no longer being misled. A second is that the courts should not be burdened with having to determine the relative merits of competing products.

A comparison of the following two cases should emphasize the importance of the competitor's privilege. In *Pendleton* v. *Time, Inc.* an erroneous claim by *Life* magazine that a portrait of Harry S. Truman was the first painted of him was held to disparage the first actual portrait, even though there were no specific assertions of unfavorable fact. Because the parties were not competitors, the privilege was not available to avoid liability. In *Quinby and Co.* v. *Funston* the defendant made a similar claim of exclusivity at the plaintiff's expense by advertising that a particular investment plan was the first of its kind and was not obtainable elsewhere. The plaintiff, who had a similar plan in effect at the time, was awarded neither damages nor an injunction. The court held that the defendant's claims came within the purview of privileged utterances as defined by the *Restatement*. The statements were found to be simply extravagant claims, or puffing, and not capable of misleading anyone. The defendant's competitive relationship with the plaintiff saved him from a result similar to that of the *Pendleton* case.

There is a corollary to the competitor's privilege doctrine which should be mentioned, the principle of self-defense. When it is impossible to obtain the aid of the court, a competitor may indulge in self-help in order to prevent imminent and irreparable damage. Where the court has refused to recognize a publication against a competitor as disparagement, the injured party may protect himself by embarking upon a similar course of advertising. If a particular type of puffing is not disparagement, then neither will be a similar brand of counterpuffing.

Finally, as we have already seen, a rival claimant has a conditional privilege. He may protect his interests by issuing good-faith warnings against patent, trade-mark, or copyright infringement. In the language of the *Restatement,* Section 647, a rival claimant is privileged to make "an honest assertion of an inconsistent legally protected interest in himself."

Means of Disparagement

It is the purpose of this section to explore the various forms in which disparagement has appeared. Many of the cases discussed so far have involved direct attacks upon product quality, but as we have seen, some methods are more subtle and no less devastating.

Indirect. The disparagement may be indirect, as in the *Advance Music* case, in which the plaintiff was damaged by the defendant's inaccurate representations as to the relative popularity of the plaintiff's songs, or as in *Pendleton* v. *Time, Inc.,* where an erroneous claim by *Life* magazine that a portrait of Harry S. Truman was the first ever painted of him was held to disparage the first actual portrait. Similarly, misrepresentations as to the share of the listening audience that a radio station had, or false quality ratings in a restaurant guide book could constitute indirect disparagement. In a recent case, *L'Aiglon Apparel, Inc.* v. *Lana Lobell, Inc.,* the defendant's advertisements represented that its $6.95 dress was identical to a $17.95 dress made by the plaintiff, thereby causing buyers to believe that they could purchase the same dress for the lower amount from the defendant. In fact, the defendant's copy was cheaper in material and workmanship, and thus damaged the plaintiff's reputation for producing quality goods.

Inference. The famous case of *National Refining Co.* v. *Benzo Gas Motor Fuel Co.* provides an excellent example of inferential disparagement. The plaintiff was the only producer and seller of a benzol-gasoline motor fuel in Kansas City. The defendant circulated leaflets which falsely stated that benzol's harmful qualities caused bearing, cylinder, and valve damage to internal combustion engines, but did not mention the plaintiff by name. Because the plaintiff was the sole producer of benzol in the area, the judge allowed the jury to infer that the leaflets were directed against the plaintiff and awarded him damages. (The damage award was subsequently reversed for a failure to show special damages.) It is the generally accepted rule that the failure specifically to mention the plaintiff by name is irrelevant, but the absence of specific reference introduces an additional problem of proof. The plaintiff must show that the persons to whom the statements were made knew that they referred to him, his business, or his goods.

"Bait and Switch." Unauthorized and undisclosed substitution of one article for another ("bait and switch") may give rise to disparagement. In the recent New York case of *Electrolux Corp.* v. *Val-Worth, Inc.* the defendant advertised rebuilt Electrolux vacuum cleaners for sale at low prices in order to invite inquiry by prospective customers. The defendant disparaged the rebuilt machines in order to switch to a more costly machine not built by the plaintiff. More than direct disparagement was found in this case. The court made the interesting observation that disparagement occurred indirectly when, after the people came into the store thinking in terms of Electrolux as a result of the extensive advertising campaign, they were disappointed by the attempted "switch." The court enjoined further damage to the plaintiff's good will. In *Admiral Corp.* v. *Price Vacuum Stores, Inc.* it was indicated that trade-mark

infringement may also involve disparagement of the plaintiff's goods, especially when the product sold by the defendant under the infringing trade-mark is inferior to the plaintiff's.

Pictures. Factual assertions do not have to be verbal; they can be communicated through signs and pictures and are thus actionable if untrue. Though the case law is scanty, *Paramount Pictures, Inc.* v. *Leader Press, Inc.* provides a good illustration. In that case the plaintiff motion picture producer created its own artistic advertising accessories and leased them to theaters playing Paramount films. The defendant manufactured and sold advertising materials in competition with the displays leased by the plaintiff. The evidence allegedly showed that the defendant's descriptions of the films and pictorial portrayals of the stars were inferior and inaccurate, thereby disparaging the plaintiff's movies. The court held that these allegations of misrepresentation stated a cause of action upon which injunctive relief could be granted.

Comparison. In competitive advertising, product comparisons are among the most effective means of influencing the consuming public. As a result, comparative misrepresentation is a route frequently chosen by business rivals. Yet of all the forms of disparagement, this one is often the most difficult to describe in terms of what is or is not actionable. Of course, where a suit involves a comparison in which the defendant has made specific assertions of untrue fact about a competitor's product, there is little doubt as to the outcome. For instance, an injunction was granted in *Rosenberg* v. *J. C. Penney Co.* prohibiting the defendant from displaying in its store window the plaintiff's garment, to which a placard making invidious comparisons had been attached. The signs alleged that in comparison to the defendant's product the plaintiff's "garment is either a poorly made second or prison-made merchandise. . . . 25% of the weight of the cloth is starch and filler." That such false assertions about the product of a competitor are actionable is obvious. But problems arise when the comparisons contain specific misrepresentations solely about the utterer's own product.

If a party falsely claims that his product is superior to another, is equal to a more expensive product, or possesses some unique advantages, it is a form of disparagement, because it implies that a competitor's product is of an inferior grade or does not possess something that the defendant has. These false claims may be protected by the competitor's puffing privilege, which makes complex an otherwise straightforward area of the law. The privilege is extended by *Restatement,* Section 649, to unduly favorable comparisons made by a competitor about his own products. It has been suggested that one of the rationales for this rule is that extravagant claims about the merits of one's own product have become so commonplace that the consumer is no longer misled by them. Here lies the rub, for if a court can be convinced that consumers have been mis-led, the justification for the privilege disappears. Consequently, absent hard-and-fast rules by which to guide his course of conduct, a seller may be compelled to defend each and every comparative advertisement, with the possibility of a different conclusion being reached in each state.

Following are two recent cases in which the particular comparisons involved were held to be not within the ambit of the permissible "puff." The defendants in *L'Aiglon Apparel, Inc.* v. *Lana Lobell* used a picture of their competitor's expensive dress in advertising their own poor imitation at a lower price, thus falsely implying that the plaintiff's product was comparatively no better than the defendant's, that is, was of cheap quality. In *Davis Electronics Co.* v. *Channel Master Corp.* the defendant pictured the plaintiff's television antenna in its advertisement and then claimed it was "outperformed" by the antennas made by Channel Master. The plaintiff sought a temporary injunction, in response to which the defendant made a motion to dismiss on the ground that the claims, even if in fact false, were excusable as mere trade puffing. The court refused to dismiss the action. One observer has read the case to stand for the proposition that, "it is more than mere puffing when the seller asserts that his goods are better than those of a designated competitor." However, a careful reading of the decision indicates that the privilege will be denied by the court only where there is proof of malicious intent.

It is still an open question in the state courts as to what types of comparative misrepresentations are actionable. Some commentators reject the dictum in *National Refining Co.* v. *Benzo Gas Motor Fuel Co.,* which accepted the more permissive English view of puffing. One writer stated, "The English doctrine has been defended on the psychological assumption that 'statements by a trader vaunting the superiority of his goods are not likely to influence the conduct of possible customers. . . .' If this were true a businessman would not spend his money on such advertisements."

European laws of commercial disparagement require that in the interest of honest competition, all comparisons be left to the public. Several American commentators have suggested adoption of this rule with the exception of necessary comparisons, that is, where the features of an article cannot be brought to the attention of the customer unless it is compared with the article of a competitor. Technical improvements or the existence of a particular ingredient absent in competitive products are examples of the exception.

Despite the widespread use of inaccurate product comparisons as an advertising device, they have seldom been challenged in private suits. This result can best be explained by the fact that most businessmen utilizing the comparative method measure their product against those of the entire industry, not just against the product of a particular competitor.

Thus, damages would be next to impossible to prove. For this reason, and because of the puffing privilege, the responsibility for preventing the deceptive use of this practice has fallen upon the FTC.

STATE LEGISLATION

We have already noted that the state legislative schemes to control the myriad methods of unfair competition and deceptive advertising practices have generally been, at best, inadequate. The state laws governing commercial disparagement are no exception. Against this background of ineffective enforcement, however, some courts have attempted to broaden the heretofore narrow proscriptions of existing laws.

The Uniform Deceptive Practices Act has a specific section covering disparagement. Section 2(a) (8) proscribes the disparagement of "the goods, services or business of another by false or misleading representations of fact." The act also follows the lead taken by a few states in authorizing private parties to enjoin the deceptive practices covered by the act.

DISPARAGEMENT AND THE FEDERAL TRADE COMMISSION

Because of the difficulties encountered in attempting to obtain private judicial relief from commercial disparagement, the importance of the commission's authority under Section 5 of the Federal Trade Commission Act cannot be overstated. The scope of protection under Section 5 is significantly broader than has been the case in the state courts. For example, truth is not always a defense. Moreover, the commission may be able to intervene in those cases where the courts are reluctant to recognize a private remedy, for example, where the disparager's attack is directed against a group or industry rather than an individual competitor.

Early in the commission's history it accepted the right of a competitor to puff. But as the commission expanded its concepts of what constituted disparagement, there has been a concomitant erosion of the puffing privilege. As a result, under the Federal Trade Commission Act today, a competitor who falsely claims the superiority of his product over another is more likely to be found guilty of indirect disparagement. The commission categorizes this form of deceptive advertising as comparative misrepresentation. The distinction appears to be that "disparagement," for its purposes, is limited to specific assertions of untrue facts about a competitor's product, whereas "comparative misrepresentation" includes only deceptive assertions about one's own product in comparison to a competitor's. Following the dichotomy established by the commission, the discussion in the following section shall be limited to disparagement. Indirect disparagement by comparative misrepresentation will be dealt with in a subsequent section.

Truth as a Defense

Truth is an absolute defense under American case law. But the FTC has recognized that acts and practices which are truthful may also be unfair or deceptive. In *Gordon-Van Tine Co.* the commission ordered the respondent to cease using an advertisement which incompletely summed up the consequences of an FTC proceeding against a competitor. The stipulation accepted in the case went even further by prohibiting the use of any orders or records of the commission, even in their full and exact wording, for the purpose or with the effect of disparaging the business of a competitor who had complied with the order. The commission prevented the use of unquestionably true materials because they were objectively irrelevant to the question of product quality and therefore misleading. Additionally, the commission ruled in *U.S. Products Co.* that the respondent could not advertise that charges had been filed with the FTC, together with the nature of the assertions. Again truth was no defense to the charge of disparagement.

The commission was slow in expanding its campaign against truthful disparagements to attacks upon a competitor's product. The courts were unquestionably responsible for this delay. Because the commission must rely upon the courts for enforcement of its orders, it cannot proceed at a pace faster than the judiciary is willing to accept. In *Philip Carey Mfg. Co.* v. *FTC* the respondent informed prospective purchasers that a petition of bankruptcy had been filed against a competitor. Despite his unethical conduct, the court reversed the commission order, holding truth to be an absolute defense. "[W]e know of no standard which forbids the telling of truth, even about a competitor."

In subsequent years the courts became more permissive, and the commission responded with the "doctrine of significance," which appeared first in *Columbia Appliance Corp.* Presented there was the question of whether or not a particular solvent, one of a number used in synthetic dry-cleaning machines, was properly characterized as more toxic, poisonous, or dangerous than other competing brands. The commission decided that because all the solvents were toxic to some extent, the broad distinctions as to their relative safety or dangerous propensities were not justified. This result was reached despite the finding that in scientific circles the distinctions as to the harmful characteristics of each brand were justified. In order to avoid consumer deception, the commission ruled that advertisements containing references to a competitor's products must describe only significant differences between the two. This doctrine was applied in the *Lorillard* case.

Subsequent cases reflect the increasing demand for nondeceptive truth. The *Eugene Agee* decision saw the commission once again attack statements as disparaging because of their objective irrelevance. The respondent, who compiled a "Directory of Private Business Schools in the United States," stated that a certain competing school was undesirable because its student body was comprised of many young girls from rural communities, old men, and Negroes. Those remarks were ruled logically invalid because they bore no relation whatsoever to the quality of work or standing of the school. They were unfairly disparaging because they appealed to one's prejudices, not his intellect.

The *Bostwick Laboratories* case provides another example of unlawful truthful disparagement. The respondent was engaged in the manufacture and sale of various insecticides. In advertising his products he said that competitive insect killers which contained DDT might be a danger to health. This statement was true only if the insecticides were indiscriminately used in a manner contrary to the cautions expressed in the directions. The commission held that this important omission from the respondent's words made them deceptive and disparaging.

Additional Examples of Disparagement

Some of the most interesting FTC disparagement cases have involved television advertisements. However, the importance of these decisions warrants their being reviewed in a separate chapter. The materials in this section will be limited to nontelevision practices.

The advertisements employed by various manufacturers of stainless steel cookery to attack competing types of utensils have been among those frequently censored by the commission. We have already encountered Perma-Maid's efforts: "Did you ever find maggots in your aluminum pans? Do you know that such pans may be full of the most deadly bacteria known to science?" Other advertisements have also relied upon health scares in disparaging aluminum and enamel cooking utensils. At least two alleged that such utensils cause cancer, ulcers, appendicitises, tumors, and anemia.

The Zenith Radio Corporation took a more subtle approach in an attempt to boost the sales of its hearing aid. The corporation owned a magazine called *Better Hearing* which purported to be an independent publication. In this magazine Zenith compared one of its current models with a discontinued model of a competitor's hearing aid without disclosing that fact. Under the guise of being a disinterested evaluator, the magazine disparaged its rival's product by making false representations concerning its construction. Zenith agreed to cease and desist from these practices.

COMPARATIVE MISREPRESENTATIONS

Puffing and Technical Truth

Comparative misrepresentation is the type of disparagement most frequently encountered in the FTC cases. Nowhere are the commission's departures from the common law attitudes toward truth and puffing more important.

The erosion of the competitor's puffing privilege is not a recent development in the commission's interpretation of Section 5. It dates back at least to the early 1940's, as the *Moretrench* case demonstrates. The respondent in that case manufactured pumps, pipes, and wellpoints designed to drain wet places preparatory to building. One of its advertisements pictured several wellpoints of various makes plus its own. The words below the picture exclaimed, "One Moretrench wellpoint is as good as any five others . . . say experienced contractors." The commission held that this claim was not mere puffing but was deceptive and therefore unlawful. On appeal, the United States Court of Appeals for the Second Circuit said, "It is extremely hard to believe that any buyers of such machinery could be misled by anything which was patently no more than the exuberant enthusiasm of a satisfied customer, but in such matters we understand that we are to insist upon the most literal truthfulness." Though dismayed by the results, the court deferred to the commission's judgment and affirmed the cease and desist order.

A more recent case, *Steelco* v. *FTC,* provides some insight as to the present limitations upon the right to puff. Though the case involved disparagement and not comparative misrepresentation, the following general statement on puffing by the United States Court of Appeals for the Seventh Circuit is helpful, "It seems plain that the representations were made in order to induce the purchase of the petitioner's product. . . . Statements made for the purpose of deceiving prospective purchasers . . . cannot be properly categorized as 'puffing.' "

This statement is an accurate description of the law under the Federal Trade Commission Act as it is today and represents a significant departure from the law adhered to in the state courts. Whereas the puffing privilege as originally formulated allowed false assertions of fact about one's own product, the commission has adopted the more restrictive test of whether or not the false statement has the capacity to mislead the public. If it does, then the statement is not a permissible puff. The recent

Liggett & Myers case provides a good example of this rule as it applies to comparative misrepresentation. As that case demonstrates, it may well be that the puffing privilege has almost disappeared from the FTC's lexicon of available defenses to an action for comparative misrepresentation.

In contrast to the judicial acceptance of the commission's restrictions upon puffing, the early attempts to introduce the doctrine of significance as a limitation upon the defense of truth were thwarted by the courts. In the *International Parts* case the respondent had employed the following advertisement: "Warning! To protect yourself against leaking carbon monoxide gas, be sure your muffler is made with continuous Electric-Welded Seams throughout . . . not locked, crimped, or spotwelded." Basing its conclusion on expert testimony that there was no danger of leaking fumes from any muffler that was properly made, the FTC found the advertisement deceptive and untrue. However, the United States Court of Appeals for the Seventh Circuit rejected this view on the basis of additional expert testimony which revealed that a muffler with a continuous, electrically welded seam throughout was less likely to leak than one that had been spotwelded, locked, or crimped. Although the incidence of leaking mufflers of any kind was very low, the respondent's comparisons were technically true, and thus permissible in the eyes of the court.

The commission's first breakthrough with the courts in this area of truth in comparisons came several years later in the *Lorillard* case. There a scientific study of major cigarettes investigating the relative quantities of nicotine, tars, and resins was sponsored by *Reader's Digest*. Accompanying the text was a chart which revealed that the quantitative differences between the brands were insignificant in terms of physiological harm to the smoker. The tenor of the article was that one cigarette can just about nail down the smoker's coffin as well as another. But because the chart revealed that Old Gold cigarettes ranked lowest in these deleterious substances (albeit a quantitatively insignificant difference), Lorillard amassed an advertising campaign in which the results of the study were heralded as follows, "Old Golds found lowest in nicotine; Old Golds found lowest in throat irritating tars and resins. See Impartial Test by *Reader's Digest* July Issue. . . . [O]ld Gold was best among all seven cigarettes tested."

The commission found fault with this advertising because it did not print all that the *Reader's Digest* article said. The small portion that it reprinted was found to have created an entirely false and misleading impression. The purpose of the *Digest's* chart was to indicate an absence of substantial difference between cigarettes, not to demonstrate that Old Gold was of a superior quality.

The United States Seventh Circuit Court of Appeals upheld the FTC's rejection of technical truth. "The important criterion is the net impression which the advertisement is likely to make upon the general populace." The statements must be true as the ignorant, unthinking, and credulous consumer views them. Anyone reading these advertisements "would have gained the very definite impression that Old Gold cigarettes were less irritating to the throat and less harmful than other leading brands. . . . The truth was exactly the opposite." Both the omissions and the absence of medically significant differences were fatal to these claims. Furthermore, the defendant was not saved by a reference to the sources of his statistics. In the court's words, "few would have troubled to look up the *Reader's Digest* to see what it really had said."

A few months later the R. J. Reynolds Tobacco Co. adopted a similar approach in advertising its Camel brand of cigarettes. The commission's order to cease and desist from representing that Camels contain less nicotine than do the four other largest-selling brands of cigarettes was affirmed by a federal court. It is not clear from the opinion whether or not the respondent's claims were at least technically true. Had they been, however, the result would have been the same. The commission rejected the ads on the basis that the tobacco constituents of Camels were like those of other leading brands. Reynolds made other comparative claims which bear mentioning here even though the "technical truth" issue was not involved. It was contended that Camels relieved fatigue, created or released bodily energy, did not impair the "wind" or physical condition of athletes, and aided digestion by increasing the alkalinity of the digestive tract. These representations were prohibited by the United States Seventh Circuit Court of Appeals.

The Liggett & Myers Tobacco Co. was another cigarette manufacturer whose advertising practices were challenged by the commission. The subject in controversy in this case was an advertisement, which, among other things, said: "Buy Chesterfield—*Much Milder.*" For twenty years the term *milder* had been in wide use by cigarette manufacturers. This case appears to be the first in which its use was challenged. In disposing of the respondent's defense that this was mere puffing, the commission followed a pattern established by earlier cases. In its view, the word *milder* was a clear and positive affirmation of the quality of Chesterfield cigarettes, made to induce their purchase; therefore, it was not a puff. Once again a drastic blow was struck at this common law privilege. Because it is reasonable to assume that all advertising is designed to induce sales, and because comparative advertisements generally contain positive affirmations as to quality, the reasoning of the commission leads to one inescapable conclusion, that little, if any, false comparative advertising can be defended as mere puffing.

Thus, the only remaining issue was the truth of the respondent's assertion. It is here that the complex problems arose. The advertisement was either true in the sense that it was an expression of *opinion,* or false, if viewed as an expression of *fact.* Relying upon a dictionary definition of the word, the hearing examiner accepted the contention made by Liggett & Myers that *milder* related only to such sensory feelings as taste and smell. In other words, it merely connoted a quality product, "a well-blended, pleasant-tasting cigarette." Under this view, which essentially treated *milder* as an expression of pure opinion, the statement could not be untrue even from the consumer's viewpoint, because there is no objective standard of falsity by which to measure it. Thus, it could not be considered misleading.

The commission, however, disagreed with the findings of the hearing examiner. It emphasized that in determining whether a particular advertisement is misleading, "regard must be had not to fine spun [dictionary] distinctions and arguments that may be made in excuse, but to the effect which, in its overall context, it might reasonably be expected to have on the general public." Taking into consideration the other statements contained within the advertisement—for example, the alleged findings by medical specialists that Chesterfields do not adversely affect the nose and throat—the FTC was of the opinion that the term *milder* inferentially related to a physiological condition and constituted an announcement that Chesterfields were "less irritating" to the nose and throat than other cigarettes. Because the expert testimony had previously established that Chesterfield smoke was "not significantly different . . . from other brands," the commission's decision as to the meaning of *milder* was the turning point of the case. A word that had not been objectionable when characterized as opinion was found false and misleading when held to be a factual assertion. The respondent was found to have engaged in comparative misrepresentation.

It is interesting to note that the advertisement also stated that Chesterfields "contain tobaccos of better quality and higher price than any other king-sized cigarette." The commission did not challenge this comparison.

Within the past few years the FTC has challenged several comparative bread advertisements. Commission decisions in two of these cases, *National Bakers Services, Inc.* v. *FTC* and *Bakers Franchise Corp.* v. *FTC*, were upheld by the federal courts. The advertisements used by National frequently contained a picture of a glamorous motion picture star in a full-length pose. These ads generally displayed a loaf of bread called Hollywood, along with such words as *reducing diets, panther slim, leopard lithe, tigress trim,* and *diet wisely.* The statement "only about 46 calories in an 18 gram slice" was always present. The commission was of the opinion that this amounted to a claim that Hollywood bread was substantially lower in calories than ordinary bread. In fact, it was merely cut into thinner slices. Even though it was true that each 18-gram slice contained only 46 calories, the implication was deceiving. Consequently, truth was not a defense. According to the FTC the consuming public has no conception of the gram weight or calorie content of a slice of regular bread. Therefore, these representations as to calories per slice, when made in the context of other statements advocating keeping slim, led the public to believe that this particular bread would effect a weight loss or prevent weight gain. The commission's order, which was affirmed by the United States Court of Appeals for the Seventh Circuit, prohibited the respondents from claiming that Hollywood had fewer calories than a slice of ordinary bread unless it was also advertised that the Hollywood bread was sliced thinner.

Similarly, in the *Baker's Franchise* case, the United States Third Circuit Court of Appeals upheld a commission order requiring the respondent to desist from falsely representing that its Lite-Diet was a lower-calorie bread. The respondent accurately claimed that his bread contained only 45 calories per slice but neglected to mention that its bread weighed 17 grams per slice as opposed to regular bread's 23. When considered in the context of the bread's name and such statements as "Who'd ever think such delicious bread could help keep you slim," the ad was found to create in the mind of the public an erroneous impression of a higher caloric content in competing breads. Once again technical truth was no defense.

Having discussed cigarettes and breads, we turn to toothpaste, a subject that bears a sequential relationship to the previous two items. Many readers have seen the advertisements for Crest in which the representatives of two groups of children are interviewed with respect to their cavities. Those using Crest received anywhere from 25 to 49 per cent fewer cavities than the group using "regular" toothpaste. These results were accurate and significant. But the commission was not satisfied. The "regular" toothpaste was Crest minus the ingredient stannous fluoride, a toothpaste formula unlike those used in competing brands of toothpaste. It was felt that the expression *regular toothpaste* was generally understood to refer to brands of commercially available toothpaste competing with Crest. In the commission's view, the consumer was being misled by the failure to state that Crest was competing with a nonexistent product. The respondents agreed to cease using this technically true but deceptive advertisement.

A truthful assertion may also fail to meet the commission's rigid standards because of a lack of specificity. In the *Tounecraft Industries* case, the respondent claimed that its "waterless" method of cooking with stainless steel utensils was better for one's health than cooking in aluminum pots

and pans. Though the "waterless" method was found to be more beneficial in some respects, the respondent was required by the FTC to
specify the precise manner in which its wares promoted better health.

So far only cases in which the commission has prevailed have been
examined. The result in *FTC* v. *Sterling Drug, Inc.* should serve to
demonstrate that under certain circumstances technical truth may be
available as a defense to an alleged violation of the Federal Trade Commission Act. There the controversy had its roots in an issue of the
American Medical Association journal which carried an article written
by medical experts on the comparative merits of five analgesic compounds or pain relievers—Bayer aspirin, St. Joseph's aspirin, Bufferin,
Anacin, and Excedrin. Giving the results of their tests in statistical detail,
the authors noted that the data failed to demonstrate any significant
difference among any of the drugs. In view of the various claims by
competitors that their products were less upsetting, or "twice as fast as
aspirin," or "50% stronger than aspirin," Sterling Drug was understand-
ably anxious to make the most out of the A.M.A. journal's report. Thus,
it embarked upon an extensive advertising campaign which utilized these
findings. Included in these advertisements was the statement, "The study
shows that there is no significant difference among the products tested in
rapidity of onset, strength, or duration of relief. Nonetheless, it is interesting to note that within just fifteen minutes, Bayer Aspirin had a
somewhat higher pain relief score than any of the other products."

The commission sought to enjoin these advertisements, attacking,
among other things, the last sentence of the preceding paragraph as
improperly representing that Bayer aspirin gave greater short-run relief
than its competitors. The statement was technically true. Nowithstand-
ing the fact that the statistical margin of error in the study was greater
than the difference between the rapidity of onset scores of Bayer and
its nearest competitor, meaning that the second place drug might fare
as well as or better than Bayer over the long run of statistical tests,
Sterling's product relieved pain faster in this particular test. The United
States Court of Appeals for the Second Circuit, in ruling against the
commission, noted that although a close examination of the charts drawn
up by the medical experts revealed a lack of significant difference between the drugs tested, the Bayer advertisement had stated just that in the
sentences preceding its excursion into the specifics of the pain-relief
scores. The court distinguished these facts from those in *P. Lorillard Co.*
v. *FTC*, upon which the commission had relied heavily. There, although
literally true, the statements were used to convey an impression dia-
metrically opposed to that intended by the writer of the article. Here
Serling Drug had not conveyed a misleading impression as to either the
spirit or the specifics of the article. Thus, the commission failed to make

a proper showing that it had reason to believe the advertisement deceptive.

CONCLUSION

The FTC has demonstrated that its concern is not with technical truth, but with truth as the consumer views it. The law is not made for the protection of experts, but for the public; and to protect the public the advertising must be relevant, fair, and relate to significant differences between the competing products. Only then is truth a defense to a charge of deceptive comparisons.

18

Business, Employment, and Sales Schemes

More than any other deceptive commercial practice, with the possible exception of fictitious pricing, the result of unfair or deceptive advertising as to business, sales, and employment opportunities is felt in the victim's pocketbook. Furthermore, the particular segment of the consuming public so affected is the one least able to afford it: the uneducated, the poor man looking for a better job. But who wants a poor-paying job with no fringe benefits? What seller of an opportunity, then, will be prone to disparage or to reveal the less attractive aspects of the one he offers?

Yet such an offer, unlike the areas outlined in Chapter 9 in which the FTC has determined that certain facts are material and, therefore, must be revealed, is not subject to a general rule of disclosure. Although a more exacting standard as to what the consumer needs to know would seem appropriate for the reason that an employment-opportunity or a self-improvement correspondence course usually involve both a sizable investment by the buyer and a commodity which cannot be seen or examined—or even, in most instances, reasonably related to anything of which the buyer has knowledge—the practice has been that disclosure will not be ordered unless the advertisement of the service or course cannot be structured truthfully and nondeceptively without it.

The Federal Trade Commission's approach, generally, to career-opportunity advertising was revealed recently in a case involving the Cinderella Career College and Finishing Schools of Washington, D.C. Although the commission reviewed representations with respect to job placement and educational loans, the long opinion (characterized by one commissioner as making a "federal case" out of the situation) dealt primarily with the school's claims as to what its courses of instruction would do for the "graduate." Ordinarily, the test of deception is the advertisement read as a whole, or the overall impression; but in the advertisements under review, the commission appeared to pinpoint the word *career* as crucial and, in conjunction therewith, *training.*

One advertisement appeared in the "educational directory" of a Washington newspaper under the subheading *Air Career,* and stated in part, "Air Career Training is now available at Cinderella Career School. . . . Prepare for a Stewardess or Reservationist position." Another invited the reader to mail in for a "free brochure on an airline career"; yet another read "Careers in . . . Retail Buying" and claimed "comprehensive training in buying" and described (vividly, according to the commission) the glamorous activities of buyers and their remuneration.

Cinderella also distributed a pamphlet, entitled "Wonderful things happen to a Cinderella Girl," which contained the following paragraph:

> miracles
> after
> sundown
> Drab little typist becomes lovely airline stewardess! Overweight order clerk now a fashion counselor! "No-date" steno becomes belle of the office! High school graduate wins success in television! Middle-age widow looks ten years younger—gets exciting new job! Shy librarian gets three raises *and* a beau! Factory worker becomes studio receptionist.

Rejecting the contention that the advertisements emphasized "personal improvement," the commission concluded that they represented directly or by implication that the courses *qualify* the student to become buyers and airline stewardesses. These claims, according to the commission, "are not subtle innuendos, but direct representations which promise the prospective student that upon taking this course she will qualify as a buyer, which simply is not true." They falsely promise such careers, the commission concluded.

There was apparently little evidence as to how these advertisements had been read by consumers. Obviously, Cinderella hoped that students would be lured by the prospect that the school could do much to improve them in a number of ways. However, for the "drab little typist" who learns to style her hair or for the "order clerk" who is assisted in a weight-reducing program, the commission apparently detected no unfair claims. But because airlines require that their stewardesses attend the schools that they themselves maintain, and because Cinderella had stipulated that completion of its course would not qualify a student to be a buyer (the student whose chances for these careers could be only enhanced and not guaranteed by the training offered), the commission concluded that Cinderella had made a promise it could not deliver.

The commission agreed that the training given by the school may enhance the student's chance to be accepted for training by one of the airlines. It could be added that the trainee in retail buying might also stand a better chance of working up through the ranks of sales clerks to buyer, the traditional road to that position. Nevertheless, having read a "promise" of a career into the advertisements, the commission would not settle for mere enhancement. In its view, the two were "poles apart."

Apparently the record was insufficient for an examination of the school's representations with respect to the training offered in modeling and secretarial skills. Yet, with reference thereto, the commission said, "as a general rule [such positions] would entail considerably more experience and knowledge than respondent would be able to impart to their students during one of these courses."

Difficulties inhere in the decision. Seemingly, the use of the words *training* and *career* together will be read as a promise that the former guarantees the latter. Although there is a natural tendency to join the concepts of training or education with career or material advancement, how it is to be done without promising more than such schools can deliver is a big question. To require that advertisers tell all, including the obvious limitations inherent in such courses, is a possible solution; but from this case, at least, it would seem that the FTC is not yet ready to go that far.

The *Cinderella* case was remanded to the commission for further consideration by the United States Court of Appeals for the District of Columbia, for due process and procedural reasons and without review by the court of the merits of the commission's decision. At this writing it appears likely that further proceedings and review may follow. However, the commission's analysis of the record is helpful in predicting its views on such matters in the future.

The advertising practices of correspondence course sellers have been scrutinized even more closely than the "in-residence" type. Here the written word is the only contact between buyer and seller, and judging from the amount of FTC activity in this area, these words account for a substantial portion of the deceptive practices involving employment and business opportunities. The penchant of these sellers to misdescribe themselves as "schools," "colleges," "institutes," and other traditional educational facilities has been discussed in Chapter 16. Here we are concerned with their overstatements as to what their training can do for the buyer of the home-study course.

Operating on the reasonable assumption that studies will be undertaken for an economic benefit, many purveyors of unsupervised do-it-yourself courses concentrate their advertising claims in the areas of placement facilities, vacancies available, fringe benefits attendant to a particular position, and salaries to be expected. *Hundreds of men and women needed,* and *openings in this area* are familiar eye-catching lures. Women and retired persons are enticed by the possibility of spare-time employment and, as one advertiser claimed, "independent wealth." Courses are offered in a variety of activities, from air-conditioning to welding, and including candy manufacturing, cooking, detective systems, foot culture, meat slaughtering, motel management, hypnology—even law. Preparation for civil service examinations for federal, state, and municipal employment is very often the subject of a correspondence course found to have been advertised in a deceptive manner.

One of the major complaints against the sellers of these courses is that they aim their representations at all takers without pointing out certain features which might narrow the field of interested persons, as for example, that some civil service positions do not require an examination at all or are reserved for veterans or experienced and specially trained technicians; or that government certification may be needed to fill the position for which the training is offered and the course will not necessarily entitled the "graduate" to it; or that, with respect to a civil service examination course, there is only one course of instruction regardless of the position sought. The representation "whatever job you seek, we will coach you for it successfully," provoked the United States Fifth Circuit Court of Appeals to agree with the FTC that the advertiser's claims "far exceeded the potential of his material."

The thrust of the pitch of a seller of a home-study course in television electronics was the uniqueness of an opportunity to get in on the ground floor of an industry "still in its infancy." Unfortunately for the advertiser, his enthusiasm was found to be a bit premature in the early 1940's, because commercial development of television had not yet been authorized by the FCC. Hence, to represent the industry as "already with us" and "developing rapidly" was to mislead unfairly as to the employment opportunities in the industry.

The salary or earnings to be expected once the home student has completed the course of instruction is another topic frequently exaggerated. In advertisements featuring franchise operations and profit-sharing schemes or other "be-your-own-boss" opportunities, it is usually the major point to be made. More often than not the salary or earnings described are exceptional and not to be expected generally, or are available only to the more highly skilled and experienced. Where anticipated earnings are alluded to, the FTC insists that the sum specified must be (1) a true representation of the average earnings *consistently* made by a *substantial* number of salesmen in the ordinary course of business under normal conditions, and (2) *net* earnings. If not, the advertiser must disclose that the specified sum is unusual. And where sales of a device are absolutely dependent upon the successful demonstration of the product, the fact that skill and experience are necessary prerequisites to achieve the wage level described may also have to be revealed.

Neither are advertisers permitted to hedge upon the extent of success to be expected. In this connection the commission has prohibited an advertiser from enticing prospects with phrases like *independent wealth* and *sizable business,* unless such success has been achieved customarily by salesmen under normal conditions and in the due course of business. Moreover, if the earnings represented are attributable to the designer and manufacturer of the product, it cannot be said to be either customary or normal.

Growing mushrooms in your basement or raising mink in your back yard may be less rewarding that the advertiser would have the reader believe because of difficulties inherent in such projects. Prospective buyers cannot be misled, but sellers, in addition, may have to disclose affirmatively the drawbacks to financial success.

In addition to the earnings that can be expected from a given business opportunity, advertisers have played up other factors to enhance the prospect to potential buyers. If the sale of a product is involved, the demand is often overstated so as to imply that neither sales effort nor technical know-how are required. Selling the product will be like falling off a log! One advertiser backed up such a claim with letters signed by shopkeepers when the product had been placed with them, but *before* they had time to verify the statements in the letter. This was deemed by the commission to be as unfair as falsely claiming that ninety-nine out of every 100 prospective customers have purchased.

An exclusive territory for the salesman may be promised. The commission, however, will view the claim somewhat unenthusiastically if the territory has already been worked over by others. And, of course, the offer is patently false if the territory is "exclusive" to another salesman as well.

Another gimmick used to make the prospective salesman believe he has found the soft job is to claim, without foundation, that he will receive assistance in obtaining leads and contacts or liberal financial aid for living expenses or expansion of business, or that extensive advertising will back him up. Similarly, "vanity" publishers, whose standard operating procedure is to publish books for which the printing costs are paid in advance by the author, have been found to be unduly expansive as to the amount of assistance they will give in the promotion and sale of the book. Too often such things as television guest appearances and motion picture rights were promises that the publisher could not fulfill.

Finally, where the salesman is required to purchase the wares he will sell or to make a deposit therefor—that is, to commit himself to a greater extent than the ordinary employee—the FTC will demand that these facts be revealed or at least that the products not be misrepresented as "free."

One device that has been utilized by practically every seller of a business, career, or sales opportunity, including Cinderella Career and Finishing School, is to advertise in the help-wanted columns of newspapers as though employment was being offered when, in fact, the sole purpose is to obtain leads to persons having the purchase price for a course of instruction or for an investment. Cinderella's advertisement was a typical one: "Model-Type women wanted, exp. not necessary, training avail. Call 628-1950, Cinderella Career College." One consumer witness told the FTC that she responded to the notice, expecting to be interviewed for a job, and was enrolled in the school. With neither a job available nor the intention to fill a position, the commission felt this was a "blatant ruse" to lure young women into the premises where they could be persuaded to enroll in a course.

Another help-wanted notice to come to the attention of the commission was more specific as to the position to be filled: "To refill and collect money from our Hershyette candy and sport card machines." The salary was quoted and a cash requirement was disclosed. But again the purpose of the advertisement was to acquire leads to persons who would buy the machines rather than to service ones owned by the advertiser, with the cash directed only to an inventory of merchandise to be dispensed by the machines. The vending machine distributor was ordered to discontinue use of the help-wanted columns for the purpose of securing purchasers rather than employees. The Fred Astaire Dance Studio, of Washington, D.C., was rebuked similarly when its advertised offer to pay $3 per hour to dancing instructors was found to be a ruse to sell more dance courses. Applicants were informed that the offer of employment was applicable only to instructors holding the Fred Astaire "Gold Award"—a level of achievement which takes three years of training to obtain.

False employment offers are frequently used by sellers of correspondence courses to attract women at home. One advertiser highlighted his notice with "Pleasant hand work—no experience necessary," when, in fact, he was selling a home-study course in reweaving. Another sought women to sew ready-cut garments at home and earn from $17.40 to $26.10 a dozen. What the help-wanted notice did not state, of course, was that the seamstress must not only purchase the precut fabric but sell the finished garment as well in order to earn any money.

FTC GUIDES FOR VOCATIONAL AND HOME STUDY SCHOOLS

On July 7, 1970, the FTC gave notice of a public hearing and opportunity to submit views, suggestions, or objections regarding proposed guides on vocational and home study schools. In announcing this development, the FTC stated that the scope of the guides was extended to cover both types of schools because the commission has found that both have used the same sort of unfair or deceptive acts and practices and that guidance for one will be relevant to the operations of the other.

In further identifying current legal problems in this area of trade regulation and the scope of the proposed guides the FTC stated:

> While many of the provisions of the proposed guides are based on the trade practice rules for the private home study schools, others have been formulated from the numerous orders the Commission has issued in cases involving members of this industry. Particular emphasis has been placed upon such matters as use of the term "accreditation," the effect of the negotiation of instruments of indebtedness executed by students to pay for the courses they have purchased, misleading collection practices, and matters associated with refund and cancellation policies. The latter were viewed with particular importance because of the frequency with which students attempt to terminate their enrollment prior to completion of the course, and the difficulties they encounter in doing so. In recognition of the absence of accreditation of schools of this type at the Federal level and because the various states have differing requirements regarding the maintenance of academic, training or educational standards by these schools, the proposed guides require a great many affirmative disclosures of material facts by industry members prior to the enrollment of students. These are all designed to insure that the prospective student is not deceived or otherwise deprived of the information he should have in order to make an informed decision as to whether a course will provide him with the knowledge, skills, or other benefits which he has been led to

expect, and whether all of the terms of the contract are acceptable to him.

The proposed guides may be found in Appendix XIII of this book for readers who may be interested in more detailed information on the subject. The final guides, which are unlikely to differ much from those proposed, should be available by early 1971. Any reader of this book with a problem in this area of trade regulation should obtain a copy from the FTC or from other published sources, including the *Federal Register*.

19

Deceptive Credit Practices

Purchasing goods on credit has now become an integral part of the American consumer market. The availability of deferred payment plans and the terms of these plans are frequently a major promotional factor in marketing retail goods. Charge accounts, credit cards, and other means of consumer credit have grown at a phenomenal rate, accounting for over $122 billion of debt in 1969. Credit availability, a commonplace market ingredient, is frequently taken for granted by the consuming public. Unfortunately, a number of misleading and deceptive practices have developed around the extension of credit for retail purchases.

The cost of credit in a credit transaction has been a constant source of consumer deception. Complex accounting and legal terms embodied in deferred-payment plans, installment-purchase contracts, and other consumer loan printed forms have often been employed to trap the unwary. The common law has proved woefully inadequate in dealing with credit disclosure problems experienced by the unsophisticated consumer. As the small print in contracts has become smaller and the desire for credit purchasing has increased, traditional legal remedies and/or defenses too often have proved ineffectual in preventing abuses in deferred payment purchasing.

FEDERAL TRUTH-IN-LENDING LAW

To deal with these problems, the Congress, on May 29, 1968, enacted the Consumer Credit Protection Act, Title I of which contains the Truth-in-Lending Act. This act is no doubt the most significant federal legislation dealing with deceptive credit practices in the consumer credit area.

The Board of Governors of the Federal Reserve System is directed "to prescribe regulations to carry out the purposes" of the Truth-in-Lending Act, as necessary to "prevent circumvention" and to "facilitate compliance." Pursuant to this Congressional mandate, the Federal Reserve promulgated what is now known as Federal Reserve Regulation Z, which, like the act, became effective July 1, 1969. It is important at this point to note that this regulation is not to be considered as a mere guideline to the act, but as a legislative supplement. A copy of the act is included in the appendix of this book. Copies of Regulation Z are available on request from any Federal Reserve Bank.

The primary purpose of Truth-in-Lending is "to assure a meaningful disclosure of credit terms so that the consumer will be able to compare more readily the various credit terms available to him and avoid the uninformed use of credit." In order to achieve this purpose, standard terminology is now required. It must be remembered that the act does not fix interest rates or charges involved in obtaining credit, nor does it prescribe accounting procedures. It is primarily a disclosure law. Essentially, the act is designed to bring hidden charges into the open, so that consumers can be made aware of all costs incidental to their deferred-payment purchases.

The law, as supplemented by Regulation Z, applies to any person or organization who in the ordinary course of business regularly extends or arranges for the extension of credit to consumers for personal, family, household, or agricultural purposes if a finance charge is imposed or if payment is to be made in more than four installments.

The law specifically exempts all commercial transactions, personal credit over $25,000 (except for real estate purchases), securities or commodities or sales by a broker registered with the Securities and Exchange Commission, and certain charges made by public utility companies whose rates and charges are governed by a governmental authority. The act, as well as Regulation Z, is explicit in requiring certain disclosures and the use of specific terminology (which must be placed in clear and conspicuous type and cannot be abbreviated).

Nine federal agencies have been charged with enforcing the act, with the Federal Trade Commission being responsible for all general retailers, consumer finance companies, and all other creditors not regulated by other agencies. It must always be remembered that credit practices not covered by Truth-in-Lending can still be reached by the FTC if they are found to be deceptive or unfair trade practices as defined in Section 5(a) of the Federal Trade Commission Act.

Truth-in-Lending creates a right of action for consumers against creditors who have failed to make the requisite disclosures. Civil liability is fixed by the statute at twice the amount of the finance charge (minimum $100, maximum $1,000) plus litigation costs and a reasonable attorney's fee. The consumer has one year in which to file suit. If a creditor willfully and knowingly violates the law, the act provides for a fine of not more than $5,000 and/or imprisonment of up to one year. Creditors are required to keep records of all transactions for two years in order to evidence compliance. The consumer has no such obligation. Records required to be kept by the creditor include written disclosure statements, contracts, perhaps invoices, and any other source material that will reflect compliance.

The two most significant disclosures required by Truth-in-Lending are the finance charge and the annual percentage rate. The finance charge is defined in the regulation "as the sum of all charges, payable directly or indirectly by the customer, and imposed directly or indirectly by the creditor as an incident to or as a condition of the extension of credit." In short, the finance charge is the cost of credit.

The finance charge is not limited to the classic concept of interest, but now includes interest, service or carrying charges, loan fees, points, discounts, and many other such fees and costs incidental to obtaining credit. The cost of insurance (credit life, accident, health, or loss of income) if required by the creditor, must be included in the finance charge. Certain charges are excludable providing they are itemized and disclosed; these include fees or charges required by law and paid to public officials; taxes; and license, title, or registration fees imposed by law. Also excludable from the finance charge are bona fide late-payment, delinquency, or default charges, provided that these charges are the result of an unanticipated occurrence. In other words, if a seller permits a buyer to continue purchasing after the account is past due and imposes a continuing late-payment or service charge to the account, the additional charge may become a finance charge. The continuity of the relationship, after default, becomes vital in determining whether a late charge is unanticipated.

The importance of computing the finance charge accurately cannot be overstated. If the finance charge is calculated inaccurately then the second most important disclosure in Truth-in-Lending, the annual percentage rate, will also be inaccurate. Basically, the annual percentage rate represents the relationship of the finance charge to the amount financed.

The act recognizes that there are different kinds of credit plans available and therefore speaks in terms of two major categories of credit transactions, open-end credit and credit other than open-end. The act and the Regulation define "open-end credit" but are silent on just what constitutes "credit other than open-end." Therefore, a creditor must evaluate his particular credit plan in order to ascertain exactly which category is applicable. Each category is subject to specific required disclosures and requisite terminology.

"Open-end credit" is best illustrated by the typical department store revolving charge account. In an "open-end" situation credit is extended, under a plan which permits the consumer to make purchases or obtain loans by using a credit card or other similar device. The customer has the privilege of paying the balance in full or in installments, in which case a finance charge is computed at intervals on the outstanding balance. Determining the annual percentage rate on these accounts is a relatively simple matter. Essentially, the finance charge is divided by the unpaid balance to which it applies giving the rate per month (or other relevant time period). The result is then multiplied by the number of periods per year (usually 12) and the product expressed as a percentage is the annual percentage rate. This is known as the quotient method.

For example, if a department store charges 2 per cent per month on the unpaid balance, this figure multiplied by 12 would result in an annual percentage rate of 24 per cent. However, if the store has a policy of charging 2 per cent on all balances up to $500 and 1 per cent on all balances over $500, the creditor has an option. Let us assume an unpaid balance of $1,000 in the account. The calculation would be as follows:

$$\frac{\$500 \text{ at } 2\% = \$10.00}{\$500 \text{ at } 1\% = \quad 5.00}$$
$$\overline{\$1,000} \qquad \overline{\$15.00}$$
(unpaid balance) (finance charge)

The first option is to compute the annual percentage rate mathematically using the quotient method, that is,

$15 \div 1,000 = .015 \times 100 = 1.5\% \times 12 = 18\%$ annual percentage rate

If this method is used it may mean that the creditor would have to compute the annual percentage rate each month for each account. However, the second option permits preprinting of forms, disclosing

First $500 @ 2% per month = 24%
Over $500 @ 1% per month = 12%

The 24 per cent and 12 per cent must be designated as *annual percentage rate*.

When a department store imposes a minimum finance charge per month of not more than 50 cents, the annual percentage rate need not be individually computed by the quotient method and disclosure of the periodic rate and its attendant annual percentage rate will be sufficient. Let us assume that our department store, in the preceding example, imposes a finance charge of 2 per cent on the unpaid balance, with a minimum charge of 50 cents, and the account has a $2 balance, the annual percentage rate can be disclosed as 24 per cent. However, if the minimum charge is more than 50 cents, the annual percentage rate must be computed by the quotient method. Let us assume the minimum charge to be 70 cents, the computation would be as follows:

$$.70 \div 2 = .35 \times 100 = 35\% \times 12 = 420\% \text{ annual percentage rate}$$

Thus, it can be said that even though the act or regulation does not set rates or accounting methods, it indirectly deters creditors from imposing minimum finance charges in excess of 50 cents because of the high annual percentage rate which would result therefrom.

Credit other than open-end includes consumer loans or purchases in which credit is extended for a given period of time. In these transactions the total amount of the obligation, number of payments, and due date are usually evidenced by contract between the creditor and his customer. Most consumer loans (banks, finance companies, credit unions, and so on) big-ticket items (washing machines, television sets, and so on), and real estate transactions are made or sold in this manner, with the creditor or seller arranging for the extension of credit.

The annual percentage rate for transactions involving credit other than open-end must be computed in accordance with the actuarial method or U.S. rule; however, because accuracy is required to the nearest $\frac{1}{4}$ per cent, there is no real advantage in one method over the other. The Federal Reserve Board has compiled annual percentage rate tables disclosing the finance charge per $100 of the amount financed that can be used for these calculations. Before the tables can be used, the creditor must know (1) the amount of the finance charge, (2) the total amount financed, and (3) the number of payments.

For example, let's take a transaction involving a finance charge of $35 with a total amount financed of $200 payable in twenty-four months. The formula would be

$$\$35 \div \$200 = .1750 \times \$100 = \$17.50 \text{ (finance charge per \$100)}$$

Tables available from the Federal Reserve Board and the Federal Reserve Banks contain these calculations. The annual percentage rate of our example is 16 per cent.

It is noteworthy that in a consumer credit transaction classified as credit other than open-end the finance charge need not be expressed as an annual percentage rate if it does not exceed $5 on an amount financed not exceeding $75 or $7.50 on amounts exceeding $75. However, all other required disclosures *as applicable* must be made.

The protection intended by Truth-in-Lending would be nonexistent if the consumer were legally bound by contractual obligations before he was made aware of the extent of the credit terms. Therefore, all required disclosures must be made before the obligation is incurred. For open-end credit the required disclosures must be made when the account is opened or before it is used for the first time. Creditors are obligated to furnish periodic statements which contain specific terminology to identify the activity in the billing cycle. Certain disclosures in specific terms are required to be made on the face of the statement (such as previous balance, purchases, payments, credits, finance charge, new balance, and annual percertage rate). Other required disclosures can be made on the front or reverse side. The Regulation should be consulted for the exact location of the items as applicable to an individual creditor's plan.

For transactions involving credit other than open-end, all required disclosures must be made "before the transaction is consummated." Local law usually determines at what point in time the transaction is consummated, that is, when it is binding on the persons to the agreement. Again certain required language must be used, as applicable, such as *cash price, cash downpayment, trade in, unpaid balance, amount financed, finance charges,* and so on. Periodic statements on credit other than open-end are permissible and not mandatory. It must be remembered that discounts for prompt payment fall within the category of credit other than open-end. Since the advent of Truth-in-Lending many creditors have reconsidered their offering of cash discounts to consumers because of the complexities of computing the annual percentage rate. Recognizing the problem involved, on August 11, 1969, the Federal Reserve amended Regulation Z §226.8(0) so as to exempt computations of the annual percentage rate if the amount of the discount does not exceed 5 per cent. For example, if a creditor offers a consumer a 2 per cent cash discount if his bill is paid within ten days, full amount due in thirty days (assume a $1,000 purchase), the $20 discount, considered a finance charge, would not have to be reflected as an annual percentage rate. However, if the discount is 6 per cent/ten days, net thirty, the following computation would have to be made in arriving at the required annual percentage rate.

$$\frac{60}{940} \times 100 \times \frac{12}{1} = 76.56\%, \text{ or } 76\frac{1}{2}\% \text{ (annual percentage rate)}$$

This amendment contains other disclosure provisions applicable to "discount for prompt payment" transactions and should be thoroughly digested by creditors involved with same.

There are special protective provisions in Truth-in-Lending for credit transactions which will create a security interest in the consumer residence. In other words, if a creditor obtains a security interest in real estate used as a residence, the consumer must be given written notification by the creditor that such an interest will be created and that he has the right to rescind the transaction within three business days. If a consumer elects to rescind, he must do so in writing directed to the creditor's place of business. If a customer elects to rescind by mail, notification is considered given at the time the notice is mailed; if by telegram, at the time the notice is filed for transmission.

The form of the notice of the right to rescind given the consumer by the creditor is set out in the Regulation. The consumer must receive two copies of this notice, one of which he can use to rescind the transaction. In a genuine emergency situation, a consumer may waive his right to rescind, providing it is done through a signed and dated personal statement setting forth the reasons for so doing. The law forbids the use of printed waiver forms for this purpose.

Truth-in-Lending applies not only to the credit transaction itself but also to the advertising of credit terms. When credit terms are to be included in an advertisement, the general rule is simple: If any credit term (except the annual percentage rate) is stated specifically, then all credit terms must be included and so stated. The credit terms must be clearly and conspicuously set out and detailed on the face of the advertisement; however, multipage ads and catalogues are considered one advertisement, and disclosures, if made prominently, need only be made once.

General statements contained in advertisements, such as *easy credit, just say "charge it," charge accounts available, all major credit cards honored, open a revolving budget account,* do not require statement of all the terms. However, specific statements, such as *no money down, no downpayment, $50 down, pay $9 a month, only $5 a month,* do require full disclosure. The disclosures need not be lengthy so long as they are complete.

It should be remembered that any broadly stated advertisement relating to credit availability, which may not be subject to Truth-in-Lending, will still be covered by Section 5(a) of the Federal Trade Commission Act. Therefore, terms such as *liberal credit* and *easy credit* must mean what they say. In other words, one who uses such advertisements must ordinarily extend credit to persons whose ability to pay is generally below typical standards (of credit worthiness) without changing any of the terms of the transaction. The law specifically exempts from liability the media through which advertising is disseminated to the general public.

STATE LAW AND CREDIT TRANSACTIONS

The majority of states have some form of Truth-in-Lending law. Where present, such law may be substituted for Federal Truth-in-Lending, provided the Federal Reserve Board grants permission to do so. One consideration is whether the state law has effective enforcement provisions. Only the Federal Reserve Board may grant such an exemption. Until an exception is granted, federal law governs.

Where state law requires a creditor to make disclosures that are either inconsistent with or broader than federal law, both sets of disclosures may be made. When both disclosures are required, the state requirements should either immediately follow the federal disclosures, with a clear line of demarcation separating the two, or appear on a separate sheet of paper. It must be kept in mind that federal disclosures are required to be made in a clear, conspicuous, and meaningful sequence. Any attempt to obscure or hide the required information is a violation of the act.

State laws vary considerably in the extent to which they regulate credit transactions. At the very minimum all states have usury laws fixing the maximum interest collectible on certain kinds of loans. Not only do interest rates vary, but the kinds of transactions subject to the penalties for usury vary also. For the most part loans only are covered; installment sales are generally not included in the usury laws.

Retail installment sales laws of one kind or another are also found in many states. These laws, which primarily cover sales involving consumer goods of all types, including motor vehicles, present the same confusing variety as the usury laws. These laws usually fix maximum and minimum finance charges permissible, maximum delinquency charges, and the time when such charges may be assessed. Often contract formalities, such as who must sign and whether a writing is required, are also covered.

Some state statutes in the credit field cover a great variety of specific practices, such as home solicitation, judgment notes, assignments of wages, and collateral held by creditors. These statutes were enacted piecemeal in individual states when particular abusive credit practices appeared. Many of these statutes go far beyond Truth-in-Lending in attempting to eliminate deceptive practices in the credit area.

To codify and clarify this confusion the National Conference of Commissioners on Uniform State Laws in 1968 approved the final draft of the Uniform Consumer Credit Code (UCCC). Thus far the UCCC has been enacted in only Oklahoma and Utah; however, it can be expected that the code will receive the same universal acceptance as its cousin, the Uniform Commercial Code. If widely accepted, this statute would represent the most significant and comprehensive regulation of credit to date.

The UCCC was drawn to conform to the rules of the Federal Consumer Protection Act but goes far beyond it in establishing a uniform system of rules governing all aspects of the law of consumer credit. It would also include many of the provisions presently enacted and embodied in state statutes.

FAIR CREDIT REPORTING

Congress is presently considering amending the Consumer Credit Protection Act by adding the Fair Credit Reporting Act. Like Truth-in-Lending, this bill aims only at consumer credit and will not cover business reports or business insurance reports. The necessity for such regulation is obvious. Credit bureaus in the United States now maintain files on over 110 million individuals in this country. With the computer making these files easily and quickly available the necessity for control is clear. Unfavorable credit reports can often have a disastrous effect on a consumer. As a result of inaccurate or arbitrary credit information, credit sources can dry up. The consumer may not know how or why. The fear that such may result has occasionally led consumers to pay bills that, in fact, they did not owe or, more commonly, about which there is a legitimate dispute. The consumer is presently without recourse to ensure accurate credit reporting.

The proposed bill will regulate credit reports on consumers limiting the furnishing of reports to five uses: (1) credit, (2) insurance, (3) employment, (4) obtaining a governmental license or other license or other benefit, and (5) other legitimate business needs involving a business transaction with a consumer.

With certain limited exceptions the law would prohibit reporting adverse information more than seven years old; this period would be extended to fourteen years for bankruptcy. A very important provision in the law would require that effective procedures be maintained to preserve confidentiality and proper use of information obtained. This is a necessary step, given the size and scope of the credit industry.

The most significant result such legislation would have would be to remove the secrecy from the credit report. At the consumer's request he could learn the nature and substance of all information on file concerning him as well as obtain a list of those who have received reports on him for the two preceding years. Credit-reporting agencies would be required by law to establish effective procedures for allowing the consumer to include in his file and in all future credit reports his position on any disputed item. To aid in ensuring that accurate, unbiased information is collected, credit reporters would be required to maintain a current evaluation of "public record information." These last steps will go a long way toward creating credit records that represent an objective analysis of a consumer's credit history by including more than just the reports furnished by satisfied or dissatisfied creditors.

DECEPTIVE COLLECTION PRACTICES

The last step in the credit transaction is settlement of the account. An unfortunate adjunct of an easy-credit, time-payment economy is the customer who defaults on his bill. Debt collection, by its very nature, is an unpleasant business. However, the unscrupulous practices of some who engage in this business have made it a great deal more unpleasant than it need be. Fortunately, the unscrupulous in the debt collection business are few; most operate ethically and fairly.

When the Federal Trade Commission directed its attention to the practices of the debt collection industry, it was clear that the deceptive practices it sought to eliminate were not only those that harassed the unfortunate buyer who through inadvertence or lack of sophistication had overextended himself. Deceptive collection schemes that were aimed at collecting even legitimately owed debts were also to be eliminated. This includes the least sympathetic character in the credit society, the "skip," a debtor who runs out on his debts.

The courts that have spoken out on this issue have agreed with the commission's view. The deceptive practices must be abandoned in the public interest. The public interest does not dissolve merely because the schemes, which ranged from the merely deceptive to the unconscionable, were aimed at collecting legitimately owed debts from persons refusing to pay. Commenting on a case before it that involved one of the more flagrant violations, the United States Ninth Circuit Court of Appeals said, "Petitioner's scheme is a cheap swindle, and the argument that it is less so because it may in certain cases trap swindling debtors is not pleasant to entertain."

At the outset it should be made clear that the deceptive practices to be discussed here involve only those aimed at the collection of debts from the debtor. The practices engaged in by some collection agencies to solicit business from creditors have also received the attention of the courts and the FTC. However, these practices are amply covered in the chapters dealing with misrepresentation, and the law does not alter significantly because there is a collection agency involved. It should also be noted that the most abusive practices involved in collecting debts through threats and/or illegal repossession are subject to redress in the state civil and criminal courts. Cases of this type are fortunately rare. However, an action in tort will lie for collection techniques that involve harassment and threats to a degree that the debtor suffers physical consequences or serious invasion of privacy. Criminal courts of the states can deal with the downright illegal violations, such as breaking and entering or assault.

Deceptive collection practices involve not only independent collection agencies but also the collection "department" used by the creditor himself. It is a violation of Section 5 of the Federal Trade Commission Act for a creditor to represent that a debt has been turned over to an independent third party when, in fact, it has not. A creditor may not, by the use of separate letterheads or other communications, misrepresent that these communications come from a third party when, in fact, they come from the creditor himself. Even when the collection agency is a corporate subsidiary of the creditor, it is a misrepresentation to assert that the collector is an innocent third party. The same is true of heading collection communications as emanating from the creditor's claims department if, in fact, no such department exists. Moreover, a creditor may not represent that uncollected debts will be turned over to a third party when he has no intention of so doing.

In order to collect debts it is often necessary to locate a missing debtor. The so-called skip-tracer forms were developed to serve this need. Deceptive skip-tracer forms involve communications addressed to the debtor's friends, relatives, employers, or his own last known address seeking to elicit information by subterfuge. The *sine qua non* of these communications is that if their true purpose were known, the addressee would probably not respond. The communications, often disguised as questionnaires, official surveys, or other inquiries, usually contain requests for information ostensibly to "verify" the addressee's identification. When completely filled out, the correspondence supplies the collector with information to aid in debt collection—present address; employment; bank, if any; property owned that could be subject to seizure, such as automobiles or home; wife's name and employment, if any; and other relevant information.

One common scheme was to send announcements that a prepaid package for the named debtor was in the possession of the writer. The card, if filled out and returned, would enable the writer to mail the package.

Clearly the most offensive scheme of this type has been the communication that implied that it emanated from a branch of the government. One such case brought by the FTC involved a California collector who used IBM cards, punched and colored green, to resemble government checks. These cards, which requested the usual information, were sent by the collector to an office in Washington, D.C., from which they were mailed to the debtor. The cards' titles, "Employment Verification Request—Area A, Department of Claims and Settlement, Department of Vehicle Verification Records," plus the Washington return address went far to create the impression that these were official government communications.

In 1959 Congress enacted a statute making it a criminal offense for a collection agency to use in its name the words *national, federal, United States,* or the initials *U.S.,* with an intent to mislead the public. The Department of Justice enforces this statute. The previously described scheme, which does not violate this law, remains under the jurisdiction of the Federal Trade Commission.

The Federal Trade Commission takes the view that in order for a skip-tracer form not to be deceptive it must affirmatively disclose that its purpose is to collect a debt. Mere literal truth is not sufficient if the entire impact of the form is deceptive. Although there is not a significant number of court decisions on this point, the FTC position has not always been upheld. The United States Court of Appeals for the Seventh Circuit ruled that affirmative disclosures should be required only in the case of flagrant abuse. The court reasoned that the collection agency would face the possibility of libel suits if communications addressed to relatives and employers asserted that the named party owned a debt.

The FTC originally codified its position in *Guides Against Debt Collection Deception,* adopted June 30, 1965. In these guides, affirmative disclosure of the purpose to collect a debt, whether a communication was addressed to the debtor himself or third parties, was required only if the communication suggested that it was for other than debt collection purposes. The guides were amended in June 1968, and now the commission requires affirmative disclosure stated clearly and conspicuously on all communications, written or oral, to debtors or third parties.

Aside from skip-tracer forms suggesting government affiliation, forms that simulate legal process were often used. These forms, of the same general size, type, and character as court documents, usually demanded immediate payment. The commission has taken the position, upheld by the courts, that such forms violate Section 5.

HOLDER IN DUE COURSE

One area yet to be dealt with extensively by either the legislatures or the commission is the doctrine of the holder in due course. Briefly stated, this means that one who holds commercial paper, such as a promissory note to secure an installment contract, holds it free of claims by the debtor if the holder has purchased the paper without knowing such claims exist. In short, if the buyer receives defective merchandise from a seller but the seller has negotiated the obligation to the holder, then the buyer is obligated to pay the holder without regard to any available contractual defenses. Claims based on defects in the merchandise must be settled between seller and buyer. Because the seller has already been, in effect, paid in full when he negotiated the obligation to the holder, there is little possibility that the buyer will have his claim settled if the seller is unscrupulous. This doctrine developed to assure the negotiability of commercial paper in a commercial situation. It is of doubtful utility in the area of consumer credit. State legislatures and state courts have recently turned their attention to this problem, and the commission is beginning to move in this area. The FTC has adopted a policy that in cease and desist orders or assurances of voluntary compliance resulting from matters involving deceptive practices by a business that negotiates commercial paper to third parties, the order or assurance shall contain a prohibition against renegotiation unless the instrument bears a legend that the assignee received them subject to all defenses that the debtor may have against the assignor, where such defenses arise from conduct of the assignor which violates the Federal Trade Commission Act or any other law administered by the commission.

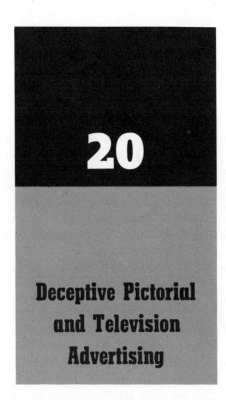

20

Deceptive Pictorial and Television Advertising

Misrepresentation can occur not only directly and indirectly through verbal and written statements, but also through pictorialization and characterization. One may be scrupulously honest with words and still be fostering deception by means of pictures and sketches that insinuate or blatantly present a falsehood.

The range of pictorial deception is potentially as wide as the whole gamut of false advertising and perhaps more dangerous. The printed word speaks to the mind, it asks a potential customer to believe a claim. A picture "proves" to the mind, through the eye, the validity of that claim. The following analysis is not exhaustive, for man can conceive of many ways to deceive, but it will give a general idea of the methods deemed unlawful.

Pictorial misrepresentation has two forms which overlap somewhat. Historically, the oldest form is deceptive and misleading illustrations and photographs. With the advent of the television, new forms of deceptive depiction were devised and discovered.

PHOTOGRAPHS AND ILLUSTRATIONS

The purpose of advertising is to acquaint the public with new products and new methods, to create, it is hoped, a market for the specific product advertised. A purchaser will decide among products based on their advertised claims, even when those claims are false. Deceptive pictures as well as statements can be used to lure potential customers into their first purchase. Such deceptive lures come in a variety of forms. A common practice is to picture products in advertising layouts that are not actually in stock or are not even available to be sold. The Federal Trade Commission has issued cease and desist orders in many circumstances. For example, a manufacturer of desk accessories agreed to stop running advertisements with pictorial representations of a desk pad with panels bearing an embossed design, when such a desk pad was not offered for sale or carried in stock.

In a similar matter, a cease and desist order was issued against a furrier, whose advertisements showed models wearing fur garments of a grade and quality not available in his store at any price, much less the stated price. Such a practice closely resembles the illegal bait-and-switch schemes discussed in another chapter. Although this is a milder form of the bait and switch, for no overt representations are made, the practice is, nonetheless, illegal. The pictures are a lure to potential customers. Once in the store the salesman can start his pitch.

Similar to this scheme is the dressing up of the advertised product. An automobile advertisement showed a four-door sedan equipped with bumper, bumper guards, and the figure $395. In much smaller type was "f.o.b. factory Toledo—for standard coupe—other models higher." The car pictured was much more expensive, and the car delivered when ordered from this advertisement came without bumpers and other parts required by law for operational use. The FTC, thus, ordered this advertisement stopped. Similar treatment has been accorded to clothing advertisers who have pictured their wares as tailor-fit, cleaned or new, when they are selling unrepaired secondhand clothing.

The deception can be heightened by the addition of words to a seemingly innocent picture. A hearing aid was pictured as a one-piece outfit with the words *one tiny unit is all you wear,* when in fact the entire outfit required many more parts to be functional. Such omissions from the product description are as deceptive as the window-dressing additions.

Children are particularly susceptible to deceptive pictorial advertising, because they are credulous and inclined to believe fantastic claims. Consequently, advertising that is directed to a juvenile audience must be scrupulously honest. The toy area has proved to be a fruitful pocket of deception and patent dishonesty. An excellent example can be seen by the facts behind a recent cease and desist order. The manufacturer ran multicolored advertisements in newspapers, periodicals, and other media. The pieces (soldiers, cannons, and so on) in the "204 Revolutionary War Soldiers" kit were pictured as being 4 inches long, multicolored, and three-dimensional. The cannons and rifles were seen shooting with emissions of smoke and fire. In reality, the pieces were not 4 inches long, came only in red *or* blue, were not three-dimensional, and merely stood, not emitting anything. The manufacturer ran similar deceptive advertisements for his "104 Kings Knights," "147 Famous Automobiles," and "Aircraft Carrier." Deceptive toy advertisements, "claiming that the toy can do more than it is able, be more than it is, or be better than it is," have been enjoined by the commission on many occasions.

Fabric misidentification has been discussed at length in another chapter. It will suffice here to say that a picture can also convey (with or without words) a misconception as to fabric content. A picture of an antelope removes any doubt from your mind that the trade-mark *Koranteloup* indicates antelope hide. Similarly, pictures of sheep and lambs remove any confusion from *Duro-Persian,* leaving one with a totally erroneous idea that the rayon and cotton cloth is actually Persian lamb.

Collateral misrepresentation can be accomplished easily through the use of pictures. Nonexistent endorsements, awards, and connections can be accomplished through pictorial innuendos and canards. A cigar company was ordered to cease using the term *Exposicion de Paris* with the year *1870* and a pictorial representation of a medal that falsely implied an award was received from the Paris Exposition. One can also not incorrectly infer that one has received recognition from an accepted authority. A picture of a locomotive on a watch implies that the watch is acceptable as a railroad watch—a renowned precision instrument. When such is not the case, the picture is deceptive.

The most frequent offenders in this field are the white-suited gentlemen, the doctor image. "Doctors" have been used to endorse baldness cures, mattresses, stomach-ache remedies, and many others. In a typical advertisement involving mattresses, the words read, "Orthopedic, Deluxe. Citation. Scientifically constructed for proper support." A woman was pictured reclining on a mattress. Standing to one side was a man in a white jacket, ostensibly a doctor, writing a prescription. Contrary to the impression created, the mattresses were not specifically designed or constructed to afford substantial healthful benefits, and doctors did not prescribe them. The practice was, consequently, enjoined.

Being sponsored, or approved, or connected with the United States government is considered a fine selling point. Often, therefore, misrepresentations will imply such a situation. A picture of Boulder Dam was used to imply that a certain waterproofing product was used in its construction. A fertilizer company, using before-and-after pictures asserted that they were taken by the Atomic Energy Commission during tests. Because both of the preceding representations were false, both were ordered stopped. A more blatant example is the use of the *United States* in the trade name, with attached depictions of American symbols. A credit bureau, United States Association of Credit Bureaus, used as a trade symbol an American eagle and a shield, the upper portion of which contained stars on a blue background and the lower portion of which bore the legend *U S A of C B* on a red background. This false designation was stopped in *United States Association of Credit Bureaus* v. *FTC*, a 1962 decision of the United States Seventh Circuit Court of Appeals.

Disparagement through pictures is devastatingly effective. Showing a competitor's product either compared to yours or in its own bad light tells a story worth a thousand name-calling words. A steel file cabinet manufacturer ran advertisements showing its own filing case and a similar competitive product. The latter was in disorder, implying that the case would necessarily occupy such space as represented. It was consequently ordered halted.

Before-and-after pictures tell a short story of the marvels of a product. When truthful, they advise the public of results that can be expected from a product. When false, they merely mislead. The fertilizing company mentioned before used its "Atomic Energy Commission" photographs as before-and-after exhibits to show the power of its plant food only fifteen minutes after application to the plant. In reality, the photographs were taken one hour apart, not the asserted fifteen minutes, and gave, therefore, the erroneous impression of quick-acting effectiveness. This practice was halted, along with the government-connection statements.

The public likes to deal with large concerns, well-established firms, original manufacturers, and large operations. Letterheads of company stationery are a popular place to picture one's building, office, or factory —a matter of pride to the owner. But the picture should be that of the building owned and not, as in one case, of the Merchandise Mart in Chicago. Users of two floors of a building, or even just the loft, should be wary of picturing the entire twelve-story building as their own.

A flagrant example of this type of deception involved representations made by a cigar manufacturer. By use of pictures of a large factory, tropical scenes, seagoing vessels, persons hand-wrapping cigars, and an executive smoking a cigar, the letterhead represented that the concern was an importer of tobacco which it handmade itself, in a large factory, and that it controlled the cigar process from seeding to smoking. In reality, the concern had the basement and one floor of a building from which it sold premade American cigars.

This same company practiced another important form of deception. Trading on the public's preference for British tobacco and pipes it called its firm House of Winchester, Ltd. (printed in Old English Gothic type), exhibited the British royal coat of arms, and had a depiction of a Gothic cathedral or abbey. Because it was a United States firm, this was blatant misrepresentation. The same is true whether it is perfume impliedly from France, radios from Japan, caviar from Russia, or linen from Ireland.

The use of the seal and emblem of Great Britain's coat of arms with the word *Canadian* and the trade name *Canadian Fur Trappers Corp.* is misleading as to source of origin (United States dealer) and mode of manufacturing (not trapped in Canada). Pictures of women spinning at looms to imply that machine-made articles are handmade, and pictures of American Indians to indicate that souvenirs are made by Indians, where such were actually made in Japan, are equally deceptive and forbidden.

The pictorial deceptions need not be so blatant or even so bald. The innuendo and scare ad are just as vulnerable. Thus, it has been found to be an FTC violation to run pictures of a woman shampooing her hair, with a frightened expression on her face and the words *don't burn your hair with detergent*. This was found to be a scare tactic, as well as a disparagement, and was unfounded in fact.

These few examples show the wide range of possible deceptions. The best rule to follow in the use of pictures is that what cannot be said or left out in words cannot be pictured.

TELEVISION ADVERTISING

As Another Dimension to the Still Picture

An announcer is seen talking to the audience on the television screen. In the background another actor winds up and pitches a ball straight at the announcer. But to the amazement of the audience, the announcer is not hit, the ball bounces off and is deflected by an invisible plastic shield. The announcer then tells the audience that this is how Gardol works. Gardol forms an invisible protective shield around your teeth and prevents tooth decay.

This very successful toothpaste advertising campaign ran for a substantial time on television before the FTC finally ordered it stopped. The commission claimed and proved that the impression given the viewing public through the use of words and pictures was that Gardol was able to afford *complete* protection, the same as the plastic shield. This impression was created not only through the use of the invisible shield routine but also by a caricaturization of an invisible Gardol shield around a tooth. The FTC complaint with the advertisement was this claim of complete protection, such protection being impossible. Because the claim was untrue and misleading, it had to cease.

Television is a most important area of consideration for the commission. Considering the high number of television sets owned per capita in this country (approximately 53.5 million television families) and the large amounts of viewing time spent by an average American family (approximately six hours, twenty-seven minutes per day per family), television is a most potent weapon in an advertiser's arsenal. Many people can be reached with this medium and a great variety of selling schemes can be devised, with unique and clever formats. There is also a wide area of possible deception opened up. We shall here consider those deceptive schemes that are merely the same form of deception, as is the case with still pictures but with an additional dimension, movement. Later we will consider a problem unique to television, the mock-up.

The first form of deception concerns demonstrations of the product purporting to prove nonexistent abilities or properties. A liquid cleaner was shown sitting on a radiator, on a kitchen stove, and near a candle, with no apparent fear by the actors of its catching fire. No verbal claims were made that the product was inflammable, but the demonstrations gave this impression. Because the cleaner was dangerously flammable, the use of these demonstrations, which insinuated that the cleaner could be used safely near a flame, were dangerously deceptive. Just as the commission requires disclosure of the combustible nature of the product, so too it cannot allow insinuations of the converse.

The same can be said for the representation that a hair spray can change straight hair to curly. While the audio extolled the virtues of the product and its ability to change hair structure, the video showed old-fashioned soda straws breaking when bent and the newer ones bending with ease. The commission ordered this practice halted because of the inability of the product to alter the hair structure so as to make straight hair curly.

Telling and depicting nonexistent abilities applies equally to disparaging competitor's products as well as to bolstering one's own product. In comparing the durability and strength of competing food wraps and demonstrating their relative preserving powers, it is deceptive to wrinkle and tear the competitors' products. It is equally deceptive to use two separate ham hocks in the test. To use an already aged ham to wrap in a competitor's foil stacks the cards against a fair comparison. Such deceptions have been ordered ceased.

Again, children are an audience for deception. They are the main consumers of television time, consequently, a lot of advertising time, as well as programing time, is directed at them. An example of the potential of television deception can be seen by the case of the Robot Commando. The depiction showed a child speaking to the robot through a microphone, and the robot responding. In reality the robot responded to blowing into the microphone and setting the dial at the appropriate action desired. The robot would walk straight ahead if the dial were set to that designation no matter what was said into the microphone, or if nothing at all were said. The implication that the robot responded to verbal commands was totally erroneous and deceptive, and an appropriate cease and desist order was entered.

A second form of the usual deception can be practiced best in the television medium. The moving picture with sound lends itself perfectly to tests and demonstrations; it is a more desirable before-and-after depiction, for it is a running account. The pitfall, though, is the use of demonstrations whether they prove a meaningfully relevant proposition or not. A safety razor ad showed the announcer shaving two boxing gloves with two separate razors, the advertised brand and the brand X nonsafety variety. The latter sliced through the boxing glove leaving a long gash; the safety razor did not. The purpose of the demonstration was to show the danger to a man's face from using nonsafety razors. Unfortunately for the manufacturer, the demonstration merely proved which razor was best for shaving boxing gloves, for the test did not in any way duplicate actual use. The results were that the ads unduly frightened people and unnecessarily disparaged competing razors. Because the test did not prove what it purported to prove, that safety razors are safer for people, it was ordered halted.

A similar cease and desist order was entered against a cigarette advertiser whose filter absorbency demonstrations, water flowing through two competing filters, had no relationship to how much tar and nicotine would be filtered out in a normal smoke.

The nonconclusive demonstration is not limited, however, to the unusual use of a product, such as shaving a boxing glove or "smoking" water. It has been practiced by merely showing one's own product. A margarine company, trying to imply that its product tasted more like butter than other margarines, had all three placed in a row—advertised margarine, butter, and brand X margarine. Flavor gems, which were in reality drops added by the prop man, appeared on the sponsored brand and the butter, but not on brand X. Over and above the fact that the flavor gems were deceptively added, they did not prove flavor or quality as claimed—and, therefore, the likeness of the brand to butter—but were basically undesirable characteristics of margarine, avoided at all costs by the industry. This "demonstration" not only did not prove the truth of the statement nor could it have, for the drops were fake, but could be said to prove just the reverse.

To understand what is deceptive in this confusing field it would be wise to see what is considered not deceptive. A toothpaste advertisement showed a smoking machine deposit fresh tobacco stains on a white plate.

It also showed the stain being removed by the sponsor's product. The original FTC decision ordered the practice halted, but on review the case was dismissed. The commission reasoned that the surface of the plate was a close enough simulation of tooth enamel to present a valid test. It also was reasoned that no representation was made as to long-accumulated stains, which the toothpaste could probably not remove, for the test was performed only on the new stain deposited by the smoking machine.

Similarly, the commission dismissed a complaint against a "flaming car" advertisement. After the advertised car wax was applied to the car's surface, gasoline was poured over it and lit. Cold water was splashed on and put out the fire. The purpose of the test was to show the heat-and-cold resistance of the wax. Although it was possible that the flames did not burn long enough significantly to raise the temperature on the car surface, the commission failed to prove that this was so; therefore, the advertisement was allowed to continue as proof of the claims.

The final area need only be mentioned—the area of collateral misrepresentation and scare tactics—for it is the same as for still pictures. In referring to the men in the white jackets, the commission has said that the representation that a product is recommended by doctors is prohibited "unless limited to the number of doctors not greater than has been proven to be the fact."

As a New Problem Inherent to Television

In the *Carter Products* case the United States Court of Appeals for the Fifth Circuit said:

> Everyone knows that on television all that glitters is not gold. On a black and white screen white looks grey and blue looks white; the lily must be painted. Coffee looks like mud. Real ice cream melts much more quickly than the firm but false sundae. The plain fact is, except by props and mock-ups, some objects cannot be shown on television as the viewer, in his mind's eye, knows the essence of the object.

A mock-up is an object to aid in the creation of a desired effect. Specifically, its use in a television commercial is to simulate a real object which, because of technical requirements of the medium, is impractical or impossible to use in the commercial. The advertising industry has been most ingenious in its solution to television's inherent weaknesses. By key lighting on one of two shirts, sheets or towels, it can make one appear lighter than the other. Glycerine is used to give a frosty appearance to soft drink and beer containers. Tea is made triple strength, so that it appears as normal rather than as water. Grenadine is added to orange juice to keep it from looking like milk. Color corrections are made—blue appears white, and white appears gray. Shampoo or other foamy substances are used to give a lasting head to beer, and ice cream is often whipped potatoes, which of course will not melt.

Mock-ups can be divided into three categories: (1) those devices which can be termed theatrical or technical devices to make a product seem to perform as it actually would before the naked eye under normal conditions; (2) those devices containing contrived effects to present the product as attractively as possible, such as "cosmetic glorification"; and (3) those devices used in such a way as to imply properties or performance characteristics for the product that it does not possess and that are of sufficient importance to be likely to affect a decision to purchase.

The commission and the courts have vacillated in their opinion as to the proper use of mock-ups. The question for the present, however, was decided by the United States Supreme Court in 1965.

The earlier cases (pre-1961) only forbade the use of mock-ups that materially misrepresented the nature of the advertised product or a competitor's products but did not take the position that mock-ups were illegal per se. An example of this was the cease and desist order entered against a kitchen knife company. The challenged advertisements showed a knife cutting through a nail. After the cutting, the knife was shown to be as sharp as before. The advertisement was deceptive because the nail was precut, which could not be seen by the viewing audience, and because two separate knives were used for the before and after shots. This simple form of a mock-up was held to be deceptive because the substitution misrepresented the basic nature of the product. The use of a mock-up, as such, was not held to be a violation.

Around 1961 the commission reversed its policy and began to insist that the mock-up not only must represent accurately and honestly what was to be portrayed, but also must be a genuine depiction if that depiction (test or demonstration) was to be used as a selling point. In other words, if the object for which the mock-up was to be substituted was a selling point in the advertisement, it would be illegal to allow any mock-up at all, even if it were to give an accurate depiction through the television screen. Initially, the court declined to accept the commission's approach. The second most famous shaving cream commercial case, *Carter Products,* is a good example. An actor was seen shaving with ordinary brand X lather. He applied it to his face, but the lather dried out rapidly, so that he was seen shaving in discomfort. He was next seen shaving with the advertised brand, in great comfort, for the cream was rich, moist, and comfortable. So far this might appear not to be improper; it is merely an apparent comparison between two brands of shaving cream. But what the viewing audience does not see is the hidden mock-up. A mixture of 90 per cent H_2O and 10 per cent ultrawet 60L, a foaming agent which dries out and disappears upon contact with the air, was used as a mockup replacement for the brand X lather. The mixture was in no way a soap, for it contained no fatty acids, and broke down much easier than a soap would upon contact with the air. The commercial, therefore, falsely disparaged competing lathers. There was also no need for the company to use the mock-up; if its own product could be photographed, so could the competitor's.

The FTC cease and desist order in this case was very broad. It proscribed the depiction of the superiority of any product over competing products when the portrayal or depiction was not a *genuine* or *accurate* comparison of the product. To comply with this order not only must the comparison be true, but the genuine substances themselves must be used, no mock-up.

On appeal, the United States Court of Appeals for the Fifth Circuit refused to go along with what it considered to be an overbroad order. The court agreed with the commission on the necessity of accuracy and the truthfulness of the representation. But the court went on to say that where the *only* untruth is that the substance the audience sees is artificial and where the visual appearance is otherwise a correct and accurate representation of the product itself, the public is not injured. The public is not buying the particular substance it sees in the studio, but the product itself, as seen by the audience on the television screen. If the public receives the product as it understood it to be, then there has been no material deception. The court remanded the case to the commission for consideration of allowing recognition of the validity of mock-ups which merely compensate fairly for the technical limitations of television and communicate fairly to the viewers the actual qualities and characteristics of the object which are simulated. The court did agree, however, to the prohibition of mock-ups which distort actual qualities or characteristics of the simulated product.

The Sandpaper Shaving Commercial

In 1961 the FTC instituted the sandpaper shaving commercial case, *Colgate Palmolive Co.* v. *FTC,* which was eventually to proceed through two FTC cease and desist orders, two remands from the United States First Circuit Court of Appeals, and finally to the United States Supreme Court. The case is instructive not only because of the dispositive treatment given mock-ups, but also because of the fact that it presents the course of an FTC order from inception to eventual end.

The commercial began with a famous football star holding a mask of sandpaper in front of his face. The audio asks, "Who is the man behind the sandpaper mask?" The commercial progresses by the analogy between the tough, "sandpaper" beard and a real piece of coarse, heavy sandpaper. Eventually the announcer demonstrated his shaving cream's super moisturizing power by shaving the sandpaper. He applied the lather and whisked off a clean stroke almost immediately. The audio at the same time was "apply [pause] soak [pause] off in a stroke." The commission cited the advertisement as deceptive on two grounds. First, the shaving cream could not have shaved even fine sandpaper in this short length of time. In order to accomplish the clean stroke, the sandpaper had to be soaked over an hour. The second point that the commission cited was the fact that the shaved sandpaper was not sandpaper at all, but a plexiglass mock-up with sand sprinkled on it to give it the televised appearance of sandpaper. The mock-up was used, as the company indicated, because regular sandpaper appeared as plain colored paper on the television screen. The initial order by the hearing examiner dismissed the complaint. It referred to the first misrepresentation as harmless exaggeration, or puffing, because the shaving cream did have the ability eventually to shave sandpaper. Great stress was laid upon the announcer's "apply . . . *soak* . . . off in a stroke," which truthfully admitted that soaking was necessary. The second point, the use of the mock-up per se, he dismissed because of the technical problems peculiar to television. He decided that reasonable latitude in the use of mock-ups or props should be permitted, provided, of course, that such use is not misleading in a material respect as to the actual properties or qualities of the product advertised.

Upon appeal to the full commission, the ruling was reversed unanimously, prohibiting all use of camera trickery in demonstrating the qualities of a product offered for sale. The commission observed that the advertisement made two statements: (1) sandpaper can be shaved immediately because of the supermoisturizing quality of the cream, and (2) don't just take the sponsor's word for it, see for yourself. The first was determined to be patently false and deceptive, as all successive courts and commission orders agreed. As to the second, the commission said:

> Even if [the commercials fairly and truthfully described the shaving cream's effectiveness in shaving the sandpaper], the commercials would be deceptive, within the meaning of the statute, in the manner in which they deliberately misinform the viewers that what he sees being shaved is genuine "tough, dry sandpaper," rather than a plexiglass mock-up. There is no dispute that this is untrue. Did it tend to mislead the public and was it an unfair advertising practice? We hold that it did, and it was.

The commission held that even if the claim were true and, therefore, no customer would be deceived as to getting what he wants, the practice would still be deceptive. The commission likened this to phony testimonials and erroneous indications of sources of product. In each of these two cases, the deceptive use is the falsification of a fact, extrinsic to the objective value of the product, a fact which essentially does not affect the intrinsic value of the product. These collateral extrinsic misrepresentations are considered to be selling points to the public and are often relied on; consequently, they must be totally honest.

The commission expressed little sympathy for the inherent limitations of the television medium and for the inability to project all substance across the screen. The limitations are merely limitations and no license to lie. In explanation of its apparent outlawry of mock-ups, the commission gave the following example and reasoning. It would be permissible under the order to use wine as coffee (for instance, in a background scene) but not to use wine as coffee and then point out to the viewing audience the rich color of the coffee. The difference is the distinction between a misstatement of truth that is material to the inducement of a sale (the latter) and one that is not.

A significant side note in this case, as well as in many other deceptive advertising cases, is the citation of the advertising agency as a corespondent. The commission often holds the agency liable whether it acts in its own interest or not, or with intention to deceive or not.

The United States Court of Appeals for the First Circuit remanded to the commission on the ground that the scope of the order was too ambiguous. The court said that the order read so that only truthful *and genuine* representations could be made, prohibiting in essence mock-ups in demonstrations. The court incredulously refused to believe that the FTC meant anything that drastic, and hence remanded for a narrowing of the order. The court felt that accuracy to the viewer, and not genuineness in the studio, was all that was important or necessary.

On remand, however, the commission refused to waiver. Rather, it reiterated its former position, adding that if a misrepresentation is calculated to affect a buyer's judgment, it does not make it a fair business practice to say the judgment was capricious.

The second commission order required the respondent to cease and desist:

> Unfairly and deceptively advertising any product by presenting a test, experiment or demonstration that is represented to be actual proof of a claim made for a product, and is not in fact a genuine test, experiment or demonstration being conducted as represented and does not constitute actual proof of the claim because of undisclosed use and substitution of a mock-up or prop.

The First Circuit Court of Appeals again refused to accede to the commission's positions, holding that, be it test or otherwise, if the depiction is an accurate portrayal of the product's attributes or performance, then no deceit is being practiced.

Finally, in 1965, the case reached the end of the journey, the United States Supreme Court. The question the Supreme Court asked itself was,

"Is it a deceptive practice within Section 5 of the Federal Trade Commission Act to represent falsely that a televised test, experiment, or demonstration provides a viewer with visual proof of a product claim, regardless of whether the product claim is itself true?" The answer was yes. The Court did not deal directly with the problem of dishonest representations (for example, a demonstration which "proves" a nonexistent fact), for all through the long appellate procedure this was conceded to be a Section 5 violation.

The Court quoted with approval from its prior decision in the *Algoma Lumber Co.* case: "The public is entitled to get what it chooses, though the choice be dictated by caprice or by fashion or perhaps by ignorance." According to the Court there is little difference between the use of false testimonials and invented testing agency certificates and the use of a mock-up in a demonstration to show even a true representation.

> In each the seller has used misrepresentation to break down what he regards to be an annoying or irrational habit of the buying public. . . . In each case the seller reasons that when the habit is broken the buyer will be satisfied with the performance of the product he receives. Yet, a misrepresentation has been used to break the habit and . . . a misrepresentation for such an end is not permitted.

In answering the advertising industry's dismayed cry that the standards would be too tough to follow, the Court said,

> If, however, it becomes impossible or impractical to show simulated demonstrations on television in a truthful manner, this indicates that television is not a medium that lends itself to this type of commercial, not that the commercial must survive at all costs.

Since this definitive pronouncement on the use of undisclosed mock-ups, the commission and a federal court of appeals have had another chance to review the decision, and have affirmed it, the court saying "that the undisclosed use of mock-ups [is] a deceptive practice even though the test, experiment or demonstration actually prove[s] the product claim." Thus, in *Libby-Owens-Ford Glass Co.* v. *FTC*, an automobile glass company was accused of using undisclosed mock-ups unfairly to disparage competing products. By use of different camera angles, more oblique for the competitor's product, and Vaseline smeared on the competitor's glass, the advertiser "successfully" demonstrated the heightened distortion of all brand X glass. The commission, in a decision which was upheld by the United States Sixth Circuit Court of Appeals, concluded that even if by use of these "tricks" the result appeared as truthful, the practice was deceptive because of the undisclosed mock-ups. The result is that if an advertiser is going to ask the public to believe a claim and to test that belief by seeing, then he must be totally truthful and use only the genuine product.

CONCLUSION

The result of this line of cases has been the creation of a hard-and-fast rule with ambiguities. In order to be deceptive, (1) the mock-up must be presented as actual proof of a claim made for the product (not merely as scenery); (2) the claim must be a material inducement to the product's sale (the commission includes in this category any number of collateral representations); and (3) the demonstration is not in fact a genuine test; because of (4) the use of an undisclosed mock-up (disclosure in some form, for instance, by the use of the word *simulation* or the like, would take the commercial out of the prohibition).

There are problems left, but they are not insoluble. The main one is the use of a genuine product which does not give an accurate representation (for example, the telecast of a milk product over the screen making it look thicker and creamier, or showing a white sheet washed in a competitor's soap, which naturally appears gray over the television). Because the commission has stressed accuracy as well as genuineness, this practice seems to be precluded.

But by requiring both accuracy and genuineness, certain products cannot be used or visual claims made because of the inherent television difficulties. Presumably, resourcefulness and imagination will be able to overcome this high barrier and result in more truthful but, nonetheless, forceful advertising.

Essentially, in the whole area of television advertising (conventional and mock-ups), the problem is the same as it is in nonpictorial advertising. Added to the truthfulness requirement, however, is the requirement of total genuineness.

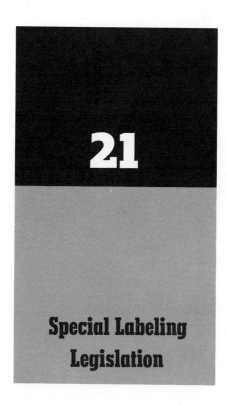

21

Special Labeling Legislation

A comprehensive body of rules for the labeling, invoicing, and advertising of wools, textiles, and furs is found in the Wool Products Labeling Act, the Textile Product Identification Act, and the Fur Product Labeling Act. Principally, these laws require the truthful labeling of the products covered. They are designed to protect manufacturers and distributors as well as the ultimate consumer against misbranding or deceptive practices. The statutes are similar in several respects; however, the textile and fur laws are generally broader than the wool law. The detailed requirements of each of the laws are found in the rules and regulations promulgated thereunder. It would seem that little has been left to guesswork.

Prior to the passage of these laws, attacks on the misrepresentation or misdescription of wool, textile, and fur products had been pursued by the Federal Trade Commission under Section 5 of the Federal Trade Commission Act. Under these labeling laws, too, the FTC is the administrative agency charged with their enforcement. The FTC is authorized to issue cease and desist orders against violators, to instigate injunction proceedings, and when wool or fur products are involved, to seize the misbranded product by condemnation. Willful violators are liable to a fine and/or imprisonment.

Generally, the laws provide for the furnishing of various types of guarantees by those who would otherwise be liable for the sale or transportation of a misbranded wool, fur, or textile product. Certain persons (for example, common carriers and exporters) are specifically exempt from the labeling and other requirements; some products are also excluded. Possible exculpation is found in the "unavoidable variations in manufacture" language so often used by the FTC and included in the recent Fair Packaging and Labeling Act, to be discussed later in this chapter.

The labeling rules are applicable, generally, at all levels of the production and distribution system, from the original producer on down to the retail level, provided the requisite interstate commerce elements are present. The textile and fur laws, however, more extensively cover practices at the retail level of distribution. These two statutes cover the misbranding of products which already have been shipped in interstate commerce. The wool law, on the other hand, covers only the misbranding of a product which will move in interstate commerce, or is moving in interstate commerce. However, the label must remain on, once jurisdiction has attached.

Each of the laws specifies the information which must appear on labels. The failure to include the required information is unlawful, as is the failure to affix a label to the product. Advertising is regulated only as to textile and fur products, but the invoicing of all three types of products is covered. Wool invoicing is covered under Section 5 of the Federal Trade Commission Act. The removal or mutilation of a required label is unlawful unless it is for the purpose of substituting one which would conform to the requirements of the particular law.

THE WOOL PRODUCTS LABELING ACT OF 1939

The stated purpose of the Wool Products Labeling Act of 1939 (WPLA) is to protect producers, manufacturers, distributors, and consumers from the unrevealed presence of substitutes and mixtures in spun, woven, knitted, felted, or otherwise manufactured wool products. Misbranding of wool products, then, is the prohibited practice. As Senator Chavez of New Mexico is reported to have said, "if one asks for a wool blanket it shall be a wool blanket. That is all there is to the bill." Essentially, that is all there is to the act; and anyone, except common carriers and exporters who handle a misbranded wool product that is moving or will move in interstate commerce, is subject to the act. Actual knowledge by the original manufacturer of ultimate destination is not essential; it is no defense that he did not know that the wool product that he shipped intrastate would be introduced into commerce by customers, or that wool products sold to an out-of-state buyer were shipped to an associate corporation of the purchaser located in the same state as the seller. It is equally immaterial that one, subject to Section 3, had no title to goods that were misbranded and delivered for shipment in commerce. As to foreign-manufactured wool products, the responsibility for truthful labeling rests with the importer, and that person may not escape liability by asserting that the false label was affixed prior to his receipt of the wool product.

Wool Product

But what is a wool product? The statutory definition is broad and encompasses any product, or portion thereof, which contains or is represented as containing either wool or reprocessed wool or reused wool. *Wool* is defined as the unreclaimed fiber from the fleece of sheep or lamb or from the hair of the Angora or Cashmere goat, the camel, alpaca, llama, and vicuna. *Reprocessed wool* refers to that fiber which results from the process of reducing the wool in a wool product to a fibrous state. *Reused wool,* on the other hand, refers to a similarly resulting fiber whose source was a wool product which may also have contained reprocessed wool and which had been utilized, to an unnamed extent, by the ultimate customer.

It should be noted, however, that these definitions, although fairly well delineating what the content of a wool product shall be, fail to define *product.* That was the crucial question in *Carr* v. *FTC.* Petitioner was a garnetter, that is, one who reverts clippings and other waste wool materials to a mass, called garnett, comparable in appearance and substance with the original wool prior to carding. The commission had required that a label be affixed to the garnett in accordance with the Wool Act on the ground that it was a "product," containing wool and reprocessed wool, the finished result of the manufacturing process performed by the respondent.

The United States First Circuit Court of Appeals, however, looked to the dictionary meaning of garnetting ("to reduce waste to fiber") and the Latin derivation of the word *product* (*pro ducere,* "to lead forward"), concluding:

> We cannot but be struck by the antithetical meanings of producing and reducing the fiber for the purpose of starting over again. The

qualities of an article, and hence whether it is a "product," must be judged by what it is, not by what it may once have been.

Although the court in the *Carr* case did expressly leave the door open for the FTC to argue this matter further on the basis of the administrative history of the definition, Garnett, for the time, is wool and not a wool product. If it is composed of wool which has been processed, it is reprocessed wool but not a product of reprocessed wool. Similarly, bales of waste materials containing woolen rugs and cuttings left by garment and fabric manufacturers are not a wool product though they may ultimately be used in a wool product.

On the other hand, wool batting used in the manufacture of quilted goods and fur fibers separated from the skins of the guanaco (a South American mammal related to the camel but lacking a dorsal hump) and the quanaquito for use by fabric manufacturers *are* wool products and must be labeled with the information as required by the act. By operation of Rule 22 of the Rules and Regulations under the act, samples, swatches, and specimens of articles to be sold therefrom are also wool products and must be labeled.

Though they may contain wool, carpets, rugs, mats, and upholsteries are exempted from the labeling requirements.

Misbranding

Under Section 4 of the act, a wool product will be deemed to be misbranded by

1. Failing to affix a stamp, tag, label or other identification as to the name or amount of the constituent fibers. (In *Susquehanna Woolen Mills,* the commission found as an acceptable reason for failure to comply with the labeling requirements the policy of the Navy Department, during the period covered by the complaint, to require no tags or marks on its blankets other than "U.S.N." or "U.S.N. Medical.")
2. Falsely or deceptively so stamping, tagging or labeling the product.
3. Affixing a stamp, tag, or label which neglects to show all the information set forth in the statute and the rules and regulations thereunder and in the manner there prescribed.

The second category contemplates the prohibition of such things as Cashmora as a brand name for a product containing no cashmere, or King Camel for one not made of camel hair. False implication by reason of symbols or pictures on labels is also prohibited. Likewise, fictitious prices on labels have been prohibited.

The information required on the required label is set forth in Section 4(a)(2)(A), (B), and (C). The label, tag, or whatever must show a breakdown, in percentages of the total weight of the wool product, of the constituent fibers exclusive of ornamentation that does not exceed 5 per cent of the total. The breakdown must include the fiber content of

1. Wool, reprocessed, and reused wool.
2. Any nonwoolen fiber which exceeds 5 per cent of the total weight.
3. Nonwoolen fibers which amount to less than 5 per cent of the total with the percentage thereof stated in the aggregate.

With a reasonable tolerance permitted by the act (the FTC has said that 5 per cent is the maximum variance contemplated by the statute), it would seem, nevertheless, that Section 4(a)(1) and (2) contemplates an accurate representation of the fiber content of a wool product. An *under-estimation* of the wool content, however, apparently is not a violation of the act.

The FTC had issued a cease and desist order against a blanket manufacturer who had labeled his blankets as containing less wool than was found actually to exist (in one instance, the variance was 9 per cent; in another, only $\frac{1}{10}$ of 1 per cent) and had failed to indicate in exactly correct proportions the character of the nonwoolen fibers. Both were deemed to be misbranding under Section 4(a)(1) and (2)(A). The United States Court of Appeals for the Second Circuit set aside the order in *Marcus* v. *FTC*. In the .1 per cent matter, the real basis of the complaint was the substitution of 90 per cent wool, 10 per cent nylon labels for the manufacturer's labels of 90 per cent wool, 10 per cent undetermined fibers.

The court pointed to the purpose of the WPLA as expressed in the preamble thereto, to protect consumers and others from the "unrevealed presence of substitutes and mixtures," that is, substitutes *for wool* in a product claimed to be made wholly or partially of wool. Clearly, Congress had intended to protect against an inferior wool substitute. The "substitute" whose presence in the blankets was unrevealed was wool itself, a superior fiber. Indeed, one commission witness had testified that "a high wool content is a mark of a better product in blankets." The court, therefore, was compelled to conclude that "the labeling requirement is not applicable where the percentage of wool is underestimated."

The "labeling requirement" of the act, of course, includes nonwoolen fibers which the manufacturer has also misrepresented.

If the court meant to say that the WPLA was not intended to encompass a situation in which the consumer is getting something more (or better) than he bargained for, the decision seems soundly based. Equally plausible is its characterization of the "focus" of the act as being *on wool*. It clearly is. But the court's dictum with respect to the accuracy of statements about nonwool fibers—when the percentage of *wool* is *correctly stated*—is not so easily accepted. It would leave the control of deceptive practices as to these constituent fibers to Section 5 of the Federal Trade Commission Act, because "Congress in passing the WPLA was not interested in labeling *per se*. . . ." That may be true. If it were controlling, however, it would give manufacturers license to miss the mark totally in statements as to nonwoolen fibers, with respect both to their character and amount. One would wonder whether Section 4(a)(2)(A) is that purposeless? It is worth noting that the FTC staff regards the *Marcus* case as the law.

An answer is perhaps unnecessary. The FTC pursues labels which are inaccurate in their wool and nonwool fiber content information. Furthermore, the advent of the later textile, fur, and packaging statutes, as well as the continuing amendments to the rules under the WPLA, would seem to indicate that the focus, generally, is on better and *more* information on product labels. This may not be "labeling"; it is consistent, nevertheless, with a concern for the consumer, initiated largely in 1939 with the WPLA and continuing to this day with growing momentum.

The Required Label

The rules are replete with directions for complying with the labeling requirement of Section 4. For instance, naming the constituent fiber is important. Generally speaking (because combinations and exceptions are provided for), the common generic name of the fiber is to be used. For manufactured fibers, reference must be made to the names established under the Textile Fiber Products Identification Act. By rule, a *nonwoolen* fiber present in the amount of less than 5 per cent of the total weight *may not* be designated by its generic name; only "other fiber (or fibers)" may be used.

Under Section 4 of the act, two other bits of information must also appear on the label along with the fiber content information: (1) the maximum percentage of the total weight of any nonfibrous loading, filling, or adulterating matter and (2) the name or registered identification number of the manufacturer or of the one or more persons offering for sale or transporting or distributing the wool product.

On August 1, 1949 the FTC published a pamphlet for the use of all persons concerned with the proper labeling of wool products under the WPLA of 1939 and the rules and regulations relating thereto. Some illustrations of acceptable labels and tags are therein provided. For example, a relatively uncomplicated wool product might bear this label:

Doe Manufacturing Co.
(or)
WPL 98
   50% Wool
   25% Rayon
   25% Cotton
Exclusive of Ornamentation

The following is suggested for an all wool blanket with a binding of different fiber content:

WPL 98
100% Wool
Binding All Rayon

The several sections of a wool product may differ as to fiber content. Sectional disclosure is mandatory where deception would result if an overall disclosure were made. The following example is illustrative of the proper form:

WPL 98
Front: 100% Wool
Back and Sleeves: 100% Cotton

Knitted Sections
50% Wool
50% Rayon

The rules also permit the use of the term *fur fiber* when the wool product is composed of the hair or fur fiber of any animal or animals other than those defined under *wool* in Section 2(b), provided such fur fiber exceeds 5 per cent of the total weight. An example will show the proper way to disclose this information where the animal producing the fur fiber is either of the nonspecialty group or of the specialty group included in Section 2(b).

   60% Wool
   40% Fur Fiber
      (or)
   60% Wool
   30% Fur Fiber
   10% Angora Rabbit

The fiber content information must be attached to the product so as to meet the requirements of permanency, conspicuity, and legibility. Where this is done, however, the rules permit imprinting the fiber content information on the wool product itself rather than tagging or otherwise affixing a label. According to an advertisement in a trade journal, the Wool Bureau was to spend over half its 1968 advertising budget on television to tell American consumers the advantages of the permanently *sewn-in* wool-mark label over the temporary paper hang-tags: "Pure virgin wool is the quality fiber and it deserves a prestige label. A label that lasts the life of the product. A label that stays with the consumer instead of getting thrown away before the garment is even worn." The value of such information to the consumer for the life of the product is considerable in light of the difficulty even experts experience in identifying textile content. Proper cleaning and storage, for example, depend on the availability of this information. The WPLA, however, requires no more than that it be disclosed all along the line of distribution up to, and including, the final disposition to the ultimate consumer.

Whether or not "labeling" is the thrust of this legislation, proper structuring of the label has been deemed to be, at least, a reasonable means of fulfilling the purpose of the WPLA. Accordingly, everything from arrangement of the required information to the type of print to be used has been set forth in the rules. The English language must be used and abbreviations, ditto marks, and the like, are forbidden.

"Ornamentation" is not considered as part of the required fiber content information under Section 4(a)(2)(A). The term is not there further explained, however. Rule 16 supplies the essential detail. As seen in the preceding labeling illustration "Exclusive of Ornamentation" is proper to indicate that the fiber content information does not include a percentage designation for ornamentation under 5 per cent. If, however, ornamentation does exceed 5 per cent of the total fiber weight or if it constitutes a distinct and separate section of the wool product, percentages must be given.

One other category has been exempted by the act from the fiber content disclosure requirements. With provisos, there is no requirement to designate the fiber content of linings, paddings, stiffenings, trimmings, and facings. As parts of wool products, they are unexposed and ordinarily for structural purposes only. But the rules make some rather obvious distinctions and bring within the labeling requirements certain wool products that would otherwise be classified as linings, paddings, and so forth. They are (1) those which are sold for use as linings and paddings, (2) those which contain linings or paddings, but are not articles of wearing apparel, and (3) linings incorporated for warmth or represented as being for that purpose. Authorization for such classification by the FTC is expressly given in Section 4(d) of the act.

Imported Wool Products

Unless an imported wool product was manufactured more than twenty years prior to importation, it is subject to the labeling requirements under the WPLA and the rules in approximately the same manner as domestic products. In addition, invoices for imports must contain the same required information as well as complying with the Tariff Act of 1930. Omission or falsification may result in a denial of importation rights.

Even so, it was felt that an inequality existed in the administration of the act for domestic and imported wool products. Nothing similar to the records showing fiber content of wool products required of domestic manufacturers and the possibility of FTC inspections and tests could be imposed upon foreign manufacturers. Enforcement efforts have to be directed, if at all, at other than the manufacturing level. Then, in February, 1968, the commission promulgated an amendment to the rules and regulations under the act. Commissioner Elman dissented to the issuance of the rule, the European Economic Community protested that it was discriminatory as a "very harsh and costly control system for all United States imports of wool products," and importers and a trade association filed suit in the Federal District Court for the District of Columbia to enjoin enforcement of the rule by the FTC. FTC Chairman Paul Rand Dixon defended the rule as doing "no more than remove the disadvantages under which domestic manufacturers now operate and place them on a fair competitive basis with foreign manufacturers."

The controversy was based on the obligations imposed on importers before their wool products could be released from customs under an FTC "notice of release." Forms in quadruplicate specifying certain information was the primary condition precedent; but whenever the FTC had "reason to believe that any wool products subject to this section may be misbranded," testing could be required to show that the product was correctly labeled. Testing, either by the commission or in laboratories approved by it, was at the importer's expense. He would also have to bear storage costs during the delay.

Pre-entry clearance was possible, however. Paper work again presented a problem, but clearance would preclude the delay which considerably worried importers. Otherwise, release of the imports from customs was by the aforementioned "notice" or under bond such as an "immediate delivery and consumption entry bond." One importer had his own idea for solving the situation and recommended that other countries indulge in some testing of their own: "They ought to check every car and every refrigerator for thickness of enamel and gauge of steel. That might get quick results."

In 1969 the District of Columbia Circuit Court of Appeals enjoined enforcement of the rule in *Textile and Apparel Group* v. *FTC*. Appellants had applied for a pre-enforcement injunction at the district court level which had been rejected for want of a justiciable case or controversy. The appellate court held the question was ripe for review and granted a permanent injunction against the rule. On the merits the court found the rule to be unwarranted under the Wool Act of 1939 and violative of due process as formulated by the commission. Thus, the prerule controversy has been reperpetuated with its dichotomy in testing between domestic and foreign products.

THE FUR PRODUCTS LABELING ACT

Modeled on, but broader than, the Wool Products Labeling Act of 1939, the Fur Act (FPLA) was passed to provide similar protection to consumers and scrupulous merchants engaged in a trade which in 1951, the year of its enactment, amounted to $500 million a year. The statute was also seen as affording protection to the infant domestic fur-farming industry against unscrupulous competition arising out of the use of "false and glamorized designations for cheap imported furs." As written and as enforced, the act would seem to cover both areas well.

Again interstate commerce is the legal pivot. Accordingly, under Section 3 it is unlawful to distribute or advertise in commerce any fur product or fur that has been misbranded or falsely advertised or invoiced, or any fur product *made of fur* that has been shipped in commerce and is misbranded or falsely or deceptively advertised or invoiced. As under the Wool Act, removal of the required label (except to substitute an appropriate one) is prohibited and imported furs are included under the labeling and invoicing requirements.

Misbranding and False Advertising and Invoicing

Under Section 4 a fur product is misbranded if it is (1) falsely or deceptively labeled or identified (or if the label contains any form of misrepresentation with respect to the fur product), or (2) a label is not affixed to the fur product with certain information, or (3) the required label uses an animal name other than as provided in the *Name Guide* established by rules.

The act requires the following facts to be disclosed on the label: the name of the animal that produced the fur, the fact that the fur is used, the fact of artificial coloring or bleaching, the use of waste fur (ears and throats) or paws, tails, or bellies, the name or registered identification number of the manufacturer, and the name of the country of origin if the fur is imported. ("Russian Sable" is permitted as descriptive of fur but it will not satisfy required disclosure of country of origin; that must be added.) By operation of the rules and regulations under the FPLA, other items become "required information" and all such information must appear on the label to avoid a charge of misbranding.

Advertising and invoicing of furs and fur products are covered in Section 5. Again the act and the rules set forth the "required information" to be contained in an advertisement (or any public notice intended to effect the sale of a fur product) or invoice. An advertisement or invoice deficient as to any of the items is "false" within the meaning of the statute. A retail sales slip is an *invoice* within the FPLA, which defines the term [Section 2(f)] as a "written account, memo" issued in connection with "any commercial dealing in fur products or furs" which describe the product "delivered to a purchaser." A fur product is falsely invoiced, then, if the retail sales slip does not contain the required information because a sales slip is a "written account" or "memo," a retail sale is plainly a "commercial dealing," and a customer of a retailer is a "purchaser." Generally, the required information covers the same ground as is required on labels. Rule 38(b) has the effect of requiring a specific statement of country of origin. An institutional type of advertisement which is not intended to effect the sale is not subject to the "required information" disclosures unless reference is made to color that is artificial. To be certain, however, that the FTC's antideception policy is fully implemented, Rule 49 would seem to cover everything that could be eliminated under Section 5 of the FTCA. This rule reads: "No furs or fur products shall be labeled, invoiced or advertised in any manner which is false, misleading or deceptive in any respect."

As under the Wool Act, the rules provide for the proper structuring of fur product labels, even to their minimum dimensions (1¾ inches by 2¾ inches). "Indelible ink" [Rule 29(b)] is the medium prescribed and handwriting (but not handprinting) is prohibited.

There is one aspect of the FPLA which the summary treatment given here fails to point out sufficiently. At least the fact that it has created litigation would seem to make it worthy of more detailed discussion. The statute clearly distinguishes between fur products and furs in declaring, in Section 3, those activities which are unlawful. Subsection (b) prohibits, among other things, the advertisement of a misbranded fur product made of fur which has been shipped and received in commerce. The language is deemed to confer jurisdiction over the local marketing of every misbranded fur product processed from furs that theretofore had moved in commerce. Where, however, that subsection is relied upon for jurisdiction, there must be evidence that the furs themselves, before they were made into fur products, were shipped and received in commerce. Jurisdiction will not rest solely on the fact that a *fur product* was purchased in commerce.

Section 3(a), among other activities, makes it unlawful to advertise *in commerce* a misbranded *fur product*. In order to pursue the alleged misbranding, the nexus, of course, is the advertising in a newspaper or other medium with an interstate circulation. It is now established that to constitute a violation of Section 3(a) the fur product found to be misbranded must be specifically referred to in the advertisements in commerce. An advertisement featuring properly labeled fur products although "essentially . . . a storewide promotion" is insufficient to embrace other products of the advertiser that are found to be misbranded under the act.

THE TEXTILE FIBER PRODUCTS IDENTIFICATION ACT

Again, in the tradition of the Wool Products Labeling Act of 1939 and the Fur Products Labeling Act, this legislation (TFPIA) is a "disclosure" statute. The principle underlying these acts recognizes that, although the government should not seek to set product quality standards, the purchaser should be protected to the extent of a label containing basic information about wool, fur, and textile products, the composition of which is not readily apparent.

Broader in application than the Wool Act, the Textile Products Identification Act is closer in scope to the Fur Act in its coverage of advertising as well as labeling and invoicing. Radio and television advertisements, however, are not subject to the provisions of the act, a "serious loophole" in the opinion of the FTC.

Textile Product

The product (or "textile fiber product" as it is denominated throughout the act) to which the disclosure provisions apply includes the fibers, yarns, or fabrics (in a finished or unfinished state) to be used in household textile articles and the articles themselves, whether they be wholly or only in part composed of yarns or fabrics. Carpets, rugs, upholsteries and mats, which were excluded under the WPLA, are covered here. The act, however, does not change the requirements for other wool products. They remain subject only to the WPLA. For the few wool products covered by the TFPIA the commission has provided for the affirmative disclosure of wool and reprocessed and reused wool "because these terms not only have acquired a generic status but also it was necessary to assure consistency with the use of the terms under the Wool Products Labeling Act."

Textile products to be exported are specifically exempted from the labeling requirements as are those that are unfinished, that is, not ready for use by the ultimate consumer. An unfinished product, however, must be invoiced as to the fiber content in each marketing transaction "in order to establish a complete chain of truthful content disclosure for the raw fibers to the finished consumer product." The invoice must also bear the name of the person or concern responsible for designation of fiber content.

Under Section 12 and by regulation pursuant thereto, many special textile fiber products are excluded from the statutory requirements. These range from stuffings and linings to sewing threads, bandages, and textile products incorporated in footwear, handbags, toys, and diapers.

Prohibited Activities

The language of Section 3 is broad and simply stated. The misbranding and false advertising of textile fiber products are prohibited whether (1) the product will move in commerce, (2) the product has been advertised or offered for sale in commerce, or (3) the product, or its textile fiber content, has been shipped and received in commerce. In other words, it is unlawful and a deceptive practice to use the channels of interstate *commerce* for any textile fiber product that is misbranded or falsely and deceptively advertised and to market any misbranded or falsely and deceptively advertised product that has been offered for sale or advertised in such commerce or that is offered, advertised, or sold after interstate shipment.

In addition, the act declares the removal or mutilation of the required stamp, tag, or label, after shipment in commerce and before sale to the ultimate consumer, to be unlawful. Where a package bearing the required information is broken before sale to the consumer, the information must be affixed to each unit in the broken package. By operation of a rule, the one who initially packages a textile product in a container that commonly would be broken for sale shall affix the required information to each unit. The rule is applicable to handkerchiefs, for example.

Misbranding

As under the statutes previously discussed, a textile fiber product is misbranded if it is falsely or deceptively labeled, invoiced, advertised, or otherwise identified and if the product is not identified, by whatever means is chosen, so as to include the information required by the act and the rules thereunder. Under Section 4(f) the fiber content information need not be affixed to a portion of a fabric, *when sold at retail,* severed from properly labeled bolts or pieces of fabric. Under certain conditions, however, samples, swatches, or specimens of textile fiber products used to effect the sale of the product must be labeled.

The following information is required by the act:

1. The percentage of each (natural or manufactured) constituent fiber present in amounts of 5 per cent or more of the total weight of the

fiber content in order of predominance by weight (fibers present in amounts of less than 5 per cent must be designated as other fibers, unless they have a definite functional significance which is stated on the label along with the generic name).

2. Identification of each fiber by its generic name.

3. The name or registered identification number of the manufacturer or other person subject to the act.

4. The name of the country of manufacture or process, from which the textile fiber product is imported (the required information must also appear on the original invoice of imported textile products).

The rules and regulations promulgated under the TFPIA detail the structuring of the required label. Again the thrust is durability, legibility, and accessibility throughout the chain of distribution of the textile product.

The innovation of pile textile fabrics that simulate fur has given rise to some stringent rules for labeling and advertising. They are, nonetheless, consistent with the traditional Federal Trade Commission Act anti-deception policy and implemental to the Fur Products Labeling Act. The strong resemblance to fur of many of these "fake furs" is, of course, the deception to be eliminated. Accordingly, Rule 9 forbids absolutely the use in labeling or advertising of any names, words, depictions, symbols or descriptive matter suggesting a fur-bearing animal unless the product is a fur product within the meaning of the Fur Act. Names of animals, alone or in combination with another word, such as *Beaverton,* as well as terms commonly used to describe animal hair or fleece (for example, mutation) are prohibited. The rules do permit, however, the use, on such textile products, of animal names when that animal's fur is not commonly or commercially used in fur products. *Kitten soft* and *Bear Brand* would be, for example, permissibly descriptive of a textile product simulating real fur.

The statute deals summarily with the advertising of these fake furs. Under Section 4(g), an advertisement is declared to be false and deceptive if the name or symbol of a fur-bearing animal is used in connection with a product that is not a fur product, permitting, however, the disclosure of the presence of fur hairs or fibers in a textile product.

On October 2, 1964, in a letter to Senator Magnuson of the Senate Commerce Committee, the FTC interpreted Section 4(g) as embodying an unqualified prohibition against the use of fur or animal names in advertising nonfur products. The commission announced, however, that it would not prohibit truthful and nondeceptive ads for fake furs as outlined in the preceding discussion and according to the amended Rule 9, which became effective in January, 1963.

False and Deceptive Advertising

As mentioned earlier, a falsely or deceptively advertised textile product is misbranded under the act. There is no requirement, however, to set out in an advertisement the fiber content information required on the label and other forms of identification so long as no reference is made to the fiber content either by generic name, word, trade-mark or terms connoting the name or presence of textile fibers. Once that is done (for example, percale sheets) the advertisement must set forth the names of the constituent fibers in order of predominance by weight. The respective percentages, however, need not be given. The manufacturer's name or country of origin for imported products are also not required in advertisements.

Guaranties

No detailed discussion of guaranties has been given under the other labeling statutes, primarily because the TFPIA is more comprehensive, providing for three types whereas only two are permitted under the Wool Act and the Fur Act. Otherwise, the significance and effect is the same and the forms, found in the respective rules, are similar if not identical. The purpose of these guaranties, of course, is protection for intermediary marketers.

All three statutes permit the use of a continuing guaranty, filed with he FTC, applicable to all products handled by the guarantor. The separate guaranty, that is, one designating a specific product (textile, wool, or fur) of the guarantor, is also permitted under each of the labeling acts.

The guaranty peculiar to the Textile Fiber Product Identification Act is the continuing guaranty given by the seller to the buyer as to all textile fiber products sold to, or to be sold to, the buyer by the seller-guarantor.

As should be obvious from the standpoint of FTC jurisdiction, an importer cannot make use of a guaranty from the manufacturer of the product he imports for sale. The responsibility for complying with all labeling and advertising requirements is strictly his own.

Separate Guaranty. "We guarantee [or, based upon a guaranty received . . .] that the textile fiber product(s) specified herein are not misbranded nor falsely or deceptively advertised or invoiced under the provisions of the Textile Fiber Products Identification Act and Rules and Regulations thereunder." The printed name and address on the invoice or paper will suffice to meet the signature and address requirement. The disclosure of required information on label or invoice or other paper relating to the marketing and handling of the textile fiber product is not considered a form of separate guaranty.

Continuing Guaranty from Seller to Buyer

We, the undersigned, guarantee that all textile fiber products, now being sold or which may hereafter be sold or delivered to _____ _____ are not, and will not be, misbranded nor falsely nor deceptively advertised or invoiced under the provisions of the Textile Fiber Product Identification Act and Rules and Regulations thereunder. This guaranty effective until _____.

Dated, signed, and executed this _____ day of _____.
19____ at _____, _____.

          (city)   (State or Territory)

_____

      (Name under which business is conducted)

_____

Corporate seal if applicable

_____

      (Signature of proprietor, partner, or authorized official)

Continuing Guaranty Filed with the FTC. The prescribed form is set forth in the rules, but preprinted forms are available upon request to the commission. It must be executed in duplicate and each copy acknowledged before a notary public.

With such guaranty on file, notice of the fact is sufficient by setting forth, on the invoice or other paper covering the marketing or handling of the product guaranteed, the following statement: "Continuing guaranty under the Textile Fiber Products Identification Act filed with the Federal Trade Commission."

FLAMMABLE FABRICS ACT

The purpose of the Flammable Fabrics Act (FFA) is to protect the public from the danger surrounding the use of highly flammable textiles and related materials of the type that have caused bodily injury or death to individuals. The act originally covered only wearing apparel and fabrics intended or sold for use in wearing apparel. In 1967 the law was amended to include interior furnishings, and fabrics and related materials used in wearing apparel and interior furnishings.

Even prior to the enactment of the Flammable Fabrics Act, the FTC proceeded against persons placing flammable fabrics and garments in interstate commerce. On the theory that sale of such fabrics or garments without disclosing that they were highly flammable was an unfair practice under Section 5 of the Federal Trade Commission Act, the commission issued cease and desist orders prohibiting sales without such disclosures. But under the Federal Trade Commission Act, the FTC could proceed only *after* the flammable articles were introduced into the market. It could not forestall such introduction. Accordingly, the Federal Trade Commission favored legislation that would make it possible to prevent effectively the purchase by the ultimate consumer of the dangerous merchandise. As its Chairman Mead commented, in a letter to the Chairman of the House Committee on Interstate and Foreign Commerce, March 19, 1953:

> Once the merchandise leaves the factory it quickly becomes so scattered into various channels of trade that instances of burning of consumers are bound to occur because of the inability adequately to trace the articles or have them removed from sale. This points up the importance of the prophylactic character of the bill.

The FTC is authorized to enforce the Flammable Fabrics Act by its cease and desist orders, by suits to enjoin violation of the act, and by libel suits for the seizure and confiscation of articles in violation of the law. Willful violators are liable to a fine and imprisonment. However, persons receiving items from others may protect themselves (Section 8) from criminal prosecution for violation of the act by securing, in good faith, a guarantee that the article or fabric is not so highly flammable as to be dangerous.

Persons or Activities Covered by the FFA

Consistent with its purpose to prevent the introduction or movement in interstate commerce of highly flammable merchandise, the manufacture, sale, and importation of such merchandise is prohibited by Section 3.

The provisions of the act do not apply to common or contract carriers or to freight forwarders when they ship or deliver for shipment into commerce items in the ordinary course of business. Neither does the act apply to any converter, finisher, or processor who, under contract or commission, performs services for any person subject to the act, providing he does not affect the flammability of any item contrary to the terms of the contract or the act. Under Section 11(c) items shipped or delivered for shipment into commerce, to be finished or processed so as to conform to the flammability standards of the FFA, will not be subject thereto, provided delivery is made directly to the person who will perform the flammability treatment and records of such delivery and of the completed treatment are maintained. As the commission has explained in a "note" appended to Rule 14, this exemption does no violence to the force and effect of other sections of the act.

> In particular, Section 11(c) does not authorize the sale or offering for sale of any article of wearing apparel or textile fabric which is in fact dangerously flammable at the time of sale or offering for sale, even though the seller intends to ship the article for treatment prior to delivery to the purchaser or has already done so. Moreover, under Sec-

tion 3 of the Act a person is liable for a subsequent sale or offering for sale if, despite the purported completion of treatment to render it not dangerously flammable, the article in fact remains dangerously flammable.

Under Section 15 exports intended for foreign consumption also are exempted from the provisions of the FFA providing such products bear a tag or other stamp stating they are to be exported and, in fact, they are exported. Items, although essentially exports, to be shipped to American installations outside the continental limits are subject to the act, as are items imported for dyeing and other finishing (therefore using "commerce") and then exported from the United States.

The use of the channels of interstate commerce for imports not conforming to an applicable standard of flammability is unlawful under Section 9. But again, in an effort to forestall their introduction, delivery from customs is expressly dependent on compliance with the Tariff Act of 1930 and/or the giving of a bond. In the event delivery is made, subsequent redelivery may be demanded where it is found that the import is so highly flammable as to be dangerous when worn by individuals.

Articles of Wearing Apparel

By statutory definition an article of wearing apparel is any costume or article of clothing worn or intended to be worn by individuals. A partial exemption existed for hats and gloves (provided they were less than 14 inches in length and were not affixed to an article of clothing so as to form an integral part thereof) and for footwear, provided it was not hosiery or affixed so as to form an integral part of another garment.

With respect to hats, although bridal veils clearly fall within the prescribed test of "covering, veils and veilings," those that merely decorate hats do not. Neither, of course, are they, when so used, includable as a "fabric" for an article of wearing apparel. Recognizing, nonetheless, a hazard if the veils were flammable, the FTC decided in one case to determine the question of wearing apparel on a case-by-case basis. But only a short time later the commission amended the rules and regulations to bring certain ornamental veils within the "covering" test.

Effective May, 1967, Rule 6, subsection (b), made it necessary to affix to fabrics intended for use in hats, gloves, and footwear an invoice specifying the intended use. Moreover, if such fabrics would be so highly flammable as to be dangerous within the meaning of the FFA, the rule required anyone marketing such fabrics and the manufacturer using such fabrics to maintain records reflecting acquisition, disposition, and intended use.

Similar provisions are found in subsection (a) of the rule for the maintenance of records for statute-exempted fabrics used in interlinings (unless such interlining fabric is used or intended to be used for another purpose) and other *unexposed* parts of wearing apparel.

Subsection (d) excludes handkerchiefs as an article of wearing apparel provided, when finished, the size does not exceed 24 inches on any side or 576 square inches in area. On the other hand, a handkerchief which is a decoration or trimming (or the fabric used therefor) is subject to the requirements of the act. A subsequent "Interpretation" by the FTC erased any idea that mere size or description could alone be determinative. It clearly left room for a "handkerchief" to be a "covering" if such was the use or intended purpose. Scarves, of course, are articles of wearing apparel.

In August, 1967, the problem of ornamental veilings was solved. When used as part of a hat, such veils would cause the hat to be included with the definition of article of wearing apparel as a "covering" if, from the tip of the crown of the hat, the veil measured 9 inches or more and extended more than 2 inches beyond the brim. Similarly, an all-veiling "hat" would be included if such material was more than 9 inches in width and extended more than 9 inches from the tip of the crown of the completed hat.

The FTC has determined, also, that baby receiving blankets which are principally used to wrap an infant are not subject to the FFA. But a corsage made of wood fiber chips is subject, as an article of wearing apparel, within the meaning of the statute.

Flammability Standards

In the original 1953 act Section 4 was the "Standard of Flammability" section. Directed at fabrics and articles of wearing apparel that burn rapidly and intensely, it adopted existing commercial standards established through the Department of Commerce providing the conditions and the manner in which such products would be tested. Under the standards to which the act made reference, determination of flammability that would render the products tested unsuitable for clothing was to be based on two factors: the ease of ignition and the speed of flame spread. These factors would help to discriminate between (as the legislative history reflects the purpose of the framers) "the conventional fabrics that present moderate and generally recognized hazards and the special types of fabrics which present unusual hazards and are highly dangerous." The major hazards were considered to be

1. Those cotton and rayon (which ignite and burn more readily than wool) fabrics with fuzzy or furlike surfaces which flash—and burn with great rapidity.

2. Synthetic fabrics which melt when heated with a resultant molten

material capable of producing serious burns when coming in contact with the skin.

Under Section 4 of the law as amended in 1967 the references to specific standards were deleted in light of new procedures for the establishment or updating of standards, under the Secretary of Commerce, by amendment or regulation, including labeling (for fabrics, related materials, wearing apparel, and interior furnishing) needed to protect the public against unreasonable risk of the occurrence of fire leading to death or personal injury or significant property damage. The old Commercial Standards, however, will continue to be applicable to wearing apparel and fabrics to be used therefor until superseded or modified by the Secretary of Commerce.

Pre-emption

Under Section 16, added to the act in 1967, the Flammable Fabrics Act is intended to supersede any law of any state or political subdivision inconsistent therewith.

FAIR PACKAGING AND LABELING

On November 3, 1966, Congress passed the Fair Packaging and Labeling Act. The act authorizes the Secretary of Health, Education and Welfare to promulgate regulations concerning labels of food, drugs, devices, and cosmetics. With the exception of some few excluded commodities enumerated in Section 10 of the act, the Federal Trade Commission has been granted the power to write regulations concerning all other consumer commodities as that term is defined by the act. Primarily, the products controlled by the FTC are those sold in the supermarket or drugstore.

Regulations for food took effect on July 1, 1968, for drugs, cosmetics, and devices on December 31, 1969, and for all other consumer commodities on September 10, 1969. The act provided that the regulations would not preclude the orderly disposal of packages in inventory or with the trade as of these effective dates of the regulations.

The purpose of the law is to facilitate value comparisons and to enable consumers to obtain accurate information about the quantity of the contents in a package. The act is aimed at eliminating confusing or obscure statements of quantity on labels, preventing the use of superfluous adjectives, as in such terms as *giant quart* or *full gallon,* defining meaningful use for the terms *small, medium,* and *large* used to characterize package sizes, and stopping the misuse of "economy" or "cents-off" claims.

Product coverage is not entirely clear, particularly for those consumer commodities under FTC jurisdiction. Certain items—meats, poultry, tobacco, pesticides, prescription drugs, alcoholic beverages, and seeds— are expressly excluded. Senator Magnuson, chairman of the Senate Inter- state and Foreign Commerce committee, said the bill was not intended to cover durable articles; textiles or items of apparel; any household appliance, equipment, or furnishing; bottled gas for heating or cooking purposes; paints and kindred products; flowers, fertilizers, plants or shrubs, garden and lawn supplies; pet-care supplies; and stationery and writing supplies, gift wraps, fountain pens, and mechanical pencils and kindred products. There was an attempt on the Senate floor to extend the bill to cover all commodities a consumer might buy at retail sale, but this amendment was defeated.

The act requires the label to bear a specification of the identity of the commodity. The regulations implement this by requiring that the specifi- cation of identity be in terms of any name required by federal law or regulation or, in the absence of such a name, the common or usual name of the commodity, or, in the absence thereof, the generic name or other appropriately descriptive term, such as a statement of function.

The act likewise requires the label to bear the name and place of busi- ness of the manufacturer, packer, or distributor. In implementing this requirement of the act, the regulations specify that for a corporation, the actual corporate name must be used, and unless the name appearing on the label is that of the manufacturer, the name shall be qualified by a phrase revealing the connection of the person with the product. The regulations also require the place of business of the manufacturer, packer, or distributor to include the zip code.

The act requires a net quantity of contents to be separately stated on the label in a prescribed form. Essentially, on packages of at least 1 pound or 1 pint but less than 4 pounds or 1 gallon, a dual declaration ex- pressing ounces or fluid ounces and parenthetically largest whole units (pounds, pints, quarts) is required.

The quantity-of-contents statement by regulations must appear on the principal display panel of the label, with prescribed separation from other labeling information. Unless the principal display panel of the label is less than 5 square inches in area, the prescribed quantity-of-con- tents statement must appear in the lower 30 per cent of the label. A minimum type size for use in expressing the quantity-of-contents statement is specified, and the minimum is determined by the size of the package surface bearing the principal display panel. When the label gives the number of servings, uses, or applications of the quantity of contents, the regulations prescribe the manner of such representations. Many consumer commodities, especially those subject to the FTC, are quantified in terms of dimensions or area rather than weight or volume. The FTC regulations include the forms of expressing the measure of such commodities.

Exempted from the requirements of the FPLA, by virtue of the definition of *package,* are shipping containers used solely for transportation of consumer commodities in bulk or in quantity to manufacturers, packers, or processors and outer wrappings used by retailers to deliver consumer commodities, if such outer wrappings are devoid of printed matter pertaining to any particular commodity.

The act also grants to the administrating agencies the authority to issue regulations relating to: (1) standards characterizing sizes of packages enclosing consumer commodities; (2) the placement on a package of printed matter representing retail offerings at prices lower than the ordinary or customary retail sale price; (3) the declaration on the label of each package of the common or usual name of the consumer commodity, or if it consists of more than one component, the common or usual name of each in the order of decreasing predominance; (4) nonfunctional slack fill.

A violation of the FPLA regulations issued by the FTC constitutes a false and deceptive act or practice in violation of Section 5(a) of the Federal Trade Commission Act and is subject to the enforcement provisions of Section 5 (b) of the Federal Trade Commission Act.

CIGARETTE LABELING AND ADVERTISING

Congress, in enacting the Federal Cigarette Labeling and Advertising Act, declared its policy and purpose to be that of establishing a federal program to warn the public that cigarette smoking may be hazardous to health by including a warning to that effect on each package of cigarettes. In accordance with this stated purpose and to avoid nonuniform and confusing labeling, the act pre-empts any other authority from requiring any other health warning statements.

This act, effective January 1, 1966, is a labeling, advertising, and reporting statute and requires that all cigarette packages contain the statement:

CAUTION: Cigarette Smoking May Be
Hazardous to Your Health

The statement must appear in a conspicuous place and in legible type on every cigarette package. The act makes it unlawful for any person to manufacture, import, or package cigarettes for sale or distribution within the United States whose package does not bear the required warning. Packages of cigarettes designed for export from the United States or for consumption beyond the jurisdiction of the internal revenue laws of the United States are exempt from the act. However, cigarettes packaged and destined for sale and distribution to members of the U.S. Armed Forces located outside the United States are not exempt.

The "advertising" part of this legislation is curious, and is, in part at least, explainable by the general role of the Federal Trade Commission with respect to its policing of false and deceptive advertising and its eager jump into the subject of cigarette advertising before Congress acted. The commission, on June 22, 1964, promulgated a trade regulation rule which required that, commencing January 1, 1965, all cigarette packages contain an affirmative warning that cigarette smoking is dangerous to health and may cause death from cancer and other diseases and that after July 1, 1965, all cigarette advertising contain a like warning. However, Congress, on July 27, 1965, passed the Federal Cigarette Labeling and Advertising Act, which established a moratorium on health warning requirements in advertising. Thus, for a period terminating July 1, 1969, the commission could not require an affirmative statement relating to smoking and health in cigarette advertising.

The commission's authority with respect to false and misleading advertising was not impaired by the act, even though it vacated the requirement of its trade regulation rule on July 28, 1965. Any statement in an advertisement that might tend to alter or dilute the required warning, express or implied, is subject to appropriate commission action.

Since the *Report of the Surgeon General's Advisory Committee on Smoking and Health* was published on January 11, 1964, there have been many scientific studies and evaluations of the impact of cigarette smoking on health. Since passage of the act, the trend has been toward stronger cigarette health warnings on both labels and in advertising.

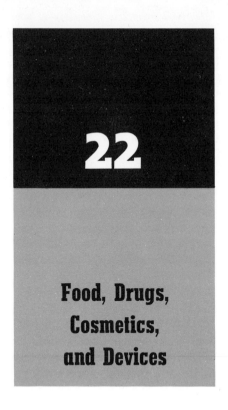

22

Food, Drugs, Cosmetics, and Devices

Food, drugs, cosmetics, and therapeutic devices have been more closely scrutinized and thoroughly regulated by congressional legislation than any other household products. The history of the legislation is long, complex, and even confused. New laws overlap old laws and areas of agency enforcement are entangled.

The clearest explanation is the historical one. At the end of the nineteenth century, laws were passed to prevent importation of adulterated foods. But it was not until 1906, and largely at the urging of an official of the Department of Agriculture, that the first interstate pure food and drug law was passed. The primary evil the law sought to eradicate was the health threat posed by adulterated food, but the legislation was drafted only in part in terms of adulteration. Much of the law was directed at misbranding and provided for control over labels or labeling.

The reasons for such a law seem patently obvious today, but to a generation believing in *laissez-faire* free enterprise, even a can of putrid

384

chicken was a matter of *caveat emptor,* and protection of health and safety were not considered to be a concern of government. Several magazines, principally *Collier's* and the *Lady's Home Journal,* aided by the muckrakers, uncovered some of the revolting practices of the food industry. The city dweller was vulnerable. No longer was he able to rely on his own fastidiousness in his farmyard or garden, but he was forced instead to accept what came from the grocery shelves, New methods of processing and preserving, new additives, transportation from distant points, and unknown manufacturers made it impossible for him to check what he was consuming. States had attempted regulation, but this was of little use where the bulk of food moved interstate. Because, as a matter of federal law, state regulation is not permitted to burden interstate commerce, state legislation resulted in only piecemeal regulation.

The federal act of 1906 covered adulterated and misbranded food, drugs, liquors, and medicines. This meant regulation of labels and labeling, but not of advertising. Advertising was placed under the aegis of the Federal Trade Commission, upon its creation in 1914, specifically under Section 5, which prohibits "unfair methods of competition in commerce." Many of the FTC's early cases involved food and drug advertisements, including the very first commission order reviewed by the courts.

Then in 1931 the Supreme Court handed down the *Raladam* decision, holding that the FTC was without jurisdiction unless there was proof that the advertisement injured competitors. Raladam was a reducing remedy of dubious efficacy, containing desiccated thyroid that could easily have injured and deceived consumers. But the wording of the Federal Trade Commission Act, as it read in 1931, prohibited only "unfair methods of *competition* in commerce." This holding restricted the commission's activity in areas where only the consumer and not the competitor was injured by the trade practice.

The year 1938, however, saw a new Federal Food, Drug, and Cosmetic Act and an amended Federal Trade Commission Act.

WHEELER-LEA AMENDMENTS

The 1938 amendments to the Federal Trade Commission Act, often referred to as the Wheeler-Lea amendments, closed the loophole of the *Raladam* decision by inserting "unfair and deceptive acts or practices in commerce" so that Section 5 now reads, "Unfair methods of competition in commerce and unfair or deceptive acts or practices in commerce are hereby declared unlawful."

The purpose of the Wheeler-Lea amendments was "first to broaden the power of the FTC over unfair methods of competition by extending its jurisdiction to cover unfair or deceptive acts in commerce," and second, to provide more effective control over false advertising of food, drugs, devices, and cosmetics.

Under Section 12(a) of the amended act, it is unlawful to disseminate or cause to be disseminated any false advertisement for the purpose of inducing or with the likelihood of inducing the purchase of food, drugs, devices, or cosmetics if the advertisement is sent through the United States mail, or is in commerce, or if the purchase is in commerce. Commerce is defined under Section 4 of the Federal Trade Commission Act. No matter how incidental the existence of one of the three events, the FTC has power to act. If the advertisement is in a newspaper shipped across a state line, if only a few copies fall into commerce, or if the advertisement is mailed intrastate but through the U.S. mails, the commission has jurisdiction.

The act of sending a false advertisement that violates Section 12(a) is also an unfair and deceptive act under Section 5. The commission can choose alternate routes of issuing its own complaints under Section 5 or seeking court remedies under Section 13 or Section 14.

If the commission proceeds under Section 5, its own cease and desist orders become final in sixty days unless there is court review. A violation of a final order is subject to a $5,000 fine. Sections 13 and 14 provide court proceedings for injunctions, criminal fines of $5,000, or imprisonment of six months, where there has been a false advertisement of a food, drug, device, or cosmetic. The criminal penalty is to be applied only when the product is injurious to health or when there is an intent to defraud.

The injunction can be brought either before or after the FTC issues its complaint on the basis of a "proper showing" that it has "reason to believe" that Section 12 has been violated. Occasionally, the court makes an independent judgment of "reasons to believe" and may deny the FTC's request for injunction.

Publishers, radio broadcasters, and advertising agencies are exempted from liability under Section 14(b), unless they refuse to furnish the name of the one who issued the false advertisement. Also, no newspaper or periodical is subject to an injunction for a deceptive advertisement if the injunction would unreasonably delay its publication.

Section 15 defines *false advertisement,* and false advertisement of margarine, as well as *food, drug, device, cosmetics,* and *margarine.* These words have been defined by statute and judicial construction to a point that some of their distinctions would not be recognized in common usage. For clarity, the statutory definitions will be given later in the chapter where the topic is more fully discussed. The definition of false advertising was intentionally made very broad. It was supposed to cover anything the human mind could devise. Fraudulent intent was not a necessary element; it was sufficient to show that the advertising was materially misleading.

FEDERAL FOOD, DRUG, AND COSMETIC ACT

The Federal Food, Drug, and Cosmetic Act of 1938 corrected some of the loopholes of the 1906 act and its subsequent amendments. The 1906 act required fraudulent intent of misbranding; the 1938 act demanded only likelihood to deceive. Under the 1906 act a food with a fanciful or distinctive name was exempted from the standards of adulteration. Since the 1938 act such mixtures or compound foods are no longer immune from attack. In the area of drugs, since 1938 a difference of medical opinion about a drug is a material fact that must be stated on the label. Failure to do so may amount to misbranding. Cosmetics and devices were included in the act for the first time, although toilet soap is expressly excluded.

With the new legislation the two agencies continued to have contiguous and in some cases overlapping control over food, drugs, cosmetics, and devices. Apparently the duplication was intentional. Senator Lea saw advertisements as economic problems, not as health problems. Because the FTC was established to regulate trade practices, it should continue to regulate advertising. On the other hand, the Food and Drug Administration was assumed to have the expertise and scientific staff to test therapeutic claims and establish standards for health and safety.

WORKING AGREEMENT

The critical words on which the jurisdiction of the two agencies turn are *labeling* and *advertising*. The Federal Food, Drug, and Cosmetic Act defines labeling as including all labels and other written, printed, or graphic matter (1) on any article or any of its containers or wrappers, or (2) accompanying such an article. If an article is alleged to be misbranded because the labeling is misleading, then in determining whether this is true there shall be taken into account (among other things) not only representations made or suggested by statement, word, design, devices, or any combination thereof, but also the extent to which the labeling fails to reveal facts material in the light of such representations or material with respect to consequences that may result from the use of the article.

The Federal Trade Commission Act defines *false advertisement* for purposes of Sections 12, 13, and 14, as follows:

> The term false advertisement means an advertisement, other than labeling, which is misleading in a material respect, and in determining whether any advertisement is misleading, there shall be taken into account (among other things) not only representations made or suggested by statement, word, design, device, sound or any combination, therefor, but also the extent to which the advertisement fails to reveal facts material in the light of such representations or material, with respect to consequences which may result from the use of the commodity to which the advertisement relates under the conditions prescribed in said advertisement or under such conditions as are customary or usual. No advertisement of a drug shall be deemed to be false if it is disseminated only to members of the medical profession, contains no false representation of a material fact and includes or is accompanied in each instance by truthful disclosure of the formula showing quantitatively each ingredient of such drug.

No one drafting the 1938 acts foresaw how interrelated the two concepts could be. The dual jurisdiction and the distinction between the two powers can be briefly stated by reference to the Working Agreement between the Federal Trade Commission and the Food and Drug Administration.

The Federal Food, Drug, and Cosmetic Act is directed toward any article of food, drug, device, or cosmetic that is adulterated or misbranded while introduced into or in interstate commerce, or while held for sale after shipment in interstate commerce. The FDA having discovered a violation of the act reports it to the Justice Department with a recommendation for seizure, criminal prosecution, or injunction.

An article is misbranded if the labeling is false or misleading in any particular. Drugs or devices are misbranded if there are inadequate directions for use. Drugs are also misbranded if there are inadequate warnings against use by those with pathological conditions or by children where its use may be dangerous to health. Misbranding occurs also where there are inadequate warnings against an unsafe dosage or methods of administration or duration of treatment or manner of application on whatever form as is necessary to protect the users.

Section 12 of the Federal Trade Commission Act makes a false advertisement of food, drugs, devices, or cosmetics a deceptive practice. A false advertisement under Section 15(a)(1) is an advertisement other than labeling which is misleading in a material respect. In considering the advertisement, the commission can take into account not only the representation made and suggested by the statement, word, design, device, sound, or combination, but also the extent to which the advertisement fails to reveal facts material in the light of such representations or material with respect to consequences that may result from the use of the commodity.

Labeling, as defined in the Federal Food, Drug, and Cosmetic Act includes written, printed, or graphic matter which accompanies a food, drug, device or cosmetic which is held for sale after shipment or delivery in interstate commerce.

Any written, printed, or graphic matter describing a food, drug, device, or cosmetic can be both an advertisement or labeling depending on whether it is being used to advertise or to accompany the article.

More recent amendments to the Federal Food and Drug Act have been the Kefauver–Harris Drug Amendments of 1962, giving the FDA control over prescription drug advertising. Finally, there is the Fair Packaging and Labeling Act, discussed in another chapter, which imposes new standards on packages and labels to aid the consumer in making value per ounce comparisons.

LABELING AND ADVERTISING

The distinction between labeling and advertising is important and troubling because the sanctions and procedures of the two agencies are different. The Federal Food, Drug, and Cosmetic Act calls a product misbranded if its labeling is false or misleading *in any particular*. The FTC must find the advertisement to be *materially* misleading. The FTC can order affirmative disclosure only when it is needed to balance an impression of misleading material fact in the advertisement, but the FDA can demand an affirmative disclosure no matter what has been said.

The usual penalty of the FTC is an order to cease and desist, which comes after the often time-consuming procedure of a complaint, hearing, initial order, appeal, final order, and court review. Its power to issue injunctions and impose sentences and fines under Section 14 is limited to fraudulent or injurious advertisement of food, drugs, devices, and cosmetics. The FDA has more drastic methods and speedier ones: seizure, injunction, and criminal prosecution.

A reviewing court is less likely to disturb the findings of the FTC, which proceeds through a hearing examiner and then on appeal to the full commission, than the findings of the FDA, which relies on the Justice Department to bring actions in the federal district courts. The former is held to the standards for review of administrative decisions (the court must affirm if there is substantial evidence in the record to sustain the agency's decision); the latter to the standards of evidence in the federal courts, which gives the appellate court wider scope in reviewing a lower court's decision.

The standards determining what constitutes deception are similar in both agencies. Those most likely to be deceived are those to whom the product appeals. If those persons are shown to have been deceived, a sufficient showing of deception has been made, even if the reasonable man would not be interested. It is the message as a whole that is considered and it can be deceptive even if word by word the message is accurate. Improper emphasis or ambiguity can be also deceptive.

Labeling was originally considered to consist of the directions for use and information accompanying the food, drug, device, or cosmetic; its definition included the more limited term *label*. Advertisements were considered to be the promotional and persuasive sales talk in media separate and distinct from the product. Had they remained so simply isolated, the dichotomy of health and safety under the FDA and economic regulations and trade practices under the FTC would have been a simple rule to apply. The information glued to the bottle is the label. The paper accompanying the bottle of aspirin is the labeling. If the labeling failed to give adequate directions for use or warnings, or did not list its active ingredients in the order of quantity, the product would be misbranded and subject to the FDA sanctions.

On the other hand, if radio and television commercials and magazines and newspaper spreads proclaimed this aspirin as a marvelous new product, a cure for rheumatism or arthritis, or a panacea, it would be a case for the FTC, because these are advertisements.

But if a company is engaged in an unfair and deceptive practice involving production of substandard jams that are labeled fresh fruit preserves, and there is no showing of interstate advertising, but only of false labels and labelings, can the FTC take the jurisdiction? In *Fresh Grown Preserve Corp.* v. *FTC* the Second Circuit Court of Appeals answered in the affirmative. The commission's Section 5 jurisdiction is much broader than the Section 12 powers. If it can show unfair and deceptive trade practices (and deceptive labels are evidence of this), then it can proceed under Section 5 alone without relying on Section 12 and the Section 15 definition of false advertisement. Section 15(a) defines advertisement to exclude labeling, but Section 15(a) applies only to Section 12 violations, not to Section 5 powers. This power of the FTC has been restated in *Houbigant, Inc.* v. *FTC*. Conversely, the FDA can use advertisements to show evidence of misbranding, thereby subjecting the product to seizure. The FDA ultimately pursues the product, not the graphic or written material. *Labeling* and *accompanying* have been given a functional test definition to allow the FDA to reach harmful products.

Situations have arisen in which the textual information has been shipped separately from the product, or where the information alone has been shipped, or where a book or pamphlet has been displayed near a product.

The functional test, as stated by the Seventh Circuit in the *Kordel* case, is "not of physical contiguity, but of textual relationship. . . ." The products and literature were interdependent because without the latter, the former lacked the labeling necessary to inform the public. Therefore, accompaniment need not mean that the material is in the package or container.

Both agencies are constantly bringing actions against health books, health foods, and advertisements for either the book or the food. Under the Federal Food and Drug Act, pamphlets can constitute labeling. In one case, Kordel was the sole source and author of the pamphlets and the drugs, which were distributed together through health stores. On seven occasions the pamphlets were in the same carton as the drugs; on thirteen occasions they were shipped separately. One was shipped eighteen months after the drug. All the pamphlets were replete with references to Kordel products, explaining their uses and furnishing a price list. The pamphlets themselves were sometimes price-marked for sale, sometimes given away gratuitously, sometimes fitted for mailing with blank address spaces. In the stores they were displayed near the drugs. The court said that the Federal Food, Drug, and Cosmetic Act could not be circumvented by the easy device of a "sale" of advertising matter where the advertising performs the function of labeling.

In *United States* v. *Urbeteit* the rule in *Kordel* was applied in a case involving a therapeutic device. Here again Urbeteit was the source of both the manual and the drug. The manual, although shipped separately, was needed to explain how to use the device. The court found the two transactions integrated by "functional standards" although the two articles were mailed separately.

A complaint alleging that a joint shipment of a book and molasses misbranded the molasses was insufficient to make the book the labeling of the black strap molasses in *United States* v. *8 Cartons,* but the complaint was amended to show that the book commended the molasses as a source of vitamins and therapeutic for certain diseases, and that the recipient of both had a window display with a magazine article by the same author and an offer to supply the molasses and the book which he was displaying together, and that he told customers to look up molasses in the index of the book.

In another case the $1 booklet bore the title *About Honey*. The health store displayed it above the honey jars. The labels on the honey jars themselves bore no deceptive language. However, under the test of *Kordel* the court found a functional relationship between the booklet and the honey and held the booklet to be a label.

The Second Circuit took a different view in a case involving Sterling Honey and Vinegar. Here again the labels on the bottles themselves were faultless. There was a book giving a recipe which mislabeled this concoction of honey and vinegar, and the book mentioned the brand name Sterling Honey. Nevertheless, there was no evidence of a joint promotion. In fact, the book sales far exceeded the honey and vinegar sales. The claimant stocked both, but the court held the book was not a label.

A book entitled *Calories Don't Count* got a tremendous reception from many who are torn between a weakness for fried foods and rich sauces and a desire to be thinner. The book advocates safflower oil. Soon capsules of safflower oil were being marketed, and the book was rewritten in sections to mention the capsules. The book was displayed along with the packages of capsules in a New York department store with a sign linking the two. The court found that the book was "genuinely independent" of the capsules. It had been on sale for two months before the capsules were available. The capsules had adequate directions for use. There were no joint sales, tie-ins, or joint prices.

The FTC faced the question whether an advertisement for a health book claiming unverified therapeutic benefits is a deceptive advertisement, and it answered in the affirmative:

> [I]t is quite irrelevant whether the treatment being advertised is in the form of a pill encased in a box or in the form of a particular regimen described in a book or other writing. Literalness and exactitude and perhaps understatement must be the earmarks of promotions connected with health remedies. Advertisers must be scrupulously careful not only as respects the literal truthfulness of the message, but as respects all of the implications, innuendos and suggestions which are conveyed in the advertising message!

In an earlier case, the commission had decided that the FTC prohibits deceptive advertisements of all products including books. Even if the advertisement is truthful in describing the book's contents and merely repeats the "promises of therapeutic benefits" contained in the book, such an advertisement is deceptive, because if the promises are false, the advertisement is deceptive. But because only the advertisement and not the book was challenged, the proceeding did not involve censorship of the book.

There is lurking in all these agency actions against books a constitutional question. The first amendment right of free speech is preciously guarded, but courts have not been troubled by restricting such health books when used as labels or as advertisements. The short answer is that commercial advertising is not protected by the first amendment. The longer answer weighing the beliefs and rituals of the health cult against other protected beliefs, including religious beliefs, often similarly motivated and similarly reasuring, has not as yet been expounded by the courts. The constitutional argument is often voiced by the defendants, but generally is dismissed summarily by the commission or court.

FOOD

Besides the general statutory provisions, the FDA and the FTC have specific powers with respect to food.

Margarine is defined by statute and by regulation. The FTC has repeatedly prohibited advertisements suggesting that margarine is a dairy product. Under Section 15(a)(2) of the Federal Trade Commission Act, which defines the false advertisement of margarine, a company cannot use the word butter, "in its advertisement to imply that its margarine contains butter and therefore is superior to other brands of margarine." The subtler sales pitch of "churned to a delicate, sweet creamy goodness," or "country fresh," or "the same day to day freshness which characterizes our other dairy products" also violates Section 15(a)(2).

The purpose of the section, according to the legislative history, was to prevent any advertisement of margarine which gave the consumer the impression he was buying butter or a dairy product. The section was passed in 1950, as a legislative compromise upon the repeal of the margarine excise tax which had been imposed since 1886.

The FDA has the power to establish standards for a food. Any food not living up to the standard is deemed an imitation. If it is not so labeled, it is misbranded and subject to sanctions. The standards can be for the consistency of canned corn, the toughness of the fibers in string-beans, the amount of fruit in a cherry pie, the amount of bread in frozen breaded fish sticks—or for the characteristics of hundreds of other products.

Peanut butter is one of the products for which standards have been set lately. The FDA currently demands that peanut butter must contain 90 per cent peanuts. The manufacturers claim that this produces too sticky a mass for the average consumer, who prefers fewer peanuts and easier spreading consistency. The smoother consistency is created by decreasing the peanuts and increasing the vegetable oil and preservatives. The lengthy hearing have been going on for eleven years and are not yet completed.

Many new products have involved litigation concerning the right to exist as an independent food or to disappear as a misbranded imitation. Coffee-Rich, the frozen nondairy creamer, resembling half-and-half (that is, half milk and half cream) has occasioned actions in Massachusetts, Kansas, Michigan, Virginia, and Wisconsin. These actions were brought in state courts under state law, modeled on Section 403(g) of the Federal Food and Drug Act, relating to the promulgation of standards. The manufacturers of Coffee-Rich were able to prove that it possessed attributes of its own, that it had lower cholesterol and fewer calories and was longer lasting. Furthermore, it was clearly labeled and identifiable.

Therefore, it was held to be a new and different product and not an imitation.

Recently, the question arose whether margarine, an imitation product, could have an imitation, a low-calorie margarine. Because of all the statutory and regulatory definitions, the government argued that margarine could not have an imitation. The court disagreed, pointing out that the margarine was catering to the consumer preference for low-calorie foods.

Other foods that have been seized for misbranding include a chicken and almond sauce mix. The vignette showed a plate of noodles with a piece of chicken, but the FDA found so little chicken in the sauce that it would not be subject to the Poultry Products and Inspection Act administered by the Department of Agriculture.

The FTC has ordered that the mere fact that a loaf of bread is sliced thinner is insufficient grounds for proclaiming it as low calorie. There was a proliferation of so-called diet breads advertised as low calorie, some even insinuating that eating them alone without more self-control would lead to a more slender figure. Actually, ounce by ounce these breads had as many calories as standard bread. The only difference was that they had been sliced thinner so that the diner would be given a smaller portion. The commission ordered that the companies cease and desist marketing the bread under such deceptive names as Slimette.

The FDA has proposed new regulations for dietary foods. The reaction to the regulations was violent, often more misguided than helpful to the FDA. Advocates of vitamin supplements and health foods thought their lifeblood would be destroyed by the new restrictions.

The FDA hoped to educate the consumer away from four great nutritional myths: (1) that our soil is depleted, (2) that modern processing removes all nutritional value from our foods, (3) that most of us suffer from a subclinical nutritional deficiency, and (4) that it is virtually impossible to get all the minerals and vitamins we need from our daily diet.

The widespread use of MDR—minimum daily requirement—confuses the consumer, who commonly believes that if that is the minimum, twice as much would be twice as beneficial. Many minerals for which no nutritional need has been established are frequently added to food or vitamin pills. The proposed regulations would permit marketing of food supplements supplying established needs in amounts ranging from one-half to one and one-half times the daily requirement.

Contrary to many peoples' expectations, excess amounts of vitamins are not beneficial; in fact, they can be harmful. The FDA has requested removal of vitamin D supplements from some common foods.

There is a legitimate argument concerning the regulations because they were drafted under a section of the act [403(j)] which refers only to information on the label and not to restrictions on the contents. Later, the regulations were drafted so that vitamins are deemed both food and drugs. As food (because they have nutritional value) the FDA can promulgate standards under Section 201(f); and as drugs (because they possess curative powers) the FDA can demand strict labeling and manufacturing standards under Section 201(g). The regulations are drafted under both Section 403(j) and Section 201. It is proposed that the label should state, "Except for persons with special medical needs, there is no scientific basis for recommending routine use of a dietary supplement."

Vitamins and tonics have also posed a problem for the FTC. The typical advertisement lists a myriad of symptoms—tiredness, weakness, depression, fatigue, listlessness, nervousness, edginess (the kind of feelings most of us have had one or more times in our lives). Supposedly, a concoction of vitamins and minerals will cure the ailments. The advertisements have neglected to reveal that only rarely does tiredness stem from a simple iron or vitamin deficiency. In one case the commission found an advertising campaign had been directed at the entire population, of whom only 10 per cent had an iron deficiency and less than 1 per cent a vitamin deficiency. The vast majority suffered from tiredness due to psychological or physical ills which cannot be cured by a tonic.

Similarly, the FDA found vitamins to be misbranded when their labeling suggested that men and women required different dosages, that many conditions could be cured by this vitamin product, and that there were ingredients in these tablets that could be obtained naturally only by eating vast amounts of food. The FDA also found that the implication that the tablets contained nutritionally significant ingredients was false, because there were only minute traces of the ingredients, which made no impact on a person's system.

DEVICES

Some of the devices that have been subjected to FDA or FTC jurisdiction are humorless, outrageous, pathetic, and beyond the credibility of many ordinary men. Devices were included in the 1938 Food and Drug Act. The definition given was "instruments, apparatus, and contrivances, including their parts and accessories, intended (1) for use in diagnosis, cure, mitigation, treatment, or prevention of disease in man or other animals; or (2) to affect the structure or any function of the body of man or other animals."

It is the intent presented in the directions which determines whether the device is subject to the Food and Drug Act. For example, a child's toy or adult game, Slim Twist, which is a platform on a swivel base, was recently seized because its labeling suggested it was a weight-reducing device. A chin vibrator was similarly seized for false and misleading therapeutic claims. Weird and fantastic machines using heat and electricity, reducing machines, bed-wetting remedies, and bust developers are only a few of the gadgets that have been seized under the act.

COSMETICS

Cosmetics were included in the 1938 Food and Drug Act because the proponents of the bill recognized that "in many instances cosmetics are injurious to health and produce physical injuries to the body." Cosmetics are defined as "(1) articles to be rubbed, poured, sprinkled, or sprayed on, introduced into, or otherwise applied to the human body or any part thereof intended for cleansing, beautifying, promoting attractiveness, or altering the appearance and (2) articles intended for use as a component of any such article; except that such term shall not include soap."

The Color Additives Act of 1960 established standards for approved safe color additives, so that now coal tar dyes are not permitted in any product except hair dyes.

In this field it is sometimes hard to distinguish whether an article is a drug or a cosmetic. Because the statutory regulation of drugs is more thorough, the FDA attempts to prove that articles sold as cosmetics are actually drugs, under the statutory definition, and are therefore subject to regulation as drugs.

Much turns on the labeling and the implications flowing from the directions for use. A suntan lotion can be a cosmetic if its purpose is to glamorize by tanning, but it can be a drug if it is used to prevent sunburn. A deodorant claiming to neutralize odor passes as a cosmetic; if it claims to chemically alter the body's system of manufacturing perspiration and odor, it becomes a drug.

Standards of advertising are harder to establish in the cosmetic field, because hyperbole is rampant. The purchaser of a cosmetic wants glamor and identifies with the suggestions of dramatic change and irresistible attractiveness. "Rejuvenescence" was held too big a claim for a beauty cream and the company was ordered to cease and desist its deceptive advertising. A hair spray which represented that it made straight hair curly was held deceptive.

In the area of male vanity, a company advertising a baldness claim was ordered to disclose that its treatment could only aid a sufferer of "nonmale pattern baldness," and over 95 per cent of baldness was male pattern, so that most sufferers of baldness responding to the advertisement would not be helped by the treatment.

A cosmetic containing a dangerous ingredient can be taken off the market, as occurred recently when the FDA seized some nail strengthener containing formaldehyde.

If the ingredient in question is not unsafe, but only not generally recognized as safe and effective, the FDA proceeds against it as a drug.

The FDA seized a wrinkle remover named Sudden Change for not having a new drug application—the article was misbranded, it was alleged, because it did not bear the established name of each active ingredient. This is a requirement for drugs, under Section 352(e)(1)(A)(ii), but until the passage of the Fair Packaging and Labeling Act, it was not required for cosmetics. Moreover, the label contained false statements that could mislead the middle-aged woman into believing the cream would restore her face to a wrinkle-free state. The face-lift cream gave only a temporary effect, not the dramatic permanent one suggested by the labeling. Also, the labeling left the impression that the cream was newly discovered.

DRUGS

Drugs are divided into nonprescription or over-the-counter drugs (OTC) and prescription drugs. The FTC regulates the advertising of OTC drugs; since 1962 the FDA has regulated prescription-drug advertising. The FDA promulgates standards of safety and efficacy for both sorts of drugs, old drugs as well as new, the finished product as well as the ingredients, and scrutinizes the labels and labeling.

First, for both the FTC and the FDA a drug is defined as

(1) articles recognized in the official United States Pharmacopoeia, official Homeopathic Pharmacopoeia of the United States, or official National Formulary, or any supplement to any of them; and (2) articles intended for use in the diagnosis, care, mitigation, treatment, or prevention of any disease in man or other animals; and (3) articles (other than food) intended to affect the structure or any function of the body of man or other animals; and (4) articles intended for use as a component of any article specified in clause (1), (2), or (3); but does not include devices or their components, parts, or accessories.

Drugs are marketed for every conceivable ailment. Ailments for which no definitive medical treatment has been found have numerous alleged remedies: arthritis, cancer, skin disorders, dandruff, acne and psoriasis, colds, aches, pains and headaches, and stomach upsets. Sadly enough, anyone afflicted by these diseases will spend thousands of dollars on remedies and will believe claims in advertising that no reasonable man would accept. It is that susceptible group of gullible persons "the aged and the infirm, who are especially vulnerable to the inflated promises of curative powers of drugs" that the FTC is most interested in protecting. They, because of their misery, may have lost their objectivity.

An advertisement proclaiming as safe a medication that turns out to have a label full of precautionary statements is false. An advertisement proclaiming lasting relief of diseases which at present have no cure is deceptive.

All tablets containing aspirin are recurrently subject to agency regulation. Aspirin is one of the oldest, yet still one of the most effective pain relievers. It is sold under many brand names and in many combinations. Each brand has used a variety of marketing slogans, some of which the FTC has found to be deceptive. Recently, it charged Bufferin with making misleading statements with respect to arthritis research. Bufferin showed tests indicating that Bufferin brought relief from swelling and inflammation to arthritis sufferers separate and distinct from its general pain-killing properties. The hearing examiner ruled for the respondent and recommended dismissal of the complaint because the FTC failed to prove that the wording of the advertisement would be misunderstood by the reader.

A new aspirin product, a time-release capsule, was subjected to FDA review when it appeared that some of the clinical reports of its investigational testing had been falsified. The companies filed amended applications and labels not claiming eight-hour relief, which the FDA accepted. The FDA then proposed to permit the aspirin makers to show that a double-strength aspirin would be safe and effective. This would mean that producers of ordinary aspirin could double their dosage, thereby lessening the competitive edge of the time-release aspirin.

There is an FTC-proposed trade-regulations rule, now in litigation, "prohibiting one company from claiming that its aspirin product is any more effective as a pain reliever than any other product containing an equal amount of aspirin."

The industrywide attack by the FTC on hemorrhoid preparations resulted in a finding of deceptive advertising that relief would be anything more than temporary.

The FDA required that antibiotics no longer be added to throat lozenges because virtually all respiratory nose and throat troubles are viral and antibiotics do not work against viruses.

The FTC investigated the claims of Outgro, a remedy for ingrown toenails. Outgro did toughen the skin, but it made much more sweeping claims and failed to reveal facts the commission considered material. Outgro was claimed to cure the ingrown toenail, but it could not. Moreover, it was not to be used if infection had set in. The commission ordered the company to cease and desist making unqualified claims and to make affirmative disclosures of the limitations of Outgro. However, the commission allowed the company to keep the name Outgro because of the recognition that had been built up around the well-established trade name.

PRESCRIPTION DRUGS

Prescription drug advertising has boomed in the last decade. The simplest explanation is the recent discovery of the new drugs now on the market. Of the drugs sold today 90 per cent were unknown twenty-five years ago, 80 per cent unknown fifteen years ago, and 50 per cent unknown ten years ago.

Virtually all prescription drug advertising appears in professional journals aimed at selling the doctor. Some major drug companies advertise in regular journals to promote their institutional image, but the sales talk for prescription drugs must be made to doctors. Although it is often said that the purposes of prescription drug advertising are different from those of regular consumer advertising, a glance at the glossy layouts leaves little doubt that the need to promote consumer perference is as great here as with cornflakes.

Until 1962, however, prescription drug advertising was exempt from FTC control under Section 15, and was subject only to the FDA labeling requirements. Senator Kefauver's investigation of drug prices resulted in the passage of the 1962 Kefauver–Harris drug amendments, which gave the FDA regulatory power over prescription drug advertising. The amendments include the following language:

(n) In the case of any prescription drug distributed or offered for sale in any State, unless the manufacturer, packer, or distributor thereof includes all advertisement and other descriptive printed matter issued or caused to be issued by the manufacturer, packer or distributor with respect to that containing a true statement of (1) prominently and in type at least half as large as that used for any trade or brand name thereof (2) the formula showing quantitatively, each ingredient of such drug to the extent required for labels—Sec. 502(e) and (3) such other information in brief summary relating to side effects, contraindications and effectiveness as shall be required in regulations which shall be issued by the Secretary in accordance with the procedure specified in Sec. 701(e) of this Act; provided, that (A) except in extraordinary circumstances, no regulation issued under this paragraph shall require prior approval by the Secretary of the content of any advertisement, and (B) no advertisment of a prescription drug, published after the effective date of regulations issued under this paragraph applicable to advertisement of prescription drugs shall, with respect to the matters specified in this paragraph or covered by such regulations, be subject to the provisions of S. 12–17 of the F.T.C.A. as amended (15 U.S.C. 52–57). This paragraph (n) shall not be applicable to any printed matter which the Secretary determines to be labeling as defined in Section 201(m) of this Act.

The basic purposes of the law, according to William W. Goodrich, Assistant General Counsel of the Department of Health, Education, and Welfare were

(1) to improve the quality of all drugs, to familiarize the professional and the public with the established name.

(2) to improve the reliability or safety of new drugs by closer control of investigation and use of the drugs and better data on safety and substantial evidence to support therapeutic claims.

(3) to improve the "follow up" system of reports and procedures for removal.

(4) to create a better system of control over prescription drug ads and promotional material, so that the physician has accurate information. Accurate information means—a balanced presentation of the usefulness of the drug, the limitations on its effectiveness, its side effects, contra-indications, adverse reactions, and warnings of its dangers.

(5) to subject all antibiotics to certification; because of the threat to life of threatening infections and because of their method of production, there is a need for a government laboratory check for greater assurance of safety and effectiveness.

(6) to have comprehensive inspection powers.

For the first time prescription drug advertising was subject to government control. The FDA's supervisory control was spelled out in the regulations to prohibit:

(1) fanciful proprietary names;

(2) featuring of inert or inactive ingredients;

(3) confusing proprietary names; and

(4) to require the use of the established name in the advertisement.

The established name is that name found in the United States Homeopathic Pharmacopoeia. Although the FDA controls prescription drug advertising, it does not control the detail men who come to the doctor's office to sell him new drugs. These and the oral affirmations they make are assumedly under the jurisdiction of the FTC. The FDA has considerable control over a new drug under its New Drug Application procedures (NDA) and over antibiotics under its certification procedures.

New drugs and antibiotics may be advertised only for those conditions which were listed on the labeling which the FDA accepted in the NDA or antibiotic application for certification. One of the sixty-two amendments required that drugs be shown to be safe and effective. A showing of effectiveness was not required before. By a clause, commonly called the Grandfather Clause, any drugs commercially available October 9, 1962 that were not new drugs and that had never been covered by a new drug application could continue to be marketed by anyone without proof of safety and effectiveness as long as only old claims were used for them and for products of identical composition.

The Grandfather Clause thrusts at efficacy. Drugs were and continue to be withdrawn if they are shown to be no longer safe. Also, companies may be penalized if the labeling claims are false and misleading and are not corrected within a reasonable time. But now, in addition, the FDA can suspend a drug if it is not shown to be effective. By the regulatory scheme, all new drugs must have applications on file with the FDA. If there is a violation by the manufacturer, the FDA can suspend the NDA. Then if a drug is marketed without an NDA, that is a prohibited act and the FDA can recommend that the Justice Department prosecute.

Any product formerly covered by an NDA and all similar products, although they themselves were never specifically subject to an NDA, are subject to the requirements of efficacy. Therefore, the manufacturer has the responsibility of showing its drug's effectiveness both for the claims it expressly promotes and for those that the public and the medical profession infer from its promotion.

The use of the established name, or the generic name, has touched off a controversy. The regulations demand that the generic name appear prominently in direct conjunction and each time the proprietary name appears. It has not been resolved whether the generic name must appear immediately after the trade name each time the trade name is used in an advertisement. The issue was raised in *Abbott Labs* v. *Gardner,* which has settled the procedural point that drug companies can seek preliminary declaratory relief in the courts, although the merits of the case have not been reached.

Obviously *equal prominence* is a relative matter, depending on the layout. *Direct conjunction* is interpreted to allow a trade-mark symbol between the two words, and *prominently* means only as the layman would understand it.

The FDA indicates that it is sufficient to give only a summary of all uses, dosages, side effects, contraindications, and hazards when stated in the advertisements, but such information must be in full in the labeling, brochures, mailing pieces, detailing pieces, file cards, price lots, and catalogues.

The drug companies are worried that use of the established name each time the proprietary name is used will only extend the copy to the point that it is not read. They question the vagueness of such terms as *fair summary, fair balance, reasonably close association.* Comments by the staff of the FDA indicate that fair balance does not mean that the photographs must show the successful case along with the one who has been afflicted with all the severe side effects.

The regulations require that the labeling of prescription drugs show the established name of the drug, and the established name of all active ingredients. With nonprescription drugs, also, the label must show the established name of the drug and of the ingredients, but there is no requirement that the labeling show the established name even if the proprietary name is used. Prescription drugs must carry the established name one half as large as the proprietary name and in direct conjunction. This is not necessary for nonprescription drugs; the only requirement is that the established name be prominent.

If certain ingredients are used, the quantity must be stated on both prescription and nonprescription drugs, whether the ingredient is active or not. In addition, the labels of prescription drugs must have the quantity of every active ingredient.

The FDA operates by means of a letter informing the manufacturer that its advertisement is misleading. Twelve manufacturers received such a letter between February and November, 1967. They admitted error and sent out a correctional letter to physicians, commonly referred to as the Dear Doctor letter.

The FDA has instituted a new uniform system of marking envelopes used to mail drug information to doctors. A red background means an important drug hazard warning is inside. A drug labeling change comes in a blue background. Brown means an important correction of drug information. These were used to proclaim labeling changes in March, 1967. Also, the FDA has published the *Compendium of Medical Advertising,* which contains all the pertinent information on drug advertising from the law to speeches and correspondence.

Commissioner Goddard has listed seven common deceptive practices in prescription drug advertisements.

1. Quotations out of context, using favorable quotations from one author while omitting unfavorable quotations by the same man. For example, an arthritis advertisement used only portions of a report which contained the sentence, "excellent results have also been obtained on some cases of rheumatoid arthritis. . . . there have been striking failures as well."

2. "Halo" quotations, which leave the impression that the study was representative of a much larger and more general experience with a drug.

3. The lack of balance problem, where one physician's recommendations are used and no reference is made to criticism by equally experienced physicians.

4. The use of "old stuff," where old research is used to support a claim when later and better research exists to modify and discount the claim.

5. Simply selecting mediocre research when better research information is available.

6. Examples of too selective research or the presentation of only those research papers heavily unbalanced in favor of the claims.

7. Extensions and distortions of claims for usefulness of the drugs beyond claims approved by the Food and Drug Administration.

In an advertising seminar, one commentator used ten specific advertisements as examples. One used the catch phrase *behavioral drift* in recommending a drug as therapy for cases of "behavioral drift." It was unclear from the advertisement whether the drug was a tranquilizer or an antidepressant. The phrase *behavioral drift* has no psychiatric validity, but it leaves the impression that a variety of symptoms can be cured by the drug, and therefore it is likely to be prescribed for more ailments than it was tested for and verified by scientific research.

Each oral contraceptive, in fighting for a share of a lucrative market, proclaims itself to produce fewer side effects than the others. At present there is no scientific support for the promises that one causes less weight gain, or has less hormone substance. One oral contraceptive advertised itself as the first sequential contraceptive when actually it had only been approved thirteen days before the second sequential oral contraceptive.

An arthritis remedy was advertised as permitting safe long-term dosage, and continued to advertise this after the labeling of the drug had been revised to include new cautionary information with respect to long-term uses. The drug had also been featured in a magazine article as a general drug for bursitis, tennis elbow, and trick knees, using only users' testimonials for verification of claims.

A new antibiotic advertised its absence of side effects, without mentioning two it did have—hematologic toxicity and frequent severe diarrhea. Another antibiotic was marketed as particularly safe for children without substantial evidence that this was true. A new penicillin was misleadingly advertised as an everyday penicillin for common bacterial respiratory infections. Its real value was in fighting penicillin-resistant staph infections. The FDA thought that any advertisement should clearly disclose that it was of maximum benefit to doctors who, having diagnosed infections as penicillin resistant, needed to shift the patient from regular penicillin to this variety.

Finally, the commentator criticized appetite depressants, because there has been no conclusive showing that any drug works effectively on the human satiety center.

Any claim of safety without modifying language is regarded with suspicion, especially when applied to a powerful drug. Any claim of lengthy therapy for an illness for which science has established no cure is subject to scrutiny.

Drugs proclaiming themselves newer, better, different from other similar drugs often mislead. The advertisements which suggest the drugs for ills which can best be described as the "frustrations of daily living" or any drug suggesting itself as a panacea are generally criticized.

At the time of this writing, only two drugs, Peritrate and Serax, had been seized by the FDA for failure to provide a "fair balance" on their advertisements. In both cases, however, the misleading advertisement was discontinued immediately.

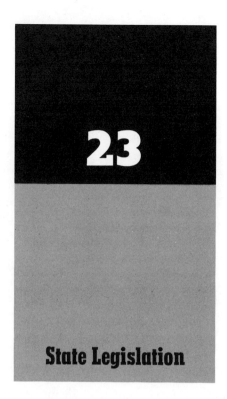

23

State Legislation

We have discussed various aspects of the state laws dealing with unfair and deceptive business practices in the various substantive chapters dealing with specific forms of unlawful practices. Our purpose here is to examine the various types of state statutes in their entirety and to focus particularly on two recent model statutes, the Uniform Deceptive Trade Practices Act and the Uniform Consumer Credit Code.

CRIMINAL LEGISLATION

As we saw in Chapter 2 the first comprehensive effort at the state level to cope with the augmenting abuses of the advertising industry at the turn of the century was the *Printers' Ink* Statute drafted in 1911 by Harry Nims for the advertising journal, *Printers' Ink*. Eventually adopted in forty-four states, the statute was a response to the inadequacies of the common law and the absence of effective motivation to bring individual law suits because of the small amount of money usually involved. The criminal statute which appeared in *Printers' Ink* was designed to fill this gap and provide an effective means for state regulation of advertising.

The model act requires proof of three elements in order to find a person guilty of a misdemeanor: (1) the intent to sell or dispose of merchandise or services; (2) the making or publishing, whether directly or indirectly, of an advertisement regarding such products; and (3) a representation of fact in such advertisement which is misleading, deceptive, or untrue. As originally drafted, the purpose of the model act was to make the advertiser absolutely liable for what he said. The act was designed to remove three of the most serious impediments to success of a common-law cause of action, that is, (1) actual reliance by the purchaser; (2) actual knowledge of the misleading character of the advertisement by the seller; and (3) an intent to deceive by the seller. Generally, the constitutionality of the statutes based on the model act has been upheld despite the absence of knowledge and reliance requirements.

However, some state legislatures, in the course of enacting this statute, declined to go as far as the model act and required both that the advertiser must know, or be reasonably chargeable with knowledge of, the falsity of his statement and that an intent to deceive must be proved. Proof of "scienter" (guilty knowledge) and intent to deceive severely encroaches upon the effectiveness of these statutes. Not only do they pose substantial evidentiary barriers to conviction, but they make the cost of proof much greater, thus inhibiting the states' prosecution of all but the more serious offenses.

Additionally, some courts have been disinclined to allow a radical departure from the common-law concepts and have imposed their own limitations upon these statutes. For example, there is some authority for the proposition that, as at common law, statements of opinion or prediction are not actionable. In the New York case of *People* v. *Clarke* an indictment charged that the defendant had advertised that "the guarantee of the company was issued only on mortgages carefully and wisely selected;" that "the properties on which the mortgages were given were worth more than the mortgages to cover the interest charges, [and] taxes . . . ;" and that the guarantees made the mortgages absolutely safe. These representations were held to be mere opinion and not actionable under the statute. Thus, the distinction between fact and opinion can be important in determining the applicability of the statute in a given case. It has been stated that the growing tendency today is to interpret so-called opinions as facts, thus broadening the scope of these criminal statutes.

Another limitation has been the requirement imposed by some courts that the misleading statements must refer very specifically to the goods or services offered for sale. Thus a shopkeeper, desiring the patronage of shoppers sympathetic to the demands of organized labor, who falsely claimed to pay high wages to his employees was held to be immune from prosecution. To similar effect, one who claimed that a sale was held by order of a bankruptcy court, which was in fact not true, could not be prosecuted. These results have been criticized for ignoring the basic purpose of the original statute, namely, to proscribe all false statements "which tend to induce action by the reader or listener." This criticism notwithstanding, the "specific reference" requirement still stands as a judicial limitation upon the *Printers' Ink* type of statute in many states.

The efficacy of these statutes is further impaired by the fact that, as in the case of penal statutes generally, they are strictly and narrowly construed. Questions have arisen as to whether or not less direct forms of deception, such as "bait" advertising (that is, offering goods for sale with an intent not to sell them, but to lure prospective customers into the store), come within the ambit of the statutory proscriptions. Partly because of the general feeling that "bait" advertising is not within the general terms of the statute, at least six states have amended their statutes so as specifically to make "bait" advertising a crime. Some of these amendments have gone so far as to give the state's attorney general the power to seek injunctions against continued violations of the statute.

The existence of these legislative and judicial limitations upon the *Printers' Ink* model act has resulted in making the statutes in many states applicable only to categorical misrepresentations of fact. The result has been that in these jurisdictions only the most blatant untruths are attackable under the statute. As one would expect, the number of prosecutions has been small in these jurisdictions. But infrequent prosecution has been characteristic of almost *every* jurisdiction. This result is somewhat surprising when one considers that the *Printers' Ink* statutes, absent legislative and judicial fetters, are regarded, in some circles at least, as broad enough to reach the vast majority of false and misleading advertisers. The problem in these jurisdictions has been pinpointed as one of ineffective enforcement. According to a recent survey taken of attorney generals from the forty-four states with a *Printers' Ink* type of statute, most jurisdictions have never used the statute, and only a few have brought more than a small number of actions. Aside from the problems generally associated with any criminal case, the primary reason for lack of enforcement appears to be that the energies of the law enforcement agencies are diverted to more pressing matters. In the jurisdictions exhibiting the largest number of prosecutions, special agencies have been created for enforcement.

Lest anyone think that these statutes are totally ineffective, it should be pointed out that a statute can have deterrent effect even without prosecutions thereunder. Threats of prosecution can often be more effective in eliminating unlawful practices than actual prosecution. Better Business Bureaus and other private organizations have also utilized these statutes in a similar manner.

But generally the *Printers' Ink* statute has fallen far short of the goals that were envisioned at the time of its introduction. The legislative and judicial limitations upon the original statute, plus the criminal nature of its sanction, have severely hampered its effectiveness. The failure to provide administrative machinery for enforcement has contributed to this result.

In addition to the statutes designed to cover false advertising generally, many states have enacted statutes prohibiting "sales below cost" advertising, and every state has passed legislation dealing with particular businesses and commodities. For example, there are laws regulating food, drug, bank, and insurance advertising. Some of these statutes are directed against a particular type of deceptive practice, such as improperly advertising "wholesale prices." The extremely limited application of this generally uncoordinated mass of statutes has led to the closing of few, if any, of the gaps found in the general *Printers' Ink* statutes. In the view of one noted commentator, modern advertising is not being effectively regulated by this "patch-work quilt type of enforcement." A principal weakness of state-by-state enforcement is the absence in the statutes of consumer and competitor remedies. Where the state agency entrusted with enforcement does not act, business abuses remain undeterred.

CIVIL LEGISLATION GENERALLY

Twenty-eight states have adopted laws similar to the Federal Trade Commission Act. Five of these states—Washington, Hawaii, Vermont, Massachusetts, and North Carolina—have adopted statutes reading exactly like the Federal Trade Commission Act, "unfair methods of competition and unfair or deceptive acts and practices" in trade or commerce are specifically prohibited. The other twenty-three states accomplish the same purpose, though with slightly different language. These states are Alaska, Arizona, California, Colorado, Connecticut, Delaware, Illinois, Iowa, Kansas, Maryland, Michigan, Minnesota, Missouri, New Jersey, New Mexico, New York, North Dakota, Oregon, Pennsylvania, Rhode Island, South Dakota, Texas, and Wisconsin. In addition, Arkansas, Florida, Kentucky, Maine, Ohio, Tennessee, and West Virginia have established consumer fraud bureaus, consumer complaint clearing houses, or study committees to determine whether new legislation should be enacted.

A good deal of the impetus for the increase in state legislative activity is to be found in the FTC's recent campaign urging the states to enact laws to prevent consumer deception and unfair competitive practices. The basic argument advanced by Commissioner Dixon in favor of such legislation is that it would stop unfair practices locally before they assume interstate proportions. Thus, "the need for federal action will be minimized and the people most directly affected will be deciding what constitutes unfair or deceptive practices." Additionally, if the states take on more vigorous roles in the regulation of advertising practices, the FTC will be able to devote more time to problems of regional or national significance. Another advantage of state statutes based on the FTC model is the existence of hundreds of court decisions interpreting the act.

The commission's suggested state legislation goes beyond the literal language of the Federal Trade Commision Act. Included is a provision authorizing courts to decree restitution of money or property to persons suffering damages from an unfair or deceptive trade practice, and the appointment of a receiver or revocation of the privilege of doing business in the state. The FTC has also suggested legislation permitting injured consumers to bring private or class actions with minimum recovery of $200 or, in the court's discretion, three times the actual damages, in addition to costs and attorneys' fees. Since the FTC made this recommendation in April of 1969, three states—North Carolina, Hawaii, and Massachusetts—have enacted legislation providing for private or class actions.

The FTC recommendations also include elimination of the holder in due course doctrine for consumer installment transactions. Under the laws of most states, transferees of consumers' promissory notes or other evidence of indebtedness are treated as holders in due course and are not subject to defenses that the consumer could have asserted against the original seller or lessor of the goods or services. In the FTC's view,

> eliminating the holder in due course doctrine for consumer installment transactions will help to eliminate consumer deception and the hardships which consumers suffer as a result of high-pressure selling methods. Retailers will no longer be able to secure what amounts to virtual immunity from their illegal practices by assigning the installment contracts to a finance company. At the same time, more finance companies will be encouraged to investigate the business practices of concerns from whom they buy consumer paper, which may dry up the sources of financing of those fly-by-night operators who engage in deceptive and fraudulent sales practices.

Another recommendation would authorize the assessment of civil penalties up to $2,000 for willful violations and criminal penalties up to $5,000 and one year's imprisonment for fraudulent conduct. Finally, the commission has recommended, and a number of states have enacted, statutes providing for a three-day "cooling-off" period in connection with door-to-door sales; during this period a consumer could change his mind and rescind a contract.

It is evident that, with FTC encouragement, the states are beginning to move in the area of enacting state statutes dealing with unfair and deceptive trade practices. Local practices may thus be removed locally, leaving the FTC to proceed in cases involving national and regional matters.

UNIFORM DECEPTIVE TRADE PRACTICES ACT

In August of 1964 the National Conference of Commissioners on uniform state laws approved the final draft of the Uniform Deceptive Trade Practices Act. Based in part upon the present California Civil Code (Section 3396), it is designed to remove many of the burdensome restrictions which an injured party encounters when seeking redress through one of the common-law causes of action. In the words of the act's author, "Certain objectionable practices are singled out, but the courts are left free to fix the proper ambit of the act in case-by-case adjudications." The deceptive practices which are specifically mentioned can be divided into two parts: those involving misleading trade identification, and those comprising false or deceptive advertising.

Section 2(a), the principal substantive section of the act, provides:

A person engages in a deceptive trade practice when, in the course of his business, vocation, or occupation, he:
(1) passes off goods or services as those of another;
(2) causes likelihood of confusion or of misunderstanding as to the source, sponsorship, approval, or certification of goods or services;
(3) causes likelihood of confusion or of misunderstanding as to affiliation, connection, or association with, or certification by, another;
(4) uses deceptive representations or designations of geographic origin in connection with goods or services;
(5) represents that goods or services have sponsorship, approval, characteristics, ingredients, uses, benefits, or quantities that they do not have or that a person has a sponsorship, approval, status, affiliation, or connection that he does not have;
(6) represents that goods are original or new if they are deteriorated, altered, reconditioned, reclaimed, used, or secondhand;
(7) represents that goods or services are of a particular standard quality, or grade, or that goods are of a particular style or model, if they are of another;
(8) disparages the goods, services, or business of another by false or misleading representation of fact;

(9) advertises goods or services with intent not to sell them as advertised;

(10) advertises goods or services with intent not to supply reasonably expectable public demand, unless the advertisement discloses a limitation of quantity;

(11) makes false or misleading statements of fact concerning the reasons for, existence of, or amounts of price reduction; or

(12) engages in any other conduct which similarly creates a likelihood of confusion or of misunderstanding.

As can be seen from a reading of the substantive sections, the act codifies at the state level many of the situations held by the common-law courts and the FTC to be violations of the laws against unfair and deceptive trade practices, which we have discussed in other chapters. Interpretations of the twelve subsections can thus be gleaned from the chapters dealing with each of the enumerated abuses. The principal significance of the act would thus seem to be in its remedial provisions. Thus, sections 2(b) and 3(a) add that evidence of competition between the parties, intent to deceive, actual confusion, and actual monetary damages are not prerequisites to relief under the act. Sections 2(c) and 3(c) make it clear that the act does not replace any of the available common-law remedies. This is important because of the absence of a damage remedy in the act. Thus, in cases of deliberate deceptive practices, actionable by common-law remedies for damages, the injunctive remedy provided by the act "is in addition to remedies otherwise available against the same conduct."

Section 3(a) of the act authorizes injunctive relief and accords to the courts the discretion to award attorneys' fees if the party charged with the deceptive practices has knowingly engaged in the prohibited practice or against the plaintiff if he brought the action knowing it to be groundless. Section 3(a) is also significant in its incipient nature. Actual damages are not necessary for relief. Rather, "a person *likely* to be damaged by a deceptive trade practice of another may be granted an injunction against it." (Emphasis supplied.)

Although the implications of the act to the law of unfair and deceptive business practices are first beginning to be felt in the initial cases appearing in the eight states which have thus far enacted the statute, the potential contributions of the Uniform Act would include at least three significant factors. As summarized by Professor Richard Dole, these are "a nationwide standard of actionability with respect to deceptive trade practices; an improved private remedy with respect to deceptive trade practices [which, it will be recalled, is the major disadvantage of the "little FTC acts"]; and an increased incentive for the absorption of Federal Trade Commission precedents into the law of deceptive trade practices."

UNIFORM CONSUMER CREDIT CODE

State law governing consumer credit is extensive and varied. For the most part, laws were enacted in a piecemeal fashion to correct specific abuses that reached the attention of the legislature. The proposed Uniform Consumer Credit Code would consolidate all state laws regulating consumer credit into one comprehensive statute. It was drawn specifically to clarify and modernize existing laws and to provide a uniform rule of consumer credit for all jurisdictions.

Because of its comprehensive nature, the Credit Code, if enacted by a state, supplants any existing state statutes relating to consumer credit. The Credit Code would not replace existing and developing principles of common law and equity relating to validating and invalidating causes in a credit transaction. Federal law in the consumer credit area would be undisturbed by the Credit Code. In fact, drafters of the Uniform Consumer Credit Code drew the statute specifically to be consistent with existing federal legislation.

The Federal Consumer Protection Act, which includes Truth-in-Lending, is the major federal legislation in this area. When the Credit Code and Truth-in-Lending cover the same aspect of a credit transaction, such as disclosure of terms or advertising, compliance with the federal law completely fulfills the Credit Code requirements also. However, the UCCC goes much beyond Truth-in-Lending in substantive regulation of credit transactions.

The Credit Code is meant to be the comprehensive statement of a state's consumer credit policy. Therefore, all aspects of consumer credit are included in the code. The Credit Code not only requires disclosures but sets maximum rate charges permissible, provides for licensing of certain kinds of creditors, limits or forbids specific practices, provides debtors with statutory remedies, and establishes criminal penalties for violation.

It would be impossible in a work of this size to provide a detailed analysis of the Credit Code, which is a long and complex statute. Discussion here will focus on credit practices that have in the past proved deceptive or abusive and that the Credit Code either regulates or forbids. Generalizations about the Credit Code are difficult to make, but a few points should be kept in mind.

First and most important, the Credit Code will govern only consumer credit. Consumer credit in any type of transaction is defined in much the same way as consumer credit is defined in Truth-in-Lending. The code will operate when credit, the right to defer payment, is granted by a person or organization who regularly engages in transactions of some kind to a person primarily for family, household, or agricultural purposes in an amount of not more than $25,000. The right to defer payment may be granted in connection with the sale of goods or services, sale of an interest in land, or any debt incurred. For the transaction to be covered a charge called credit service charge for sales or loan service charge for loans must be imposed or the debt must be payable in more than four installments.

The Credit Code contains two major subdivisions, sale and loan. These terms are defined by the code and in many cases go beyond traditional definitions. For example, sales include sale of services and consumer leases (bailments). The Credit Code contains over fifty definitions. Therefore, it should be remembered that words employed in this discussion are employed with reference to their code usage, though perhaps not with technical precision.

Another important general feature of the Credit Code is that its protection is mandatory. Rights and benefits conferred by the code may not be waived even by agreement of the parties (§1.107). This does not mean claims arising under the code cannot be settled. They may be, and for less than the amount claimed, subject to judicial discretion to alter in case of unconscionability.

We turn now to the Credit Code treatment of what can be termed deceptive credit practices.

(1) Multiple Agreements

For consumer sales, the Credit Code provides a graduated rate ceiling with higher rates for smaller principals financed going from an annual rate of 36 per cent on the unpaid balance for amounts of $400 or less to 15 per cent yearly on the unpaid balance for amounts more than $1,000 (§2.201). It also provides that for some kinds of sales transactions the seller need not disclose the annual percentage rate if the credit services charge is less than $5 for amounts financed under $75, or $7.50 for amounts over $75 (§2.306).

It might be tempting under these rules for a seller to split a single transaction into several in order to take advantage of one or the other of these benefits. The Credit Code, anticipating this possibility, forbids the use of multiple agreements "with intent to obtain a higher credit service charge" or "to avoid disclosure of an annual percentage rate."

(2) Balloon Payments

A credit device that is occasionally used to trap the unwary is the balloon payment. A balloon payment is a payment, usually the last, in an installment schedule that is considerably larger than the other payments on the schedule. An example would be a one-year loan of $210 with eleven $10 payments and a final payment of $100. "A balloon payment can be used to induce a buyer to enter into a burdensome contract by offering him invitingly small installment payments until the end of the contract, when the buyer is confronted with a balloon payment too large to pay."

If the debtor is unable to pay the larger payment, the creditor could either pursue his remedies for default or more likely refinance exacting higher charges and interest. The Credit Code (§2.405–§3.402) to a large extent alleviates this problem. If any scheduled payment is more than twice as large as the average of early scheduled payments, the debtor has the right to refinance at the time payment is due without penalty. "The terms of the refinancing shall be no less favorable to the debtor than the terms of the original sale or loan."

(3) Holder in Due Course and Assignment

The evils attendant to the doctrine of holder in due course have been touched upon in an earlier chapter. In a significant step forward toward balancing the financial policy of negotiability against protection of consumers, the Credit Code prohibits sellers in a consumer sale or lease from taking a negotiable instrument as evidence of the obligation. The only negotiable instrument a seller may take is a check (§2.403).

"Since the prohibition against certain negotiable instruments in consumer financing will be well known by the financial community after enactment of this Act, professional financiers buying consumer paper will normally not qualify as holders in due course with respect to instruments taken by dealers in violation of this section and negotiated to them."

Consumer sales assignment of a contract in which a clause has been inserted that the buyer will not assert any claims or defenses against the assignee of the creditor brings about indirectly the same immunity for the holder that the law of negotiable instruments accomplishes for the holder in due course. The doctrines are closely related and result in the same vice, a consumer obligated to pay but with little recourse for defective goods.

The interrelation of these doctrines can be well illustrated by the New Jersey case of *Unico* v. *Owen*. In this case the buyer entered into an installment contract to purchase 140 record albums at $698. The buyer would receive twelve albums at first payment and twelve albums every six months thereafter until the deliveries totaled 140. In addition, the buyer would receive "without separate charge" a famous-brand stereo record player. The installment contract was the usual elaborate printed form with a multiplicity of paragraphs and conditions. Attached thereto was a promissory note and included therein was a boiler-plate clause permitting the seller to assign and agreeing that the buyer would not set up against any assignee of the seller any claims or defenses against the seller. The assignee's right of payment was absolute.

The buyer did receive the stereo set and twelve record albums. No more record albums were ever delivered, and attempts by him to secure delivery proved fruitless. After making the first twelve installments the buyer stopped paying. The seller then became insolvent. The plaintiff in this case was the assignee. The promissory note had been negotiated to him and the contract assigned to him on the day it was made. The New Jersey Supreme Court held that the plaintiff under New Jersey law did not qualify as a holder in due course. However, the plaintiff argued that even if he did not qualify as a holder in due course, he could qualify because of the assignment clause.

It is clear that the underlying problems and policies in these two doctrines are very closely related. The Credit Code, in dealing with the law of assignments, offers two alternative solutions from which a legislature may choose. The first provides that an assignee will be subject to all claims and defenses of the buyer arising out of sale. However, the assignee's liability is limited to the amount owing to the assignor. The rights of the buyer cannot be asserted in an affirmative action, but only as a matter of defense or set-off against a claim by the assignee.

The second alternative would permit enforcement of the waiver clauses only if the assignee were not related to the seller and had acquired the contract in good faith and for value. The assignee must give notice of assignment to the buyer, and the waiver clause will be enforceable if he receives no notice of facts giving rise to the buyer's claim within three months of mailing the notice of assignment. Good faith is defined by the Code to exclude those assignees who from a course of dealing with the seller know that there are existent substantial complaints by other buyers or that seller does not adequately perform his contracts or remedy defaults. The same limitations on liability apply to this alternative (§2.404).

(4) Cross Collateral

It has been the practice of some installment sellers to hold as collateral for an unpaid balance all goods previously sold in a series of what ordinarily would appear to be separate transactions. As a result, a security interest was retained by the seller in all goods no matter how much had been paid by the buyer or at what point in time payments were made. The effect of these clauses is to keep a balance due on every item purchased until the balance due on all items whenever purchased was liquidated. Debt incurred at the time of purchase of each item was secured by the right to reposses all items previously purchased by the same purchaser and each new item purchased automatically became subject to a security interest arising out of the previous dealings.

In the case of *Williams* v. *Walker Thomas Furniture* the buyer in 1962 purchased a stereo for about $500. At the time of that purchase she had a balance outstanding of $164. The balance remained from a purchasing history begun in 1957 and totaling about $1,800. Of this amount $1,400 had been paid. When she defaulted on payments on the stereo, the furniture store attempted to repossess all items previously purchased.

The court held that under the Uniform Commercial Code this contract was unconscionable. However, all courts have not so found. Moreover, the time period of most cross-collateral agreements would not necesarily be as long as that in the cited cases, nor would the amount of purchase necessarily be as great. One feature would be the same, however; the buyer would own nothing until the entire debt had been paid.

The Credit Code continues to tolerate cross collateral as an acceptable form of security interest; however, it does place certain limitations upon the practice (§2.408). A seller who sells goods on credit to a buyer in more than one sale may secure the debts arising from each sale by a cross-security interest in other goods so long as the seller has an existing security interest in the other goods. If the seller has no security interest in goods previously sold, they cannot become the subject of a cross-security agreement.

When a debt is secured by cross collateral, payments received by the seller are deemed applied to purchases in the order that purchases were made (§2.409). Security interest in property terminates when payments are such that each respective item has been paid for. In short, there can be no never-ending chain.

When a seller is secured by cross collateral the rate of the credit service charge permissible will be that which would be permitted if the debts had been consolidated under the code. In effect this prevents a seller from taking the advantages of cross collateral without also offering the buyer the lower rates provided for by the code's graduated rate schedule.

(5) Wage Assignments

Another form of security often taken by sellers or lenders is an assignment of wages. Under the law of assignment, the employer when notified must set aside the assigned earnings for the benefit of a creditor assignee. This enables a creditor not only to reach a debtor's wages without a judicial proceeding for garnishment, but very often to reach amounts larger than those permissible under the state law. The code provides that a creditor may not take an assignment of earnings as security for payment of a debt. Such an assignment is unenforceable by the assignee and recoverable by the debtor if paid. In this way a debtor has the opportunity to have his debt determined by a court before his wages are reached. A voluntary revocable payroll deduction in favor of a creditor may be authorized by a debtor.

(6) Confession of Judgment

Closely akin to the wage assignment is the confession of judgment. Some states permit an arrangement whereby a debtor agrees in advance either to a judgment against him or to appointment of an agent to submit to judgment for him. The debtor is generally not summoned to court and judgment is entered pro forma. This is generally done as soon as the credit transaction is completed. When a debtor defaults, the creditor is free to execute upon the judgment immediately, whether or not a valid defense exists.

This practice is very simply prohibited by the code.

(7) Referral Sales

The typical referral scheme which would be barred by the Credit Code (§2.411) is one in which the seller, before closing the sale, offers to reduce the price by a stated amount for every name of a person the buyer supplies who will agree to buy from the seller. The inducement of the referral plan can be employed by unscrupulous sellers to make more acceptable to the buyer an inflated price tag. What results most often is that the persons named never do purchase and the buyer is bound to pay the full original contract price.

The Credit Code makes unenforceable agreements to purchase that are based upon a promise by the seller to pay value, reduce the price, to the buyer, contingent upon the occurrence of an event subsequent to the time the agreement is entered into. The evil sought to be eliminated is raising the expectations of the buyer of benefits to accrue to him from events that are to occur in the future. If benefits will accrue to the buyer at the time of the sale—if, for example, the seller will reduce the price immediately at purchase upon being given names of prospective customers—the agreement is not covered by this section of the Credit Code.

If a buyer is induced to purchase by a referral scheme that violates the Credit Code, the agreement is unenforceable by the seller. The buyer at his option may either rescind the agreement and return the goods recovering any payments made or keep the goods or benefit of services without any obligation to pay for them. Although the code is not clear on this point, most likely if the buyer elects to keep the goods, he is relieved of the obligation of further payment only. Payments previously made can be retained by the seller.

(8) Home Solicitation Sales

The Credit Code singles out for special treatment consumer credit sales in which the transaction is negotiated face to face at the buyer's place of residence. Such sales have in the past been shown to be in a significant proportion the result of high-pressure techniques. When a a sales method fits the Credit Code definition of a home solicitation sale, when it is consummated by means of a personal solicitation at the buyer's place of residence and not pursuant to a pre-existing revolving charge account or to prior negotiations between the parties at a business establishment (§2.501), then the Credit Code provides the buyer with a limited right of cancellation.

The buyer is afforded a three-day "cooling-off" period during which he has the absolute right to rescind the contract. In the case of an emergency, the buyer may not cancel if the seller in good faith has begun performance or the goods cannot be returned in as good condition as received. The seller must furnish buyer with a written notice of his right to rescind.

If the buyer elects to cancel, the seller must return to the buyer any payments made. The seller is entitled to a cancellation fee of 5 per cent of the cash price if the buyer has made a cash down payment. If no cash down payment is made or if the buyer cancels or rescinds by exercising a privilege independent of his statutory right of cancellation, the seller is entitled to no cancellation fee.

The rights set forth for home solicitation sales are designed to meet a specific set of facts and are in no way exclusive. The buyer still may cancel or rescind a sales agreement under any other rules of contract law or under other sections of the Credit Code without incurring a cancellation fee. It will be noted here that sales consummated anywhere that create a security interest in personal real estate are subject to cancellation under Truth-in-Lending and the UCCC.

24

Toward Ethical
Advertising: A Plan

Because advertising is the principal vehicle in our society for the marketing of goods and services, it is the principal source of the unfair and deceptive practices that we have discussed in the preceding pages of this book. Consequently, it would be inappropriate to conclude our remarks without examining specifically the problems of the industry and the various facets of regulatory efforts designed to ensure the proper accomplishment of its very necessary function—consumer education.

The fall of 1959 brought public confidence in advertising to a crisis. First came the astonishing revelations of the "rigged" television quiz shows. Then came the "payola" scandals. The public outcry was deafening, and cynicism was rampant. Such criticism had been heard before, albeit not to the same intense degree. In 1946 an ex-Madison Avenue copywriter named Frederic Wakeman published a novel about the advertising world and thereby touched off a full-blown literary trend. Few would accord the accolade of greatness to *The Hucksters,* but it has the distinction of being a prototype. Folk heroes live in a popular fiction, and as more and more former advertising men produce more and more novels, a new folk hero-rogue has entered the stream of national consciousness, supplanting the Mississippi River pilot, the Indian fighter, the foreign correspondent, and the young, blasé Wall Street bond salesman of the 1920's. The new hero is the bright and earnest young man-about-Madison Avenue, complete with gray flannel suit, attaché case, and the most sincere smile imaginable.

The stereotype plot goes something like this. An intelligent, earnest, idealistic, but naïve young man lands a job in a huge, glittering New York advertising agency. The young man's brilliance wins him a few early successes; then his dreams are shattered by a sudden revelation of the harsh immorality of the world of Madison Avenue. The issue is presented: will our young hero, now stripped of his naïveté, pack up his untarnished ideals and go home, or will he surrender them and worship the goddess Success unashamed? In most of the novels he chooses the latter course and then proceeds to drown himself in a sea of cynicism, alcohol, and sensuality. Our hero is not left to wallow in the Slough of Despond, however. At the final crisis the mask of cynicism is stripped from his eyes, usually with the help of a fatherly colleague or the love of a good woman. He then proceeds to deliver a ringing denunciation of Madison Avenue and all outlying advertising provinces, packs up his rejuvenated ideals and his girl, and flies away to buy a small-town newspaper or write The Great American Novel. Sometimes, if the author is unusually optimistic, the hero is allowed to remain in the world of advertising, achieving success and hanging on to his integrity at the same time.

As a result of all of this, not a few Americans have hastily concluded that advertising is wholly devoid of ethics. On the contrary, it is hereby submitted that advertising is as susceptible to principled performance as any other form of economic activity. Since the shocks of rigging and of payola, remarkable progress has been made in the provision of an ethical framework for advertising. But much yet remains to be done.

In an era when control over advertising is a serious issue, it is particularly necessary to analyze the nature and sources of the necessary controls and restraints. A society can benefit if harmful forms of activity are curbed by beneficent restraints. But a society can be mutilated if inept and unduly harsh restraints proscribe useful activity. The so-called consumer revolution is particularly instructive in this connection. The consumer, largely disfranchised for so many years, is now beginning to assert himself. All levels of government are beginning to respond with legislation to his claims for protection against business abuses. Though many of the claims and legislative responses thereto are justified, perspective and reason must not give way to the bandwagon. The passing of statute after statute in the wake of the dramatization by the mass media of consumer demands may prove not to be the most effective means of achieving ethical advertising, and may, in fact, result in such overregulation and restrictiveness as to stifle and destroy our free competitive economy. A system which has provided the highest and most equitable standard of living in the history of the world should not be so lightly discarded.

At this point, then, let us isolate the sources of restraint necessary to achieve the wholly realizable goal of ethical advertising:

1. Vigorous federal enforcement.
2. Encouragement of improved state and local enforcement.
3. A sense of professionalism and resulting self-regulation.
4. Media cooperation.
5. Consumer education.

VIGOROUS FEDERAL ENFORCEMENT

The enactment of legal prohibitions has a practical effect far beyond the mere exposition of an institutionalized ethical standard. The presence of legal mandates and a vigorous and effective program for enforcing those mandates strengthens the hand of the advertiser who is genuinely concerned with adherence to a high moral standard. There cannot be a climate favorable to elimination of deception without the certainty that the irresponsible few will be deterred. One way in which to achieve widespread ethical conduct in the advertising world is to silence those who say, "We have to hit below the belt because everybody else does." If sanctions against that tiny, willfully unscrupulous minority are swift and sure, then honest advertisers can look to their own efforts without fear of unfair competition.

For some years prior to the disclosures of rigging and payola, the Federal Trade Commission had instituted a policy of monitoring radio and television advertisements. When the crisis arose, swift and effective action was needed. Consequently, the commission's monitoring program was intensified and the staff was doubled. Attorneys were transferred from other areas of the commission's work to monitoring and investigating radio and television advertising claims. Additional investigators were assigned to the New York City area for the sole purpose of handling cases selected for full investigation. Seven trial attorneys were assigned to assist in the investigation and preparation of these cases for trial. All commercial advertising on network stations was monitored throughout the broadcast day. In December of 1959 the monitoring unit referred 519 advertisements to various other bureaus and divisions within the commission. These offices had requested all advertising dealing with particular products or entire product lines. Examples of the latter included all advertising of cigarettes, reducing devices, cold remedies, furniture, and television sets and tubes. During November and December of 1959 the monitoring unit examined nearly 41,000 commercials and screened out almost 2,800 television commercials to determine which would require full-scale investigation. As a result, several products were named in commission complaints which set forth allegations of camera trickery or the omission of important facts.

To take just one example, there was the case of the television commercial advertising a certain oleomargarine. In this commercial, drops of moisture were shown on the advertised oleo and on butter as well. A competitive oleo was shown without any such drops. The announcer claimed that the drops were indicative of the flavor and quality of the particular brand of margarine. The Federal Trade Commission disagreed. The commission found that the moisture drops had nothing at all to do with the product, but had actually been applied to the product just for purposes of the television demonstration. Furthermore, the drops were magnified. Finally, they did not determine the flavor and quality of the margarine. A cease and desist order was issued, and both the advertiser and the agency involved agreed to discontinue such deception.

The same vigorous action took place in cleaning up the disgraceful practice of payola. This practice involved a direct money payment from record manufacturers and distributors to disc jockeys and other broadcasting personnel for promoting certain records by playing them with particular frequency. Depending upon the broadcast appeal of a given disc jockey and the popularity of his show, the consideration ranged from sporadic payments of various amounts to weekly or monthly payments on a regular basis from several record manufacturers and distributors. In the Philadelphia, Boston, New York, Cleveland, and Chicago areas, investigation revealed that cash payments ran into thousands of dollars. Sometimes the inducement was other than cold cash. All sorts of arrangements were devised to secure increased program exposure of certain records.

Promptly upon obtaining the facts, the commission acted. Nearly 100 complaints were issued in the fiscal year of 1960. Fifty-seven respondents consented to the orders and agreed to terminate all forms of payola. Some of the consent orders involved large and well-known recording enterprises.

This is the sort of vigorous federal enforcement needed to clean up that minority which persists in deceptive advertising. Such enforcement supplies the answer to those who seek refuge in the justification that "everyone else is doing it." Such enforcement provides the necessary effective deterrent. Public interest demands swift elimination of any poison that creeps into the economic system. Public interest, as we have seen, created the commission, and that interest must be served by strong measures when necessary. In this way federal enforcement helps to clear the path for the great number of businessmen who believe in and practice ethical advertising.

Vigorous federal enforcement, of course, goes well beyond the area of formal complaints and orders. As we have seen in the chapter dealing with commission procedure, there are many techniques which are comparatively informal but which amount to enforcement nonetheless. The FTC recognizes a duty to encourage those who would be honest as well as a duty to correct those who would be dishonest. For example, the holding of trade practice conferences and the ultimate adoption of trade practice rules has contributed measurably to the goal of ethical advertising, as have the FTC's guides. Other conferences are held with a particular local industry, as in the case of the jewelry industry in New York City. During fiscal 1960, personnel of the commission met with over 100 representatives of the retail jewelry industry in New York City to discuss the advertising and sale of jewelry. The commission's guides program has many facets, one of which is to suggest the sanction of federal enforcement. The *Tire Advertising and Labeling Guides* were issued during fiscal 1959; in its 1960 report the commission indicated that fifty assurances had been received from the tire industry to the effect that certain deceptive practices would terminate. The *Cigarette Advertising Guides* constitute another excellent example of vigorous federal enforcement short of the iron fist. During fiscal 1960 the administration of that guide resulted, according to the commission's annual report, in the elimination of sixty-two questionable claims involving thirty different brands. Most significantly, through the guides program seven major manufacturers agreed to remove from their advertising all tar and nicotine claims. Another instance of federal activity resulting in voluntary compliance is the case of refrigerator advertising. During fiscal 1961 the FTC sent a letter to all members of the refrigerator industry calling attention to various misrepresentations of the storage capacity of particular units. The industry had represented capacity in gross terms, including space occupied by coils, panels, and so forth. As a result of the commission letter the responsible concerns promptly agreed to eliminate the deception and speak only in terms of net space.

These examples might be multiplied endlessly, but the lesson is always the same. Vigorous federal enforcement plays a vital role in helping to achieve a national standard of truth in advertising. But federal enforcement is just one part of the solution. If state and local authorities are not equally active, if the advertising industry itself does not develop the necessary professional responsibility, if self-regulatory measures do not appear from within, if media cooperation is not secured, and, finally, if consumers are not educated—then the goal of ethical advertising still remains distant.

ENCOURAGEMENT OF IMPROVED STATE AND LOCAL ENFORCEMENT

When it comes to achieving ethical advertising, there is a familiar tendency, as in all areas of the economy, to refer all problems to the federal government in Washington. The federal role is important, but we must not make the mistake of shifting the entire burden of responsibility. In this regard the development of widespread ethical standards in advertising is no different from any other American goal. State and local authorities have a vital responsibility, and their activity must constitute an integral part of any solution.

Not only is local participation essential to the maintenance of our system of free enterprise, but there are compelling practical considerations which justify an active program on the part of state and local authorities. First of all, there is a great mass of advertising that is conducted on a purely local basis. As we have seen earlier, the power of the Federal Trade Commission is properly limited by the concept of interstate commerce. Malefactors in the area of purely local advertising may be wholly beyond the reach of federal authority. Yet the annual sales volume of local concerns will often run into many thousands and even millions of dollars. Many local concerns are also engaged in activities which have vital effects upon the welfare of the community. When vigorous enforcement is necessary to weed out a few shoddy practitioners whose scope is purely local, the responsibility rests upon state and local authorities. A second practical reason for encouraging a greater role in local enforcement lies in the concrete problem of a limited federal budget. There are many cases in which the FTC could exercise jurisdiction but chooses not to expend its limited funds and personnel on matters which may more properly be handled by the states themselves.

An extensive catalogue of state laws regulating deceptive advertising is beyond the scope of this book. Let us simply examine some of the general areas of local statutory regulation and some of the problems encountered thereunder.

Beginning in 1911, the *Printers' Ink* model law was adopted in whole or with modifications in most states. Today all but four states (Arkansas, Delaware, Mississippi, and New Mexico) have on their books some form of this statute. The substance of the original model reads as follows:

Any person, firm, corporation or association, who with intent to sell
. . . anything . . . directly or indirectly, to the public . . . or with
intent to increase the consumption thereof, or to induce the public
. . . to enter into any obligation relating thereto . . . makes, publishes, disseminates, circulates or places before the public, or causes
to be placed before the public . . . an advertisement of any sort . . .
which advertisement contains any assertion, representation or statement of fact which is untrue, deceptive or misleading, shall be guilty
of a misdemeanor.

The original statutes were directed primarily at printed advertising.
Many states have by now expanded the coverage to include radio and
television. Seventeen states have added to the model, by use of the word
knowingly, a requirement of proof. In these states, in order to sustain
conviction, the prosecution must prove that the seller had knowledge
that the statement in question was false.

As we observed in the preceding chapter, there are serious problems
under these laws. The difficulty of proof under the statutes requiring
prior knowledge tends to thwart prosecutions. Indeed, *Printers' Ink* itself
has taken the position that by adding the word *knowingly* many states
have weakened the model statute. But proof is only part of the problem.
After all, these are not civil but *criminal* laws, and, as such, they embody
all the stigma of any criminal law. Local authorities are often wary of
attempting to brand the deceptive advertiser as a criminal. In addition, a
higher standard of proof, proof beyond a reasonable doubt, is imposed
by criminal statutes. Moreover, there are practical problems for the state
enforcement authorities. In virtually all cases the enforcement of *Printers'
Ink* statutes is the responsibility of the county and district attorneys or the
state attorneys general. Clearly, these officials must devote substantial portions of their time to the regular course of prosecutions involving the
usual felonies and misdemeanors. The amount of time, personnel, and
money that they can devote to the elimination of deceptive advertising is
severely limited.

Still, the statutes can and have been used effectively. Two New York
cases provide instructive examples of the sort of work which can be done
at the local level. A seller of toys in the suburban New York City area
advertised by means of signs in his store window. Several signs read, "Toy
Discount Super Market, 20% to 40% Off." The practice of the dealer was
to establish prices higher than those normally charged by his competitors
and then to mark the prices down to a competitive level. Some of his
prices, even after the "markdown," were still slightly above those of the
normal market. This seller was convicted under the New York version of
the *Printers' Ink* statute. The theory of the prosecution was simply that
he had conveyed the impression through advertising that his prices were
20 to 40 per cent less than those prevailing in the market, when in fact

his prices were either at or above the market level. Another instance is that of the New York City jeweler who advertised in his store window "1 Ct. Perfect Diamond. Platinum Setting $265." The state investigators determined that a ring so marked actually weighed only three quarters of a carat and had several imperfections. For this advertising the jeweler was convicted.

State efforts to eliminate deceptive advertising have not been limited to the *Printers' Ink* statutes. The states have moved to regulate in many specific areas of advertising—alcoholic beverages, food, drugs, cosmetics, lotteries, securities, flag advertising, outdoor advertising, political advertising, trading stamps and premiums, tax-absorption advertising, and the advertising of obscene matter. As one study observed, the state's hand is generally strongest in that area of the economy where it exercises a licensing power. This factor lies behind state efforts at control of the advertising of alcoholic beverages. Similarly, the licensing power acts as a firm control on the advertising of hairdressers, barbers, real estate dealers, and funeral directors.

Some states have acted specifically to eliminate deceptive pricing in advertising. For example, Michigan, Minnesota, Olkahoma, and Tennessee have specific statutes prohibiting the use of such words as *wholesaler, manufacturer,* or similar designations unless the seller is actually engaged in the represented trade.

A number of states have enacted laws against bait-and-switch advertising. Some of the statutes even provide for the use of injunctions to eliminate the practice.

The examples and instances set forth here are only illustrative of the vast network of state legislation aimed at the elimination of misleading and deceptive advertising. For a more extensive treatment, the reader should refer to the preceding chapter and to the sources listed in the bibliography (Appendix I) of this book. One note of caution: the intelligent businessman faced with a potential legal advertising problem cannot afford to ignore the effect of state law and must consult his legal counsel in regard to possible local liability.

Whatever may be said for the difficulties involved in state and local enforcement, the need for such activity is undisputed. Perhaps we may soon see the advent of administrative agencies organized by the state and operated on a state level. A few states have already taken this step and have thus removed much of the burden from their regular law enforcement officials. We are beginning to see state legislatures and municipal bodies devoting greater attention to the problem of deceptive advertising. A body of civil law, as distinguished from strict criminal sanction, is being developed. It is to be hoped that a greater allocation of funds and personnel at the local level can be achieved.

Ultimately, great progress can be made through state and local enforcement toward reaching the goal of ethical advertising. Increasingly vigorous enforcement at this level will add meaningfully to the effort to eliminate the fringe of persistent and willfully dishonest advertisers. Clearly, there is a competitive inequity in requiring compliance with standards of honesty on the part of merchandisers of products sold in interstate commerce when local merchants who sell only locally but compete for the same consumer's dollar may continue to use deceptive sales appeals. Vigorous and alert local enforcement can correct this inequity, and the recalcitrant minority can be silenced. Then the great number of honest advertisers will not succumb to the temptation to reply in kind. The resulting atmosphere will lend strength to all those who sincerely desire an effective ethical framework for advertising.

An examination of ethical goals for advertisers cannot end with law enforcement, for we must recognize that law does involve imposition as well as expression. If we are not to abandon the premise that ethical conduct is an individual responsibility, we must not place our sole reliance upon the law. By definition, in a free society responsibility must ultimately be assumed by individuals. Law cannot do much more than express standards and provide a favorable climate for the exercise of individual responsibility. We must turn, then, to the scope and nature of professionalism and self-regulation in the advertising industry.

A SENSE OF PROFESSIONALISM AND RESULTING SELF-REGULATION

At this moment millions of purchasers are making millions of buying decisions. It is fair to surmise that in the great bulk of these transactions the purchaser is buying a reputation. In some instances it will be the reputation of the manufacturer; in others, that of the retailer; in still others, that of an advertising media. But in each instance reputation is an important factor. Therefore, the preservation of a reputation for propriety and decency is a matter of intense self-interest. But such an effort must go even deeper; it should be and is a matter of self-respect. Temptations in the market place can be severe, but no businessman with a shred of dignity can for one moment imagine that any material gain is worth the destruction of his own pride, his own code of ethics, and his own sense of vocation. Thus, advertisers must ensure that every message bearing their imprint is a truthful message. Every medium must ensure that no false voices speak through it. And the creators of advertising must assume a special professional responsibility.

Professional responsibility extends far beyond the mere avoidance of legal penalties and observance of legal boundaries. Professionalism means a willingness to disagree respectfully with one's client; to tell one's client forthrightly that there are severe objections to a proposed course of action; to recommend an unobjectionable program; and, yes, to resign from the service of the client if he persists in violating the ethical precepts of his adviser. If advertising men and women develop this sense of professionalism and if advertisers absorb the lesson that good will and public reputation slowly and painfully acquired can easily be dissipated by an ill-advised and offensive short-term campaign, public respect for advertising will be assured.

The acceptance of professional responsibility requires courage. It also requires a sense of one's own worth and dignity, and a sense of the importance of one's work. The man who works only for money can have no true dignity. The man who is prepared to sacrifice everything for financial gain can have no pride in his work. If advertising is to become something more than the rat race described in popular novels, then each individual in the industry must demonstrate that he can exercise professional responsibility.

During the years that have elapsed since the rigging and payola scandals and the resulting highwater mark in public cynicism, a host of advertising men and women have come to appreciate the necessity for individual responsibility. It is true that these individual efforts are difficult to measure. Self-imposed restraints by individuals are tested in the privacy of offices; responsible actions induced by these restraints receive no publicity. On the other hand, harmful actions by individuals who recognize no restraints inevitably command public attention. Nevertheless, careful and impartial observers of advertising can detect a perceptible increase in the ranks of those who stand for honest advertising.

The reinvigoration and extension of the self-policing efforts of voluntary groups is more easily measured. In the past few years all segments of the advertising industry have developed self-regulatory, self-policing programs which are the broadest in scope and effectiveness that business has ever known. Let us review some of these voluntary efforts in more detail.

The American Association of Advertising Agencies (A.A.A.A.) represents, as its name implies, the nation's advertising agencies. This organization has performed a key role in the industry's step-up of self-regulation. In April of 1962, A.A.A.A. published its new *Creative Code,* embodying standards of truthfulness and good taste which would govern the production of advertising. The guidelines are set forth in this language by the association:

> Therefore, we, the members of the American Association of Advertising Agencies, in addition to supporting and obeying the laws and legal regulations pertaining to advertising, undertake to extend and

broaden the application of high ethical standards. Specifically we will not knowingly produce advertising which contains:

a. False or misleading statements or exaggerations, visual or verbal.

b. Testimonials which do not reflect the real choice of a competent witness.

c. Price claims which are misleading.

d. Comparisons which unfairly disparage a competitive product or service.

e. Claims insufficiently supported, or which distort the true meaning or practicable application of statements made by professional or scientific authority.

f. Statements, suggestions or pictures offensive to public decency.

The code goes on to provide for the expulsion of agencies for "clear and willful violations. . . ."

Further regulation is provided by the Committee for Improvement of Advertising Content, operated jointly by A.A.A.A. and the Association of National Advertisers, Inc. The latter organization (A.N.A.) has for many years maintained an over-all conscientious effort to supply leadership and direction to national advertisers in all their advertising activities. Under the procedure of the joint committee, as described in the January 15, 1963, issue of *Advertising Age,* any agency or advertiser may enter a criticism of a particular advertisement at any time. Indeed, persons in the advertising industry are asked to note objectionable advertising. The individual observing the item preserves a written advertisement or jots down the pertinent details of a radio or television advertisement. Such a report is then forwarded through a local A.A.A.A. or A.N.A. representative to the committee headquarters in New York. The identity of the person initiating the criticism is kept anonymous, and the objection is evaluated by a panel of twenty individuals—ten members from each organization. Each panel member examines the advertisement in question and a vote is taken. If a majority determines that the advertisement is "seriously objectionable," a report is sent to the responsible advertiser and agency requesting corrective action. After thirty days, *Advertising Age* explains, both the advertiser and agency must come forward with a satisfactory answer. If there is no answer, or if the answer is unsatisfactory, the committee notifies the boards of directors of A.A.A.A. and A.N.A. for "appropriate action, which can mean expulsion from either association."

Of course, this program relies on voluntary self-regulation. But it has helped bring about a large number of improvements, many of them in advertisements which have wide exposure. What is particularly significant is that much of the committee's work involves the critical problem of bad taste. This is an area generally beyond the scope of federal enforcement; the industry itself must voluntarily eliminate advertisements in bad taste.

In an effort to deal on the local level with complaints regarding truth and taste in advertising, the board of governors of the A.A.A.A. Cleveland Council devised "The Cleveland Plan for Maintaining Public Confidence in Advertising." With the cooperation of the Cleveland Advertising Club and the Cleveland Better Business Bureau, the plan was put into operation in early 1960. This plan is so significant in terms of local self-regulation that some details should be submitted for the record here.

The sponsors of the plan divided objectionable advertising into four categories and provided machinery for dealing with each. The categories are "local, untruthful," "local, bad taste," "national, untruthful," and "national, bad taste." The objective of the plan is stated this way: "to eliminate, insofar as possible, all four kinds of objectionable advertising in Cleveland—both metropolitan and suburban areas—newspapers, radio, television, outdoor and direct mail." Depending upon the category, complaints are handled by the local Better Business Bureau, the Cleveland Advertising Panel, the National Better Business Bureau, and the National A.A.A.A. Committee.

One particularly effective aspect of the plan was the way it was put before the public. Cleveland newspapers carried full-page advertisements which boldly asked the reader, "What do *you* think of advertising?" The public was asked to send in specific criticisms of specific advertisements, and form letters were even provided to facilitate the mailing of criticism. The forms called for some details of the offending advertisement, the medium carrying it, the date and time, and a statement of why the individual regarded the advertisement as objectionable.

This plan proved so successful that other A.A.A.A. Councils have used it as a model in organizing similar programs. Such plans are now in operation in Philadelphia, Pittsburgh, Dayton, Dallas, Denver, Phoenix, San Francisco, Oakland, and many other cities.

Returning now to the Association of National Advertisers, that organization has made a continuing effort to give individual advertisers a sense of their own responsibilities and to point up areas in which these responsibilities are not being met. The A.N.A. has widely disseminated the *Text of Purex Corporation's Advertising Policy* in print and from the speaker's platform. This text is one of the many good examples of the program of a national advertiser that has recognized its individual responsibilities and adopted a definite code of advertising practices. We have already noted the role of the A.N.A. on the Joint Committee for Improvement of Advertising Content. This association has also widely distributed a most valuable booklet compiled by its general counsel, Gilbert H. Weil, *Legal Rules of the Road to Honest Advertising*.

Credit must also be given to the Advertising Federation of America (A.F.A.). This is the organization which binds together the advertising clubs in nearly all major American cities. These advertising clubs, in most instances, were responsible for the local Better Business Bureau movements. The A.F.A. is thus a grass-roots organization in the fullest sense. Long before the television scandals, representatives of the A.F.A. came to officials of the Federal Trade Commission to offer cooperation in improving advertising and to urge that the government do more toward educating business in the requirements of law. These representatives requested numerous copies of the FTC advertising guides and placed the power and machinery of their organization behind wide distribution of the guides.

The Better Business Bureau movement from the beginning epitomized voluntary self-regulation and self-discipline at the grass roots. There are now over 120 local bureaus throughout the country, representing approximately 125,000 companies. The present National Better Business Bureau (N.B.B.B.) is the offspring of the former National Vigilance Committee, which was originally organized to police fraudulent advertisers. Today the N.B.B.B. operates in the sphere of national advertising, functioning, as we have seen in the example of the Cleveland Plan, as a sort of clearing house for objections to national advertising. The local bureaus, on the other hand, work to clean up deceptive advertising at the local and regional level.

The *New York Times* has described the principal work of the Better Business Bureau as "quiet investigation and patient persuasion," and this is an accurate picture. The bureaus do a large share of the donkey work of business self-regulation; this quiet, difficult work must be accomplished at the local level. There is now a closer cooperation between the advertising industry and the Better Business Bureaus than ever before. Many advertisers and agencies now consult the bureaus prior to placing advertising. This practice is proceeding at an ever-increasing pace; the number of advertising agencies contacting the N.B.B.B. in New York, for example, has greatly expanded since 1958.

Space precludes more than passing mention of many other effective efforts at industry self-regulation. There are, for example, programs of the Associated Business Publications, the Direct Mail Advertising Association, the National Association of Transportation Advertising, the National Editorial Association, National Business Publications, and the Outdoor Advertising Association of America. Laudable efforts have been made by groups in literally dozens of specific industries, such as automobile dealer groups, the Air Transport Association, the Electronics Industry Association, and so on, all of which have adopted advertising codes. One of the most intelligent and determined programs is that of the American Home Laundry Manufacturers Association. There have been a multitude of self-regulatory programs within individual businesses, including a large number of advertising agencies. Some, like McCann Erickson, have assigned a top executive to screen advertising for truth and taste. The Lennen & Newell agency has employed a scientist who is responsible for ensuring that scientific claims and demonstrations developed by the agency are factual and fair.

Many excellent publications serving the advertising industry, such as *Advertising Age, Broadcasting, Sponsor,* and *Sales Management,* have strongly supported self-regulatory programs in the industry. This has been done both through education on the problems of advertising and encouragement of voluntary solutions by the industry. *Advertising Age,* for instance, carried a series entitled "Advertising We Can Do Without," which featured advertisements forwarded by readers which seemed to cross the lines of truth and good taste. In the series the magazine reproduced the actual advertisement, thus exposing the advertiser and his defects.

Of all the trade publications, however, one deserves special mention. *Printers' Ink,* founded in 1888, has traditionally played a leading role in the movement for truth in advertising. In its earlier days, as we have seen, this publication led the successful fight for the adoption of a model advertising statute by the states. *Printers' Ink* also strongly supported the development and growth of Better Business Bureaus. In recent years it has launched other programs for truth and taste in advertising. It published a candid series of articles designed to alert advertising to the scope of the problem, to spell out the dangers of laxity, to pinpoint responsibility for action, and to show what action could be taken. These articles prove that *Printers' Ink,* which may be thought of as the editorial conscience of the advertising industry, is very much alive to its self-appointed, historical role.

To conclude this section on self-regulation in advertising, the author must remark that the entire advertising industry is on trial. It has been on trial since late in 1959; it will continue to be on trial for a long time into the future. In large measure the outcome of this trial rests with the advertising industry. If it succumbs to ineffectual handwringing or cynicism or intransigence in the face of the public interest, a bitter outcome is certain. The only way to avert that outcome is to demonstrate responsibility. In whatever way we wish to define the function of the advertising industry, that function must include as an indispensable element the duty to tell the truth in a tasteful manner.

Advertising men and women must find within themselves a belief in their capacities to meet responsibilities and the will to discharge those responsibilities. It was John Stuart Mill who said that "one person with a belief is equal to a force of ninety-nine who have only interests." As we have seen, many in advertising have demonstrated that they have beliefs. But the work cannot stop. The demonstrations must continue and increase in scope and effectiveness. Only in this way can persons in advertising show, as they must, that they are determined to be responsible citizens in a free society.

MEDIA COOPERATION

The public and moral responsibility of advertisers and those who serve the industry must in turn be shared by the advertising media—newspapers, magazines, periodicals, radio, and television. The question whether the Federal Trade Commission should hold media *legally* responsible for deceptive advertising has been a subject of much public comment. This possible extension of legal responsibility is a matter involving serious policy considerations. It is the firm hope of the author that the FTC will not find it necessary to name an advertising medium as respondent in a deceptive advertising case. If federal and state authorities engage in the sort of vigorous enforcement that is necessary, and if the whole of the advertising industry, in cooperation with all advertising media, does the proper job of intensive self-regulation, it would seem that this serious legal step need not be taken.

The mere fact that the recent crisis in public confidence had its origin in television does not mean that other media can or should relax. First of all, practical considerations of self-interest dictate against such an answer. Visual deception in a television commercial may have an immediate impact upon public confidence in all television commercials, but the cynicism thus aroused may also result in a skeptical attitude toward printed assertions of advertisers. No medium can afford complacency toward problems of other media.

Moreover, advertisers cannot lightly dismiss a decline in public confidence engendered by a scandal in a particular medium. Today many advertisers conduct campaigns in many media simultaneously in order to achieve maximum effect for a promotion. If the product is deceptively described in one medium, then public confidence in the product as well as the medium is adversely affected. The task of maintaining public confidence by insisting upon truthful advertising cannot be shrugged off merely by finding an isolated whipping boy. Anyone concerned with advertising in any of its ramifications has a duty to insist upon truthfulness. Developing a sense of professionalism and a high degree of self-regulation is as much the responsibility of the media as it is of the advertising industry itself. This responsibility must be borne as a vital part of the quest for ethical advertising.

The acid test of media self-regulation probably comes in the actual acceptance or rejection of advertising. It is here that the newspaper industry provides an excellent example. The American Newspaper Publishers Association has encouraged each of its member newspapers to fix their own advertising acceptability standards. Assistance in this task is available to newspaper executives by use of the FTC guides relating to certain types of deceptive advertising. Further help may be had from the various codes and standards adopted by the advertising industry itself. In this regard, *Advertising Age* reports that "virtually every major U.S. daily newspaper" has a guide of some sort delineating acceptable and unacceptable advertising.

That the newspapers have done their part is indicated by a survey of the Publishers Association, which stated that in the year 1958 a total of 219 newspapers rejected $8,909,766 worth of advertising. One year later the number of newspapers rose to 348, but the rejections dropped off to just over $6 million. For 1960 the Association reported that 755 newspapers rejected $7,645,408 in advertising which failed to meet the high standards of truthfulness and good taste set by the individual papers. It is significant not only that advertising is being rejected, and in vast amounts, but also that the volume of rejection has not risen in proportion to the number of papers reporting. There is no evidence of any softening of ethical fiber on the publishers' part. The Association had an explanation for this trend, and it is particularly instructive in the context of our examination of the means for achieving ethical advertising. Said the publishers:

> Hundreds of newspapers reported to ANPA that offerings of false and misleading advertisements had slowed to a trickle for two reasons: (1) Consistent adherence to high standards of truthfulness and good taste have convinced the small minority of businessmen who succumb to temptation that it is useless to try to get daily newspapers to publish their copy, and (2) Widespread public discussion of "truth in advertising" campaigns in newspapers and other media have had a beneficial effect everywhere in the public interest.

Thus, the individual publisher can and must police his columns to ensure that no false and misleading advertising ever is printed in his newspaper. When a newspaper prepares copy for its advertisers, it can ensure that the advertisement conforms to all legal and moral standards. In the last analysis, all the conscientious newspapermen need do when confronted by a questionable advertisement is to consult his own conscience. One need not be a philosopher or a lawyer to recognize truth and taste. Self-regulation may require the rejection of a small number of advertisements and some immediate monetary loss, but it would seem that such a loss will be short term. Rising standards of acceptability throughout the community and the nation will soon force all advertisers to recognize that any short-term advantage in sales resulting from a deceptive practice may be far outweighed by the long-term damage to the seller's public reputation.

Similar efforts have been made in the magazine field. In 1960 the Magazine Publishers Association organized a copy advisory committee to act in a purely advisory capacity, the individual magazines retaining all rights to accept or reject advertising. When any magazine has a question concerning the acceptability of a certain piece of copy, it may submit the copy to the committee. A collective opinion is then given on the advisability of accepting, requesting a change in, or rejecting the copy submitted. Such an opinion is solely for the guidance of the individual publisher in arriving at his own decision.

According to *Advertising Age,* most leading magazines formulate standards of advertising acceptability. For example, *The New Yorker* magazine made a concerted effort over a period of several years to eliminate superlatives and exaggerations from its advertising pages. As a result, the magazine reported that it had measurably reduced the frequency with which certain expressions appeared. As an illustration, the term *World's best* reportedly appeared 312 times during the first six months of the year 1956. For the same time period in 1961 the phrase appeared only seventy-nine times. *Advertising Age* reports further that during the first four months of 1962 *The New Yorker* rejected some $260,000 in advertising.

The downfall of rigged quiz shows and the revelations of widespread payola practices in broadcasting brought to the surface a public distrust of the broadcast media which was wider than many informed observers had suspected. Television, after all, is a peculiarly intimate medium. It brings simultaneous sight and sound into the living room before an audience of all ages. This intimacy makes television all the more vulnerable to public criticism for possible abuses of its responsibility. The entire broadcasting industry thus owes to the public and to itself a most rigorous and searching variety of self-regulation. The broadcasting industry cannot afford to shrug off public cynicism with the attitude that "it will all blow over." It has not blown over and will not blow over.

Fortunately, the great majority of people in broadcasting do not take this lighthearted approach. There is no doubt that the broadcasting industry is now engaged in good faith in a massive effort to clean its house and to maintain public good will and approval of the advertising carried by radio and television. Lest there be any doubt of this self-awakening, let us look at the statement of one expert witness, the president of the National Broadcasting Company. In early 1960, following the rigging and payola scandals, this executive said, "We in broadcasting have undergone severe criticism—*and in part it is legitimate criticism*—for deceitful and dishonest program practices that developed within our very fast growing, extremely potent medium."

The principal source of self-regulation in broadcasting is the Television Code of the National Association of Broadcasters (NAB). The code itself deals with program standards as well as advertising standards. Over 75 per cent of the individual stations, all of the television networks, and numerous film producers subscribe to the NAB Code. In an effort to check up on observance of the code, the association runs a widespread monitoring program. The standards are enforced by a Code Review Board composed of station representatives. The method of enforcement is largely persuasive, although the sanction of expulsion is always available. Member television stations are permitted to display the Seal of Good Practice, which it is hoped will become a prestigious symbol to the industry and to viewers. Code offices have been established in Washington, Hollywood, and New York to police the industry more effectively.

As a result of this program, increasing numbers of advertisers, agencies, stations, networks, and film producers are using the board's facilities for the purpose of obtaining advisory opinions on code compliance before a particular program or commercial has so far advanced in production that change is impossible. Then, too, code members are notified of important decisions made by the Federal Trade Commission and regularly receive other educational material on advertising pitfalls from various self-regulatory sources.

The other self-regulatory arm of broadcasting is the Radio Code of Good Practice, which operates on substantially the same basis as the Television Code.

The self-regulatory effort to ban illegal and tasteless advertising in broadcasting will not achieve its maximum potential until nearly 100 per cent of the nation's radio and television broadcasters become members of the code operation. Only in this way can an industrywide program of self-policing be effected. Failing such a program, police efforts will undoubtedly come from other and perhaps harsher sources. Any reasonably discerning broadcaster who wets his index finger and turns it toward the winds blowing from Washington must rapidly conclude that increased support of group self-regulation is vital.

CONSUMER EDUCATION

We have already noted the significant rise in the level of sophistication of the American public as a potent factor shaping the climate within which ethical advertising may be achieved. Everyone connected with the process of advertising—advertisers, agencies, and media alike—must re-examine their work in light of a new evaluation of the American audience. That audience grows better educated and more discerning day by day. The proverbial advertiser who, as we have observed previously, addresses his messages to twelve-year-olds continues to do so at his peril. A brief backward glance is sufficient to highlight the sharply rising level of taste and sophistication of the American audience.

James Webb Young, a great advertising pioneer, discusses a 1913 advertisement of Postum in a *Saturday Review* article. The ad points out the advantages of Postum over Brazilian coffee, attributing the following ills to coffee: "Sallow Complexions; Stomach Trouble; Bad Liver; Heart Palpitations; Shattered Nerves; Caffeine, a Drug; Weakness from Drugging." Mr. Young then quotes a judgment on the changes that forty years of education can bring: "We doubt if the present owners of Postum would OK copy like this today. Even if they did not own Maxwell House." We all realize that the incredible claims of yesterday would not be convincing today.

Every increase in cultural sophistication, every advance in education, every exposure to wider experience places an additional seal of doom on shoddy, tasteless, and irresponsible advertising. Despite the appearance in recent years of some very sophisticated institutional advertising, it still seems that advertisers are sometimes the last to weigh the American audience at its true value. It is certain that today's consumer is aware, and that he resents being patronized as an unsuspecting boob.

During the crisis in public confidence engendered by the television scandals, the author received hundreds of letters from resentful and disillusioned consumer viewers. Many letters were referred to the FTC's Bureau of Investigation as specific complaints against deceptive advertising. For obvious reasons, it would not be appropriate to quote from such letters in this book. A number of other letters, however, were general in nature, and their tone is a meaningful indication of consumer awareness. A selection follows.

From a lady in Los Angeles:

> I'd like to see a return to the straightforward advertising of quality in merchandise so that we could have some confidence in the reliability of the manufacturer.
>
> Modern merchandising is too lazy to plan and execute good things. They have apparently swallowed their own line, that the American people read, listen to or watch only the lowest, least, lousiest, most unholy, degrading kind of program. . . . The average American is better educated and of better stuff than ever before.

A housewife in Rochester, New York:

> We as a family are tired of gagging over vials of mucus, beakers of stomach acid and tubes of fatty acids during the dinner hour. . . .

Much of TV advertising is thoroughly disgusting and shows up most advertising men as cultural nitwits.

Most important for present purposes is the question of what the aware consumer will do about false or objectionable advertising. Some of the letters provide the answer.

A citizen of Richmond, Virginia:

When we see an offensive or misleading ad, we add it to our list of those products not to be bought under any circumstances. This also includes hucksters who shout their message so that you have to get up and turn down your TV set. Conversely, we reward those whose advertising is straightforward, truthful, and well within the bounds of decency.

From a New Jersey housewife:

Many people are becoming more and more disgusted by these types of commercials dealing with articles of an intimate and private nature which are not fit for discussion in mixed company. They certainly are not neceessary on television and radio.

As a woman, I deeply resent them and refuse to purchase the advertising brands. I will join the many women who are offended by them and will do my best to influence public opinion.

A Maryland housewife:

We *can* hear normal voices on television and the commercial assault on our eardrums is not only insulting—it is painful. I, for one, have registered a vow not to buy any products the merits of which are screamed at me!

From Cleveland, Ohio:

And some products I refuse to buy on account of over-emphasis.

Finally, a letter from a housewife in Red Oak, Iowa:

I agree wholeheartedly with all you have said about illegal huckstering on TV, and everyone in small towns such as mine feel the same way. Multiply the small towns by the cities and it must be the same all over the United States.

. . . We get the feeling that the sponsors are convinced that the listening public is just a bunch of morons that will swallow anything and sit raptly waiting to absorb more and more of the same.

We . . . have favorite programs that each week are looked forward to with happy expectancy, only to have the time come and be so irritated by the commercial drivel, or the loud raucous music . . . that we end the evening by hating the sponsor and his product, and almost hating the favorite program. . . . We have squirmed in our seats, and covered our ears, and shut our eyes during some of the commercials. And after that, does the sponsor think for one moment that we, the suffering public, would ever even take his product as a gift. I personally have turned against some products that I had no reason to dislike, excepting for the irritation I had to suffer over it, just to get to hear a favorite program. . . .

That consumer disillusionment with advertising has continued since my years at the FTC is verified in almost every issue of *Advertising Age*. In a recent issue of that magazine which contained a report on a panel discussion of "Selling in the American Youth Market," similar comments were echoed by participant after participant. The "dishonesty" of the few, dramatized by the filing of FTC complaints and the attendant publicity, created the assumption that advertising is "usually dishonest."

The lesson should be obvious to all those concerned with advertising. Insult the public intelligence long enough and hard enough, deceive and mislead the public often enough, and you will produce an almost devastating alienation. Further, we must not assume that because the public wrath fell upon the broadcasting field, other media are immune. In fact, much of the same objectionable material has also been disseminated through printed media in both local and national advertising campaigns.

We must, therefore, recognize the emergence of a new weapon in the war against trickery in the market place—the consumer himself. The public interest is served not only by restraining deception in selling but also by overcoming gullibility in buying. Or, in blunt language, "The gyp seller depends on the sucker buyer and can't exist without him."

Fully aware of the power represented by an aware public, the Federal Trade Commission in December of 1959 called its first Conference on Public Deception. The conference was held in Washington, with over fifty conferees present representing consumer and public service organizations from all over the nation. The conference was also fully open to the members of the press.

Topics discussed included food and drug advertising; direct-selling practices; fictitious pricing and bait advertising; labeling of wool, fur, and textile products; and misrepresentation of employment opportunities. In each area formal presentations were made by commission officials and by spokesmen from consumer and service groups. Following the statements the floor was opened for discussion. After the conference the commission kept in contact with the participants in order to report further developments as they occurred.

In addition to the federal authorities many state officials have contributed to this crucial program of consumer education. Several state attorneys general have recognized the need for coordinated discussion by representatives of law enforcement, media, and consumer groups and have as a result called conferences similar to the federal Conference on Public Deception. Such local conferences have had a strong impact in the effort to clean up deceptive advertising by alerting consumers.

Media, too, deserve credit for the exposure that they have given to various revelations of advertising and marketing trickery. Intelligent press coverage of Federal Trade Commission action, for example, has added immeasurably to the effect of the commission's work. Press coverage of the Conference on Public Deception did much to advance the objective of public education. Such national magazines as *Redbook* and *Good Housekeeping* lent their support by carrying feature articles on deceptive pricing. The award-winning articles of Miriam Ottenberg in the *Washington Star* are a splendid example of the manner in which the press can bring fraudulent schemes to the public's attention and thereby destroy such schemes. The articles dealt with racketeering in used-car sales in the District of Columbia. As a result of this disclosure, significant procedural and administrative reforms were effected, the public was alerted, and many of the shady operators were forced to close up shop. Installment credit reforms discussed in the preceding chapter are another example.

Finally, many of the self-regulatory groups in industry have themselves added to the impetus of consumer education. The Federal Trade Commission guides on such subjects as bait advertising, guarantees, tire advertising, and deceptive pricing have been reprinted by industry groups and given wide dissemination. In this way hundreds of thousands, if not millions, of consumers are made increasingly aware of a variety of illegal and deceptive tricks in advertising.

In the last analysis, the education of the consumer may truly be the best guard against the use of chicanery in the market place. For example, imagine how difficult it would be for fraudulent operators if we could alert every member of the buying public to put up his guard whenever he sees or hears one of the following six "sucker" signals:

> Buy now or lose the chance. . . .
> You have been specially selected. . . .
> It's only a legal form. . . .
> Just a few easy lessons. . . .
> You can save up to. . . .
> Yours absolutely free. . . .

An aware and intelligent consumer capable of exercising discriminating judgment is one of the essentials in the effort to achieve ethical advertising. All intelligent businessmen must recognize, as indeed most have, the importance of alert consumers who are able and willing to bring to bear upon the shoddy trickster the fiercest economic weapon of all—the simple refusal to buy.

CONCLUSION

We have analyzed the various sources from which support may be drawn in the quest for ethical advertising. Broadly, the means for achieving this societal goal can be grouped as follows:

1. Individual responsibility.
2. Voluntary group effort.
3. State and local government.
4. Federal government.

What shall be the relative contribution of these sources?

In a nation that places individual liberty at the highest point on its scale of values, it is obvious that the most desirable resolution of this issue entails a large contribution from the first source and contributions of geometrically descending proportions from the three succeeding sources. If the vast majority of individuals engaged in a given activity recognize the necessity for self-imposed restraints to prevent harm to others, then voluntary group effort is necessary only to reinforce and support the conscientious effort of individuals. If all necessary restraint could be furnished by individual responsibility and voluntary group effort, then no contribution would be necessary from government.

Descending from the ideal to the practical, we often find that a few individuals engaged in activity where restraint is necessary refuse to recognize their responsibilities. If voluntary group effort cannot impose necessary restraints upon these civic failures, then the necessity for governmental action is apparent. Historically, governmental contributions to necessary restraints have often come first from state and local governments, with a contribution from the federal government coming only after demonstration that the combined efforts of individuals, voluntary groups, and local governments have been unable to achieve a satisfactory level of beneficial restraints.

Just as nature abhors a vacuum, so does a civilized society abhor a vacuum in the imposition of needed restraints. It is important to realize that the failure of one source of necessary restraints will result only temporarily in the absence of restraint; the pressure of public opinion will soon force the needed contribution from another source.

Pressures for increased governmental control of advertising have been building in recent years. It is possible that these pressures will result in controls more extensive than really ought to be necessary to ensure that advertising's responsibilities will be met. This possibility was heightened by 1970 testimony of Assistant Attorney General Richard McLaren before a Senate subcommittee. Though noting that "the Department of Justice is cautious about extending the area of government supervision of private industry," he concluded, "The complaints have become so numerous that we believe the federal government must substantially increase its role. Certainly the federal government has a legitimate interest in insuring that the economic prosperity of the consumer should be protected in a way that is meaningful for all our citizens."

The best defense against such pressures is a demonstration that individuals and groups within the advertising industry can meet their responsibilities on a voluntary basis. The record in this regard is encouraging, but the hard work must continue.

I believe in self-regulation. A free man can and will accept responsibility as well as privilege; free men recognize that freedom means responsibility. Some advertising men have adopted a cynical attitude toward self-regulation. One of these pessimists said, "Talk of self-policing leaves me very cold." Another told a prominent magazine that only the Federal Trade Commission had the power to clean up advertising and that to suggest any other means was to invite futility. This attitude is as dangerous as it is false. Certainly, vigorous enforcement of prohibitions against false advertising by the Federal Trade Commission is a must, but individual integrity is also a must. If industry fails to accept its responsibility for truthful advertising, then we can secure truth only by massive government control. This alternative is appalling, because, at bottom, those businessmen who pass their moral responsibilities on to the government are advocating a police state. It is difficult to believe that effective trade regulation can be brought about only by a Gestapo. Individual integrity is the mortar cementing the foundations of our system of government. If the mortar cracks and crumbles in spots, it can be repaired. But the house will not stand without mortar.

In short, the goal of ethical advertising can be reached. The Federal Trade Commission and state law enforcement officials can provide the sanctions that are an indispensable part of any civilized activity. The men of advertising can, in cooperation with the media, guide their efforts by firm ethical standards, thus providing the largest contribution. Consumers and consumer protection groups, by public education and by vociferous protest against tasteless advertising, can achieve ever-higher levels of good taste. If all of these social entities perform conscientiously and efficiently, then we can provide one more illustration that the complex balance of forces that is the American system can respond to challenge without surrendering individual freedom.

Appendix I

Selected Bibliography

Chapter 1: Introduction

BIBLIOGRAPHY

Holbrook, *The Golden Age of Quackery* (1959).
Turner, *The Shocking History of Advertising* (1953).

Chapter 2: Common Law Remedies

BIBLIOGRAPHY

Oppenheim, *Unfair Trade Practices* (1965).

CASES

International News Service v. *Associated Press,* 248 U.S. 215 (1918).

Chapter 3: History of Federal Regulation

BIBLIOGRAPHY

Austern, *The Parentage and Administrative Ontogeny of the Federal Trade Commission,* in 1955 N.Y.S.B.A. Antitrust Law Symposium 83.

Baker & Baum, *Section 5 of the Federal Trade Commission Act: A Continuing Process of Redefinition,* 7 Vill. L. Rev. 517 (1962).

Creative Code of the American Association of Advertising Agencies (1962). 1916 FTC Annual Report 6.

83 Cong. Rec. 3256 (1938).

Handler, *Introduction to Symposium—The Fiftieth Anniversary of the Federal Trade Commission,* 64 Colum. L. Rev. 385, 388 (1964).

Handler, *Jurisdiction of the Federal Trade Commission Over False Advertising,* 31 Colum. L. Rev. 527, 539 (1931).

Henderson, *The Federal Trade Commission* 339 (1924).

Holbrook, *The Golden Age of Quackery* (1959).

Kintner, *Federal Trade Commission Regulation of Advertising,* 64 Mich. L. Rev. 1269 (1966).

Millstein, *The Federal Trade Commission and False Advertising,* 64 Colum. L. Rev. 439, 450 (1964).

Note, 56 Colum. L. Rev. 1018, 1022 (1956).

Simon, *The Law for Advertising and Marketing* (1956).

Turner, *The Shocking History of Advertising* (1953).

Weston, *Deceptive Advertising and the Federal Trade Commission: Decline of Caveat Emptor,* 24 Fed. B.J. 548, 550 (1964).

38 Stat. 719 (1914).

52 Stat. 114 (1938), adding 15 U.S.C. §52 (1964).

52 Stat. 115 (1938), adding 15 U.S.C. §§53, 54 (1964).

54 Stat. 1129 (1940), adding 15 U.S.C. §§68 (1964).

64 Stat. 21 (1950), amending 15 U.S.C. §55(a)(2) (1964).

65 Stat. 175 (1951), adding 15 U.S.C. §§69–69j (1964).

65 Stat. 178 (1951), adding 15 U.S.C. §69(c) (1964).

67 Stat. 111 (1953), adding 15 U.S.C. §§1191–1200 (1964).

72 Stat. 1717 (1958), adding 15 U.S.C. §§70–70K (1964).

CASES

A. Theo. Abbot & Co., 1 FTC 16 (1916).

Block & Co., 1 FTC 154 (1918).

Circle Cirk Co., 1 FTC 13 (1916).

FTC v. Gratz, 273 U.S. 421, 436–37 (1920) (dissenting opinion).

FTC v. Klesner, 280 U.S. 19 (1929).

FTC v. Raladam Co., 283 U.S. 643 (1931).

FTC v. Winstead Hosiery Co., 258 U.S. 483 (1922).

Globe Cardboard Novelty Co., Inc. v. FTC, 192 F. 2d 444 (3d Cir. 1951).

Pep Boys—Manny, Moe & Jack, Inc. v. FTC, 122 F. 2d 158 (3d Cir. 1941).

Perma-Maid Co. v. FTC, 121 F. 2d 282 (6th Cir. 1941).

Scientific Mfg. Co. v. FTC, 124 F. 2d 640 (3d Cir. 1941).

Sears, Roebuck & Co. v. FTC, 258 Fed. 307 (7th Cir. 1919).
Standard Oil Co. v. United States, 221 U.S. 1 (1911).

Chapter 4: Federal Trade Commission: Practice and Procedure

BIBLIOGRAPHY

Baker & Baum, *Enforcement, Voluntary Compliance, and the Federal Trade Commission,* 38 Ind. L. J. 322 (1963).
Burrus & Savarese, *Institutional Decision Making and the Problem of Fairness in FTC Antitrust Enforcement,* 53 Geo. L. J. 655 (1965).
Burrus & Teter, *Antitrust: Rulemaking and Adjudication in the FTC,* 54 Geo. L. J. 1106 (1966).
Dixon, "The Federal Trade Commission and the Antitrust Laws," in Van Cise, *Understanding the Antitrust Laws* (1963).

Chapter 5: General Principles

BIBLIOGRAPHY

Alexander, *Honesty and Competition* (1967).
Harper & McNeely, *A Synthesis of the Law of Misrepresentation,* 22 Minn. L. Rev. 939, 1004 (1938).
Kintner, *Federal Trade Commission Regulation of Advertising,* 64 Mich. L. Rev. 1269 (1966).
Note, *Developments in the Law—Deceptive Advertising,* 80 Harv. L. Rev. 1008 (1967).

CASES

Alberty Food Products, Inc., 44 FTC 475, 513–514 (1948), *modified,* 182 F. 2d 36 (D.C. Cir.), *cert. denied,* 340 U.S. 818 (1950).
Atlantic Sponge & Chamois Corp., 52 FTC 500 (1955).
Aronberg v. *FTC,* 132 F. 2d 165 (1943).
Bockenstette v. *FTC,* 134 F. 2d 369 (10th Cir. 1943).
Buchsbaum & Co. v. *FTC,* 160 F. 2d 121 (7th Cir. 1947).
Carlay Co. v. *FTC,* 153 F. 2d 493 (7th Cir. 1946).
Charles of Ritz Distributors v. *FTC,* 143 F. 2d 676 (2d Cir. 1944).
Deming v. *Darling,* 20 N.W. 107 (Mass. 1889).
DDD Corp v. *FTC,* 125 F. 2d 679 (7th Cir. 1942).
Dr. W. B. Caldwell, Inc. v. *FTC,* 111 F. 2d 889 (7th Cir. 1940).
Excelsior Laboratories, Inc. v. *FTC,* 171 F. 2d 488 (2d Cir. 1948).
R. H. Fechtel, 38 FTC 794 (1944) (Stip.)
FTC v. *Algoma Lumber Co.,* 291 U.S. 67, 81 (1934).
FTC v. *Colgate Palmolive Co.,* 380 U.S. 374 (1965).
FTC v. *Mary Carter Paint Co.,* 382 U.S. 46 (1965).
FTC v. *Standard Education Society,* 302 U.S. 112 (1937).
Grelb v. *FTC,* 144 F. 2d 580 (2d Cir. 1944).

Kalwaitys v. *FTC,* 237 F. 2d 654 (1956).
Kidder Oil Co. v. *FTC,* 117 F. 2d 892 (7th Cir. 1949).
Ostermoor & Co., Inc. v. *FTC,* 16 F. 2d 962 (2d Cir. 1927).
Personal Drug Co., 50 FTC, 828, 833–834 (1954).
Prima Products, Inc. v. *FTC,* 209 F. 2d 405 (2d Cir. 1954).

Chapter 6: Copyrights, Patents, and Trade-marks

BIBLIOGRAPHY

Nimmer, *Copyright* (1963).
Nimmer, *Copyright Publication,* 56 Colum. L. Rev. 185 (1956).
Register of Copyrights, *Report on the Copyright Law Revision,* 87th Cong., 1st Sess. (Comm. print 1961).
Ringer & Gillin, *Copyrights,* rev. ed. (1965).
Rothenberg, *Copyright and Public Performance of Music* (1954).

CASES

Bleistein v. *Donaldson Lithographing Co.,* 188 U.S. 239 (1903).
Folsom v. *Marsh,* 9 F. Cas. 342 (No. 4901) (C.C.D. Mass. 1841) (Story, J.).
Henry Holt & Co. v. *Liggett & Myers Tobacco Co.,* 23 F. Supp. 302 (E.D. Pa. 1938).
Nichols v. *Universal Pictures Corp.,* 45 F. 2d 119 (2d Cir. 1930).

Chapter 7: Trade Names, Passing Off, and Product Simulation

BIBLIOGRAPHY

Callmann, *Unfair Competition, Trademarks, and Monopolies* (1968).
Callmann, *Unfair Competition and Trademarks,* 2d ed. (1950).
Hopkins, *Trademarks, Trade Names and Unfair Competition,* 4th ed. (1924).
Kaplan & Brown, *Cases on Copyright, Unfair Competition, and Other Topics* (1960).
Le Blanc, *Trademarks and Unfair Competition* (1966).
Nimms, *The Law of Unfair Competition,* 2d ed. (1917).
Note, *Doctrine of Functionality,* 64 Colum. L. Rev. 544 (1964).

CASES

American-Marietta Co. v. *Krigsman,* 275 F. 2d 287 (2d Cir. 1960).
Bourjois v. *Hermida Laboratories, Inc.* 106 F. 2d (3d Cir. 1939).
Buck's Stove and Range Co. v. *Keichle,* 76 Fed. 758 (C.C.D. Ind. 1896).
Champion Spark Plug Co. v. *A. R. Mosler Co.,* 233 Fed. 112 (S.D. N.Y. 1916).
Champion Spark Plug Co. v. *Sanders,* 331 U.S. 125 (1947).
Cheney Bros. v. *Doris Silk Corp.,* 35 F. 2d 279 (2d Cir. 1929).
Compco Corp. v. *Day-Brite Lighting, Inc.,* 376 U.S. 234 (1964).
Double Eagle Lubricants v. *FTC,* 360 F. 2d 268 (10th Cir. 1965).
Geisel v. *Poynter Prods., Inc.,* 295 F. Supp. 331 (S.D. N.Y. 1968).

General Pool Corp. v. Hallmark Pool Corp., 259 F. Supp. 383 (N.D. Ill. 1966).

Glenn v. Advertising Publications, Inc., 148 U.S.P.Q. 645 (1966).

Hygienic Specialties Co. v. H. G. Salzman, Inc., 302 F. 2d 614 (2d Cir. 1962).

Lerner Stores Corp. v. Lerner, 162 F. 2d 160 (9th Cir. 1947).

Metropolitan New York Retail Merchants Ass'n v. City of New York, 1969 Trade Cases ¶ 72, 732 (N.Y. Sup. Ct. 1969).

Motor Improvements, Inc. v. A.C. Spark Plug Co., 80 F. 2d 385 (6th Cir. 1935).

Parkway Baking Co. v. Freihofer Baking Co., 255 F. 2d 641 (3d Cir. 1958).

Prestonettes, Inc. v. Coty, 264 U.S. 359 (1924).

Sears, Roebuck & Co. v. Stiffel Co., 376 U.S. 225 (1964).

Stork Restaurant, Inc. v. Sahati, 166 F. 2d 348 (9th Cir. 1948).

Sylvania Electric Prods., Inc. v. Dura Electric Lamp Co., 144 F. Supp. 112 (D. N.J. 1956), *aff'd,* 247 F. 2d 730 (3d Cir. 1957).

William R. Warner & Co. v. Eli Lilly & Co., 265 U.S. 526 (1924).

United Merchants & Manufacturers, Inc. v. Bromley Fabrics, Inc., 148 N.Y.S. 22 (S. Ct., Spec. Term 1955).

Chapter 8: Unfair Appropriation of and Interference with a Competitor's Business

BIBLIOGRAPHY

Callmann, *Unfair Competition, Trademarks, and Monopolies* (1968).

Callmann, *Unfair Competition and Trademarks,* 2d ed. (1950).

Hopkins, *Trademarks, Trade Names and Unfair Competition,* 4th ed. (1924).

Kaplan & Brown, *Cases on Copyright, Unfair Competition, and Other Topics* (1960).

Le Blanc, *Trademarks and Unfair Competition* (1966).

Nimms, *The Law of Unfair Competition,* 2d ed. (1917).

Note, *Doctrine of Functionality,* 64 Colum. L. Rev. 544 (1964).

CASES

International News Serv. v. Associated Press, 248 U.S. 215 (1918).

National Exhibition Co. v. Martin Fass, 143 N.Y.S. 2d 767 (Sup. Ct. 1955).

New York World's Fair 1964–1965 Corp. v. Colourpicture Publishers, Inc., 141 U.S.P.Q. 939 (N.Y. Sup. Ct. 1964).

Prest-O-Lite Co. v. Davis, 209 Fed. 917 (S.D. Ohio 1913).

RCA Manufacturing Co. v. Whiteman, 114 F. 2d 86 (2d Cir. 1940).

Ticker Cases, 119 Fed. 294 (1902).

Chapter 9: Deceptive Nondisclosure

BIBLIOGRAPHY

Advisory Opinion Digest No. 126 (FTC May 26, 1967).

Advisory Opinion Digest No. 193 (FTC February 20, 1968).

Advisory Opinion Digest No. 220 (FTC April 4, 1968).

Advisory Opinion Digest No. 222 (FTC April 4, 1968).
Advisory Opinion Digest No. 229 (FTC April 4, 1968).
Advisory Opinion Digest No. 230 (FTC April 4, 1968).
Advisory Opinion Digest No. 234 (FTC April 4, 1968).
Advisory Opinion Digest No. 307 (FTC November 25, 1968).

CASES

Adell Chemical Co., 54 FTC 1801 (1958).
Alberty v. *FTC,* 182 F. 2d 36 (D.C. Cir. 1950).
All-State Industries, 3 CCH Trade Reg. Rep. ¶ 18,740 (FTC 1969).
American Medicinal Products v. *FTC,* 136 F. 2d 426 (9th Cir. 1943).
American Merchandise Co., 28 FTC 1465 (1939).
American Tack Co., 50 FTC 202 (1953).
Assets, Inc., 57 FTC 533 (1960).
Atomic Products, 48 FTC 289 (1951).
Berkey & Gay Furniture Co. v. *FTC,* 42 F. 2d 427 (6th Cir. 1930).
Bolta Co., 44 FTC 17 (1947).
Budco, Inc., 57 FTC 652 (1960).
Carter Products, 47 FTC 1137 (1951).
Colognes, Inc., 59 FTC 872 (1961).
Copinol Co., 33 FTC 1291 (1941).
Dabrol Products Corp., 47 FTC 791 (1950).
Dermolav Laboratories, 26 FTC 902 (1938).
Double Eagle Lubricants, Inc. v. *FTC,* 1965 Trade Cases ¶ 71,613 (10th Cir. 1965).
First Buckingham Community, 3 CCH Trade Reg. Rep. ¶ 18,357 (FTC 1968).
Frontier Asthma Co., 43 FTC 117 (1946).
Frost's Industries, 51 FTC 1463 (1955).
Household Sewing Machine Co., 3 CCH Trade Reg. Rep. ¶ 18,882 (FTC 1969).
Humania Hair Goods & Specialty Co., 40 FTC 466 (1945), *modified,* 46 FTC 936 (1950).
Ideal Toy Corp. [1963–1965 Transfer Binder], Trade Reg. Rep. ¶ 16,751 (FTC 1964).
J. B. Williams Co., Inc. v. *FTC,* 381 F. 2d 884 (6th Cir. 1967).
James B. Tompkins [1963–1965 Transfer Binder], Trade Reg. Rep. ¶ 16,692 (FTC 1963).
Kenmont Hat Co., 59 FTC 971 (1961).
Kochton Plywood & Veneer Co., 55 FTC 870 (1958).
Lee Rubber & Tire Corp., 56 FTC 1026 (1960).
L. Heller & Son, 47 FTC 34 (1950).
Lincoln Dental Supply Co., 27 FTC 965 (1938).
Manco Watch Strap Co., 60 FTC 495, *modified,* 61 FTC 298 (1962).
Master Mechanic Mfg. Co., 59 FTC 792 (1961).
McK. Edwards, 37 FTC 619 (1942).
Miracle Hearing Aid, Inc., 49 FTC 1410 (1953).
Mohawk Refining Corp. v. *FTC,* 263 F. 2d 818 (3rd Cir. 1959).
National Employment Information Service [1957–1958 Transfer Binder], Trade Reg. Rep. ¶ 27,668 (FTC 1958).

National Ozone Corp. 47 FTC 816 (1950).

New American Library of World Literature, 49 FTC 220 (1952), *remanded,* 213 F. 2d 143 (2d Cir. 1954), *modified,* 49 FTC 760 (1953); 51 FTC 583 (1955); *aff'd as modified,* 227 F. 2d 384 (2nd Cir. 1955).

Northam Warren Corp. v. *FTC,* 59 F. 2d 196 (2d Cir. 1932).

Oxwall Tool Co., 59 FTC 1408 (1961).

Portwood v. *FTC,* 1969 Trade Cases ¶ 72,970 (10th Cir. 1969).

Prilex Products Co., 49 FTC 1637 (1953).

Rhodes Pharmacal Co. v. *FTC,* 208 F. 2d 382 (1953), *rev'd per curiam,* 348 U.S. 940 (1955).

Royal Baking Powder Co. v. *FTC,* 281 Fed. 744 (2d Cir. 1922).

Royal Oil Corp. v. *FTC,* 262 F. 2d 741 (4th Cir. 1959).

Royal Sewing Machine Corp., 49 FTC 1351 (1953), 56 FTC 466 (1959).

Rudolph R. Siebert Co., 49 FTC 1418 (1953).

Salyer Refining Co., 54 FTC 1026 (1958).

Samson Rosenblatt, 8 FTC 400 (1925).

Scott-Mitchell House, 53 FTC 1384 (1957) (Stipulation), 56 FTC 1488 (1960).

Segal v. *FTC,* 1944–1945 Trade Cases ¶ 57,223 (2d Cir. 1944).

Segal Optical Co., 34 FTC 218 (1941).

S. S. S. Co., Inc. v. *FTC,* 1969 Trade Cases ¶ 72,929 (9th Cir. 1969).

State Sewing Machine Corp., 48 FTC 941 (1952).

Sylvette Watch Co., 54 FTC 1795 (1958).

Ultra-Violet Products, 34 FTC 1325 (1942), *modified,* 39 FTC 105 (1944), *modified,* 40 FTC 645 (1945).

United Fibre Works, 6 FTC 101 (1923).

U.S. Ass'n of Credit Bureaus, 1962 Trade Cases ¶ 70,230 (7th Cir. 1962).

Utica Cutlery Co., 56 FTC 1186 (1960).

Vulcan Lamp Works, 32 FTC 7 (1940).

William Adams, Inc., 53 FTC 1164 (1957).

Chapter 10: Product Description, Composition, and Origin

BIBLIOGRAPHY

Advisory Opinion Digest No. 17 (FTC March 22, 1966) ("velvet" and "suede").

Advisory Opinion Digest No. 60 (FTC June 18, 1966) (diamonds as "clear, pure color").

Advisory Opinion Digest No. 69 (FTC July 6, 1966) (origin disclosure).

Advisory Opinion Digest No. 107 (FTC January 13, 1967) (vinyl as "leather").

Advisory Opinion Digest No. 120 (FTC April 15, 1967) ("new").

Advisory Opinion Digest No. 146 (FTC October 24, 1967) ("new").

Advisory Opinion Digest No. 197 (FTC February 27, 1968) ("handmade").

Advisory Opinion Digest No. 207 (FTC April 4, 1968) ("made in U.S.A.").

Advisory Opinion Digest No. 211 (FTC April 4, 1968) (origin disclosure).

Advisory Opinion Digest No. 215 (FTC April 4, 1968) (origin disclosure).

Advisory Opinion Digest No. 218 (FTC April 4, 1968) (origin disclosure).

Advisory Opinion Digest No. 219 (FTC April 4, 1968) (origin disclosure).

Advisory Opinion Digest No. 225 (FTC April 4, 1968) ("leather").

Advisory Opinion Digest No. 234 (FTC April 4, 1968) (origin disclosure).
Advisory Opinion Digest No. 236 (FTC April 4, 1968) (origin disclosure).
Advisory Opinion Digest No. 252 (FTC May 21, 1968) (origin disclosure).
Advisory Opinion Digest No. 255 (FTC May 30, 1968) (origin disclosure).
Advisory Opinion Digest No. 301 (FTC October 22, 1968) ("Danish").
Alexander, *Honesty and Competition* (1967).
Trade Practice Rule, Handkerchief Industry, 4 CCH Trade Reg. Rep. ¶ 41,181, §181.0 (1949).
Trade Practice Rule, Jewelry Industry, 4 CCH Trade Reg. Rep. ¶ 41,023, §23.22 *et seq.* (1957 as amended 1959).
Trade Practice Rule, Masonry Waterproofing Industry, 4 CCH Trade Reg. Rep. ¶ 41,169, §§169.2–169.5 (1946).
Trade Practice Rule, Watch and Watch Case Industry, 4 CCH Trade Reg. Rep. ¶ 41,170 (1947).

CASES

A. DePinna Co., 27 FTC 1238 (1938).
Alexandra de Markoff Sales Corp., 30 FTC 1533 (Stip. 2814, 1940).
Allen B. Wrisley Co. v. *FTC,* 113 F. 2d 437 (7th Cir. 1940).
Allen V. Tornek Co., 55 FTC 1770 (1959), *aff'd per curiam,* 276 F. 2d 513 (D.C. Cir. 1960).
Alva Laboratories [1963–1965 Transfer Binder], Trade Reg. Rep. ¶ 17,001 (FTC 1964).
American Hair & Felt Co., 31 FTC 1278 (1940).
American Health Society, 27 FTC 237 (1938).
American Remedy Co., 24 FTC 1128 (1937).
American Rug & Carpet Co., 37 FTC 53 (1943).
A. & M. Karagheusian, Inc., 36 FTC 446 (1943).
Anheuser-Busch, Inc., 54 FTC 277 (1957).
Arabian Toilet Goods Co., 48 FTC 354 (1951).
Arnold Constable Corp., 58 FTC 49 (1961).
Arnold Stone Co. v. *FTC,* 49 F. 2d 1017 (5th Cir. 1931), *remanding* 14 FTC 291 (1930).
Aronberg v. *FTC,* 132 F. 2d 165 (7th Cir. 1942).
Art Nat'l Mfrs. Distributing Co., 1962 Trade Cases ¶ 70,214 (2nd Cir. 1962), *enforcing* [1961–1963 Transfer Binder], Trade Reg. Rep. ¶ 15,138 (FTC 1961).
Aspironal, Co., 34 FTC 310 (1941).
Associated Laboratories, 36 FTC 626 (1943), *aff'd per curiam,* 150 F. 2d 629 (2nd Cir. 1945).
Atlantic Sponge & Chamois Corp., 52 FTC 500 (1955).
Bakers Franchise Corp. v. *FTC,* 302 F. 2d 258 (3rd Cir. 1962).
Belgarde & Frank, Inc. [1963–1965 Transfer Binder], ¶ 16,925 (FTC 1964).
Belmont Hosiery Mills, 23 FTC 1165, Stip. 1879 (1936).
Belmont Laboratories, 26 FTC 244 (1938), *aff'd,* 103 F. 2d 538 (3rd Cir. 1939).
Belmont Products Co., 23 FTC 1164, Stip. 1878 (1936).
Benot Watch Case Co., 54 FTC 634 (1957).
Ben Greenberg & Brother, 22 FTC 974, Stip. 1719 (1936).

Bengué v. *American Pharmaceutical Co.,* 280 N.Y.S. 153 (Sup. Ct. 1935).

Benrus Watch Co. v. *FTC,* 352 F. 2d 313 (8th Cir. 1965).

Berkey & Gay Furniture Co. v. *FTC,* 42 F. 2d 427 (6th Cir. 1930).

Bigelow-Sandford Carpet Co., 34 FTC 1252 (1942).

Bonwit Teller, Inc., 28 FTC 540 (1939).

Bradley-Boston, Inc., 15 FTC 20 (1931).

Burn, Pollak & Beer, 28 FTC 1169 (1939).

Burry Biscuit Corp., 33 FTC 89 (1941).

Capitol Records, 44 FTC 1347 (1948).

Capra Gem Co. [1963–1965 Transfer Binder], Trade Reg. Rep. ¶ 16,704 (FTC 1963).

Carter Products v. *FTC,* 1950–1951 Trade Cases ¶ 62,769 (7th Cir. 1950).

Celanese Corp. of America, 50 FTC 170 (1953).

Century Metalcraft Corp. v. *FTC,* 112 F. 2d 443 (7th Cir. 1940).

Chatham Research Laboratories, 56 FTC 1197 (1960); 60 FTC 1889 (1962); 60 FTC 1891 (1962).

Charles of the Ritz Distributors Corp. v. *FTC,* 143 F. 2d 676 (2nd Cir. 1944).

Charles Scribner's Sons, 20 FTC 535, Stip. 1350 (1935).

Chelsea Leathergoods Co., 58 FTC 503 (1961).

Cheston L. Eshelman Co., 53 FTC 1316, Stip. 8826 (1956).

Chicago Lock Co., 31 FTC 1623, Stip. 2854 (1940).

Colgate-Palmolive-Peet Co., 31 FTC 1630, Stip. 2867 (1940).

Colony House, Inc., 39 FTC 632, Stip. 3938 (1944).

Commercial Mfg. Co., 22 FTC 373 (1936).

Consolidated Book Publishers, 32 FTC 1003 (1941).

Contact Lens Specialists, 57 FTC 757 (1960).

Corozone Air Conditioning Corp., 23 FTC 1111, Stip. 1772 (1936).

Curtiss-Wright Corp., 58 FTC 1936 (1961).

Dahlberg Co., 56 FTC 1098 (1960).

Darling Dimple Co., 30 FTC 1534, Stip. 2815 (1940).

D.D.D. Corp. v. *FTC,* 125 F. 2d 679 (7th Cir. 1942).

Delaware Watch Co. [1963–1965 Transfer Binder], Trade Reg. Rep. ¶ 16,546 (FTC 1964), *adopting initial order* ¶ 16,454 (FTC 1963), *aff'd per curiam,* 1964 Trade Cases ¶ 71,106 (2nd Cir. 1964).

Dennison Brothers, 22 FTC 786 (1936).

D.S. & W. Hosiery Co., 22 FTC 975, Stip. 1772 (1936).

Devcon Corp. [1963–1965 Transfer Binder], Trade Reg. Rep. ¶ 16,622 (FTC 1963).

Dofan Handbag Co., 58 FTC 781 (1961).

Dolcin Corp. v. *FTC,* 219 F. 2d 742 (D.C. Cir. 1954).

Dominion Briquetts & Chemicals, Ltd., 59 FTC 175 (1961).

Edward & John Burke, Ltd. v. *Bishop,* 175 Fed. 167 (C.C.S.D. N.Y. 1910).

E. Griffiths Hughes Inc. v. *FTC,* 1932–1939 Trade Cases ¶ 55,075 (2nd Cir. 1935), *aff'd per curiam,* 18 FTC 1 (1933).

Enterprise Aluminum Co., 30 FTC 1542, Stip. 2828 (1940).

E.S. Ullmann-Allied Co., 44 FTC 170 (1947).

Ever-Lasting Products Co., 47 FTC 1598 (1951).

Excelsior Laboratory, 44 FTC 921 (1948).

Feshbach & Ackerman Fur Corp., 37 FTC 734, Stip. 3753 (1943).

Fox Film Corp. v. *FTC,* 296 Fed. 353 (2d Cir. 1924).

Franklin Shockey Co., 56 FTC 303 (1959).

Fresh Grown Preserve Corp., 31 FTC 952 (1940), *aff'd per curiam,* 139 F. 2d 200 (2d Cir. 1943).

FTC v. *Cassoff,* 38 F. 2d 790 (2d Cir. 1930).

FTC v. *Good-Grape Co.,* 45 F. 2d 70 (6th Cir. 1930).

FTC v. *Hires Turner Glass Co.,* 81 F. 2d 362 (3d Cir. 1935).

FTC v. *Morrissey,* 47 F. 2d 101 (7th Cir. 1931).

Fuld Bros., 34 FTC 1559, Stip. 3820 (1941).

Gallant Trading Co., 36 FTC 470 (1943).

Gimble Bros. v. *FTC,* 116 F. 2d 578 (2d Cir. 1941).

Gold Medal Books, 27 FTC 1304 (1938).

Gulbransen Co., 23 FTC 1147, Stip. 1842 (1936).

Hamilton Garments Co., 14 FTC 133 (1930).

Hanovia Chemical & Mfg. Co., 47 FTC 1694, Stip. 7848 (1950).

Harket Pottery Co., 23 FTC 1157, Stip. 1864 (1936).

Harry D. Koenig & Co., 55 FTC 2087, Stip. 9064 (1955).

Harry's Linoleum Co., 59 FTC 1422 (1961).

Haskelite Mfg. Corp. v. *FTC,* 127 F. 2d 765 (7th Cir. 1942).

Hawthorne Watch Co., 54 FTC 1670 (1958).

Health Violet Products, 13 FTC 134 (1929).

Heavenly Creations [1963–1965 Transfer Binder], Trade Reg. Rep. ¶ 16,818 (FTC 1964), *aff'd per curiam,* 1964 Trade Cases ¶ 71,299 (2d Cir. 1964).

Heinz W. Kirchner [1963–1965 Transfer Binder], Trade Reg. Rep. ¶ 16,664 (FTC 1963), *aff'd,* 1964 Trade Cases ¶ 71,278 (9th Cir. 1964).

Howe & Co., 36 FTC 685 (1943), *modified,* 41 FTC 371 (1945).

Huddersfield Worsted Mills Corp., 42 FTC 262 (1946).

I. B. C. Watch Case Co., 53 FTC 578 (1956).

Jacob Busch, 10 FTC 217 (1926).

J. B. Williams Co. [1965–1967 Transfer Binder], Trade Reg. Rep. ¶ 17,339 (FTC 1965).

Jean Vivadou Co., 24 FTC 124 (1936).

Jergens-Woodbury Sales Corp., 33 FTC 1267 (1941).

John F. Trommer, Inc., 36 FTC 577 (1943).

John R. Evans & Co., 32 FTC 1677, Stip. 3033 (1941).

John Solari & Co., 43 FTC 184 (1946).

Johnson Smith & Co., 36 FTC 245 (1943).

Joseph Bancroft & Sons Co., 44 FTC 1235 (1948).

Justin Haynes & Co., 26 FTC 1147 (1938).

J. Warshal & Sons, 37 FTC 710, Stip. 3717 (1943).

Karastan Rug Mills, 36 FTC 411 (1943).

Karno Tailors, 46 FTC 1201, Stip. 7921 (1949).

Ladd Knitting Mills, 55 FTC 941 (1958).

Lane v. *FTC,* 130 F. 2d 48 (9th Cir. 1942).

Latex Fiber Industries, 52 FTC 1721, Stip. 8690 (1955).

Lee Products Co., 39 FTC 637, Stip. 3945 (1945).

Lekas & Drivas, Inc., 37 FTC 9 (1943), *aff'd as modified,* 145 F. 2d 976 (2d Cir. 1944).

L. Hoffmann, 31 FTC 793 (1940).

London Handkerchief Co., 40 FTC 291 (1945).

Long-Koch Co., 10 FTC 128 (1926).

Lord & Taylor, 26 FTC 911 (1938).

Louis Batlin, 9 FTC 143 (1925).

Louis Pierce Hartley, 31 FTC 1728, Stip. 3002 (1940).

L. Silverman & Sons, 53 FTC 253 (1956).

Lustberg, Nast & Co., 35 FTC 132 (1942), *aff'd,* 1944–1945 Trade Cases ¶ 57,261 (2d Cir. 1944).

Maatschappij Tot Exploitatie Van Rademaker's Koninklijke Cacao & Chocoladefadrieken v. *Kosloff,* 45 F. 2d 94 (2d Cir. 1930).

Marshall v. *Procter & Gamble Mfg. Co.,* 170 F. Supp. 828 (D. Md. 1959).

Mary Moffet, Inc. v. *FTC,* 194 F. 2d 504 (2d Cir. 1952).

Masland Duraleather Co. v. *FTC,* 34 F. 2d. 733 (3d Cir. 1929).

Masterkraft Guild Weavers, 34 FTC 698 (1942).

Merck & Co. [1965–1967 Transfer Binder], Trade Reg. Rep. ¶ 17,503 (FTC 1966).

M.J. Gropper & Sons, 14 FTC 274 (1930).

M.N. Arnold Shoe Co., 32 FTC 771 (1941).

Monsanto Chemical Co. v. *Perfect Fit Products Mfg. Co.,* 232 F. Supp. 493 (S.D. N.Y. 1964).

Montgomery Ward & Co., 23 FTC 1166, Stip. 1880 (1936).

Morrison Knitwear Co., 56 FTC 1244 (1960).

Motloid Co., 38 FTC 661 (1944).

Mountain Grove Creamery, Ice & Electric Co., 6 FTC 426 (1923).

Muntz TV, 54 FTC 1825 (1958).

Murray Hill House, 58 FTC 71 (1961).

Nat'l Committee for Education, 39 FTC 171 (1944).

Nat'l Lacquer Mfg. Co., 35 FTC 178 (1940).

Nat'l Silver Co. v. *FTC,* 88 F. 2d 425 (2d Cir. 1937).

Necchi Sewing Machine Sales Corp., 55 FTC 2130, Stip. 9134 (1958).

N. Fluegelman & Co. v. *FTC,* 37 F. 2d 59 (2d Cir. 1930).

Northwestern Extract Co., 46 FTC 786 (1950).

N. Shure Co., 12 FTC 105 (1928).

Ohio Leather Co. v. *FTC,* 45 F. 2d 39 (6th Cir. 1930), *aff'g* 12 FTC 323 (1929).

Outdoor Supply Co., 57 FTC 361 (1960).

Ozark Creamery Co., 8 FTC 377 (1925).

Papercraft Corp. [1963–1965 Transfer Binder], Trade Reg. Rep. ¶ 16,721 (FTC 1964).

Plymouth Textiles, 48 FTC 31 (1951).

Pond's Extract Co., 33 FTC 1253 (1941).

Previcol, Inc., 47 FTC 1702, Stip. 8042 (1950).

Procter & Gamble Co. v. *FTC,* 11 F. 2d 47 (6th Cir. 1926), *aff'g* 8 FTC 148 (1924).

Product Testing Co. [1963–1965 Transfer Binder], Trade Reg. Rep. ¶ 16,806 (FTC 1964).

Providence Import Co., 58 FTC 89 (1961).

Puritan Undergarment Corp., 29 FTC 664 (1939).

Quaker Oats Co. [1963–1965 Transfer Binder], Trade Reg. Rep. ¶ 16,713 (FTC 1964).

Radio Wire Television, 34 FTC 1278 (1942).

Reliable Specialty Corp., 27 FTC 67 (1938).

Rhodes Pharmacal Co. v. *FTC,* 208 F. 2d 382 (7th Cir. 1953), *rev'd per curiam,* 348 U.S. 940 (1955).

Rieser Co., 25 FTC 402 (1937).

Ringwalt Linoleum Works, 1 FTC 436 (1919).

Roosevelt Mercantile Co., 30 FTC 807 (1940).

Rubber City Paint Co., 14 FTC 331 (1931).

Rubber Products Co., 49 FTC 1590, Stip. 8297 (1952).

Saks & Co., 30 FTC 898 (1940).

Sales on Sound Corp., 27 FTC 850 (1938).

Samuel E. Burnstein, Inc., 44 FTC 1 [1947, *modifying* 10 FTC 223 (1926)].

Sanford Mills, 33 FTC 1161 (1941).

S. Buchsbaum & Co. v. *FTC,* 160 F. 2d 121 (7th Cir. 1947).

Schweizerishe Kaeseunion Bern v. *Saul Stark, Inc.,* 293 N.Y.S. 816 (Sup. Ct. 1937).

Seaboard Paint & Varnish Co., 31 FTC 684 (1940).

Segal Lock & Paint Hardware Co., 34 FTC 1375 [1942, *aff'd,* 143 F. 2d 935 (2d Cir. 1944)].

Sheffield Silver Co., 40 FTC 354 (1952).

S. H. Kress & Co., 40 FTC 738 (1945).

Silf Skin, Inc., 55 FTC 1899 (1959).

Simpson v. *U.S.,* 241 Fed. 841 (6th Cir. 1917).

Sinnock & Sherrill, 28 FTC 46 (1939).

Smith-Kirk Candy Co., 8 FTC 130 (1924).

S. Reiffe & Sons, 34 FTC 1270 (1942).

Standard Toykraft, 3 CCH Trade Reg. Rep. ¶ 17,983 (FTC 1967).

Stephen Rug Mills, 34 FTC 958 (1942).

Stipulation No. 537, 13 FTC 456 (1930).

Stipulation No. 1057, 17 FTC 489 (1933).

Sun-Fast Textiles, 58 FTC 285 (1961).

Thomas v. *FTC,* 116 F. 2d 347 (10th Cir. 1940).

Trade Laboratories, 25 FTC 937 (1937).

U.S. Chemical & Plastics, 61 FTC 485 (1962).

U.S. v. *Schwiman,* 177 Fed. 581 (W.D. Mich. 1910).

United States Plywood Corp., 58 FTC 737 (1961).

Vanogdin, Inc., 26 FTC 930 (1938).

Virginia Products Co., 29 FTC 451 (1939).

Waltham Precision Instrument Co., 61 FTC 1027 (1962).

Winona Monument Co., 22 FTC 156 (1936).

Wood & Hyde Co., 32 FTC 1626 (1941).

Woods Mfg. Co., 30 FTC 1541, Stip. 2827 (1940).

Chapter 11: Endorsements, Testimonials, Tests, and Surveys

BIBLIOGRAPHY

Federal Trade Commission Act (Wheeler-Lea Act), 15 U.S.C. §45 (1946).
Handler, *False and Misleading Advertising*, 39 Yale L. J. 22, 35 (1929).
Note, *Liability of Advertising Endorsers*, 2 Stanford L. Rev. 496 (1950).
Note, *Testimonial Advertising and the Federal Trade Commission*, 17 Geo. Wash. L. Rev. 340 (1949).
The Uniform Deceptive Practices Act, 54 Trademark Reporter 897 (1964).

CASES

In Re All-Star Dairy Association, Inc., 58 FTC 1238, Stip. 9451 (1961).
In Re American Chemical Paint Co., 45 FTC 9 (1948).
In Re American International Industries, Inc., 57 FTC 119 (1960).
In Re American Processing and Sales Co., 49 FTC 1593, Stip. 8302 (1952).
In Re American Viscose Corp., 45 FTC 305 (1948).
In Re Ann Hartman, 51 FTC 592 (1955).
In Re Ar-Ex Cosmetics, Inc., 48 FTC 800 (1952).
Bristol-Myers Co. v. *FTC*, 185 F. 2d 58 (4th Cir. 1950).
In Re C. G. Hyre, 24 FTC 263 (1936).
Consumer Sales Corp. v. *FTC*, 198 F. 2d 404 (2d Cir. 1952).
Consumers Union of the United States, Inc. v. *Admiral Corporation*, 186 F. Supp. 800 (S.D. N.Y. 1960).
Country Tweeds, Inc. v. *FTC*, 326 F. 2d 144 (2d Cir. 1964).
Eastern Railroad Presidents Conference v. *Noerr Motor Freight, Inc.*, 365 U.S. 127 (1961).
In Re Empire Amerex Products Corp., 55 FTC 1604 (1959).
FTC v. *A.P.W. Paper Co.*, 328 U.S. 193 (1946).
FTC v. *Army and Navy Trading Company*, 88 F. 2d 776 (D.C. Cir. 1937).
FTC v. *Standard Education Society*, 302 U.S. 112 (1937).
FTC v. *Sterling Drug Company, Inc.*, 317 F. 2d 669 (2d Cir. 1963).
In Re Ford Motor Co., 58 FTC 1219, Stip. 9400 (1961).
Foster-Millburn Co. v. *Chinn*, 120 S.W. 364 (Ky. Ct. App. 1909).
Friedman v. *Sealy, Inc.*, 274 F. 2d 255 (10th Cir. 1959).
Girl Scouts of the United States of America v. *Hollingsworth*, 188 F. Supp. 707 (E.D. N.Y. 1960).
Gynex Corp. v. *Dilex Institute of Feminine Hygiene*, 85 F. 2d 103 (2d Cir. 1936).
In Re Hearst Magazines, Inc., 32 FTC 1440 (1941).
In Re Inecto, Inc., 16 FTC 198 (1932).
In Re Mayo Brothers Vitamins, Inc., 40 FTC 116 (1945).
Moretrench Corp. v. *FTC*, 127 F. 2d 792 (2d Cir. 1942).
Mytinger & Casselberry, Inc. v. *FTC*, 301 F. 2d 534 (D.C. Cir. 1962).
In Re Neuville, Inc., 53 FTC 436 (1956).
Niresk Industries, Inc. v. *FTC*, 278 F. 2d 337 (7th Cir. 1960).
Northam Warren Corp. v. *FTC*, 59 F. 2d 196 (2d Cir. 1932).
In Re Philip Morris & Company, Inc., 49 FTC 703 (1952).

In Re Procter & Gamble Co., 56 FTC 1623 (1960) (Tide Laundry Detergent).

In Re Procter & Gamble Co., 60 FTC 438 (1961) (Crest Tooth Paste).

R. J. Reynolds Tobacco Co. v. *FTC,* 192 F. 2d 535 (7th Cir. 1951).

In Re Reliable Stores Corp., 55 FTC 2101, Stip. 9083 (1958).

In Re Royal Sewing Machine Corporation, 56 FTC 467 (1959).

Stanley Laboratories, Inc. v. *FTC,* 138 F. 2d 388 (9th Cir. 1943).

In Re Theronoid, Inc., 17 FTC 298 (1933).

Thomas A. Edison, Inc. v. *Shotkin,* 69 F. Supp. 176 (D. Colo. 1946).

United States v. *John J. Fulton Co.,* 33 F. 2d 506 (9th Cir. 1929).

United States Navy Weekly, Inc. v. *FTC,* 207 F. 2d 17 (D.C. Cir. 1953).

In Re United States Safety Service Co., 55 FTC 453 (1958).

In Re United States Testing Company, Inc., 61 FTC 1312 (1963).

In Re Wilbert W. Hasse Co., Inc., 33 FTC 662 (1941).

Chapter 12: Pricing and Savings Claims

BIBLIOGRAPHY

Advisory Opinion Digest, No. 109 (FTC Jan. 24, 1967).

Advisory Opinion Digest, No. 277 (FTC August 23, 1968).

Analysis, Fictitious Pricing, Antitrust and Trade Regulations Report No. 237:B-1 (1966).

Brown, *Services to Distributors,* 26 ABA, Antitrust Section 85 (1964).

Comment, *FTC Revised Deceptive Pricing Limit Manufacturer's Liability,* 39 N.Y.U. L. Rev. 884 (1964).

Developments in the Law—Deceptive Advertising, 80 Harv. L. Rev. 1005 (1967).

Harkrader, *Fictitious Pricing and the FTC: A New Look at an Old Dodge,* 37 St. John's L. R. 1 (1962).

Kidston, *Preticketing and List Prices,* 8 Antitrust Bull. 427 (1963).

Murphy, *The Ethics of Retail Price Advertising,* 6 Antitrust Bull. 419 (1961).

Trade Practice Rule, Free Goods, 4 CCH Trade Reg. Rep. ¶ 40,210 (FTC 1953).

Trade Practice Rule, Relating to the Sale and Financing of Motor Vehicles, 4 CCH Trade Reg. Rep ¶ 41,197 (FTC 1951).

CASES

ABC Jalousie Co. of Washington, Inc., 58 FTC 232 (1961).

Alben-Harley, 4 FTC 31 (1921).

American Chicle Co. v. *Topps Chewing Gum, Inc.,* 111 F. Supp. 224 (D.C. N.Y.), *aff'd* 208 F. 2d 560 (2d Cir. 1953).

Ames, Inc., 34 FTC 1548 Stip. 3261 (1941).

Arnold Constable Corp., 58 FTC 49 (1961).

Associated Furniture Mfgrs. Warehouse Co., 9 FTC 333 (1925).

Baltimore Luggage Co. v. *FTC,* 296 F. 2d 608 (4th Cir. 1961), *cert. denied,* 369 U.S. 860 (1962).

Bankers Securities Corp. v. *FTC,* 297 F. 2d 403 (3d Cir. 1961).

Benrus Watch Co. v. *FTC,* 352 F. 2d 313 (8th Cir. 1965), *cert. denied* 384 U.S. 939 (1966).

Better Living, Inc., 54 FTC 648 (1957), *aff'd* 259 F. 2d 271 (3d Cir. 1958).

B. H. Stinemetz & Son Co., 5 FTC 424 (1923).

Big Four Grocery Co., 3 FTC 338 (1921).

Bond Vacuum Stores, Inc., 51 FTC 504 (1954).

Bulova Watch Co. [1963–1965 Transfer Binder], Trade Reg. Rep. ¶ 16,841 (FTC 1964) complaint dismissed.

Chester H. Roth Co., 55 FTC 1076 (1959).

Chicago Portrait Co. v. *FTC,* 4 F. 2d 759 (7th Cir. 1925).

Cole-Conrade Co., 2 FTC 188 (1919).

Consumer Sales Corp. v. *FTC,* 198 F. 2d 404 (2d Cir. 1952).

Continental Products, Inc. [1963–1965 Transfer Binder], Trade Reg. Rep. ¶ 16,883 (FTC 1964).

David Mann [1963–1965 Transfer Binder], Trade Reg. Rep. ¶ 16,896 (FTC 1964).

D. S. & W. Hosiery Co., 22 FTC 975, Stip. 1722 (FTC 1936).

Earl Scheit, Inc. [1963–1965 Transfer Binder], Trade Reg. Rep. ¶ 16,437 (FTC 1963).

Eastern Textile Co., 21 FTC 126 (1935).

Edward Goldstein Enterprises, Inc., 48 FTC 399 (1951).

Erwin Feather Quilt Co., 30 FTC 1079 (1940).

Estee Sleep Shops, Inc. [1963–1965 Transfer Binder], Trade Reg. Rep. ¶ 16,810, *adopted as final order,* ¶ 16,867 (FTC 1964).

Fair v. *FTC,* 272 F. 2d 609 (7th Cir. 1959).

Firestone Tire & Rubber Co., 33 FTC 282 (1941).

Ford Motor Co. v. *FTC,* 120 F. 2d 175 (6th Cir. 1941).

FTC v. *Winsted Hosiery Co.,* 258 U.S. 483 (1922).

Garland Co., 61 FTC 552 (1962).

General Motors Corp. v. *FTC,* 114 F. 2d 33 (2d Cir. 1940).

Giant Food Inc. v. *FTC,* 61 FTC 326 (1962), *aff'd,* 322 F. 2d 977 (D.C. Cir. 1963).

Gimbel Brothers [1961–1963 Transfer Binder], Trade Reg. Rep. ¶ 15,748 (FTC 1962).

Gimbel Bros., Inc. [1961–1963 Transfer Binder], Trade Reg. Rep. ¶ 16,146, *adopting,* ¶ 15,663 (FTC 1962) complaint dismissed.

Gimbel Bros., Inc. v. *FTC,* 116 F. 2d 578 (2d Cir. 1941).

Goodyear Tire & Rubber Co., 33 FTC 298 (1941).

Group Sales Corp., 32 FTC 402 (1941).

Gruen Industries, Inc. [1963–1965 Transfer Binder], Trade Reg. Rep. ¶ 16,834 (FTC 1964).

Harsam Distributors, Inc., 54 FTC 1212 (1958), *aff'd,* 263 F. 2d 396 (2d Cir. 1959).

Heavenly Creations, Inc. v. *FTC,* 339 F. 2d 7 (2d Cir. 1964), *cert. denied,* 380 U.S. 955 (1965).

Hecht Co., 36 FTC 830 (1943).

Helbros Watch Co. v. *FTC,* 310 F. 2d 868 (D.C. Cir. 1962).

Holst Publishing Co., 24 FTC 404 (1937).

Household Sewing Machine Co., 52 FTC 250 (1955).

Imperial Carpets Co., 3 CCH Trade Reg. Rep. ¶ 18,588 (FTC 1968) *adopted,* 3 CCH Trade Reg. Rep. ¶ 18,659 (FTC 1969).

International Art Co. v. *FTC,* 109 F. 2d 393 (7th Cir. 1940).

International China Co., 23 FTC 360 (1936).

J. A. Stransky Mfg. Co., 36 FTC 552 (1943).

John Surrey, Ltd. [1965–1967 Transfer Binder], Trade Reg. Rep. ¶ 17,221 (FTC 1965).

Jones Bros. Publishing Co., 21 FTC 225 (1935).

Kaiser Rand Corp., 56 FTC 886 (1960).

Koch v. FTC, 206 F. 2d 311 (6th Cir. 1953).

Leeds Travelwear, Inc. [1961–1963 Transfer Binder], Trade Reg. Rep. ¶ 15,997 (FTC 1962).

Lexington Storage Warehouse Co., 9 FTC 324 (1925).

Liberty Wholesale Grocers, 3 FTC 103 (1920).

Magnavox Corp [1963–1965 Transfer Binder], Trade Reg. Rep. ¶ 17,159 (FTC 1964).

Majestic Electric Supply Co. [1963–1965 Transfer Binder], Trade Reg. Rep. ¶ 16, 825 (FTC 1964).

Mandel Bros., Inc. v. FTC, 254 F. 2d 18 (7th Cir. 1958).

Mannis v. FTC, 293 F. 2d 774 (9th Cir. 1961).

Mary Carter Paint Co., 60 FTC 1827 (1962), *aff'd,* 382 U.S. 46 (1965).

Metropolitan Vacuum Cleaner Co., 56 FTC 357 (1959).

Midwest Sewing Center [1963–1965 Transfer Binder], Trade Reg. Rep. ¶ 17,143 (FTC 1964) complaint dismissed.

Monarch China Co., 31 FTC 775 (1940).

Nash, Inc., 61 FTC 596 (1962).

National Coin Corp., 35 FTC 312 (1942).

Niresk Industries, Inc., 55 FTC 1889 (1959), *aff'd,* 278 F. 2d 337 (7th Cir. 1960).

North American Philips Co. [1963–1965 Transfer Binder], Trade Reg. Rep. ¶ 16,865 (FTC 1964) complaint dismissed.

Plaza Luggage and Supply Co., 44 FTC 443 (1948).

Product Testing Co. [1963–1965 Transfer Binder], Trade Reg. Rep. ¶ 16,806 (FTC 1964).

Rainbow Crafts, Inc. [1963–1965 Transfer Binder], Trade Reg. Rep. ¶ 17,057 (FTC 1964) complaint dismissed.

Rayex Corp. v. FTC, 317 F. 2d 290 (2d Cir. 1963).

Regina Corp. [1961–1963 Transfer Binder], Trade Reg. Rep. ¶ 15,936 (FTC 1962).

Revco D. S., Inc. [1965–1967 Transfer Binder], Trade Reg. Rep. ¶ 17,287 (FTC 1965).

S. Benson Studios, Inc., 21 FTC 306 (1935).

Saks & Co., 30 FTC 898 (1940).

Scott & Tetzer Co., 59 FTC 132 (1961).

Scott-Mitchell House, Inc., 56 FTC 1488 (1960).

Sears, Roebuck & Co., 33 FTC 334 (1941).

Sears, Roebuck & Co. v. FTC, 258 F. 307 (7th Cir. 1919).

Sidney J. Kreiss, Inc., 56 FTC 1421 (1960).

Southern Piano Co., 54 FTC 640 (1957).

S. Reiffe & Sons, Inc., 34 FTC 1270 (1942).

Stern & Co., 59 FTC 1418 (1961).

Sure-Fit Seat Cover Center, 60 FTC 930 (1962).

Thomas v. *FTC*, 116 F. 2d 347 (10th Cir. 1940).

United States v. *George's Radio & T.V. Co.*, 1962 Trade Cases ¶70,281 (D. D.C. 1962).

Vanity Fair Mills, Inc., 3 CCH Trade Reg Rep. ¶ 18,398 (FTC 1968) consent order.

Walter J. Black, Inc., 50 FTC 225 (1953).

Waltham Watch Co. [1963–1965 Transfer Binder], Trade Reg Rep. ¶ 16,834 (FTC 1964).

Wardell Piano Co., 30 FTC 656 (1940).

World Library Guild, Inc., 23 FTC 598 (1936).

Chapter 13: Free Goods and Offers

BIBLIOGRAPHY

Advisory Opinion Digest No. 21 (FTC March 29, 1966).

Advisory Opinion Digest No. 196 (FTC February 27, 1968).

California Unfair Practices Act, Cal. Bus. & Prof. Code Ann. §17000 (Deering 1960).

Callmann, *The Law of Unfair Competition, Trademark and Monopolies* (1968).

Indiana Fair Trade Act, Ind. Stat. Ann. §66-303 (Burns Supp. 1961).

Recent Decision, *Walter J. Black*, 52 Mich. L. Rev. 1239 (1954).

Simon, *The Law for Advertising and Marketing* (1956).

Weston, *Deceptive Advertising and the Federal Trade Commission: Decline of Caveat Emptor*, 24 Fed. Bar J. 548 (1964).

Wolff, *Sales Promotion by Premiums as a Competitive Device*, 40 Colum. L. Rev. 1174 (1940).

CASES

American Industrial Rubber Co., 36 FTC 232 (1943).

Around-the-World Shoppers' Club [1963–1965 Transfer Binder], Trade Reg. Rep. ¶ 16,1805 (FTC 1964).

Atlantic Sewing Stores, 54 FTC 174 (1957).

Balzer v. *Caler*, 74 P. 2d 839 (Cal. Dist. Ct. App. 1937).

Basic Books, Inc. v. *FTC*, 276 F. 2d 718 (7th Cir. 1960).

Berkshire Textile Co., 21 FTC 710 (1935).

Bernhard v. *Savall Drug Store*, 82 N.Y.S. 2d (Sup. Ct. 1948).

Bonded Jewelers of America, 27 FTC 1429 (1938).

Book-of-the-Month Club, 48 FTC 1297 (1952), *aff'd*, 202 F. 2d 846 (2d Cir. 1953), *modified*, 50 FTC 778 (1954).

Bristol-Myers Co. v. *Lit Bros.*, 6 A. 2d 843 (Pa. 1939).

Bristol-Myers Co. v. *Piker*, 96 N.E. 2d 177 (N.Y. 1950).

Chicago Technical College, 35 FTC 569 (1942).

Chilton Greetings Co., 32 FTC 148 (1940).

Consolidated Book Publishers v. *FTC*, 53 F. 2d 942 (7th Cir. 1931).

Credit TV Service, 52 FTC 1493 (1956).

Doubleday & Co., 50 FTC 482 (1953).

DuPont de Nemours & Co. v. *Kaufmann & Chernick, Inc.,* 148 N.E. 2d 634 (Mass. Sup. Jud. Ct. 1958).

Eastern Textile Co., 21 FTC 126 (1935).

Ever-Keen Dry Shaver Co., 29 FTC 108 (1939).

Fashion Frocks, Inc., 62 FTC 1223 (1963).

General Surveys, 34 FTC 1157 (1942).

Gever v. *American Stores Co.,* 127 A. 2d 694 (Pa. 1956).

Holst Publishing Co., 24 FTC 404 (1937).

John C. Winston Co. v. *FTC,* 3 F. 2d 961 (3d Cir. 1925).

Jonas Schainuck & Son, 23 FTC 151 (1936).

Ray S. Kalwajtys, 52 FTC 721, *aff'd,* 237 F. 2d 654 (7th Cir. 1956).

Licht's Fur Factory, 24 FTC 1347 (1937).

Long Wear Hosiery Co., 26 FTC 284 (1938).

Mary Carter Paint Co., 60 FTC 1827 (1962), *aff'd,* 382 U.S. 46 (1965).

Memorial Granite Co., 35 FTC 552 (1942).

Milton Goldberg, 36 FTC 612 (1943).

Model Home Supply Co., 34 FTC 1234 (1942).

Modern Manner Clothes, 47 FTC 412 (1950), *aff'd,* 192 F. 2d 392 (2d Cir. 1951); *vacated,* 214 F. 2d 338 (2d Cir. 1954).

Modern Studios, 59 FTC 543 (1961).

Moye Photographers, 50 FTC 926 (1954).

National Publicity Bureau, 28 FTC 857 (1939).

New England Bakery Co., 2 FTC 465 (1919).

Nutri-Health, Inc., 59 FTC 1061 (1961).

Ohmlac Paint & Refinery Co., 69 FTC 419 (1962).

Old Homestead Bread Co. v. *Marx Baking Co.,* 117 P. 2d 1007 (Colo. 1941).

Ostermoor & Co. v. *FTC,* 16 F. 2d 962 (2d Cir. 1927).

People v. *Victor,* 283 N.W. 666 (Mich. 1939).

Progress Tailoring Co. v. *FTC,* 153 F. 2d 103 (7th Cir. 1946).

Puro Co., 50 FTC 454 (1953).

Rast v. *Van Deman & Lewis Co.,* 240 U.S. 342 (1916).

Samuel Stores, 27 FTC 882 (1938).

Schick, Inc. & Schick Service, Inc., 55 FTC 665 (1958).

Sidney J. Kreiss, 56 FTC 1421 (1960).

Skidmore v. *Swift & Co.,* 323 U.S. 134 (1944).

Spiegel, Inc. v. *FTC,* 1969 Trade Cases ¶ 72, 819 (7th Cir. 1969).

Sperry & Hutchinson Co., 3 Trade Reg. Rep. ¶ 18,449 (FTC 1968).

Squibb & Sons v. *Charlines' Cut Rate,* 74 A. 2d 354 (N.J. Super. Ct. 1950).

Standard Distributors, 48 FTC 1435 (1952), *aff'd,* 211 F. 2d 7 (2d Cir. 1954), *modified,* 51 FTC 677 (1955).

Standard Education Society v. *FTC,* 86 F. 2d 692 (2d Cir. 1936), *aff'd,* 302 U.S. 112 (1937).

State v. *Tankar Gas, Inc.,* 26 N.W. 2d 647 (Wis. 1947).

Supreme Sales Co., 34 FTC 1460 (1942).

Unicorn Press, 47 FTC 258 (1950).

Union Fountain Pen Co., 31 FTC 698 (1940).

Universal Industries, 32 FTC 1270 (1941).

Walside, Inc., 54 FTC 572 (1957).

Walter J. Black, Inc., 50 FTC 225 (1953).

Ward Baking Co., 1 FTC 388 (1917).

Weco Products Co. v. *Mid-City Cut Rate Drug Stores,* 131 P. 2d 856 (Cal. Dist. Ct. App. 1942).

Wellworth Sales Co., 22 FTC 405 (1941).

Wilson Chemical Co [1963–1965 Transfer Binder], Trade Reg. Rep. ¶16,749 (FTC 1964).

Chapter 14: Contests, Lotteries, and Games of Chance

BIBLIOGRAPHY

Advisory Opinion Digest, No. 40 (FTC April 30, 1966).
Advisory Opinion Digest, No. 45 (FTC May 18, 1966).
Advisory Opinion Digest, No. 78 (FTC August 2, 1966).
Advsory Opinion Digest, No. 86 (FTC August 26, 1966).
Advisory Opinion Digest, No. 87 (FTC September 2, 1966).
Advisory Opinion Digest, No. 123 (FTC May 5, 1967).
Gambling, 38 Am. Jur.2d §5.
Note, *Bank Nights and Similar Devices as Illegal Lotteries,* 50 Yale L. J. 941 (1941).
Note, *Recent Decisions,* 41 Geo. L. J. 556 (1953).
Peckett, *Contests and the Lottery Laws,* 45 Harv. L. Rev. 1196 (1932).

CASES

A. S. Douglas & Co., 16 FTC 353 (1932).
Arthur Murray, Inc., 57 FTC 306 (1960).
Atlas Sewing Centers, Inc., 57 FTC 974 (1960).
Bear Sales Co. v. *FTC,* 362 F. 2d 96 (7th Cir. 1966).
Blackburn v. *Ippolito,* 156 So. 2d 550 (Fla. App. Ct. 1963).
Boyd v. *Piggly Wiggly Southern, Inc.,* 155 S.E. 2d 630 (Ga. App. 1967).
Brockett v. *State,* 125 S.E. 513 (Ga. App. 1924).
Brooklyn Daily Eagle v. *Voorhies,* 181 Fed. 579 (E.D. N.Y. 1910).
Brother Internat'l Corp. of California, 56 FTC 434 (1959).
Calvine Cotton Mills, Inc., 51 FTC 294 (1954).
Chas. A. Brewer & Sons v. *FTC,* 158 F. 2d 74 (6th Cir. 1946).
City of Rosewell v. *Jones,* 67 P. 2d 286 (N.M. 1937).
Clark H. Geppert, 57 FTC 1199 (1960).
Clark v. *State,* 6 Div. 841 (Ala. 1955).
Commonwealth v. *Allen,* 404 S.W. 2d 464 (Ky. App. 1966).
Commonwealth v. *Emerson,* 42 N.E. 559 (Mass. 1896).
Conway Tailors, 36 FTC 835 (1943).
Conqueror Trust Co. v. *Simmon,* 162 Pac. 1098 (Okla. 1917).
Curtis-Elliott, Inc., 43 FTC 279 (1934).
D. Arnold Co., 18 FTC 279 (1934).
Dandy Products, Inc. v. *FTC,* 332 F. 2d 985 (7th Cir 1964).
Darlington Theatres, Inc. v. *Coker,* 2 S.E. 2d 782 (S.C. 1939).
D'Orio v. *Startup Candy Co.,* 266 Pac. 1037 (Utah 1928).

Dunham v. *St. Croix Soap Mfg Co.,* 34 N.B. 243 (Ala. 1897).

Eastman v. *Armstrong-Byrd Music Co.,* 212 Fed. 662 (8th Cir. 1914).

Ehrhart Conrad Co., 30 FTC 1172 (1940).

FCC v. *American Broadcasting Company, Inc.,* 347 U.S. 284 (1953).

FTC v. *F. A. Martoccio Co.,* 87 F. 2d 561 (8th Cir. 1937).

FTC v. *Gratz,* 253 U.S. 421 (1920).

FTC v. *Keppel & Brother, Inc.,* 291 U.S. 304 (1934).

FTC v. *Raladam Co.,* 283 U.S. 643 (1931).

Feitler v. *FTC,* 201 F. 2d 790 (9th Cir. 1953).

Fitzsimmons v. *United States,* 156 Fed. 477 (9th Cir. 1907).

Francis v. *United States,* 188 U.S. 375 (1903).

G. Fred Stayton, 23 FTC 657 (1936).

Garden City Chamber of Commerce v. *Wagner,* 100 F. Supp. 769 (E.D. N.Y. 1951).

Gellman v. *FTC,* 290 F. 2d 666 (8th Cir. 1961).

Great Western Distributing Co. [1963–1965 Transfer Binder], Trade Reg. Rep. ¶16,723 (FTC 1964).

Griffeth Amusement Co. v. *Morgan,* 98 S.W. 2d 844 (Tex. Civ. App. 1936).

Haven Company, 62 FTC 1009 (1963).

Hofeller v. *FTC,* 82 F. 2d 647 (7th Cir. 1936).

Holmes v. *Saunders,* 250 P. 2d 269 (Calif. App. 1952).

Iris Amusement Corporation v. *Kelly,* 8 N.E. 2d 647 (Ill. 1937).

J. C. Martin Corp., 52 FTC 1674 (1956).

J. D. Drushell, 28 FTC 795 (1939).

J. H. Allen & Co., 1 FTC 538 (1918).

John Alden Company, 21 FTC 584 (1935).

Kayden Industries, Inc. v. *Murphy,* 150 N.W. 2d 447 (Wis. 1967).

Keller v. *FTC,* 132 F. 2d 59 (7th Cir. 1942).

Las Vegas Hacienda, Inc. v. *Gibson,* 359 P. 2d 85 (Nev. 1961).

Lewis Brothers, Inc., 18 FTC 281 (1934).

Lichtenstein v. *FTC,* 194 F. 2d 607 (9th Cir. 1952).

Marvin v. *Trout,* 199 U.S. 212 (1905).

Maughs v. *Porter,* 161 S.E. 242 (Va. 1931).

Midwest Television, Inc. v. *Waaler,* 194 N.E. 2d. 653 (Ill. App. 1963).

Minges v. *City of Birmingham,* 36 So. 2d 93 (Ala. 1948).

Modernistic Candies, Inc. v. *FTC,* 145 F. 2d 454 (7th Cir. 1944).

National Candy Co. v. *FTC,* 104 F. 2d 999 (7th Cir. 1939).

National Conference on Legalizing Lotteries v. *Farley,* 96 F. 2d 861 (D.C. Cir. 1938).

National Premium Company, 31 FTC 835 (1940).

National Thrift Ass'n v. *Crews,* 241 Pac. 72 (Oregon 1925).

Ostler Candy Co. v. *FTC,* 106 F. 2d 962 (10th Cir. 1939).

People v. *Eagle Food Centers, Inc.,* 202 N.E. 2d 473 (Ill. 1964).

Phalen v. *Commonwealth of Virginia,* 49 U.S. 163 (1850).

Publix Printing Corp., 28 FTC 1715 (1939).

Quaker City Chocolate & Confectionery Company, 18 FTC 269 (1934).

R. J. Williams Furniture Co. v. *McComb Chamber of Commerce,* 112 So. 579 (Miss. 1927).

Reinhart & Newton Co., 10 FTC 110 (1926).

St. Peter v. *Pioneer Theatre Corporation,* 291 N.W. 164 (Iowa 1940).

Sherwood & Roberts-Yakima, Inc. v. *Leach,* 409 P. 2d 160 (Wash. 1966).

Simmons v. *Randforce Amusement Corporation,* 293 N.Y.S. 745 (1937).

State v. *Danz,* 250 Pac. 37 (Wash. 1926).

State v. *Fox Kansas Theatre Co.,* 62 P. 2d 929 (Kans. 1936).

State v. *Globe-Democrat Pub. Co.,* 110 S.W. 2d 705 (Mo. 1937).

State v. *ITM, Inc.,* 275 N.Y.S. 2d 303 (1966).

State v. *Powell,* 212 N.W. 169 (Minn. 1927).

United-Detroit Theatres Corp. v. *Colonial Theatrical Enterprises, Inc.,* 273 N.W. 756 (Mich. 1937).

United Jewelers' Mfg. Co. v. *Keckley,* 90 Pac. 781 (Kans. 1907).

United States v. *McKenna,* 149 Fed. 252 (W.D. N.Y. 1906).

United States v. *Rosenblum,* 121 Fed. 181 (S.D. N.Y. 1903).

United States v. *Wallis,* 58 Fed. 942 (D.C. Idaho 1893).

W. J. Thompson, Inc., 22 FTC 46 (1935).

Waite v. *Press Pub. Assoc.,* 155 Fed. 58 (5th Cir. 1907).

Wren Sales Co., Inc. v. *FTC,* 296 F. 2d 456 (7th Cir. 1961).

Yellow-Stone Kit v. *State,* 88 Ala. 196 (1890).

Chapter 15: Warranties and Guarantees

BIBLIOGRAPHY

Advisory Opinion Digest, No. 81 (FTC Aug. 12, 1966).

Advisory Opinion Digest, No. 100 (FTC Nov. 9, 1966).

Consumer Bulletin No. 1, *Pitfalls to Watch for in Mail Order Insurance Policies* (FTC 1969).

Prosser, *Torts,* §95, 3d ed. (1964).

Prosser, *The Assault Upon the Citadel,* 69 Yale L. J. 1099 (1960).

Prosser, *The Fall of the Citadel,* 50 Minn. L.R. 791 (1966).

Restatement of Torts §402(a) (Tent. Draft No. 7, 1962).

Uniform Commercial Code §§2-213–2-215, §2-318.

The Ways and Meanings of Defective Products and Strict Liability, 32 Tenn. L. R. 363.

Williston, *Sales* §181, rev. ed. (1948).

CASES

Accro Watch Co., Inc. [1963–1965 Transfer Binder], Trade Reg. Rep. ¶17,394 (FTC 1965).

Aegis Productions, Inc. v. *Arriflex Corp. of America,* 268 N.Y.S. 2d 185 (1966).

Allen v. *Brown,* 310 P. 2d 923 (Kans. 1957).

Amato v. *Worrell-Nash Motor Co.,* 7 S.W. 2d 423 (Mo. Ct. App. 1928).

American Foods, Inc. [1963–1965 Transfer Binder], Trade Reg. Rep. ¶16,904 (FTC 1964).

American Industrial Rubber Co., 36 FTC 232 (1943).

Atlas Supply Co., 55 FTC 2151 (Stip. 9178, 1959).

Baxter v. *Ford Motor Company,* 35 P. 2d 1090 (Wash. 1934).

L. E. Waterman Co., 40 FTC 563 (1945).

Lifetime, Inc., 59 FTC 1231 (1961).

Lilley v. *Manning Motor Company*, 137 S.E. 2d 847 (N.C. 1964).

Lowe v. *Lamb*, 2 Craw 125 (Crawford Cty. Pa. 1962).

Lt. Baldwin, 59 FTC 975 (1961).

Mars Electronics, Inc., 58 FTC 810 (1961).

McMeekin v. *Gimbel Brothers, Inc.*, 223 F Supp. 896 (W.D. Pa. 1963).

Midas, Inc., 57 FTC 92 (1960).

Miller v. *Andy Burger Motors, Inc.*, 370 S.W. 2d 654 (Mo. App. 1963).

Mitchell v. *Miller*, 214 A. 2d 694 (Conn. Super. Ct. 1965).

Mitchell v. *Rudasill*, 332 S.W. 2d 91 (Mo. App. 1960).

Montgomery Ward & Co. v. *FTC*, 379 F. 2d 666 (7th Cir. 1967).

Morgan Supply Co. v. *Yarborough*, 74 S.E. 2d 500 (Ga. Ct. App. 1953).

Name Brand Distributors [1961–1963 Transfer Binder], Trade Reg. Rep. ¶16,653 (FTC 1963).

Norton Buick Co. v. *E. W. Tune Company*, 351 P. 2d 731 (Okla. 1960).

Norway v. *Root*, 361 P. 2d 162 (Wash. 1961).

Parker Pen Co. v. *FTC*, 159 F. 2d 509 (7th Cir. 1946).

Pati-Port, Inc. v. *FTC*, 313 F. 2d 103 (4th Cir. 1963).

Payne v. *Valley Motor Sales, Incorporated*, 124 S.E. 2d 622 (W. Va. 1962).

Perlmutter v. *Beth David Hospital*, 123 N.E. 2d 792 (N.Y. Ct. App. 1951).

Randy Knitwear, Inc. v. *American Cyanamid Company*, 181 N.E. 2d 399 (N.Y. Ct. App. 1962).

Ray v. *Deas*, 144 S.E. 2d 468 (Ga. Ct. App. 1965).

Recipe Foods, Inc., 51 FTC 873 (1955).

Recoton Corp. and G. Shirmer, Inc., 56 FTC 1028 (1960).

Robert H. Carr, Inc. v. *Yarsley*, 31 D & C 2d 262 (Chester Cty. Pa. 1963).

Rose v. *Chrysler Motors*, 28 Cal. Rptr. 185 (1963).

Sans & Streiffe, Inc. [1961–1963 Transfer Binder], Trade Reg. Rep. ¶15,724 (FTC 1962).

Santor v. *A. and M. Karagheusian*, 207 A. 2d 305 (N.J. 1964).

Schipper v. *Levitt & Sons, Inc.*, 207 A. 2d 314 (N.J. 1965).

Seely v. *White Motor Company*, 403 P. 2d 145 (Cal. 1965).

Sibert v. *FTC*, 367 F. 2d 364 (2d Cir. 1966).

Simpson v. *Powered Products of Mich., Inc.*, 192 A. 2d 555 (Conn. Common Pleas 1963).

State-Farm Mut. Auto Ins. Co. v. *Anderson-Weber, Inc.*, 110 N.W. 2d 449 (Iowa 1961).

Stauffer Laboratories, Inc. v. *FTC*, 343 F. 2d 75 (9th Cir. 1965).

Sutter v. *St. Clair Motors, Inc.*, 194 N.E. 2d 674 (Ill. App. 1963).

"Tab" and Technical Apparatus Builders, 55 FTC 1677 (1959).

Tri-State Distributing [1963–1965 Transfer Binder], Trade Reg. Rep. ¶16,430 (FTC 1963).

Towel Shop, 56 FTC 1049 (1960).

The United States Bedding Company, 55 FTC 1886 (1959).

Vandermark v. *Ford Motor Company*, 391 P. 2d 168 (Cal. 1964).

Webster v. *Blue Ship Tearoom, Inc.*, 198 N.E. 2d 309 (Mass. 1964).

Weiss v. *Saffell*, 313 P. 2d 390 (Ariz. 1957).

Wesco Products Co. [1963–1965 Transfer Binder], Trade Reg. Rep. ¶16,515 (FTC 1963).

Western Radio Corporation v. *FTC*, 399 F. 2d 937 (7th Cir. 1964).

Willman v. *American Motor Sales, Inc.*, 44 Erie A.G.J. 51 (Erie Cty. Ct. Pa. 1961).

Winterbottom v. *Wright*, 10 M & W 109, 152 Eng. Rep. 402 (1842).

World-Wide Television Corporation v. *FTC*, 352 F. 2d 303 (3d Cir. 1965).

Chapter 16: Business and Trade Status

BIBLIOGRAPHY

Advisory Opinion Digest No. 127 (FTC, May 26, 1967) ("embossed").

Advisory Opinion Digest No. 130 (FTC, June 13, 1967) ("national").

Callmann, *Unfair Competition, Trademarks, and Monopolies* (1968).

FTC Guide for Avoiding Deceptive Use of Word "Mill" in Textile Industry, 2 CCH Trade Reg. Rep. ¶7,905 (1965).

Handler, *Unfair Competition in the Federal Trade Commission*, 8 Geo. Wash. L. Rev. 399 (1939).

Stevens, *Unfair Competition* (1917).

Trade Practice Rule, Braided Rug Industry, 4 CCH Trade Reg. Rep. ¶41,071 (FTC 1964)

Trade Practice Rule, Engraved Stationery and Allied Products Industry of the New York City Trade Area, 4 CCH Trade Reg. Rep. ¶41,037 (FTC 1957).

Trade Practice Rule, Handkerchief Industry, 4 CCH Trade Reg. Rep. ¶41,181 (FTC 1949).

Trade Practice Rule, Jewelry Industry, 4 CCH Trade Reg. Rep. ¶41,023 (FTC 1957).

CASES

A. Berry Seed Company, 2 FTC 427 (1920).

Adam Hat Stores v. *Scherper*, 45 F. Supp. 804 (E.D. Wis. 1942).

Affiliated Brokers, Inc., 54 FTC 97 (1957).

Alexandra de Markoff Sales Corp., 30 FTC 1533, Stip. 2814 (1940).

Adolph Castor & Bros. v. *FTC*, 138 F. 2d 824 (2d Cir. 1943).

Altman Neckwear Corp., 33 FTC 17 (1941).

Ambassador East, Inc. v. *Orsatti*, 257 F. 2d 79 (3d Cir. 1958).

Ambassador East, Inc. v. *Shelton Corners, Inc.*, 120 F. Supp. 551 (S.D. N.Y. 1954).

American Bank Machinery Co., 23 FTC 714 (1936), *modified*, 27 FTC 1485 (1936).

American Field Seed Co., 27 FTC 583 (1938).

American Marketing Associates, 3 CCH Trade Reg. Rep. ¶18,182 (FTC 1968).

American Mushroom Industries, 25 FTC 1179 (1937).

American Music Guild, Inc. [1965–1967 Transfer Binder], Trade Reg. Rep. ¶17,288 (FTC 1965).

American Registry of Doctor's Nurses, 56 FTC 941 (1960).

American Steel Foundries v. *Robertson*, 269 U.S. 372 (1926).

Armour & Co., 1 FTC 430 (1919).

Artistic Tailoring Co., 28 FTC 1242 (1939).

Associated Perfumers v. *Andelman,* 55 N.E. 2d 209 (Mass. 1944).

Averbach Co., 29 FTC 879 (1939), *modified,* 39 FTC 306 (1944).

Aviation Institute of U.S.A., 15 FTC 249 (1931).

Bargain Barn, Inc. v. *Zipper,* 189 N.Y.S. 2d (1959).

Bear Mill Mfg. Co. v. *FTC,* 98 F. 2d 67 (2d Cir. 1938).

Bengué v. *American Pharmaceutical Co.,* 280 N.Y.S. 153 (1935).

Bennett v. *FTC,* 200 F. 2d 362 (D.C. Cir. 1952).

Benton Announcements, Inc. v. *FTC,* 130 F. 2d 254 (2d Cir. 1942).

Blackstone-Marshall Publishing Co., 32 FTC 1741, Stip. 3146 (1941).

Block v. *Standard Distilling & Distributing Co.,* 95 Fed. 978 (S.D. Ohio 1899).

Branch v. *FTC,* 141 F. 2d 31 (7th Cir. 1944).

Brondabrooke Publishers, Inc. [1963–1965 Transfer Binder], Trade Reg. Rep. ¶16,620 (FTC 1963).

Bronson Shoe Co., 21 FTC 384 (1935).

Brown Fence & Wire Co. v. *FTC,* 64 F. 2d 934 (6th Cir. 1933).

Browning King Co. of New York v. *Browning King Co.,* 176 F. 2d 105 (3d Cir. 1949).

Burrell Cutlery Co., 41 FTC 405, Stip. 4116 (1945).

Burtley Co., 33 FTC 455 (1941).

Business Opportunities Co., 53 FTC 119 (1956).

California Apparel Creators v. *Wieder of California,* 162 F. 2d 893 (2d Cir. 1947).

Carpet & Rug Mills, Inc. [1965–1967 Transfer Binder], Trade Reg. Rep. ¶17,785 (FTC 1966) (consent order).

Cheri, 14 FTC 416 (1931).

Cheshill Mfg. Co., 32 FTC 475 (1941).

Christmas Club, 25 FTC 1116 (1937).

Clark Thread Co. v. *Armitage,* 67 Fed. 896 (S.D. N.Y. 1895), *aff'd,* 74 F. 936 (2d Cir. 1896).

Colonial Academy, Inc., 57 FTC 1241 (1960).

Colman v. *Flavel,* 40 Fed. 854 (D.C. Ore. 1886).

Columbia Pants Mfg. Co., 13 FTC 61 (1929).

Conrad Schickerling Research Laboratory, 30 FTC 1105 (1940).

Consolidated Book Publishers v. *FTC,* 53 F. 2d 942 (7th Cir. 1931).

Consumers Products of America, Inc., 3 CCH Trade Reg. Rep. ¶18,059 (FTC 1967).

Consumers Union of United States v. *Lane,* 9 N.Y.S. 2d 873 (1939).

C. O. Taylor Distributing Company, 23 FTC 900 (1936).

Couristan, Inc., 57 FTC 794 (1960).

Dakota Seed & Grain Co. [1963–1965 Transfer Binder], Trade Reg. Rep. ¶ 17,096, *adopting,* ¶ 17,403 (FTC 1964).

David P. Barry Corp., 34 FTC 1595, Stip. 3335 (1941).

Deer v. *FTC,* 152 F. 2d 65 (2d Cir. 1945).

Delco Carpet Mills [1965–1967 Transfer Binder], Trade Reg. Rep. ¶17,804, *adopting,* ¶ 17,762 (FTC 1966).

DeNobili Cigar Co. v. *Nobile Cigar Co.,* 56 F. 2d 324 (1st Cir. 1932).

Distinctive Emblem & Uniform Corp., 53 FTC 744 (1957).

Dorothy Gray Salons v. *Mills Sales Co.,* 295 N.Y.S. 204 (1937).

Downes v. *Culbertson,* 275 N.Y.S. 233 (1934).

Dunshee v. *Standard Oil Co.,* 132 N.W. 371 (Iowa 1911).

E. D. Muller & Co., 33 FTC 24 (1941).

Educators Ass'n v. *FTC,* 108 F. 2d 470 (2d Cir. 1939).

Emerson Electric Mfg. Co. v. *Emerson Radio & Phonograph Corp.,* 105 F. 2d 908 (2d Cir. 1939).

Esquire, Inc. v. *Esquire Bar,* 37 F. Supp. 875 (S.D. Fla. 1941).

Etablissements Rigaud, Inc. v. *FTC,* 125 F. 2d 590 (2d Cir. 1942).

Family Wholesale Drug Plan, Inc., A.T.R.R. No. 279: A-14 (Nov. 15, 1966).

Federated Bureau of Installment Credit, 3 CCH Trade Reg. Rep. ¶18,061 (FTC 1967).

Federated Nationwide Wholesalers Service, 3 CCH Trade Reg. Rep. ¶17,995 FTC 1967).

Fidelity Bond & Mortgage Co. v. *Fidelity Mortgage Co.,* 12 F. 2d 582 (6th Cir. 1926).

Fioret Sales Co. v. *FTC,* 100 F. 2d 358 (2d Cir. 1938).

Fleischmann Co., 1 FTC 119 (1918).

Flora v. *Flora Shirt Co.,* 283 Pac. 1013 (Okla. 1930).

Folding Furniture Works, 34 FTC 921 (1942).

Ford Motor Co. v. *Helms,* 25 F. Supp. 698 (E.D. N.Y. 1938).

Ford Motor Co. v. *Wilson,* 223 Fed. 808 (D.C. R.I. 1915).

FTC v. *Army & Navy Trading Co.,* 88 F. 2d 776 (D.C. Cir. 1937).

FTC v. *Cassoff,* 38 F. 2d 790 (2d Cir. 1930).

FTC v. *Civil Service Training Bureau,* 79 F. 2d 113 (6th Cir. 1935).

FTC v. *Good-Grape Co.,* 45 F. 2d 70 (6th Cir. 1930).

FTC v. *Maisel Trading Post,* 77 F. 2d 246, *modified and aff'd,* 79 F. 2d 127, *opinion modified,* 84 F. 2d 768 (10th Cir. 1936).

FTC v. *Midwest Mills,* 90 F. 2d 723 (7th Cir. 1937).

FTC v. *Pure Silk Hosiery Mills,* 3 F. 2d 105 (7th Cir. 1925).

FTC v. *Real Products Corp.,* 90 F. 2d 617 (2d Cir. 1937).

FTC v. *Royal Milling Co.,* 288 U.S. 212 (1933).

Gallant Trading Co., 36 FTC 470 (1943).

Gelfo Mfg. Co., 50 FTC 1159, Stip. 8526 (1954).

G. H. Bass & Co., 57 FTC 1567, Stip. 9368 (1960).

Globe Tool & Eng. Co., 19 FTC 554, Stip. 1265 (1934).

Bouchman v. *Strauch,* 91 N.Y.S. 223 (1904).

Goldtone Studios v. *FTC,* 183 F. 2d 257 (2d Cir. 1950).

Goodman v. *FTC,* 244 F. 2d 584 (9th Cir. 1957).

Gotham Sales Co., 21 FTC 457 (1935).

Greening Nursery Co., 36 FTC 273 (1943).

Guarantee Veterinary Co. v. *FTC,* 285 Fed. 853 (2d Cir. 1922).

Haglett v. *Pollack Stogey Co.,* 188 Fed. 494 (W.D. Pa.), *aff'd,* 195 Fed. 28 (3d Cir. 1912).

Hair & Scalp Clinic, Inc., 50 FTC 721 (1954).

Hall Gentry Studios, 31 FTC 1610, Stip. 2834 (1940).

Hanson v. *Triangle Publications,* 163 F. 2d 74 (8th Cir. 1947).

Harper Mfg. Co., 33 FTC 1610 (1941).

Helbrose Watch Co. v. *FTC,* 310 F. 2d 868 (D.C. Cir. 1962).

Herzfeld v. *FTC,* 140 F. 2d 207 (2d Cir. 1944).

Hiram Carter, Inc., 34 FTC 514 (1942).

Holland Furnace Co. v. *FTC,* 295 F. 2d 302 (7th Cir. 1961).

Holzappel's Compositions Co. v. *Rahtjen's American Composition Co.,* 183 U.S. 1 (1901).

Horlick's Malted Milk Corp. v. *Horlick,* 50 F. Supp. 417 (E.D. Wis. 1943).

Howard E. Jones & Co., 31 FTC 1538 (1940).

H. Pettus Randall, 41 FTC 393, Stip. 4097 (1945).

Hunt Potato Chip Co. v. *Hunt,* 164 N.E. 2d 335 (Mass. 1960).

Hygenic Fleeced Underwear Co. v. *Way,* 137 Fed. 592 (3d Cir. 1905).

Industrial Heat Systems, 58 FTC 1231, Stip. 9433 (1961).

In Re Floersheim, 316 F. 2d 423 (9th Cir. 1963).

Institute of Hydraulic Jack Repair [1963–1965 Transfer Binder], Trade Reg. Rep. ¶16,499 (FTC 1963).

International Silver Co. v. *Oneida Community Limited,* 73 F. 2d 69 (2d Cir. 1934).

Jacob Seigel Co. v. *FTC,* 150 F. 2d 751 (3d Cir. 1944), 327 U.S. 608 (1946).

Jennings v. *Johnson,* 34 Fed. 364 (D.C. Me. 1888).

J. J. Berliner & Staff, 55 FTC 154 (1958).

Josten Mfg. Co., 36 FTC 307 (1943).

Julius C. Schwartz, 41 FTC 120 (1945).

Kaumagraph Co., 20 FTC 1 (1934).

Keith M. Merik Co., 57 FTC 1255 (1960).

Kennerley v. *Simonds,* 247 Fed. 822 (S.D. N.Y. 1917).

Kidd v. *Johnson,* 100 U.S. 617 (1888).

Korber Hats, Inc. v. *FTC,* 1963 Trade Cases. ¶70,597 (1st Cir. 1962).

Lakeland Nursery Sales Corp. [1965–1967 Transfer Binder], Trade Reg. Rep. ¶17,362 (FTC, 1965).

Lane v. *FTC,* 130 F. 2d 48 (9th Cir. 1942).

LaSalle Extension University, 50 FTC 1083 (1954).

L. & C. Mayers Co. v. *FTC,* 97 F. 2d 365 (2d Cir. 1938).

Leonard Custom Tailors Co., 36 FTC 105 (1943).

Lifetime, Inc., 59 FTC 1231 (1961).

Lighthouse Rug Co. v. *FTC,* 35 F. 2d 163 (7th Cir. 1929).

Lincoln Chair & Novelty Co., 33 FTC 693 (1941).

Lower Main Street Merchants Ass'n v. *Paul Geller & Co.,* 171 A. 2d 21 (N.J. 1961).

Macher v. *FTC,* 126 F. 2d 420 (2d Cir. 1942).

Maisel Trading Post, 18 FTC 30 (1933).

Mantle Lamp Co. of America v. *Aladdin Mfg. Co.,* 78 F. 2d 426 (7th Cir. 1935).

Marlin Fire Arms Co., 29 FTC 130 (1939).

Master Artists Ass'n, 36 FTC 365 (1943).

Mennen Co. v. *FTC,* 288 Fed. 774 (2d Cir. 1923).

Melwood Distilling Co. v. *Harper,* 167 Fed. 389 (W.D. Ark. 1908).

M. Lober & Associates Co., 59 FTC 375 (1961).

Morris White Mfg. Co., 28 FTC 333 (1939).

National Blind Industries, Inc., 50 FTC 372 (1953).

National Drug Plan, Inc., 59 FTC 170 (1961).

National Laboratories of St. Louis [1963–1965 Transfer Binder], Trade Reg. Rep. ¶16,608 (FTC 1963).

National Research Corp. [1963–1965 Transfer Binder], Trade Reg. Rep. ¶17,108 (FTC 1964).

Nebraska Seed & Grain Co. [1963–1965 Transfer Binder], Trade Reg. Rep. ¶16,808 (FTC 1964).

N. Fluegelman & Co. v. FTC, 37 F. 2d 59 (2d Cir. 1930).

Northwest Film Ad Service, Inc., 36 FTC 207 (1943).

N.Y. World's Fair v. World's Fair News, 297 N.Y.S. 923 (1937).

Olan Mills Portrait Studios, 37 FTC 732, Stip. 3740 (1943).

Pan American Cigar Co., 3 CCH Trade Reg. Rep. ¶18,045 (1967).

Parke, Austin & Lipscomb v. FTC, 142 F. 2d 437 (2d Cir. 1944).

Pennsylvania Whiskey Distributing Co., 26 FTC 97 (1937).

Perfection Mfg. Co. v. B. Coleman Silver's Co., 270 Fed. 576 (7th Cir. 1921).

Peterson Core Oil & Mfg. Co., 32 FTC 1152 (1941).

Philip Morris & Co., 32 FTC 278 (1940).

Platell Shoe Co., 22 FTC 695 (1936).

Plattner Distributing Co., 39 FTC 239 (1944).

Pioneer Mattress Co., 33 FTC 583 (1941).

Pioneer Merchandise Co., 34 FTC 302 (1941).

Pioneer Paper Co., 7 FTC 316, *et seq.* (1924).

Post Graduate Hospital School of Nursing, Inc., 53 FTC 432 (1956).

Post Graduate School of Nursing [1963–1965 Transfer Binder], Trade Reg. Rep. ¶16,911, *dismissing,* ¶16,781 (FTC 1964).

Pratt Furniture Co., 58 FTC 1123 (1961).

Preservaline Mfg. Co. v. Heller Chemical Co., 118 Fed. 103 (N.D. Ill. 1902).

Primsit Textile Co., 31 FTC 1423 (1940).

Professional Reminder Service, 48 FTC 753 (1952).

Progress Tailoring Co. v. FTC, 153 F. 2d 103 (7th Cir. 1946).

Providence Import Co., 58 FTC 89 (1961).

Regency Thermographers, 52 FTC 1703, Stip. 8653 (1955).

Reho Rubber Co., 34 FTC 457 (1941).

Reid v. St. John, 229 Pac. 863 (D.C. App. Cal. 1924).

Robert H. Cristman, 43 FTC 787, Stip. 7577 (1947).

Rudin & Roth, 53 FTC 207 (1956).

Rugs of the Blind, Inc., 50 FTC 117 (1953).

Safeway Stores v. Sklar, 75 F. Supp. 98 (E.D. Pa. 1947).

Sally's Furs, Inc., 36 FTC 325 (1943).

Seaboard Chemical Co., 35 FTC 871, Stip. 3558 (1943).

Sidney J. Kreiss, Inc., 56 FTC 1421 (1960).

Singer Mfg. Co. v. June Mfg. Co., 163 U.S. 169 (1896).

Société Comptoir de L'Industrie Cotonnière, Etablissements Boussac v. Alexander's Dept Stores, 109 F. Supp. 594 (S.D. N.Y. 1961), *aff'd,* 299 F. 2d 33 (2d Cir. 1962).

Southern Pacific Salvage Co. [1965–1967 Transfer Binder], Trade Reg. Rep. ¶17,438 (FTC 1966).

Standard Mills, Inc. [1963–1965 Transfer Binder], Trade Reg. Rep. ¶ 16,607 (FTC 1963).

Standard Oil Co. of New Mexico v. *Standard Oil Co. of Cal.,* 56 F. 2d 973 (10th Cir. 1932).

Stanley Laboratories v. *FTC,* 138 F. 2d 388 (9th Cir. 1943).

St. Louis Lightning Rod Co., 3 FTC 327 (1921).

Stipulation No. 28, 8 FTC 573 (1925).

Stipulation No. 562, 13 FTC 470 (1930).

Stork Restaurant v. *Sahati,* 166 F. 2d 348 (9th Cir. 1948).

Son-Bath Textiles, Inc., 58 FTC 285 (1961).

Sun Valley Air College, Inc., 55 FTC 1596 (1959).

Sure-Fit Seat Cover Center, 60 FTC 930 (1962).

Surf Club v. *Tatum Surf Club,* 10 F. 2d 554 (Fla. 1942).

Thayer Pharmacal Co., 18 FTC 219 (1934).

Theophilus J. Craig, 36 FTC 90 (1943).

Travelodge Corp. v. *Siragusa,* 228 F. Supp. 238 (N.D. Ala. 1964).

Union Pencil Co., 59 FTC 1092 (1961).

United Silk Co., 23 FTC 368 (1936).

U.S. Ass'n of Credit Bureaus v. *FTC,* 299 F. 2d 220 (7th Cir. 1962).

U.S. Business Card Co., 30 FTC 1340 (1940).

U.S. v. *Hindman,* 179 F. Supp. 926 (D. N.J. 1960).

United States Navy Weekly v. *FTC,* 207 F. 2d 17 (D.C. Cir. 1953).

U.S. Retail Credit Ass'n, 57 FTC 1510 (1960).

U.S. Retail Credit Ass'n v. *FTC,* 300 F. 2d 212 (4th Cir. 1962).

Virginia Dare Stores Corp. [1963–1965 Transfer Binder], Trade Reg. Rep. ¶ 16,823 (FTC 1964).

Volkswagenwerk v. *Frank,* 198 F. Supp. 916 (D. Colo. 1961).

Wallach Bros. v. *Wallack,* 192 N.Y.S. 723 (Sup. Ct. 1922).

Walter Kidde & Co., 36 FTC 431 (1943).

Waltham Watch Co. v. *FTC,* 318 F. 2d 28 (7th Cir. 1963).

West Coast Claim Adjusters [1965–1967 Transfer Binder], Trade Reg. Rep. ¶ 17,258 (FTC 1965) (consent order).

Western European Import Co., 59 FTC 504 (1961).

Westville Refinery, Inc., 36 FTC 402 (1943).

World's Star-Malloch, Inc., 36 FTC 76 (1943).

Yale & Towne Mfg. Co. v. *Haber,* 7 F. Supp. 791 (E.D. N.Y. 1934).

Chapter 17: Disparagement and Comparisons

BIBLIOGRAPHY

Black, *The Bill of Rights,* 35 N.Y.U. L. Rev. 882 (1960).

Comment, *The Law of Commercial Disparagement: Business Defamation's Impotent Ally,* 63 Yale L. J. 65 (1953).

Restatement (Second) of Torts §§626–628, 633, 647, 649 (1960).

The Uniform Deceptive Practices Act, §2(a)(8), 54 Trademark Reporter 897, 901 (1964).

CASES

Admiral Corp. v. *Price Vacuum Stores, Inc.,* 141 F. Supp. 796 (E.D. Pa. 1956).

Advance Music Corp. v. *American Tobacco Co.,* 290 N.Y. 79 (1946).

Bakers Franchise Corp. v. *FTC,* 302 F. 2d 258 (3d Cir. 1962).

Black & Yates, Inc. v. *Mahogony Ass'n, Inc.,* 129 F. 2d 227 (3d Cir. 1942).

Bostwick Laboratories, 49 FTC 1244 (1953).

Burnet v. *Wells,* 12 Mod. 420.

Carter v. *Knapp Motor Co.,* 11 So. 2d 383 (Ala. 1943).

Columbia Appliance Corp., 45 FTC 379 (1948).

Davis Electronics Co. v. *Channel Master Corp.,* 116 F. Supp. 919 (S.D. N.Y. 1953).

Drug Research Corp. v. *Curtis Publishing Co.,* 7 N.Y. 2d 435 (Sup. Ct. 1960).

Electrolux Corp. v. *Val-Worth, Inc.,* 190 N.Y.S. 2d 977 (1959).

Emack v. *Kane,* 34 Fed. 46 (N.D. Ill. 1888).

Eugene Agee, 48 FTC 820 (1952).

FTC v. *Gordon-Van Tine Co.,* 1 FTC 316 (1919).

FTC v. *Sterling Drug, Inc.,* 317 F. 2d 669 (2d Cir. 1963).

FTC v. *U.S. Products Co.,* 7 FTC 301 (1924).

Fowler v. *Curtis Publishing,* 182 F. 2d 377 (D.C. Cir. 1950).

Frawley Chemical Corp. v. *A. P. Larson Co., Inc.,* 86 N.Y.S. 2d 710 (1949).

Greyhound Securities, Inc. v. *Greyhound Corp.,* 207 N.Y.S. 2d 383 (1960).

Harwood Pharmacal Co., Inc. v. *National Broadcasting Co., Inc.,* 9 N.Y. 2d 460 (Sup. Ct. 1961).

Hopkins C. Co. v. *Read Drug & C. Co.,* 124 Md. 210 (1914).

Houston Chronicle Pub. Co. v. *Martin,* 64 S.W. 2d 816 (Tex. Civ. App. 1933).

International Parts Corp. v. *FTC,* 133 F. 2d 883 (7th Cir. 1943).

L'Aiglon Apparel, Inc. v. *Lana Lobell, Inc.,* 214 F. 2d 649 (3d Cir. 1954).

Larson v. *Brooklyn Daily-Eagle,* 150 N.Y.S. 464 (1914).

Liggett & Myers Tobacco Co., 55 FTC 354 (1958).

Marlin Firearms Co. v. *Shields,* 171 N.Y. 384 (1902).

Maytag Co. v. *Meadows Mfg. Co.,* 35 F. 2d 403 (7th Cir. 1929), *cert. denied,* 281 U.S. 737 (1930).

McMorries v. *Hudson Sales Corp.,* 233 S.W. 2d 938 (Tex. Civ. App. 1950).

Menard v. *Houle,* 298 Mass. 546 (1937).

Moretrench Corp. v. *FTC,* 127 F. 2d 792 (2d Cir. 1942).

National Bakers Services, Inc. v. *FTC,* 329 F. 2d 365 (7th Cir. 1964).

National Refining Co. v. *Benzo Gas Motor Fuel Co.,* 20 F. 2d 763 (8th Cir. 1927), *cert. denied,* 275 U.S. 570 (1927).

P. Lorillard Co. v. *FTC,* 186 F. 2d 52 (4th Cir. 1950).

Paramount Pictures, Inc. v. *Leader Press, Inc.,* 106 F. 2d 229 (10th Cir. 1939).

Pendleton v. *Time, Inc.,* 339 Ill. App. 188 (1949).

Perma-Maid Co. v. *FTC,* 121 F. 2d 282 (6th Cir. 1941).

Philip Carey Mfg. Co. v. *FTC,* 29 F. 2d 49 (6th Cir. 1928).

Quinby & Co. v. *Funston,* 177 N.Y.S. 2d 736 (1958).

R. J. Reynolds Tobacco Co. v. *FTC,* 192 F. 2d 535 (7th Cir. 1951).

Rosenberg v. *J. C. Penney Co.,* 30 Cal. App. 2d 609 (1939).

Royer v. *Stoody Co.,* 192 F. Supp. 949 (W.D. Okla. 1961).

Scientific Mfg. Co., Inc. v. *FTC,* 124 F. 2d 640 (3d Cir. 1941).

Shevers Ice Cream Co. v. *Polar Products Co.,* 194 N.Y.S. 44 (1921).

Steelco Stainless Steel Co. v. *FTC*, 187 F. 2d 693 (7th Cir. 1951).

Tounecraft Industries, 55 FTC 225 (1958).

Valentine v. *Chrestensen,* 316 U.S. 52 (1942).

Chapter 18: Business, Employment, and Sales Schemes

CASES

Accurate Style Mfg. Co. [1957–1958 Transfer Binder], Trade Reg. Rep. ¶ 17,289 (FTC 1958) (consent order).

Allied Specialties, Inc., 32 FTC 1544 (1941).

Atlantic Jet Training, Inc. [1961–1963 Transfer Binder], Trade Reg. Rep. ¶ 15,362 (FTC 1961) (consent order).

Blackstone College of Law, 50 FTC 1070 (1954).

Capitol Service, Inc. [1954–1955 Transfer Binder], Trade Reg. Rep. ¶ 25,167 (FTC 1954).

Cinderella Career College and Finishing School, 3 CCH Trade Reg. Rep. ¶ 18,576 (FTC 1968).

Commercial Mfg. Co., 22 FTC 373 (1936).

Coronado Mfg. Co., 28 FTC 1400 (1939).

Dean Ross Piano Studios [1954–1955 Transfer Binder], Trade Reg. Rep. ¶ 25,485 (FTC 1955) (consent order).

De Forest's Training, Inc. v. *FTC,* 134 F. 2d 819 (7th Cir. 1943).

Elite Publishing Co., 28 FTC 1680 (1939).

Exposition Press, Inc. v. *FTC,* 295 F. 2d 869 (2d Cir. 1961).

Fred Astaire Dance Studios Corp. [1963–1965 Transfer Binder], Trade Reg. Rep. ¶ 16,829 (FTC 1964).

Hobart Steel Co., 60 FTC 459 (1962) (consent order).

Inter-Communication System of America, Inc., 45 FTC 361 (1948).

International Motels, Inc. [1956–1957 Transfer Binder], Trade Reg. Rep. ¶ 25,963 (FTC 1956) (consent order).

Invisible Reweaving Institute [1956–1957 Transfer Binder], Trade Reg. Rep. ¶ 26,292 (FTC 1956) (consent order).

Joseph G. Branch Institute of Engineering & Science, 36 FTC 1 (1943), *aff'd,* 141 F. 2d 31 (7th Cir. 1944).

Marcel Co., 59 FTC 1182 (1961).

Mid-Continent Training Service, 59 FTC 1312 (1961) (consent order).

Motor Equipment Specialty Co., 28 FTC 1341 (1939).

National Laboratories of St. Louis [1963–1965 Transfer Binder], Trade Reg. Rep. ¶ 16,608 (FTC 1963).

North Central Training Service, 59 FTC 220 (1961).

Parker Bouldin Co., 38 FTC 763 (1944) (Stipulation).

P. Lorillard Co. v. *FTC,* 186 F. 2d 52 (7th Cir. 1950).

Rushing v. *FTC,* 320 F. 2d 280 (5th Cir. 1963).

Sure Laboratories, 34 FTC 563 (1942).

Von Schrader Mfg. Co., 33 FTC 58 (1941).

Ward Laboratories, Inc. v. *FTC,* 276 F. 2d 952 (2d Cir. 1960).

Chapter 19: Deceptive Credit Practices

BIBLIOGRAPHY

Address, Sheldon Feldman, Chief, Division of Consumer Credit, Federal Trade Commission, May 26, 1969.

Consumer Credit Protection Act, 15 U.S.C. §1601.

Fair Credit Reporting Act, 115 Cong. Rec., S. 13905 (Remarks of Senator Proxmire, 1969).

Fair Credit Reporting Act, S. Rep. No. 91–517, 91st Cong., 1st Sess. S. 823 (1969).

Federal Reserve Board Regulation Z, 12 C.F.R. §226.

FTC Release, October 3, 1969.

FTC Release, October 13, 1969.

Kintner, Henneberger, & Neill, *A Primer on Truth in Lending*, 13 St. Louis Univ. L. J. 501 (1969).

Uniform Consumer Credit Code.

Willier & Hart, *Consumer Credit Handbook* (1969).

CASES

Business & Professional, Inc., 63 FTC 234 (1963).

Family Publications Service, Inc., 63 FTC 971 (1963).

Mohr v. *FTC*, 1959 Trade Cases ¶ 69,528 (9th Cir. 1959).

Silverman v. *FTC*, 1944–45 Trade Cases ¶ 57,300 (9th Cir. 1944).

United States Ass'n. of Credit Bureaus, Inc. v. *FTC*, 1962 Trade Cases ¶ 70,230 (7th Cir. 1962).

Chapter 20: Deceptive Pictorial and Television Advertising

BIBLIOGRAPHY

Comment, *Advertising—Undisclosed Use of Simulations in Television Commercials—a Deceptive Practice*, 18 Vand. L. Rev. 2008 (1965).

Note, *A New Antitoxin to Advertising Artifice—Television Advertising and the Federal Trade Commission*, 37 Notre Dame Lawyer 524 (1962).

Note, *Illusion or Deception: The Use of "Props" and "Mock-Ups" in Television Advertising*, 72 Yale L. J. 145 (1962).

Note, *Rapid Shave in the First Circuit Court of Appeals—Television Advertising and the Federal Trade Commission (Part II)*, 38 Notre Dame Lawyer 350 (1963).

Note, *Trade Regulation—Use of Undisclosed Mock-Up in Television Commercial Demonstration Held to be Deceptive Practice in Violation of Federal Trade Commission Act*, 34 Fordham L. Rev. 362 (1965).

CASES

In Re Abe Sandhaus, 45 FTC 856, Stip. 7750 (1949).

In Re Adell Chemical Co., Inc., 54 FTC 1801 (1958).

Algoma Lumber Co. v. *FTC*, 291 U.S. 67 (1934).

In Re Aluminum Co. of America, 58 FTC 265 (1961).

In Re American Chicle Co., 54 FTC 1625 (1958).

In Re AMT Corp., FTC Dkt. C-633 (December 24, 1963).

In Re Becker Clock Co., Inc., 31 FTC 1520 (1940).

In Re Bloom Brothers Co., 23 FTC 1157, Stip. 1862 (1936).

In Re Brown & Williamson Tobacco Corp., 56 FTC 956 (1960).

In Re Canadian Fur Trappers Corp., 31 FTC 859 (1940).

Carter Products, Inc. v. *FTC,* 323 F. 2d 523 (5th Cir. 1963).

In Re Colgate-Palmolive Co., 58 FTC 422 (1961) (Colgate Tooth Paste).

Colgate-Palmolive Co. v. *FTC,* 380 U.S. 374 (1965).

In Re Concrete Materials Corp., 46 FTC 152 (1949).

Concrete Materials Corp. v. *FTC,* 189 F. 2d 359 (7th Cir. 1951).

In Re Crystex of Florida, Inc., 29 FTC 1462, Stip. 2529 (1939).

In Re Edwin Cigar Co., 32 FTC 1596 (1941).

Erickson v. *FTC,* 272 F. 2d 318 (7th Cir. 1959).

In Re Eversharp, Inc., 57 FTC 841 (1960).

In Re Frank & Meyer Neckwear Co., 39 FTC 573 (1944).

In Re Garden Research Laboratories, 50 FTC 424 (1953).

In Re Halsam Products Co., FTC Dkt. C-690 (January 21, 1964).

In Re Harold Greenberg, 59 FTC 1071 (1961).

In Re Hiram Carter, Inc., 34 FTC 514 (1942).

In Re Hutchinson Chemical Corp., 55 FTC 1942 (1959).

In Re Ideal Toy Corp., FTC Dkt. 8530 (January 20, 1964).

In Re Interwoven Stocking Co., 31 FTC 1062 (1940).

In Re Isidore Gendelmen, 43 FTC 320 (1947).

In Re Johnson Smith & Co., 36 FTC 245 (1943).

Keele Hair & Scalp Specialists, Inc. v. *FTC,* 275 F. 2d 18 (5th Cir. 1960).

In Re Koret, Inc., 41 FTC 340 (1945).

In Re L. Hoffman, 27 FTC 1499, Stip. 2227 (1938).

In Re Lanolin Plus, Inc., 54 FTC 446 (1957).

In Re Lever Brothers Co., 61 FTC 1013 (1962).

Libby-Owens-Ford Glass Co. v. *FTC,* 352 F. 2d 415 (6th Cir. 1965).

In Re Lucky Products, Inc., FTC Dkt. C-608 (October 16, 1963).

In Re M. L. Fernandez & Brothers, 34 FTC 1579, Stip. 3311 (1941).

In Re Max Factor & Co., 55 FTC 1328 (1959).

In Re The Mennen Co., 58 FTC 676 (1961).

In Re New York Handkerchief Mfg. Co., 35 FTC 721 (1942).

Ostermoor & Co., Inc. v. *FTC,* 16 F. 2d 962 (2d Cir. 1927).

In Re Progress Tailoring Co., 37 FTC 277 (1943).

In Re R. H. Macy & Co., 27 FTC 1508, Stip. 2244 (1938).

In Re Ralph Dweck, 47 FTC 1048 (1951).

In Re Rapaport Bros., Inc., 53 FTC 1322, Stip. 8832 (1956).

In Re Rochester Acoustical Lab, Inc., 50 FTC 1138, Stip. 8487 (1953).

In Re Runsafe Sales Co., 24 FTC 1455, Stip. 1967 (1937).

In Re Samuel Smith, 43 FTC 447 (1947).

In Re Stamp & Album Co. of America, 50 FTC 1137, Stip. 8484 (1953).

In Re Standard Brands, Inc., 56 FTC 1491 (1960).

In Re Steel Storage File Co., 32 FTC 1680, Stip. 3038 (1941).

In Re United States Association of Credit Bureaus, Inc., 58 FTC 1044 (1961).

In Re Willys-Overland Motors, Inc., 27 FTC 498 (1938).
In Re Winston Sales Co., Inc., FTC Dkt. 8531 (November 22, 1963).
In Re Yale Engineering Co., 56 FTC 1745, Stip. 9305 (1960).
In Re Zlotnick, the Furrier, Inc., 48 FTC 1068 (1952).
In Re 2361 State Corp., FTC Dkt. C-735 (April 21, 1964).

Chapter 21: Special Labeling Legislation

BIBLIOGRAPHY

Advisory Opinion Digest, No. 148 (FTC Nov. 7, 1967).

Fair Packaging and Labeling Act, 15 U.S.C. §1453.

Fair Packaging and Labeling Act, H.R. Rep. No. 449, 89th Cong., 2d Sess., H.R. 3014 (1965).

Federal Cigarette Labeling and Advertising Act, 15 U.S.C. §1331.

Federal Hazardous Substances Labeling Act, 15 U.S.C. §1261.

Federal Hazardous Substances Labeling Act, H.R. Rep. No. 1861, 86th Cong., 2d Sess., S. 1283 (1960).

FTC Issues Revision of Rule Designed to Prevent Misbranding of Wool Imports, 338 Antitrust and Trade Reg. Rep. A-9 (1968).

FTC is Temporarily Enjoined from Enforcing New Imported-Wool-Labeling Rule, 345 Antitrust and Trade Reg. Rep. A-5 (1968).

FTC Release, July 24, 1953.

FTC Release, August 26, 1941.

FTC Release, September 2, 1941.

FTC Release, September 9, 1958.

Flammable Fabrics Act, 15 U.S.C. §1191.

Flammable Fabrics Act, S. Rep. No. 400, 83d Cong., 1st Sess., H.R. 5069 (1953).

Fur Products Labeling Act, 15 U.S.C. §69.

Government Files First Civil Penalty Suit Involving Fabrics-Act Order, 265 Antitrust Trade Reg. Rep. A-10 (1966).

Illustration of Certain Forms of Acceptable Tags or Labels Under the Wool Products Labeling Act and the Rules and Regulations as Amended and Issued by the Commission Thereunder (FTC August 1, 1949).

Regulations for the Enforcement of the Federal Food, Drug & Cosmetic Act and the Fair Packaging and Labeling Act, 21 C.F.R. §1.

Rules and Regulations under Flammable Fabrics Act, 16 C.F.R. §302.

Rules and Regulations under Fur Products Labeling Act, 16 C.F.R. §301.

Rules and Regulations under the Textile Fiber Products Identification Act, 16 C.F.R. §303.

Rules and Regulations under the Wool Products Labeling Act of 1939, 16 C.F.R. §300.

Textile Fiber Products Identification Act, 15 U.S.C. §70.

Textile Fiber Products Identification Act, S. Rep. No. 1658, 85th Cong., 2d Sess., H.R. 469 (1959).

Wool Products Labeling Act of 1939, 15 U.S.C. §68.

Women's Wear Daily, September 13, 1968, pp. 34–35.

Women's Wear Daily, September 15, 1968, p. 68.

CASES

Alscap, Inc., 60 FTC 275 (1962).

Benton Furs, 54 FTC 203 (1957).

Courtaulds (Alabama) Inc. v. *Dixon,* 294 F. 2d 899 (D.C. Cir. 1961).

David D. Doniger & Co., 43 FTC 432 (1947).

Diamond Debs, Inc., 58 FTC 1209, Stip. 9373 (1961).

Elliott Knitwear, 59 FTC 893 (1961).

Europe Craft Imports, Inc., 58 FTC 599 (1961).

FTC v. *Mandel Brothers, Inc.,* 358 U.S. 812 (1959).

Fiber Enterprises, Inc., 56 FTC 1360 (1960).

G. Sherman Corporation, 56 FTC 783 (1960).

Gorodetzer & Stillman, Inc. v. *Hunter Mills Corp.,* 1962 Trade Cases ¶ 70,430 (N.Y. App. Div. 1962).

Hoving Corp., 57 FTC 690 (1960).

Last Wool Stock Corporation, 58 FTC 487 (1961).

Madame E, 59 FTC 383 (1961).

Marcus v. *FTC,* 354 F. 2d 85 (2d Cir. 1965).

Merrimack Textile Fibres, Inc., 59 FTC 432 (1961).

Mortons, Inc., 58 FTC 704 (1961).

Nichols & Co., Inc., 58 FTC 113 (1961).

Novick & Co., Inc. [1961–1963 Transfer Binder], Trade Reg. Rep. ¶ 16,298 (FTC 1963).

Pelta Furs, 52 FTC 1307 (1956).

Susquehanna Woolen Mills, 39 FTC 574 (1943).

Target Sportswear, Inc., 54 FTC 1454 (1957).

Textile & Apparel Group, American Importers Ass'n v. *FTC,* 1969 Trade Cases ¶ 72,753 (D.C. Cir. 1969).

Textron, Inc., 59 FTC 1008 (1961).

The Fair v. *FTC,* 1959 Trade Cases ¶ 69,548 (7th Cir. 1959).

United Felt Co., 56 FTC 412 (1959).

Chapter 22: Food, Drugs, Cosmetics, and Devices

BIBLIOGRAPHY

Advisory Opinion Digest, No. 102 (FTC Nov. 11, 1966).

Note, *Drug Amendments of 1962,* 38 N.Y.U. L. Rev. 1082 (1963).

FDA Release No. 67-58, May 10, 1967 (thiazide-potassium chloride).

FDA Release No. 67-88, July 28, 1967 (Golden Grain Macaroni Co.).

Food and Drug Administration, Proposal, August 17, 1963 [1963–1967 Transfer Binder], F. D. Cosm. L. Rep. ¶ 80,037 (FDA 1963).

Food and Drug Administration, *Report on Enforcement and Compliance,* October, 1963 [1963–1967 Transfer Binder], F. D. Cosm. L. Rep. ¶ 40,069 (FDA 1963).

Address by James L. Goddard, Commissioner of Food and Drugs, February 8, 1967 [1963–1967 Transfer Binder], F. D. Cosm. L. Rep. ¶ 80,161 (FDA 1967).

Goddard, *Guidelines,* 28 FDC Reports No. 22, May 30, 1966 (FDA).

Goodrich, *A Look into the Nooks and Corners of the Kefauver-Harris Drug Amendments of 1962,* 19 The Business Lawyer 187 (1963).

Goodrich, 1967 Food, Drug and Cosmetic L. J., 46.

Statement of William W. Goodrich, Asst. General Counsel for Food and Drugs [1963–1967 Transfer Binder], F. D. Cosm. L. Rep. ¶ 60,079 (FDA 1964).

HEW Release, HEW-A97, April 30, 1964 (Helene Curtis).

H. R. Rep. No. 1613, 75 Cong., 1st. Sess. S. 1077 (1937).

H. R. Rep. No. 1731, 81 Cong., 2d Sess. (1950).

Remarks of Senator Lea, 83 Cong. Rec. 410 (1938).

Editorial, *Wall Street Journal,* Dec. 29, 1967, p. 6.

CASES

Abbott Laboratories v. *Celebrezze,* 352 F. 2d 286 (3d Cir. 1965).

American Home Products [1963–1965 Transfer Binder], Trade Reg. Rep. ¶ 16,606 (FTC 1963).

Bakers Franchise Corp. v. *FTC,* 302 F. 2d 258 (3d Cir. 1962).

Bristol-Myers, 3 CCH Trade Reg. Rep. ¶ 18,109 (FTC 1967).

Charles of the Ritz Dist. Corp. v. *FTC,* 143 F. 2d 676 (2d Cir. 1944).

Coffee-Rich, Inc. v. *McDowell* [1963–1967 Transfer Binder], F. D. Cosm. L. Rep. ¶ 40,047 (Wis. 1963).

Coffee-Rich, Inc. v. *Michigan Dept. of Agriculture,* 135 N.W. 2d 594 (Mich. Ct App. 1965).

E. F. Drew & Co., Inc. v. *FTC,* 235 F. 2d 735 (2d Cir. 1956).

FTC v. *Raladam Co.,* 283 U.S. 643 (1931).

FTC v. *Sterling Drug, Inc.,* 317 F. 2d 669 (2d Cir. 1963).

Fresh Grown Preserve Corp. v. *FTC,* 125 F. 2d 917 (2d Cir. 1942).

Grove Laboratories, Inc., 3 CCH Trade Reg. Rep. ¶ 17,985 (FTC 1967).

Houbigant, Inc. v. *FTC,* 139 F. 2d 1019 (2d Cir.), *cert. denied,* 323 U.S. 763 (1944).

J. B. Williams Company v. *FTC,* 381 F. 2d 884 (6th Cir. 1967).

Keele Hair & Scalp Specialists, Inc. v. *FTC,* 275 F 2d 18 (5th Cir. 1960).

Kordel v. *U.S.,* 335 U.S. 345 (1948).

Max Factor & Co., 55 FTC 1328 (1959).

Mueller v. *U.S.,* 262 F. 2d 443 (5th Cir. 1958).

National Bakers Services, Inc. v. *FTC,* 329 F. 2d 365 (7th Cir. 1964).

Reddi-Spred Corporation v. *FTC,* 229 F. 2d 557 (3d Cir. 1956).

Rodale Press, Inc. [1965–1967 Transfer Binder], Trade Reg. Rep. ¶ 17,236 (FTC 1965).

S. I. Research Co., 3 CCH Trade Reg. Rep. ¶ 17,988 (FTC 1967).

S.S.S. Co., 3 CCH Trade Reg. Rep. ¶ 18,087 (FTC 1967).

Sears, Roebuck & Co. v. *FTC,* 258 Fed. 307 (7th Cir. 1919).

Shafe v. *FTC,* 256 F. 2d 661 (6th Cir. 1958).

Spaulding Bakeries, Inc. [1963–1965 Transfer Binder], Trade Reg. Rep. ¶ 16,591 (FTC 1963).

Sterling Drug, Inc. [1963–1965 Transfer Binder], Trade Reg. Rep. ¶ 16,815 (FTC 1964).

United States v. *8 Cartons, More or Less, Molasses,* 97 F. Supp. 313 (W.D. N.Y. 1951).

United States v. *250 Jars Cal's Tupelo Blossom U.S. Fancy Pure Honey,* 218 F. Supp. 208 (E.D. Mich. 1963).

United States v. *856 Cases, More or Less, labelled "Demi",* 254 F. Supp. 57 (N.D. N.Y. 1966).

United States v. *Fred Urbuteit,* 335 U.S. 355 (1948).

United States v. *Herman Taller* [1963–1967 Transfer Binder], F. D. Cosm. L. Rep. ¶ 80,168 (E.D. N.Y. 1967).

United States v. *Vitasafe Corporation,* 345 F. 864 (3rd Cir.), *cert. denied,* 382 U.S. 918 (1965).

Valentine v. *Chrestensen,* 316 U.S. 52 (1942).

Ward Laboratories, Inc. v. *FTC,* 276 F. 2d 952 (2d Cir. 1960).

Witkower Press, Inc., 57 FTC 145 (1960).

Wybrant System Products Corporation v. *FTC,* 266 F. 2d 571 (2d Cir. 1959).

Chapter 23: State Legislation

BIBLIOGRAPHY

California Civil Code, Section 3396.

1 Callmann, *Unfair Competition and Trademarks,* 314 (2d Ed. 1950).

Dole, *The Uniform Deceptive Trade Practices Act,* 51 Minn. L. Rev. 1005 (1967).

Dole, *Uniform Deceptive Trade Practices Act,* 54 T. M. Rep. 435 (1964).

FTC News Release, July 7, 1966.

Gotschall, "States Act to Protect Consumers Against Deceptive and Unfair Trade Practices," address on September 26, 1969.

Note, *The Regulation of Advertising,* 56 Colum. L. Rev. 1018 (1956).

Uniform Consumer Credit Code.

Uniform Deceptive Trade Practices Act.

Chapter 24: Toward Ethical Advertising: A Plan

BIBLIOGRAPHY

Advertising Age, XXXIV (January 15, 1963).

Holbrook, *The Golden Age of Quackery* (1959).

Note, *Federal Regulation of Deceptive Packaging: The Relevance of Technological Justifications,* 72 Yale L. J. 788 (1963).

Note, *The Regulation of Advertising,* 56 Colum. L. Rev. 1018 (1956).

Simon, *The Law for Advertising and Marketing* (1956).

Turner, *The Shocking History of Advertising* (1953).

Appendix II

Printer's Ink Model
State Statute

Any person, firm, corporation or association who, with intent to sell or in any wise dispose of merchandise, securities, services, or anything offered by such person, firm, corporation or association, directly or indirectly, to the public for sale or distribution, or with intent to increase the consumption thereof, or to induce the public in any manner to enter into any obligation relating thereto, or to acquire title thereto, or an interest therein, makes, publishes, disseminates, circulates, or places before the public, or causes, directly or indirectly, to be made, published, disseminated, circulated, or placed before the public, in this State, in a newspaper or other publication, or in the form of a book, notice, handbill, poster, bill, circular, pamphlet, or letter, or in any other way, an advertisement of any sort regarding merchandise, securities, service, or anything so offered to the public, which advertisement contains any assertion, representation or statement of fact which is untrue, deceptive or misleading, shall be guilty of a misdemeanor.

Appendix III

Illinois Uniform Deceptive Trade Practices Act

(Approved August 5, 1965; effective January 1, 1966)

AN ACT *defining and prohibiting deceptive trade practices and providing remedies to those persons likely to be damaged by such practices.*

Be it enacted by the People of the State of Illinois, represented in the General Assembly:

Section 1. Definitions.

As used in this Act unless the context otherwise requires:

(1) "article" means a product as distinguished from a trademark, label or distinctive dress in packaging;

(2) "certification mark" means a mark used in connection with the goods or services of a person other than the certifier to indicate geographic origin, material, mode of manufacture, quality, accuracy or other characteristics of the goods or services or to indicate that the work or labor on the goods or services was performed by members of a union or other organization;

(3) "collective mark" means a mark used by members of a cooperative, association or other collective group or organization to identify goods or services and

distinguish them from those of others or to indicate membership in the collective group or organization;

(4) "mark" means a word, name, symbol, device or any combination of the foregoing in any form or arrangement;

(5) "person" means an indivdual, corporation, government or governmental subdivision or agency, business trust, estate, trust, partnership, unincorporated association, 2 or more of any of the foregoing having a joint or common interest or any other legal or commercial entity;

(6) "service mark" means a mark used by a person to identify services and to distinguish them from the services of others;

(7) "trademark" means a mark used by a person to identify goods and to distinguish them from the goods of others;

(8) "trade name" means a word, name, symbol, device or any combination of the foregoing in any form of arrangement used by a person to identify his business, vocation or occupation and distinguish it from the business, vocation or occupations of others.

Section 2. Deceptive trade practices.

A person engages in a deceptive trade practice when, in the course of his business, vocation or occupation, he:

(1) passes off goods or services as those of another;

(2) causes likelihood of confusion or of misunderstanding as to the source, sponsorship, approval or certification of goods or services;

(3) causes likelihood of confusion or of misunderstanding as to affiliation, connection or association with or certification by another;

(4) uses deceptive representations or designations of geographic origin in connection with goods or services;

(5) represents that goods or services have sponsorship, approval, characteristics, ingredients, uses, benefits or quantities that they do not have or that a person has a sponsorship, approval, status, affiliation or connection that he does not have;

(6) represents that goods are original or new if they are deteriorated, altered, reconditioned, reclaimed, used or secondhand;

(7) represents that goods or services are a particular standard, quality or grade or that goods are a particular style or model, if they are of another;

(8) disparages the goods, services or business of another by false or misleading representation of fact;

(9) advertises goods or services with intent not to sell them as advertised;

(10) advertises goods or services with intent not to supply reasonably expectable public demand, unless the advertisement discloses a limitation of quantity;

(11) makes false or misleading statements of fact concerning the reasons for, existence of or amounts of price reductions;

(12) engages in any other conduct which similarly creates a likelihood of confusion or of misunderstanding.

In order to prevail in an action under this Act, a complainant need not prove competition between the parties or actual confusion or misunderstanding.

This Section does not affect unfair trade practices otherwise actionable at common law or under other statutes of this State.

Section 3. Person damaged granted injunction—costs and attorneys' fees assessed against defendant.

A person likely to be damaged by a deceptive trade practice of another may be granted an injunction against it in accordance with the principles of equity and upon terms that the court considers reasonable. Proof of monetary damage, loss of profits or intent to deceive is not required. Relief granted for the copying of an article shall be limited to the prevention of confusion or misunderstanding as to source.

Costs or attorneys' fees or both may be assessed against a defendant only if the court finds that he has wilfully engaged in a deceptive trade practice.

The relief provided in this Section is in addition to remedies otherwise available against the same conduct under the common law or other statutes of this State.

Section 4. When Act does not apply.

This Act does not apply to:

(1) conduct in compliance with the orders or rules of or a statute administered by a federal, state or local governmental agency;

(2) publishers, broadcasters, printers or other persons engaged in the dissemination of information or reproduction of printed or pictorial matter who publish, broadcast or reproduce material without knowledge of its deceptive character; or

(3) actions or appeals pending on the effective date of this Act.

Subsections (2) and (3) of Section 2 do not apply to the use of a service mark, trademark, certification mark, collective mark, trade name or other trade identification that was used and not abandoned before the effective date of this Act, if the use was in good faith and is otherwise lawful except for this Act.

Section 5. Act construed.

This Act shall be construed to effectuate its general purpose to make uniform the law of those states which enact it.

Section 6. Act cited.

This act may be cited as the Uniform Deceptive Trade Practices Act.

Section 7. Severability.

If any provision of this Act or the application thereof to any person or circumstances is held invalid, the invalidity does not affect other provisions or applications of the Act which can be given effect without the invalid provision or application, and to this end the provisions of this Act are severable.

Section 8. Effective date.

This Act takes effect January 1, 1966.

Appendix IV

Federal Trade
Commission Act

[Public No. 203—63d Congress, as amended by Public—No. 447—75th Congress, as amended by Public—No. 459—81st Congress, as amended by Public—No. 542—82d Congress, as amended by Public—No. 85–791– 85 Congress, as amended by Public—No. 85–909 85th Congress] [1]

[H.R. 15613, S. 1077, H.R. 2023, H.R. 5767, H.R. 6788 and H.R. 9020]

An Act To create a Federal Trade Commission, to define its powers and duties, and for other purposes.

Be it enacted by the Senate and House of Representatives of the United States of America in Congress assembled, That a commission is hereby created and established, to be known as the Federal Trade Commission (hereinafter referred to as the commission), which shall be composed of five commissioners, who shall

[1] The Act is published as also amended by Public No. 706, 75th Congress and by Public No. 542, 82d Congress (see footnote 7), and as further amended, as above noted, by Public No. 459, 81st Congress, Ch. 61, 2d Session, H.R. 2023 (An Act to regulate oleomargarine, etc.), approved March 16, 1950, and effective July 1, 1950 (see footnotes 9, 12, and 13).

be appointed by the President, by and with the advice and consent of the Senate. Not more than three of the commissioners shall be members of the same political party. The first commissioners appointed shall continue in office for terms of three, four, five, six, and seven years, respectively, from the date of the taking effect of this Act, the term of each to be designated by the President, but their successors shall be appointed for terms of seven years, except that any person chosen to fill a vacancy shall be appointed only for the unexpired term of the commissioner whom he shall succeed: *Provided, however,* That upon the expiration of his term of office a Commissioner shall continue to serve until his successor shall have been appointed and shall have qualified. The commission shall choose a chairman from its own membership.[2]

No commissioner shall engage in any other business, vocation, or employment. Any commissioner may be removed by the President for inefficiency, neglect of duty, or malefeasance in office. A vacancy in the commission shall not impair the right of the remaining commissioners to exercise all the powers of the commission.

The commission shall have an official seal, which shall be judicially noticed.

Sec. 2. That each commissioner shall receive a salary of $10,000 a year, payable in the same manner as the salaries of the judges of the courts of the United States.[3] The commission shall appoint a secretary, who shall receive a salary of $5,000 a year,[4] payable in like manner, and it shall have authority to employ and fix the compensation of such attorneys, special experts, examiners, clerks and other employees as it may from time to time find necessary for the proper performance of its duties and as may be from time to time appropriated for by Congress.[5]

With the exception of the secretary, a clerk to each commissioner, the attor-

[2] Under the provisions of Section 3 of Reorganization Plan No. 8 of 1950, effective May 24, 1950 (as published in the Federal Register for May 25, 1950, at page 3175) the functions of the Commission with respect to choosing a chairman from among the membership of the Commission was transferred to the President. Under said plan, prepared by the President and transmitted to the Senate and House on March 13, 1950, pursuant to the provisions of the Reorganization Act of 1949, approved June 20, 1949, there were also transferred to the Chairman of the Commission, subject to certain limitations, "the executive and administrative functions of the Commission, including functions of the Commission with respect to (1) the appointment and supervision of personnel employed under the Commission, (2) the distribution of business among such personnel and among administrative units of the Commission, and (3) the use and expenditure of funds."

[3] The salary of the Chairman was fixed at $20,500 and the salaries of the other four Commissioners at $20,000 by Sec. 105 (9) and Sec. 106 (a) (45), respectively, of Public Law 854, 84th Congress, Chapter 804, 2d, Session, H.R. 7619 (An Act To adjust the rates of compensation of the heads of the executive departments and of certain other officials of the Federal Government, and for other purposes), approved July 31, 1956. [Since this amendment, the salaries have been raised again.]

[4] The salary of the Secretary is controlled by the provisions of the Classification Act of 1923, approved March 4, 1923, 42 Stat. 1488, as amended, which likewise generally controls the compensation of the employees.

[5] See preceding footnote.

neys, and such special experts and examiners as the commission may from time to time find necessary for the conduct of its work, all employees of the commission shall be a part of the classified civil service, and shall enter the service under such rules and regulations as may be prescribed by the commission and by the Civil Service Commission.

All of the expenses of the commission, including all necessary expenses for transportation incurred by the commissioners or by their employees under their orders, in making any investigation, or upon official business in any other places than in the city of Washington, shall be allowed and paid on the presentation of itemized vouchers therefor approved by the commission.

Until otherwise provided by law, the commission may rent suitable offices for its use.

The Auditor for the State and Other Departments shall receive and examine all accounts of expenditures of the commission.[6]

Sec. 3. That upon the organization of the commission and election of its chairman, the Bureau of Corporations and the offices of Commissioner and Deputy Commissioner of Corporations shall cease to exist; and all pending investigations and proceedings of the Bureau of Corporations shall be continued by the commission.

All clerks and employees of the said bureau shall be transferred to and become clerks and employees of the commission at their present grades and salaries. All records, papers, and property of the said bureau shall become records, papers, and property of the commission, and all unexpended funds and appropriations for the use and maintenance of the said bureau, including any allotment already made to it by the Secretary of Commerce from the contingent appropriation for the Department of Commerce for the fiscal year nineteen hundred and fifteen, or from the departmental printing fund for the fiscal year nineteen hundred and fifteen, shall become funds and appropriations available to be expended by the commission in the exercise of the powers, authority, and duties conferred on it by this Act.

The principal office of the commission shall be in the city of Washington, but it may meet and exercise all its powers at any other place. The Commission may, by one or more of its members, or by such examiners as it may designate, prosecute any inquiry necessary to its duties in any part of the United States.

Sec. 4. The words defined in this section shall have the following meaning when found in this Act, to wit:

"Commerce," means commerce among the several States or with foreign nations, or in any Territory of the United States or in the District of Columbia, or between any such Territory and another, or between any such Territory and any States or foreign nation, or between the District of Columbia and any State or Territory or foreign nation.

"Corporation" shall be deemed to include any company, trust, so-called Massachusetts trust, or association, incorporated or unincorporated, which is organized to carry on business for its own profit or that of its members, and has shares of

[6] Auditing of accounts was made a duty of the General Office by the Act of June 10, 1921, 42 Stat. 24.

capital or capital stock or certificates of interest, and any company, trust, so-called Massachusetts trust, or association, incorporated or unincorporated, without shares of capital or capital stock or certificates of interest, except partnerships, which is organized to carry on business for its own profit or that of its members.

"Documentary evidence" includes all documents, papers, correspondence, book of account, and financial and corporate records.

"Acts to regulate commerce" means the Act entitled "An Act to regulate commerce," approved February 14, 1887, and all Acts amendatory thereof and supplementary thereto and the Communications Act of 1934 and all Acts amendatory thereof and supplementary thereto.

"Antitrust Acts," means the Act entitled "An Act to protect trade and commerce against unlawful restraints and monopolies," approved July 2, 1890; also sections 73 to 77, inclusive, of an Act entitled "An Act to reduce taxation, to provide revenue for the Government, and for other purposes," approved August 27, 1894; also the Act entitled "An Act to amend sections 73 and 76 of the Act of August 27, 1894, entitled 'An Act to reduce taxation, to provide revenue for the Government, and for other purposes,'" approved February 12, 1913; and also the Act entitled "An Act to supplement existing laws against unlawful restraints and monopolies, and for other purposes," approved October 15, 1914.

Sec. 5. (a) (1) Unfair methods of competition in commerce, and unfair or deceptive acts or practices in commerce, are hereby declared unlawful.

(2) Nothing contained in this Act or in any of the Antitrust Acts shall render unlawful any contracts or agreements prescribing minimum or stipulated prices, for the resale of a commodity which bears, or the label or container of which bears, the trade-mark, brand, or name of the producer or distributor of such commodity and which is in free and open competition with commodities of the same general class produced or distributed by others, when contracts or agreements of that description are lawful as applied to intrastate transactions under any statute, law, or public policy now or hereafter in effect in any State, Territory, or the District of Columbia in which such resale is to be made, or to which the commodity is to be transported for such resale.

(3) Nothing contained in this Act or in any of the Antitrust Acts shall render unlawful the exercise or the enforcement of any right or right of action created by any statute, law, or public policy now or hereafter in effect in any State, Territory, or the District of Columbia, which in substance provides that willfully and knowingly advertising, offering for sale, or selling any commodity at less than the price or prices prescribed in such contracts or agreements whether the person so advertising, offering for sale, or selling is or is not a party to such a contract or agreement, is unfair competition and is actionable at the suit of any person damaged thereby.

(4) Neither the making of contracts or agreements as described in paragraph (2) of this subsection, nor the exercise or enforcement of any right or right of action as described in paragraph (3) of this subsection shall constitute an unlawful burden or restraint upon, or interference with, commerce.

(5) Nothing contained in paragraph (2) of this subsection shall make lawful contracts or agreements providing for the establishment or maintenance of mini-

mum or stipulated resale prices on any commodity referred to in paragraph (2) of this subsection, between manufacturers, or between producers, or between wholesalers, or between brokers, or between factors, or between retailers, or between person, firms, or corporations in competition with each other.

(6) The Commission is hereby empowered and directed to prevent persons, partnerships, or corporations, except banks, common carriers subject to the Acts to regulate commerce, air carriers, and foreign air carriers subject to the Civil Aeronautics Act of 1938, and persons, partnerships, or corporations insofar as they are subject to the Packers and Stockyards Act, 1921, as amended, except as provided in section 406 (b) of said Act, from using unfair methods of competition in commerce and unfair or deceptive acts or practices in commerce.[7]

[7] Public No. 542, 82d Cong., Ch. 745, 2d Session, H.R. 5767, approved July 14, 1952 (the McGuire Act, 15 U.S.C. 45,66 Stat. 631), amended Sec. 5(a) of this Act, by inserting in lieu thereof Sec. 5 (a)(1) through (6).

Therefore, by subsection (f) of Section 1107, of the "Civil Aeronautics Act of 1938," approved June 23, 1938, Public No. 706, 75th Congress, Ch. 601, 3d Sess., S. 3845, 52 Stat. 1028, the language of former Sec. 5(a) was amended by inserting immediately following the words "to regulate commerce," the words "air carriers and foreign air carriers subject to the Civil Aeronautics Act of 1938," as above set out in Sec. 5(a) (6).

Public No. 85-909, 85th Cong., H.R. 9020, approved September 2, 1958, amended the Packers and Stockyards Act, 1921, as amended (7 U.S.C. 226, 227 and 72 Stat. 1749, 1750) by striking out subsection (b) of Section 406 and inserting in lieu thereof the following:

"(b) The Federal Trade Commission shall have power and jurisdiction over any matter involving meat, meat food products, livestock products in unmanufactured form, or poultry products, which by this Act is made subject to the power or jurisdiction of the Secretary, as follows:

"(1) When the Secretary in the exercise of his duties of the Commission that it make investigations and reports in any case.

"(2) In any investigation of, or proceeding for the prevention of, an alleged violation of any act administered by the Commission, arising out of acts or transactions involving meat, meat products, livestock products in unmanufactured form, or poultry products, if the Commission determines that effective exercise of its power or jurisdiction with respect to retail sales of any such commodities is or will be impaired by the absence of power or jurisdiction over all acts or transaction involving such commodities in such investigation or proceeding. In order to avoid unnecessary duplication of effort by the Government and burdens upon the industry, the Commissioner shall notify the Secretary of such determination, the reasons therefor, and the acts or transactions involved, and shall not exercise power or jurisdiction with regard to acts or transactions (other than retail sales) involving such commodities if the Secretary within ten days from the date of receipt of the notice notifies the Commission that there is pending in his Department an investigation of, or proceeding for the prevention of, an alleged violation of this Act involving the same subject matter.

"(3) Over all transactions in commerce in margarine or oleomargarine and over retail sales of meat, meat food products, livestock products in unmanufactured form, and poultry products.

"(c) The Federal Trade Commission shall have no power or jurisdiction over any matter which by this Act is made subject to the jurisdiction of the Secretary, except as provided in subsection (b) of this section."

(b) Whenever the Commission shall have reason to believe that any such person, partnership, or corporation has been or is using any unfair method of competition or unfair or deceptive act or practice in commerce, and if it shall appear to the Commission that a proceeding by it in respect thereof would be in the interest of the public, it shall issue and serve upon such person, partnership, or corporation a complaint stating its charges in that respect and containing a notice of a hearing upon a day and at a place therein fixed at least thirty days after the service of said complaint. The person, partnership, or corporation so complained of shall have the right to appear at the place and time so fixed and show cause why an order should not be entered by the Commission requiring such person, partnership, or corporation to cease and desist from the violation of the law so charged in said complaint. Any person, partnership or corporation may make application, and upon good cause shown may be allowed by the Commission to intervene and appear in said proceeding by counsel or in person. The testimony in any such proceeding shall be reduced to writing and filed in the office of the Commission. If upon such hearing the Commission shall be of the opinion that the method of competition or the act or practice in question is prohibited by this Act, it shall make a report in writing in which it shall state its findings as to the facts and shall issue and cause to be served on such person, partnership, or corporation an order requiring such person, partnership, or corporation to cease and desist from using such method of competition or such act or practice. Until the expiration of the time allowed for filing a petition for review, if no such petition has been duly filed within such time, or, if a petition for review has been filed within such time then until the record in the proceeding has been filed in a court of appeals of the United States, as hereinafter provided, the Commission may at any time, upon such notice and in such manner as it shall deem proper, modify or set aside, in whole or in part, any report or any order made or issued by it under this section.[7a] After the expiration of the time allowed for filing a petition for review, if no such petition has been duly filed within such time, the Commission may at any time, after notice and opportunity for hearing, reopen and alter, modify, or set aside, in whole or in part, any report or order made or issued by it under this section, whenever in the opinion of the Commission conditions of fact or of law have so changed as to require such action or if the public interest shall so require: *Provided, however,* That the said person, partnership, or corporation may, within sixty days after service upon him or it of said report or order entered after such a reopening, obtain a review thereof in the appropriate circuit court of appeals of the United States, in the manner provided in subsection (c) of this section.

(c) Any person, partnership, or corporation required by an order of the Commission to cease and desist from using any method of competition or act or

---

The same Public Law also amended Subsection 6 of Section 5(a) of the Federal Trade Commission Act (15 U.S.C. 45(a)(6) and 38 Stat. 719) by substituting "person, partnerships, or corporations insofar as they are subject to the Packers and Stockyards Act, 1921, as amended, except as provided in Section 406(b) of said Act" for "persons, partnerships, or corporations subject to the Packers and Stockyards Act, 1921, except as provided in Section 406(b) of said Act."

[7a] This sentence was amended by Public Law 85–791, 85th Cong., H.R. 6788, approved August 28, 1958, 72 Stat. 942.

practice may obtain a review of such order in the circuit court of appeals of the United States, within any circuit where the method of competition or the act or practice in question was used or where such person, partnership, or corporation resides or carries on business, by filing in the court, within sixty days [8] from the date of the service of such order, a written petition praying that the order of the Commission be set aside. A copy of such petition shall be forthwith transmitted by the clerk of the court of the Commission, and thereupon the Commission shall file in the court the record in the proceeding, as provided in section 2112 of title 28, United States Code. Upon such filing of the petition the court shall have jurisdiction of the proceeding and of the question determined therein concurrently with the Commission until the filing of the record and shall have power to make and enter a decree affirming, modifying, or setting aside the order of the Commission, and enforcing the same to the extent that such order is affirmed and to issue such writs as are ancillary to its jurisdiction or are necessary in its judgment to prevent injury to the public or to competitors pendente lite.[8a] The findings of the Commission as to the facts, if supported by evidence, shall be conclusive. To the extent that the order of the Commission is affirmed, the court shall thereupon issue its own order commanding obedience to the terms of such order of the Commission. If either party shall apply to the court for leave to adduce additional evidence, and shall show to the satisfaction of the court that such additional evidence is material and that there were reasonable grounds for the failure to adduce such evidence in the proceeding before the Commission, the court may order such additional evidence to be taken before the Commission and to be adduced upon the hearing in such manner and upon such terms and conditions as to the court may seem proper. The Commission may modify its findings as to the facts, or make new findings as to the facts, or make new findings, by reason of the additional evidence so taken, and it shall file such modified or new findings, which, if supported by evidence, shall be conclusive, and its recommendation, if any, for the modification or setting aside of its original order, with the return of such additional evidence. The judgment and decree of the court shall be final, except that the same shall be subject to review by the Supreme Court upon certiorari, as provided in section 240 of the Judicial Code.

(d) Upon the filing of the record with it the jurisdiction of the court of appeals of the United States to affirm, enforce, modify, or set aside orders of the Commission shall be exclusive.[8b]

(e) Such proceedings in the circuit court of appeals shall be given precedence over other cases pending therein, and shall be in every way expedited. No order of the Commission or judgment of court to enforce the same shall in anywise relieve or absolve any person, partnership, or corporation from any liability under the Antitrust Acts.

[8] Section 5(a) of the amending Act of 1938 provides:

Sec. 5. (a) In case of an order by the Federal Trade Commission to cease and desist, served on or before the date of the enactment of this Act, the sixty-day period referred to in section 5(c) of the Federal Trade Commission Act, as amended by this Act, shall begin on the date of the enactment of this Act.

[8a] The above two sentences were also amended by Public Law 85-791.

[8b] The above section was also amended by Public Law 85-791.

(f) Complaints, orders, and other processes of the Commission under this section may be served by anyone duly authorized by the Commission, either (a) by delivering a copy thereof to the person to be served, or to a member of the partnership to be served, or the president, secretary, or other executive officer or a director of the corporation to be served; or (b) by leaving a copy thereof at the residence or principal office or place of business of such person, partnership, or corporation; or (c) by registering and mailing a copy thereof addressed to such person, partnership, or corporation at his or its residence or principal office or place of business. The verified return by the person so serving said complaint, order, or other process setting forth the manner of said service shall be proof of the same, and the return post office receipt for said complaint, order, or other process registered and mailed as aforesaid shall be proof of the service of the same.

(g) An order of the Commission to cease and desist shall become final

(1) Upon the expiration of the time allowed for filing a petition for review, if no such petition has been duly filed within such time; but the Commission may thereafter modify or set aside its order to the extent provided in the last sentence of subsection (b); or

(2) Upon the expiration of the time allowed for filing a petition for certiorari, if the order of the Commission has been affirmed, or the petition for review dismissed by the circuit court of appeals, and no petition for certiorari has been duly filed; or

(3) Upon the denial of a petition for certiorari, if the order of the Commission has been affirmed or the petition for review dismissed by the circuit court of appeals; or

(4) Upon the expiration of thirty days from the date of issuance of the mandate of the Supreme Court, if such Court directs that the order of the Commission be affirmed or the petition for review dismissed.

(h) If the Supreme Court directs that the order of the Commission be modified or set aside, the order of the Commission rendered in accordance with the mandate of the Supreme Court shall become final upon the expiration of thirty days from the time it was rendered, unless within such thirty days either party has instituted proceedings to have such order corrected to accord with the mandate, in which event the order of the Commission shall become final when so corrected.

(i) If the order of the Commission is modified or set aside by the circuit court of appeals, and if (1) the time allowed for filing a petition for certiorari has expired and no such petition has been duly filed, or (2) the petition for certiorari has been denied, or (3) the decision of the court has been affirmed by the Supreme Court, then the order of the Commission rendered in accordance with the mandate of the circuit court of appeals shall become final on the expiration of thirty days from the time such order of the Commission was rendered, unless within such thirty days either party has instituted proceedings to have such order corrected so that it will accord with the mandate, in which event the order of the Commission shall become final when so corrected.

(j) If the Supreme Court orders a rehearing; or if the case is remanded by the circuit court of appeals to the Commission for a rehearing, and if (1) the time allowed for filing a petition for certiorari has expired, and no such petition has been duly filed, or (2) the petition for certiorari has been denied, or (3) the decision of the court has been affirmed by the Supreme Court, then the order of the Commission rendered upon such rehearing shall become final in the same manner as though no prior order of the Commission had been rendered.

(k) As used in this section the term "mandate," in case a mandate has been recalled prior to the expiration of thirty days from the date of issuance thereof, means the final mandate.

(l) Any person, partnership, or corporation who violates an order of the Commission to cease and desist after it has become final, and while such order is in effect, shall forfeit and pay to the United States a civil penalty of not more than $5,000 for each violation, which shall accure to the United States and may be recovered in a civil action brought by the United States. Each separate violation of such an order shall be a separate offense, except that in the case of a violation through continuing failure or neglect to obey a final order of the Commission each day of continuance of such failure or neglect shall be deemed a separate offense.[9]

Sec. 6. That the commission shall also have power [10]—

(a) To gather and compile information concerning, and to investigate from time to time the organization, business, conduct, practices, and management of any corporation engaged in commerce, excepting banks and common carriers subject to the Act to regulate commerce, and its relation to other corporations and to individuals, associations, and partnerships.

(b) To require, by general or special orders, corporations engaged in commerce, excepting banks, and common carriers subject to the Act to regulate commerce, or any class of them, or any of them, respectively, to file with the commission in such form as the commission may prescribe annual or special, or both annual and special, reports or answers in writing to specific questions, furnishing to the commission such information as it may require as to the organization, business, conduct, practices, management, and relation to other corporations, partnerships, and individuals of the respective corporations filing such reports or answers in writing. Such reports and answers shall be made under oath, or otherwise, as the commission may prescribe, and shall be filed with the commission within such reasonable period as the commission may prescribe, unless additional time be granted in any case by the commission.

(c) Whenever a final decree has been entered against any defendant corporation in any suit brought by the United States to prevent and restrain any violation of the antitrust Acts, to make investigation, upon its own initiative, of the manner in which the decree has been or is being carried out, and upon the application of the Attorney General it shall be its duty to make such investiga-

---

[9] Foregoing sentence added by subsection (c) of Sec. 4, Public No. 459, 81st Congress. (See footnote 1.)

[10] Public No. 78, 73d Cong., approved June 16, 1933, making appropriations for the fiscal year ending June 30, 1934, for the "Executive Office and sundry independent bureaus, boards, commissions," etc., made the Commission contingent upon the provision (48 Stat. 291; 15 U.S.C.A., sec. 46a) that "hereafter no new investigations shall be initiated by the Commission as the result of a legislative resolution, except the same be a concurrent resolution of the two Houses of Congress."

tion. It shall transmit to the Attorney General a report embodying its findings and recommendations as a result of any such investigation, and the report shall be made public in the discretion of the commission.

(d) Upon the direction of the president or either House of Congress to investigate and report the facts relating to any alleged violations of the antitrust Acts by any corporation.

(e) Upon the application of the Attorney General to investigate and make recommendations for the readjustment of the business of any corporation alleged to be violating the antitrust Acts in order that the corporation may thereafter maintain its organization, management, and conduct of business in accordance with law.

(f) To make public from time to time such portions of the information obtained by it hereunder, except trade secrets and names of customers, as it shall deem expedient in the public interest; and to make annual and special reports to the Congress and to submit therewith recommendations for additional legislation; and to provide for the publication of its reports and decisions in such form and manner as may be best adapted for public information and use.

(g) From time to time to classify corporations and to make rules and regulations for the purpose of carrying out the provisions of this Act.

(h) To investigate, from time to time, trade conditions in and with foreign countries where associations, combinations, or practices of manufacturers, merchants, or traders, or other conditions, may affect the foreign trade of the United States, and to report to Congress thereon, with such recommendations as it deems advisable.

Sec. 7. That in any suit in equity brought by or under the direction of the Attorney General as provided in the antitrust Acts, the court may, upon the conclusion of the testimony therein, if it shall be then of opinion that the complainant is entitled to relief, refer said suit to the commission, as a master in chancery, to ascertain and report an appropriate form of decree therein. The commission shall proceed upon such notice to the parties and under such rules of procedure as the court may prescribe, and upon the coming in of such report such exceptions may be filed and such proceedings had in relation thereto as upon the report of a master in other equity causes, but the court may adopt or reject such report, in whole or in part, and enter such decree as the nature of the case may in its judgment require.

Sec. 8. That the several departments and bureaus of the Government when directed by the President shall furnish the commission, upon its request, all records, papers, and information in their possession relating to any corporation subject to any of the provisions of this Act, and shall detail from time to time such officials and employees to the commission as he may direct.

Sec. 9. That for the purposes of this Act the commission, or its duly authorized agent or agents, shall at all reasonable times have access to, for the purpose of examination, and the right to copy any documentary evidence of any corporation being investigated or proceeded against; and the commission shall have power to require by subpoena the attendance and testimony of witnesses and the production of all such documentary evidence relating to any matter under investigation. Any member of the commission may sign subpoenas, and members and examiners of the commission may administer oaths and affirmations, examine witnesses, and receive evidence.

Such attendance of witnesses, and the production of such documentary evidence, may be required from any place in the United States, at any designated place of hearing. And in case of disobedience to a subpoena the commission may invoke the aid of any court of the United States in requiring the attendance and testimony of witnesses and the production of documentary evidence.

Any of the district courts of the United States within the jurisdiction of which such inquiry is carried on may, in case of contumacy or refusal to obey a sub-poena issued to any corporation or other person, issue an order requiring such corporation or other person to appear before the commission, or to produce documentary evidence if so ordered, or to give evidence touching the matter in question; and any failure to obey such order of the court may be punished by such court as a contempt thereof.

Upon the application of the Attorney General of the United States, at the request of the commission, the district courts of the United States shall have jurisdiction to issue writs of mandamus commanding any person or corporation to comply with the provisions of this Act or any order of the commission made in pursuance thereof.

The commission may order testimony to be taken by deposition in any pro-ceeding or investigation pending under this Act at any stage of such proceeding or investigation. Such depositions may be taken before any person designated by the commission and having power to administer oaths. Such testimony shall be reduced to writing by the person taking the deposition, or under his direction, and shall then be subscribed by the deponent. Any person may be compelled to appear and depose and to produce documentary evidence in the same manner as witnesses may be compelled to appear and testify and produce documentary evidence before the commission as hereinbefore provided.

Witnesses summoned before the commission shall be paid the same fees and mileage that are paid witnesses in the courts of the United States, and witnesses whose depositions are taken, and the person taking the same shall severally be entitled to the same fees as are paid for like services in the courts of the United States.

No person shall be excused from attending and testifying or from producing documentary evidence before the commission or in obedience to the subpoena of the commission on the ground or for the reason that the testimony or evidence, documentary or otherwise, required of him may tend to criminate him or sub-ject him to a penalty or forfeiture. But no natural person shall be prosecuted or subjected to any penalty or forfeiture for or on account of any transaction, mat-ter, or thing concerning which he may testify, or produce evidence, documentary or otherwise, before the commission in obedience to a subpoena issued by it: *Provided,* That no natural person so testifying shall be exempt from prosecution and punishment for perjury committed in so testifying.

Sec. 10 That any person who shall neglect or refuse to attend and testify, or to answer any lawful inquiry, or to produce documentary evidence, if in his power to do so, in obedience to the subpoena or lawful requirement of the commission, shall be guilty of an offense and upon conviction thereof by a court of competent jurisdiction shall be punished by a fine of not less than $1,000 nor more than $5,000, or by imprisonment for not more than one year, or by both such fine and imprisonment.

Any person who shall willfully make, or cause to be made, any false entry or statement of fact in any report required to be made under this Act, or who shall willfully make, or cause to be made, any false entry in any account, record, or memorandum kept by any corporation subject to this Act, or who shall willfully neglect or fail to make, or cause to be made, full, true, and correct entries in such accounts, records, or memoranda of all facts and transactions appertaining to the business of such corporation, or who shall willfully remove out of the jurisdiction of the United States, or willfully mutilate, alter, or by any other means falsify any documentary evidence of such corporation, or who shall willfully refuse to submit to the commission or to any of its authorized agents, for the purpose of inspection and taking copies, any documentary evidence of such corporation in his possession or within his control, shall be deemed guilty of an offense against the United States, and shall be subject, upon conviction in any court of the United States of competent jurisdiction, to a fine of not less than $1,000 nor more than $5,000 or to imprisonment for a term of not more than three years, or to both such fine and imprisonment.

If any corporation required by this Act to file any annual or special report shall fail so to do within the time affixed by the commission for filing the same, and such failure shall continue for thirty days after notice of such default, the corporation shall forfeit to the United States the sum of $100 for each and every day of the continuance of such failure which forfeiture shall be payable into the Treasury of the United States, and shall be recoverable in a civil suit in the name of the United States brought in the district where the corporation has its principal office or in any district in which it shall do business. It shall be the duty of the various district attorneys, under the direction of the Attorney General of the United States, to prosecute for the recovery of forfeitures. The costs and expenses of such prosecution shall be paid out of the appropriation for the expenses of the courts of the United States.

Any officer or employee of the commission who shall make public any information obtained by the commission without its authority, unless directed by a court, shall be deemed guilty of a misdemeanor, and, upon conviction thereof, shall be punished by a fine not exceeding $5,000, or by imprisonment not exceeding one year, or by fine and imprisonment, in the discretion of the court.

Sec. 11. Nothing contained in this Act shall be construed to prevent or interfere with the enforcement of the provisions of the antitrust Acts or the Acts to regulate commerce, nor shall anything contained in the Act be construed to alter, modify, or repeal the said antitrust Acts to regulate commerce or any part or parts thereof.

Sec. 12. (a) It shall be unlawful for any person, partnership, or corporation to disseminate, or cause to be disseminated, any false advertisement—(1) By

United States mails, or in commerce by any means, for the purpose of inducing, or which is likely to induce, directly or indirectly the purchase of food, drugs, devices or cosmetics; or (2) By any means, for the purpose of inducing, or which is likely to induce, directly or indirectly, the purchase in commerce of food, drugs, devices, or cosmetics.

(b) The dissemination or the causing to be disseminated of any false advertisement within the provisions of subsection (a) of this section shall be an unfair or deceptive act or practice in commerce within the meaning of section 5.

Sec. 13. (a) Whenever the Commission has reason to believe—(1) that any person, partnership, or corporation is engaged in, or is about to engage in, the dissemination or the causing of the dissemination of any advertisement in violation of section 12, and (2) that the enjoining thereof pending the issuance of a complaint by the Commission under section 5, and until such complaint is dismissed by the Commission or set aside by the court on review, or the order of the Commission to cease and desist made thereon has become final within the meaning of section 5, would be to the interest of the public, the Commission by any of its attorneys designated by it for such purpose may bring suit in a district court of the United States or in the United States court of any Territory, to enjoin the dissemination or the causing of the dissemination of such advertisement. Upon proper showing a temporary injunction or restraining order shall be granted without bond. Any such suit shall be brought in the district in which such person, partnership, or corporation resides or transacts business.

(b) Whenever it appears to the satisfaction of the court in the case of a newspaper, magazine, periodical, or other publication, published at regular intervals —(1) that restraining the dissemination of a false advertisement in any particular issue of such publication would delay the delivery of such issues after the regular time therefor, and (2) that such delay would be due to the method by which the manufacture and distribution of such publication is customarily conducted by the publisher in accordance with sound business practice, and not to any method or device adopted for the evasion of this section or to prevent or delay the issuance of an injunction or restraining order with respect to such false advertisement or any other advertisement, the court shall exclude such issue from the operation of the restraining order or injunction.

Sec. 14. (a) Any person, partnership, or corporation who violates any provision of section 12(a) shall, if the use of the commodity advertised may be injurious to health because of results from such use under the conditions prescribed in the advertisement thereof, or under such conditions as are customary or usual, or if such violation is with intent to defraud or mislead, be guilty of a misdemeanor, and upon conviction shall be punished by a fine of not more than $5,000 or by imprisonment for not more than six months, or by both such fine or imprisonment; except that if the conviction is for a violation committed after a first conviction of such person, partnership, or corporation, for any violation of such section, punishment shall be by a fine of not more than $10,000 or by imprisonment for not more than one year, or by both such fine and imprisonment: *Provided,* That for the purposes of this section meats and meat food products duly inspected, marked, and labeled in accordance with rules and regulations issued under the Meat Inspection Act approved March 4, 1907, as amended, shall be conclusively presumed not injurious to health at the time the same leave official "establishments." [11]

(b) No publisher, radio-broadcast licensee, or agency or medium for the dissemination of advertising, except the manufacturer, packer, distributor, or seller of the commodity to which the false advertisement relates, shall be liable under this section by reason of the dissemination by him of false advertisement, unless he has refused, on the request of the Commission, to furnish the Commission the name and post-office address of the manufacturer, packer, distributor, or advertising agency, residing in the United States, who caused him to disseminate such advertisement. No advertising agency shall be liable under this section by reason of the causing by it of the dissemination of any false advertisement, unless it has refused, on the request of the Commission, to furnish the Commission the name and post-office address of the manufacturer, packer, distributor, or seller, residing in the United States, who caused it to cause the dissemination of such advertisement.

Sec. 15. For the purposes of sections 12, 13, and 14—

(a) (1) The term "false advertisement" means an advertisement, other than labeling, which is misleading in a material respect; and in determining whether any advertisement is misleading, there shall be taken into account (among other things) not only representations made or suggested by statement, word, design, device, sound, or any combination thereof, but also the extent to which the advertisement fails to reveal facts material in the light of such representations or material with respect to consequences which may result from the use of the commodity to which the advertisement relates under the conditions prescribed in said advertisement, or under such conditions as are customary or usual. No advertisement of a drug shall be deemed to be false if it is disseminated only to members of the medical profession, contains no false representation of a material fact, and includes, or is accompanied in each instance by truthful disclosure of, the formula showing quantitatively each ingredient of such drug.

(2) In the case of oleomargarine or margarine an advertisement shall be deemed misleading in a material respect if in such advertisement representations are made or suggested by statement, word, grade designation, design, device, symbol, sound, or any combination thereof, that such oleomargarine or margarine is a dairy product, except that nothing contained herein shall prevent a truthful, accurate, and full statement in any such advertisement of all the ingredients contained in such oleomargarine or margarine.[12]

(b) The term "food" means (1) articles used for food or drink for man or other animals, (2) chewing gum, and (3) articles used for components of any such article.

[11] Section 5(b) of the amending Act of 1938 provides:

Section. 5. (b) Section 14 of the Federal Trade Commission Act, added to such Act by section 4 of this Act, shall take effect on the expiration of sixty days after the date of the enactment of this Act.

[12] Subsection (a) of Sec. 4 of Public No. 459, 81st Congress (see footnote 1), amended sec. 15 of this Act by inserting " (1)" after the letter " (a)" in subsection (a) above, and by adding the end of such subsection new paragraph (2), above set out.

(c) The term "drug" means (1) articles recognized in the official United States Pharmacopoeia, official Homeopathic Pharmacopoeia of the United States, or official National Formulary, or any supplement to any of them; and (2) articles intended for use in the diagnosis, cure, mitigation, treatment, or prevention of disease in man or other animals; and (3) articles (other than food) intended to affect the structure or any function of the body of man or other animals; and (4) articles intended for use as a component of any article specified in clause (1), (2), or (3); but does not include devices or their components, parts, or accessories.

(d) The term "device" (except when used in subsection (a) of this section) means instruments, apparatus, and contrivances, including their parts and accessories, intended (1) for use in the diagnosis, cure, mitigation, treatment, or prevention of disease in man or other animals; or (2) to affect the structure or any function of the body of man or other animals.

(e) The term "cosmetic" means (1) articles to be rubbed, poured, sprinkled, or sprayed on, introduced into, or otherwise applied to the human body or any part thereof intended for cleansing, beautifying, promoting attractiveness, or altering the appearance, and (2) articles intended for use as a component of any such article; except that such term shall not include soap.

(f) For the purposes of this section and section 407 of the Federal Food, Drugs, and Cosmetic Act, as amended, the term "oleomargarine" or "margarine" includes—

(1) all substances, mixtures, and compounds known as oleomargarine or margarine;

(2) all substances, mixtures, and compounds which have a consistence similar to that of butter and which contain any edible oils or fats other than milk fat if made in imitation or semblance of butter.[13]

Sec. 16. Whenever the Federal Trade Commission has reason to believe that any person, partnership, or corporation is liable to a penalty under section 14 or under subsection (1) of section 5, it shall certify the facts to the Attorney General, whose duty it shall be to cause appropriate proceedings to be brought for the enforcement of the provisions of such section or subsection.

Sec. 17. If any provision of this Act, or the application thereof to any person, partnership, corporation, or circumstance, is held invalid, the remainder of the Act and the application of such provision to any other person, partnership, corporation, or circumstance, shall not be affected thereby.

Sec. 18. This Act may be cited as the "Federal Trade Commission Act."
Original, approved September 26, 1914.
Amended and approved March 21, 1938.[14]

[13] Subsection (b) of Sec. 4. of Public No. 495, 81st Congress (see footnote 1) further amended sec. 15 of this Act, by adding at the end thereof the new subsection (f) as above set out.
[14] See footnote 1.

Appendix V

Fair Packaging and Labeling Act

Public Law 89–755; 80 Stat. 1296
[S. 985]

An Act to regulate interstate and foreign commerce by preventing the use of unfair or deceptive methods of packaging or labeling of certain consumer commodities distributed in such commerce, and for other purposes.

Be it enacted by the Senate and House of Representatives of the United States of America in Congress assembled, That:

This Act may be cited as the "Fair Packaging and Labeling Act."

DECLARATION OF POLICY

Sec. 2. Informed consumers are essential to the fair and efficient functioning of a free market economy. Packages and their labels should enable consumers to obtain accurate information as to the quantity of the contents and should facilitate value comparisons. Therefore, it is hereby declared to be the policy of the Congress to assist consumers and manufacturers in reaching these goals in the marketing of consumer goods.

PROHIBITION OF UNFAIR AND DECEPTIVE PACKAGING AND LABELING

Sec. 3. (a) It shall be unlawful for any person engaged in the packaging or labeling of any consumer commodity (as defined in this Act) for distribution in commerce, or for any person (other than a common carrier for hire, a contract carrier for hire, or a freight forwarder for hire) engaged in the distribution in commerce of any packaged or labeled consumer commodity, to distribute or to cause to be distributed in commerce any such commodity if such commodity is contained in a package, or if there is affixed to that commodity a label, which does not conform to the provisions of this Act and of regulations promulgated under the authority of this Act.

(b) The prohibition contained in subsection (a) shall not apply to persons engaged in business as wholesale or retail distributors of consumer commodities except to the extent that such persons (1) are engaged in the packaging or labeling of such commodities, or (2) prescribe or specify by any means the manner in which such commodities are packaged or labeled.

REQUIREMENTS AND PROHIBITIONS

Sec. 4. (a) No person subject to the prohibition contained in section 3 shall distribute or cause to be distributed in commerce any packaged consumer commodity unless in conformity with regulations which shall be established by the promulgating authority pursuant to section 6 of this Act which shall provide that—

(1) The commodity shall bear a label specifying the identity of the commodity and the name and place of business of the manufacturer, packer, or distributor;

(2) The net quantity of contents (in terms of weight, measure, or numerical count) shall be separately and accurately stated in a uniform location upon the principal display panel of that label;

(3) The separate label statement of net quantity of contents appearing upon or affixed to any package—

(A) (i) if on a package containing less than four pounds or one gallon and labeled in terms of weight or fluid measure, shall, unless subparagraph (ii) applies and such statement is set forth in accordance with such subparagraph, be expressed both in ounces (with identification as to avoirdupois or fluid ounces) and, if applicable, in pounds for weight units, with any remainder in terms of ounces or common or decimal fractions of the pound; or in the case of liquid measure, in the largest whole unit (quarts, quarts and pints, or pints, as appropriate) with any remainder in terms of fluid ounces or common or decimal fractions of the pint or quart;

(ii) if on a random package, may be expressed in terms of pounds and decimal fractions of the pound carried out to not more than two decimal places;

(iii) if on a package labeled in terms of linear measure, shall be expressed both in terms of inches and the largest whole unit (yards, yards and feet, or feet, as appropriate) with any remainder in terms of inches or common or decimal fractions of the foot or yard;

(iv) if on a package labeled in terms of measure of area, shall be expressed both in terms of square inches and the largest whole square unit (square yards, square yards and square feet, or square feet, as appropriate) with any remainder in terms of square inches or common or decimal fractions of the square foot or square yard;

(B) shall appear in conspicuous and easily legible type in distinct contrast (by typography, layout, color, embossing, or molding) with other matter on the package;

(C) shall contain letters or numerals in a type size which shall be (i) established in relationship to the area of the principal display panel of the package, and (ii) uniform for all packages of substantially the same size; and

(D) shall be so placed that the lines of printed matter included in that statement are generally parallel to the base on which the package rests as it is designed to be displayed; and

(4) The label of any package of a consumer commodity which bears a representation as to the number of servings of such commodity contained in such package shall bear a statement of the net quantity (in terms of weight, measure, or numerical count) of each such serving.

(5) For purposes of paragraph (3) (A) (ii) of this subsection the term "random package" means a package which is one of a lot, shipment, or delivery of packages of the same consumer commodity with varying weights, that is, packages with no fixed weight pattern.

(b) No person subject to the prohibition contained in section 3 shall distribute or cause to be distributed in commerce any packaged consumer commodity if any qualifying words or phrases appear in conjunction with the separate statement of the net quantity of contents required by subsection (a), but nothing in this subsection or in paragraph (2) of subsection (a) shall prohibit supplemental statements, at other places on the package, describing in nondeceptive terms the net quantity of contents: *Provided,* That such supplemental statements of net quantity of contents shall not include any term qualifying a unit of weight, measure, or count that tends to exaggerate the amount of the commodity contained in the package.

ADDITIONAL REGULATIONS

Sec. 5. (a) The authority to promulgate regulations under this Act is vested in (A) the Secretary of Health, Education, and Welfare (referred to hereinafter as the "Secretary") with respect to any consumer commodity which is a food, drug, device, or cosmetic, as each such term is defined by section 201 of the Federal Food, Drug, and Cosmetic Act (21 U.S.C. 321); and (B) the Federal Trade Commission (referred to hereinafter as the "Commission") with respect to any other consumer commodity.

(b) If the promulgating authority specified in this section finds that, because of the nature, form, or quantity of a particular consumer commodity, or for other good and sufficient reasons, full compliance with all the requirements otherwise applicable under section 4 of this Act is impracticable or is not necessary for the adequate protection of consumers, the Secretary or the Commission (whichever the case may be) shall promulgate regulations exempting such commodity from those requirements to the extent and under such conditions as the promulating authority determines to be consistent with section 2 of this Act.

(c) Whenever the promulating authority determines that regulations containing prohibitions or requirements other than those prescribed by section 4 are necessary to prevent the deception of consumers or to facilitate value comparisons as to any consumer commodity, such authority shall promulate with respect to that commodity regulations effective to—

(1) establish and define standards for characterization of a size of a package enclosing any consumer commodity, which may be used to supplement the label statement of net quantity of contents of packages containing such commodity, but this paragraph shall not be construed as authorizing any limitation on the size, shape, weight, dimensions, or number of packages which may be used to enclose any commodity;

(2) regulate the placement upon any package containing any commodity, or upon any label affixed to such commodity, of any printed matter stating or representing by implication that such commodity is offered for retail sale at a price lower than the ordinary and customary retail sale price or that a retail sale price advantage is accorded to purchasers thereof by reason of the size of that package or the quantity of its contents;

(3) require that the label on each package of a consumer commodity (other than one which is a food within the meaning of section 201(f) of the Federal Food, Drug, and Cosmetic Act) bear (A) the common or usual name of such consumer commodity, if any, and (B) in case such consumer commodity consists of two or more ingredients, the common or usual name of each such ingredient listed in order of decreasing predominance, but nothing in this paragraph shall be deemed to require that any trade secret be divulged; or

(4) prevent the nonfunctional-slack-fill of packages containing consumer commodities.

For purposes of paragraph (4) of this subsection, a package shall be deemed to be nonfunctionally slack-filled if it is filled to substantially less than its capacity for reasons other than (A) protection of the contents of such package or (B) the requirements of machines used for enclosing the contents in such package.

(d) Whenever the Secretary of Commerce determines that there is undue proliferation of the weights, measures, or quantities in which any consumer commodity or reasonably comparable consumer commodities are being distributed in packages for sale at retail and such undue proliferation impairs the reasonable ability of consumers to make value comparisons with respect to such consumer commodity or commodities, he shall request manufacturers, packers, and distributors of the commodity or commodities to participate in the development of a voluntary product standard for such commodity or commodities under the procedures for the development of voluntary products standards established by the Secretary pursuant to section 2 of the Act of March 3, 1901 (31 Stat. 1449, as amended; 15 U.S.C. 272). Such procedures shall provide adequate manufacturer, packer, distributor, and consumer representation.

(e) If (1) after one year after the date on which the Secretary of Commerce first makes the request of manufacturers, packers, and distributors to participate in the development of a voluntary product standard as provided in subsection (d) of this section, he determines that such a standard will not be published pursuant to the provisions of such subsection (d), or (2) if such a standard is published and the Secretary of Commerce determines that it has not been observed, he shall promptly report such determination to the Congress with a statement of the efforts that have been made under the voluntary standards program and his recommendation as to whether Congress should enact legislation providing regulatory authority to deal with the situation in question.

PROCEDURE FOR PROMULGATION OF REGULATIONS

Sec. 6. (a) Regulations promulgated by the Secretary under section 4 or section 5 of this Act shall be promulgated, and shall be subject to judicial review, pursuant to the provisions of subsections (e), (f), and (g) of section 701 of the Federal Food, Drug, and Cosmetic Act (21 U.S.C. 371(e), (f) and (g). Hearings authorized or required for the promulgation of any such regulations by the Secretary shall be conducted by the Secretary or by such officer or employee of the Department of Health, Education, and Welfare as he may designate for that purpose.

(b) Regulations promulgated by the Commission under section 4 or section 5 of this Act shall be promulgated, and shall be subject to judicial review, by proceedings taken in conformity with the provisions of subsections (e), (f) and (g) of section 701 of the Federal Food, Drug, and Cosmetic Act (21 U.S.C. 371(e), (f) and (g)) in the same manner, and with the same effect, as if such proceedings were taken by the Secretary pursuant to subsection (a) of this section. Hearings authorized or required for the promulgation of any such regulations by the Commission shall be conducted by the Commission or by such officer or employee of the Commission as the Commission may designate for that purpose.

(c) In carrying into effect the provisions of this Act, the Secretary and the Commission are authorized to cooperate with any department or agency of the United States, with any State, Commonwealth, or possession of the United States, and with any department, agency, or political subdivision of any such State, Commonwealth, or possession.

(d) No regulation adopted under this Act shall preclude the continued use of returnable or reusable glass containers for beverages in inventory or with the trade as of the effective date of this Act, nor shall any regulation under this Act preclude the orderly disposal of packages in inventory or with the trade as of the effective date of such regulation.

ENFORCEMENT

Sec. 7. (a) Any consumer commodity which is a food, drug, device, or cosmetic, as each such term is defined by section 201 of the Federal Food, Drug, and Cosmetic Act (21 U.S.C. 321), and which is introduced or delivered for introduction into commerce in violation of any of the provisions of this Act, or the regulations issued pursuant to this Act, shall be deemed to be misbranded within the meaning of chapter III of the Federal Food, Drug, and Cosmetic Act, but the provisions of section 303 of that Act (21 U.S.C. 333) shall have no application to any violation of section 3 of this Act.

(b) Any violation of any of the provisions of this Act, or the regulations issued pursuant to this Act, with respect to any consumer commodity which is not a food, drug, device, or cosmetic, shall constitute an unfair or deceptive act or practice in commerce in violation of section 5(a) of the Federal Trade Commission Act and shall be subject to enforcement under section 5(b) of the Federal Trade Commission Act.

(c) In the case of any imports into the United States of any consumer commodity covered by this Act, the provisions of sections 4 and 5 of this Act shall be enforced by the Secretary of the Treasury pursuant to section 801(a) and (b) of the Federal Food, Drug, and Cosmetic Act (21 U.S.C. 381).

REPORTS TO THE CONGRESS

Sec. 8. Each officer or agency required or authorized by this Act to promulgate regulations for the packaging or labeling of any consumer commodity, or to participate in the development of voluntary product standards with respect to any consumer commodity under procedures referred to in section 5(d) of this Act, shall transmit to the Congress in January of each year a report containing a full and complete description of the activities of that officer or agency for the administration and enforcement of this Act during the preceding fiscal year.

COOPERATION WITH STATE AUTHORITIES

Sec. 9. (a) A copy of each regulation promulgated under this Act shall be transmitted promptly to the Secretary of Commerce, who shall (1) transmit copies thereof to all appropriate State officers and agencies, and (2) furnish to such State officers and agencies information and assistance to promote to the greatest practicable extent uniformity in State and Federal regulation of the labeling of consumer commodities.

(b) Nothing contained in this section shall be construed to impair or otherwise interfere with any program carried into effect by the Secretary of Health, Education, and Welfare under other provisions of law in cooperation with State governments or agencies, instrumentalities, or political subdivisions thereof.

DEFINITIONS

Sec. 10. For the purposes of this Act—

(a) The term "consumer commodity", except as otherwise specifically provided by this subsection, means any food, drug, device, or cosmetic (as those terms are defined by the Federal Food, Drug, and Cosmetic Act), and any other article, product, or commodity of any kind or class which is customarily produced or distributed for sale through retail sales agencies or instrumentalities for consumption by individuals, or use by individuals for purposes of personal care or in the performance of services ordinarily rendered within the household, and which usually is consumed or expended in the course of such consumption or use. Such term does not include—

> (1) any meat or meat product, poultry or poultry product, or tobacco or tobacco product;

> (2) any commodity subject to packaging or labeling requirements imposed by the Secretary of Agriculture pursuant to the Federal Insecticide, Fungicide, and Rodenticide Act, or the provisions of the eighth paragraph under the heading "Bureau of Animal Industry" of the Act of March 4, 1913 (37 Stat. 832–833; 21 U.S.C. 151–157), commonly known as the Virus-Serum-Toxin Act;

(3) any drug subject to the provisions of section 503(b) (1) or 506 of the Federal Food, Drug, and Cosmetic Act (21 U.S.C. 353(b) (1) and 356);

(4) any beverage subject to or complying with packaging or labeling requirements imposed under the Federal Alcohol Administration Act (27 U.S.C. 201 et seq.); or

(5) any commodity subject to the provisions of the Federal Seed Act (7 U.S.C. 1551–1610).

(b) The term "package" means any container or wrapping in which any consumer commodity is enclosed for use in the delivery or display of that consumer commodity to retail purchasers, but does not include—

(1) shipping containers or wrappings used solely for the transportation of any consumer commodity in bulk or in quantity to manufacturers, packers, or processors, or to wholesale or retail distributors thereof;

(2) shipping containers or outer wrappings used by retailers to ship or deliver any commodity to retail customers if such containers and wrappings bear no printed matter pertaining to any particular commodity; or

(3) containers subject to the provisions of the Act of August 3, 1912 (37 Stat. 250, as amended; 15 U.S.C. 231–233), the Act of March 4, 1915 (38 Stat. 1186, as amended; 15 U.S.C. 234–236), the Act of August 31, 1916 (39 Stat. 673 as amended; 15 U.S.C. 251–256), or the Act of May 21, 1928 (45 Stat. 685, as amended; 15 U.S.C. 257–257i).

(c) The term "label" means any written, printed, or graphic matter affixed to any consumer commodity or affixed to or appearing upon a package containing any consumer commodity.

(d) The term "person" includes any firm, corporation, or association.

(e) The term "commerce" means (1) commerce between any State, the District of Columbia, the Commonwealth of Puerto Rico, or any territory or possession of the United States, and any place outside thereof, and (2) commerce within the District of Columbia or within any territory or possession of the United States not organized with a legislative body, but shall not include exports to foreign countries.

(f) The term "principal display panel" means that part of a label that is most likely to be displayed, presented, shown, or examined under normal and customary conditions of display for retail sale.

SAVING PROVISION

Sec. 11. Nothing contained in this Act shall be construed to repeal, invalidate, or supersede—

(a) the Federal Trade Commission Act or any statute defined therein as an antitrust Act;

(b) the Federal Food, Drug, and Cosmetic Act; or

(c) the Federal Hazardous Substances Labeling Act.

EFFECT UPON STATE LAW

Sec. 12. It is hereby declared that it is the express intent of Congress to supersede any and all laws of the States or political subdivisions thereof insofar as they may now or hereafter provide for the labeling of the net quantity of contents of the package of any consumer commodity covered by this Act which are less stringent than or require information different from the requirements of section 4 of this Act or regulations promulgated pursuant thereto.

EFFECTIVE DATE

Sec. 13. This Act shall take effect on July 1, 1967: *Provided,* That the Secretary (with respect to any consumer commodity which is a food, drug, device, or cosmetic, as those terms are defined by the Federal Food, Drug, and Cosmetic Act), and the Commission (with respect to any other consumer commodity) may by regulation postpone, for an additional twelve-month period, the effective date of this Act with respect to any class or type of consumer commodity on the basis of a finding that such a postponement would be in the public interest.

Approved November 3, 1966.

Appendix VI

Consumer Credit Protection Act

Public Law 90–321
90th Congress, S. 5
May 29, 1968
An Act

To safeguard the consumer in connection with the utilization of credit by requiring full disclosure of the terms and conditions of finance charges in credit
transactions or in offers to extend credit; by restricting the garnishment of
wages; and by creating the National Commission on Consumer Finance to study
and make recommendations on the need for further regulation of the consumer
finance industry; and for other purposes.

*Be it enacted by the Senate and House of Representatives of the United
States of America in Congress assembled,*
§ 1. Short title of entire Act
   This Act may be cited as the Consumer Credit Protection Act.

TITLE I—CONSUMER CREDIT COST DISCLOSURE

CHAPTER 1—GENERAL PROVISIONS

§ 101. Short title

This title may be cited as the Truth in Lending Act.

§ 102. Findings and declaration of purpose

The Congress finds that economic stabilization would be enhanced and the competition among the various financial institutions and other firms engaged in the extension of consumer credit would be strengthened by the informed use of credit. The informed use of credit results from an awareness of the cost thereof by consumers. It is the purpose of this title to assure a meaningful disclosure of credit terms so that the consumer will be able to compare more readily the various credit terms available to him and avoid the uninformed use of credit.

§ 103. Definitions and rules of construction

(a) The definitions and rules of construction set forth in this section are applicable for the purposes of this title.

(b) The term "Board" refers to the Board of Governors of the Federal Reserve System.

(c) The term "organization" means a corporation, government or governmental subdivision or agency, trust, estate, partnership, cooperative, or association.

(d) The term "person" means a natural person or an organization.

(e) The term "credit" means the right granted by a creditor to a debtor to defer payment of debt or to incur debt and defer its payment.

(f) The term "creditor" refers only to creditors who regularly extend, or arrange for the extension of, credit for which the payment of a finance charge is required, whether in connection with loans, sales of property or services, or otherwise. The provisions of this title apply to any such creditor, irrespective of his or its status as a natural person or any type of organization.

(g) The term "credit sale" refers to any sale with respect to which credit is extended or arranged by the seller. The term includes any contract in the form of a bailment or lease if the bailee or lessee contracts to pay as compensation for use a sum substantially equivalent to or in excess of the aggregate value of the property and services involved and it is agreed that the bailee or lessee will become, or for no other or a nominal consideration has the option to become, the owner of the property upon full compliance with his obligations under the contract.

(h) The adjective "consumer", used with reference to a credit transaction, characterizes the transaction as one in which the party to whom credit is offered or extended is a natural person, and the money, property, or services which are the subject of the transaction are primarily for personal, family, household, or agricultural purposes.

(i) The term "open end credit plan" refers to a plan prescribing the terms of credit transactions which may be made thereunder from time to time and under the terms of which a finance charge may be computed on the outstanding unpaid balance from time to time thereunder.

(j) The term "State" refers to any State, the Commonwealth of Puerto Rico, the District of Columbia, and any territory or possession of the United States.

(k) Any reference to any requirement imposed under this title or any provision thereof includes reference to the regulations of the Board under this title or the provision thereof in question.

(l) The disclosure of an amount or percentage which is greater than the amount or percentage required to be disclosed under this title does not in itself constitute a violation of this title.

§ 104. Exempted transactions

This title does not apply to the following:

(1) Credit transactions involving extensions of credit for business or commercial purposes, or to government or governmental agencies or instrumentalities, or to organizations.

(2) Transactions in securities or commodities accounts by a broker-dealer registered with the Securities and Exchange Commission.

(3) Credit transactions, other than real property transactions, in which the total amount to be financed exceeds $25,000.

(4) Transactions under public utility tariffs, if the Board determines that a State regulatory body regulates the charges for the public utility services involved, the charges for delayed payment, and any discount allowed for early payment.

§ 105. Regulations

The Board shall prescribe regulations to carry out the purposes of this title. These regulations may contain such classifications, differentiations, or other provisions, and may provide for such adjustments and exceptions for any class of transactions, as in the judgment of the Board are necessary or proper to effectuate the purposes of this title, to prevent circumvention or evasion thereof, or to facilitate compliance therewith.

§ 106. Determination of finance charge

(a) Except as otherwise provided in this section, the amount of the finance charge in connection with any consumer credit transaction shall be determined as the sum of all charges, payable directly or indirectly by the person to whom the credit is extended, and imposed directly or indirectly by the creditor as an incident to the extension of credit, including any of the following types of charges which are applicable:

(1) Interest, time price differential, and any amount payable under a point, discount, or other system of additional charges.

(2) Service or carrying charge.

(3) Loan fee, finder's fee, or similar charge.

(4) Fee for an investigation or credit report.

(5) Premium or other charge for any guarantee or insurance protecting the creditor against the obligor's default or other credit loss.

(b) Charges or premiums for credit life, accident, or health insurance written in connection with any consumer credit transaction shall be included in the finance charge unless

(1) the coverage of the debtor by the insurance is not a factor in the approval by the creditor of the extension of credit, and this fact is clearly disclosed in writing to the person applying for or obtaining the extension of credit; and

(2) in order to obtain the insurance in connection with the extension of credit, the person to whom the credit is extended must give specific affirmative written indication of his desire to do so after written disclosure to him of the cost thereof.

(c) Charges or premiums for insurance, written in connection with any consumer credit transaction, against loss of or damage to property or against liability arising out of the ownership or use of property, shall be included in the finance charge unless a clear and specific statement in writing is furnished by the creditor to the person to whom the credit is extended, setting forth the cost of the insurance if obtained from or through the creditor, and stating that the person to whom the credit is extended may choose the person through which the insurance is to be obtained.

(d) If any of the following items is itemized and disclosed in accordance with the regulations of the Board in connection with any transaction, then the creditor need not include that item in the computation of the finance charge with respect to that transaction:

(1) Fees and charges prescribed by law which actually are or will be paid to public officials for determining the existence of or for perfecting or releasing or satisfying any security related to the credit transaction.

(2) The premium payable for any insurance in lieu of perfecting any security interest otherwise required by the creditor in connection with the transaction, if the premium does not exceed the fees and charges described in paragraph (1) which would otherwise be payable.

(3) Taxes.

(4) Any other type of charge which is not for credit and the exclusion of which from the finance charge is approved by the Board by regulation.

(e) The following items, when charged in connection with any extension of credit secured by an interest in real property, shall not be included in the computation of the finance charge with respect to that transaction:

(1) Fees or premiums for title examination, title insurance, or similar purposes.

(2) Fees for preparation of a deed, settlement statement, or other documents.

(3) Escrows for future payments of taxes and insurance.

(4) Fees for notarizing deeds and other documents.

(5) Appraisal fees.

(6) Credit reports.

§ 107. Determination of annual percentage rate

(a) The annual percentage rate applicable to any extension of consumer credit shall be determined, in accordance with the regulations of the Board,

(1) in the case of any extension of credit other than under an open end credit plan, as

(A) that nominal annual percentage rate which will yield a sum equal to the amount of the finance charge when it is applied to the unpaid balances of the amount financed, calculated according to the actuarial method of allocating payments made on a debt between the amount financed and the amount of the finance charge, pursuant to which a payment is applied first to the accumulated finance charge and the balance is applied to the unpaid amount financed; or

(B) the rate determined by any method prescribed by the board as a method which materially simplifies computation while retaining reasonable accuracy as compared with the rate determined under subparagraph (A).

(2) in the case of any extension of credit under an open end credit plan, as the quotient (expressed as a percentage) of the total finance charge for the period to which it relates divided by the amount upon which the finance charge for that period is based, multiplied by the number of such periods in a year.

(b) Where a creditor imposes the same finance charge for balances within a specified range, the annual percentage rate shall be computed on the median balance within the range, except that if the Board determines that a rate so computed would not be meaningful, or would be materially misleading, the annual percentage rate shall be computed on such other basis as the Board may by regulation require.

(c) The annual percentage rate may be rounded to the nearest quarter of 1 per centum for credit transactions payable in substantially equal installments when a creditor determines the total finance charge on the basis of a single add-on, discount, periodic, or other rate, and the rate is converted into an annual percentage rate under procedures prescribed by the Board.

(d) The Board may authorize the use of rate tables or charts which may provide for the disclosure of annual percentage rates which vary from the rate determined in accordance with subsection (a)(1)(A) by not more than such tolerances as the Board may allow. The Board may not allow a tolerance greater than 8 per centum of that rate except to simplify compliance where irregular payments are involved.

(e) In the case of creditors determining the annual percentage rate in a manner other than as described in subsection (c) or (d), the Board may authorize other reasonable tolerances.

(f) Prior to January 1, 1971, any rate required under this title to be disclosed as a percentage rate may, at the option of the creditor, be expressed in the form of the corresponding ratio of dollars per hundred dollars.

§ 108. Administrative enforcement

(a) Compliance with the requirements imposed under this title shall be enforced under

(1) section 8 of the Federal Deposit Insurance Act, in the case of

(A) national banks, by the Comptroller of the Currency.

(B) member banks of the Federal Reserve System (other than national banks), by the Board.

(C) banks insured by the Federal Deposit Insurance Corporation (other than members of the Federal Reserve System), by the Board of Directors of the Federal Deposit Insurance Corporation.

(2) section 5(d) of the Home Owners' Loan Act of 1933, section 407 of the National Housing Act, and sections 6(i) and 17 of the Federal Home Loan Bank Act, by the Federal Home Loan Bank Board (acting directly or through the Federal Savings and Loan Insurance Corporation), in the case of any institution subject to any of those provisions.

(3) the Federal Credit Union Act, by the Director of the Bureau of Federal Credit Unions with respect to any Federal credit union.

(4) the Acts to regulate commerce, by the Interstate Commerce Commission with respect to any common carrier subject to those Acts.

(5) the Federal Aviation Act of 1958, by the Civil Aeronautics Board with respect to any air carrier or foreign air carrier subject to that Act.

(6) the Packers and Stockyards Act, 1921 (except as provided in section 406 of that Act), by the Secretary of Agriculture with respect to any activities subject to that Act.

(b) For the purpose of the exercise by any agency referred to in subsection (a) of its powers under any Act referred to in that subsection, a violation of any requirement imposed under this title shall be deemed to be a violation of a requirement imposed under that Act. In addition to its powers under any provision of law specifically referred to in subsection (a), each of the agencies referred to in that subsection may exercise, for the purpose of enforcing compliance with any requirement imposed under this title, any other authority conferred on it by law.

(c) Except to the extent that enforcement of the requirements imposed under this title is specifically committed to some other Government agency under subsection (a), the Federal Trade Commission shall enforce such requirements. For the purpose of the exercise by the Federal Trade Commission of its functions and powers under the Federal Trade Commission Act, a violation of any requirement imposed under this title shall be deemed a violation of a requirement imposed under that Act. All of the functions and powers of the Federal Trade Commission Act are available to the Commission to enforce compliance by any person with the requirements imposed under this title, irrespective of whether that person is engaged in commerce or meets any other jurisdictional tests in the Federal Trade Commission Act.

(d) The authority of the Board to issue regulations under this title does not impair the authority of any other agency designated in this section to make rules respecting its own procedures in enforcing compliance with requirements imposed under this title.

§ 109 Views of other agencies

In the exercise of its functions under this title, the Board may obtain upon request the views of any other Federal agency which, in the judgment of the Board, exercises regulatory or supervisory functions with respect to any class of creditors subject to this title.

§ 110. Advisory committee

The Board shall establish an advisory committee to advise and consult with it in the exercise of its functions under this title. In appointing the members of the committee, the Board shall seek to achieve a fair representation of the interests of sellers of merchandise on credit, lenders, and the public. The committee shall meet from time to time at the call of the Board, and members thereof shall be paid transportation expenses and not to exceed $100 per diem.

§ 111. Effect on other laws

(a) This title does not annul, alter, or affect, or exempt any creditor from complying with, the laws of any State relating to the disclosure of information in connection with credit transactions, except to the extent that those laws are inconsistent with the provisions of this title or regulations thereunder, and then only to the extent of the inconsistency.

(b) This title does not otherwise annul, alter or affect in any manner the meaning, scope or applicability to the laws of any State, including, but not limited to, laws relating to the types, amounts or rates of charges, or any element or elements of charges, permissible under such laws in connection with the extension or use of credit, nor does this title extend the applicability of those laws to any class of persons or transactions to which they would not otherwise apply.

(c) In any action or proceeding in any court involving a consumer credit sale, the disclosure of the annual percentage rate as required under this title in connection with that sale may not be received as evidence that the sale was a loan or any type of transaction other than a credit sale.

(d) Except as specified in sections 125 and 130, this title and the regulations issued thereunder do not affect the validity or enforceability of any contract or obligation under State or Federal law.

§ 112. Criminal liability for willful and knowing violation

Whoever willfully and knowingly

(1) gives false or inaccurate information or fails to provide information which he is required to disclose under the provisions of this title or any regulation issued thereunder,

(2) uses any chart or table authorized by the Board under section 107 in such a manner as to consistently understate the annual percentage rate determined under section 107(a)(1)(A), or

(3) otherwise fails to comply with any requirement imposed under this title,

shall be fined not more than $5,000 or imprisoned not more than one year, or both.

§ 113. Penalties inapplicable to governmental agencies

No civil or criminal penalty provided under this title for any violation thereof may be imposed upon the United States or any agency thereof, or upon any State or political subdivision thereof, or any agency of any State or political subdivision.

§ 114. Reports by Board and Attorney General

Not later than January 3 of each year after 1969, the Board and the Attorney General shall, respectively, make reports to the Congress concerning the administration of their functions under this title, including such recommendations as the Board and the Attorney General, respectively, deem necessary or appropriate. In addition, each report of the Board shall include its assessment of the extent to which compliance with the requirements imposed under this title is being achieved.

CHAPTER 2—CREDIT TRANSACTIONS

§ 121. General requirement of disclosure

(a) Each creditor shall disclose clearly and conspicuously, in accordance with the regulations of the Board, to each person to whom consumer credit is extended and upon whom a finance charge is or may be imposed, the information required under this chapter.

(b) If there is more than one obligor, a creditor need not furnish a statement of information required under this chapter to more than one of them.

§ 122. Form of disclosure; additional information

(a) Regulations of the Board need not require that disclosures pursuant to this chapter be made in the order set forth in this chapter, and may permit the use of terminology different from that employed in this chapter if it conveys substantially the same meaning.

(b) Any creditor may supply additional information or explanations with any disclosures required under this chapter.

§ 123. Exemption for State-regulated transactions

The Board shall by regulation exempt from the requirements of this chapter any class of credit transactions within any State if it determines that under the law of that State that class of transactions is subject to requirements substantially similar to those imposed under this chapter, and that there is adequate provision for enforcement.

§ 124. Effect of subsequent occurrence

If information disclosed in accordance with this chapter is subsequently rendered inaccurate as the result of any act, occurrence, or agreement subsequent to the delivery of the required disclosures, the inaccuracy resulting therefrom does not constitute a violation of this chapter.

§ 125. Right of rescission as to certain transactions

(a) Except as otherwise provided in this section, in the case of the consumer credit transaction in which a security interest is retained or acquired in any real property which is used or is expected to be used as the residence of the person to whom credit is extended, the obligor shall have the right to rescind the transaction until midnight of the third business day following the consummation of the transaction or the delivery of the disclosures required under this section and all other material disclosures required under this chapter, whichever is later, by notifying the creditor, in accordance with regulations of the Board, of his intention to do so. The creditor shall clearly and conspicuously disclose, in accordance with regulations of the Board, to any obligor in a transaction subject to this section the rights of the obligor under this section. The creditor shall also provide, in accordance with regulations of the Board, an adequate opportunity to the obligor to exercise his right to rescind any transaction subject to this section.

(b) When an obligor exercises his right to rescind under subsection (a), he is not liable for any finance or other charge, and any security interest given by the obligor becomes void upon such a rescission. Within ten days after receipt of a notice of rescission, the creditor shall return to the obligor any money or property given as earnest money, downpayment, or otherwise, and shall take any action necessary or appropriate to reflect the termination of any security interest created under the transaction. If the creditor has delivered any property to the obligor, the obligor may retain possession of it. Upon the performance of the creditor's obligations under this section, the obligor shall tender the property to the creditor, except that if return of the property in kind would be impracticable or inequitable, the obligor shall tender its reasonable value. Tender shall be made at the location of the property or at the residence of the obligor, at the option of the obligor. If the creditor does not take possession of the property within ten days after tender by the obligor, ownership of the property vests in the obligor without obligation on his part to pay for it.

(c) Notwithstanding any rule of evidence, written acknowledgment of receipt of any disclosures required under this title by a person to whom a statement is required to be given pursuant to this section does no more than create a rebuttable presumption of delivery thereof.

(d) The Board may, if it finds that such action is necessary in order to permit homeowners to meet bona fide personal financial emergencies, prescribe regulations authorizing the modification or waiver of any rights created under this section to the extent and under the circumstances set forth in those regulations.

(e) This section does not apply to the creation or retention of a first lien against a dwelling to finance the acquisition of that dwelling.

§ 126. Content of periodic statements

If a creditor transmits periodic statements in connection with any extension of consumer credit other than under an open end consumer credit plan, then each of those statements shall set forth each of the following items:

(1) The annual percentage rate of the total finance charge.

(2) The date by which, or the period (if any) within which, payment must be made in order to avoid additional finance charges or other charges.

(3) Such of the items set forth in section 127(b) as the Board may by regulation require as appropriate to the terms and conditions under which the extension of credit in question is made.

§ 127. Open end consumer credit plans

(a) Before opening any account under an open end consumer credit plan, the creditor shall disclose to the person to whom credit is to be extended each of the following items, to the extent applicable:

(1) The conditions under which a finance charge may be imposed, including the time period, if any, within which any credit extended may be repaid without incurring a finance charge.

(2) The method of determining the balance upon which a finance charge will be imposed.

(3) The method of determining the amount of the finance charge, including any minimum or fixed amount imposed as a finance charge.

(4) Where one or more periodic rates may be used to compute the finance charge, each such rate, the range of balances to which it is applicable, and the corresponding nominal annual percentage rate determined by multiplying the periodic rate by the number of periods in a year.

(5) If the creditor so elects,

(A) the average effective annual percentage rate of return received from accounts under the plan for a representative period of time; or

(B) whenever circumstances are such that the computation of a rate under subparagraph (A) would not be feasible or practical, or would be misleading or meaningless, a projected rate of return to be received from accounts under the plan.

The Board shall prescribe regulations, consistent with commonly accepted standards for accounting or statistical procedures, to carry out the purposes of this paragraph.

(6) The conditions under which any other charges may be imposed, and the method by which they will be determined.

(7) The conditions under which the creditor may retain or acquire any security interest in any property to secure the payment of any credit extended under the plan, and a description of the interest or interests which may be so retained or acquired.

(b) The creditor of any account under an open end consumer credit plan shall transmit to the obligor, for each billing cycle at the end of which there is an outstanding balance in that account or with respect to which a finance charge is imposed, a statement setting forth each of the following items to the extent applicable:

(1) The outstanding balance in the account at the beginning of the statement period.

(2) The amount and date of each extension of credit during the period, and, if a purchase was involved, a brief identification (unless previously furnished) of the goods or services purchased.

(3) The total amount credited to the account during the period.

(4) The amount of any finance charge added to the account during the period, itemized to show the amounts, if any, due to the application of percentage rates and the amount, if any, imposed as a minimum or fixed charge.

(5) Where one or more periodic rates may be used to compute the finance charge, each such rate, the range of balances to which it is applicable, and, unless the annual percentage rate (determined under Section 107(a)(2)) is required to be disclosed pursuant to paragraph (6), the corresponding nominal annual percentage rate determined by multiplying the periodic rate by the number of periods in a year.

(6) Where the total finance charge exceeds 50 cents for a monthly or longer billing cycle, or the pro rata part of 50 cents for a billing cycle shorter than monthly, the total finance charge expressed as an annual percentage rate (determined under section 107(a)(2)), except that if the finance charge is the sum of two or more products of a rate times a portion of the balance, the creditor may, in lieu of disclosing a single rate for the total charge, disclose each such rate expressed as an annual percentage rate, and the part of the balance to which it is applicable.

(7) At the election of the creditor, the average effective annual percentage rate of return (or the projected rate) under the plan as prescribed in subsection (a)(5).

(8) The balance on which the finance charge was computed and a statement of how the balance was determined. If the balance is determined without first deducting all credits during the period, that fact and the amount of such payments shall also be disclosed.

(9) The outstanding balance in the account at the end of the period.

(10) The date by which, or the period (if any) within which, payment must be made to avoid additional finance charges.

(c) In the case of any open end consumer credit plan in existence on the effective date of this subsection, the items described in subsection (a), to the extent applicable, shall be disclosed in a notice mailed or delivered to the obligor not later than thirty days after that date.

§ 128. Sales not under open end credit plans

(a) In connection with each consumer credit sale not under an open end credit plan, the creditor shall disclose each of the following items which is applicable:

(1) The cash price of the property or service purchased.

(2) The sum of any amounts credited as downpayment (including any trade-in).

(3) The difference between the amount referred to in paragraph (1) and the amount referred to in paragraph (2).

(4) All other charges, individually itemized, which are included in the amount of the credit extended but which are not part of the finance charge.

(5) The total amount to be financed (the sum of the amount described in paragraph (3) plus the amount described in paragraph (4)).

(6) Except in the case of a sale of a dwelling, the amount of the finance charge, which may in whole or in part be designated as a time-price differential or any similar term to the extent applicable.

(7) The finance charge expressed as an annual percentage rate except in the case of a finance charge

(A) which does not exceed $5 and is applicable to an amount financed not exceeding $75, or

(B) which does not exceed $7.50 and is applicable to an amount financed exceeding $75.

A creditor may not divide a consumer credit sale into two or more sales to avoid the disclosure of an annual percentage rate pursuant to this paragraph.

(8) The number, amount, and due dates or periods of payments scheduled to repay the indebtedness.

(9) The default, delinquency, or similar charges payable in the event of late payments.

(10) A description of any security interest held or to be retained or acquired by the creditor in connection with the extension of credit, and a clear identification of the property to which the security interest relates.

(b) Except as otherwise provided in this chapter, the disclosures required under subsection (a) shall be made before the credit is extended, and may be made by disclosing the information in the contract or other evidence of indebtedness to be signed by the purchaser.

(c) If a creditor receives a purchase order by mail or telephone without personal solicitation, and the cash price and the deferred payment price and the terms of financing, including the annual percentage rate, are set forth in the creditor's catalog or other printed material distributed to the public, then the disclosures required under subsection (a) may be made at any time not later than the date the first payment is due.

(d) If a consumer credit sale is one of a series of consumer credit sales transactions made pursuant to an agreement providing for the addition of the deferred payment price of that sale to an existing outstanding balance, and the person to whom the credit is extended has approved in writing both the annual percentage rate or rates and the method of computing the finance charge or charges, and the creditor retains no security interest in any property as to which he has received payments aggregating the amount of the sales price including any finance charges attributable thereto, then the disclosure required under subsection (a) for the particular sale may be made at any time not later than the date the first payment for that sale is due. For the purposes of this subsection, in the case of items purchased on different dates, the first purchased shall be deemed first paid for, and in the case of items purchased on the same date, the lowest priced shall be deemed first paid for.

§ 129. Consumer loans not under open end credit plans

(a) Any creditor making a consumer loan or otherwise extending consumer credit in a transaction which is neither a consumer credit sale nor under an open end consumer credit plan shall disclose each of the following items, to the extent applicable:

(1) The amount of credit of which the obligor will have the actual use, or which is or will be paid to him or for his account or to another person on his behalf.

(2) All charges, individually itemized, which are included in the amount of credit extended but which are not part of the finance charge.

(3) The total amount to be financed (the sum of the amounts referred to in paragraph (1) plus the amounts referred to in paragraph (2)).

(4) Except in the case of a loan secured by a first lien on a dwelling and made to finance the purchase of that dwelling, the amount of the finance charge.

(5) The finance charge expressed as an annual percentage rate except in the case of a finance charge

(A) which does not exceed $5 and is applicable to an extension of consumer credit not exceeding $75, or

(B) which does not exceed $7.50 and is applicable to an extension of consumer credit exceeding $75.

A creditor may not divide an extension of credit into two or more transactions to avoid the disclosure of an annual percentage rate pursuant to this paragraph.

(6) The number, amount, and the due dates or periods of payments scheduled to repay the indebtedness.

(7) The default, delinquency, or similar charges payable in the event of late payments.

(8) A description of any security interest held or to be retained or acquired by the creditor in connection with the extension of credit, and a clear identification of the property to which the security interest relates.

(b) Except as otherwise provided in this chapter, the disclosures required by subsection (a) shall be made before the credit is extended, and may be made by disclosing the information in the note or other evidence of indebtedness to be signed by the obligor.

(c) If a creditor receives a request for an extension of credit by mail or telephone without personal solicitation and the terms of financing, including the annual percentage rate for representative amounts of credit, are set forth in the creditor's printed material distributed to the public, or in the contract of loan or other printed material delivered to the obligor, then the disclosures required under subsection (a) may be made at any time not later than the date the first payment is due.

§ 130. Civil liability

(a) Except as otherwise provided in this section, any creditor who fails in connection with any consumer credit transaction to disclose to any person any information required under this chapter to be disclosed to that person is liable to that person in an amount equal to the sum of

(1) twice the amount of the finance charge in connection with the transaction, except that the liability under this paragraph shall not be less than $100 nor greater than $1,000; and

(2) in the case of any successful action to enforce the foregoing liability, the costs of the action together with a reasonable attorney's fee as determined by the court.

(b) A creditor has no liability under this section if within fifteen days after discovering an error, and prior to the institution of an action under this section or the receipt of written notice of the error, the creditor notifies the person concerned of the error and makes whatever adjustments in the appropriate account are necessary to insure that the person will not be required to pay a finance charge in excess of the amount or percentage rate actually disclosed.

(c) A creditor may not be held liable in any action brought under this section for a violation of this chapter if the creditor shows by a preponderance of evidence that the violation was not intentional and resulted from a bona fide error notwithstanding the maintenance of procedures reasonably adapted to avoid any such error.

(d) Any action which may be brought under this section against the original creditor in any credit transaction involving a security interest in real property may be maintained against any subsequent assignee of the original creditor where the assignee, its subsidiaries or affiliates were in a continuing business relationship with the original creditor either at the time the credit was extended or at the time of the assignment, unless the assignment was involuntary, or the assignee shows by a preponderance of evidence that it did not have reasonable grounds to believe that the original creditor was engaged in violations of this chapter, and that it maintained procedures reasonably adapted to apprise it of the existence of any such violations.

(e) Any action under this section may be brought in any United States district court, or in any other court of competent jurisdiction, within one year from the date of the occurrence of the violation.

§ 131. Written acknowledgment as proof of receipt

Except as provided in section 125(c) and except in the case of actions brought under section 130(d), in any action or proceeding by or against any subsequent assignee of the original creditor without knowledge to the contrary by the assignee when he acquires the obligation, written acknowledgment of receipt by a person to whom a statement is required to be given pursuant to this title shall be conclusive proof of the delivery thereof and, unless the violation is apparent on the face of the statement, of compliance with this chapter. This section does not affect the rights of the obligor in any action against the original creditor.

CHAPTER 3 — CREDIT ADVERTISING

Sec.

141. Catalogs and multiple-page advertisements.
142. Advertising of downpayments and installments.
143. Advertising of open end credit plans.
144. Advertising of credit other than open end plans.
145. Nonliability of media.

§ 141. Catalogs and multiple-page advertisements

For the purposes of this chapter, a catalog or other multiple-page advertisement shall be considered a single advertisement if it clearly and conspicuously displays a credit terms table on which the information required to be stated under this chapter is clearly set forth.

§ 142. Advertising of downpayments and installments

No advertisement to aid, promote, or assist directly or indirectly any extension of consumer credit may state

(1) that a specific periodic consumer credit amount or installment amount can be arranged, unless the creditor usually and customarily arranges credit payments or installments for that period and in that amount.

(2) that a specified downpayment is required in connection with any extension of consumer credit, unless the creditor usually and customarily arranges downpayments in that amount.

§ 143. Advertising of open end credit plans

No advertisement to aid, promote, or assist directly or indirectly the extension of consumer credit under an open end credit plan may set forth any of the specific terms of that plan or the appropriate rate determined under section 127(a)(5) unless it also clearly and conspicuously sets forth all of the following items:

(1) The time period, if any, within which any credit extended may be repaid without incurring a finance charge.

(2) The method of determining the balance upon which a finance charge will be imposed.

(3) The method of determining the amount of the finance charge, including any minimum or fixed amount imposed as a finance charge.

(4) Where periodic rates may be used to compute the finance charge, the periodic rates expressed as annual percentage rates.

(5) Such other or additional information for the advertising of open end credit plans as the Board may by regulation require to provide for adequate comparison of credit costs as between different types of open end credit plans.

§ 144. Advertising of credit other than open end plans

(a) Except as provided in subsection (b), this section applies to any advertisement to aid, promote, or assist directly or indirectly any consumer credit sale, loan, or other extension of credit subject to the provisions of this title, other than an open end credit plan.

(b) The provisions of this section do not apply to advertisements of residential real estate except to the extent that the Board may by regulation require.

(c) If any advertisement to which this section applies states the rate of a finance charge, the advertisement shall state the rate of that charge expressed as an annual percentage rate.

(d) If any advertisement to which this section applies states the amount of the downpayment, if any, the amount of any installment payment, the dollar amount of any finance charge, or the number of installments or the period of repayment, then the advertisement shall state all of the following items:

(1) The cash price or the amount of the loan as applicable.

(2) The downpayment, if any.

(3) The number, amount, and due dates or period of payments scheduled to repay the indebtedness if the credit is extended.

(4) The rate of the finance charge expressed as an annual percentage rate.

§ 145. Nonliability of media

There is no liability under this chapter on the part of any owner or personnel, as such, of any medium in which an advertisement appears or through which it is disseminated.

TITLE II—EXTORTIONATE CREDIT TRANSACTIONS

Sec.

201. Findings and purpose.

§ 201. Findings and purpose

(a) The Congress makes the following findings:

(1) Organized crime is interstate and international in character. Its activities involve many billions of dollars each year. It is directly responsible for murders, willful injuries to person and property, corruption of officials, and terrorization of countless citizens. A substantial part of the income of organized crime is generated by extortionate credit transactions.

(2) Extortionate credit transactions are characterized by the use, or the express implicit threat of the use, of violence or other criminal means to cause harm to person, reputation, or property as a means of enforcing repayment. Among the factors which have rendered past efforts at prosecution almost wholly ineffective has been the existence of exclusionary rules of evidence stricter than necessary for the protection of constitutional rights.

(3) Extortionate credit transactions are carried on to a substantial extent in interstate and foreign commerce and through the means and instrumentalities of such commerce. Even where extortionate credit transactions are purely intrastate in character, they nevertheless directly affect interstate and foreign commerce.

(4) Extortionate credit transactions directly impair the effectiveness and frustrate the purposes of the laws enacted by the Congress on the subject of bankruptcies.

(b) On the basis of the findings stated in subsection (a) of this section, the Congress determines that the provisions of chapter 42 of title 18 of the United States Code are necessary and proper for the purpose of carrying into execution the powers of Congress to regulate commerce and to establish uniform and effective laws on the subject of bankruptcy.

§ 202. Amendments to title 18, United States Code.

(a) Title 18 of the United States Code is amended by inserting the following new chapter immediately after chapter 41 thereof:

"CHAPTER 42 — EXTORTIONATE CREDIT TRANSACTIONS

"Sec.

"891. Definitions and rules of construction.

"892. Making extortionate extensions of credit.

"893. Financing extortionate extensions of credit.

"894. Collection of extensions of credit by extortionate means.

"895. Immunity of witnesses.

"896. Effect on State laws.

"§ 891. Definitions and rules of construction

"For the purposes of this chapter:

"(1) To extend credit means to make or renew any loan, or to enter into any agreement, tacit or express, whereby the repayment or satisfaction of any debt or claim, whether acknowledged or disputed, valid or invalid, and however arising, may or will be deferred.

"(2) The term 'creditor', with reference to any given extension of credit, refers to any person making that extension of credit, or to any person claiming by, under, or through any person making that extension of credit.

"(3) The term 'debtor', with reference to any given extension of credit, refers to any person to whom that extension of credit is made, or to any person who guarantees the repayment of that extension of credit, or in any manner undertakes to indemnify the creditor against loss resulting from the failure of any person to whom that extension of credit is made to repay the same.

"(4) The repayment of any extension of credit includes the repayment, satisfaction, or discharge in whole or in part of any debt or claim, acknowledged or disputed, valid or invalid, resulting from or in connection with that extension of credit.

"(5) To collect an extension of credit means to induce in any way any person to make repayment thereof.

"(6) An extortionate extension of credit is any extension of credit with respect to which it is the understanding of the creditor and the debtor at the time it is made that delay in making repayment or failure to make repayment could result in the use of violence or other criminal means to cause harm to the person, reputation, or property of any person.

"(7) An extortionate means is any means which involves the use, or an express or implicit threat of use, of violence or other criminal means to cause harm to the person, reputation, or property of any person.

"(8) The term 'State' includes the District of Columbia, the Commonwealth of Puerto Rico, and territories and possessions of the United States.

"(9) State law, including conflict of laws rules, governing the enforceability through civil judicial processes of repayment of any extension of credit or the performance of any promise given in consideration thereof shall be judicially noticed. This paragraph does not impair any authority which any court would otherwise have to take judicial notice of any matter of State law.

"§ 892. Making extortionate extensions of credit

"(a) Whoever makes any extortionate extension of credit, or conspires to do so, shall be fined not more than $10,000 or imprisoned not more than 20 years, or both.

"(b) In any prosecution under this section, if it is shown that all of the following factors were present in connection with the extension of credit in question, there is prima facie evidence that the extension of credit was extortionate, but this subsection is nonexclusive and in no way limits the effect or applicability of subsection (a):

"(1) The repayment of the extension of credit, or the performance of any promise given in consideration thereof, would be unenforceable, through civil judicial processes against the debtor

"(A) in the jurisdiction within which the debtor, if a natural person, resided or

"(B) in every jurisdiction within which the debtor, if other than a natural person, was incorporated or qualified to do business at the time the extension of credit was made.

"(2) The extension of credit was made at a rate of interest in excess of an annual rate of 45 per centum calculated according to the actuarial method of allocating payments made on a debt between principal and interest, pursuant to which a payment is applied first to the accumulated interest and the balance is applied to the unpaid principal.

"(3) At the time the extension of credit was made, the debtor reasonably believed that either

"(A) one or more extensions of credit by the creditor had been collected or attempted to be collected by extortionate means, or the nonrepayment thereof had been punished by extortionate means; or

"(B) the creditor had a reputation for the use of extortionate means to collect extensions of credit or to punish the nonrepayment thereof.

"(4) Upon the making of the extension of credit, the total of the extensions of credit by the creditor to the debtor then outstanding, including any unpaid interest or similar charges, exceeded $100.

"(c) In any prosecution under this section, if evidence has been introduced tending to show the existence of any of the circumstances described in subsection (b)(1) or (b)(2), and direct evidence of the actual belief of the debtor as to the creditor's collection practices is not available, then for the purpose of showing the understanding of the debtor and the creditor at the time the extension of credit was made, the court may in its discretion allow evidence to be introduced tending to show the reputation as to collection practices of the creditor in any community of which the debtor was a member at the time of the extension.

"§ 893. Financing extortionate extensions of credit

"Whoever willfully advances money or property, whether as a gift, as a loan, as an investment, pursuant to partnership or profit-sharing agreement, or otherwise, to any person, with reasonable grounds to believe that it is the intention of that person to use the money or property so advanced directly or indirectly for the purpose of making extortionate extensions of credit, shall be fined not more than $10,000 or an amount not exceeding twice the value of the money or property so advanced, whichever is greater, or shall be imprisoned not more than 20 years, or both.

"§ 894. Collection of extensions of credit by extortionate means

"(a) Whoever knowingly participates in any way, or conspires to do so, in the use of any extortionate means

"(1) to collect or attempt to collect any extension of credit, or

"(2) to punish any person for the nonrepayment thereof,

shall be fined not more than $10,000 or imprisoned not more than 20 years, or both.

"(b) In any prosecution under this section, for the purpose of showing an implicit threat as a means of collection, evidence may be introduced tending to show that one or more extensions of credit by the creditor were, to the knowledge of the person against whom the implicit threat was alleged to have been made, collected or attempted to be collected by extortionate means or that the nonrepayment thereof was punished by extortionate means.

"(c) In any prosecution under this section, if evidence has been introduced tending to show the existence, at the time the extension of credit in question was made, of the circumstances described in section 892(b)(1) or the circumstances described in section 892(b)(2), and direct evidence of the actual belief of the debtor as to the creditor's collection practices is not available, then for the purpose of showing that words or other means of communication, shown to have been employed as a means of collection, in fact carried an express or implicit threat, the court may in its discretion allow evidence to be introduced tending to show the reputation of the defendant in any community of which the person against whom the alleged threat was made was a member at the time of the collection or attempt at collection.

"§ 895. Immunity of witnesses

"Whenever in the judgment of a United States attorney the testimony of any witness, or the production of books, papers, or other evidence by any witness in any case or proceeding before any grand jury or court of the United States involving any violation of this chapter is necessary to the public interest, he, upon the approval of the Attorney General or his designated representative, may make application to the court that the witness be instructed to testify or produce evidence subject to the provisions of this section. Upon order of the court the witness shall not be excused from testifying or from producing books, papers, or other evidence on the ground that the testimony or evidence required of him may tend to incriminate him or subject him to a penalty or forfeiture. But no such witness may be prosecuted or subjected to any penalty or forfeiture for or on account of any transaction, matter, or thing concerning which he is compelled, after having claimed his privilege against self-incrimination, to testify or produce evidence, nor may testimony so compelled be used as evidence in any criminal proceeding against him in any court, except a prosecution for perjury or contempt committed while giving testimony or producing evidence under compulsion as provided in this section.

"§ 896. Effect on State laws

"This chapter does not preempt any field of law with respect to which State legislation would be permissible in the absence of this chapter. No law of any State which would be valid in the absence of this chapter may be held invalid or inapplicable by virtue of the existence of this chapter, and no officer, agency, or instrumentality of any State may be deprived by virtue of this chapter of any jurisdiction over any offense over which it would have jurisdiction in the absence of this chapter."

(b) The table of chapters captioned "Part I—Crimes" at the beginning of part I of title 18 of the United States Code is amended by inserting

"42. Extortionate credit transactions .... 891" immediately above

"43. False personation .... 911".

§ 203. Reports by Attorney General

The Attorney General shall make an annual report to Congress of the activities of the Department of Justice in the enforcement of chapter 42 of title 18 of the United States Code.

TITLE III—RESTRICTION ON GARNISHMENT

305. Exemption for State-regulated garnishments.
306. Enforcement by Secretary of Labor.
307. Effect on State laws.

§ 301. Findings and purpose

(a) The Congress finds:

(1) The unrestricted garnishment of compensation due for personal services encourages the making of predatory extensions of credit. Such extensions of credit divert money into excessive credit payments and thereby hinder the production and flow of goods in interstate commerce.

(2) The application of garnishment as a creditors' remedy frequently results in loss of employment by the debtor, and the resulting disruption of employment, production, and consumption constitutes a substantial burden on interstate commerce.

(3) The great disparities among the laws of the several States relating to garnishment have, in effect, destroyed the uniformity of the bankruptcy laws and frustrated the purposes thereof in many areas of the country.

(b) On the basis of the findings stated in subsection (a) of this section, the Congress determines that the provisions of this title are necessary and proper for the purpose of carrying into execution the powers of the Congress to regulate commerce and to establish uniform bankruptcy laws.

§ 302. Definitions

For the purposes of this title:

(a) The term "earnings" means compensation paid or payable for personal services, whether denominated as wages, salary, commission, bonus, or otherwise, and includes periodic payments pursuant to a pension or retirement program.

(b) The term "disposable earnings" means that part of the earnings of any individual remaining after the deduction from those earnings of any amounts required by law to be withheld.

(c) The term "garnishment" means any legal or equitable procedure through which the earnings of any individual are required to be withheld for payment of any debt.

§ 303. Restriction on garnishment

(a) Except as provided in subsection (b) and in section 305, the maximum part of the aggregate disposable earnings of an individual for any workweek which is subjected to garnishment may not exceed

(1) 25 per centum of his disposable earnings for that week, or

(2) the amount by which his disposable earnings for that week exceed thirty times the Federal minimum hourly wage prescribed by section 6(a)(1) of the Fair Labor Standards Act of 1938 in effect at the time the earnings are payable,

whichever is less. In the case of earnings for any pay period other than a week, the Secretary of Labor shall by regulation prescribe a multiple of the Federal minimum hourly wage equivalent in effect to that set forth in paragraph (2).

(b) The restrictions of subsection (a) do not apply in the case of

(1) any order of any court for the support of any person.

(2) any order of any court of bankruptcy under Chapter XIII of the Bankruptcy Act.

(3) any debt due for any State or Federal tax.

(c) No court of the Unnted States or any State may make, execute, or enforce any order or process in violation of this section.

§304. Restriction on discharge from employment by reason of garnishment

(a) No employer may discharge any employee by reason of the fact that his earnings have been subjected to garnishment for any one indebtedness.

(b) Whoever willfully violates subsection (a) of this section shall be fined not more than $1,000, or imprisoned not more than one year, or both.

§ 305. Exemption for State-regulated garnishments

The Secretary of Labor may by regulation exempt from the provisions of section 303(a) garnishments issued under the laws of any State if he determines that the laws of that State provide restrictions on garnishment which are substantially similar to those provided in section 303(a).

§ 306. Enforcement by Secretary of Labor

The Secretary of Labor, acting through the Wage and Hour Division of the Department of Labor, shall enforce the provisions of this title.

§ 307. Effect on State laws

This title does not annul, alter, or affect, or exempt any person from complying with, the laws of any State

(1) prohibiting garnishments or providing for more limited garnishments than are allowed under this title, or

(2) prohibiting the discharge of any employee by reason of the fact that his earnings have been subjected to garnishment for more than one indebtedness.

TITLE IV—NATIONAL COMMISSION ON CONSUMER FINANCE

Sec.

§ 401. Establishment

There is established a bipartisan National Commission on Consumer Finance, referred to in this title as the "Commission".

§ 402. Membership of the Commission

(a) The Commission shall be composed of nine members, of whom

(1) three are Members of the Senate appointed by the President of the Senate;

(2) three are Members of the House of Representatives appointed by the Speaker of the House of Representatives; and

(3) three are persons not employed in a full-time capacity by the United States appointed by the President, one of whom he shall designate as Chairman.

(b) A vacancy in the Commission does not affect its powers and may be filled in the same manner as the original appointment.

(c) Five members of the Commission constitute a quorum.

§ 403. Compensation of members

(a) Members of Congress who are members of the Commission shall serve without compensation in addition to that received for their services as Members of Congress; but they shall be reimbursed for travel, subsistence, and other necessary expenses incurred by them in the performance of the duties vested in the Commission.

(b) Each member of the Commission who is appointed by the President may receive compensation at a rate of $100 for each day he is engaged upon work of the Commission, and shall be reimbursed for travel expenses, including per diem in lieu of subsistence as authorized by law (5 U.S.C. 5703) for persons in the Government service employed intermittently.

§ 404. Duties of the Commission

(a) The Commission shall study and appraise the functioning and structure of the consumer finance industry, as well as consumer credit transactions generally. The Commission, in its report and recommendations to the Congress, shall include treatment of the following topics:

(1) The adequacy of existing arrangements to provide consumer credit at reasonable rates.

(2) The adequacy of existing supervisory and regulatory mechanisms to protect the public from unfair practices, and insure the informed use of consumer credit.

(3) The desirability of Federal chartering of consumer finance companies, or other Federal regulatory measures.

(b) The Commission may make interim reports and shall make a final report of its findings, recommendations, and conclusions to the President and to the Congress by January 1, 1971.

§ 405. Powers of the Commission

(a) The Commission, or any three members thereof as authorized by the Commission, may conduct hearings anywhere in the United States or otherwise secure data and expressions of opinion pertinent to the study. In connection therewith the Commission is authorized by majority vote

(1) to require, by special or general orders, corporations, business firms, and individuals to submit in writing such reports and answers to questions as the Commission may prescribe; such submission shall be made within such reasonable period and under oath or otherwise as the Commission may determine.

(2) to administer oaths.

(3) to require by subpena the attendance and testimony of witnesses and the production of all documentary evidence relating to the execution of its duties.

(4) in the case of disobedience to a subpena or order issued under paragraph (a) of this section to invoke the aid of any district court of the United States in requiring compliance with such subpena or order.

(5) in any proceeding or investigation to order testimony to be taken by

deposition before any person who is designated by the Commission and has the power to administer oaths, and in such instances to compel testimony and the production of evidence in the same manner as authorized under subparagraphs (3) and (4) above.

(6) to pay witnesses the same fees and mileage as are paid in like circumstances in the courts of the United States.

(b) Any district court of the United States within the jurisdiction of which an inquiry is carried on may, in case of refusal to obey a subpena or order of the Commission issued under paragraph (a) of this section, issue an order requiring compliance therewith; and any failure to obey the order of the court may be punished by the court as a contempt thereof.

(c) The Commission may require directly from the head of any Federal executive department or independent agency available information which the Commission deems useful in the discharge of its duties. All departments and independent agencies of the Government shall cooperate with the Commission and furnish all information requested by the Commission to the extent permitted by law.

(d) The Commission may enter into contracts with Federal or State agencies, private firms, institutions, and individuals for the conduct of research or surveys, the preparation of reports, and other activities necessary to the discharge of its duties.

(e) When the Commission finds that publication of any information obtained by it is in the public interest and would not give an unfair competitive advantage to any person, it may publish the information in the form and manner deemed best adapted for public use, except that data and information which would separately disclose the business transactions of any person, trade secrets, or names of customers shall be held confidential and shall not be disclosed by the Commission or its staff. The Commission shall permit business firms or individuals reasonable access to documents furnished by them for the purpose of obtaining or copying those documents as need may arise.

(f) The Commission may delegate any of its functions to individual members of the Commission or to designated individuals on its staff and to make such rules and regulations as are necessary for the conduct of its business, except as otherwise provided in this title.

§ 406. Administrative arrangements

(a) The Commission may, without regard to the provisions of title 5, United States Code, relating to appointments in the competitive service or to classification and General Schedule pay rates, appoint and fix the compensation of an executive director. The executive director, with the approval of the Commission, shall employ and fix the compensation of such additional personnel as may be necessary to carry out the functions of the Commission, but no individual so appointed may receive compensation in excess of the rate authorized for GS–18 under the General Schedule.

(b) The executive director, with the approval of the Commission, may obtain services in accordance with section 3109 of title 5 of the United States Code, but at rates for individuals not to exceed $100 per diem.

(c) The head of any executive department or independent agency of the

Federal Government may detail, on a reimbursable basis, any of its personnel to assist the Commission in carrying out its work.

(d) Financial and administrative services (including those related to budgeting and accounting, financial reporting, personnel, and procurement) shall be provided the Commission by the General Services Administration, for which payment shall be made in advance, or by reimbursement, from funds of the Commission in such amounts as may be agreed upon by the Chairman of the Commission and the Administrator of General Services. The regulations of the General Services Administration for the collection of indebtedness of personnel resulting from erroneous payments apply to the collection of erroneous payments made to or on behalf of a Commission employee, and regulations of that Administration for the administrative control of funds apply to appropriations of the Commission.

(e) Ninety days after submission of its final report, as provided in section 404(b), the Commission shall cease to exist.

§ 407. Authorization of appropriations

There are authorized to be appropriated such sums not in excess of $1,500,000 as may be necessary to carry out the provisions of this title. Any money so appropriated shall remain available to the Commission until the date of its expiration, as fixed by section 406(e).

TITLE V—GENERAL PROVISIONS

Sec.

501. Severability.

502. Captions and catchlines for reference only.

503. Grammatical usages.

504. Effective dates.

§ 501. Severability

If a provision enacted by this Act is held invalid, all valid provisions that are severable from the invalid provision remain in effect. If a provision enacted by this Act is held invalid in one or more of its applications, the provision remains in effect in all valid applications that are severable from the invalid application or applications.

§ 502. Captions and catchlines for reference only

Captions and catchlines are intended solely as aids to convenient reference, and no inference as to the legislative intent with respect to any provision enacted by this Act may be drawn from them.

§ 503. Grammatical usages

In this Act:

(1) The word "may" is used to indicate that an action either is authorized or is permitted.

(2) The word "shall" is used to indicate that an action is both authorized and required.

(3) The phrase "may not" is used to indicate that an action is both unauthorized and forbidden.

(4) Rules of law are stated in the indicative mood.

§ 504. Effective dates

(a) Except as otherwise specified, the provisions of this Act take effect upon enactment.

(b) Chapters 2 and 3 of title I take effect on July 1, 1969.

(c) Title III takes effect on July 1, 1970.

Approved May 29, 1968.

Appendix VII

FTC Guides Against Bait Advertising

(Nov. 24, 1959)

The following guides have been adopted by the Federal Trade Commission for the use of its staff in the evaluation of bait advertising [1] and related switch practices. While the guides do not purport to be all inclusive, they enumerate the major indications of bait and switch schemes. They have been released to the public in the interest of consumer education and to obtain voluntary, simultaneous and prompt cooperation by those whose practices are subject to the jurisdiction of the Federal Trade Commission.

Adversary actions against those who engage in bait advertising, and whose practices are subject to Commission jurisdiction, are brought under the Federal Trade Commission Act (15 U.S.C. Secs. 41–58). Section 5 of the Act declares unlawful, "unfair methods of competition in commerce, and unfair or deceptive acts or practices in commerce."

[1] For the purpose of these Guides "advertising" includes any form of public notice however disseminated or utilized.

The Guides

BAIT ADVERTISING DEFINED

Bait advertising is an alluring but insincere offer to sell a product or service which the advertiser in truth does not intend or want to sell. Its purpose is to switch consumers from buying the advertised merchandise, in order to sell something else, usually at a higher price or on a basis more advantageous to the advertiser. The primary aim of a bait advertisement is to obtain leads as to persons interested in buying merchandise of the type so advertised.

1. BAIT ADVERTISEMENT

No advertisement containing an offer to sell a product should be published when the offer is not a bona fide effort to sell the advertised product.

2. INITIAL OFFER

No statement or illustration should be used in any advertisement which creates a false impression of the grade, quality, make, value, currency of model, size, color, usability, or origin of the product offered, or which may otherwise misrepresent the product in such a manner that later, on disclosure of the true facts, the purchaser may be switched from the advertised product to another.

Even though the true facts are subsequently made known to the buyer, the law is violated if the first contact or interview is secured by deception.

3. DISCOURAGEMENT OF PURCHASE OF ADVERTISED MERCHANDISE

No act or practice should be engaged in by an advertiser to discourage the purchase of the advertised merchandise as part of a bait scheme to sell other merchandise.

Among acts or practices which will be considered in determining if an advertisement is a bona fide offer are:
- (a) the refusal to show, demonstrate, or sell the product offered in accordance with the terms of the offer,
- (b) the disparagement by acts or words of the advertised product or the disparagement of the guarantee, credit terms, availability of service, repairs or parts, or in any other respect, in connection with it,
- (c) the failure to have available at all outlets listed in the advertisement a sufficient quantity of the advertised product to meet reasonably anticipated demands, unless the advertisement clearly and adequately discloses that supply is limited and/or the merchandise is available only at designated outlets,
- (d) the refusal to take orders for the advertised merchandise to be delivered within a reasonable period of time,
- (e) the showing or demonstrating of a product which is defective, unusable or impractical for the purpose represented or implied in the advertisement,
- (f) use of a sales plan or method of compensation for salesmen or penalizing salesmen, designed to prevent or discourage them from selling the advertised product.

4. SWITCH AFTER SALE

No practice should be pursued by an advertiser, in the event of sale of the advertised product, of "unselling" with the intent and purpose of selling other merchandise in its stead.

Among acts or practices which will be considered in determining if the initial sale was in good faith, and not a strategem to sell other merchandise, are:

(a) accepting a deposit for the advertised product, then switching the purchaser to a higher-priced product,

(b) failure to make delivery of the advertised product within a reasonable time or to make a refund,

(c) disparagement by acts or words of the advertised product, or the disparagement of the guarantee, credit terms, availability of service, repairs, or in any other respect, in connection with it,

(d) the delivery of the advertised product which is defective, unusable or impractical for the purpose represented or implied in the advertisement.

(NOTE: SALES OF ADVERTISED MERCHANDISE)

Sales of the advertised merchandise do not preclude the existence of a bait and switch scheme. It has been determined that, on occasions, this is a mere incidental by-product of the fundamental plan and is intended to provide an aura of legitimacy to the over-all operation.

Nothing contained in these Guides relieves any party subject to a Commission cease and desist order or stipulation from complying with the provisions of such order or stipulation. The Guides do not constitute a finding in and will not affect the disposition of any formal or informal matter before the Commission.

Robert M. Parrish,
Secretary.

Appendix VIII

FTC Guides Against Deceptive Advertising of Guarantees

(April 26, 1960)

The following Guides have been adopted by the Federal Trade Commission for the use of its staff in evaluation of the advertising of guarantees. They have been released to the public in the interest of education of the businessman and the consumer and to obtain voluntary, simultaneous and prompt cooperation by those whose practices are subject to the jurisdiction of the Federal Trade Commission.

The Guides enumerate the major principles applicable to the advertising of guarantees although they do not purport to be all-inclusive and do not attempt to define the exact border lines between compliance with and violation of the law.

The Federal Trade Commission Decisions, upon which these Guides are based, indicate that the major difficulty with this type of advertising has been the failure to state adequately what the guarantee is. Concerning this, an appellate court stated: "Ordinarily the word, guarantee, or warrantee, is incomplete unless it is used in connection with other explanatory words. To say a . . . [product] or other subject is guaranteed is meaningless. What is the guarantee? The answer to this question gives meaning to the word, 'guaranteed.' "

535

The Guides have application not only to "guarantees" but also to "warranties," to purported "guarantees" and "warranties," and to any promise or representation in the nature of a "guarantee" or "warranty."

Adversary actions against those who engage in deceptive advertising of guarantees and whose practices are subject to Commission jurisdiction are brought under the Federal Trade Commission Act (15 U.S.C., Secs. 41-58). Section 5 of the Act declares unlawful "unfair methods of competition in commerce and unfair or deceptive acts or practices in commerce."

The Guides

In determining whether terminology and direct or implied representations concerning guarantees, however made, i.e., in advertising or otherwise, in connection with the sale or offering for sale of a product, may be in violation of the Federal Trade Commission Act, the following general principles will be used:

I—GUARANTEES IN GENERAL

In general, any guarantee in advertising shall *clearly and conspicuously disclose—*
(a) *The nature and extent of the guarantee.*
This includes disclosure of—
> (1) What product or part of the product is guaranteed,
> (2) What characteristics or properties of the designated product or part thereof are covered by, or excluded from, the guarantee,
> (3) What is the duration of the guarantee,
> (4) What, if anything, any one claiming under the guarantee must do before the guarantor will fulfill his obligation under the guarantee, such as return of the product and payment of service or labor charges;

and
(b) *The manner in which the guarantor will perform.*
This consists primarily of a statement of exactly what the guarantor undertakes to do under the guarantee. Examples of this would be repair, replacement, refund. If the guarantor or the person receiving the guarantee has an option as to what may satisfy the guarantee this should be set out;
and
(c) *The identity of the guarantor.*
The identity of the guarantor should be clearly revealed in all advertising, as well as in any documents evidencing the guarantee. Confusion of purchasers often occurs when it is not clear whether the manufacturer or the retailer is the guarantor.

II—PRORATA ADJUSTMENT OF GUARANTEES

Many guarantees are adjusted by the guarantor on a pro rata basis. The advertising of these guarantees should clearly disclose this fact, the basis on which they will be prorated, e.g., the time for which the guaranteed product has been used, and the manner in which the guarantor will perform.

If these guarantees are to be adjusted on the basis of a price other than that paid by the purchaser, this price should be clearly and conspicuously disclosed.*

Example: "A" sells a tire with list price of $48 to "B" for $24, with a 12 months guarantee. After 6 months use the tire proves defective. If "A" adjusts on the basis of the price "B" paid, $24, "B" will only have to pay ½ of $24, or $12, for a new tire. If "A" instead adjusts on the basis of list price, "B" will owe ½ of $48, or $24, for a new tire. The guarantor would be required to disclose here the following: that this was a 12 months guarantee, that a list price of $48 would be used in the adjustment, that there would be an adjustment on the basis of the time that the tire was used, and that he would not pay the adjusted amount in cash, but would make an adjustment on a new tire.

* (*Note:* Guarantees which provide for an adjustment based on a fictitious list price should not be used even where adequate disclosure of the price used is made.)

III—"SATISFACTION OR YOUR MONEY BACK" REPRESENTATIONS

"Satisfaction or Your Money Back," "10 Day Free Trial," or similar representations will be construed as a guarantee that the full purchase price will be refunded at the option of the purchaser.

If this guarantee is subject to any conditions or limitations whatsoever, they shall be set forth as provided for in Guide I.

Example: A rose bush is advertised under the representation "Satisfaction or Your Money Back." The guarantor requires return of the product within one year of purchase date before he will make refund. These limitations, i.e., "return" and "time" shall be clearly and conspicuously disclosed in the ad.

IV—LIFETIME GUARANTEES

If the words "Life," "Lifetime," or the like, are used in advertising to show the duration of a guarantee, and they relate to any life other than that of the purchaser or original user, the life referred to shall be clearly and conspicuously disclosed.

Example: "A" advertised that his carburetor was guaranteed for life, whereas his guarantee ran for the life of the car in which the carburetor was originally installed. The advertisement is ambiguous and deceptive and should be modified to disclose the "life" referred to.

V—SAVINGS GUARANTEES *

Advertisements frequently contain representations of guarantees that assure prospective purchasers that savings may be realized in the purchase of the advertiser's products.

Some typical advertisements of this type are "Guaranteed to save you 50%," "Guaranteed never to be undersold," "Guaranteed lowest price in town."

These advertisements should include a clear and conspicuous disclosure of what the guarantor will do if the savings are not realized, together with any time or other limitations that he may impose.

* (*Note:* The above guarantees may constitute affirmative representations of fact and, in this respect, are governed by Guide VII.)

Example: "Guaranteed lowest price in town" might be accompanied by the following disclosure:

"If within 30 days from the date that you buy a sewing machine from me, you purchase the identical machine in town for less and present a receipt therefor to me, I will refund your money."

VI—GUARANTEES UNDER WHICH THE GUARANTOR DOES NOT OR CANNOT PERFORM

A seller or manufacturer should not advertise or represent that a product is guaranteed when he cannot or does not promptly and scrupulously fulfill his obligations under the guarantee.

A specific example of refusal to perform obligations under the guarantee is use of "Satisfaction or your money back" when the guarantor cannot or does not intend promptly to make full refund upon request.

VII—GUARANTEE AS A MISREPRESENTATION

Guarantees are often employed in such a manner as to constitute representations of material facts. If such is the case, the guarantor not only undertakes to perform under the terms of the guarantee, but also assumes responsibility under the law for the truth of the representations made.

Example 1: "Guaranteed for 36 months" applied to a battery is a representation that the battery can normally be expected to last for 36 months and should not be used in connection with a battery which can normally be expected to last for only 18 months.

Example 2: "Guaranteed to grow hair or money back" is a representation that the product will grow hair and should not be used when in fact such product is incapable of growing hair.

Example 3: "Guaranteed lowest prices in town" is a representation that the advertiser's prices are lower than the prices charged by all others for the same products in the same town and should not be used when such is not the fact.

Example 4: "We guarantee you will earn $500 a month" is a representation that prospective employees will earn a minimum of $500 each month and should not be used unless such is the fact.

Nothing contained in these Guides relieves any party subject to a Commission cease and desist order or stipulation from complying with the provisions of such order or stipulation. The Guides do not constitute a finding in and will not affect the disposition of any formal or informal matter before the Commission.

Robert M. Parrish,
Secretary.

Appendix IX

FTC Guides Against Deceptive Pricing*

(January 8, 1964)

Introduction

These Guides are designed to highlight certain problems in the field of price advertising which experience has demonstrated to be especially troublesome to businessmen who in good faith desire to avoid deception of the consuming public. Since the Guides are not intended to serve as comprehensive or precise statements of law, but rather as practical aids to the honest businessman who seeks to conform his conduct to the requirements of fair and legitimate merchandising, they will be of no assistance to the unscrupulous few whose aim is to walk as close as possible to the line between legal and illegal conduct. They are to be considered as *guides,* and not as fixed rules of "do's" and "don'ts" or detailed statements of the Commission's enforcement policies. The fundamental spirit of the Guides will govern their application.

* Inquiries concerning these Guides and requests for copies should be addressed to the Bureau of Industry Guidance, Federal Trade Commission, Washington, D.C. 20580.

The basic objective of these Guides is to enable the businessman to advertise his goods honestly, and to avoid offering the consumer nonexistent bargains or bargains that will be misunderstood. Price advertising is particularly effective because of the universal hope of consumers to find bargains. Truthful price advertising, offering real bargains, is a benefit to all. But the advertiser must shun sales "gimmicks" which lure consumers into a mistaken belief that they are getting more for their money than is the fact.

GUIDE I—FORMER PRICE COMPARISONS

One of the most commonly used forms of bargain advertising is to offer a reduction from the advertiser's own former price for an article. If the former price is the actual, *bona fide* price at which the article was offered to the public on a regular basis for a reasonably substantial period of time, it provides a legitimate basis for the advertising of a price comparison. Where the former price is genuine, the bargain being advertised is a true one. If, on the other hand, the former price being advertised is not *bona fide* but fictitious—for example, where an artificial, inflated price was established for the purpose of enabling the subsequent offer of a large reduction—the "bargain" being advertised is a false one; the purchaser is not receiving the unusual value he expects. In such a case, the "reduced" price is, in reality, probably just the seller's regular price.

A former price is not necessarily fictitious merely because no sales at the advertised price were made. The advertiser should be especially careful, however, in such a case, that the price is one at which the product was openly and actively offered for sale, for a reasonably substantial period of time, in the recent, regular course of his business, honestly and in good faith—and, of course, not for the purpose of establishing a fictitious higher price on which a deceptive comparison might be based. And the advertiser should scrupulously avoid any implication that a former price is a selling, not an asking price (for example, by use of such language as, "Formerly sold at $ _____"), unless substantial sales at that price were actually made.

The following is an example of a price comparison based on a fictitious former price. John Doe is a retailer of Brand X fountain pens, which cost him $5 each. His usual markup is 50% over cost; that is, his regular retail price is $7.50. In order subsequently to offer an unusual "bargain," Doe begins offering Brand X at $10 per pen. He realizes that he will be able to sell no, or very few, pens at this inflated price. But he doesn't care, for he maintains that price for only a few days. Then he "cuts" the price to its usual level—$7.50—and advertises: "Terrific Bargain: X Pens, Were $10, Now Only $7.50!" This is obviously a false claim. The advertised "bargain" is not genuine.

Other illustrations of fictitious price comparisons could be given. An advertiser might use a price at which he never offered the article at all; he might feature a price which was not used in the regular course of business, or which was not used in the recent past but at some remote period in the past, without making disclosure of that fact; he might use a price that was not openly offered to the public, or that was not maintained for a reasonable length of time, but was immediately reduced.

If the former price is set forth in the advertisement, whether accompanied or not by descriptive terminology such as "Regularly," "Usually," "Formerly," etc., the advertiser should make certain that the former price is not a fictitious one. If the former price, or the amount or percentage of reduction, is not stated in the advertisement, as when the ad merely states, "Sale," the advertiser must take care that the amount of reduction is not so insignificant as to be meaningless. It should be sufficiently large that the consumer, if he knew what it was, would believe that a genuine bargain or saving was being offered. An advertiser who claims that an item has been "Reduced to $9.99," when the former price was $10.00, is misleading the consumer, who will understand the claim to mean that a much greater, and not merely nominal, reduction was being offered.

GUIDE II—RETAIL PRICE COMPARISONS; COMPARABLE VALUE COMPARISONS

Another commonly used form of bargain advertising is to offer goods at prices lower than those being charged by others for the same merchandise in the advertiser's trade area (the area in which he does business). This may be done either on a temporary or a permanent basis, but in either case the advertised higher price must be based upon fact, and not be fictitious or misleading. Whenever an advertiser represents that he is selling below the prices being charged in his area for a particular article, he should be reasonably certain that the higher price he advertises does not appreciably exceed the price at which substantial sales of the article are being made in the area—that is, a sufficient number of sales so that a consumer would consider reduction from the price to represent a genuine bargain or saving. Expressed another way, if a number of the principal retail outlets in the area are regularly selling Brand X fountain pens at $10, it is not dishonest for retailer Doe to advertise: "Brand X Pens, Price Elsewhere $10, Our Price $7.50."

The following example, however, illustrates a misleading use of this advertising technique. Retailer Doe advertises Brand X pens as having a "Retail Value $15.00, My Price $7.50," when the fact is that only a few small suburban outlets in the area charge $15. All of the larger outlets located in and around the main shopping areas charge $7.50, or slightly more or less. The advertisement here would be deceptive, since the price charged by the small suburban outlets would have no real significance to Doe's customers, to whom the advertisement of "Retail Value $15.00" would suggest a prevailing, and not merely an isolated and unrepresentative, price in the area in which they shop.

A closely related form of bargain advertising is to offer a reduction from the prices being charged either by the advertiser or by others in the advertiser's trade area for other merchandise of like grade and quality—in other words, comparable or competing merchandise—to that being advertised. Such advertising can serve a useful and legitimate purpose when it is made clear to the consumer that a comparison is being made with other merchandise and the other merchandise is, in fact, of essentially similar quality and obtainable in the area. The advertiser should, however, be reasonably certain, just as in the case of comparisons involving the same merchandise, that the price advertised as being the price of comparable merchandise does not exceed the price at which such merchandise is being offered by representative retail outlets in the area. For example, retailer

Doe advertises Brand X pen as having "Comparable Value $15.00." Unless a reasonable number of the principal outlets in the area are offering Brand Y, an essentially similar pen, for that price, this advertisement would be deceptive.

GUIDE III—ADVERTISING RETAIL PRICES WHICH HAVE BEEN ESTABLISHED OR SUGGESTED BY MANUFACTURERS (OR OTHER NON-RETAIL DISTRIBUTORS)

Many members of the purchasing public believe that a manufacturer's list price, or suggested retail price, is the price at which an article is generally sold. Therefore, if a reduction from this price is advertised, many people will believe that they are being offered a genuine bargain. To the extent that list or suggested retail prices do not in fact correspond to prices at which a substantial number of sales of the article in question are made, the advertisement of a reduction may mislead the consumer.

There are many methods by which manufacturers' suggested retail or list prices are advertised: large scale (often nation-wide) mass-media advertising by the manufacturer himself; pre-ticketing by the manufacturer; direct mail advertising; distribution of promotional material or price lists designed for display to the public. The mechanics used are not of the essence. These Guides are concerned with *any* means employed for placing such prices before the consuming public.

There would be little problem of deception in this area if all products were invariably sold at the retail price set by the manufacturer. However, the widespread failure to observe manufacturers' suggested or list prices, and the advent of retail discounting on a wide scale, have seriously undermined the dependability of list prices as indicators of the exact prices at which articles are in fact generally sold at retail. Changing competitive conditions have created a more acute problem of deception than may have existed previously. Today, only in the rare case are *all* sales of an article at the manufacturer's suggested retail or list price.

But this does not mean that all list prices are fictitious and all offers of reductions from list, therefore, deceptive. Typically, a list price is a price at which articles are sold, if not everywhere, then at least in the principal retail outlets which do not conduct their business on a discount basis. It will not be deemed fictitious if it is the price at which substantial (that is, not isolated or insignificant) sales are made in the advertiser's trade area (the area in which he does business). Conversely, if the list price is significantly in excess of the highest price at which substantial sales in the trade area are made, there is a clear and serious danger of the consumer being misled by an advertised reduction from this price.

This general principle applies whether the advertiser is a national or regional manufacturer (or other non-retail distributor), a mail-order or catalog distributor who deals directly with the consuming public, or a local retailer. But certain differences in the responsibility of these various types of businessmen should be noted. A retailer competing in a local area has at least a general knowledge of the prices being charged in his area. Therefore, before advertising a manufacturer's list price as a basis for comparison with his own lower price, the retailer should ascertain whether the list price is in fact the price regularly charged by principal outlets in his area.

In other words, a retailer who advertises a manufacturer's or distributor's suggested retail price should be careful to avoid creating a false impression that he is offering a reduction from the price at which the product is generally sold in his trade area. If a number of the principal retail outlets in the area are regularly engaged in making sales at the manufacturer's suggested price, that price may be used in advertising by one who is selling at a lower price. If, however, the list price is being followed only by, for example, small suburban stores, house-to-house canvassers, and credit houses, accounting for only an insubstantial volume of sales in the area, advertising of the list price would be deceptive.

On the other hand, a manufacturer or other distributor who does business on a large regional or national scale cannot be required to police or investigate in detail the prevailing prices of his articles throughout so large a trade area. If he advertises or disseminates a list or pre-ticketed price in good faith (i.e., as an honest estimate of the actual retail price) which does not appreciably exceed the highest price at which substantial sales are made in his trade area, he will not be chargeable with having engaged in a deceptive practice. Consider the following example:

> Manufacturer Roe, who makes Brand X pens and sells them throughout the United States, advertises his pen in a national magazine as having a "Suggested Retail Price $10," a price determined on the basis of a market survey. In a substantial number of representative communities, the principal retail outlets are selling the product at this price in the regular course of business and in substantial volume. Roe would not be considered to have advertised a fictitious "suggested retail price." If retailer Doe does business in one of these communities, he would not be guilty of a deceptive practice by advertising, "Brand X Pens, Manufacturer's Suggested Retail Price, $10.00, Our Price, $7.50."

It bears repeating that the manufacturer, distributor or retailer must in every case act honestly and in good faith in advertising a list price, and not with the intention of establishing a basis, or creating an instrumentality, for a deceptive comparison in any local or other trade area. For instance, a manufacturer may not affix price tickets containing inflated prices as an accommodation to particular retailers who intend to use such prices as the basis for advertising fictitious price reductions.

GUIDE IV—BARGAIN OFFERS BASED UPON THE PURCHASE OF OTHER MERCHANDISE

Frequently, advertisers choose to offer bargains in the form of additional merchandise to be given a customer on the condition that he purchase a particular article at the price usually offered by the advertiser. The forms which such offers may take are numerous and varied, yet all have essentially the same purpose and effect. Representative of the language frequently employed in such offers are "Free," "Buy One—Get One Free," "2-For-1 Sale," "Half Price Sale," "1¢ Sale," "50% Off," etc. Literally, of course, the seller is not offering anything "free" (i.e., an unconditional gift), or ½ free, or for only 1¢, when he makes such an offer, since the purchaser is required to purchase an article in order to receive the "free" or "1¢" item. It is important, therefore, that where such a form of offer is used, care be taken not to mislead the consumer.

Where the seller, in making such an offer, increases his regular price of the article required to be bought, or decreases the quantity and quality of that article, or otherwise attaches strings (other than the basic condition that the article be purchased in order for the purchaser to be entitled to the "free" or "1¢" additional merchandise) to the offer, the consumer may be deceived.

Accordingly, whenever a "free," "2-for-1," "half price sale," "1¢ sale," "50% off" or similar type of offer is made, all the terms and conditions of the offer should be made clear at the outset.

GUIDE V—MISCELLANEOUS PRICE COMPARISONS

The practices covered in the provisions set forth above represent the most frequently employed forms of bargain advertising. However, there are many variations which appear from time to time and which are, in the main, controlled by the same general principles. For example, retailers should not advertise a retail price as a "wholesale" price. They should not represent that they are selling at "factory" prices when they are not selling at the prices paid by those purchasing directly from the manufacturer. They should not offer seconds or imperfect or irregular merchandise at a reduced price without disclosing that the higher comparative price refers to the price of the merchandise if perfect. They should not offer an advance sale under circumstances where they do not in good faith expect to increase the price at a later date, or make a "limited" offer which, in fact, is not limited. In all of these situations, as well as in others too numerous to mention, advertisers should make certain that the bargain offer is genuine and truthful. Doing so will serve their own interest as well as that of the public.

These Guides supersede the Guides Against Deceptive Pricing adopted October 2, 1958.

Adopted: December 20, 1963.

Joseph W. Shea,
Secretary.

Appendix X

FTC Guides Against Debt Collection Deception

(June 14, 1968)

The Commission is cognizant that many and varied ruses are often employed in obtaining information relative to debts and debtors that would not otherwise have been furnished had the true purpose of the requests for such information been disclosed and that subterfuges are sometimes used to induce settlement of claims. The Commission does not, of course, condone avoidance of payment of honest debts, but neither can it countenance the use of false or misleading means in collecting them. These guides are intended to serve as practical aids to the honest businessman who seeks to conform his conduct to the requirements of fair and legitimate business practices.

The primary objectives of these guides are (1) the prevention of deception in connection with collection or attempted collection of debts and (2) the maintenance of fair competition among those engaged in the business of collecting debts.

It is expected that these guides will encourage voluntary compliance with the law by industry members. Mandatory proceedings to prevent deceptive practices in the collection of debts may be brought under the Federal Trade Commission Act (15 U.S.C., Secs. 41–58) against those whose practices are subject to the jurisdiction of the Commission. The courts have held that the use of interstate channels of communication in promoting and carrying out deceptive collection schemes is sufficient to bring these matters within the Commission's jurisdiction.

The Guides as adopted by the Federal Trade Commission are hereinafter set forth.

Inquiries and requests for copies of the guides should be directed to the Bureau of Industry Guidance, Federal Trade Commission, Washington, D. C. 20580.

The Guides

DEFINITIONS OF TERMS AS USED IN THESE GUIDES:

"Industry Member" shall mean any person, firm, partnership, corporation, organization, association and any other legal entity engaged in the practice of collecting or attempting to collect any and all kinds of money debts for itself or others, or any person, firm, partnership, corporation, organization, association or any other legal entity which places in the hands of others through sale or otherwise, or distributes for itself or others, any kind of material used or to be used in connection with collecting or attempting to collect such debts or seeking information concerning debtors, commonly called skip-tracing.

"Debt" shall mean money which is due or alleged to be due from one to another.

"Debtor" shall mean one who owes or is alleged to owe a money debt.

"Creditor" shall mean one to whom a money debt is due or is alleged to be due.

"Credit Bureau"—any person, firm, partnership, corporation, organization, association or any other legal entity engaged in gathering, recording and disseminating favorable as well as unfavorable information relative to the credit worthiness, financial responsibility, paying habits and character of individuals, firms, corporations, and any other legal entity being considered for credit extension, so that a prospective creditor may be able to make a sound decision in the extension of credit.

"Collection Agency"—any person, firm, partnership, corporation, organization, association and any other legal entity which collects money debts for others.

GUIDE 1—DECEPTION (GENERAL)

An industry member shall not use any deceptive representation or deceptive means to collect or attempt to collect debts or to obtain information concerning debtors.

(*Note:* The Commission has found that in the collection of debts some industry members either disguise the purpose for which information is desired or hold out an inducement to debtors to furnish information which is not in their interest to supply and which they normally would not voluntarily furnish. In connection with the collection or attempted collection of debts or the seeking of information concerning debtors, the Commission has prohibited, *among others,* the following misrepresentations:

1. that an industry member was seeking information in connection with a survey.

2. that an industry member is in the business of a casting service for the motion picture or television industry.

3. that an industry member has a prepaid package for the debtor.

4. that a sum of money or valuable gift will be sent to the addressee if the required information is furnished.

5. that accounts have been turned over to innocent purchasers for value.

6. that debts have been turned over to an attorney or an independent organization engaged in the business of collecting past-due accounts.

7. that documents are legal process forms.)

GUIDE 2—DISCLOSURE OF PURPOSE

(a) An industry member shall not use or cause to be used in his behalf in connection with the collection of or the attempt to collect a debt or in connection with obtaining or attempting to obtain information concerning a debtor, any forms, letters, questionnaires, or other material printed or written which do not clearly and conspicuously disclose that such are used for the purpose of collecting or attempting to collect a debt or to obtain or attempt to obtain information concerning a debtor. (This affirmative disclosure also applies to all forms of communication, oral or otherwise.)

(b) An industry member shall not, through sale or otherwise, place in the hands of others for use in connection with the collection of or attempt to collect a debt or in connection with obtaining or attempting to obtain information concerning a debtor, any forms, letters, questionnaires or other material printed or written which do not clearly and conspicuously reveal thereon that such are used for the purpose of collecting or attempting to collect a debt or to obtain or attempt to obtain information concerning a debtor.

GUIDE 3—GOVERNMENT AFFILIATION

An industry member shall not use any trade name, address, insignia, picture, emblem, or any other means which creates a false impression that such industry member is connected with or is an agency of government.

GUIDE 4—ORGANIZATIONAL TITLE

An industry member which is not in fact a "Credit Bureau" as defined in these Guides shall not use the term "Credit Bureau" in its corporate or trade name; nor shall it use any other term of similar import or meaning in its corporate or trade name, or in any other manner, as to create the false impression that such industry member is a credit bureau.

GUIDE 5—TRADE STATUS

In collecting or attempting to collect debts due him, an industry member shall not, through the use of any designation or by any other means, create the impression that he is a collection agency, unless he is such as defined in these Guides.

GUIDE 6—SERVICES

In the solicitation of accounts for collection or for ascertainment of credit status, an industry member shall not directly, or by implication, misrepresent the services he renders.

(*Note:* Guide 6 is general in nature since the varied misrepresentations used in connection with the solicitation of accounts for collection are numerous. Listed below are a few specific examples of representations which have been prohibited by the Commission because they were false or deceptive:

1. that the industry member's organization is separated into functional divisions, such as credit reporting, analytical, tracing, and collecting.

2. that the industry member employs local representatives, regional investigators, and lawyers on his personnel staff in various States and throughout the world.

3. that collection fees are less than what the industry member actually charges.

4. that no charges will be made for accounts unless they are collected.

5. that the industry member makes personal calls on debtors to collect accounts.

6. that the industry member will furnish credit reports to parties who assign accounts to him for collection.)

Effective: September 20, 1965.

Joseph W. Shea,
Secretary.

Appendix XI

FTC Proposed "Free" Goods Guide

In order to stimulate consumer sales, attract new customers or introduce new merchandise into the marketplace, advertisers have often found the offer of free merchandise, contingent upon the purchase of some other article of merchandise or service, to be a useful and valuable marketing tool. However, because the purchasing public continually searches for the best buy, and regards the offer of free merchandise to be the ultimate bargain, advertisers must be extremely careful to avoid any possibility that consumers will be misled or deceived by such offers. Representative of the language frequently used in such offers are "Free", "Buy 1, Get 1 Free", "2-for-1 sale", "50% Off With Purchase of 2", etc. Related representations that raise many of the same questions include "Half-Price Sale", "1¢ Sale", "½ Off", etc.

The public understands that, except in the case of introductory offers, the advertiser who makes an offer of free merchandise has established a regular price for the merchandise or service which must be purchased by consumers in order to avail themselves of that which is represented to be "free". In other words, when the purchaser is told that an article is "free" to him if another article is purchased, the word "free" indicates that he is paying nothing for that article and only the regular price for the other. Thus, a purchaser has a right to believe that the merchant will not directly and immediately recover, in whole or in part, the cost of the "free" merchandise by marking up the price of the article which he must purchase or by substitution of inferior merchandise.

When using the word "free" or other words of similar import or meaning in advertising, all the terms, conditions and obligations upon which receipt and retention of a free item of merchandise (or service) are contingent should be set forth, clearly and conspicuously, *at the outset* so as to leave no reasonable probability that the terms of the advertisement or offer might be misunderstood. Stated differently, all of the terms, conditions and obligations should appear in close conjunction with the word "free", or similar words, in advertising. Disclosure of the terms of the offer, set forth in a footnote of an advertisement to which reference is made by an asterisk or other symbol placed next to the word "free" is not regarded as making disclosure at the outset.

In advertising that an article of merchandise is "free" upon the purchase of some other merchandise, the advertisers must insure (1) that the price charged for the merchandise which must be purchased is not increased, (2) that there is no reduction in the quantity, quality, or size of the merchandise which must be purchased before obtaining the "free" gift, and (3) that no other strings or conditions are attached to the offer (other than the basic condition that the article be purchased in order for the purchaser to be entitled to the "free" or "1¢ additional" merchandise).

Only the advertiser's own regular price for the merchandise to be purchased may be used as the basis for a "free" offer. Consequently, it would be deceptive to advertise an offer of "free" merchandise based on a price which is in excess of the advertiser's regular price for merchandise required to be purchased. Likewise, it would be deceptive to advertise a "free" offer and attempt to justify it on the basis of a price being charged by others in a trade area for the same or similar merchandise, when such price is in excess of the advertiser's regular price.

A regular price is the price at which an article of merchandise (or service) is openly and actively sold by the advertiser to the public on a regular basis for a reasonably substantial period of time in the recent and regular course of business. A price which (1) is not the advertiser's actual selling price, (2) is a price which was not used in the recent past but at some remote period in the past, or (3) is a price which has been used only for a short period of time, is not a regular price.

Some products are almost never sold at a single regular price but are instead sold by means of individual negotiated transactions. The seller of such products is not precluded from making a "free" offer if the product is offered at the *lowest* price at which the seller has actually sold it in the recent past.

Continuous "free" offers or the frequent repetition of such offers should be avoided. Continuous or frequently repeated offers of the type in question are false and misleading since the advertiser's regular price for merchandise to be purchased by consumers in order to avail themselves of "free" merchandise will, by lapse of time, become the regular price for the "free" merchandise together with the merchandise required to be purchased. Under such circumstances, therefore, any offer of "free" merchandise is merely illusory.

Introductory offers of "free" merchandise may be advertised on a temporary basis when advertisers expect, in good faith, to discontinue the offer after a limited time and commence selling the newly introduced merchandise separately from that which was described as "free" at a price which is not in excess of the price that prevailed during the introductory period.

This Guide does not preclude the use of non-deceptive "combination" offers in which two or more items or services, for example, toothpaste and a toothbrush, or soap and deodorant, or clothing and alterations, are offered for sale as a single unit at a single stated price, and in which no representation is made that the price is being paid for one item and the other is "free". Similarly, sellers are not precluded from setting a price for a product or service which also includes furnishing the purchaser with a second distinct product or service at one inclusive price—again where no representation is made that the latter is free.

Offers of "free" merchandise which may be deceptive for failure to meet the provisions of this Guide, may not be corrected by the substitution, for the word "free" of such similar words and terms as "gift", "given without charge", "bonus" or other words and terms which tend to convey to the consuming public the impression that an article of merchandise (or service) is "free".

(*Note:* If adopted and promulgated by the Commission, the provisions of the Guide set forth above will supersede those contained in the trade practice rule or use of the word "free", released by the Commission on December 3, 1953. In addition, provisions of those Guides and trade practice rules dealing with use of the term "free" will be construed in light of the foregoing proposed Guide.)

Appendix XII

FTC Trade Regulation Rules

Games of Chance in the Food Retailing and Gasoline Industries

The Federal Trade Commission, pursuant to the Federal Trade Commission Act, as amended, 15 U. S. C. 41, et seq., and the provisions of Part 1, Subpart B of the Commission's procedures and rules of practice, 16 CFR 1.11, et seq., has conducted a proceeding for the promulgation of a trade regulation rule relating to games of chance in the food retailing and gasoline industries. Notice of this proceeding, including two proposed rules, was published in the FEDERAL REGISTER on January 7, 1969 (34 F. R. 218). Interested parties were thereafter afforded opportunity to participate in the proceeding through the submission of written data, views, and arguments and to appear and orally express their views as to the proposed rules and to suggest amendments, revisions and additions thereto.

The Commission has now considered all matters of fact, law, policy, and discretion, including the data, views, and arguments presented by interested parties in response to the notice and has determined that the adoption of the trade regulation rule and statement of its basis and purpose set forth herein is in the public interest.

<h2 style="text-align:center">C<small>ONTENTS</small></h2>

The rule.
Statement of basis and purpose.
Separate statement of Commissioner MacIntyre.
Separate statement of Commissioner Nicholson.
Dissenting statement of Commissioner Elman.
Interpretations.

§ 419.1 The Rule.

The Commission, on the basis of the findings made by it in this proceeding, as set forth in the accompanying Statement of Basis and Purpose, hereby promulgates as a Trade Regulation Rule its determination that in connection with the use of games of chance in the food retailing and gasoline industries, it constitutes an unfair and deceptive act or practice for users, promoters, or manufacturers of such games to:

(a) Engage in advertising or other promotions which misrepresent by any means, directly or indirectly, participants' chances of winning any prize.

(b) Engage in any advertising, including newspaper and broadcast media advertising, or other promotions such as store signs, window streamers, banners, or display materials, or issue any game piece if such game piece refers, on the exposed portion thereof, in any manner to prizes or their number or availability, which fail to disclose clearly and conspicuously:

(1) The exact number of prizes in each category or denomination to be made available during the game program and the odds of winning each such prize made available, this disclosure, for prizes in the amount or value of $25 or more, to be revised each week a game extends beyond 30 days to reflect the number of such unredeemed prizes still available and the odds existing of winning each such unredeemed prize; and

(2) The geographic area covered by the game (e.g., "Nation-wide," "Washington, D.C. metropolitan area," etc); and

(3) The total number of retail outlets participating in the game; and

(4) The scheduled termination date of the game.

(c) Fail to mix, distribute, and disperse all game pieces totally and solely on a random basis throughout the game program and throughout the geographic area covered by the game, and fail to maintain such records as are necessary to demonstrate to the Commission that total randomness was used in such mixing, distribution, and dispersal.

(d) Promote, sell, or use any game which is capable of or susceptible to being solved or "broken" so that winning game pieces or prizes are predetermined or preidentified by such methods rather than by random distribution of the participating public.

(e) Fail to furnish the Commission at the conclusion of each game, and fail to post clearly and conspicuously in each retail outlet which used the game:

(1) A complete list of the names and addresses of the winners of each prize and the amount or value of the prizes won by each;

(2) The total number of game pieces distributed;

(3) The total number of prizes in each category or denomination which were made available; and

(4) The total number of prizes in each category or denomination which were awarded.

(f) Promote or use any new game without a break in time between the new game and any game previously employed in the same establishment equivalent to the duration of the game previously employed.

NOTE: Under this paragraph (f) a retail establishment which has promoted a game for 60 days may not employ a new game without a 60-day interval between the two.

(g) Terminate any game, regardless of the scheduled termination date, prior to the distribution of all game pieces to the partcipating public.

(h) Add additional winning game pieces during the course of a game, or in any manner replenish the prize structure of a game in progress. (34 *Federal Register* 13302, August 16, 1969, effective October 17, 1969 (Part II-E of the Statement of Basis and Purpose).)

Appendix XIII

Proposed FTC Guides for Private Vocational and Home Study Schools

§ 254.1 Definitions.

(a) *Industry member.* Any person, firm, corporation, or organization engaged in the operation of a privately owned school which offers resident or correspondence courses or training or instruction purporting to prepare or qualify individuals for employment in any occupation or trade or in work requiring mechanical, technical, artistic, or clerical skills or which is for the purpose of enabling a person to improve his appearance, social aptitude, personality, or other attributes is considered to be an industry member. However, those engaged in the operation of resident public or bona fide nonprofit primary or secondary schools, or public or private nonprofit institutions of higher education which offer at least a 2-year program of accredited college level studies for resident students, shall not be considered industry members.

(b) *Accredited.* For the purpose of this part, the term "accredited" means that a course or school to which the term is applied has been evaluated through the use of established criteria by an accrediting agency or associations recognized by the U.S. Commissioner of Education of the U.S. Department of Health, Education, and Welfare, as reliable authority as to the quality of the training offered.

(c) *Approved.* For the purpose of this part, the term "approved" means that a school or course has been recognized by a State or Federal agency as meeting educational standards or other related qualifications as prescribed by that agency for the school or course to which the term is applied. It is not and should not be used interchangeably with "accredited", and the term "approved" is not justified by the mere grant of a corporate charter to operate, or license to do business as a school and should not be used unless the represented "approval" has in fact been affirmatively required or authorized by State or Federal law.

§ 254.2 Deceptive trade or business names.

(a) An industry member should not use any trade, business name, label, insignia, or designation which has the capacity and tendency or effect of misleading or deceiving students or prospective students with respect to the character of the school, its courses of instruction, its accreditation, or any other material fact.

(b) An industry member should not falsely represent directly or indirectly by the use of a trade or business name or in any other manner, that:

(1) It is a part of, or connected with, a branch, bureau, or agency of the U.S. Government, or of any State, or a Civil Service Commission;

(2) It is an employment agency or that it is an employment agent or authorized training facility for another industry or member of such industry, or otherwise deceptively conceal the fact that it is a school;

(3) It is a university, college, institute, high school, seminary, or a society or other nonprofit institution of learning.

(c) If an industry member conducts its instruction primarily by correspondence or home study or does not conduct resident instruction, a clear and conspicuous disclosure should be made in immediate conjunction with its trade or business name that it is a correspondence or home study school.

§ 254.3 Misrepresentation of extent or nature of accreditation or approval.

(a) An industry member should not misrepresent directly or indirectly the extent or nature of any accreditation or approval its school may have received from a State agency or from a nationally recognized accrediting agency, or association. Illustratively, an industry member should not:

(1) Unqualifiedly represent that its school is accredited unless all of its courses of study have in fact been accredited by an accrediting agency recognized by the U.S. Commissioner of Education of the U.S. Department of Health, Education, and Welfare, or

(2) Represent that its school or a course is approved, unless the nature, extent, and purpose of that approval are disclosed together with the identity of the approving authority, for example, "This course approved for veterans training by the (name of the State agency)". If the school or course is not also accredited by a nationally recognized accrediting agency or association such fact should be clearly and conspicuously disclosed.

(b) An industry member should not represent that students successfully completing a course or courses may transfer credit therefor to an accredited institution of higher learning or by virtue of completion thereof become qualified for admission to such an institution if such credit is not so transferable, or if the student must successfully complete a validation period of study at the accredited institution or if the student must pass an examination conducted by other educational authorities as a prerequisite to admission to such institution of higher learning.

(c) An industry member should not represent that a course of instruction has been approved by a particular industry, or that successful completion thereof qualifies the student for admission to a labor union or similar organization, or for the receipt of a State or Federal license to perform certain functions, unless such is the fact.

(d) An industry member should not represent that its courses are recommended by vocational counselors, high schools, colleges, educational organizations, employment agencies, or members or officials of a particular industry, or that it has been the subject of unsolicited testimonials or endorsements from former students or anyone else unless such is the fact. Testimonials or endorsements which do not accurately reflect current practices of the school, or current conditions or employment opportunities in the industry or occupation for which the training pertains, should not be used.

§ 254.4 Misrepresentation of facilities, services, qualifications of instructors, and status.

(a) An industry member should not misrepresent directly or indirectly in its advertising, promotional materials, or in any manner the size, location, facilities, or equipment of its school or the number or educational qualifications of its faculty and other personnel. Illustratively, an industry member should not:

(1) Use or refer to fictional organization divisions or position titles or make any representation which has the tendency or capacity to mislead or deceive students or prospective students, as to the size or importance of the school, its divisions, faculty, personnel, or officials, or in any other material respect.

(2) Misrepresent directly or indirectly the size, importance, location, facilities, or equipment of the school through use of photographs, illustrations, or any other depictions in catalogs, advertisements, or other promotional materials. For example, photographs or illustrations which purport to show school equipment should not be used if the school does not use such equipment in the conduct of its courses.

(3) Represent that the school owns, operates, or supervises a dormitory, eating, or other living accommodations unless such is the fact.

(4) Falsely or deceptively represent the location or locations at which its courses will be conducted.

(5) Misrepresent the nature, or efficacy, of its courses, training devices, methods or equipment or the number, qualifications, training, or experience of its faculty or personnel, whether by means of endorsements or otherwise.

(6) Falsely represent that it has a placement service or deceptively represent the effectiveness of its efforts to secure jobs for its graduates, or the nature or degree of assistance furnished to persons completing its courses in obtaining employment.

(7) Falsely represent that it will provide or arrange for part or full-time employment while the student is undergoing instruction; or misrepresent in any manner, directly or by implication, the availability of such employment or any other form of financial assistance.

(8) Deceptively represent the nature of any relationship which the school or

any of its officers, employees, or instructors may have with the United States Government or any of its agencies or any agency of a State or local government, or that by virtue of such a relationship or any prior relationship its students will receive preferred consideration in obtaining employment with such a government or any of its agencies.

(9) Represent directly or indirectly that certain individuals or classes of individuals are bona fide working members of its faculty, or are members of its advisory board, or have played an active part in the preparation of its instruction materials, unless such is the fact, or misrepresent in any manner, directly or by implication, the extent or nature of the association of any person with the school or the courses offered.

(10) Misrepresent the nature and extent of any personal instruction, guidance, assistance, or other attention it will provide for its students either during a course or after completion of a course.

(b) An industry member should not represent directly or indirectly that it is a nonprofit organization if it is in fact engaged in business for profit for itself or for its owners, members, or stockholders.

(c) An industry member should not falsely represent that it is affiliated with or otherwise connected with a public or private religious or charitable organization.

(d) An industry member should not falsely or deceptively represent that a course has been recently revised, or that it has a revision system or service, or misrepresent in any manner, its facilities, procedures, or ability to keep a course current.

§ 254.5 Misrepresentation of enrollment qualifications or limitations.

(a) An industry member should not misrepresent the nature or extent of any prerequisites it has established for enrollment in a course or courses. For example, it should not:

(1) Represent that a course is available only to those having a high school diploma or other specific educational qualifications, unless the sale of such a course is limited to persons possessing generally acceptable evidence of such a diploma or educational qualifications.

(2) Represent that only those who make an acceptable grade or complete successfully a certain test or examination will be admitted, if in fact enrollments are not thus limited.

(3) Falsely represent that it will accept for enrollment only a limited number of persons or a limited number of persons from a certain geographical area.

(4) Falsely represent that applications for enrollment will be considered for only a limited period of time, or that they must be submitted by a certain date.

(b) An industry member should not falsely represent that the lack of a high school education or prior training or experience is not a handicap or impediment to successful completion of a course.

(c) An industry member should take appropriate measures to insure that applicants are informed of any necessary prerequisites to the successful completion of the course, and it should insure that applicants who are not qualified for a particular course, by reason of intelligence, education, or other condition, are not enrolled therein.

§ 254.6 Misrepresentation of future employment opportunities.

(a) An industry member should not misrepresent directly or indirectly the opportunities for employment which will be available to students who successfully complete a course or courses. Illustratively, an industry member should not:

(1) Misrepresent the nature or extent of any demand for its graduates; or represent that a certain proportion or number of its graduates have obtained employment unless it has ascertained on the basis of reliable information that such is the fact.

(2) Falsely represent that its graduates will be placed in jobs in the geographical area of their choice.

(3) Misrepresent the amount of any starting or other salaries which its graduates may be likely to receive by virtue of completion of a course or courses.

(4) Represent that its graduates will be able to secure top positions in a particular field because of their completion of a particular course or courses when, in fact, such positions are available only to persons who have had additional training for or experience in such positions. Thus an industry member should not represent, for example, that "* * * salaries up to $12,000 are available" when in fact the entry level salaries are much lower.

(5) Represent that persons completing its courses will be qualified for and able to obtain employment in certain positions or industries without further training or experience when in fact such persons must serve apprenticeships, or satisfy other qualifications, or undergo additional training.

(6) Falsely represent that it has made or will make arrangements with employment agencies or industry members for interviews or preferred consideration for employment of its graduates.

(7) Falsely represent that by virtue of successful completion of a course or courses of instruction that the student will receive a raise in pay in his present position or be qualified for promotion to a higher position.

(b) An industry member should not misrepresent directly or indirectly the job security of persons engaged in certain types of employment or of its graduates.

(c) An industry member should not deceptively represent that completion of a course or courses will enable the student to pass a Civil Service examination for a particular job.

(d) An industry member should not, unless it promptly and scrupulously fulfills any obligations stated therein, use a "money-back" or similar guarantee which guarantees that:

(1) The student will pass a future Government or Civil Service examination or test, or any other form of examination or test given by any organization not affiliated with the school;

(2) The student will be placed on a list of eligibles for employment;

(3) The student will secure employment within the field of training to which the course pertains.

(e) An industry member should not condition a guarantee upon any other contingency which has the capacity, tendency or effect of misleading or deceiving students or prospective students regarding the efficacy of the course or the existence of employment opportunities, or any other material matter.

NOTE: The Commission's Guides Against Deceptive Advertising of Guarantees afford further guidance in this area. Copies are available upon request.

(f) An industry member which purports to offer training for a particular occupation, trade, profession, or other endeavor must ascertain the prerequisites to, qualifications for, or limitations on employment therein in each State in which the course is offered or sold. If a course is designed to prepare a student for a particular occupation, trade, profession, or other endeavor, students who, by reason of a lack of prior education, age, physical, mental or other condition or circumstance, are unqualified to perform such duties should not be enrolled therein unless the existence of such disqualification is affirmatively disclosed to the applicant. If those pursuing such a course must also satisfy requirements imposed by any Federal or State law or regulation, such as but not limited to the successful completion of an examination or the obtaining of a license, the existence of such requirements must also be affirmatively disclosed, together with the name of the Federal agency and/or State(s) by which such requirements have been imposed. If completion of the course will not qualify the prospective student to take a required examination or to obtain a license in one or more of the States in which the course is offered or sold without further training or education, such facts should be affirmatively disclosed together with the names of such States and such additional requirements or qualifications as may have been established by each.

§ 254.7 Deceptive use of diplomas, degrees, or certificates.

(a) An industry member should not issue a diploma, certificate of completion, or any document of similar import, which misrepresents directly or indirectly the subject matter, substance or content of the course of study or any other material fact concerning the course for which it was awarded or the accomplishments of the student to whom it was awarded.

(b) An industry member should not offer or confer an academic or professional degree, certificate, or diploma such as but not limited to bachelor of arts, bachelor of science, associate in arts, or those degrees which entitle the possessor to seek admission to or apply for a license to practice, teach, or enter the profession indicated therein such as doctor of medicine, bachelor of pharmacy, bachelor of laws, bachelor of arts or science. The term "degree" as used in this section means any academic, professional, or honorary degree or title, or any designation, mark, appellation, series of letters or words such as, but not limited to, associate, bachelor, master, doctor, or fellow, which signifies, purports to be, or is generally taken to signify satisfactory completion of the requirements of an academic, educational, or professional program of study beyond the secondary school level or is a recognized honorary title conferred for some meritorious recognition.

(c) An industry member should not offer or confer a high school diploma unless it has been authorized to confer such a diploma by the authorities of the State in which the school is situated or in which the diploma will be awarded and in which the student pursued the course of study. If a course is designed or intended to prepare the student for a G.E.D. or similar examination to be administered by State or other educational authorities, that fact should be disclosed, together with any conditions or limitations on the eligibility of a person to take such examinations.

§ 254.8 Deceptive sales practices.

(a) In obtaining leads to prospective students, an industry member should not use advertisements or promotional material which is classified or designated as "Help Wanted", "Employment", "Business Opportunities", or by words or terms of similar import, so as to represent directly or by implication that employment is being offered.

(b) An industry member should not deceptively designate or refer to its sales representatives as "registrars," "counselors," "advisors," or by words of similar import or misrepresent in any other manner, the title qualifications, training, experience or status of its salesmen, agents, employees, or other representatives.

(c) The advertising or promotional materials of an industry member which are used to provide leads for prospective students should include the full name and address of the school and the fact that it is a school if such is not apparent from its name. In addition if those who respond to such an advertisement will be contacted by a salesman, the advertisement should contain a clear and conspicuous disclosure that a salesman will call.

(d) In obtaining leads to prospective students, an industry member should not represent that it is conducting a talent hunt, contest, or similar tests, unless such is the fact and such representation is accompanied by a clear and conspicuous disclosure of the industry member's name and address conducting the test and the fact that it is a school if such is not apparent from its name and whether the course to which it pertains will be conducted in residence or by correspondence. The results of the contest or test and the percentage of participants in the contest or test who were winners or who passed should be disclosed to such prospective students prior to enrollment.

§ 254.9 Deceptive pricing and misuse of the word "Free."

(a) An industry member should not represent directly or indirectly in advertising or otherwise that a course or courses may be taken for a specified price, or at a saving, or at a reduced price, when such is not the fact; or otherwise deceive students or prospective students with respect to the cost of a course or any equipment, books or supplies associated therewith or furnish any means or instrumentality by which others engaged in obtaining enrollments may make such representations. Illustratively, an industry member should not represent:

(1) That veterans, or other stated classes of persons may be enrolled at a reduced or special rate unless such is the fact;

(2) That a specific amount is its usual and customary price for a course unless such amount is the price at which the course has been usually and customarily sold in the recent regular course of business;

(3) That any saving is afforded in the price of a course from the member's regular price unless the price at which the course is offered constitutes a reduction from the price at which the course has been usually and customarily sold in the recent regular course of business;

(4) That books, training materials or training aids are furnished at reduced rates,

(i) Unless the prices therefor have been reduced from the prices at which they were usually and customarily sold by the member in the recent and regular course of business; or

(ii) Unless the prices therefor have been reduced from the prices at which they were usually and customarily sold at retail by principal outlets in the trade area.

(b) An industry member should not misrepresent that the total cost of the course to a prospective student or falsely represent that it offers scholarships which pay for all or part of the course.

(c) An industry member should not represent that any course material, training device, or service is free unless it is in fact provided without cost or obligation to the student.

NOTE: The Commission's "Guides Against Deceptive Pricing" and "Guides Concerning Use of the Word 'Free' and Similar Representations," afford further guidance in this area. Copies are available upon request.

§ 254.10 Deceptive or unfair collection practices.

(a) An industry member should not use any deceptive representations or deceptive means to collect or attempt to collect tuition or other charges from its students.[1]

(b) An industry member should not falsely represent that a delinquent account has been or will be referred to an independent collection agency or misrepresent in any other manner that someone other than the industry member is or will be attempting to collect the amount allegedly due.

(c) An industry member should not seek to enforce or obtain a judgment or otherwise attempt to collect on any contract or other instrument between itself and a student, or transfer or assign such contract or other instrument to a third party for the purpose of collection or of enforcing or obtaining a judgment on said contract or instrument, where the member or its employees or representatives orally misrepresented the nature or the terms of said contract or instrument at the time or prior to the time the contract or instrument was signed.

§ 254.11 Credit transactions.

(a) An industry member should not use any contract provision, oral or written representation, or other device or means to deny or abridge the benefits of any applicable federal or state law intended to protect consumers or credit purchasers.

(b) An industry member should not negotiate or assign a trade acceptance, conditional sales contract, promissory note or other instrument of indebtedness executed by or on behalf of a student without first endorsing on the face thereof a legend stating: "Any holder takes this instrument subject to the terms and conditions of the contract which gave rise to the debt evidenced hereby."

§ 254.12 Cancellation and refund policies.

(a) In connection with the offering for sale, or the enrollment of students in their respective homes or places of abode, an industry member should not:

(1) Contract for any sale whether in the form of trade acceptance, conditional sales contract, promissory note, or otherwise which shall become binding

---

[1] The Commission's "Guides Against Debt Collection Deception" afford further guidance in this area. Copies are available upon request.

on the purchaser prior to midnight of the third day, excluding Sundays and legal holidays, after date of execution.

(2) Fail to disclose, orally prior to the time of sale and in writing on any trade acceptance, conditional sales contract, promissory note, or other instrument executed by the purchaser with such conspicuousness and clarity as is likely to be observed and read by such purchaser that the purchaser may rescind or cancel the sale directing or mailing a notice of cancellation to the members' address prior to midnight of the third day, excluding Sundays and legal holidays, after the date of the sale. Upon such cancellation the burden shall be on the industry member to collect any books or other materials left in the purchaser's home and to return any payments received from the purchaser. Nothing contained in these right-to-cancel provisions shall relieve the purchaser of the responsibility for taking reasonable care of the books or materials prior to cancellation and during a reasonable period following cancellation.

(3) Fail to provide a separate and clearly understandable form which the purchaser may use as a notice of cancellation.

(4) Negotiate any trade acceptance, conditional sales contract, promissory note, or other instrument of indebtedness to a finance company or other third party prior to midnight of the fifth day, excluding Sundays and legal holidays, after the date of execution by the purchaser.

Provided, however, That nothing contained in this section shall relieve an industry member of any additional obligations respecting contracts made in the home imposed either by Federal law, the law of the State in which the student resides, or the law of the State which governs the transaction between the parties.

(b) All industry members should have a definite established policy for the settlement of obligations in any instance in which a student desires to cancel, discontinue or otherwise terminate his enrollment after execution of the contract and prior to completion of the course. This settlement policy should provide both for refunds or reduction of the amount due under the contract, as appropriate, regardless of whether the student terminates his enrollment before or after payment of the contract price.

(c) With respect to any home study (correspondence) course, the settlement policy must as a minimum permit withdrawal or termination at any time prior to completion of the course with the right to a refund or of cancellation of the obligation for not less than the pro rata cost of the uncompleted portion of the course, but subject to a reasonable, nonrefundable enrollment fee.

(d) With respect to any resident training course, the settlement policy must as a minimum permit withdrawal or termination on a pro rata basis (similar to that set forth in paragraph (c) of this section) at any time during the first one-third ($1/3$) of the course, and in no case must it detract or diminish any right which such student might have under applicable law in the event of suit for unliquidated damages under the law of the State which governs the contract.

(e) The terms and conditions of such policy, including the form of notice which the student must give and the method or criteria used to determine the amount of money to be refunded or the amount of the unpaid obligation to be remitted as the case may be, subject to the provisions of paragraphs (c), (d), and (f) of this section, should be clearly and conspicuously

(1) Disclosed in all catalogs and similar documents containing a description of the school or course offered, and

(2) Made a part of the enrollment contract.

The contract provision which incorporates the settlement provisions should also provide that the right of the student to a refund or to a reduced obligation shall not be abrogated or in any way diminished as a result of the assignment or other transfer of the industry member's interest in the contract or evidence of debt to any third party, and that such right shall be assertable against any such future party in interest.

(f) If a student has been materially and substantially misled or deceived by an industry member's failure to comply with this part, and if by reason of such failure the student wishes to withdraw from or terminate his enrollment, he should be refunded all moneys paid and any further obligation shall be canceled notwithstanding any contract provisions made pursuant to paragraphs (c) and (d) of this section; *Provided,* That the student must give notice of withdrawal or termination promptly upon becoming aware of the deception. Should the student not discover such failure until after completion of the course, he shall be entitled to total refund upon giving notice as required above.

(g) At the time the application and other documents referred to in paragraph (c) of this section are executed, the purchaser should be furnished with a copy thereof together with instructions as to the name and address of the person to whom notice of his intention to cancel the contract should be sent.

(h) An industry member that uses salesmen to visit prospective students and solicit enrollments should require such salesmen to make an oral explanation of the member's cancellation policy prior to the execution of the enrollment contract.

(i) An industry member should clearly and conspicuously disclose to prospective students prior to enrollment that the collection of student accounts may be undertaken by a designated agency, if such is the fact, and whether such action will affect the student's rights to withdraw or otherwise discontinue the course, or affect any affirmative defenses which may be available to him.

§ 254.13 Affirmative disclosure prior to enrollment.

(a) In order to prevent deception the Commission may require the affirmative disclosure of material facts concerning a school or any of its courses, which if known to prospective student or students would influence their decision to purchase the course or to enroll. The failure to disclose such information as may be required is an unfair trade practice violative of section 5 of the Federal Trade Commission Act. Virtually all of this part imposes requirements regarding affirmative disclosures. Unless otherwise specified such disclosures should be made in a clear and conspicuous manner so as to be likely to be perceived by the student or prospective student prior to enrollment. In addition to those disclosures this section provides in summary form a description of additional disclosures which should be made to prospective students, or to the parents or guardians of prospective students who are minors, prior to the execution of the enrollment contract or contract of sale.

(b) Before obtaining the signature of a prospective student or his parent or guardian on an enrollment contract or contract of sale, an industry member should furnish to that person a written statement, catalog, or bulletin which contains the following information:

(1) The name of the industry member, and its mailing address;

(2) The industry member's policy and regulations on enrollment and specific entrance requirements for each course (See also § 254.5);

(3) The industry member's policy and regulations relative to makeup work, delay or delinquency in meeting course requirements, and standards required of the student for achieving satisfactory progress;

(4) A detailed schedule of fees, charges for tuition, books, supplies, tools, rentals, and other charges. (See also § § 254.8, 254.9, and 254.11);

(5) A course outline for each course offered showing subjects or units in the course, type of work or skill to be learned, and approximate time and clock hours required to complete each subject or unit (See also § § 254.6 and 254.7); and

(6) A description of the available space, facilities, equipment, and similar information. (See also § 254.4).

Issued: July 7, 1970.

By direction of the Commission.

[SEAL]   JOSEPH W. SHEA,
                                          Secretary.

Appendix XIV

Digests of Selected FTC Advisory Opinions

No. 1 Use of Terms *Chamoislike* or *Chamois Type*

The Commission was requested to express an opinion concerning the legality of describing unsplit sheepskin as "Chamois-like Sheepskin" or "Chamois-type Sheepskin" on the basis, it is claimed, that the product looks and feels like chamois leather, and possesses the same qualities as the genuine product.

This problem has been before the commission in different forms on several occasions. In each instance the commission has taken the position that it will prohibit the branding or labeling of leather products as *Chamois, Chamois Type* or *Chamoislike* unless such products are made (a) from the skin of the Alpine antelope, commonly known and referred to as Chamois, or (b) from sheepskin fleshers which have been oil-tanned after removal of the grain layer.

The word *chamois* has its origin in the common name of a small goatlike Alpine antelope whose skin was made into a soft, pliable leather used in the manufacture of gloves, and for polishing such articles as glass, jewelry, fine metals, and wood. It possessed the additional feature of absorbing water readily and returning, when dry, to its original state of softness and pliability. The animal became virtually extinct for commercial purposes about 1890 and since that time the word acquired a secondary meaning after being widely used commercially to designate certain leathers produced from split sheepskin fleshers.

The necessity for splitting sheepskin is to remove the impervious grain layer so as to make the underside more receptive to tanning. Because the two layers do not react at the same rate, should an amount of the grain layer remain the skin will not stretch uniformly and will eventually rip and crumble. In any event, irrespective of the relative merits of the many processes which may be employed to produce the leather, the fact remains that the grain layer must be separated from the sheepskin flesher in order that an acceptable chamois will result. This requirement the requesting party's product does not fulfill.

The claim that the subject product is equal in all respects to genuine chamois is not true, since the grain layer has not been removed. The genuine product has become firmly established in industry and elsewhere as herein defined, and such product is what the public is entitled to get when it purchases chamois even though the choice may be dictated by caprice or fashion, or perhaps by ignorance. The fact that the product is equal or will serve substantially the same purpose is wholly immaterial. (*FTC* v. *Algoma Lumber Co.,* 291 U.S. 67, 78. To the same effect see *Benton Announcements, Inc.* v. *FTC,* 1930 F. 2d. 254.)

The question posed herein is whether the word *chamois* might be a permissible designation for the subject product if qualifying terms as *like* or *type* were added. Use of the word in any manner is a representation that the product is that which has traditionally been sold as chamois and so accepted by the public after years of buying experience. Although the ordinary purchaser may not know how chamois is made, he is entitled to believe that the particular product sold under that name is in fact a chamois as it is understood in the industry, and such implication cannot be offset by qualifying words. After reading both, an ordinary consumer would still not know the truth about the product without resort to specialized information. In other words, the capacity and tendency to deceive through any other application of the word chamois would continue to exist.

The requesting party was advised that the definition of chamois has become firmly established in law, in industry, and in the public's mind to mean nothing less than those leather products made from the skin of the Alpine antelope or from the fleshers of sheepskin which have been oil-tanned after removal of the grain layer and that any other use of the word, whether or not modified by qualifying language, to describe leather made by other or incomplete processes would serve only to dilute its accepted meaning and would not be in the general public interest. Consequently, to label the subject product in the manner contemplated would be a deceptive practice and subject the requesting party to a charge of violation of Section 5, Federal Trade Commission Act.

August 7, 1964

No. 11 Foreign Origin Labeling

The Commission was requested to advise whether or not it would be permissible to label finished truss plates made from imported galvanized steel coils as a domestic product manufactured in the U.S.A. without any reference to the origin of the steel. The plates are cut and stamped to size in this country and further stamped to form tooth-like fastening devices as part of the finished plate.

The Commission advised that it would not be proper to label these plates as made in the U.S.A. because that would constitute an affirmative representation that they were entirely made in this country, which is not the fact unless, of course, the label also discloses in a clear and conspicuous manner the fact that the steel in said plates is imported.

December 17, 1965

No. 17 Use of Descriptions "Velvet" and "Suede" for a Flocked Fabric

A Federal Trade Commission advisory opinion informed a manufacturer that the unmodified terms *velvet* and *suede* could not properly be used to describe a flocked fabric.

The manufacturer had described the material in question as one formed of micro-cut flock fibers upstanding on end and adhered to a suitable backing. The resulting fabric, it was said, has the appearance and feel of velvet and suede.

The Commission believes the consuming public understands the unmodified term "suede" to connote leather and the unmodified term "velvet" to connote, among other things, a particular kind of warp pile fabric.

The fabric in question, therefore, may properly be designated only as "suede fabric," "suede cloth"; "velvet-like fabric" or "velvet-like cloth" or by words of similar import. The expressions "sueded fabric," "sueded cloth"; "velveted fabric" or "velveted cloth" or words of similar import are also unobjectionable.

March 22, 1966

No. 25 Use of Description *14K* for Item Not Entirely Gold

The Federal Trade Commission rendered an advisory opinion that it is improper to mark or describe an earring as having a "14 K post" when the post is not entirely gold.

"Under Rule 22(c) (1) of the Trade Practice Rules for the Jewelry Industry," the Commission advised, "an article may not be so designated unless it is 'composed throughout of an alloy of gold'; since this article will contain substantial electroplatings of base metals, it plainly is not composed throughout of gold."

The requesting party had stated that the earring in question would be constructed as follows:

1. The ornamental front part would be basically brass, but no quality claim is contemplated as to this part of the article.
2. The front part is attached to a post made for penetration of pierced ears and held in place by a clutch-type back made basically of brass. No quality claim for the clutch-type back is contemplated.

3. The post will be 14-karat gold. After being soldered for the ornamental front the entire article will be electroplated with copper, then electroplated with nickel, and finally electroplated with high-karat gold.

April 2, 1966

No. 33 *Made in U.S.A.* Label

The Federal Trade Commission has rendered an advisory opinion that it would not be permissible to label dental X-ray film as made in the U.S.A. if it consists in part of a raw safety-base film imported from a foreign country, with the remaining ingredients to be made in the United States.

The commission's advice was that the imported raw safety base film "is the principal and essential component of the finished product. Without it there can be no X-ray picture." The manufacturing and packaging processes described in the letter from the requesting party "would not change the basic structure or composition of the imported film to such an extent that its identity would be lost. It is concluded, therefore, that it would not be proper under Section 5 of the Federal Trade Commission Act to label the dental X-ray film as 'Made in U.S.A.' "

April 15, 1966

No. 47 Use of Leather Terms for Nonleather Product

The Federal Trade Commission has made public its advice to a marketer of gloves that it would be improper to use a leather-connoting description for gloves which in fact contain no leather, even though qualifying language is used to describe their true composition.

Noting that the gloves are to be imported from Japan and the requesting party intends to disclose their origin on the paper bands and box labels, the commission further advised that to avoid possible deception, disclosure of the Japanese origin must also be made on each pair of gloves by marking or stamping or on a label or tag affixed thereto. This disclosure must be readily visible upon casual inspection of the gloves and of such permanence as to remain on them until consummation of sale to the ultimate purchaser.

May 19, 1966

No. 58 Foreign-Origin Labeling

The commission was requested to furnish an advisory opinion concerning the labeling as to origin of toy balloons mounted on display cards. The balloons were to be imported from England mounted on 8- x 16-inch display cards, with either thirty-six or seventy-two balloons to a card, which will sell for 5 or 10 cents per balloon. The card is to be clearly marked *Made in England,* but the individual balloons will not be so marked.

The commission advised that if the display card is clearly marked *Made in England,* no real purpose would be served by requiring each individual balloon to be similarly marked so long as the balloons are not removed from the card prior to sale.

June 17, 1966

No. 60 Advertising of Diamonds as "Clear, Pure Color"

The Federal Trade Commission has advised a jewelry firm proposing to advertise diamonds as "clear, pure color" that a substantial segment of the purchasing public would understand the claim to mean a top grade white or colorless diamond, and that it should not be used to describe a diamond which shows any color when viewed under normal, north daylight or its equivalent.

June 18, 1966

No. 61 Use of Terms *Gold Filled* or *Rolled Gold Plate*

The Federal Trade Commission has informed a marketer of jewelry that it would be improper to use terms such as *gold filled* or *rolled gold plate* in describing gold-filled jewelry articles which are electroplated with nickel and finished with either gold flash or gold electroplate.

The commission said that a purchaser of such an article would not get the type of performance expected from gold-filled articles because points of wear would expose the coating of white nickel at a very early stage and the ornamental value would be seriously reduced.

"Being electroplated with nickel," the Commission said, the "gold filled material would not service its function and a person buying the article on that basis would not get what he had been led to believe he was getting. In fact, Rule 22(b)(4) of the Trade Practice Rules for the Jewelry Industry specifically contemplates that the *surface* coating, not the inner portion, be made of 'gold filled' or 'rolled gold plates.' "

June 18, 1966

No. 63 Guarantee Advertising

A television station has been advised by the Federal Trade Commission that it would be improper in commercials it produces for local automobile dealers to mention the manufacturer's guarantee to refer viewers to the manufacturer's national advertising for a description of the guarantee's terms.

"In brief," the commission's advisory opinion stated,

the law requires that when a guarantee is mentioned in the advertising of a product all the material terms and conditions of the guarantee must be clearly and conspicuously disclosed in the same advertisement. The objective is to avoid the possibility of a reader or hearer being misled by concluding, erroneously, that the guarantee is broader or affords more protection than is in fact the case, and, obviously, this objective is not attained by a mere reference in the advertisement to the fact that one may ascertain the terms and conditions of the guarantee by looking elsewhere.

The Commission is aware of the fact that the advertising of automobile guarantees may present complications because of the numerous conditions which the guarantees contain. But this factor alone makes the disclosure all the more important in order to avoid deception of consumers.

June 22, 1966

No. 84 Proper Labeling of Rebuilt Fuses

The Federal Trade Commission made public an advisory opinion concerning the proper labeling of rebuilt fuses to be used by public utilities and commercial consumers of electricity.

The requesting company inquired as to whether it will be necessary to label a fuse as "rebuilt" or "remanufactured" if it is broken down to its smallest components and all parts that are used are inspected to meet new parts standards.

Advising that the concern's "rebuilt fuses would have to be labeled as such," the Commission cited its frequent holding,

in connection with a variety of products, that in the absence of an adequate disclosure to the contrary, merchandise which resembles and has the appearance of merchandise composed of new materials but which is, in fact, composed of reclaimed materials, will be regarded by purchasers as being entirely new and that a substantial segment of the consuming public has a preference for merchandise which is composed of new and unused materials. This has been held to be so without regard to the comparative quality of the new and rebuilt products, for in such matters the public is entitled to get what it chooses no matter what dictates the choice.

Answering other questions posed by the company, the Commission stated:

[All] advertising material promoting the sale of these fuses should also contain a disclosure of their used or rebuilt nature, [but] it is not necessary, once this disclosure is clearly and conspicuously made, to repeat the word over and over again even where technical instructions are being given. Technical instructions for the use of these fuses are not ordinarily part of the advertising designed to induce customers to buy and, if not, there would be no requirement for disclosure in the instructions as distinguished from advertising.

Generally speaking, * * * the disclosure must be on the cartons, invoices and in advertising literature, as well as on the fuses themselves. However, the disclosure need not be placed on the fuses themselves if you can establish that the disclosure on the bags, boxes or other containers is such that the ultimate purchasers, at the point of sale, are informed that they are rebuilt fuses. The question of informing the ultimate purchasers here becomes important in the event any of your customers also resell the fuses to others under circumstances where those ultimate purchasers are not informed as to their rebuilt nature.

August 19, 1966

No. 98 Removal of Foreign-Origin Disclosure and Use of Word *Manufacturing*

The Commission announced it had advised a distributor of imported time clocks that the "removal or obliteration of foreign origin disclosures on imported products is under certain circumstances a violation of the Tariff Act which is administered by the Bureau of Customs" and invited the distributor to contact that Bureau on this particular point. The distributor wanted permission to remove the foreign origin label prior to reselling the time clocks in the United States. "Regardless of the position of that Bureau," the Commission added, "such removal or obliteration in the circumstances you describe may result in a deception of the purchasing public as to the country of origin" and might be found to be in violation of the FTC Act.

Permission was also requested to use the word *manufacturing* in the trade name of the company and in advertising, even though the time clocks are imported in their finished state. The commission was of the opinion that the use of such word "would have the tendency to lead consumers and others into the belief, contrary to fact, that they are dealing directly with the manufacturer and so to mislead or deceive them. In these circumstances, it would not be proper to use the word 'manufacturing' or any other word of similar import in your trade name or in your advertising or to otherwise represent your company as a manufacturer."

Finally, the distributor wanted to know if it would be proper to represent his company as a manufacturer if it performed a "small part" of the manufacturing process on the time clocks. In regard to this question, the Commission reached the following conclusion:

> The amount of manufacturing which a concern must engage in to justify representing itself as a manufacturer will vary from case to case, depending on the specific circumstances. Your question, however, indicates you intend to operate as a manufacturer only in the technical sense and not in a substantive way, in an attempt to justify the use of a term not otherwise a correct description of your business. We likewise do not believe, in these circumstances, that it would be proper to represent your company as a manufacturer.

October 31, 1966

No. 100 "Lifetime Guarantee" Advertising

A seller of aluminum siding requested the commission to render an advisory opinion concerning the legality of its proposed use of a "lifetime guarantee" for aluminum siding.

The proposed guarantee would represent that the siding will not rust, peel, blister, flake, chip, or split under conditions of normal weathering for the lifetime of the original owner. If, after inspection, the seller determines that a claim is valid under the guarantee the seller will within three years after installation furnish all materials and labor necessary to repair or replace, at the seller's option, all siding at no cost to the owner. For the next seven years, the seller will furnish all materials and labor at a cost to the owner of 8 per cent of the then current price for each year or part thereof after the third year. For the next ten years the seller will furnish all materials and labor at a cost to the owner of an additional 3 per cent of the then current price for each year or part thereof after the tenth year. Thereafter, the seller will furnish only the material necessary to repair or replace, at the seller's option, at a cost to the seller of 10 per cent of the then current price. The owner must assume all other costs, including 90 per cent of the cost of materials and 100 per cent of the cost of labor.

In addition, the seller furnished the results of extensive laboratory and field testing of house siding since 1948 under every type of environment which would lead to the conclusion that no aluminum siding, no matter what its finish, will last for a lifetime. In fact, the evidence submitted, if accepted as true, would establish that the maximum life expectancy of such siding under normal conditions would come closer to twenty years and would be considerably less under more extreme circumstances. This is based upon experience indicating that even if it does not rust, peel, blister, flake, chip, or split, the finish will weather to such an extent as to require repainting within that time.

The commission made it plain that it has not conducted its own investigation in order to verify the accuracy of this evidence and that the comments set forth in its opinion were based upon the facts as presented and upon the assumption that those facts were correct. On this basis, the commission advised that it would not be legal for the seller to employ a guarantee to represent that the siding will last for a lifetime or for any other period beyond what can reasonably be expected.

The opinion pointed out that both the trade practice rules for the residential aluminum siding industry and the commission's *Guides Against Deceptive Advertising of Guarantees* contain the principle that a guarantee shall not be used which exaggerates the life expectancy of a product. In such a case, the guarantee itself constitutes a misrepresentation of fact even though all required disclosures of material terms and conditions might be made in all advertising of the guarantee. This simply recognizes the principle that a guarantee can be used as a representation of an existing fact as well as a guarantee. Viewed in this light, use of this guarantee would constitute an affirmative representation that the siding will last for the lifetime of the owner when the evidence furnished would indicate this is not true. The gravamen of the offense would be the affirmative misrepresentation of the life expectancy of the product and this could not be corrected by a mere disclosure that what is represented to be a fact is not actually true.

Of equal importance in the commission's view was the fact that the seller here proposed to couple two basically inconsistent provisions in the same guarantee. One was the use of the lifetime representation and the other was the prorated feature. The commission stated its opinion to be that it is conceptually impossible to combine the two in the same guarantee when the proration period virtually terminates at the end of twenty years. A guarantee cannot be for a lifetime if it terminates after twenty years. Undoubtedly, many owners will live far beyond that period of time and so the guarantee cannot help but confuse even though a careful reading of its terms might show that it states all relevant facts and even though all advertisements make the required disclosures.

Literally speaking, some benefit may be claimed for the remainder of the owner's life after the expiration of the twenty year period, for the seller will still assume 10 per cent of the cost of materials. But this would appear to be more a matter of form than substance. The owner would be given a mere pittance in order to furnish some color of justification for the claim that the guarantee is for a lifetime. The situation is that the owner must pay more than 90 per cent of all costs in order to receive the benefit of the remaining 10 per cent of the cost of materials, which does not leave him with anything of substantial value to justify the representation of lifetime warranty. In the commission's view, the purchaser must be afforded something of substantial value for his lifetime in order to support the representation and the Commission did not feel that less than 10 per cent of all costs was of substantial value.

Finally, the commission noted that the proposed guarantee excludes damages resulting from normal weathering of surfaces. In view of the fact that this appears to be the most prevalent cause for repainting aluminum siding, the commission also advised that this is a material term or condition which not only should be set forth in the guarantee, for whatever period of time it runs, but also should be clearly and conspicuously set forth in all advertising which mentions the guarantee.

November 9, 1966

No. 120 Description of a Product as New

The commission was requested to render an advisory opinion as to the permissible period of time during which an advertiser could continue to describe a new product as being new.

The commission pointed out that the word *new* may be properly used only when the product so described is either entirely new or has been changed in a functionally significant and substantial respect. A product may not be called new when only the package has been altered or some other change made that is functionally insignificant or insubstantial.

Assuming that a particular product could truthfully be described as "new" in the first instance, the opinion noted that there is little precedent for determining how long an advertiser may truthfully continue to describe it as new. The commission stated it was aware, of course, that the word has been frequently abused and that it is in the interest of all advertisers to have established ground rules for its use. However, the time period during which a particular product may be called new will depend upon the circumstances and is not subject to precise limitations; any selection of a fixed period of time or a rigid cut-off date would have to be arbitrary in nature. Further, any such attempt would not only fence in all advertisers without regard to the circumstances, but would fence in the commission as well, and deprive it of all flexibility in dealing with individual situations.

Instead, the commission felt it would be preferable, considering the absence of precedents, to establish a tentative outer limit for use of the claim, while leaving itself free to take into consideration unusual situations which may arise. Thus, the commission's position was that until such a time as later developments may show the need for a different rule, it would be inclined to question use of any claim that a product is new for a period of time longer than six months. This general rule would apply unless exceptional circumstances warranting a period either shorter or longer than six months were shown to exist.

April 15, 1967

No. 138 Use of Symbols and Names Having Fur-Bearing Animal Connotations in Labeling Textile Fiber Products

The commission was requested to render an opinion with respect to the labeling of textile fiber products manufactured so as to simulate a fur or fur product.

The requesting party proposed using a label which would bear the depiction for a fur-bearing animal commercially used in fur products, a trade name and trade-mark having a fur-bearing animal connotation, and the required fiber content disclosures.

The commission pointed out that the rules and regulations promulgated under authority of the Textile Fiber Products Identification Act provide, in Rule 9, that the label of a textile fiber product shall not contain a name, word, depiction, descriptive matter, or other symbol which connotes or signifies a fur-bearing animal, unless such product is a fur product within the meaning of the Fur Products Labeling Act. Subject to this proviso, a textile fiber product may not be described on the label with the name or part of a name of a fur-bearing animal, whether as a single or combination word similar to a fur-bearing animal name, for example, *Broadtail*.

The rules permit the nondeceptive use on textile fiber products of fur-bearing animal names but only where the animal fur is not commonly or commercially used in fur products, as for example, *Bear*. Further, the rules do not prevent or prohibit the nondeceptive use of a trade-mark or trade name containing the name, symbol, or depiction of a fur-bearing animal unless "the textile fiber product in connection with which such trade-mark or trade name is used simulates a fur or fur product."

The commission advised that it would not be proper, in the labeling of textile fiber products, to use a label bearing the depiction of a fur-bearing animal or a trade-mark and trade name having fur-bearing animal connotations. Such labeling, with or without the required fiber content disclosures, of a textile fiber product manufactured so as to simulate the fur of an animal commonly or commercially used in fur products would have the tendency and capacity of inducing prospective customers into the mistaken belief that the textile fiber product to which such label is affixed contains the fur of the animal depicted or fur fibers from such animal.

August 24, 1967

No. 139 Advertising Claims For Personal Deodorant Spray

The commission announced it had rendered an advisory opinion in regard to some proposed advertising claims for a personal deodorant spray.

Specifically, the commission considered the propriety of the following two claims: (1) that the product meets the U.S. government requirements for safety and effectiveness and (2) that no other medicated personal deodorant spray equals its safety and effectiveness.

In regard to the first claim, the commission said there were no specific standards or requirements officially recognized by the U.S. government relating to the safety and effectiveness of personal deodorant sprays. Under these circumstances, therefore, the commission said it would be improper to claim that such requirements exist and that the product meets those requirements.

With respect to the second claim, the commission said that opinion evidence indicated there are other medicated deodorant sprays on the market which are equally as safe and effective as the product in question. In view of this opinion evidence, and in the absence of reports of properly controlled studies establishing the validity of the claim, the commission said that it could not give its approval to the second claim.

August 30, 1967

No. 161 Advertising Promoting Sale of Information and a Product

The commission issued its advisory opinion concerning proposed advertising offering for sale for $1 a pamphlet which (1) advises a method for curing athlete's foot and (2) recommends the use of a specific proprietary product for this purpose. The advertiser has no financial interest in the product in question. He does not himself propose to sell the product.

The commission stated that use of the proposed advertising would be violative of Sections 5 and 12 of the Federal Trade Commission Act in that it implies, contrary to fact, that all cases of athlete's foot can be eliminated or cured by use of the advertised method and product "within a very short time" and with "patience and a little care." The commission believes that the proposed advertising implies, contrary to fact, that through it some new facts as to the care and cure of athlete's foot are now available which have hitherto been withheld from the public.

Its opinion concluded with the following statement:

> The laws against deceptive advertising apply equally to those who are selling advice or information and to those who are selling products. In either case the test is whether the advice (or product) being offered will in fact achieve the results claimed for it in the advertising. If the advice recommends the use of

a product, the efficacy of the product for the use recommended must of course also be considered.

This opinion in no way relates to the question of whether your proposal would constitute the practice of medicine or to the legality of your doing so.

Commissioner Elman dissents. He does not agree that selling advice is in the same category as selling a product. Recognizing that a good deal of foolish and worthless advice is being peddled to the American people, and not merely in the field of medicine or health, Commissioner Elman does not believe that Congress intended that the Federal Trade Commission or any other government agency should set itself up as a board of review examining into the validity or worth of ideas, opinions, beliefs, and theories disseminated to the public.

January 18, 1968

No. 190 Random Distribution of "Bonus Certificates" with Purchase

The commission in an advisory opinion stated that the random inclusion of "bonus certificates" in egg cartons would be violative of Section 5 of the Federal Trade Commission.

The seller proposed to include "bonus certificates" in cartons of eggs offered for sale. The certificates were described as being worth "so many eggs or $5.00 in cash." They would be randomly distributed so that some cartons would contain eggs plus a certificate of value, while others would contain eggs only, or eggs plus a certificate of little or no value.

The commission was of the view that this would be merchandising by lottery, a practice which the commission has long held to be unfair within the meaning of Section 5 of the Federal Trade Commission Act.

February 16, 1968

No. 202 Jobbers and Wholesalers

The commission issued an advisory opinion to an applicant who (1) asked for a definition of the words "jobber" and "wholesaler," and (2) asked the commission's views as to the propriety of a proposed revision in price lists.

In response the Commission stated:

As a working rule, one might suppose that, in a three level system, wholesalers are closer to producers and jobbers are closer to retailers in the distribution of a producer's goods. Traditionally, producers sell to wholesalers who sell at a higher price to jobbers who sell at a higher price to retailers.

The controlling element in your problem, however, as in similar problems arising under the amended Clayton Act, is whether or not resale competition actually exists as between and among these various resellers rather than the names they use to describe themselves. If in fact a so-called wholesaler competes with a so-called jobber in the redistribution of goods, the difference in names is of no consequence; the fact of competition is.

In *F.T.C.* v. *Ruberoid,* 343 U.S. 470 (1952) the Supreme Court stressed that actual competition in resale operations is decisive rather than nomenclature and approved the Commission's disregard of "ambiguous labels, which might be used to cloak discriminatory discounts to favored customers."

What you plan, as we understand it, is to sell your middlemen, whether "wholesalers" or "jobbers," at one price, while selling certain selected retailers at a higher price.

In the circumstances you present, you may properly do this provided the "wholesalers" and "jobbers" are functioning at the same distribution level and are not themselves engaged in retail operations competitive with the selected retailers.

March 14, 1968

No. 204 Guarantee Advertising

In an advisory opinion rendered to a watch manufacturer, the commission ruled that a guarantee which has conditions and limitations, other than as to time, may not be represented as an unconditional guarantee. It also advised the requesting party that a guarantee which lasts for only three years cannot be described as a lifetime guarantee. Moreover, the commission objected to the guarantee being described as "4-Ever."

With respect to the claim *unconditional,* the commission said that it would be proper to claim that a product is "Unconditionally guaranteed for three years" if in fact no other conditions existed. However, where there are conditions other than time, such as were present in the case presented for review, the commission said that it would be improper under Section 5 of the FTC Act to claim that the guarantee is unconditional. The reason for this, it was concluded, is that the term *unconditional* means there are no conditions attached, and it is a contradiction in terms rather than an attempt at modification to permit use of the claim *unconditional* provided the conditions are disclosed.

Under the terms of the guarantee that was the subject of the commission's opinion, the purchaser of the watch had the option to renew the original guarantee which expired at the end of three years by paying a service fee of $5 on an annual basis. By having to pay the $5 service fee, the commission said, the purchaser no longer has a "lifetime guarantee" but a service or insurance policy that is renewable at his expense on an annual basis.

The commission also ruled that it is necessary to disclose the life being referred to whenever it is claimed that the duration of the guarantee is for a lifetime. For example, is it the life of the original purchaser, the original user, or the life of the product? Thus, even if the requesting party resolved the first objection and offered a guarantee for life rather than for three years, it would still be necessary to disclose clearly and conspicuously the life to which reference was being made.

In the opinion the commission also objected to the term *4-Ever* because, contrary to fact, the product was not guaranteed forever.

Finally, the commission stated that it was not ruling upon the "waterproof" claim because it currently has under consideration a possible revision of trade practice rules relating to the term *Waterproofing* as applied to watches.

April 3, 1968

No. 239 Labeling of Mesquite Chips

The commission announced it had rendered an advisory opinion to a manufacturer of mesquite chips, a product designed to flavor food cooked with charcoal.

In the advisory opinion, the commission dealt with two questions. The first question involved Section 5 of the FTC Act and the propriety of such claims in labeling as whether the product will impart "real western barbecue" flavor to food and whether it may properly be labeled as mesquite chips. Second, under Section 4 of the Fair Packaging and Labeling Act, is it proper to state the net weight as "32 oz. (2 lbs.)" if the weight may vary as much as 2 ounces either way after it is shipped into interstate commerce, depending upon the presence or absence of humidity, and the package in fact contains 32 ounces when it is packed?

Passing upon the first question, the commission said that it had no objection to the proposed claims in the labeling insofar as Section 5 of the FTC Act is concerned.

With respect to the second question, the commission ruled that the proposed declaration of net weight complies with Section 4 of the Fair Packaging and Labeling Act and comes within the variations in stated weight permitted under Section 500.22(b) of its regulations. This section permits: "Variations from the stated weight . . . when caused by customary and ordinary exposure, after the commodity is introduced into interstate commerce, to conditions which normally occur in good distribution practice and which unavoidably result in change of weight or measure."

In arriving at this conclusion, the commission said that it has assumed that good distribution practices will be followed in the marketing of the product which unavoidably result in the change of weight in a relatively small percentage of cases, and that an overage is as likely to occur as often as a loss in weight.

The commission's opinion also advised the requesting party of certain technical requirements of its regulations, such as the location of the declaration of net weight, the exact size of the declaration in relation to the area of the principal display panel, and other information relating to the identity and location of the manufacturer of the product.

April 30, 1968

No. 255 Foreign Origin Labeling of Flatware Imported in Substantial Part

The commission rendered an advisory opinion in regard to the proper marking of the origin of flatware that is imported in substantial part. Specifically, the following three questions were ruled upon by the commission.

First, can flatware which is gold plated in the United States be marketed without disclosing the foreign origin of the imported stainless steel blanks, if it is sold under a trade name consisting of a company name suggesting domestic origin hyphenated with the word *American*? (The gold plating will cost from 30 to 50 per cent of the total cost of the finished product.)

Second, if the trade name referred to in the first question is not used, will it then be necessary to disclose the foreign origin of the imported stainless steel blanks?

Third, if a disclosure is required, must it be stamped on the flatware itself or can it be placed on a string tag attached to the flatware or on the container?

In response to the first question, the commission said that the use of the proposed trade name would constitute an affirmative representation, contrary to fact, that the entire product was made in the United States. Because a substantial portion originates in a foreign country, it will then be necessary to disclose clearly the country of origin of the imported stainless steel blanks in immediate connection with the trade name wherever it is used, both in advertising and labeling.

In response to the second and third questions, the commission said that disclosure of the origin of the imported components would be required even though the company elected not to market the flatware under the proposed trade name. The commission also stated that the disclosure may be made on the flatware itself, or on a string attached thereto, or on the container, provided the disclosure is of that degree of conspicuity and permanency as will likely be observed by prospective purchasers making a casual inspection of the merchandise prior to, not after, the purchase thereof.

May 30, 1968

Index

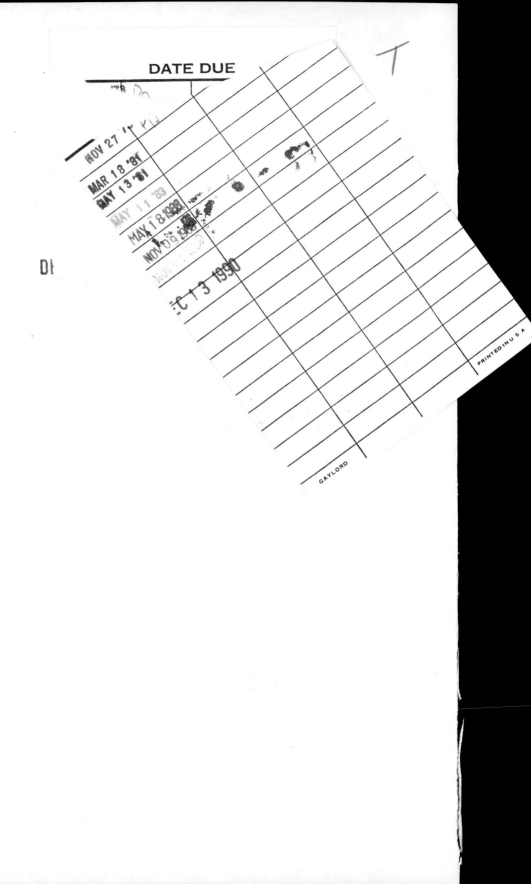